McGraw-Hill Education

Catholic High School Entrance Exams

Fourth Edition

McGraw-Hill Education

Catholic High School Entrance Exams

Fourth Edition

Wendy Hanks • Mark Alan Stewart • Judy Unrein

New York   Chicago   San Francisco   Athens   London   Madrid
Mexico City   Milan   New Delhi   Singapore   Sydney   Toronto

1 2 3 4 5 6 7 8 9   LHS   22 21 20 19 18 17

ISBN   978-1-259-83706-7
MHID   1-259-83706-8

e-ISBN   978-1-259-83707-4
e-MHID   1-259-83707-6

McGraw-Hill Education books are available at special quantity discounts to use as premiums and sales promotions or for use in corporate training programs. To contact a representative, please visit the Contact Us pages at www.mhprofessional.com.

CONTENTS

▓ PART 5. PRACTICE TESTS

INTRODUCTION

This book provides all the tools you need to get ready for the COOP, HSPT, or TACHS. The book is divided into five parts.

The book is organized by skills rather than by exam type, since all three exams have similar content. The *Contents* page indicates which sections and chapters apply to each exam. Most of the chapters apply to all three exams, but if a chapter applies only to one or two of the exams, the listing will indicate which of the three exams it covers. For example, if a listing says:

Chapter 8. Analogies (COOP, HPST)

Then that chapter applies to only the COOP and HSPT exams. If you are preparing for the TACHS exam, you should skip that chapter.

The easiest way to see exactly what you need to do to prepare for your specific exam is to follow the Study Plan for that exam. Simply complete the tasks listed on your study plan in the order they are listed and you will be fully prepared for your exam. See pages 5–8 for the study plans.

Part 1. Getting Started

Start here for answers to basic questions about the three exams.

Part 2. Diagnostic Tests

Take an exam-style mini-test to familiarize yourself with your test and to determine your strengths and weaknesses up front—so you know where to focus your exam prep. Each of the three diagnostic tests (COOP, HSPT, and TACHS) contains all the various question types you're most likely to see on your exam.

Learn test-taking rules and procedures, tips for preparation, and basic test-taking strategies. Choose a study plan to help you prepare for your exam.

Part 3. Verbal Skills

Prepare for reading, vocabulary, language, and other question types that test your verbal skills. Learn a step-by-step approach to handling each question type. After each lesson, apply what you've learned to a series of exam-style practice questions. At the end of Part 3 you'll find a handy review of all the basic rules of grammar and writing mechanics you need to know for your exam.

Part 4. Math and Quantitative Skills

Prepare for math computation, quantitative reasoning, and other question types that test your knowledge of math concepts and your math problem-solving skills. Learn a step-by-step approach to handling each question type. After each lesson, apply what you've learned to a series of exam-style practice questions. At the end of Part 4 you'll find a handy math review covering all the math topics you need to know for your exam.

Part 5. Practice Tests

In Part 5, you apply all you've learned in the book's lessons to two full-length practice COOP exams, two full-length practice HSPT exams, or two full-length practice TACHS exams. Be sure to read the explanations to the questions you answer incorrectly, so that you can avoid making similar mistakes on exam day.

OBTAINING UPDATED TEST INFORMATION

This book provides much of the information you need to know about the three tests—especially when it comes to test preparation and practice. However, you should not rely solely on this book for your information. The high school to which you're applying for admission can probably provide up-to-date information about test registration procedures and about testing fees, locations, and dates. You can also contact the test developers directly for this information:

Cooperative Admissions
Examination Office
CTB/McGraw-Hill
20 Ryan Ranch Road
Monterey, CA 93940
(800)538-9547
www.ctb.com

HSPT
Scholastic Testing Service
480 Meyer Road
Bensenville, IL 60106-1617
(800)642-6STS
www.ststesting.com

TACHS
TACHS Examination Office
P.O. Box 64675
Eagan, MN 55164-9522
(866)6IT-ACHS
www.tachsinfo.com

McGraw-Hill Education

Catholic High School Entrance Exams

Fourth Edition

PART

1 GETTING STARTED

Overview of the COOP, HSPT, and TACHS

COOP, HSPT, and TACHS are the abbreviated names of three different standardized tests given to eighth-grade students for parochial high school admission and placement. Here are the full names of the three tests:

COOP (Cooperative Admissions Examination)
HSPT (High School Placement Test)
TACHS (Test for Admission into Catholic High Schools)

Each high school decides which of these three tests (if any) applicants must take for admission and placement. (Some schools don't require scores for any of these tests.) Of the three tests, the HSPT has been in use the longest time and is by far the most widely used among the high schools. In contrast, the TACHS was new in 2005 and is given only to students applying in the New York State Diocese schools.

The three tests all use a multiple-choice question format to measure math, verbal, English language, and reasoning skills. Each of the three tests is divided into several sections, or subtests. However, each of the three tests contains its own distinct question types. The number of sections and questions varies as well.

Tips for COOP, HSPT, and TACHS Preparation

To make sure you've done all you can to prepare for the COOP, HSPT, or TACHS, follow the suggestions in this section.

Work on your weaknesses. After taking the COOP, HSPT, or TACHS diagnostic test in Part 2 of this book, you'll have a good idea which areas are your strongest, and which are your weakest. Use the time before your exam to focus on your weaknesses. Pay special attention to the lessons that will help you overcome them.

Practice under exam conditions. Be sure to take the practice tests in this book under testing conditions. Limit your time to the exam's time limits, and fill in the answer sheet (provided in this book) as you go, just as you will during the real exam. Also, don't take more than a 2- or 3-minute break between any two sections.

Try to reduce test-taking anxiety. Anxiety and panic are the two factors that can hurt your test performance the most. Although it's natural to be a bit nervous during an important test, you can minimize test anxiety by following these suggestions:

- On the day before the test, try not to talk about the test, or even think about it. Keep yourself busy with other activities.
- Just before the test, try stretching, deep breathing, or anything else that helps you stay calm.

The Day Before the Test

- Make sure you know how to get to the testing site and how long it will take to get there.
- Pack your testing materials: your admission card and identification, several sharp pencils with clean erasers, and a light sweater or jacket in case the testing room is cold.
- Try not to talk about the test or even think about it. Keep yourself busy with other activities.
- Go to bed a little early so that you get plenty of sleep.

The Morning of the Test

- Eat a light, healthy breakfast that includes some protein. Do not eat a heavy breakfast, or you might get sleepy during the test.
- Bring your testing materials. Make sure you are not wearing a digital watch that might beep. Do not bring any electronics into the testing room. Do not bring scratch paper.
- Just before the test, do some stretching or deep breathing to calm yourself and help you focus.

Give yourself a second chance to take the test (HSPT only). The HSPT is given twice each year—once in the spring and once in the fall. Because you're allowed to take the HSPT twice, take the test in the fall of eighth grade so you can take it again if you don't perform well the first time. (Students are allowed to take the COOP or TACHS only once, and so this strategy does not apply to those tests.)

Testing Procedures and Rules

The following procedures and rules apply to all three tests—the COOP, HSPT, and TACHS:

- The use of calculators is prohibited.
- For the COOP and HSPT, you may write in your test booklet. However, no additional scratch paper is allowed. For the TACHS, you may not write in your test booklet, but scratch paper will be provided.
- You mark your responses by filling in ovals ("bubbles") on the answer sheet provided. (Selections you mark in your test booklet are not scored.)
- The time allowed for each test section (subtest) is strictly enforced.
- During a timed test section (subtest), you are not allowed to work ahead to another test section or return to a previous section.
- No electronics may be brought into the testing room. This includes calculators, cell phones, and digital watches.
- Listen carefully to the test directions, and be sure that you understand the directions before you begin the exam.

Basic Test-Taking Strategies

The basic test-taking strategies you'll learn here apply to all three tests: the COOP, HSPT, and TACHS.

Answer each and every test question, even if you need to guess. There are no point deductions or penalties for incorrect answers. For any question, as long as you select a choice on your answer sheet, your chances of earning credit for a correct response are at least 1 in 4. On the other hand, if you leave a blank on your answer sheet, you have no chance of earning credit for a correct answer.

Use process of elimination to increase your odds. Don't expect to be 100% sure of your answer to every test question. If you're not sure what the correct answer is, narrow the choices by eliminating any choice you know is wrong. For the TACHS, since you may not mark on the test booklet, use your scratch paper for process of elimination. Write the letters of the answers on your scratch paper, and then cross off the letters of the choices you eliminate.

Answer easy questions first. The easiest questions generally appear first in a section, while the toughest ones tend to appear near the end. But there might be some easy questions toward the end as well. All test questions, easy and tough ones alike, are worth one point each. So make sure you answer all the easy questions first. Don't spend too much time dwelling on the "toughies"; earmark them, and then come back to them later if you have time.

Really use your pencil. Don't be reluctant to write all over the test booklet or scratch paper. (For the COOP and HSPT, you can write on the test booklet. For the TACHS, you cannot mark on the test booklet, but you will be given scratch paper.) Using a pencil helps you to focus on the question at hand and to think clearly. Use your pencil freely to

- make notes and write down key words
- underline or circle things (on the COOP or HSPT)
- use process of elimination to cross off answers you know are wrong
- do calculations
- solve equations

Note: On the TACHS, there's a separately timed portion of the Mathematics test that covers estimation. You will NOT be permitted to scratch out computations during this part.

Fill in your answer sheet as you go—even for answers you don't know. Mark your answer sheet for each question before you move ahead to the next question, even if you're not sure what the correct answer is. If a question stumps you, make your best guess, and then earmark the question (put a bold question mark next to the question number or write down the question number) to return to later if you have time. You can always erase your previous answer on your answer sheet.

Pace yourself. Time is a factor on every section of the COOP, HSPT, and TACHS. After every 5 minutes or so, check the time remaining during the current timed section. If you're falling behind pace, speed up a bit so that you have enough time to attempt every question in the section. If it looks like you're going to finish the section with time to spare, that's fine. You'll have time at the end to go back and check your work. (A great way to determine your best pace is to take the practice tests in Part 5 of this book under timed conditions.)

Study Plan for COOP, HSTP, and TACHS Preparation

COOP Study Plan (4 Weeks)

*This study plan is for a four-week preparation. It can easily be modified for either shorter or longer preparation times. Simply complete the tasks listed, in order, at whatever pace your preparation time requires.

Week One

■ Read the Introduction and Chapter 1: Overview.
■ Read and work through Chapter 2: The COOP.
■ Take the "COOP Diagnostic Test."

Week Two

■ Read and work through Chapter 5: Reading Comprehension.
■ Read and work through Chapter 7: Sentence and Paragraph Composition (read the entire chapter and do questions 11–20 on pages 138–140).
■ Read and work through Chapter 12: Mathematics—Concepts and Problem Solving.
■ Read and work through Chapter 13: Sequences (read the entire chapter and do questions 6–20 on pages 212–213).
■ Read and work through Chapter 14: COOP Quantitative Reasoning.

Week Three

■ Read and work through Chapter 6: Vocabulary (pages 115–117 overview; read "Necessary Element" Questions and Word-Grouping Questions on pages 118–120; do the "COOP Practice Questions" on pages 121–122).
■ Read and work through Chapter 8: Analogies (skip "HSPT Analogies—Step by Step" on pages 143–144; do questions 1–10 on pages 153–155).
■ Read and work through Chapter 9: Verbal Logic (page 159 overview; pages 160–166; do questions 11–20 on pages 167–168).
■ Read and work through Chapter 11: Review of Grammar and Writing Mechanics.
■ Read and work through Chapter 16: Review of Mathematics.

Week Four

■ Take "COOP Practice Test 1."
■ Review "COOP Practice Test 1" (even the questions you answered correctly).
■ Take "COOP Practice Test 2."
■ Review "COOP Practice Test 2" (even the questions you answered correctly).
■ Review the "Tips for Preparation, Testing Procedures and Rules," and "Basic Test-Taking Strategies" in Chapter 1.

HSPT Study Plan (4 Weeks)

*This study plan is for a four-week preparation time. It can easily be modified for either shorter or longer preparation times. Simply complete the tasks listed, in order, at whatever pace your preparation time requires.

Week One

■ Read the Introduction and Chapter 1: Overview.
■ Read and work through Chapter 3: The HSPT.
■ Take the "HSPT Diagnostic Test."

Week Two

■ Read and work through Chapter 5: Reading Comprehension.
■ Read and work through Chapter 7: Sentence and Paragraph Composition (read the entire chapter and do questions 1–10 on pages 137–138).

- Read and work through Chapter 12: Mathematics—Concepts and Problem Solving.
- Read and work through Chapter 13: Sequences (skip sections on letter and picture sequences; do questions 1–5 on pages 211–212).
- Read and work through Chapter 15: HSPT Quantitative Reasoning.

Week Three

- Read and work through Chapter 6: Vocabulary (skip "Necessary Element" Questions on pages 121–122; do the "HSPT Practice Questions" on pages 124–125).
- Read and work through Chapter 8: Analogies (skip "COOP Picture Analogies" and "COOP Word Analogies" on pages 153–155; do questions 11–20 on pages 155–156).
- Read and work through Chapter 9: Verbal Logic (pages 159–166; do questions 1–10 on pages 166–167).
- Read and work through Chapter 10: Usage and Writing Mechanics.
- Read and work through Chapter 16: Review of Mathematics.

Week Four

- Read and work through Chapter 11: Review of Grammar and Writing Mechanics.
- Take "HSPT Practice Test 1."
- Review "HSPT Practice Test 1" (even the questions you answered correctly).
- Take "HSPT Practice Test 2."
- Review "HSPT Practice Test 2" (even the questions you answered correctly).
- Review the "Tips for Preparation, Testing Procedures and Rules," and "Basic Test-Taking Strategies" in Chapter 1.

TACHS Study Plan (4 Weeks)

*This study plan is for a four-week preparation. It can easily be modified for either shorter or longer preparation times. Simply complete the tasks listed, in order, at whatever pace your preparation time requires.

Week One

- Read the Introduction and Chapter 1: Overview.
- Read and work through Chapter 4: The TACHS.
- Take the "TACHS Diagnostic Test."

Week Two

- Read and work through Chapter 5: Reading Comprehension.
- Read and work through Chapter 7: Sentence and Paragraph Composition.
- Read and work through Chapter 10: Usage and Writing Mechanics.
- Read and work through Chapter 12: Mathematics—Concepts and Problem Solving.

Week Three

- Read and work through Chapter 6: Vocabulary (read the introduction on page 115; read "Word-in Context Questions" on pages 117–118; read "Vocabulary—Heads Up!" on page 120; do the "TACHS Practice Questions" on page 127).
- Read and work through Chapter 11: Review of Grammar and Writing Mechanics.
- Read and work through Chapter 16: Review of Mathematics.

Week Four

- Take "TACHS Practice Test 1."
- Review "TACHS Practice Test 1" (even the questions you answered correctly).
- Take "TACHS Practice Test 2."
- Review "TACHS Practice Test 2" (even the questions you answered correctly).
- Review the "Tips for Preparation, Testing Procedures and Rules," and "Basic Test-Taking Strategies" in Chapter 1.

The COOP

The COOP (Cooperative Admissions Examination) is a multiple-choice test administered to eighth-grade students to help parochial high schools evaluate them for admission and placement. The test is developed by CTB/McGraw-Hill (an independent publisher), which makes the test available to the high schools for testing prospective students. The COOP is given twice a year—in October and November. Students may take the exam only once. Students or their parents should contact high schools directly for information about the school's COOP requirements and to obtain registration materials.

The COOP covers a variety of verbal, math, reading, language, and general reasoning skills. The exam is multiple choice only. However, the precise format (number and types of questions) of the test varies some-what from year to year. This book prepares the student for all the areas the test covers.

Format of the COOP

The COOP consists of approximately 180 multiple-choice questions. The total testing time is approximately 2 hours, 20 minutes. The COOP consists of seven subtests, which vary in the number of questions and time allotted. The following table shows the breakdown in time and the order in which the seven subtests often appear on the exam:

Subtest	Number of Questions	Time
Sequences	20	15 minutes
Analogies	20	7 minutes
Quantitative Reasoning	20	15 minutes
Verbal Reasoning—Words	20	15 minutes
Verbal Reasoning—Context	20	15 minutes
Reading and Language Arts	40	40 minutes
Mathematics	40	35 minutes

(*Note:* The table above indicates the format of some previously administered COOP exams. On your exam, the sequence of subtests, as well as the exact number of questions and time allowed on any subtest, might differ.)

All questions have four answer choices. In *odd*-numbered questions, the four answer choices are lettered A, B, C, and D. In *even*-numbered questions, the four answer choices are lettered F, G, H, and J. You're allowed to write in your test booklet. However, you must mark your answers on a separate answer sheet, which is provided. On this sheet, you fill in ovals with your pencil to indicate your selections. The testing service uses the answer sheet to determine your test scores. Next, we'll look at each of the seven subtests more closely.

Test 1: Sequences

This test measures your ability to recognize patterns in number, letter, and picture sequences. This subtest contains three distinct question types:

■ *Number Sequence* (continuing or completing a series or other pattern of numbers)
■ *Letter Sequence* (continuing or completing a series or other pattern of letters)
■ *Picture Sequence* (continuing or completing a series or other pattern of pictures)

Directions: Choose the response that continues the pattern or sequence.

1. A, D, G, J, _____
   A K
   B L
   C M
   D N

The correct answer is choice C. The alphabetic pattern skips two letters after each letter shown, so after J the pattern would skip K and L, and the next letter shown would be M.

2. Choose the response that completes the pattern in the chart below.

1	1
2	4
3	
4	16
5	25

   F 6
   G 7
   H 9
   J 12

The correct answer is choice H. The numbers in the column on the right are the squares of the numbers in the column on the left. $3^2 = 9$.

3. Choose the response that continues the pattern or sequence.

A ⇧

B ☆

C ⇩

D ☆☆

The correct answer is choice A. The pattern is two stars and an arrow, but each time the arrow repeats it alternates position from pointing up to pointing down. At this point in the sequence the last arrow was pointing down, so the next item should be an arrow pointing up.

Test 2: Analogies

This test measures your ability to understand relationships between objects and ideas presented in picture form.

Directions: Choose the picture that would go in the empty box so that the bottom two pictures are related in the same way the top two are related.

1.

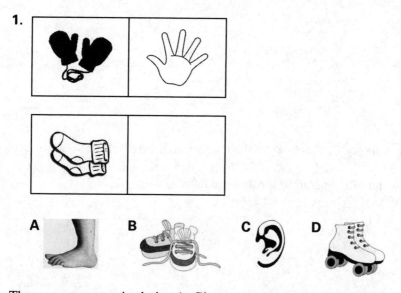

The correct answer is choice A. Gloves are worn on a person's hands, and socks are worn on a person's feet.

Test 3: Quantitative Reasoning

This test is designed to gauge your ability to think about numbers in ways that you normally wouldn't.

Here are the three types of questions you're most likely to see on this test (and the ones we'll cover in this book):

- *Missing Operation* (identifying the mathematical operation that links one number to another)
- *Geometric Fractions* (calculating fractions that represent darkened portions of geometric grids)
- *Scale Balancing* (comparing weighted number values based on a visual representation)

Directions: Find the fraction of the grid that is colored black.

1.

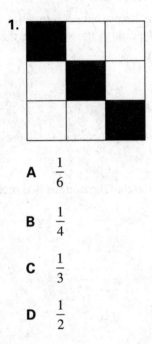

A $\dfrac{1}{6}$

B $\dfrac{1}{4}$

C $\dfrac{1}{3}$

D $\dfrac{1}{2}$

The correct answer is choice C. Three out of the nine squares are black, so $\dfrac{3}{9} = \dfrac{1}{3}$.

Directions: Find the missing operation for this equation:

2. $(4 + 3)$ _____ $3 = 21$
   F $+$
   G $-$
   H $\times$
   J $\div$

The correct answer is choice H. $4 + 3 = 7$ and $7 \times 3 = 21$.

Directions: Find what needs to be added to balance the second scale.

3.

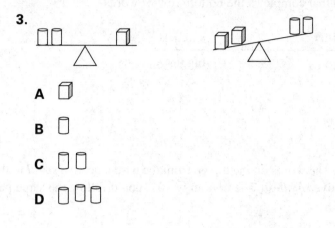

A

B

C

D

The correct answer is choice C. Since the first scale is balanced, two cans equal one box. The second scale has two boxes, so it would need four cans to balance. Two cans must be added.

Test 4: Verbal Reasoning—Words

This test measures your vocabulary, your ability to understand relationships between words, and your aptitude for recognizing key relationships among words in groups. The test contains a variety of question types. Here are the four types you're most likely to encounter (and the ones we'll cover in this book):

■ *Essential Element* (understanding inherent characteristics of the idea or object signified by a particular word)
■ *Analogy* (understanding relationships between words and groups of words)
■ *Verbal Classification—Exclusion* (identifying a word that doesn't belong in the same group with three others)
■ *Verbal Classification—Inclusion* (identifying a word that belongs in the same group with three others)

Directions: Find the word that is most similar to the underlined words.

1. <u>apple</u>   <u>orange</u>   <u>banana</u>
 A fruit
 B sweet
 C peach
 D cucumber

The correct answer is choice C. Each of the underlined words is a type of fruit. Among the answer choices, only *peach* is a type of fruit.

Directions: The words in the top row are related in a certain way. The words in the bottom row are related in the same way. Find the word that completes the bottom row of words.

2. small   smaller   smallest
_____

big   biggest

    F size
    G bigger
    H larger
    J medium

The correct answer is choice G. The words on the top go from the base adjective *small* to the comparative *smaller* and then to the superlative *smallest*. The bottom words should follow the same pattern from *big* to *bigger* to *biggest*.

Directions: Choose the word that does not belong with the others.

3.
    A run
    B jog
    C swim
    D skip

The correct answer is choice C. Each of the other three words describes a way to move on land with one's legs.

Directions: Choose the word that names a part of the underlined word.

4. <u>airplane</u>
    F fly
    G captain
    H ticket
    J wing

The correct answer is choice J. The wing is a part of an airplane.

Test 5: Verbal Reasoning—Context

This test measures your verbal logic and reasoning skills. This subtest contains only one question type, in which you evaluate conclusions based on a series of other statements.

Directions: Find the statement that is true according to the given information.

1. All dogs are mammals. Jake is a dog.
    A Jake is a Labrador retriever.
    B Jake is a mammal.
    C A mammal is a dog.
    D Cats are also mammals.

The correct answer is choice B. If Jake is a dog and all dogs are mammals, then Jake must be a mammal.

Test 6: Reading and Language Arts

This test measures your ability to understand and interpret ideas presented in brief reading passages. It also covers various aspects of English language use—diction (how words are used), grammar, and punctuation, as well as composing and organizing sentences and paragraphs.

The reading passages cover a wide variety of topics, ranging from social studies to the natural sciences to popular culture and current events. Passages are drawn from many different sources, including textbooks, magazine articles, speeches, novels, and short stories. To answer the questions, you won't need to know anything about the topics except what's in the passages.

Directions: The following is an excerpt from Mark Twain's *Life on the Mississippi*. Read the passage and answer questions 1–4.

The Mississippi is well worth reading about. It is not a commonplace river, but on the contrary is in all ways remarkable. Considering the Missouri its main branch, it is the longest river in the world—four thousand three hundred miles. It seems safe to say that it is also the crookedest river in the world, since in one part of its journey it uses up one thousand three hundred miles to cover the same ground that the crow would fly over in six hundred and seventy-five. It discharges three times as much water as the St. Lawrence, twenty-five times as much as the Rhine, and three hundred and thirty-eight times as much as the Thames. No other river has so vast a drainage basin: it draws its water supply from twenty-eight States and Territories; from Delaware, on the Atlantic seaboard, and from all the country between that and Idaho on the Pacific slope—a spread of forty-five degrees of longitude. The Mississippi receives and carries to the Gulf water from fifty-four subordinate rivers that are navigable by steamboats, and from some hundreds that are navigable by flats and keels. The area of its drainage basin is as great as the combined areas of England, Wales, Scotland, Ireland, France, Spain, Portugal, Germany, Austria, Italy, and Turkey; and almost all this wide region is fertile; the Mississippi valley, proper, is exceptionally so.

It is a remarkable river in this: that instead of widening toward its mouth, it grows narrower; grows narrower and deeper. From the junction of the Ohio to a point half way down to the sea, the width averages a mile in high water: thence to the sea the width steadily diminishes, until, at the "Passes," above the mouth, it is but little over half a mile. At the junction of the Ohio the Mississippi's depth is eighty-seven feet; the depth increases gradually, reaching one hundred and twenty-nine just above the mouth.

The difference in rise and fall is also remarkable—not in the upper, but in the lower river. The rise is tolerably uniform down to Natchez (three hundred and sixty miles above the mouth)—about fifty feet. But at Bayou La Fourche the river rises only twenty-four feet; at New Orleans only fifteen, and just above the mouth only two and one half.

An article in the New Orleans *Times-Democrat*, based upon reports of able engineers, states that the river annually empties four hundred and six million tons of mud into the Gulf of Mexico—which brings to mind Captain Marryat's rude name for the Mississippi—"the Great Sewer." This mud, solidified, would make a mass a mile square and two hundred and forty-one feet high.

The mud deposit gradually extends the land—but only gradually; it has extended it not quite a third of a mile in the two hundred years which have elapsed since the river took its place in history. The belief of the scientific people is that the mouth used to be at Baton Rouge, where the hills cease, and that the two hundred miles of land between there and the Gulf was built by the river.

[Source: Project Gutenberg. This text is in the public domain.]

1. Which of the following would make the best title for this passage?

   A Steamboat Life

   B The Mighty Mississippi

   C The Formation of the Mississippi Delta

   D American Rivers

The correct answer is choice B. The passage focuses on the remarkable characteristics of the Mississippi River.

2. Which of the following cities does the Mississippi River run through?

   F Natchez, Mississippi

   G Columbus, Ohio

   H Dallas, Texas

   J Gulfport, Mississippi

The correct answer is choice F. The passage states that the rise of the river "is tolerably uniform down to Natchez."

3. Here are two sentences from the passage:

The Mississippi is well worth reading about.

It is not a commonplace river, but on the contrary is in all ways remarkable.

Choose the answer that best combines the two sentences into one sentence.

   A The Mississippi is not a commonplace river.

   B The Mississippi is well worth reading about because it is in all ways remarkable.

   C The remarkable Mississippi is not commonplace.

   D Read about the Mississippi because it is not common.

The correct answer is choice B. Choice B includes the information from both sentences and correctly joins them with *because*.

4. Choose the sentence that is written correctly.

   F The Mississippi is the most longest river in the world.

   G The river rised only twenty-four feet at Bayou La Fourche.

   H A river often gets their name from a nearby city.

   J It discharges three times as much water as the St. Lawrence.

The correct answer is choice J. Choice F uses an incorrect superlative: *most longest* rather than simply *longest*. Choice G uses an incorrect verb form: *rised* instead of *rose*. Choice H uses a plural pronoun to refer to river: *their* instead of *its*.

Test 7: Mathematics

This test measures how well you understand and apply the rules and concepts of math, elementary algebra, and basic geometry. Some questions focus mainly on concepts, while others focus on solving quantitative problems accurately and efficiently.

Directions: The chart below shows students' grades on a spelling test. Use this information to answer questions 1 and 2.

Student Name	Test Score
Noah	96
Matthew	64
Isabella	92
Elena	76
Isaac	72
Gabriel	80
Alexia	88

1. How would you find the average test score for the class?
   A Add up all the scores and divide by 7.
   B Add the highest score and the lowest score and divide by 2.
   C Subtract the lowest score from the highest score.
   D Put the scores in order from least to greatest. The average is the middle number.

The correct answer is choice A. To find this average, you would find the total of the scores and divide by the number of students.

2. The total number of points a student could earn on the test is 100. If the spelling test had 25 questions and each question was worth 4 points, how many questions did Noah miss?
   F 1
   G 2
   H 3
   J 4

The correct answer is choice F. Since Noah made a 96 out of 100 and each question is worth 4 points, he must have missed only one question.

3. In a bowl of peanuts, pecans, and almonds, there are 15 peanuts, 6 pecans, and 11 almonds. If Kevin picks one nut out of the bowl without looking, what is the probability that he will pick a peanut?

   A $\dfrac{15}{17}$

   B $\dfrac{17}{32}$

   C $\dfrac{11}{21}$

   D $\dfrac{15}{32}$

The correct answer is choice D. There are 15 peanuts out of 32 total nuts, so the probability of choosing a peanut is $\dfrac{15}{32}$.

4. Kendra took a trip to the zoo, which was 20 miles away. If she drove without stopping, at an average speed of 40 miles per hour, how long did it take her to get to the zoo?

   F 15 minutes
   G 20 minutes
   H 30 minutes
   J 40 minutes

The correct answer is choice H. Use the formula distance = rate × time. 20 miles = 40 mph × t. Solve for t by dividing both sides of the equation by 40. $\frac{20}{40} = \frac{1}{2} = t$. Since time is expressed in hours, $\frac{1}{2}$ hour = 30 minutes.

How the COOP Is Scored

First, your *raw score* is calculated. This score is simply the total number of correct responses. No points are deducted for incorrect responses. Based on your raw score, a *scaled score* is then calculated according to a certain formula. You also receive a *percentile rank* for each subtest and for the test as a whole. A percentile rank indicates the percentage of test takers scoring lower than you. For example, a percentile ranking of 70 means that you scored higher than 70 percent of all other test takers.

The testing service reports your scaled score *and* your percentile rankings (but not your raw score) to the schools that need them to evaluate you. There is no "passing" or "failing" score for the COOP. Each school then decides for itself how to use the scores to compare you with other applicants.

The HSPT

The HSPT (High School Placement Test) is a multiple-choice test administered to eighth-grade students to help parochial high schools evaluate them for admission and placement. The test is developed and scored by Scholastic Testing Service (an independent publisher of standardized tests), which makes the test available to high schools for testing prospective students. The HSPT is given twice a year—in the spring and fall. Students have two (and only two) chances to take the exam—once in the fall and once in the following spring.

The basic HSPT consists of five multiple-choice sections, which cover a variety of verbal, math, reading, and language skills. A school can also choose to require an additional part—Mechanical Aptitude, Science, or Catholic Religion. Because only a small number of schools require an additional part score, this book does not cover these optional testing areas.

Students or their parents should contact parochial high schools directly for information about their HSPT requirements and to obtain registration materials.

Format of the HSPT

The HSPT consists of 298 multiple-choice questions. The questions are numbered sequentially from 1 through 298. The total testing time is 2 hours, 21 minutes. The HSPT consists of five parts, called "subtests," which vary in number of questions and time allotted. The following table shows the breakdown in time and the order that the five subtests usually appear on the exam:

Subtest	Number of Questions	Time
Verbal Skills	60	16 minutes
Quantitative Skills	52	30 minutes
Reading	62	25 minutes
Mathematics	64	45 minutes
Language	60	25 minutes

(*Note:* The table above indicates the format of previously administered HSPT exams. On your exam, the sequence of subtests, as well as the exact number of questions and time allowed on any subtest, might differ.)

Questions have four answer choices lettered A, B, C, and D, except for some questions on the Verbal Skills subtest that have only three answer choices, lettered A, B, and C. You're allowed to write in your test booklet. However, you must mark your answers on a separate answer sheet, which is provided. On this sheet you fill in ovals with your pencil to indicate your selections. The testing service uses the answer sheet to determine your test scores. Next, we'll look at each of the five HSPT subtests more closely.

Subtest 1: Verbal Skills

The Verbal Skills subtest measures your vocabulary, your ability to understand relationships between words, and your verbal reasoning skills. It contains a variety of question types, all mixed together. Here are the five types you're most likely to encounter (and the ones we'll cover in this book):

- *Synonym* (pairing words that are close in meaning)
- *Antonym* (pairing words that are opposite in meaning)
- *Analogy* (understanding relationships between words and word pairs)
- *Verbal Classification* (identifying a word that doesn't belong with others in the group)
- *Verbal Logic* (evaluating a conclusion based on two other statements)

Synonym
Each synonym question presents you with a word and four answer choices. You are to choose the answer choice that has the meaning closest to that of the original word. Be careful that you do not get confused between synonym and antonym questions.

1. Content most nearly means
  A satisfied
  B excited
  C bored
  D tired

The correct answer is choice A. Content means satisfied.

Antonym
Each antonym question presents you with a word and four answer choices. You are to choose the answer choice that has the *opposite* meaning of the original word. Be careful that you do not get confused between antonym and synonym questions. There might be a choice that is a perfect synonym for the word, but if you are supposed to find the antonym, that will be an incorrect choice.

2. Figurative means the *opposite* of
  A solid
  B literal
  C symbolic
  D truthful

The correct answer is choice B. Figurative means metaphorical or symbolic. The opposite of figurative is literal. Notice that a synonym of figurative (symbolic) is also a choice. Read the question carefully to avoid falling into a trap.

Analogy
Each analogy question presents you with a pair of words that have a relationship. Determine what that relationship is. Then you are presented with another word and four answer choices. You are to choose the answer choice that has the *same relationship* with the original word that the pair of words have.

3. Stanza is to poem as chapter is to
  A essay
  B song
  C story
  D book

The correct answer is choice D. A stanza is a section of a poem, just as a chapter is a section of a book.

Verbal Classification

In this question type, you are asked to examine a group of four words. Three of the words share something in common. You are to choose the word that does *not* belong with the other three.

4. Which word does *not* belong with the others?
  A hickory
  B maple
  C carrot
  D beech

The correct answer is choice C. Hickory, maple, and beech are all types of trees. Carrot is a vegetable and does not belong in that group.

Verbal Logic

In this question type, you are given three statements. The first two statements are true. You are to determine whether the third statement is true, false, or whether its truth cannot be determined with the information given.

5. Aaron left for school before Vivian. Evelyn left for school before Vivian. Evelyn left for school before Aaron. If the first two statements are true, the third is
  A true
  B false
  C uncertain

The correct answer is choice C. You know that both Aaron and Evelyn left before Vivian, but have no information about when Aaron and Evelyn left in relation to each other.

Subtest 2: Quantitative Skills

The Quantitative Skills subtest measures your understanding of the relationships between numbers and between geometric features, as well as your ability to combine numbers using the four basic operations—addition, subtraction, multiplication, and division. This subtest contains a variety of question types, all mixed together. Here are the four types you're most likely to encounter (and the ones we'll cover in this book):

  Number Sequence (continuing or completing a series or other pattern of numbers)
  Geometric Comparison (comparing areas, angles, or other geometric features)
  Nongeometric Comparison (comparing the values of numerical expressions)
  Number Manipulation (combining and simplifying numbers by applying the four basic operations)

1. What is the missing number in the following series: −5, −2, 1, 4, 7, ___, 13?

   A 8
   B 9
   C 10
   D 11

The correct answer is choice C. Each term is found by adding 3 to the previous term. 7 + 3 = 10.

2. Look at the temperature chart below.

Weekday	High Temperature (Celcius)
Monday	25.1
Tuesday	23.7
Wednesday	20.3
Thursday	21.8
Friday	21.5
Saturday	20.3
Sunday	22.6

Compare the following three expressions and then choose the correct answer.

   (a) the mode of the data set
   (b) the mean of the data set
   (c) the range of the data set
   A (a) < (b) < (c)
   B (c) < (b) < (a)
   C (b) < (a) < (c)
   D (c) < (a) < (b)

The correct answer is choice D. The mode of the data set is 20.3 because that temperature occurred twice and each of the others only occurred once. The mean of the data set is 22.2 (add the 7 values and divide by 7). The range of the data set is 4.8 because 25.1 − 20.3 = 4.8. Since 4.8 < 20.3 < 22.2, that means (c) < (a) < (b).

3. Examine the figure below and then choose the correct statement.

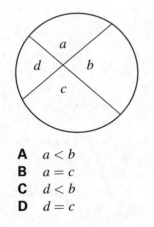

   A $a < b$
   B $a = c$
   C $d < b$
   D $d = c$

The correct answer is choice B. Vertical angles are equal.

4. What is $\frac{1}{2}$ of 20% of 72?

A 36

B 14.4

C 12.2

D 7.2

The correct answer is choice D. 20% of 72 = 14.4. $\frac{1}{2}$ of 14.4 = 7.2.

Subtest 3: Reading

The Reading subtest measures your ability to understand and interpret ideas presented in brief reading passages, as well as your ability to recognize the meanings of words in the context of brief phrases. This subtest is divided into two parts (we'll cover both in this book):

▨ *Reading Comprehension.* This first part consists of a series of brief reading passages (typically six or seven), each followed by several questions. The passages cover a wide variety of topics, ranging from social studies to the natural sciences to popular culture and current events. Passages are drawn from many different sources, including textbooks, magazine articles, speeches, novels, and short stories. To answer the questions, you won't need to know anything about the topics except what's in the passages.

▨ *Word-in-Context.* In this part, you determine the meaning of words as they're used in brief phrases.

Directions: The following is an excerpt from *Peter Pan* by James M. Barrie. Read the passage and answer questions 1–3.

After a few days' practice they could go up and down as gaily as buckets in a well. And how ardently they grew to love their home under the ground; especially Wendy. It consisted of one large room, as all houses should do, with a floor in which you could dig for worms if you wanted to go fishing, and in this floor grew stout mushrooms of a charming color, which were used as stools. A Never tree tried hard to grow in the center of the room, but every morning they sawed the trunk through, level with the floor. By tea time it was always about two feet high, and then they put a door on top of it, the whole thus becoming a table; as soon as they cleared away, they sawed off the trunk again, and thus there was more room to play. There was an enormous fireplace, which was in almost any part of the room where you cared to light it, and across this Wendy stretched strings, made of fiber, from which she suspended her washing. The bed was tilted against the wall by day, and let down at 6:30, when it filled nearly half the room; and all the boys slept in it, except Michael, lying like sardines in a tin. There was a strict rule against turning round until one gave the signal, when all turned at once. Michael should have used it also, but Wendy would have desired a baby, and he was the littlest, and you know what women are, and the short and long of it is that he was hung up in a basket.

It was rough and simple, and not unlike what baby bears would have made of an underground house in the same circumstances. But there was one recess in the wall, no larger than a bird cage, which was the private apartment of Tinker Bell. It could be shut off from the rest of the house by a tiny curtain, which Tink, who was most fastidious [particular], always kept drawn when dressing or undressing. No woman, however large, could have had a more exquisite boudoir [dressing room] and bed chamber combined. The couch, as she always called it, was a genuine Queen Mab, with club legs; and she varied the bedspreads according to what fruit blossom was in season. Her mirror was a Puss-in-Boots, of which there are now only three, unchipped, known to fairy dealers; the washstand was Pie-crust and reversible, the chest of drawers an authentic Charming the Sixth, and the carpet and rugs the best (the early) period of Margery and Robin. There was a chandelier from Tiddlywinks for the look of the thing, but of course she lit the residence herself. Tink was very contemptuous of the rest of the house, as indeed was perhaps inevitable, and her chamber, though beautiful, looked rather conceited, having the appearance of a nose permanently turned up.

[Source: Project Gutenberg. This text is in the public domain.]

1. The Never tree has the ability to
   A   grow at a fast rate
   B   spread through all the rooms
   C   function as a bed for the children
   D   warm the house at night

The correct answer is choice A. The passage describes how the children cut the tree to the floor and it grows about two feet by teatime.

2. Based on the passage, which of the following is most probably true?
   A   Michael is an infant.
   B   The floor of the house was made of woven grasses.
   C   Each child does his or her own laundry.
   D   Wendy sometimes treats Michael like a baby.

The correct answer is choice D. The passage says that Michael should sleep in the bed with the rest of the boys but that Wendy hangs him in a basket like a baby.

3. As it is used in the last sentence, the word <u>conceited</u> most nearly means
   A   pretty
   B   vain
   C   mean
   D   sad

The correct answer is choice B. *Conceited* means vain.

Subtest 4: Mathematics

The Mathematics subtest measures how well you understand and apply the rules and concepts of math, elementary algebra, and basic geometry. This subtest is divided into two parts:

- *Concepts* (understanding and applying the rules and terminology of math, elementary algebra, and basic geometry)
- *Problem Solving* (solving quantitative problems accurately and efficiently)

1. What is the area of a circle with a diameter of 6?
   A 6π
   B 9π
   C 12π
   D 36π

The correct answer is choice B. The formula for area of a circle is $A = \pi r^2$. If the diameter is 6, then the radius is 3. $3^2 = 9$, so the area is 9π.

2. What is the value of x if $2x + 7 = 10$?
   A   .5
   B   1
   C   1.5
   D   2

The correct answer is choice C. Subtract 7 from both sides of the equation to get $2x = 3$. Then divide both sides of the equation by 2 to find $x = 1.5$.

3. Find the sum of the distinct prime factors of 12.
   A   2
   B   3
   C   5
   D   8

The correct answer is choice C. The prime factorization of $12 = 2 \times 3 \times 3$. The *distinct* prime factors are 2 and 3. The sum of $2 + 3 = 5$.

4. The following chart shows the composition of a box of popsicles.

Cherry	6
Grape	5
Lime	4
Orange	5

What percent of the popsicles are grape?
   A   5
   B   10
   C   20
   D   25

The correct answer is choice D. There are 20 popsicles total, and 5 of them are grape. $\frac{x}{100} \times 20 = 5$.

Solve for x. Multiply both sides by 100 to eliminate the fraction. $20x = 500$. Divide both sides by 20 to isolate the variable. $x = 25$.

5. Lakeville Academy promises a student-teacher ratio of no more than 12:1. If there are 462 students in the school, what is the minimum number of teachers needed?

   A   38
   B   39
   C   40
   D   42

The correct answer is choice B. Divide 462 by 12 to get 38.5. Since the ratio must be no more than 12:1, the school will need 39 teachers.

Subtest 5: Language

The Language subtest covers various aspects of English language use—diction (how words are used), grammar, punctuation, capitalization, and spelling, as well as composing and organizing sentences and paragraphs. This subtest is organized into three parts:

- *Usage* (identifying word usage, capitalization, and punctuation mistakes in sentences)
- *Spelling* (identifying spelling errors in sentences)
- *Composition* (writing effective sentences, combining sentences, and composing effective paragraphs)

Usage

Usage questions typically give you three sentences and ask you to determine whether one of them has an error in usage, capitalization, or punctuation.

Directions: For the following question, choose the sentence that contains an error in punctuation, capitalization, or usage. If you find no mistakes, select choice D.

1.
- **A** My mother was born in Birmingham, Alabama.
- **B** My mother was born on May 24, 1965.
- **C** She attended The University of St. Thomas in Houston Texas.
- **D** No mistake.

The correct answer is choice C. That sentence has a punctuation error. There should be a comma between the city and state.

Spelling

Spelling questions typically present you with three sentences and ask you to determine whether one of them contains a spelling error.

Directions: For the following question, choose the sentence that contains a spelling error. If you find no spelling errors, select choice D.

2.
- **A** F. Scott Fitzgerald was truely one of the greatest American writers, and he received many awards.
- **B** It is usually necessary to separate your laundry into whites and colors.
- **C** I definitely need to do some maintenance on my bicycle.
- **D** No mistake.

The correct answer is choice A. The correct spelling is *truly*.

Composition

Composition questions may ask you to combine two phrases or sentences in the most effective way, or ask you about the best way to write a single sentence. They may also ask you about the best order of sentences in a paragraph or to supply the best transition from one idea to another.

3. Choose the best word or words to join the thoughts together.

My sister Kim likes to shop for clothes on the weekend, _____ I like to play with my friends.
A but
B and
C since
D that

The correct answer is choice A. Since these are contrasting ideas, you should join them with a contrasting conjunction such as *but*.

How the HSPT Is Scored

In scoring your HSPT exam, the testing service will first determine your *raw score*, which is simply the total number of correct responses (out of 298). No points are deducted for incorrect responses. Based on your raw score, the testing service will then calculate a *scaled score* from 200 to 800 points. The service will also determine your *percentile rank*, which indicates the percentage of test takers scoring lower than you. For example, a percentile ranking of 70 means that you scored higher than 70 percent of all other test takers.

The testing service reports your scaled score *and* your percentile rank (but not your raw score) to the schools that need them in order to evaluate you. There is no "passing" or "failing" score for the HSPT. Each school decides for itself how to use the scores to compare you with other applicants.

The TACHS

The TACHS (Test for Admission into Catholic High Schools) was introduced in 2005 and is given only to eighth-grade students applying for admission to high schools of the Archdiocese of New York and the Diocese of Brooklyn/Queens, to help these schools evaluate applicants for admission and placement. Like the COOP and HSPT, the TACHS is multiple choice only, and it's designed to measure a wide variety of math, verbal, English language, and reasoning skills. The TACHS is developed and scored by an independent testing service on behalf of the diocese.

Currently, the TACHS is given only once a year—in late October or early November. (A second testing date, in spring, might be added in the future.) Students may take the TACHS only once. Testing locations include many high schools throughout the New York Archdiocese and the Diocese of Brooklyn/Queens. The particular school where a student takes the exam has no bearing on which school(s) the student may choose to apply to for admission.

Format of the TACHS

The TACHS consists of approximately 200 multiple-choice questions. Some questions have four answer choices, while others have five answer choices. Expect the total testing time to be approximately two and a half hours.

The TACHS consists of five parts, or subtests. The following table shows the breakdown in time and one possible order in which the subtests might appear on the exam:

Subtest	Number of Questions (Approximate)	Time (Approximate)
Reading (Part 1): Vocabulary	20	10 minutes
Reading (Part 2): Comprehension	30	25 minutes
Written Expression	50	30 minutes
Mathematics	50	40 minutes
Ability	50	50 minutes

(*Note:* The table above indicates one possible format. On your exam, the sequence of subtests, as well as the exact number of questions and time allowed on any subtest, might differ.)

You are not allowed to make any marks in the test booklet itself. You will be provided with scratch paper to use for all portions of the test except a portion of the Mathematics subtest called *Estimation*. You must mark your answers on a separate answer sheet, which is provided. On this sheet, you fill in ovals with your pencil to indicate your selections. The testing service uses the answer sheet to determine your test scores. Note that on the TACHS, for odd-numbered questions the answer choices are labeled A, B, C, and D, while for even-numbered questions they are labeled J, K, L, and M.

Next, take a closer look at each of the five TACHS subtests—the skills and knowledge areas each subtest covers, the test directions, and examples of the kinds of questions to expect on each subtest.

Reading Subtest (Part 1): Vocabulary

This subtest is designed to measure your knowledge of words and their meanings. Each question consists of a brief phrase, part of which is underlined, along with four answer choices. (The underlined part might be a single word, or it might be a two-word phrase.) Your task is to find another word or phrase that is close in meaning to the underlined part, as it is used in the phrase. Underlined words include nouns, verbs, and adjectives.

Directions: For each question, decide which of the four answer choices is closest in meaning to that of the underlined word(s). Choose the best answer.

1. <u>Humid</u> weather
  A sunny
  B cold
  C pleasant
  D damp

The correct answer is choice D. The word *humid* means "damp or moist."

2. To <u>embark</u> on a trip
  J look forward to
  K begin
  L plan
  M return from

The correct answer is choice K. To *embark* is to commence or begin a course of action, usually a journey.

Reading Subtest (Part 2): Comprehension

This subtest measures your ability to understand and interpret ideas presented in a series of reading passages. Expect six to eight passages, each followed by several questions. Some questions test you simply on whether you recall and understand certain information in a passage. Most questions, however, require you to do more than that. Expect most questions to focus on the following:

  ▪ what certain information in the passage implies (but does not state explicitly)
  ▪ conclusions that can be drawn from particular information in the passage
  ▪ the author's main purpose or concern in the passage
  ▪ the passage's central idea, or theme
  ▪ the meaning of certain words as used in the passage
  ▪ the author's attitude, perspective, or opinion regarding a subject of the passage

TACHS reading passages vary in length. Although a length of three or four paragraphs is typical, you might encounter a brief, one-paragraph passage or one that runs nearly an entire page. The passages cover a wide variety of topics, ranging from social studies to the natural sciences to popular culture and current events.

Passages are drawn from many different sources, including textbooks, magazine articles, speeches, novels, and short stories, and perhaps even fables and poems. To answer the questions, you won't need to know anything about the topics except what's in the passages.

Following is a typical reading passage, which is an excerpt from a fictional work, along with five questions based on the passage. Try to answer each question, and then read the explanation that follows it.

Directions: Read the passage below. Then, for each question that follows it, decide which of the four answer choices is better than the others.

I am a single old woman. I should say at once, without being at all afraid of the name, I am an old maid; only that I am older than the phrase would express. The time was when I had my love-trouble, but, it is long and long ago. He was killed at sea when I was twenty-five.

I have all my life, since ever I can remember, been deeply fond of children. I have always felt such a love for them, that I have had my sorrowful and sinful times when I have fancied something must have gone wrong in my life—something must have been turned aside from its original intention I mean—or I should have been the proud and happy mother of many children, and a fond old grandmother this day.

Charley was my youngest brother, and he went to India. He married there, and sent his gentle little wife home to me to be confined, and she was to go back to him, and the baby was to be left with me, and I was to bring it up. It never belonged to this life. It took its silent place among the other incidents in my story that might have been, but never were. I had hardly time to whisper to her "Dead my own!" or she to answer, "Ashes to ashes, dust to dust! O lay it on my breast and comfort Charley!" when she had gone to seek her baby at Our Saviour's feet.

I went to Charley, and I told him there was nothing left but me, poor me; and I lived with Charley, out there, several years. He was a man of fifty, when he fell asleep in my arms. His face had changed to be almost old and a little stern; but, it softened, and softened when I laid it down that I might cry and pray beside it; and, when I looked at it for the last time, it was my dear, untroubled, handsome, youthful Charley of long ago.

1. The passage's narrator regrets that she _____.
   A moved to India
   B never bore children
   C was unkind to Charley's wife
   D never married

The correct answer is choice B. The second paragraph as a whole conveys the idea that the narrator wished she had borne children because she is so fond of them and that she can't help feeling that she would have had children of her own had she not taken some wrong turn in life.

2. The passage's narrator considers Charley to be _____.
   J pitiful
   K childlike
   L good-looking
   M even-tempered

The correct answer is choice L. Twice in the passage the narrator refers to Charley as "handsome."

3. What is probably true about the passage's narrator?
A She is older than a typical old maid.
B She was wild when she was younger.
C She is responsible for the deaths of her loved ones.
D Her vacation at sea ended in tragedy.

The correct answer is choice A. In the first paragraph, the narrator admits that she is an "old maid," and that she is even older than "the phrase [old maid] would express."

4. The narrator once loved a man who _____.
J left her for another woman
K died at the age of twenty-five
L refused to marry her
M died at sea

The correct answer is choice M. In the first paragraph, the narrator tells us that her lover was killed at sea when *she* was twenty-five years old.

5. Based on the passage, which of the following is most probably true?
A Charley sometimes fell asleep in the narrator's arms.
B Charley's wife fell ill on her trip from India.
C Charley died from heartache over his wife's death.
D Charley's wife died soon after their child died.

The correct answer is choice D. The narrator tells us that she "had hardly time to whisper to [Charley's wife]" . . . "when she had gone to seek her baby at Our Saviour's feet"—meaning that the death of Charley's wife occurred shortly after her baby's death.

Written Expression Subtest

The Written Expression subtest covers the following aspects of English composition:

- *Spelling* (recognizing words that are misspelled)
- *Capitalization* (recognizing words that should, or should not, be capitalized)
- *Punctuation* (end-of-sentence and other punctuation, including apostrophes and quotation marks)
- *Word Usage* (whether words are used properly in the context of particular sentences)
- *Expression* (recognizing clear, concise, and grammatically correct sentences)
- *Paragraph Composition* (transitions from one sentence to another, and paragraph organization and unity)

Each of these areas is covered by a different group of questions. Each group has its own directions.

Spelling

Each spelling question lists four words. Your job is to decide which word, if any, is spelled incorrectly. If there are no spelling errors, you should select the fifth choice *(No mistakes)*. Look for any of the following types of spelling errors: substituting an incorrect letter, reversing two consecutive letters, omitting a necessary letter, or adding an unnecessary letter.

Directions: Look for any mistake in spelling.

1.

    A brush
    B activety
    C package
    D automatic
    E *(No mistakes)*

The correct answer is choice B. The correct spelling is *activity*.

Capitalization

Each capitalization question includes three lines of text—either one or two sentences. Each line of text corresponds to a different answer choice. Your job is to decide which line of text, if any, contains a capitalization error. If there are no mistakes, you should select the fourth choice *(No mistakes)*. These questions cover capitalization of names, titles, dates, holidays, organizations, as well as other proper nouns.

Notice that each of the following examples involves one three-line sentence, which is typical of this question type.

Directions: Look for any mistake in capitalization.

1.

    A Noah received the Pulitzer prize in
    B honor of his outstanding report about
    C auto safety for *Newsweek* magazine.
    D *(No mistakes)*

The correct answer is choice A. The word *prize* is part of the proper noun *Pulitzer Prize*, and so it should be capitalized.

Punctuation

Like capitalization questions, each punctuation question includes three lines of text—either one or two sentences. Your job is to decide which line of text, if any, contains a punctuation mistake. If there are no mistakes, you should select the fourth choice *(No mistakes)*. These questions cover end-of-sentence punctuation, as well as the use of commas, colons, semicolons, apostrophes, quotation marks, and dashes.

Notice that each of the following examples involves one three-line sentence, which is typical of this question type.

Directions: Look for any mistake in punctuation.

1.

    A After Dad finished trimming the tree,
    B he joked, "You've all been naughty this
    C year, and so you won't get any presents".
    D *(No mistakes)*

The correct answer is choice C. At the end of the sentence, the quotation mark should come after the period, not before it.

2.

    J   Gary's a quick runner, and is on the

    K   school track team, while his brother Ken,

    L   who's very tall, is on the basketball team.

    M   *(No mistakes)*

The correct answer is choice J. The comma in the first line should be omitted.

Usage and Expression

In one type of usage-and-expression question, you read three lines of text and then decide which line contains a mistake in usage or expression. If you find no mistakes, you should select the fourth answer choice *(No mistakes)*. Notice that the two sentences in the following example are related, which is typical of this question type.

Directions: Look for any mistake in usage or expression.

1.

    A   Deciding which house to buy is difficult.

    B   Our house's location is very important because

    C   my family wants to live near by good schools.

    D   *(No mistakes)*

The correct answer is choice C. The two-word phrase *near by* is improper. One way to correct the mistake is simply to omit the word *by*.

Another type of usage-and-expression question provides four alternative versions of a sentence. Your job is to decide which one *best* expresses the sentence's idea. These questions focus mainly on the overall structure of a sentence, not on how specific words are used. The best version should be clear and concise, rather than wordy, repetitive, awkward, or confusing. The best version must also be free of grammatical errors. Unlike the other questions on the Language subtest, these questions do NOT include "No mistakes" as an answer option.

Directions: Choose the best way of expressing the idea.

1.

    A   Dru will arrive at the airport in less than one hour and then go straight to the hotel.

    B   At the airport, Dru will arrive in less than one hour and go straight to the hotel.

    C   Before going straight to the hotel, Dru will arrive at the airport in less than one hour.

    D   Dru will arrive at the airport, he'll arrive in less than one hour, and then he'll go straight to the hotel.

The correct answer is choice A. This version is clear, concise, and graceful. The problem with sentence B is that it conveys the idea that Dru will already be at the airport when he arrives there, which of course makes no sense. Sentence C is awkward and confusing. Sentence D is wordy and repetitive.

Paragraph Composition

For these questions, you first read a brief paragraph in which each sentence is numbered. Then, you answer two to four questions based on the paragraph. Most questions focus on sentence transitions, paragraph organization, unity (theme). Some questions may cover grammar, usage, and expression. Following is a typical paragraph, along with two questions based on the paragraph.

Directions: Questions 1 and 2 are based on the following paragraph. Choose the best answer to each question.

[1]One of the most famous Americans of the twentieth century was Dr. Martin Luther King, Jr. [2]Dr. King was born in 1929. [3]He lived most of his life in Atlanta, Georgia, where he was a minister. [4]Racial discrimination has been a problem in the United States from the time this nation was founded. [5]Dr. King is most well known for his advocacy of civil rights for African Americans. [6]His "I Have a Dream" speech is familiar to most Americans. [7]The speech has been an inspiration to people who share his desire for equal treatment of all people.

1. Which is the best way to combine sentences 2 and 3?
   A Since Dr. King was born in 1929, he lived most of his life in Atlanta, Georgia, where he was a minister.
   B Atlanta, Georgia was where Dr. King was born in 1929, was a minister, and lived most of his life.
   C Dr. King was born in 1929, but he lived most of his life in Atlanta, Georgia, where he was a minister.
   D Dr. King was born in 1929 and lived most of his life in Atlanta, Georgia, where he was a minister.

The correct answer is choice D. This version combines the two sentences in a logical and graceful way. In sentence A, the word *since* implies that Dr. King lived in Atlanta *because* he was born in 1929, which makes little sense. The way sentence B is constructed implies that Dr. King was born in Georgia, but the paragraph doesn't tell us this. Sentence C is wrong because using the word *but* to connect the ideas in the two sentences doesn't make sense.

2. Which sentence should be left out of this paragraph?
   J Sentence 1
   K Sentence 4
   L Sentence 5
   M Sentence 6

The correct answer is choice K. The topic of the paragraph is Dr. King. Sentence 4 is off this topic.

Mathematics Subtest

This test measures how well you understand and apply the rules and concepts of math, elementary algebra, basic statistics, and basic geometry. The Mathematics test is divided into two *separately timed* parts. One part covers the first three skill areas listed below, while a separate, shorter part covers the fourth area (estimation).

- *Understanding Concepts* (understanding principles and terminology of real numbers, math, elementary algebra, basic statistics, and basic geometry)
- *Problem Solving* (solving quantitative problems, including story problems, accurately and efficiently)
- *Data Interpretation* (analyzing and making computations based on quantitative information displayed in charts, tables, and graphs)
- *Estimation* (estimating answers to math problems by rounding numbers and applying your knowledge of place value, etc.)

Remember: No calculators are permitted during the TACHS, including the Mathematics test. Also, you are NOT permitted to use your pencil to answer estimation questions (a separately timed part of the Mathematics test).

All questions on the Mathematics subtest have four answer choices. Following are four examples of the types of questions you'll see on the long part of the Mathematics subtest, which focuses on concepts, problem solving, and data interpretation.

Directions: For each question, choose the best of the four answers given.

1. How many non-zero integers are less than 20 but greater than −22?
  A 21
  B 39
  C 40
  D 41

The correct answer is choice C. Don't count zero (0), 20, or −22. There are 19 integers from 1 to 19, and there are 21 integers from −21 to −1. The total number of integers in the range (not counting zero) is 40.

2. What is the area of a rectangle whose length is 4 meters (m) and whose width is one-third its length?
  J 5 m²
  K $\dfrac{16}{3}$ m²
  L 4 m²
  M $\dfrac{15}{4}$ m²

The correct answer is choice K. The rectangle's width is $\dfrac{16}{3}\left(\dfrac{1}{3}\times 4\right)$. To find the rectangle's area, multiply its width by its length: $\dfrac{4}{3}\times 4 = \dfrac{16}{3}$.

3. What is the value of x if $\dfrac{4}{x}+3=\dfrac{1}{x}$ is a true statement?
  A −1
  B $\dfrac{1}{3}$
  C $\dfrac{3}{10}$
  D $\dfrac{1}{2}$

The correct answer is choice A. You can find the correct answer by plugging each answer choice in turn into the equation. (With the correct value, the equation will hold true.) Or, you can solve the problem algebraically by isolating x on one side of the equation (first multiply all terms by x, as shown here):

$$\frac{4}{x} + 3 = \frac{1}{x}$$
$$4 + 3x = 1$$
$$3x = -3$$
$$x = -1$$

4. The following graph shows the ethnic composition of the population of State X:

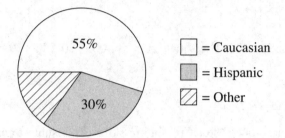

What is the ratio of State X's Hispanic population to its Caucasian population?
  J   6:11
  K   2:5
  L   3:7
  M   2:1

The correct answer is choice J. Hispanics and Caucasians account for 30% and 55%, respectively, of State X's population. The ratio is 30 to 55, which you can express as the fraction $\frac{30}{55}$, or $\frac{6}{11}$.

Now, look at some examples of estimation questions (a separately timed part of the Mathematics test).

Directions: For each question, estimate the answer; do not try to compute exact answers. You must do all work in your head; no pencil work is allowed.

1. The closest estimate of $909 - 797$ is ____.
  A   100
  B   125
  C   150
  D   175

The correct answer is choice A. Round 909 to 900, and round 797 to 800. $900 - 800 = 100$. Among the four choices, choice A provides the closest estimate: 100.

2. The closest estimate of 86×34 is ____.

J   2,500
K   2,700
L   3,300
M   3,400

The correct answer is choice K. Round 86 up to 90, round 34 down to 30, and then multiply: $90 \times 30 = 2,700$. Among the four choices, choice K provides the closest estimate: 2,700.

3. The closest estimate of $\sqrt{360}$ is ____.

A   6
B   12
C   20
D   36

The correct answer is choice C. Round 360 to 400. The square root of 400 is 20. ($20 \times 20 = 400$.)

Ability Subtest

The Ability subtest is designed to measure your abstract reasoning skills. This subtest consists of three distinct groups of "items" (they're not really questions):

▪ *Figure Classification* (recognizing common characteristics among figures)
▪ *Figure Matrices* (identifying how a figure is changed in a vertical column, how it is changed in a horizontal column, and predicting how the final figure will appear)
▪ *Spatial Reasoning* (recognizing how a folded paper with holes will appear when unfolded)

Except for the directions, the Ability subtest consists entirely of pictures. You've probably never seen a test like this in school (and you wouldn't see similar items on either the HSPT or the COOP). Let's look more closely at each of the three question types.

Figure Classification

In this type of question, your job is to examine three figures, determine how they are alike, and then decide which of five other figures is like the first three in the same ways. (Each item comes with five answer choices.) In looking for key similarities among the figures, you'll need to focus on features such as:

▪ how many sides or line segments they consist of
▪ whether a figure consists of straight or curved lines
▪ whether they are hollow, striped, or shaded
▪ the direction in which each figure "points"
▪ how a figure is divided into segments

Following are four typical examples.

Directions: The first three figures are alike in certain ways. From the five answer choices, select the figure that is most like the first three figures in the same ways.

1.

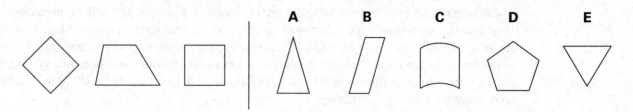

The correct answer is choice B. All figures have four sides.

2.

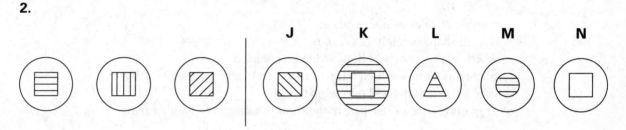

The correct answer is choice J. At the center of each circle is a small striped square.

3.

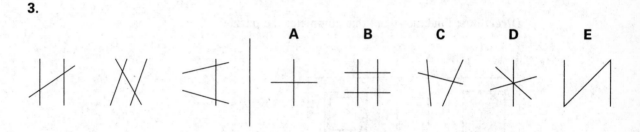

The correct answer is choice C. Each figure consists of three line segments, one of which intersects both of the other two line segments.

4.

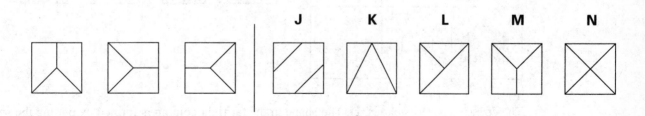

The correct answer is choice M. A "Y" divides each square into three sections.

Figure Matrices

In this type of question, you are basically putting together a puzzle. You will be presented with a matrix, or grid, of three rows and three columns of shapes, with the bottom right one missing. Your job is to figure out what the final shape will look like. The figures change according to a pattern going from left to right across the rows. They also change according to a pattern going from top to bottom down the columns. This gives you two ways to figure out what the final figure will look like. In handling these test items, you'll need to focus on changes involving:

- the addition or deletion of a certain feature
- overall size
- number of sides or line segments
- overall shape (straight or curved)
- whether the figure is hollow, striped, or shaded
- orientation (the direction a figure faces, vertically and horizontally)
- how a figure is divided into segments
- proportion (size of one part of the figure compared to another part)

Following are two typical examples.

Directions: Find the figure that completes the puzzle.

1.

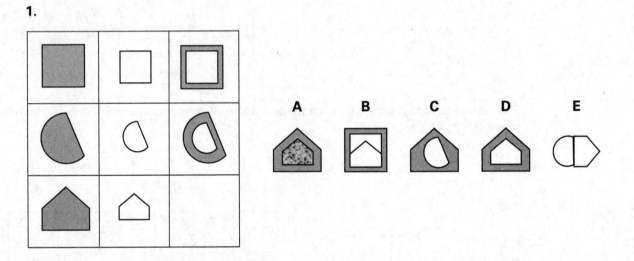

The correct answer is choice D. The shape in the far right column is formed by putting the smaller white center shape within the solid gray shape from the left column.

2.

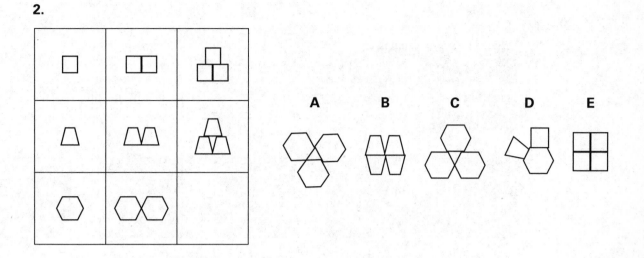

The correct answer is choice C. The figures in the rows change by adding additional identical pieces, first one on the right of the original and then another centered on top of the first two.

Spatial Reasoning (Paper Folding)

This is probably the most unusual test item on the TACHS.

Directions: In the top line of pictures, a piece of paper is folded, and one or more holes are punched through all layers. Select the figure in the bottom row that shows how the punched paper would appear unfolded.

Now, look carefully at the following example. Notice that the first picture in the top row shows how the paper is folded in half (the arrow indicates the direction of folding), while the next picture in the top row shows the folded paper (the shaded half) and where two holes are punched in it. The bottom row shows five alternative pictures; one of the five pictures correctly shows how the unfolded, punched paper would appear. The other four alternatives are inaccurate. The explanation following the example tells you how to figure out which picture is accurate.

1.

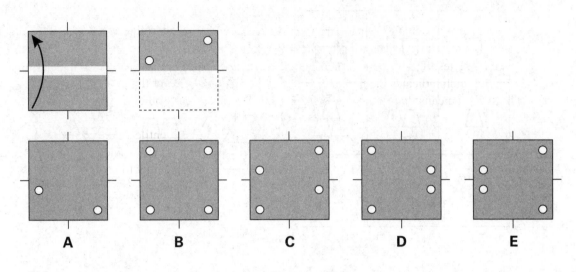

The correct answer is choice E. Two holes are punched through two layers, and so there are *four* holes altogether in the unfolded paper. You can eliminate choice A, which shows only two holes. Because the paper was folded up, each pair of matching holes is aligned vertically. The bottom half of the unfolded paper should appear as a *mirror image* of the top half. The left-hand holes are near the center, and the right-hand holes are near the outer edges. Choice E accurately shows the two mirror images.

A more challenging paper-folding question might involve folding a piece of paper *twice*. In the next example, notice that the second picture in the top row shows the paper folding in half again, while the third picture shows one hole punched through all *four* layers. The explanation that follows the example tells you how to handle it.

2.

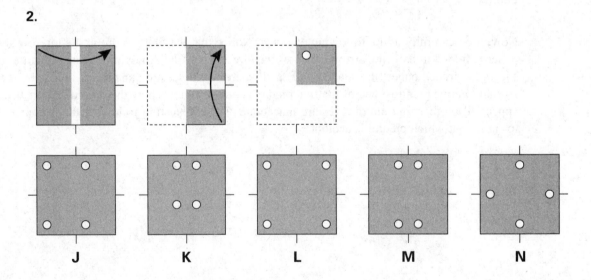

The correct answer is choice M. Because the paper is folded in half twice, the hole is punched through four layers. As a result, there are four holes. You can eliminate choice N, which shows *five* holes. The hole is punched near the paper's edge, but away from the corner, and so each of the four holes will be near an edge but not a corner. Choice M accurately shows the location of all four holes. Choices J and L are wrong because they show holes near the corner, and choice K is wrong because it shows holes near the center.

How the TACHS Is Scored

In scoring your TACHS exam, the testing service will first determine your *raw score*, which is simply the total number of correct responses. No points are deducted for incorrect responses. Based on your raw score, the testing service will then calculate a *scaled score*. The service will also determine your *percentile rank*, which indicates the percentage of test takers scoring lower than you. For example, a percentile ranking of 70 means that you scored higher than 70 percent of all other test takers.

The testing service reports your scaled score *and* your percentile rank (but not your raw score) to the schools that need them in order to evaluate you. As with the HSPT and COOP, there is no "passing" or "failing" score for the TACHS. Each school decides for itself how to use the scores to compare you with other applicants.

DIAGNOSTIC TESTS

COOP DIAGNOSTIC TEST

This COOP diagnostic test consists of 45 questions and is divided into seven parts, just like the actual COOP exam. Keep in mind, however, that the actual COOP exam is much longer (approximately 180 questions altogether).

Mark your answers where indicated on the Answer Sheet. Do not limit your time on this diagnostic test, and do not hurry through it. Instead, pay attention to which types of questions you find especially easy, and which ones you find difficult. After completing the test, read the answers and explanations that follow it. Then, use the rest of this book to prepare for the types of questions you find most difficult.

COOP DIAGNOSTIC TEST

Answer Sheet

Directions: For each answer that you select, blacken the corresponding oval on this sheet.

Sequences

1. Ⓐ Ⓑ Ⓒ Ⓓ
2. Ⓕ Ⓖ Ⓗ Ⓙ
3. Ⓐ Ⓑ Ⓒ Ⓓ
4. Ⓕ Ⓖ Ⓗ Ⓙ
5. Ⓐ Ⓑ Ⓒ Ⓓ

Analogies

1. Ⓐ Ⓑ Ⓒ Ⓓ
2. Ⓕ Ⓖ Ⓗ Ⓙ
3. Ⓐ Ⓑ Ⓒ Ⓓ
4. Ⓕ Ⓖ Ⓗ Ⓙ
5. Ⓐ Ⓑ Ⓒ Ⓓ

Quantitative Reasoning

1. Ⓐ Ⓑ Ⓒ Ⓓ
2. Ⓕ Ⓖ Ⓗ Ⓙ
3. Ⓐ Ⓑ Ⓒ Ⓓ
4. Ⓕ Ⓖ Ⓗ Ⓙ
5. Ⓐ Ⓑ Ⓒ Ⓓ

Verbal Reasoning—Words

1. Ⓐ Ⓑ Ⓒ Ⓓ
2. Ⓕ Ⓖ Ⓗ Ⓙ
3. Ⓐ Ⓑ Ⓒ Ⓓ
4. Ⓕ Ⓖ Ⓗ Ⓙ
5. Ⓐ Ⓑ Ⓒ Ⓓ

Verbal Reasoning—Context

1. Ⓐ Ⓑ Ⓒ Ⓓ
2. Ⓕ Ⓖ Ⓗ Ⓙ
3. Ⓐ Ⓑ Ⓒ Ⓓ
4. Ⓕ Ⓖ Ⓗ Ⓙ
5. Ⓐ Ⓑ Ⓒ Ⓓ

Reading and Language Arts

1. Ⓐ Ⓑ Ⓒ Ⓓ
2. Ⓕ Ⓖ Ⓗ Ⓙ
3. Ⓐ Ⓑ Ⓒ Ⓓ
4. Ⓕ Ⓖ Ⓗ Ⓙ
5. Ⓐ Ⓑ Ⓒ Ⓓ
6. Ⓕ Ⓖ Ⓗ Ⓙ
7. Ⓐ Ⓑ Ⓒ Ⓓ
8. Ⓕ Ⓖ Ⓗ Ⓙ
9. Ⓐ Ⓑ Ⓒ Ⓓ
10. Ⓕ Ⓖ Ⓗ Ⓙ

Mathematics

1. Ⓐ Ⓑ Ⓒ Ⓓ
2. Ⓕ Ⓖ Ⓗ Ⓙ
3. Ⓐ Ⓑ Ⓒ Ⓓ
4. Ⓕ Ⓖ Ⓗ Ⓙ
5. Ⓐ Ⓑ Ⓒ Ⓓ
6. Ⓕ Ⓖ Ⓗ Ⓙ
7. Ⓐ Ⓑ Ⓒ Ⓓ
8. Ⓕ Ⓖ Ⓗ Ⓙ
9. Ⓐ Ⓑ Ⓒ Ⓓ
10. Ⓕ Ⓖ Ⓗ Ⓙ

COOP DIAGNOSTIC TEST

Sequences

Directions: For questions 1–5, choose the answer that will best continue the sequence or pattern.

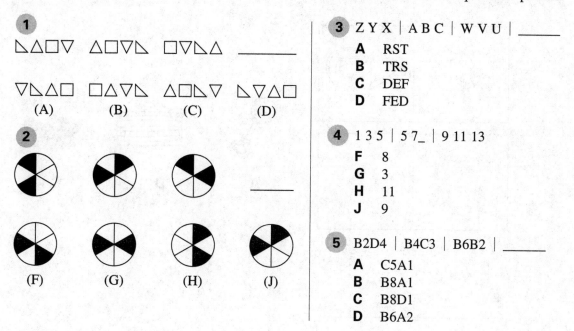

1

△△□▽ △□▽△ □▽△△ _____

▽△△□ □△▽△ △□△▽ △▽△□
(A)   (B)   (C)   (D)

2

(F)   (G)   (H)   (J)

3 Z Y X | A B C | W V U | _____

A RST
B TRS
C DEF
D FED

4 1 3 5 | 5 7 _ | 9 11 13

F 8
G 3
H 11
J 9

5 B2D4 | B4C3 | B6B2 | _____

A C5A1
B B8A1
C B8D1
D B6A2

Analogies

Directions: For questions 1–5, the two upper pictures are related in some way. Select a picture that fills in the space so that the two lower pictures are related in the same way.

1

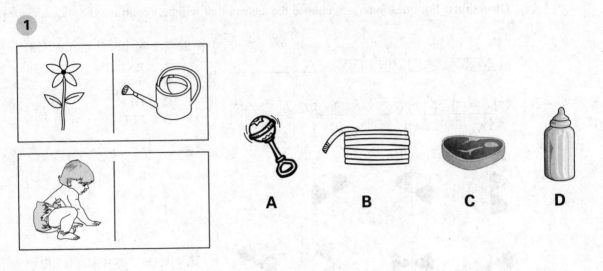

2

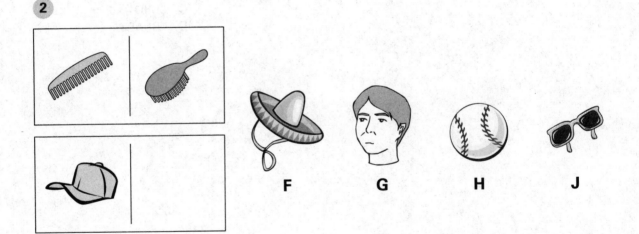

Analogies *(continued)*

3

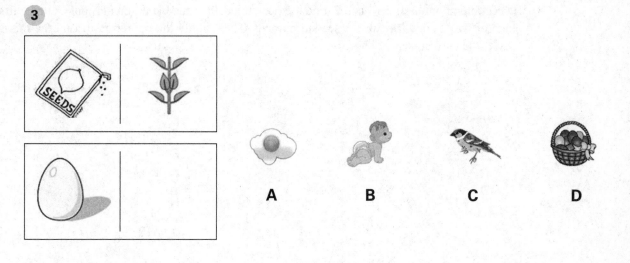

A   **B**   **C**   **D**

4

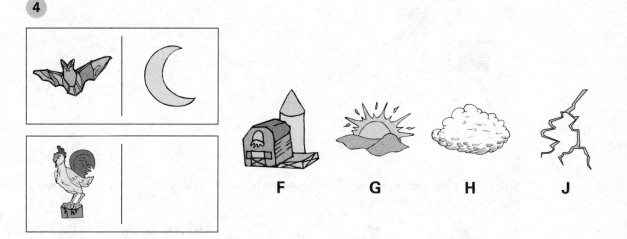

F   **G**   **H**   **J**

5

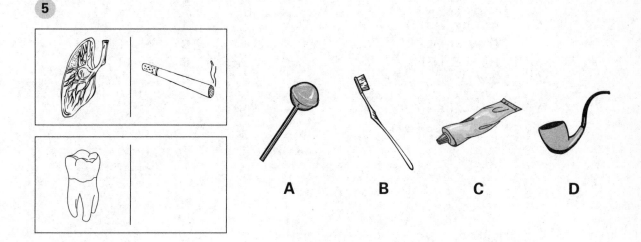

A   **B**   **C**   **D**

Quantitative Reasoning

Directions: For questions 1 and 2, find the operation (fill in the blank) that is applied to the first number in each of two pairs to obtain the second number. Then, apply the operation to find the missing number. Select the correct answer choice.

1 $7 \rightarrow \underline{} \rightarrow 4$
    $12 \rightarrow \underline{} \rightarrow 9$
    $4 \rightarrow \underline{} \rightarrow ?$

    A 7
    B 13
    C 1
    D 6

2 $1 \rightarrow \underline{} \rightarrow 6$
    $4 \rightarrow \underline{} \rightarrow 24$
    $\dfrac{3}{2} \rightarrow \underline{} \rightarrow ?$

    F 9
    G 18
    H $\dfrac{25}{2}$
    J 12

Directions: For question 3, find the fraction of the grid that is darkened.

3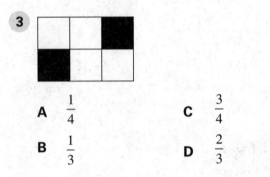

    A $\dfrac{1}{4}$ **C** $\dfrac{3}{4}$

    B $\dfrac{1}{3}$ **D** $\dfrac{2}{3}$

Directions: For questions 4 and 5, examine the balanced scale. Then, select another arrangement of objects that would also balance the scale.

4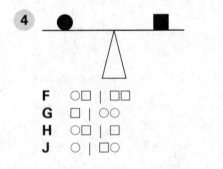

    F ○□ | □□
    G □ | ○○
    H ○□ | □
    J ○ | □○

5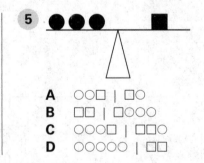

    A ○○□ | □○
    B □□ | □○○○
    C ○○○□ | □□○
    D ○○○○○ | □□

Verbal Reasoning—Words

Directions: For questions 1 and 2, find the word that names a necessary element of the underlined word.

1 <u>calendar</u>
- **A** schedule
- **B** time
- **C** month
- **D** year

2 <u>magnet</u>
- **F** magnifying
- **G** attracting
- **H** combining
- **J** experimenting

Directions: In question 3, the words in the top line are related in some way. The words in the bottom line should be related in the same way. Find the word that completes the bottom row of words.

3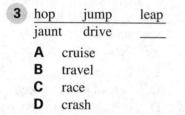
- **A** cruise
- **B** travel
- **C** race
- **D** crash

Directions: For question 4, find the word that does not belong with the others.

4
- **F** knead
- **G** chop
- **H** stir
- **J** bake

Directions: For question 5, find the word that is most like the underlined words.

5 <u>create</u> <u>make</u> <u>produce</u>
- **A** invent
- **B** act
- **C** write
- **D** illustrate

Verbal Reasoning—Context

Directions: For questions 1–5, find the statement that is most probably true according to the given information.

1 Peter is taller than Oliver, but Oliver is older than Peter.

- **A** Peter is still growing.
- **B** Oliver is heavier than Peter.
- **C** Oliver is shorter than most people his age.
- **D** Peter is younger than Oliver.

2 Mosquitoes are attracted to bright lights. Tim keeps his kitchen light on at night.

- **F** Tim's house attracts more mosquitoes than his neighbors' houses.
- **G** There are few mosquitoes near Tim's house during the daytime.
- **H** There are mosquitoes outside Tim's kitchen window at night.
- **J** Mosquitoes are not attracted to Tim's bedroom window.

3 Scott feels sleepy and tired in the morning unless he has coffee. Scott did not drink coffee this morning.

- **A** Scott is feeling tired.
- **B** Scott slept very well last night.
- **C** Scott did not want to drink coffee today.
- **D** Scott is out of coffee.

4 Yoga class meets on Monday, Wednesday, and Friday. Yoga class also meets on either Saturday or Sunday, but not both. The week begins on Sunday, and today is Thursday. Yoga class has met twice this week.

- **F** Yoga class will not meet this weekend.
- **G** Yoga class will meet this Saturday.
- **H** Yoga class met this Tuesday.
- **J** Yoga class met this Sunday.

5 The air is cold. I see children building a snowman.

- **A** There is snow on the ground.
- **B** It is snowing.
- **C** School is not in session.
- **D** It is too cold to play outside.

Reading and Language Arts

Directions: Questions 1–10 are based on a reading passage, additional sentences, and a brief essay. For each question, select the best answer.

Questions 1–5 are based on the following passage:

The main function of a building is to provide a safe shelter and living space. Beyond this function, however, what should be the goal of architecture? To impress people? To glorify the architect or owner? To create something new for its own sake? An increasing number of architects today—myself included—believe that the main goal should be to elevate the human spirit. Architecture designed with this goal in mind is known as *organic* architecture. While the "organic" label is new, the principle is centuries old. The current revival of organic architecture actually began in the middle of the twentieth century with the work of architects such as Frank Lloyd Wright and Spain's Antonio Gaudi.

Organic architecture should not be confused with *green* architecture, in which the primary design concern is with a structure's environmental cost in terms of the natural resources used to build and maintain it. Also, unlike *feng shui* design, which dictates that a building should conform to certain rules of proportion and direction, there's no objective test for whether a building is organic. If people feel more alive in and around it, or even just looking at pictures of it, then it passes as organic.

1 In the passage, the author's main purpose is to

A compare various forms of architecture

B explain the meaning of "organic architecture"

C describe a typical organic building

D criticize green architecture

2 The author of the passage is

F an architect

G a student

H a professional writer

J the owner of an organic house

3 A building designed to use energy only from the sun is an example of

A organic architecture

B natural architecture

C green architecture

D elemental architecture

4 Frank Lloyd Wright

F incorporated *feng shui* principles into his designs

G was a strong advocate of green architecture

H worked with architect Antonio Gaudi in designing houses

J helped revive the concept of organic architecture

5 Which of the following would probably be most important to an architect applying *feng shui* to a building's design?

A how to heat and cool the inside of the building

B whether the building looks like nearby structures

C a room's ceiling height compared to its length and width

D the personal tastes and preferences of the building's owner

Reading and Language Arts *(continued)*

6 Choose the sentence that is written correctly.

   F Organic buildings are often designed to be "green" as well.

   G Organic buildings are often also designed as "green," too.

   H Organic buildings are designed to often be "green" as well.

   J Frequently, organic buildings are often designed to be "green."

7 Choose the sentence that is written correctly.

   A Frank Lloyd Wright, among all modern architects, was more influential than them all.

   B More influential than any modern architect was architect Frank Lloyd Wright.

   C More than any modern architect, architect Frank Lloyd Wright was influential.

   D Frank Lloyd Wright was more influential than any other modern architect.

Here is a brief essay a student wrote about energy conservation. There are a few mistakes that need correcting. Read the essay, and then answer questions 8–10.

[1]Electricity is expensive. [2]Where I live, electricity is made by burning coal. [3]Burning coal is a major cause of global warming. [4]To save electricity, we turn off the lights when we don't need them. [5]Also we use extra blankets at night instead of turning up the heater.

8 Which is the best way to combine sentences 2 and 3?

   F Where I live, electricity is made by a major cause of global warming: burning coal.

   G Although where I live electricity is made by burning coal, burning coal is a major cause of global warming.

   H Electricity is made by burning coal where I live, and burning coal is a major cause of global warming.

   J Where I live, electricity is made by burning coal, which is a major cause of global warming.

9 Which sentence contains a punctuation error?

   A sentence 2

   B sentence 3

   C sentence 4

   D sentence 5

10 Which of the following is the best concluding sentence for the essay?

   F Also, our windows have two layers of glass, which helps keep the cold out.

   G It would be even better if we could use solar power in our house.

   H This way, my family saves money and helps the environment.

   J Although we can afford lots of electricity, we try to conserve it, anyway.

Mathematics

Directions: Choose the best answer to each question.

1 Five percent of $\frac{1}{5}$ is equal to

A $\frac{1}{25}$

B $\frac{1}{10}$

C 1

D $\frac{1}{100}$

2 $34 - 12 \times 3 + 2 =$

F 68

G 0

H 7

J -4

3 How many non-zero even integers are less than 20 but greater than -22?

A 21

B 20

C 19

D 39

4 Find the measure of interior angle *BCA* in the figure below.

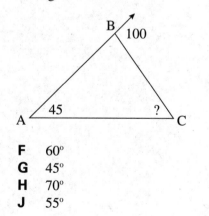

F 60°

G 45°

H 70°

J 55°

5 $\frac{13^4}{13^3} =$

A 169

B 13

C 26

D $\frac{1}{13}$

6 Kendra swam one lap in *S* seconds, faster than Paul by 4 seconds. Which of the following represents the average lap time of the two swimmers?

F $S + 2$

G $S - 2$

H $S - 1$

J $S + 4$

7 If *x* and *y* are consecutive non-zero integers, then it must be true that

A xy is odd

B $x^2 + y$ is even

C $x + xy$ is odd

D $x + y$ is odd

8 What is the area of a rectangle whose length is 4 meters and whose width is one-third its length?

F 5 m²

G $\frac{16}{3}$ m²

H 4 m²

J $\frac{15}{4}$ m²

Mathematics (continued)

9 For which value of x does $\dfrac{4}{x} + 3 = \dfrac{1}{x}$?

  A -1

  B $\dfrac{1}{3}$

  C $\dfrac{3}{10}$

  D $\dfrac{1}{2}$

10 Among 10 playing cards, two are spades, one is a heart, three are diamonds, and the rest are clubs. What is the probability of randomly selecting a card that is a club?

  F $\dfrac{3}{10}$

  G $\dfrac{1}{3}$

  H $\dfrac{2}{5}$

  J $\dfrac{1}{2}$

COOP DIAGNOSTIC TEST

Answer Key

Sequences
1. **A**
2. **H**
3. **C**
4. **J**
5. **B**

Analogies
1. **D**
2. **F**
3. **C**
4. **G**
5. **A**

Quantitative Reasoning
1. **C**
2. **F**
3. **B**
4. **F**
5. **B**

Verbal Reasoning—Words
1. **B**
2. **G**
3. **C**
4. **J**
5. **A**

Verbal Reasoning—Context
1. **D**
2. **H**
3. **A**
4. **G**
5. **A**

Reading and Language Arts
1. **B**
2. **F**
3. **C**
4. **J**
5. **C**
6. **F**
7. **D**
8. **J**
9. **D**
10. **H**

Mathematics
1. **D**
2. **G**
3. **C**
4. **J**
5. **B**
6. **F**
7. **D**
8. **G**
9. **A**
10. **H**

COOP DIAGNOSTIC TEST

Answers and Explanations

Sequences

1. **A** From frame to frame, each object moves to the left one position. (The object farthest to the left jumps to the far right.)

2. **H** From one frame to the next, each of the two shaded segments rotates in a clockwise direction by one position.

3. **C** Continuing from the first frame to the third (skipping the second frame), the sequence lists letters of the alphabet in reverse order (beginning with Z). The second frame lists letters in order beginning with A, and so it's logical for this sequence to continue (beginning with D) in the fourth frame.

4. **J** Within each frame, 2 is added to yield the next number.

5. **B** Each frame contains four elements. The first element (B) remains constant from frame to frame. Otherwise, corresponding elements run in sequential order from one frame to the next: 2-4-6-8 (second element), D-C-B-A (third element), and 4-3-2-1 (fourth element).

Analogies

1. **D** To nurture a flower, you water it using a watering can. Similarly, to nurture an infant, you give it milk using a baby bottle.

2. **F** A comb serves the same purpose as a hairbrush but generally passes through fewer strands of hair. Similarly, a baseball cap serves the same essential function as a sombrero but covers less area.

3. **C** Seeds, when properly nurtured, will produce a plant. Similarly, an egg, when properly nurtured, will produce a bird.

4. **G** Bats generally fly at nighttime (when the moon is out). Similarly, roosters generally crow at sunrise.

5. **A** Smoking cigarettes can damage one's lungs. Similarly, eating candy can damage one's teeth.

Quantitative Reasoning

1. **C** You subtract 3 from the first number to obtain the second one: $4 - 3 = 1$.

2. **F** You multiply the first number by 6 to obtain the second one: $\frac{3}{2} \times 6 = \frac{18}{2}$, or 9.

3. **B** The figure is divided into 6 congruent rectangles. Two of these rectangles, which make up $\frac{2}{6}$, or $\frac{1}{3}$ of the figure, are shaded.

4. **F** □ and ○ are equal in weight (the □:○ ratio is 1:1). Thus, as long as the same total number of total icons (of either type) appears on the left as on the right, as in choice F only, the weights balance. Otherwise, they won't.

5. **B** The scale shows that the □:○ weight ratio is 3:1. Assign a weight of 3 units to □ and a weight of 1 unit to ○. In choice B, the total on the left side equals the total on the right side: $(3 + 3) = (3 + 1 + 1 + 1)$.

Answers and Explanations *(continued)*

Verbal Reasoning—Words

1. **B** By its very definition, a calendar involves *time* segments; the segments might be years, months, days, or some other unit of time.

2. **G** By definition, a magnet draws or pulls something else toward it. In other words, magnets *attract*.

3. **C** A *hop* is a small *jump;* at the other extreme, a *leap* is a large jump. Similarly, a *jaunt* is a slow, leisurely *drive* while, at the other extreme, a *race* is characterized by fast, intense driving.

4. **J** All four words name steps in food preparation. However, unlike the other three words, *bake* does not involve the physical handling of food.

5. **A** The word *invent* and the three underlined words all refer to the act of doing, devising, or generating something new that did not exist before.

Verbal Reasoning—Context

1. **D** According to the premise, Peter is younger than Oliver. Therefore, Oliver must be older than Peter. (These are two ways of stating the same fact.)

2. **H** Because bright light attracts mosquitoes, a kitchen light left on at night (when most other lights are off) would no doubt attract them. The statements say nothing about neighboring houses, nor do they provide enough information for us to conclude whether mosquitoes are attracted to Tim's bedroom window, or to his house at all, during the daytime.

3. **A** If Scott does not have coffee, he feels tired. Because Scott has not had coffee, he must be feeling tired. The statement in choice A must be true. The statements in the three other answer choices each try to explain why Scott might not have had coffee this morning. But each one is a mere guess, because the premises offer no clue as to the true reason.

4. **G** The week begins on Sunday, and today is Thursday. Because yoga class has met twice so far this week, those two meetings must have been on Monday and Wednesday. Therefore, class did not meet on Sunday. (Otherwise, class would have met three times already this week.) Because yoga class meets either Saturday or Sunday, the class must meet on Saturday.

5. **A** It is impossible to build a snowman without snow that has fallen to the ground.

Reading and Language Arts

1. **B** In the first paragraph, the author provides a basic definition of the term. Then, in the second paragraph, the author distinguishes organic architecture from green architecture and *feng shui* to help the reader understand what organic architecture is—and what it is not.

2. **F** In the first paragraph, the author refers to herself as an architect ("... a number of architects today—myself included—...").

3. **C** The goal of green architecture is to design a building in a way that helps conserve natural resources. Using solar energy would be consistent with that goal.

4. **J** According to the passage, Wright was at least partially responsible for the renewed interest in organic architecture in the twentieth century.

5. **C** The author tells us that one of the principles of *feng shui* has to do with a building's proportions. The height of a room's ceiling compared to its other dimensions is a good example of the issue of proportion.

Answers and Explanations *(continued)*

6. **F** The sentence in choice F conveys the point clearly and without redundancy or grammatical error. The sentence in choice G contains a redundancy: The words *also* and *too* convey the same idea. In choice H, the word *often* is misplaced; the sentence implies that an organic building might sometimes be green while at other times *not* be green. The sentence in choice J suffers from a different redundancy: The words *frequently* and *often* convey the same idea.

7. **D** The best version of the sentence should make it clear that Wright was a modern architect and must compare Wright to *other* modern architects. Only choice D fits the bill.

8. **J** In choice J, using the word *which* to link the two ideas together makes for a smooth and graceful sentence that's clear in meaning. Choice F is a bit awkward and confusing, especially compared to choice J. Choice G is needlessly repetitive (. . . *burning coal, burning coal* . . .). There are two problems with choice H. The structure of the first clause conveys the nonsensical idea that the student lives in the one place where all electricity is produced. Also, the word *and* doesn't connect the two ideas very effectively.

9. **D** A comma should be inserted immediately after the first word of sentence 5 (*Also, we use* . . .).

10. **H** In the essay, the student points out two problems with using electricity where he lives (it's expensive, and it harms the environment) and lists two ways his family reduces their electricity use. The sentence in choice H ties these ideas together very nicely, and the sentence flows naturally from the preceding one (sentence 5).

Mathematics

1. **D** Because the answer choices are expressed as fractions, convert 5% to a fraction, then find the product of the two terms:

$$5\% \times \frac{1}{5} = \frac{1}{20} \times \frac{1}{5} = \frac{1}{100}.$$

2. **G** Multiply first, then perform addition and subtraction (in either order): $34 - (12 \times 3) + 2 = 34 - 36 + 2 = -2 + 2 = 0$.

3. **C** Don't count either 20 or -22. There are 10 even integers from -20 to -2, and there are 9 even integers from 2 to 18. The total number of even integers in the range is 19.

4. **J** Interior angle ABC is supplemental to a $100°$ angle; in other words, they combine to form a straight line, which contains $180°$ altogether. Thus, $m\angle ABC = 80°$. In any triangle, the sum of the three interior angles is $180°$. Thus, $m\angle BCA = 55°$ ($180° - 45° - 80°$).

5. **B** In this fraction, because the base numbers match (both are 13), you can factor out 13^3 from both the numerator and the denominator, leaving $\frac{13^1}{1}$, or 13.

6. **F** Apply the arithmetic mean (simple average) formula:

$$AM = \frac{S + (S + 4)}{2} = \frac{2S + 4}{2} = S + 2$$

7. **D** Since x and y are consecutive non-zero integers, one is odd and the other is even. The sum of an odd and even integer is always odd.

8. **G** The rectangle's width is $\frac{4}{3}$ m $\left(\frac{1}{3} \times 4\right)$. To find the rectangle's area, multiply its width by its length: $\frac{4}{3} \times 4 = \frac{16}{3}$.

Answers and Explanations *(continued)*

9. **A** You can find the correct answer by plugging each answer choice in turn into the equation. (With the correct value, the equation will hold true.) Or, you can solve the problem algebraically, by isolating x on one side of the equation (first multiply all terms by x, as shown here):

$$\frac{4}{x} + 3 = \frac{1}{x}$$
$$4 + 3x = 1$$
$$3x = -3$$
$$x = -1$$

10. **H** Of 10 cards, four are clubs. Thus, the probability of selecting a club is 4 in 10. You can express this probability as the fraction $\frac{4}{10}$, or $\frac{2}{5}$.

HSPT DIAGNOSTIC TEST

This HSPT diagnostic test consists of 50 questions and is divided into five parts, just like the actual HSPT exam. Keep in mind, however, that the actual exam is much longer (approximately 298 questions).

Mark your answers where indicated on the Answer Sheet. Do not limit your time on this diagnostic test, and do not hurry through it. Instead, pay attention to which types of questions you find especially easy, and which ones you find difficult. After completing the test, read the answers and explanations that follow it. Then, use the rest of this book to prepare for the types of questions you find most difficult.

HSPT DIAGNOSTIC TEST

Answer Sheet

Directions: For each answer that you select, blacken the corresponding oval on this sheet.

Verbal Skills

1. Ⓐ Ⓑ Ⓒ Ⓓ
2. Ⓐ Ⓑ Ⓒ Ⓓ
3. Ⓐ Ⓑ Ⓒ Ⓓ
4. Ⓐ Ⓑ Ⓒ Ⓓ
5. Ⓐ Ⓑ Ⓒ Ⓓ
6. Ⓐ Ⓑ Ⓒ Ⓓ
7. Ⓐ Ⓑ Ⓒ Ⓓ
8. Ⓐ Ⓑ Ⓒ Ⓓ
9. Ⓐ Ⓑ Ⓒ Ⓓ
10. Ⓐ Ⓑ Ⓒ Ⓓ

Reading

21. Ⓐ Ⓑ Ⓒ Ⓓ
22. Ⓐ Ⓑ Ⓒ Ⓓ
23. Ⓐ Ⓑ Ⓒ Ⓓ
24. Ⓐ Ⓑ Ⓒ Ⓓ
25. Ⓐ Ⓑ Ⓒ Ⓓ
26. Ⓐ Ⓑ Ⓒ Ⓓ
27. Ⓐ Ⓑ Ⓒ Ⓓ
28. Ⓐ Ⓑ Ⓒ Ⓓ
29. Ⓐ Ⓑ Ⓒ Ⓓ
30. Ⓐ Ⓑ Ⓒ Ⓓ

Language

41. Ⓐ Ⓑ Ⓒ Ⓓ
42. Ⓐ Ⓑ Ⓒ Ⓓ
43. Ⓐ Ⓑ Ⓒ Ⓓ
44. Ⓐ Ⓑ Ⓒ Ⓓ
45. Ⓐ Ⓑ Ⓒ Ⓓ
46. Ⓐ Ⓑ Ⓒ Ⓓ
47. Ⓐ Ⓑ Ⓒ Ⓓ
48. Ⓐ Ⓑ Ⓒ Ⓓ
49. Ⓐ Ⓑ Ⓒ Ⓓ
50. Ⓐ Ⓑ Ⓒ Ⓓ

Quantitative Skills

11. Ⓐ Ⓑ Ⓒ Ⓓ
12. Ⓐ Ⓑ Ⓒ Ⓓ
13. Ⓐ Ⓑ Ⓒ Ⓓ
14. Ⓐ Ⓑ Ⓒ Ⓓ
15. Ⓐ Ⓑ Ⓒ Ⓓ
16. Ⓐ Ⓑ Ⓒ Ⓓ
17. Ⓐ Ⓑ Ⓒ Ⓓ
18. Ⓐ Ⓑ Ⓒ Ⓓ
19. Ⓐ Ⓑ Ⓒ Ⓓ
20. Ⓐ Ⓑ Ⓒ Ⓓ

Mathematics

31. Ⓐ Ⓑ Ⓒ Ⓓ
32. Ⓐ Ⓑ Ⓒ Ⓓ
33. Ⓐ Ⓑ Ⓒ Ⓓ
34. Ⓐ Ⓑ Ⓒ Ⓓ
35. Ⓐ Ⓑ Ⓒ Ⓓ
36. Ⓐ Ⓑ Ⓒ Ⓓ
37. Ⓐ Ⓑ Ⓒ Ⓓ
38. Ⓐ Ⓑ Ⓒ Ⓓ
39. Ⓐ Ⓑ Ⓒ Ⓓ
40. Ⓐ Ⓑ Ⓒ Ⓓ

HSPT DIAGNOSTIC TEST

Verbal Skills

Directions: For questions 1–10, choose the best answer.

1. Authentic most nearly means
   A   old
   B   real
   C   neat
   D   bossy

2. Flourish most nearly means
   A   dampen
   B   absorb
   C   prosper
   D   fan

3. Subtle means the *opposite* of
   A   direct
   B   guilty
   C   flexible
   D   durable

4. Prompt means the *opposite* of
   A   impolite
   B   dark
   C   cheerful
   D   late

5. Which word does *not* belong with the others?
   A   fall
   B   roost
   C   land
   D   perch

6. Which word does *not* belong with the others?
   A   schedule
   B   itinerary
   C   plan
   D   calendar

7. Bobbie is older than Trent. Suene is older than Bobbie. Trent is younger than Suene. If the first two statements are true, the third is
   A   true
   B   false
   C   uncertain

8. Mariah is a cheerleader. Some cheerleaders are popular and are good students. Mariah is popular. If the first two statements are true, the third is
   A   true
   B   false
   C   uncertain

9. Shell is to tortoise as tire is to
   A   tricycle
   B   wheel
   C   car
   D   rubber

10. Victory is to trophy as engagement is to
    A   love
    B   date
    C   ring
    D   award

Quantitative Skills

Directions: For questions 11–20, choose the best answer.

11. 40% of what number is 60% of 12?

    A   18
    B   48
    C   26
    D   12

12. A certain number divided by 3 is 15. If you subtract 15 from the original number, the result is

    A   15
    B   30
    C   22.5
    D   −10

13. What number is the product of 27 and the cube root of 27?

    A   108
    B   9
    C   81
    D   27

14. What is the next number in the following series: 5, −5, 10, −10, 15, −15, . . . ?

    A   20
    B   10
    C   25
    D   −20

15. What is the missing number in the following series: 2, 3, 6, 7, __, 11, 14?

    A   12
    B   9
    C   8
    D   10

16. What are the next two numbers in the following series: 2, 0, 1, 5, 3, 4, 8, 6, . . . ?

    A   9, 7
    B   7, 10
    C   8, 7
    D   7, 11

17. Compare the following three expressions, and then choose the correct answer.

    (a)   0.025
    (b) 0.5×0.05
    (c) $(0.05)^2$

    A   (a) is equal to (b), and (b) is equal to (c)
    B   (c) is equal to (a), and (c) is less than (b)
    C   (a) is equal to (b) and greater than (c)
    D   (b) is less than (a) and greater than (c)

18. Compare the following three expressions, and then choose the correct answer.

    (a)   the arithmetic mean (simple average) of −4 and 8
    (b)   the least common denominator of $\dfrac{3}{4}$ and $\dfrac{3}{2}$
    (c)   the greatest prime factor of 48

    A   (a) < (b) < (c)
    B   (a) < (c) < (b)
    C   (b) > (a) > (c)
    D   (c) = (b) < (a)

Quantitative Skills *(continued)*

19. Examine figures (a), (b), and (c), and then choose the correct statement.

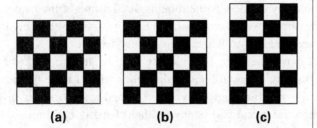

(a)   **(b)**   **(c)**

A The number of white squares in figure (a) is equal to the number of black squares in figure (c).

B The number of black squares in figure (b) is greater than the number of white squares in figure (a).

C The number of white squares in figure (b) is equal to the number of black squares in figure (c).

D The number of black squares in figure (a) is greater than the number of black squares in figure (c).

20. Examine the figure below, and then choose the correct answer.

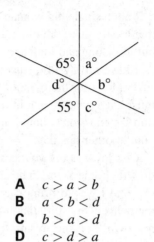

A $c > a > b$
B $a < b < d$
C $b > a > d$
D $c > d > a$

Reading

Directions: Questions 21–27 are based on the following reading passage, which is an excerpt from a fictional work written before 1900. Read the passage and select the best answer to each question.

I am a single old woman. I should say at once, without being at all afraid of the name, I am an old maid; only that I am older than the phrase would express. The time was when I had my love-trouble, but, it is long and long ago. He was killed at sea when I was twenty-five.

I have all my life, since ever I can remember, been deeply fond of children. I have always felt such a love for them, that I have had my sorrowful and sinful times when I have fancied something must have gone wrong in my life—something must have been turned aside from its original intention I mean—or I should have been the proud and happy mother of many children, and a fond old grandmother this day.

Charley was my youngest brother, and he went to India. He married there, and sent his gentle little wife home to me to be confined, and she was to go back to him, and the baby was to be left with me, and I was to bring it up. It never belonged to this life. It took its silent place among the other incidents in my story that might have been, but never were. I had hardly time to whisper to her "Dead my own!" or she to answer, "Ashes to ashes, dust to dust! O lay it on my breast and comfort Charley!" when she had gone to seek her baby at Our Saviour's feet.

I went to Charley, and I told him there was nothing left but me, poor me; and I lived with Charley, out there, several years. He was a man of fifty, when he fell asleep in my arms. His face had changed to be almost old and a little <u>stern</u>; but, it softened, and softened when I laid it down that I might cry and pray beside it; and, when I looked at it for the last time, it was my dear, untroubled, handsome, youthful Charley of long ago.

21. The passage's narrator regrets that she
    A   moved to India
    B   never bore children
    C   was unkind to Charley's wife
    D   never married

22. The passage's narrator considers Charley to be
    A   pitiful
    B   childlike
    C   good-looking
    D   even-tempered

23. What is probably true about the passage's narrator?
    A   She is older than a typical old maid.
    B   She was wild when she was younger.
    C   She is responsible for the deaths of her loved ones.
    D   Her vacation at sea ended in tragedy.

24. The narrator once loved a man who
    A   left her for another woman
    B   died at the age of twenty-five
    C   refused to marry her
    D   died at sea

25. Based on the passage, which of the following is most probably true?
    A   Charley sometimes fell asleep in the narrator's arms.
    B   Charley's wife fell ill on her trip from India.
    C   Charley died from heartache over his wife's death.
    D   Charley's wife died soon after their child died.

Reading *(continued)*

26. As it is used in the last paragraph of the passage, the word <u>stern</u> most nearly means

  A harsh

  B ugly

  C freckled

  D old

27. The narrator can best be described as

  A bitter

  B sad

  C loving

  D wealthy

Directions: For questions 28–30, choose the word that is nearest in meaning to the underlined word.

28. to <u>defer</u> enrollment

  A decrease

  B discourage

  C seek

  D postpone

29. an <u>elliptical</u> orbit

  A curved

  B distant

  C unpredictable

  D unknown

30. scattered <u>debris</u>

  A people

  B gas

  C rubbish

  D thoughts

Mathematics

Directions: For questions 31–40, choose the best answer to each question.

31. $34 - 12 \times 3 + 2 =$

A 68
B 0
C 7
D −4

32. How many non-zero even integers are less than 20 but greater than −22?

A 21
B 20
C 19
D 39

33. Find the measure of interior angle *BCA* in the figure below.

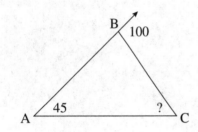

A 60°
B 45°
C 70°
D 55°

34. $\dfrac{13^4}{13^3} =$

A 169
B 13
C 26
D $\dfrac{1}{13}$

35. Kendra swam one lap in *S* seconds, faster than Greg by 1 second, but slower than Paul by 7 seconds. Which of the following represents the average lap time of the three swimmers?

A $S + 2$
B $S - 2$
C $S - 1$
D $S + 4$

36. If *x* and *y* are consecutive non-zero integers, then it must be true that

A xy is odd
B $x^2 + y$ is even
C $x + xy$ is odd
D $x + y$ is odd

37. What is the area of a rectangle whose length is 4 meters and whose width is one-third its length?

A 5 m²
B $\dfrac{16}{3}$ m²
C 4 m²
D $\dfrac{15}{4}$ m²

38. For which value of *x* does $\dfrac{4}{x} + 3 = \dfrac{1}{x}$?

A −1
B $\dfrac{1}{3}$
C $\dfrac{3}{10}$
D $\dfrac{1}{2}$

Mathematics *(continued)*

39. The following graph shows the ethnic composition of the population of State X:

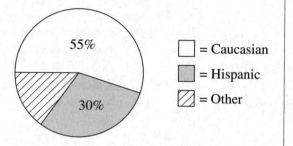

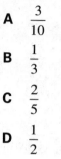

= Caucasian

= Hispanic

= Other

What is the ratio of State X's Hispanic population to its Caucasian population?

A 6:11
B 2:5
C 3:7
D 2:1

40. In a card game, Alex has 10 playing cards; two are spades, one is a heart, three are diamonds, and the rest are clubs. If he randomly selects one of his cards, what is the probability that Alex will select a club?

A $\dfrac{3}{10}$

B $\dfrac{1}{3}$

C $\dfrac{2}{5}$

D $\dfrac{1}{2}$

Language

Directions: For questions 41–45, choose the sentence that contains an error in punctuation, capitalization, or usage. If you find no mistakes, select choice D.

41.
A   A sloth can sit motionless for hours on end.
B   Wait to swim until 20 minutes after eating.
C   The train arrives somewhere between 1:00 and 1:30.
D   No mistake.

42.
A   Morning is my favorite time of day.
B   Store shelves are well stocked this season.
C   It's my fault, not yours.
D   No mistake.

43.
A   I could of won if I'd tried harder.
B   Theresa bought a Middle Eastern rug today.
C   Which of you wants the last bite?
D   No mistake.

44.
A   The question is, "Why did you fail"?
B   Balding is a inherited characteristic.
C   David beat Mike at billiards.
D   No mistake.

45.
A   Pasta is the restaurant's specialty.
B   I didn't recognize you at first.
C   Who's car is making that noise?
D   No mistake.

Directions: For questions 46 and 47, choose the sentence that contains a spelling error. If you find no spelling errors, select choice D.

46.
A   Stan faces quite an ordeal ahead.
B   Tolerance is needed in any democracy.
C   Her birthday coincided with her aniversary.
D   No mistake.

47.
A   Erica rejected his marriage proposal.
B   The restroom looked unsanitary.
C   The king reigned for one decade.
D   No mistake.

Language *(continued)*

Directions: For questions 48–50, follow the directions for each question.

48. Choose the best word or words to join the thoughts together.

I brush my teeth twice a day; _____, I floss at least once daily.

A for example
B besides
C however
D in addition

49. Which of the following expresses the idea most clearly?

A Nicotine, caffeine, and sugar have all been proven to be physically addictive.
B The physical addictiveness of nicotine, of caffeine, and of sugar has been proven.
C It's all been proven: Nicotine, caffeine, and sugar are physically addictive.
D Nicotine, caffeine, and sugar are all physically addictive, a fact that's proven.

50. Choose the phrase that best completes the sentence.

In order to grow and thrive, _____.

A often the plants must be watered
B the plants must be watered often
C watering the plants must be often
D the plants being watered must often occur

HSPT DIAGNOSTIC TEST

Answer Key

Verbal Skills

1.	**B**	6.	**D**
2.	**C**	7.	**A**
3.	**A**	8.	**C**
4.	**D**	9.	**B**
5.	**A**	10.	**C**

Quantitative Skills

11.	**A**	16.	**D**
12.	**B**	17.	**C**
13.	**C**	18.	**B**
14.	**A**	19.	**C**
15.	**D**	20.	**D**

Reading

21.	**B**	26.	**A**
22.	**C**	27.	**C**
23.	**A**	28.	**D**
24.	**D**	29.	**A**
25.	**D**	30.	**C**

Mathematics

31.	**B**	36.	**D**
32.	**C**	37.	**B**
33.	**D**	38.	**A**
34.	**B**	39.	**A**
35.	**B**	40.	**C**

Language

41.	**C**	46.	**C**
42.	**D**	47.	**B**
43.	**A**	48.	**D**
44.	**B**	49.	**A**
45.	**C**	50.	**B**

HSPT DIAGNOSTIC TEST

Answers and Explanations

Verbal Skills

1. **B** *Authentic* means "genuine or legitimate"—in other words, just the opposite of counterfeit or fake. The word *real* is a good synonym.

2. **C** To *flourish* is to thrive, succeed, or prosper.

3. **A** *Subtle* means "suggestive or indirect"—contrary to the meaning of *direct*.

4. **D** *Prompt* means "timely or punctual," just the opposite of *late*.

5. **A** Birds are said to *roost, land,* or *perch* when they set down on something (such as a tree branch or rooftop) after flight. The word *fall* does not fit this idea.

6. **D** A *schedule, itinerary,* and *plan* all refer to a scheme or design for future activities. A calendar is used as the framework for the schedule, itinerary, or plan.

7. **A** We know that Trent is younger than Bobbie, and that Bobbie is younger than Suene. Therefore, Trent must be younger than Suene.

8. **C** We know that "some" cheerleaders are popular; but we do not know if Mariah is in that group.

9. **B** A shell covers and protects a tortoise, just as a tire covers and protects a wheel.

10. **C** A trophy is a symbol of victory, much like a ring is a symbol of an engagement (to be married).

Quantitative Skills

11. **A** Convert the verbal expression to an algebraic equation, and then solve:

$$0.4x = 0.6 \times 12$$
$$0.4x = 7.2$$
$$4x = 72$$
$$x = 18$$

12. **B** The original number is $15 \times 3 = 45$. Subtract 15 from this number: $45 - 15 = 30$.

13. **C** The cube root of 27 is 3 ($3 \times 3 \times 3 = 27$). To find the product of 27 and 3, multiply: $27 \times 3 = 81$.

14. **A** Each pair of successive terms provides the next positive and negative multiple of 5. Thus, the next two numbers in the series would be 20 followed by -20.

15. **D** To progress from each term to the next, alternate between two operations: adding 1 and adding 3.

16. **D** Each group of three terms contains three consecutive integers. The greatest number is listed first, followed by the smallest number, which is followed by the middle number. Each successive group of three numbers contains the next three integers: (2, 0, 1), (5, 3, 4), (8, 6, 7), (11, 9, 10), . . .

17. **C** $0.5 \times 0.05 = 0.025$; $(0.05)^2 = (0.05)(0.05) = 0.0025$. Thus, (a) = (b), and (a) and (b) are both greater than (c).

Answers and Explanations *(continued)*

18. **B** The average of -4 and $8 = \dfrac{-4+8}{2} = \dfrac{4}{2} = 2$.

    The least common denominator of $\dfrac{3}{4}$ and $\dfrac{3}{2}$ is 4. The greatest prime factor of 48 is 3.

19. **C** The number of white and black squares in each of the three figures are as follows:

    Figure (a): 12 black, 13 white
    Figure (b): 13 black, 12 white
    Figure (c): 12 black, 12 white

    As you can see, the number of white squares in figure (b) is equal to the number of black squares in figure (c).

20. **D** Angle d is supplementary to 65° and 55° angles. In other words, the three angles combine to form a straight line, and their measures must total 180°. Thus, $d = 60$. Also, each angle in the figure is congruent to its vertical angle (the angle directly across the common vertex). Thus, $b = 50$, $c = 65$, and $a = 55$.

Reading

21. **B** The second paragraph as a whole conveys the idea that the narrator wished she had borne children because she is so fond of them, and that she can't help feeling that she would have had children of her own had she not taken some wrong turn in life.

22. **C** Twice in the passage the narrator refers to Charley as "handsome."

23. **A** In the first paragraph, the narrator admits that she is an "old maid," and that she is even older than "the phrase [old maid] would express."

24. **D** In the first paragraph, the narrator tells us that her lover was killed at sea when *she* was twenty-five years old.

25. **D** The narrator tells us that she "had hardly time to whisper to [Charley's wife]" ... "when she had gone to seek her baby at Our Saviour's feet"—meaning that the death of Charley's wife occurred shortly after her baby's death.

26. **A** As it is used in the sentence, the word *stern* means "hard, harsh, or severe." The next sentence provides a useful clue to the word's meaning; Charley's face softening implies that it was harder, or harsher, previously.

27. **C** In the passage, we learn that the narrator would have wanted to have children of her own; that she planned to take care of her brother's child; that she helped Charley's wife; and that she looked after Charley even as he was dying. All of these details paint a portrait of a loving person.

28. **D** To *defer* is to postpone, put off, or delay.

29. **A** *Elliptical* means "oval-shaped or oblong."

30. **C** *Debris* means "wreckage, rubbish, or trash."

Mathematics

31. **B** Multiply first, then perform addition and subtraction (in either order): $34 - (12 \times 3) + 2 = 34 - 36 + 2 = -2 + 2 = 0$.

32. **C** Don't count either 20 or -22. There are 10 even integers from -20 to -2, and there are 9 even integers from 2 to 18. The total number of even integers in the range is 19.

33. **D** Interior angle *ABC* is supplemental to a 100° angle; in other words, they combine to form a straight line, which contains 180° altogether. Thus, $m\angle ABC = 80°$. In any triangle, the sum of the three interior angles is 180°. Thus, $m\angle BCA = 55°$ $(180° - 45° - 80°)$.

Answers and Explanations *(continued)*

34. **B** In this fraction, because the base numbers match (both are 13), you can factor out 13^3 from both the numerator and the denominator, leaving $\dfrac{13^1}{1}$, or 13.

35. **B** Apply the arithmetic mean (simple average) formula:

$$AM = \frac{S+(S+1)+(S-7)}{3} = \frac{3S-6}{3} = S-2$$

36. **D** Because x and y are consecutive non-zero integers, one is odd and the other is even. The sum of an odd and even integer is always odd.

37. **B** The rectangle's width is $\dfrac{4}{3}$ m $\left(\dfrac{1}{3} \times 4\right)$. To find the rectangle's area, multiply its width by its length: $\dfrac{4}{3} \times 4 = \dfrac{16}{3}$.

38. **A** You can find the correct answer by plugging each answer choice in turn into the equation. (With the correct value, the equation will hold true.) Or, you can solve the problem algebraically, by isolating x on one side of the equation (first multiply all terms by x, as shown here):

$$\frac{4}{x}+3 = \frac{1}{x}$$
$$4+3x = 1$$
$$3x = -3$$
$$x = -1$$

39. **A** Hispanics and Caucasians account for 30% and 55%, respectively, of State X's population. The ratio is 30 to 55, which you can express as the fraction $\dfrac{30}{55}$, or $\dfrac{6}{11}$.

40. **C** Of 10 cards, four are clubs. Thus, the probability of selecting a club is 4 in 10. You can express this probability as the fraction $\dfrac{4}{10}$, or $\dfrac{2}{5}$.

Language

41. **C** The word *somewhere* should refer to a place rather than a time. The word *sometime* should be used instead here.

42. **D** There are no mistakes.

43. **A** The phrase *could of* is not correct. The phrase *could have* (or its contraction *could've*) should be used instead.

44. **B** Because "inherited" starts with a vowel sound, the article *an,* rather than *a,* should precede it.

45. **C** The contraction *Who's* (*Who is*) is used incorrectly here and should be replaced with the relative pronoun *Whose.*

46. **C** The correct spelling is *anniversary.*

47. **B** The correct spelling is *unsanitary.*

48. **D** The second thought continues in the same vein as the first—arguing that the speaker takes good care of her teeth. The phrase *in addition* works well here to signal a continuation of the same general idea. (Two other connectors that would work well here are *also* and *moreover.*)

49. **A** Sentence A is clear and effective. (The phrase *been proven to be* is idiomatic.) Sentence B suffers from two problems: the awkward word *addictiveness* (*addictive quality* would be better) and the unnecessary repetition of the word *of.* In sentence C, the opening clause (especially the use of the word *all*) is confusing and inappropriate. In sentence D, the final phrase—*a fact that's been proven*—is awkward and redundant.

50. **B** Because the first clause clearly refers to (or modifies) *the plants,* the second clause should begin with *the plants.* You can eliminate choices A and C. The phrase in choice D is wordy and awkward. That leaves the phrase in choice B, which helps convey the sentence's meaning clearly and gracefully.

TACHS DIAGNOSTIC TEST

This TACHS diagnostic test consists of 60 questions and is divided into four parts: Reading, Language, Mathematics, and Ability. It is shorter than the actual TACHS exam, which contains approximately 200 questions. Since, on the real test, you will not be allowed to write in your test booklet, do not write on the pages of the Diagnostic Test. Instead, get a few blank pieces of paper to use as scratch paper.

Mark your answers where indicated on the Answer Sheet. Do not limit your time on this diagnostic test, and do not hurry through it. Instead, pay attention to which types of questions you find especially easy, and which ones you find difficult. After completing the test, read the answers and explanations that follow it. Then, use the rest of this book to prepare for the types of questions you find most difficult.

TACHS DIAGNOSTIC TEST

Answer Sheet

Directions: For each answer that you select, blacken the corresponding oval on this sheet.

Reading

1. Ⓐ Ⓑ Ⓒ Ⓓ
2. Ⓙ Ⓚ Ⓛ Ⓜ
3. Ⓐ Ⓑ Ⓒ Ⓓ
4. Ⓙ Ⓚ Ⓛ Ⓜ
5. Ⓐ Ⓑ Ⓒ Ⓓ
6. Ⓙ Ⓚ Ⓛ Ⓜ
7. Ⓐ Ⓑ Ⓒ Ⓓ
8. Ⓙ Ⓚ Ⓛ Ⓜ
9. Ⓐ Ⓑ Ⓒ Ⓓ
10. Ⓙ Ⓚ Ⓛ Ⓜ
11. Ⓐ Ⓑ Ⓒ Ⓓ
12. Ⓙ Ⓚ Ⓛ Ⓜ
13. Ⓐ Ⓑ Ⓒ Ⓓ
14. Ⓙ Ⓚ Ⓛ Ⓜ
15. Ⓐ Ⓑ Ⓒ Ⓓ

Mathematics

1. Ⓐ Ⓑ Ⓒ Ⓓ
2. Ⓙ Ⓚ Ⓛ Ⓜ
3. Ⓐ Ⓑ Ⓒ Ⓓ
4. Ⓙ Ⓚ Ⓛ Ⓜ
5. Ⓐ Ⓑ Ⓒ Ⓓ
6. Ⓙ Ⓚ Ⓛ Ⓜ
7. Ⓐ Ⓑ Ⓒ Ⓓ
8. Ⓙ Ⓚ Ⓛ Ⓜ
9. Ⓐ Ⓑ Ⓒ Ⓓ
10. Ⓙ Ⓚ Ⓛ Ⓜ
11. Ⓐ Ⓑ Ⓒ Ⓓ
12. Ⓙ Ⓚ Ⓛ Ⓜ
13. Ⓐ Ⓑ Ⓒ Ⓓ
14. Ⓙ Ⓚ Ⓛ Ⓜ
15. Ⓐ Ⓑ Ⓒ Ⓓ

Ability

1. Ⓐ Ⓑ Ⓒ Ⓓ Ⓔ
2. Ⓙ Ⓚ Ⓛ Ⓜ Ⓝ
3. Ⓐ Ⓑ Ⓒ Ⓓ Ⓔ
4. Ⓙ Ⓚ Ⓛ Ⓜ Ⓝ
5. Ⓐ Ⓑ Ⓒ Ⓓ Ⓔ
6. Ⓙ Ⓚ Ⓛ Ⓜ Ⓝ
7. Ⓐ Ⓑ Ⓒ Ⓓ Ⓔ
8. Ⓙ Ⓚ Ⓛ Ⓜ Ⓝ
9. Ⓐ Ⓑ Ⓒ Ⓓ Ⓔ
10. Ⓙ Ⓚ Ⓛ Ⓜ Ⓝ
11. Ⓐ Ⓑ Ⓒ Ⓓ Ⓔ
12. Ⓙ Ⓚ Ⓛ Ⓜ Ⓝ
13. Ⓐ Ⓑ Ⓒ Ⓓ Ⓔ
14. Ⓙ Ⓚ Ⓛ Ⓜ Ⓝ
15. Ⓐ Ⓑ Ⓒ Ⓓ Ⓔ

Written Expression

1. Ⓐ Ⓑ Ⓒ Ⓓ Ⓔ
2. Ⓙ Ⓚ Ⓛ Ⓜ Ⓝ
3. Ⓐ Ⓑ Ⓒ Ⓓ Ⓔ
4. Ⓙ Ⓚ Ⓛ Ⓜ
5. Ⓐ Ⓑ Ⓒ Ⓓ
6. Ⓙ Ⓚ Ⓛ Ⓜ
7. Ⓐ Ⓑ Ⓒ Ⓓ
8. Ⓙ Ⓚ Ⓛ Ⓜ
9. Ⓐ Ⓑ Ⓒ Ⓓ
10. Ⓙ Ⓚ Ⓛ Ⓜ
11. Ⓐ Ⓑ Ⓒ Ⓓ
12. Ⓙ Ⓚ Ⓛ Ⓜ
13. Ⓐ Ⓑ Ⓒ Ⓓ
14. Ⓙ Ⓚ Ⓛ Ⓜ
15. Ⓐ Ⓑ Ⓒ Ⓓ

TACHS DIAGNOSTIC TEST

Reading (15 questions)

Directions: For questions 1–8, decide which of the four answer choices is closest in meaning to the underlined word(s). Choose the best answer.

1 To <u>relinquish</u> power

  A give up

  B fear

  C exercise

  D gain

2 A <u>minute</u> portion

  J whole

  K fast

  L tiny

  M hungry

3 An ugly <u>grimace</u>

  A scene

  B facial expression

  C monster

  D picture

4 Blind <u>justice</u>

  J boldness

  K greed

  L honesty

  M fairness

5 <u>Erratic</u> behavior

  A illegal

  B inconsistent

  C secretive

  D polite

6 To <u>defer</u> a decision

  J hope for

  K come to

  L disagree with

  M put off

7 <u>Elliptical</u> orbit

  A curved

  B distant

  C unpredictable

  D unknown

8 To <u>comply with</u> a rule

  J break

  K change

  L obey

  M learn

Reading (continued)

Directions: Questions 9–15 are based on the passage below. Read the passage. Then, for each question decide which of the four answers choices is better than the others.

The main function of a building is to provide a safe shelter and living space. Beyond this function, however, what should be the goal of architecture? To impress people? To glorify the architect or owner? To create something new for its own sake? An increasing number of architects today—myself included—believe that the main goal should be to elevate the human spirit. Architecture designed with this goal in mind is known as *organic* architecture. While the "organic" label is new, the principle is centuries old. The current <u>revival</u> of organic architecture actually began in the middle of the twentieth century with the work of architects such as Frank Lloyd Wright and Spain's Antonio Gaudi.

Organic architecture should not be confused with *green* architecture, which is concerned mainly with a structure's environmental cost in terms of the natural resources used to build and maintain it. Also, unlike *feng shui* design, which dictates that a building should conform to certain rules of proportion and direction, there's no objective test for whether a building is organic. If people feel more alive in and around it, or even just looking at pictures of it, then it passes as organic.

9 The author of the passage is _____.

   A   the owner of an organic house
   B   a student
   C   a professional writer
   D   an architect

10 Which of the following would the author agree is most important in designing a building?

   J   its effect on a person's mood
   K   how energy efficient it is
   L   its overall appearance
   M   how much it costs to build

11 A building designed to use energy only from the sun is an example of _____.

   A   organic architecture
   B   natural architecture
   C   green architecture
   D   elemental architecture

12 Based on the passage, what do we know about Frank Lloyd Wright?

   J   He incorporated *feng shui* principles into his designs.
   K   He was a strong advocate of green architecture.
   L   He worked with architect Antonio Gaudi in designing houses.
   M   He helped make organic architecture popular again.

13 Which of the following would probably be most important to an architect applying *feng shui* to a building's design?

   A   how to heat and cool the inside of the building
   B   whether the building looks like nearby structures
   C   a room's ceiling height compared to its length and width
   D   the personal tastes and preferences of the building's owner

14 As it is used in the passage, what does the word <u>revival</u> mean?

   J   respect
   K   rebirth
   L   design
   M   construction

15 In the passage, the author's main purpose is to _____.

   A   compare various forms of architecture
   B   explain the meaning of "organic architecture"
   C   describe a typical organic building
   D   criticize green architecture

Written Expression (15 questions)

Directions: For questions 1–3, look for mistakes in <u>spelling</u>.

1
- A coussin
- B empty
- C system
- D industry
- E *(No mistakes)*

2
- J machine
- K orange
- L challenge
- M orchard
- N *(No mistakes)*

3
- A announce
- B imperfect
- C refered
- D prophet
- E *(No mistakes)*

Directions: For questions 4–6, look for mistakes in <u>capitalization</u>.

4
- J On a clear fall night, especially in
- K October, you can see Jupiter, but only if
- L you are away from New York's city lights.
- M *(No mistakes)*

5
- A The quickest way to travel from San
- B Francisco to Marin county is to drive
- C across the Golden Gate Bridge.
- D *(No mistakes)*

6
- J Jan was the first girl from the Davis
- K family to go to College, where she
- L earned a Bachelor's degree in English.
- M *(No mistakes)*

Directions: For questions 7 and 8, look for mistakes in <u>punctuation</u>.

7
- A Jill, Valerie, and I all went to camp
- B in August 2003, just one month before my
- C family moved to Madison Wisconsin.
- D *(No mistakes)*

8
- J "Of course I want to go to the dance!"
- K exclaimed Curt; but what Curt had forgotten
- L was that he didn't know how to dance.
- M *(No mistakes)*

Directions: For questions 9–11, look for any mistake in <u>usage or expression</u>.

9
- A Of all the art I have ever
- B seen, Picasso's *Guernica* is
- C the most unique.
- D *(No mistakes)*

Written Expression *(continued)*

10

J   Out of the band's first two
K   albums, the second one sold
L   the most copies.
M   *(No mistakes)*

11

A   When I answered the phone,
B   the caller asked for Ms. Jones.
C   I replied, "This is she."
D   *(No mistakes)*

Directions: Questions 12–15 are based on the following paragraph. Choose the best answer to each question.

¹Electricity is generated in many different ways—by wind power, solar, and water power, as well as by nuclear fission and burning coal. ²No matter how it's produced, electricity is almost always expensive for consumers. ³Where I live, electricity is made by burning coal. ⁴Burning coal is a major cause of global warming. ⁵To save electricity, we turn off the lights in our house when we don't need them. ⁶We use extra blankets at night instead of turning up the heater.

12   What is the best way to write the underlined part of sentence 1?

J   wind, solar power, and by water
K   wind power, by solar power, and water power
L   wind, solar, and water power
M   *(No change)*

13   Which is the best way to combine sentences 3 and 4?

A   Where I live, electricity is made by a major cause of global warming: burning coal.
B   Although where I live electricity is made by burning coal, burning coal is a major cause of global warming.
C   Electricity is made by burning coal where I live, and burning coal is a major cause of global warming.
D   Where I live, electricity is made by burning coal, which is a major cause of global warming.

14   What is the best way to write the underlined part of sentence 6?

J   Because we use
K   We also use
L   We can use
M   *(No change)*

15   Which of the following is the best concluding sentence for this paragraph?

A   Also, our windows have two layers of glass, which helps keep the cold out.
B   It would be even better if we could use solar power in our house.
C   This way, my family saves money and helps the environment.
D   Although we can afford lots of electricity, we try to conserve it, anyway.

Mathematics (15 questions)

Directions: For questions 1–8, choose the best answer to each question.

1 5% of $\frac{1}{5}$ is equal to

A $\frac{1}{100}$

B $\frac{1}{25}$

C $\frac{1}{10}$

D 1

2 $34 - 12 \times 3 + 2 =$

J −4

K 0

L 7

M 68

3 If q is an odd integer, then which of the following must also be an odd integer?

A $\frac{1}{q}$

B $2q$

C $3q$

D $q + 1$

4 $\frac{13^4}{13^3} =$

J $\frac{1}{13}$

K 13

L 26

M 169

5 Use the following table to answer question 5.

Train Schedule

Train destinations	Charleston	Aiken	Greenville
Departure times	9:03 a.m.	9:30 a.m.	10:00 a.m.
Arrival times	11:07 a.m.	10:46 a.m.	12:11 a.m.

If you caught the train to Aiken, about what time would you need to ask someone to meet you at the station in Aiken?

A 11:00 p.m.

B 11:00 a.m.

C 12:15 p.m.

D 10:45 a.m.

6 Kendra swam one lap in S seconds, faster than Paul by 4 seconds. Which of the following represents the average lap time of the two swimmers?

J $S - 2$

K $S - 1$

L $S + 2$

M $S + 4$

7 Which of the following is a prime number?

A 15

B 21

C 26

D 31

8 In a card game, Alex has 10 playing cards; two are spades, one is a heart, three are diamonds, and the rest are clubs. If he randomly selects one of his cards, what is the probability that Alex will discard a club?

J $\frac{3}{10}$

K $\frac{1}{3}$

L $\frac{2}{5}$

M $\frac{1}{2}$

9 Find the measure of interior angle *BCA* in the figure below.

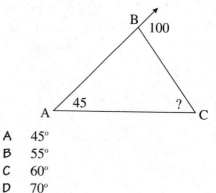

A 45°

B 55°

C 60°

D 70°

Mathematics *(continued)*

Directions: For questions 10–15, <u>estimate</u> the answer; do not try to compute exact answers. You must do all work in your head; no pencil work is allowed.

10 The closest estimate of 4,832 − 3,027 is ____.
- J   100
- K   1,000
- L   1,500
- M   2,000

11 The closest estimate of 16,285 + 1,685 is ____.
- A   10
- B   1,000
- C   18,000
- D   19,000

12 The closest estimate of 226,905 ÷ 5 is ____.
- J   45,000
- K   50,000
- L   55,000
- M   110,000

13 The closest estimate of 387 × 7 is ____.
- A   2,100
- B   2,800
- C   3,500
- D   5,600

14 The closest estimate of 333 + 7,361 is ____.
- J   7,500
- K   7,700
- L   8,200
- M   10,000

15 The closest estimate of 85^2 is ____.
- A   1,700
- B   5,400
- C   7,200
- D   8,500

Ability (15 questions)

Directions (items 1–6): The first three figures are alike in certain ways. From the five answer choices, select the figure that is most like the first three figures in the same ways.

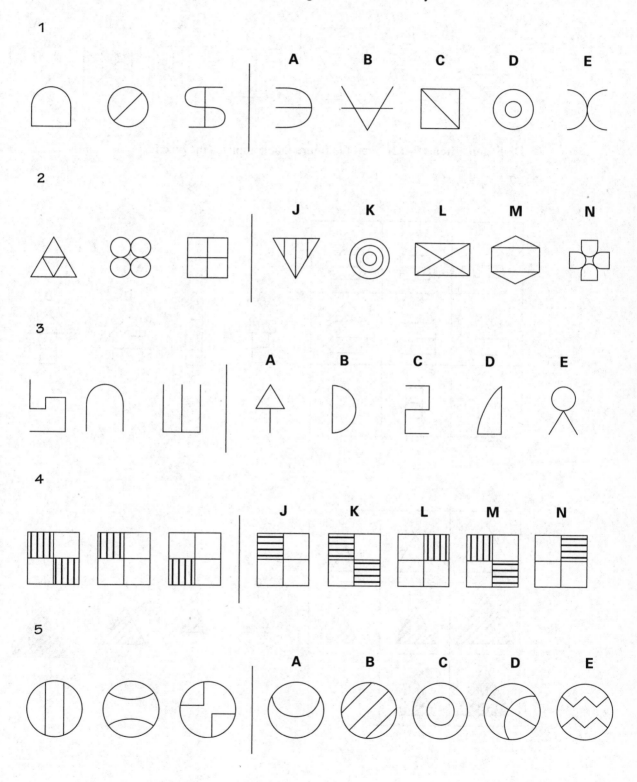

Ability (continued)

6

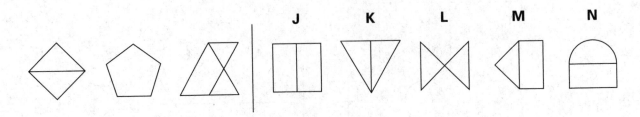

Directions (items 7–12): Find the figure that completes the puzzle.

7

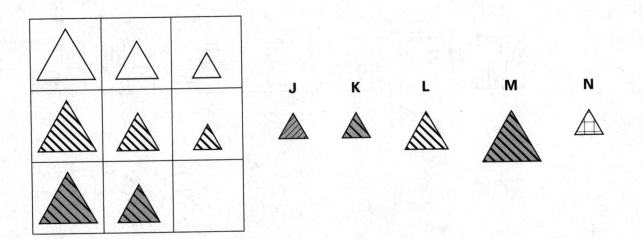

8

Ability (continued)

9

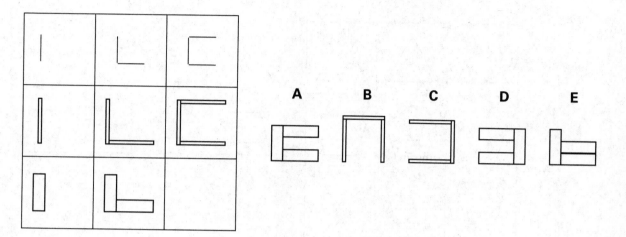

10

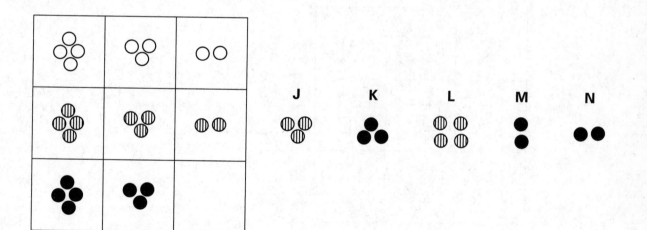

Ability (continued)

11

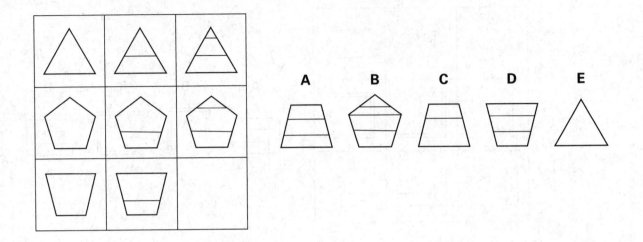

12

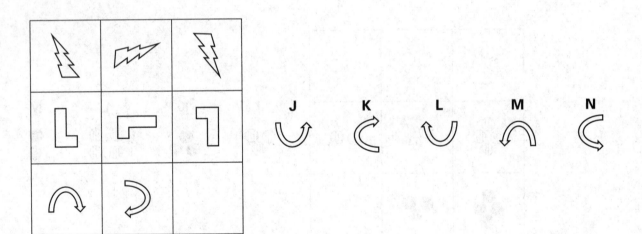

Ability (continued)

Directions (items 13–15): In the top line, a piece of paper is folded, and one or more holes are punched through all layers. Select the figure in the bottom row that shows how the punched paper would appear unfolded.

13

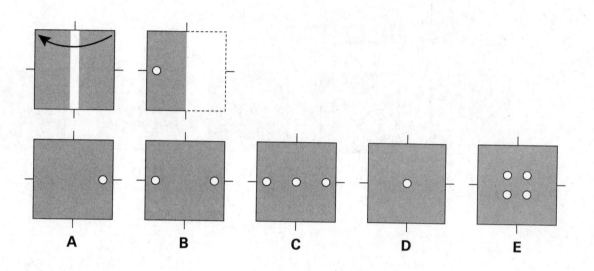

14

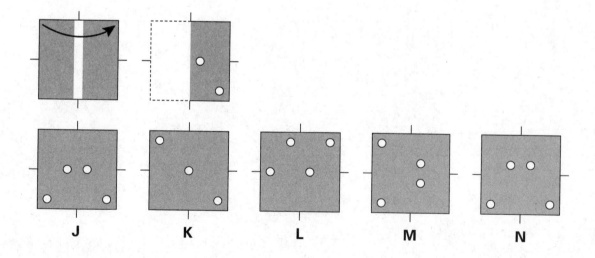

Ability *(continued)*

15

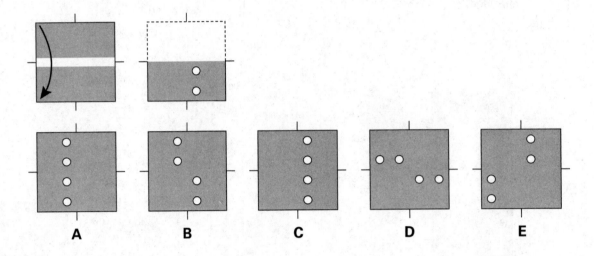

A   B   C   D   E

TACHS DIAGNOSTIC TEST

Answer Key

Reading

1.	A	9.	D
2.	L	10.	J
3.	B	11.	C
4.	M	12.	M
5.	B	13.	C
6.	M	14.	K
7.	A	15.	B
8.	L		

Written Expression

1.	A	9.	C
2.	N	10.	L
3.	C	11.	D
4.	M	12.	L
5.	B	13.	D
6.	K	14.	K
7.	C	15.	C
8.	K		

Mathematics

1.	A	9.	B
2.	K	10.	M
3.	C	11.	C
4.	K	12.	J
5.	D	13.	B
6.	L	14.	K
7.	D	15.	C
8.	L		

Ability

1.	A	9.	A
2.	N	10.	N
3.	C	11.	D
4.	L	12.	L
5.	E	13.	B
6.	J	14.	J
7.	D	15.	C
8.	K		

TACHS DIAGNOSTIC TEST

Answers and Explanations

Reading

1. **A** To *relinquish* is to abandon or give up.

2. **L** The word *minute,* used here as an adjective, means "very small."

3. **B** A *grimace* is a sneering or smirking facial expression.

4. **M** The word *justice* (used most often in law) means "fairness."

5. **B** The word *erratic* means "random, unpredictable, or inconsistent."

6. **M** To *defer* is to postpone, put off, or delay.

7. **A** *Elliptical* means "oval-shaped or oblong."

8. **L** To *comply with* is to agree to, conform to, go along with, or obey.

9. **D** In the first paragraph, the author refers to herself as an architect (". . . a number of architects today—myself included—. . .").

10. **J** In the first paragraph, the author tells us that, like a growing number of architects today, she believes that one of the chief goals of architecture is to elevate the human spirit. Accordingly, the author would probably agree that how a building affects a person's mood is very important.

11. **C** The goal of green architecture is to design a building in a way that helps conserve natural resources. Using solar energy would be consistent with that goal.

12. **M** According to the passage, Wright was at least partially responsible for the renewed interest in organic architecture in the twentieth century.

13. **C** The author tells us that one of the principles of *feng shui* has to do with a building's proportions. The height of a room's ceiling compared to its other dimensions is a good example of the issue of proportion.

14. **K** This choice provides the only word that makes sense in the context of the sentence as well as the passage as a whole. (The word *revival* means "rebirth or resurgence.")

15. **B** In the first paragraph, the author provides a basic definition of the term. Then, in the second paragraph, the author distinguishes organic architecture from green architecture and *feng shui* to help the reader understand what organic architecture is—and what it is not.

Written Expression

1. **A** The correct spelling is *cousin.*

2. **N** There are no spelling mistakes.

3. **C** The correct spelling is *referred.*

4. **M** There are no capitalization errors.

5. **B** The word *county* is part of the proper noun *Marin County,* and so it should be capitalized.

6. **K** The word *college* does not refer to any particular school, and so it should not be capitalized.

7. **C** A comma should be inserted between *Madison* and *Wisconsin.*

8. **K** There should be a comma before *but* rather than a semicolon.

9. **C** The phrase *most unique* is redundant. Unique is an absolute, so *most* is not needed.

Answers and Explanations *(continued)*

10. **L** The word *more* is needed instead of *most*, since only two things are being compared.

11. **D** The sentence is correct as written.

12. **L** The list of three different types of power should be grammatically parallel. Only choice C accomplishes this goal.

13. **D** The correct answer is D. Using the word *which* to link the two ideas makes for a smooth and graceful sentence that's clear in meaning. Choice A is a bit awkward and confusing, especially compared to choice D. Choice B is needlessly repetitive (. . . *burning coal, burning coal* . . .). There are two problems with choice C. The structure of the first clause conveys the nonsensical idea that the student lives in the one place where all electricity is produced. Also, the word *and* doesn't connect the two ideas very effectively.

14. **K** The correct answer is choice K. In the previous sentence (sentence 5), the writer indicates one way that he saves electricity. In sentence 6, the writer mentions two additional ways. To connect the two sentences' ideas so that that the two sentences flow logically from one to the other, it makes sense to begin sentence 6 with *We also use.*

15. **C** The correct answer is choice C. In the paragraph, the writer points out two problems with using electricity where he lives (it's expensive, and it harms the environment) and lists two ways his family reduces their electricity use. The sentence in choice C ties these ideas together very nicely, and the sentence flows naturally from the preceding one (sentence 6).

Mathematics

1. **A** Because the answer choices are expressed as fractions, convert 5% to a fraction, then find the product of the two terms: $5\% \times \dfrac{1}{5} = \dfrac{1}{20} \times \dfrac{1}{5} = \dfrac{1}{100}$.

2. **K** Multiply first, then perform addition and subtraction (in either order): $34 - (12 \times 3) + 2 = 34 - 36 + 2 = -2 + 2 = 0$.

3. **C** The product of two odd integers (for example, *q* and 3) is always an odd integer.

4. **K** In this fraction, because the base numbers match (both are 13), you can factor out 13^3 from both the numerator and the denominator, leaving $\dfrac{13^1}{1}$, or 13.

5. **D** According to the table, the train arrives at Aiken at 10:46 a.m.

6. **L** Apply the arithmetic mean (simple average) formula:
$$AM = \frac{S + (S + 4)}{2} = \frac{2S + 4}{2} = S + 2$$

7. **D** A *prime number* is a positive integer that is not divisible by any integer other than itself and 1. The integer 31 is a prime number. (15 is divisible by 3 and 5, 21 is divisible by 3 and 7, and 26 is divisible by 2 and 13.)

8. **L** Of 10 cards, four are clubs. Thus, the probability of selecting a club is 4 in 10. You can express this probability as the fraction $\dfrac{4}{10}$, or $\dfrac{2}{5}$.

Answers and Explanations *(continued)*

9. **B** Interior angle *ABC* is supplemental to a 100° angle; in other words, they combine to form a straight line, which contains 180° altogether. Thus, m∠*ABC* = 80°. In any triangle, the sum of the three interior angles is 180°. Thus, m∠*BCA* = 55° (180° − 45° − 80°).

10. **M** Round 4,822 to 4,800. Round 3,047 to 3,000. 4,800 − 3,000 = 1,800. Among the four choices, M provides the closest estimate: 2,000.

11. **C** Round 16,285 to 16,000. Round 1,685 to 1,600. 16,000 + 1,600 = 17,600. Among the four choices, C provides the closest estimate: 18,000.

12. **J** Rounding 228,905 to 225,000, the quotient is equal to the value of the fraction $\frac{225,000}{5}$. Ignoring the zeros for a moment, $\frac{225}{5} = 45$. To account for the zeros, shift the decimal place to the right three places—to 45,000.

13. **B** Round 387 to 400, and then multiply: 400 × 7 = 2,800. Among the four choices, choice B provides the closest estimate: 2,800.

14. **K** Round 333 up to 350, and round 7,361 down to 7,350. 350 + 7,350 = 7,700. Among the four choices, choice K provides the closest estimate: 7,700.

15. **C** $85^2 = 85 \times 85$. To estimate the product, round one number up and the other down: 80 × 90 = 7,200.

Ability

1. **A** Each figure consists of a curved line and a straight line.

2. **N** Each figure consists of four congruent smaller figures (identical in shape and size).

3. **C** All figures are "open," in other words, they contain no enclosures.

4. **L** All figures have only vertical stripes.

5. **E** All figures are divided into three sections.

6. **J** To create each figure, you draw exactly five line segments.

7. **D** Each figure in the left column is joined with another identical figure in the middle column. Then a right angle figure is put on top, like a roof, in the right column.

8. **K** Each figure gets smaller as you look from left to right. The figures in the middle row add stripes, and the figures on the bottom row both have stripes and are shaded gray. That means the missing figure should be a small, gray, striped triangle. The strips in choice J are too small and do not match.

9. **A** The left column figures are all versions of a vertical line. In the middle column, this vertical line is joined with a horizontal line at the bottom. Then another horizontal line is added at the top, forming a sort of "C" shape, with the legs going out toward the right.

10. **N** Each figure has one fewer circle as you look from left to right. The figures in the middle row add stripes and the figures on the bottom row are solid black. That means the missing figure should be a set of two solid black circles.

Answers and Explanations *(continued)*

11. **D** Each figure in the left column has a vertical line added about 1/3 of the way up the figure in the middle column. Then another vertical line is added about 2/3 of the way up the figure in the right column. Choice A has the proper shape, but it is upside down.

12. **L** Each figure in the left column has been rotated 90° in the middle column. Then the figures in the right column are rotated another 90°. Only choice L has the correct orientation, with the arrow pointing in the correct direction.

13. **B** One hole is punched through two layers, so there are two holes. The two holes are directly across the fold from each other, near the center.

14. **J** Two holes are punched through two layers, so there are four holes. Because the paper was folded left to right, each pair of matching holes is aligned horizontally. The upper holes are near the center, and the lower holes are near the outer edges.

15. **C** Two holes are punched through two layers, so there are four holes. Because the paper was folded down and one hole was punched directly above the other, all four holes are aligned vertically, just right of center.

Reading Comprehension

COOP | HSPT | TACHS

Reading Comprehension questions test your ability to understand the ideas that are stated and implied in a series of brief reading passages. Here's where you'll find these questions on the three tests:

- COOP: Reading and Language Arts test
- HSPT: Reading subtest
- TACHS: Part 2 of the Reading subtest

All three tests include several short reading passages (six or seven is most common), along with several questions based on each passage. On the COOP, these questions are mixed in with Language Arts questions, which cover paragraph structure, sentence structure, and grammar.

To handle reading passages and questions, follow this six-step approach:

Step 1: Read the questions (but *not* the answer choices), which tell you what the passage is about and what the questions cover.
Step 2: Read the passage; highlight or make notes of specific areas that you know the questions cover.
Step 3: Sum up the passage for yourself, in a sentence or two.
Step 4: For each question, try to predict what the best answer might look like, and then scan the choices for the best match. (Answer the questions in order; there's no reason to skip around.)
Step 5: Look again at any questions you weren't sure about; reread the passage as needed.
Step 6: On your answer sheet, mark your selections for all the questions in the group.

Reading Comprehension—Step by Step

Now, let's look more closely at this step-by-step approach and apply it to a typical reading passage and group of questions.

Step 1: During step 1, your goal is to figure out what the passage is all about and what information you'll need to pay special attention to when you read the passage. Here are a series of question "stems" (which do not include the answer choices) for the passage you'll read during step 2. As you can see, most of these stems are actually sentences that you complete (with one of the answer choices). As you read them, look for clues they provide about the passage on which they're based.

1. At Wolgan Gap, where did the white powder used for stenciling come from?
2. Wolgan Gap is located in _____.
3. At Wolgan Gap, the artists probably stained the rock with iron oxide in order to _____.

4 The author implies that the stencilings on cave walls in southern France ____.

5. As it is used in the passage, the word <u>emulate</u> most nearly means ____.

6. Spatterwork is similar to modern-day ____.

7. The stencilings at Wolgan Gap survive to this day probably because ____.

8. A good title for the passage is _____.

What do these eight questions tell us about the passage we're about to read? Quite a bit! Several of the questions refer to "stencilings" (which sounds like a form of art); question 3 even refers to the "artists" who produced them. Questions 1 and 3 also tell us that white powder and iron oxide were used in the process of making stencilings. Questions 6 and 7 provide clues that this art form (stencilings) is quite old—perhaps ancient—and that it has survived to this day (maybe because it has found in caves—see question 4). Several of the questions mention a place called Wolgan Gap; so, it's a good bet that this is a place where the stencilings were found. Finally, question 6 refers to something called "spatterwork." Could it be that this is the name of the art form used to create these stencilings?

As you can see, we're already focusing on the passage's topic, anticipating what we'll need to know to answer the questions. In short, we're already well on our way to answering the questions!

Step 2: Now, read the passage on which the eight questions are based. As you read, underline or circle key areas that you already know the questions will ask about.

At various spots in eastern Australia, curious works of art appear on sandstone cliffs, especially on over-hanging rocks that long ago served as shelters for the aborigines—the original inhabitants of the region—and that no doubt protected their works of art from the elements.

At one such spot, Wolgan Gap, the artists stained coarse sandstone almost black with iron oxide derived from ironstone. In nearby rock is a band of shale, disintegrated into a white powder at its exposed edge. The artist would put some of this white powder in his mouth, place his hand or foot on the rock, and blow the moistened powder around his outstretched fingers or toes, a process we call *spatterwork* today. Removing the hand or foot revealed an outline on the rock. In some cases, both hands or a whole arm and hand are stenciled together. The moist powder found its way into small cavities in the coarse and pitted sandstone, where it has remained despite the erosive activities of several generations. The residual powder appears as a halo around the object.

Archaeologists are not entirely sure what the purpose of these stencil works was. The natives may have been instructed as youths to make the stencilings; or they may have been marking territory, the way boys today carve their names on benches or rocks. Since the stenciling materials were readily at hand, once one person set an example, others could easily <u>emulate</u> it. Similar stencilings of hands appear on the walls of caves in southern France. Evidently, spatterwork is no modern pastime.

Step 3: Before looking at the questions, ask yourself: What's the main idea, point, or message that the passage's author is trying to convey? Here's one way you might sum up the passage as a whole:

Spatterwork is an ancient art form used to create stencilings in places such as Wolgan Gap. Although the purpose of the stencilings isn't known for sure, we have a good idea how they were made and what materials were used.

Step 4: Now it's time to tackle the eight questions. For each one, we'll try to formulate (or predict) a good answer, and then we'll scan the answer choices for a close match. First, question 1.

1. At Wolgan Gap, where did the white powder used for stenciling come from?

In the second paragraph, the author tells us: "In nearby rock is a band of shale, disintegrated into a white powder at its exposed edge." So, look for an answer choice that's similar to *nearby rock* or *a band of shale*. Now scan the four answer choices:

A ironstone
B overhanging rocks
C native flowers
D nearby shale

As you can see, choice D jumps out as the correct answer. Circle D in your test booklet, and go to the next question.

2. Wolgan Gap is located in ____.

In the first paragraph, the author tells us that the location of the spatterwork is on various cliffs in eastern Australia. Then, the author refers to Wolgan Gap as "one such spot," implying that Wolgan Gap is located in that part of the world. So, the correct answer should either be Australia or, more specifically, eastern Australia. Now, scan the four answer choices:

A northern Afghanistan
B eastern Australia
C southern France
D New Zealand

As you can see, choice B provides exactly what we were looking for. Circle B in your test booklet, and go to the next question.

3. At Wolgan Gap, the artists probably stained the rock with iron oxide in order to ____.

This question is tougher than the first two because the passage's author does not come right out and tell us why the artists stained the rock black. But think about it. Doesn't it make sense that by staining the rock black before stenciling on it, the white stenciling would show up more clearly against the dark background? Okay, let's look for an explanation that matches this one. Here are the four choices:

A clean the surface before stenciling on it
B hide their stenciling from view during the daytime
C create a contrasting background for the spatterwork
D form a border around their hands

Choice C provides an explanation that closely matches ours. Circle C in your test booklet, and go to the next question.

4. The author implies that the stencilings on cave walls in southern France ____.

Go back to the passage and read what the author told us about southern France at the end of the passage. Immediately after telling us that hand stencils also appear in the caves of southern France, the author concludes that "[E]vidently, spatterwork is no modern pastime." You need to "read between the lines" to understand what the author's point is here—that the stencil works were created long ago. Okay, so that's what the author has to say about the cave stencilings in southern France. A correct answer choice might say simply that they were not created recently. Don't rack your brains trying to conjure up more possibilities. Let's scan the choices to see if anything rings true:

A were created long ago
B were created by young boys
C form outlines of toes
D have been discovered only recently

Sure enough, choice A provides essentially what we predicted the correct answer might be. Circle A in your test booklet, and go to question 5.

5. As it is used in the passage, the word <u>emulate</u> most nearly means _____.

Go back to the passage and reread the sentence where the word "emulate" appears. "Since the stenciling materials were readily at hand, once one person set an example, others could easily <u>emulate</u> it." Even if you don't already know what the word means, you can certainly guess its meaning based on this sentence. When a person sets an example, isn't the idea that the person is creating a model for others to copy? In fact, if you substitute the word "copy" for emulate, the sentence makes good sense. Okay, let's scan the answer choices for a word or phrase that means copy:

A paint
B erase
C imitate
D spit

Choice C isn't exactly the word we were looking for, but *imitate* is a good synonym of *copy*. Test this answer choice just to make sure. By substituting *imitate* (copy or mimic) for *emulate,* the sentence does indeed make perfect sense; one boy might observe another boy stenciling his hand on a rock, and then, since the materials were right there, imitate the process he had observed. Circle C in your test booklet, and go to the next question.

6. Spatterwork is similar to modern-day _____.

After reading the passage, we know that spatterwork is the process of creating a stencil that the author describes. Does the passage tell us what activity today is similar to spatterwork? No, it doesn't. It's difficult to fill in this blank without looking at the answer choices. Rather than spinning our wheels trying to think of something, let's read the answer choices:

A graffiti
B advertising
C archaeology
D oil painting

Hmm, we'll need to ponder these a bit. Think again about what the author has to say about the purpose of spatterwork. In the third paragraph, the author theorizes that spatterwork might have been an artistic way that boys marked their territory long ago. Aha! Isn't this similar to how a modern-day gang member might spray paint *graffiti* in order to mark a neighborhood as the gang's territory? Yes! Circle choice A, and go to the next question.

7. The stencilings at Wolgan Gap survive to this day probably because _____.

In the second paragraph, the author tells us why the stencilings have survived: The rock on which the powder was blown was coarse (rough) and pitted rather than smooth. As a result, the powder wasn't directly exposed to elements such as wind and water, and so it resisted erosion. So, we're looking for an answer choice that tells us either that the stencilings were created on a pitted surface or that they were sheltered from the natural elements. Now, read the four choices:

A they were created deep inside caves
B the rock on which they were created was rough
C they have been preserved by archaeologists
D they were discovered for the first time only recently

Choice B expresses one of our two predictions quite nicely. Circle B in your test booklet, and go to the last question.

8. A good title for the passage is _____.

A good title would convey the passage's main idea. To complete this sentence, let's review the summary of the passage that we formulated during step 2. Here's our summary again:

Spatterwork is an ancient art form used to create stencilings in places such as Wolgan Gap. Although the purpose of the stencilings isn't known for sure, we have a good idea how they were made and what materials were used.

Okay, rather than try to conjure up a good title, let's check the four answer choices to see which one reflects this summary:

A "How Cave People Drew Pictures"
B "The Tools of Ancient Artists"
C "An Ancient Art Form Revealed"
D "Cave Paintings of Southern France"

Hmm, all four answer choices have something to do with the passage, don't they? Let's dig a little deeper. First, choice A: Is the passage about drawing pictures? Not exactly; spatterwork isn't drawing, and the result really isn't a picture. So, look for a better title. Next, choice B: The passage does describe tools and materials used in spatterwork, but not in any other ancient art. So, B seems too broad for the passage. Let's look for a better title. Next, choice C: Spatterwork is indeed an ancient art form, and the passage does reveal the process and materials used, as well as speculating about why the stencilings were made. So, C would probably be a good title for the passage. Let's check choice D to see if it's as good. Wolgan Gap is in eastern Australia, and so you can easily eliminate D as the worst of the four titles. That leaves C as the best title. Circle C in your test booklet.

Step 5: If you're unsure about any of your answers, now's the time to go back and think about them again, and possibly read certain parts of the passage again, if you have enough time. Otherwise, go to step 6.

Step 6: Now that you've answered all the questions based on this passage, mark your selections (which you circled along the way) on your answer sheet.

Question Types and Wrong-Answer Traps

Most reading questions on the COOP, HSPT, and TACHS fall into one the following four basic categories:

- Recap (summary)
- Recall
- Inference
- Vocabulary-in-Context

Let's look at each type, along with how the test makers create wrong answers that can easily trip you up if you're not ready for them.

Recap Questions

To answer a recap question, you need to recognize the passage's overall scope and its main emphasis. In other words, you job is to sum up, or *recap,* what the passage is about as a whole. Recap questions typically look like one of the following:

The main idea of the passage is ____.
In the passage, the author's primary concern is ____.
A good title for the passage is ____.

When handling these questions, look out for the following two types of wrong answers (these are the test makers' favorites):

Too broad. The answer covers ideas beyond what the passage covers.
Too narrow. The answer focuses on only a certain portion of the passage.

The group of questions we answered earlier in this lesson includes one recap question. Here it is again (we've identified wrong-answer types):

8. A good title for the passage is ____.
   A "How Cave People Drew Pictures" *(too broad)*
   B "The Tools of Ancient Artists" *(too broad)*
   C "An Ancient Art Form Revealed" *(correct answer)*
   D "Cave Paintings of Southern France" *(too narrow)*

Recall Questions

These questions are usually pretty easy because all you need to do is either remember or find the information in the passage that answers them. These questions often start with phrases such as these:

"Which of the following is an example of . . . ?"
"According to the passage, . . ."

When handling these questions, look out for the following two types of wrong answers (these are the test makers' favorites):

Misplaced detail. The passage mentions this detail, but it has nothing to do with the question at hand.
Not mentioned in the passage. If you don't remember reading it in the passage, it probably isn't there! Trust your memory, and eliminate this wrong answer.

The group of questions we answered earlier in this lesson includes two simple recall questions. Here they are again (we've identified wrong-answer types):

1. At Wolgan Gap, where did the white powder used for stenciling come from?
   A ironstone *(mentioned but not relevant to the question)*
   B overhanging rocks *(mentioned but not relevant to the question)*
   C native flowers *(not mentioned)*
   D nearby shale *(correct answer)*

2. Wolgan Gap is located in ____.
   A northern Afghanistan *(not mentioned)*
   B eastern Australia *(correct answer)*
   C southern France *(mentioned but not relevant to the question)*
   D New Zealand *(not mentioned)*

Inference Questions

Inference questions test your ability to recognize what the author implies but does not come right out and say. To answer the question, you need to "read between the lines"—to see a logical connection between two bits of information. Sometimes, to see what's implied you need to look at more than one sentence. These questions often include words such as *infer, imply,* or *suggest.* For example:

"The author of the passage implies that ____."
"Based on the passage's description of . . . , we can infer that ____."
"In the passage, the author seems to suggests that ____."

When handling these questions, look out for the following three types of wrong answers (these are the test makers' favorites):

Too speculative. The answer makes some sense, but the passage information does not support it strongly.
Nonsense. The answer is completely unsupported in the passage and makes little or no common sense.
Contradicts the passage. The answer provides information that the passage contradicts.

The group of questions we answered earlier in this lesson includes three inference questions. Here they are again (we've identified wrong-answer types):

3. At Wolgan Gap, the artists probably stained the rock with iron oxide in order to ____.
   A clean the surface before stenciling on it *(nonsense)*
   B hide their stenciling from view during the daytime *(nonsense)*
   C create a contrasting background for the spatterwork *(correct answer)*
   D form a border around their hands *(nonsense)*

4. The author implies that the stencilings on cave walls in southern France ____.
  A were created long ago *(correct answer)*
  B were created by young boys *(too speculative)*
  C form outlines of toes *(too speculative)*
  D have been discovered only recently *(too speculative)*

7. The stencilings at Wolgan Gap survive to this day probably because ____.
  A they were created deep inside caves *(contradicts the passage)*
  B the rock on which they were created was rough *(correct answer)*
  C they have been preserved by archaeologists *(too speculative)*
  D they were discovered for the first time only recently *(too speculative)*

Vocabulary-in-Context Questions

These questions test your vocabulary and your ability to understand how certain words are used in the passage. If you don't know what the word means, try each answer choice as a substitute for the word. The one that makes the most sense is probably the best one. The question stem will look similar to this one:

"As it is used in the passage, the word [*word*] most nearly means ____."

When handling these questions, look out for the following two types of wrong answers (these are the test makers' favorites):

Off-the-wall. The answer is not even close to the word's meaning and would make little, if any, sense in the context of the sentence where the word appears.
Misplaced detail. This answer mentions a detail from elsewhere in the passage that makes no sense in the context of the sentence at hand.

The group of questions we answered earlier in this lesson includes one vocabulary-in-context question. Here it is again (we've identified wrong-answer types):

5. As it is used in the passage, the word <u>emulate</u> most nearly means ____.
  A paint *(misplaced detail)*
  B erase *(off-the-wall)*
  C imitate *(correct answer)*
  D spit *(misplaced detail)*

Reading Comprehension—Heads Up!

■ Annotate and take notes as you read. This will help you keep the passage's details straight in your mind and help you find information in the passage you need as you answer the questions.
■ Sum up the passage after you read it. Chances are, you'll be able to answer at least one or two of the questions based just on your recap.
■ Try to predict an answer before reading the answer choices. This way, you can zero in on the best answer, and you won't be confused and distracted by wrong answers. Just remember: Some question stems might not give you enough to go on.
■ Always be on the lookout for the types of wrong answers you learned about in this lesson.

Practice

Directions: Questions 1–15 are based on reading passages. Read the passages and answer the questions.

Questions 1–7 are based on the following passage:

Is there a foolproof way to detect a lie? Most of us have heard of the *polygraph test,* more commonly known as a lie-detector test. In this test, a pair of plates that can sense and measure <u>subtle</u> increases in sweating is attached to a person's fingers, while at the same time other devices monitor increases in blood pressure and pulse rate as well as breathing depth. However, factors such as hunger or alcohol use can cause misleading polygraph results. Minor self-inflicted pain during the test can also result in false positives, and so can the truthful statements of pathological liars.

Another technology, the electroencephalograph (ECG), is also used to detect lies, but in quite a different way. As it turns out, one particular brain wave, which researchers have isolated and can graph, surges whenever we see something we recognize. It's impossible for any person to voluntarily suppress this surge. So, when a crime suspect wearing a special headband hooked up to an ECG machine is shown images or words connected with the crime, if that brain wave suddenly spikes, the suspect's brain is essentially shouting, "I'm guilty!"

A newer form of lie detector is far simpler than any other technology, aside from simply observing body language. People cannot help hesitating ever so briefly just before telling a lie. With modern computer technology, we can now detect and measure the briefest such pauses, which tell us when someone is lying.

1. According to the passage, when people lie they often
   A speak more softly
   B hold their breath
   C stare unnaturally
   D sweat more

2. According to the passage, pathological liars
   A are more likely than other people to commit crimes
   B can fool polygraph examiners
   C are often used to test polygraph equipment
   D rarely volunteer for polygraph tests

3. As used in the passage, the word <u>subtle</u> most nearly means
   A sweaty
   B slight
   C normal
   D sudden

4. During an electroencephalograph (ECG) test, the test taker
   A answers questions
   B wears finger plates
   C wears a special headband
   D repeats words after the examiner

5. In a polygraph test of a crime suspect, a false positive occurs when the
   A plates slip off the suspect's fingers
   B examiner asks the wrong question
   C suspect does not know the answer to a question
   D test misinterprets a truthful statement

6. The electroencephalograph (ECG) test might detect
   A a lie before it is told
   B subtle body language
   C brief pauses in speech
   D changes in blood pressure

7. A good title for the passage is
   A "How to Cheat on a Lie Detector Test"
   B "Do Polygraph Tests Always Reveal Lies?"
   C "In Search of the Perfect Lie Detector"
   D "The Technology of Crime Investigation"

Questions 8–15 are based on the following passage:

In Iraq and Syria, the lower Euphrates and Tigris rivers traverse the Euphrates valley, a wide plain that slopes gradually from 800 feet above sea level to its depths at the southern end of the Persian Gulf. The northern region of this valley is stony with only sparse vegetation, except in spring, while the southern region is characterized by deep soil in which even a pebble is rare. Except in the valley's extreme south, rainfall is minimal and the air is dry. However, when the winter snows that accumulate in the upper river basins melt in spring, the rivers rapidly rise and overflow their banks, covering the plain with a vast inland sea.

The Nile River valley also overflows from snow runoff each year. However, there are important differences between the Nile and Euphrates valleys. The time of the annual flood is reversed; the Nile's level is highest in autumn and winter, and lowest in spring and early summer. Also, while the overflows of the Nile are regulated by large lake basins in the south, there are no such lakes between the upper basins of the Tigris and Euphrates and the lower parts of these two rivers. Heavy rain or an unusually quick thaw in the Euphrates uplands results in a sudden rush of so much water that not even the rapid Tigris River, let alone its more sluggish companion, can carry it off in time to prevent violent and dangerous overflows.

8. The Euphrates valley as a whole can accurately be described as
   A dry
   B wide
   C green
   D rocky

9. As used in the passage, the word traverse most nearly means
   A irrigate
   B form
   C begin at
   D pass through

10. What is the main cause of flooding in the Euphrates valley?
   A large waves resulting from earthquakes
   B runoff of melted snow
   C lack of properly constructed dams
   D excessive rainfall

11. In what way are the Euphrates and Nile valleys similar?
   A Their rivers overflow their banks each year.
   B They flood at the same time of the year.
   C Their average elevation, or altitude, is about the same.
   D They receive about the same amount of annual rainfall.

12. The author implies that the water level in the Tigris River is
   A higher than the level of the Nile River
   B lowest in spring and summer
   C lowest in autumn and winter
   D highest in winter and spring

13. The southern end of the Euphrates valley
   A floods less often than the valley's central region
   B is higher in elevation than the valley's northern end
   C receives more rain than the rest of the valley
   D resembles the Nile River region

14. As used in the passage, the word sluggish most nearly means
   A slow
   B rocky
   C cold
   D wet

15. In which of the following would the passage most likely appear?
   A a study about the causes and results of natural floods
   B a magazine article about the Nile River
   C a book about the history of the Middle East
   D a textbook about the geography of the world's great rivers

Practice—Answers and Explanations

1. **D** The first paragraph describes the polygraph test, in which plates are attached to fingers in order to detect any increase in sweating.

2. **B** At the end of the first paragraph, the author tells us that truthful statements of pathological liars can result in false positives, which mislead a polygraph examiner to believe that such statements are actually lies.

3. **B** A special device would not be needed to detect large, obvious changes in sweating. Thus, if you substitute the word *slight,* which means "very small," for *subtle,* the sentence makes perfect sense.

4. **C** This type of test measures brain waves detected by sensors attached to a special headband.

5. **D** A polygraph test registers a false positive when it reads what is actually a truthful statement as a lie.

6. **A** An ECG test detects brain wave surges that occur whenever a person sees something recognizable. If a crime suspect views images from the crime scene and the brain wave spikes, an investigator could then question the suspect about the crime and detect whether the suspect is lying.

7. **C** The passage begins by asking, "Is there a foolproof way to detect a lie?" Then, the passage's author proceeds to trace the development of lie-detection technology, from the less reliable polygraph to newer, more reliable tests. The title suggestion in choice C conveys the flow of the discussion in a succinct and clever way.

8. **B** In the first paragraph, the author describes the valley as a "wide and gently inclined plain." The valley is not always dry, and only the northern region is rocky. Thus, choices A and D are incorrect. Vegetation in the valley is sparse at best, and so choice C is incorrect.

9. **D** The two rivers travel (or pass) through the Euphrates valley. Thus, if you substitute the phrase *pass through* for the word *traverse* (which means "cross over"), the sentence makes good sense.

10. **B** In the second paragraph, the author tells us that "when the snows accumulated in the upper basins of the great rivers during the winter melt . . . they rapidly rise and overflow their banks, covering the alluvial plain with a vast inland sea." What the author is describing here is flooding resulting from the runoff of melted snow.

11. **A** In the first sentence of the second paragraph, the author tells us that the Euphrates valley and the Nile valley are similar in that their rivers overflow their banks each year.

12. **C** According to the passage, the Nile's water level peaks in autumn and winter, but the times of the year that the Euphrates valley floods are just the reverse of the times that the Nile floods.

13. **C** In the second paragraph's first sentence, the author tells us that "except in the valley's extreme south, rainfall is minimal," implying that the southern end receives more rainfall than the rest of the valley.

14. **A** In the second paragraph, the author compares the rapid Tigris River as the Euphrates River's "more sluggish companion." In this context, it makes sense that the word *sluggish* means "slow."

15. **D** The passage is concerned primarily with the geographical setting of the Euphrates and Tigris rivers. An additional concern is with the Nile River area. Thus, the passage would fit nicely in a textbook about the geography of the world's great rivers.

Vocabulary

COOP | HSPT | TACHS

The COOP, HSPT, and TACHS all include questions designed to test your vocabulary. Here's where you'll find these questions on the three tests:

- COOP: Verbal Reasoning—Words test
- HSPT: Verbal Skills subtest and Reading subtest
- TACHS: Part 1 of the Reading subtest

In this lesson, you'll learn a step-by-step approach to each type of vocabulary question.

Word-Definition Questions

Word-definition questions test your understanding of what words mean. Here are the different types you're most likely to see on your exam, and the ones we'll cover here:

- Synonym questions (HSPT)
- Antonym questions (HSPT)
- Word-in-context questions (HSPT and TACHS)
- "Necessary Element" questions (COOP)
- Word-Grouping Questions (COOP and HSPT)

Synonym Questions (HSPT)

A *synonym* is a word that has a similar meaning to another word. In an HSPT synonym question, your job is to decide which of four words (or brief phrases) is the closest synonym of a given word. Here's an example:

Happenstance means most nearly
 A misery
 B accident
 C authority
 D conflict

To handle a synonym question, follow these steps:

Step 1: Determine the word's part of speech (noun, verb, or adjective). If you're not sure, scan the answer choices; all four will *always* match the part of speech of the original word.
Step 2: Try to formulate a good definition and one or two good synonyms. If you're not familiar with the word, try guessing what it means based on its parts or on how it "sounds."

Step 3: Scan the answer choices for one that closely matches your definition.
Step 4: If you're not sure which answer is correct, go with your hunch, or choose one that "sounds" like it might be the best synonym.

Let's apply these steps to our example.

Step 1: Perhaps you already know what the word *happenstance* means. But let's assume that you don't. The answer choices are nouns, and so *happenstance* must also be a noun.

Step 2: Let's try guessing what *happenstance* means. Part of the word is the verb *happen,* and so the definition of *happenstance* might have something to do with an occurrence or event—in other words, a happening. The other part of the word—*stance*—means "posture, position, or opinion," as in your *stance* on a controversial issue. But, simply putting these two parts together doesn't give us a clear definition of *happenstance*. The word *happenstance* sounds a lot like the word *circumstance,* which means "situation." So perhaps *happenstance* has a similar meaning. Go to step 3.

Step 3: Scan the answer choices. The words *accident* (choice B) and *conflict* (choice D) can both be described as events, happenings, or situations. On the other hand, neither *misery* (choice A) nor *authority* (choice C) can be described this way. Eliminate choices A and C.

Step 4: Let's compare the two remaining choices. Events that simply happen are often accidents, aren't they? So, *accident* seems to make more sense than *conflict* as a possible synonym. Let's go with our hunch and select it. (Our hunch is correct; the word *happenstance* means "accident or fortune, either good or otherwise.")

Antonym Questions (HSPT)

An *antonym* is a word that has an opposite or contrary meaning to another word. In an HSPT antonym question, your job is to decide which of four words (or brief phrases) is the best antonym of a given word. Here's an example:

Grandiose means the *opposite* of
  A modest
  B bright
  C nervous
  D thin

To handle an antonym question, follow these steps:

Step 1: Determine the word's part of speech (noun, verb, or adjective). If you're not sure, scan the answer choices; all four will *always* match the part of speech of the original word.
Step 2: Try to formulate a good definition and one or two good synonyms. If you're not familiar with the word, try guessing what it means based on its parts or on how it "sounds."
Step 3: Think of one or two words that mean the opposite of the original word. Scan the answer choices for one that closely matches your word(s).
Step 4: If you're not sure which answer is correct, go with your hunch, or choose one that "sounds" like it might be the best antonym.

Let's apply these steps to our example.

Step 1: Perhaps you already know what the word *grandiose* means. But let's assume you don't. The answer choices are adjectives, and so *grandiose* must also be an adjective.

Step 2: Let's try guessing what *grandiose* means. Part of the word is the adjective *grand,* which means "very large or great." So, the definition of *grandiose* might be similar. Go to step 3.

Step 3: Words that mean the opposite of *grand* include *small* and *ordinary.* Scanning the answer choices for words similar to either one, notice the word *modest* (a good synonym of *ordinary*) and *thin* (a possible synonym of *small*). Neither of the other two choices—*bright* and *nervous*—comes even close to our guess of what the opposite of *grandiose* means. Eliminate choices B and C.

Step 4: Let's compare the two remaining choices. A modest person is quite the opposite of a person who considers himself great. But a thin person is not necessarily *not* large; the word *small* would be a better antonym. So, *modest* seems to make more sense than *thin* as a good possible antonym of *grandiose.* Let's go with our hunch and select it. (Our hunch is correct; the word *grandiose* means "pompous, haughty, or pretentious"—just the opposite of *modest.*)

Word-in-Context Questions (HSPT and TACHS)

A word-in-context question is a lot like a synonym question, except that the word appears in a brief phrase, which helps you figure out its meaning. You'll find these questions in the HSPT Reading subtest and in Part 1 of the TACHS Reading subtest. Your job is to choose the word that is nearest in meaning to the underlined word. Here's an example.

to <u>annul</u> a marriage
  A bless
  B confirm
  C cancel
  D mend

Here are the steps to handling these questions:

Step 1: Read the phrase containing the underlined word. Try to define the underlined word.
Step 2: If you know the meaning of the underlined word, scan the answer choices for a close match (a good synonym).
Step 3: If you don't know what the underlined word means, try substituting each answer choice for it in the phrase. Eliminate the choices that don't make sense.
Step 4: If you have not narrowed down your choices to only one, try looking at word parts (roots and prefixes) to guess the precise meaning of the underlined word. If you're still unsure, go with your hunch.

Let's apply these steps to our example.

Step 1: Let's assume that we do not know what *annul* means.

Step 2: Since we don't know what *annul* means, skip this step.

Step 3: Let's substitute each of the four words for *annul:*
Choice A: Does the phrase "to *bless* a marriage" make any sense? Yes.
Choice B: Does the phrase "to *confirm* a marriage" make any sense? No.
Choice C: Does the phrase "to *cancel* a marriage" make any sense? Yes; a divorce cancels a marriage, doesn't it?
Choice D: Does the phrase "to *mend* a marriage" make any sense? Yes; one meaning of *mend* is "heal," and it makes sense to speak of healing a marriage.

Step 4: The only choice we've eliminated so far is choice B. Does the word *annul* itself provide any clues about what it means? The root word *null* is used in the phrase *null set,* which in mathematics refers to an empty set (a set which contains no members). So perhaps the meaning of *annul* is similar. Of the three answer choices, only choice C comes close: To cancel a marriage would leave no marriage—in other words, nothing. Select choice C. (To *annul* is to cancel, render void, or invalidate.)

"Necessary Element" Questions (COOP)

For some COOP vocabulary questions, your job is to decide which of four words best names a "necessary element" of another word. The best way to find out what this means is to try an example.

Find the word that names a necessary element of the underlined word.
secret
  A honesty
  B trust
  C hope
  D knowledge

To handle a necessary element question, follow these steps:

Step 1: Define the underlined word.
Step 2: Examine each answer choice. For each one, ask yourself: "Is this word part of the definition (a necessary element) of the underlined word?"
Step 3: If you've answered "yes" to more than one answer choice, go back and compare those two choices to decide between them.

Let's apply these steps to our example.

Step 1: A secret is some fact a person knows but is not sharing.

Step 2: Let's examine each answer choice:
Choice A: Is *honesty* part of the definition of a secret? No; a secret doesn't necessarily have anything to do with honesty, does it?
Choice B: Is *trust* part of the definition of a secret? Not really; one person might trust another person with a secret; but a fact can be a secret without an element of trust being involved.
Choice C: Is *hope* part of the definition element of a secret? No.
Choice D: Is *knowledge* part of the definition of a secret? Yes; the person who keeps a secret *knows* something that others do not. (Otherwise, the knowledge would not be secret.)

Step 3: We've answered "yes" to our question for only one of the four answer choices, and so we don't need to compare them again.

Word-Grouping Questions (HSPT and COOP)

Both the HSPT and COOP exams include questions that ask which of four words does *not* belong with the others. All four words will be the same part of speech (noun, verb, or adjective). However, three of the words will be very similar in meaning, whereas the fourth word will not—in other words, it won't belong with the group. Here's an example.

Which word does *not* belong with the others?
A salary
B money
C fee
D wage

Here's a three-step approach for handling these questions.

Step 1: Examine all four words; try to define each one.
Step 2: Figure out the relationship between the words—what they have in common. Ask yourself which word has the *least* in common with the others; mark it as a possible correct answer choice.
Step 3: If you're still not sure which answer is correct, try making up a definition that fits the words. The word that the definition does not fit well is probably the correct answer.

Let's apply these steps to our example.

Step 1: Let's define each word (as you can see, they're all related):
Choice A: A *salary* is an amount of money paid periodically to a worker by an employer.
Choice B: *Money* is what we use to pay for goods and services (and what we receive for providing them).
Choice C: A *fee* is an amount of money someone charges, usually for a service.
Choice D: A *wage* is money earned (usually per hour) working for someone else.

Step 2: Each word has something to do with money. But, *salary, fee,* and *wage* are more specific than *money,* aren't they? All of them are ways of paying a person for work. So, *money* is probably the word that does *not* belong.

Step 3: If you're still not sure that choice B is the correct choice, think of a good definition that fits the other three words. Here's a good sentence: A ___ is one method of paying *money* in exchange for services. The words *fee, wage,* and *salary* all make sense in the blank; however, the word *money* doesn't. We've confirmed that choice B is correct.

Let's practice these steps with a tougher example.

Which word does *not* belong with the others?
A create
B produce
C devise
D imagine

Step 1: Let's try to define each word:
Choice A: To *create* is to make something that didn't exist before.
Choice B: To *produce* is to make something that didn't exist before.
Choice C: Hmm . . . you might not be familiar with this word; let's skip it for now.
Choice D: To *imagine* is to dream up something that doesn't really exist.

Step 2: Each of the three familiar words has something to do with creativity. But *create* and *produce* are good synonyms, whereas *imagine* is not a good synonym of either *create* or *produce*. So, even though we're not sure what *devise* means, *imagine* is probably the word that does *not* belong in the group.

Step 3: If you're still not sure that choice D is the correct choice, think of a definition that fits both words we know. Here's a good definition: To ___ is to make or generate something new that did not exist before. To *imagine* something, even if it is new and different, is merely to dream it up in your head rather than actually making it or generating it. Select choice D as the correct answer.

On the COOP, you'll also see the reverse of the question type we just examined. Your job is to decide which of four words best belongs with three others. Here's an example.

Find the word that is most like the underlined words.

jockey driver captain
  A rider
  B passenger
  C athlete
  D pilot

Here's a three-step approach for handling these questions.

Step 1: Examine the three underlined words; try to define each one.
Step 2: Figure out the relationship between the words—what they have in common.
Step 3: Scan the answer choices for a word that is related to all three underlined words in the same way.

Let's apply these steps to our example.

Step 1: A *jockey* is a person who rides a horse. A *driver* is a person who operates a car. A *captain* is a person who leads a team of other people—for example, on a sports team, in an army, or on a ship.

Step 2: All three words name people who navigate (set the course of) some type of vehicle.

Step 3: A *pilot* also navigates a vehicle—usually an airplane. Select choice D.

Vocabulary—Heads Up!

- If you're not familiar with a word, look at its parts (root, prefix) for clues.
- The way an unfamiliar word "sounds" might help you guess what it means, especially if it sounds like a more common word you know.
- Don't get vocabulary questions backwards. For instance, if your job is to choose the best opposite, be careful not to select a synonym instead.
- To decide which word belongs (or does not belong) with a group of other words, it helps to think of a definition or a sample sentence that fits all the words in the group.
- Many words have more than one common meaning, and many nouns can also be used as verbs. Keep this in mind when answering vocabulary questions.

COOP Practice

Directions: For questions 1–10, find the word that does not belong with the others.

1.
A fall
B roost
C land
D perch

2.
F tuba
G guitar
H violin
J piano

3.
A magnify
B enlarge
C implode
D exaggerate

4.
F bracelet
G purse
H necklace
J belt

5.
A anticipate
B foresee
C estimate
D predict

6.
F bright
G alert
H witty
J wise

7.
A talk
B see
C smell
D listen

8.
F negotiate
G mediate
H contend
J settle

9.
A shirt
B tie
C coat
D hat

10.
F inhabitants
G nations
H citizens
J populace

Directions: For questions 11–16, find the word that names a necessary element of the underlined word.

11. bird
A feather
B sky
C cage
D perch

12. counselor
A defending
B teaching
C grading
D advising

13. dessert
A snack
B ice cream
C meal
D appetizer

14. vote
A ballot
B candidate
C poll
D election

15. <u>newspaper</u>
- **A** reporter
- **B** advertisement
- **C** event
- **D** delivery

16. <u>complaint</u>
- **A** anger
- **B** dissatisfaction
- **C** determination
- **D** regret

Directions: For questions 17–21, find the word that is most like the underlined words.

17. <u>weight</u> <u>length</u> <u>height</u>
- **A** measurement
- **B** volume
- **C** mile
- **D** scale

20. <u>expect</u> <u>anticipate</u> <u>foresee</u>
- **A** estimate
- **B** remember
- **C** predict
- **D** plan

18. <u>sled</u> <u>ski</u> <u>sleigh</u>
- **A** slide
- **B** slope
- **C** snow
- **D** skate

21. <u>root</u> <u>leaf</u> <u>flower</u>
- **A** stem
- **B** pollen
- **C** tree
- **D** plant

19. <u>harmful</u> <u>poisonous</u> <u>dangerous</u>
- **A** damaging
- **B** dishonest
- **C** suspicious
- **D** greedy

COOP Practice—Answers and Explanations

1. A Birds are said to roost, land, or perch when they sit down on something (such as a tree branch or rooftop) after flight. The word *fall* does not fit this idea.

2. A A tuba is a wind instrument; the others listed are all stringed instruments.

3. C The words *magnify, enlarge*, and *exaggerate* are all used to describe the process of making something bigger. The word *implode* means just the opposite of explode and thus runs contrary to the idea of making something larger.

4. B A bracelet, a necklace, and a belt are all worn around a part of the body (the wrist, neck, and waist, respectively). However, a purse is usually carried.

5. C The words *anticipate, foresee*, and *predict* each name what people do when they think about what might happen in the future. To estimate is to approximate—to "round off" or determine a "ballpark figure," which does not necessarily have anything to do with future events.

6. **D** A bright, alert, or witty person is someone with a quick and agile mind. A wise person, however, is someone who has developed sound judgment, usually through experience and reflection.

7. **A** The words *see, smell,* and *listen* each refer to one of the five senses. However, *talk* does not.

8. **C** The words *mediate, negotiate,* and *settle* all involve reaching an agreement based on a compromise—quite the opposite of *contend,* which means "fight or wrangle."

9. **D** A hat is worn on the head, while a shirt, a tie, and a coat are all worn below the head (and above the waist).

10. **B** The words *inhabitants, citizens,* and *populace* are all used to refer to the people who have in common the place where they live, such as a *nation.*

11. **A** All birds have feathers. In other words, feathers are an inherent characteristic of birds.

12. **D** The inherent function of a counselor is to guide or advise another person—that is, to help the person make wise decisions about what to do.

13. **C** A dessert must immediately follow a main course or meal. Otherwise, it is called something else, such as a *snack.* Without a meal there can be no dessert.

14. **D** By definition, the act of voting involves a voluntary decision or choice among two or more options—in other words, an *election.*

15. **C** The inherent function of any newspaper is to provide an account of current events—in other words, news.

16. **B** By definition, a complaint is an expression of dissatisfaction—in other words, that the person complaining is not satisfied.

17. **B** The word *volume* and all three underlined words refer to different ways of measuring things.

18. **D** The word *skate* and all three underlined words refer to things designed to glide over ice or snow.

19. **A** The word *damaging* and the three underlined words are used to describe something that has the potential to hurt—in other words, to do harm or damage.

20. **C** The word *predict* and all the underlined words are used to name what people do when they think about what might happen in the future.

21. **A** The word *stem* and all three underlined words refer to specific parts of a flowering plant.

HSPT Practice

Directions: For questions 1–29, choose the best answer.

1. Apathy means most nearly
   A stupidity
   B indifference
   C compassion
   D selfishness

2. Mire means most nearly
   A partner
   B beauty
   C joy
   D swamp

3. Articulate means most nearly
   A well spoken
   B intense
   C ornate
   D well dressed

4. Obstinate means most nearly
   A intelligent
   B penniless
   C stubborn
   D fortunate

5. Meticulous means most nearly
   A humble
   B overweight
   C careful
   D sick

6. Abridge means most nearly
   A judge
   B pass
   C span
   D shorten

7. Frivolous means the *opposite* of
   A important
   B plain
   C steady
   D full

8. Surpass means the *opposite* of
   A prohibit
   B trail
   C distract
   D convince

9. Inert means the *opposite* of
   A round
   B forward
   C mobile
   D smart

10. Equitable means the *opposite* of
    A poor
    B friendly
    C unfair
    D picky

11. Disdain means the *opposite* of
    A aggression
    B deception
    C precision
    D admiration

12. Plethora means the *opposite* of
    A deficiency
    B bravery
    C celebration
    D agreement

13. Which word does *not* belong with the others?
    A fall
    B roost
    C land
    D perch

14. Which word does *not* belong with the others?
    A tuba
    B guitar
    C violin
    D piano

15. Which word does *not* belong with the others?
  A magnify
  B enlarge
  C implode
  D exaggerate

16. Which word does *not* belong with the others?
  A bracelet
  B purse
  C necklace
  D belt

17. Which word does *not* belong with the others?
  A anticipate
  B foresee
  C estimate
  D predict

18. Which word does *not* belong with the others?
  A bright
  B alert
  C witty
  D wise

19. Which word does *not* belong with the others?
  A talk
  B see
  C smell
  D listen

20. Which word does *not* belong with the others?
  A negotiate
  B mediate
  C contend
  D settle

21. Which word does *not* belong with the others?
  A shirt
  B tie
  C coat
  D hat

22. Which word does *not* belong with the others?
  A inhabitants
  B nations
  C citizens
  D populace

23. Sufficient most nearly means
  A enough
  B additional
  C stolen
  D expected

24. Nuisance most nearly means
  A injury
  B annoyance
  C visitor
  D customer

25. Irate most nearly means
  A loud
  B angry
  C frightened
  D large

26. Bolster most nearly means
  A defeat
  B join
  C support
  D quit

27. Obligatory most nearly means
  A pretty
  B inviting
  C sincere
  D required

28. Grave most nearly means
  A serious
  B frequent
  C unnoticed
  D intentional

29. Trauma most nearly means
  A crime
  B swindle
  C shock
  D disaster

HSPT Practice—Answers and Explanations

1. **B** *Apathy* means "unconcern or indifference." A person who does not care or is unconcerned is said to be apathetic.

2. **D** A *mire* is a mucky, muddy place, such as a swamp or marsh.

3. **A** An *articulate* person is someone who is well spoken or eloquent.

4. **C** An *obstinate* person is someone who is stubborn, closed-minded, or bullheaded.

5. **C** *Meticulous* means "careful and conscientious." A person is said to be meticulous if he or she pays careful attention to details.

6. **D** To *abridge* is to condense or make briefer. For example, an abridged dictionary is a condensed, or shortened, version.

7. **A** *Frivolous* means "trivial, insignificant, or irrelevant"—just the opposite of important.

8. **B** To *surpass* is to exceed, outdo, or surmount—the opposite of *trail*.

9. **C** *Inert* means "motionless, idle, or inactive"—just the opposite of *mobile*.

10. **C** *Equitable* means "just or fair"—the opposite of unfair.

11. **D** *Disdain* means "contempt or scorn," contrary to *admiration*, which means "respect."

12. **A** *Plethora* means "excess, overabundance, or surplus"—the opposite of *deficiency*, which means "lack."

13. **A** Birds are said to *roost, land,* or *perch* when they sit down on something (such as a tree branch or rooftop) after flight. The word *fall* does not fit this idea.

14. **A** A tuba is a wind instrument; the others listed are all stringed instruments.

15. **C** The words *magnify, enlarge,* and *exaggerate* are all used to describe the process of making something bigger. The word *implode* means just the opposite of *explode* and thus runs contrary to the idea of making something larger.

16. **B** A bracelet, a necklace, and a belt are all worn around a part of the body (the wrist, neck, and waist, respectively). However, a purse is usually carried.

17. **C** The words *anticipate, foresee,* and *predict* each name what people do when they think about what might happen in the future. To estimate is to approximate—to "round off" or determine a "ballpark figure," which does not necessarily have anything to do with future events.

18. **D** A bright, alert, or witty person is someone with a quick and agile mind. A wise person, however, is someone who has developed sound judgment, usually through experience and reflection.

19. **A** The words *see, smell,* and *listen* each refer to one of the five senses. However, *talk* does not.

20. **C** The words *mediate, negotiate,* and *settle* all involve reaching an agreement based on a compromise—quite the opposite of *contend*, which means "fight or wrangle."

21. **D** A hat is worn on the head, while a shirt, a tie, and a coat are all worn below the head (and above the waist).

22. **B** The words *inhabitants, citizens,* and *populace* are all used to refer to the people who have in common the place where they live, such as a *nation*.

23. A *Sufficient* means "ample or enough."

24. B A nuisance is an aggravation, annoyance, or bother.

25. B *Irate* means "furious or enraged."

26. C To bolster is to reinforce, prop up, or support. The word can be used in either a literal or figurative sense.

27. D *Obligatory* means "necessary, required, or mandatory."

28. A *Grave* means "serious, important, or critical."

29. C *Trauma* means "shock or ordeal."

TACHS Practice

Directions: For questions 1–7, choose the word that is nearest in meaning to the underlined word.

1. <u>sufficient</u> funds
  A enough
  B additional
  C stolen
  D expected

2. an unwelcome <u>nuisance</u>
  A injury
  B annoyance
  C visitor
  D customer

3. an <u>irate</u> mob
  A loud
  B angry
  C frightened
  D large

4. to <u>bolster</u> a team
  A defeat
  B join
  C support
  D quit

5. an <u>obligatory</u> smile
  A pretty
  B inviting
  C sincere
  D required

6. a <u>grave</u> mistake
  A serious
  B frequent
  C unnoticed
  D intentional

7. a <u>trauma</u> victim
  A crime
  B swindle
  C shock
  D disaster

TACHS Practice—Answers and Explanations

1. **A** *Sufficient* means "ample or enough."

2. **B** A nuisance is an aggravation, annoyance, or bother.

3. **B** *Irate* means "furious or enraged."

4. **C** To bolster is to reinforce, prop up, or support. The word can be used in either a literal or figurative sense.

5. **D** *Obligatory* means "necessary, required, or mandatory."

6. **A** *Grave* means "serious, important, or critical."

7. **C** *Trauma* means "shock or ordeal."

Sentence and Paragraph Composition

COOP | HSPT | TACHS

The COOP, HSPT, and TACHS all test your ability to compose clear and effective sentences and paragraphs. But you won't actually write them yourself. Instead, you'll compare different versions of sentences and paragraphs, and then choose the best among them. Here's where you'll find these questions on the three tests:

- COOP: Reading and Language Arts test
- HSPT: Language subtest
- TACHS: Written Expression subtest

Note: On the COOP Reading and Language Arts test, composition questions are mixed in with questions based on reading passages.

Here are the basic types of composition questions you're most likely to see on your exam (we'll cover them all in this lesson).

Comparing Sentences

- Recognizing sentences that are clear, concise, and grammatically correct

Linking and Combining Phrases and Sentences

- Choosing connecting words that help ideas flow logically from one sentence (or phrase) to another and make sense together
- Recognizing effective ways to combine two sentences—using appropriate transition words and punctuation

Organizing and Editing Paragraphs

- Determining the best place to insert an additional sentence
- Identifying an irrelevant or unnecessary sentence
- Recognizing a sentence that would fit well in the paragraph
- Identifying a good topic sentence or concluding sentence
- Recognizing an appropriate topic for a one-paragraph essay

Sentence Sense and Structure

In one type of composition question, your task is to compare four different versions of a sentence (or a part of a sentence) and decide which one is written best. An incorrect choice might contain a grammatical error; or it might be too wordy; or it might be awkward or confusing. To compare sentences, follow these three steps:

Step 1: Read the first version of the sentence (or part) carefully. Then ask yourself:

- Does the sentence contain any clear errors in grammar?
- Is the sentence wordier than necessary?
- Is the sentence clumsy or repetitive, or does it simply "sound" wrong (even if you're not sure why)?
- Is the sentence confusing (do you need to read it again to figure out what it means)?

If your answer to any of these questions is "yes," eliminate the first version of the sentence.

Step 2: Repeat step 1 for the remaining three versions. Ask yourself the same three questions as in step 1, and eliminate any choice for which your answer to any of those questions is "yes."

Step 3: If you're left with more than one choice, compare them. If you can't decide which is best, select the briefest, most concise version.

Let's practice the three steps with an example. This one presents four alternative versions of *part* of a sentence.

Choose the group of words that best completes the following sentence:

According to health experts, _____.
A the cause of lung cancer is, mainly, smoking
B those with lung cancer probably got it from smoking
C smoking is the main cause of lung cancer
D smoking mainly causes lung cancer

Step 1: Sentence A contains no grammatical errors. However, if you listen to sentence A as you read it, pausing for the word *mainly* (signified by commas) seems awkward and unnatural, doesn't it? Let's look for a better version.

Step 2: Let's repeat step 1 for the remaining three versions.

Sentence B contains no grammatical errors. But, to whom does the word *those* refer? Positioning *those* immediately after *health experts* misleads the reader to think that the writer is referring to health experts who have lung cancer—rather than to people in general, which is probably what the writer meant. If sentence B had used the word *people* instead of *those,* the sentence would have been pretty good. As it stands, however, sentence B is confusing. Let's look for a better version.

Sentence C is grammatically correct. Unlike versions A and B, there are no unnatural pauses or confusing references. It's concise and clear. So, version C might very well be the best of the four. But we need to look at version D to make sure.

Sentence D contains no grammatical errors, and there are no awkward pauses. What's more, it's shorter (more concise) than sentence C. So, perhaps version D is the best answer. Let's go to step 3.

Step 3: We've eliminated A and B, but we're not sure about choice D. Let's look at it again. Is the meaning of sentence D perfectly clear? No, it's not. The problem is how the sentence is put together. The point the writer is trying to make is that lung cancer is usually the result of smoking. But, version D implies that smoking causes more than one thing, but the main thing that it causes is lung cancer. So, sentence D distorts the point the writer probably tried to make. Eliminate D, and select C as the best choice.

Now, let's apply the steps to a slightly tougher example. This one presents four alternative versions of an entire sentence.

Which sentence is written correctly and expresses the idea most clearly?
A Like their age, the significance of the newly discovered artifacts are not known.
B The age of the newly discovered artifacts and the significance of them are not known.
C The significance of the newly discovered artifacts is not known, and their age isn't known, either.
D Neither the significance of the newly discovered artifacts nor their age is known.

Step 1: Read sentence A very carefully. Notice that the subject of this sentence is *significance,* which is considered singular (as opposed to plural). Also notice that this subject takes the plural verb *are* (rather than the singular form *is*). Because the subject is singular, the verb should be singular as well. In English grammar, this problem is called a subject-verb agreement error. Eliminate version A.

Step 2: Let's repeat step 1 for the remaining three versions.

Sentence B contains no grammatical errors. It's not wordy or repetitive, and its meaning is clear. Let's keep B in mind as a possible best version.

Sentence C contains no grammatical errors. But, notice the the writer repeats *is not known.* This problem makes sentence B better than sentence C. So, you can safely eliminate C.

Sentence D is grammatically correct. The way the sentence uses the two words *neither* and *nor* is appropriate and correct. The sentence clearly and concisely gets the point across—that neither of two certain facts about the newly discovered artifacts, their age and their significance, is known.

Step 3: We've eliminated A and C, but our choice is between B and D. Let's look at sentence B more closely. The phrase *the significance of them* is a bit clumsy, isn't it? The phrase *their significance* would be better. So sentence B does leave some room for improvement. Sentence D is a more graceful alternative. Select D as the best version.

Connecting Ideas

One type of composition question focuses on the transition from one of a sentence's clauses to the next, or from one sentence to the next. Your job might be to fill in a blank with the word(s) that provides the best link. Or, your job might be to combine two sentences into one, connecting them with a word or phrase that makes sense. To handle these questions, follow these four steps:

Step 1: Read the sentence(s). Figure out how the sentence's two parts (or the two sentences) are related.
Step 2: Think of at least one or two words (or short phrases) that connect the two ideas.
Step 3: Check the answer choices for a close match.
Step 4: Read the sentence again, and plug in your selection to make sure it works well.

Let's apply these steps to an example.

Choose the best word to join the thoughts in the following sentence:

Another devastating tsunami wave might strike at any time; _____, the government is not developing a warning system to help save lives during the next tsunami.
A also
B and
C therefore
D yet

Step 1: The first clause tells us that a disaster might occur. In view of this fact, the second clause is a bit surprising. The idea in the second clause is contradictory to the idea in the first clause.

Step 2: Let's think of a word or brief phrase that might lead logically from the first idea to the second idea, which seems to oppose the first. One good word can be derived from step 1 above: *surprisingly*. Two other words that would make sense in place of the blank are *however* and *but*.

Step 3: None of the three words we thought of is listed among the answer choices. However, one of the words, *yet,* means essentially the same thing as *but* or *however*.

Step 4: Let's plug the word *yet* into the sentence. It provides a logical link. Select choice D.

Words that connect a sentence's ideas don't always come in the middle of the sentence. Let's practice the four-step approach with a sentence that starts with a blank.

Choose the best word with which to *begin* the following sentence:

_____ sharks have trouble distinguishing between potential prey and other moving objects, they often attack sea vessels, surfboards, and even buoys bobbing along the water's surface.
A While
B Since
C Although
D After

Step 1: The first clause describes a perception problem among sharks. The second clause describes the result of that problem.

Step 2: For the first clause to lead logically to the second, with what word or phrase would you start the sentence? One that comes to mind is the word *because,* which signals the reader that the first clause (before the comma) is an explanation or reason for what follows.

Step 3: Scanning the answer choices, we see that the word *because* is not among them. However, the word *since* can be used to mean essentially the same thing as *because*.

Step 4: Read the sentence again, starting with the word *Since*. The sentence makes sense, doesn't it? The idea of the sentence as a whole is that sharks attack boats, surfboards, and buoys *because* sharks think they're prey. *Since* provides a logical link between the two ideas. Select choice B.

As the previous two examples show, a good connecting word or phrase provides a logical link between ideas and helps one idea flow naturally to the next. It steers you in the right direction by telling you what the relationship is between the idea preceding it and the one following it. Let's look at some useful connecting words and the kinds of relationships they signal.

Connecting opposing or contrasting ideas. In this relationship, two parts of a sentence (or two sentences) present opposing or contrasting ideas. Here are some words that signal that an opposing idea is just ahead:

although
though
however
but
even though
yet
conversely
on the other hand
whereas
nevertheless
despite

Example:
Treating illnesses without surgery is usually painless, _____ these treatments are often less likely than surgical procedures to result in permanent healing.
A and
B although
C also
D since

The correct answer is B. The first clause tells us about an advantage of nonsurgical treatments, while the second clause tells us about a disadvantage of these treatments. The word *although* is a good connector because it signals that the idea that follows is contrary to the idea preceding it. The connectors *and* and *also* are inappropriate to contrast two different things. The word *since* signals that a reason or explanation for what precedes it is just ahead. But that's not how the sentence's two ideas are related. In short, the connectors in choices A, C, and D simply don't get the point of the sentence across, do they?

Connecting complementary or similar ideas. In this relationship, two parts of a sentence (or two sentences) present complementary or similar ideas—in other words, the writer's ideas continue in the same basic direction. Here are some words that signal that the writer is about to support an idea with a similar one:

also
furthermore
in addition (additionally)
moreover
what's more
in fact
for example
for instance

Example:

Some artists we consider among history's greatest never saw fame or fortune during their lifetimes. ____, some of these artists were actually put to death by their government for creating the type of art they did.

A However

B For this reason

C In fact

D Meanwhile

The correct answer is C. Although the ideas in the two sentences are not the same, they complement or reinforce each other, don't they? The second sentence seems to carry the idea of the first sentence a bit further in the same direction. The phrase *in fact* is a good connector because it conveys this relationship. Choices A and D are incorrect because *However* and *Meanwhile* both signal a reversal—that an opposing idea lies just ahead. Choice B is wrong because *For this reason* signals a logical conclusion or a cause-and-effect relationship, but this isn't the writer's point at all.

Connecting premise and conclusion (or cause and effect). In this relationship, one part of a sentence (or one sentence) provides a conclusion (or effect) based on the other sentence, which provides a premise (or cause). Here are some words that signal that a premise, reason, or cause lies just ahead:

because

since

for the reason that

as a result of

Here are some words that signal a conclusion, result, effect, or outcome:

therefore

thus

and so

accordingly

as a result

consequently

Example:

I noticed that it was starting to rain outside, ____ I grabbed my umbrella.

A since

B because

C although

D and so

The correct answer is D. What's the logical connection between the two parts of the sentence? There's a cause-and-effect relationship, isn't there? Noticing that it's raining is the reason for (cause of) the writer grabbing the umbrella. So, you're looking for a word or phrase that makes this logical connection for the reader. Choice D fits the bill. The word *since* signals that what precedes it is an effect, outcome, or consequence and what follows it is the cause, reason, or explanation. Notice that choices A and B both get the logic backwards; they imply that grabbing the umbrella caused it to start raining, instead of the other way around. As for choice C, the word *although* signals that an opposing idea is just ahead, which is wrong.

Paragraph Structure and Theme

To handle questions about paragraph structure and theme, you need to know how to construct a good paragraph. Here are the key guidelines you need to know:

- The ideas that a paragraph presents should flow naturally and logically from one to the next, with appropriate connecting words (the ones you learned earlier in this lesson) to help the reader follow the writer's train of thought.
- All sentences in a paragraph should relate to a central topic, or theme.
- A paragraph's topic should be specific enough to cover in four to six sentences; if it isn't, then the topic is too broad for a single paragraph.
- A good paragraph contains a topic sentence—a general assertion or claim that all the other sentences in the paragraph support.
- A paragraph's topic sentence should be either the first or last sentence in the paragraph.

On your exam, you won't actually write your own paragraph. Instead, you'll read a brief paragraph (the sentences might be numbered), and then you'll perform tasks such as these:

- Determine the best place to insert a certain additional sentence.
- Identify which sentence doesn't belong in the paragraph—because it's either irrelevant or unnecessary.
- Decide which of four additional sentences would fit best in the paragraph.
- Choose the best topic sentence or concluding sentence among four choices.

Note: On the COOP and TACHS, other questions based on numbered paragraphs focus on grammar, sentence sense, capitalization, and combining sentences. Here, we'll focus just on questions about paragraph structure and theme.

Here are the steps to handling questions about paragraph structure and theme.

Step 1: Read the questions that follow the paragraph (but don't read the answer choices yet). Think about what you should look for when you read the paragraph.
Step 2: Read the paragraph.
Step 3: Recap the paragraph. Ask yourself: What's the paragraph's theme (main idea), and how does the writer try to develop that theme?
Step 4: For the first question about paragraph structure or theme, formulate your own answer to the question.
Step 5: Scan the answer choices for the best match. If you're not sure which is best, eliminate choices that are obviously wrong, and then compare the remaining choices.
Step 6: Repeat steps 4 and 5 for any other questions about paragraph structure or theme.

Now, let's apply these steps to an example paragraph and two questions based on it.

Step 1: Read the questions (but not the answer choices yet) based on the paragraph.

1. Which sentence does not belong in the paragraph?
2. Which of the following is the best concluding sentence for the paragraph?

These questions tell us that, when we read the paragraph, we should look for a sentence that doesn't fit very well with the overall theme. We should also keep in mind that the paragraph might end abruptly—without a good ending.

Step 2: Now, read the paragraph (keep the two questions from step 1 in mind):

¹I own cats because they are low-maintenance pets. ²All you need to do for a cat is put food out and clean a litter box once a day. ³If you want a pet that's loyal to you, get a dog, not a cat. ⁴On the other hand, dogs are like little children, always getting into trouble and needing attention. ⁵Dogs ruin furniture, dig up lawns, and disturb people with their barking.

Step 3: Let's recap the paragraph:
What's the main idea, or theme? Cats are easier to have as pets than dogs.
How does the writer try to develop this theme? By listing reasons cats are easy to care for, and then listing reasons dogs make difficult pets.

Step 4: With our recap from step 3 in mind, let's attempt each of the two multiple-choice questions. Here's question 1 again:

1. Which sentence does not belong in the paragraph?

Of the five sentences, the only one that doesn't fit the theme (cats are easier pets than dogs) is sentence 3, which mentions an advantage of owning a dog over a cat.

Step 5: Now, scan the answer choices.

A sentence 1
B sentence 3
C sentence 4
D sentence 5

Choice B is the correct answer. Select it, and go to the next question.

Step 6: Now, repeat steps 4 and 5 for the second question. Here it is again:

2. Which of the following is the best concluding sentence for the paragraph?

What would be a good way to finish this paragraph, to tie all the ideas together? Again, refer to the paragraph's theme: Cats are easier pets than dogs. Let's scan the answer choices, looking for a sentence that most closely mirrors this theme:

A Short-haired cats are easier to take care of than long-haired cats.
B Also, it costs more to feed a dog than a cat.
C Unlike cats, dogs are more trouble than they're worth, in my opinion.
D Everyone should own a cat because they bring great joy to our lives.

Sentences B and C both reflect the paragraph's overall theme, and so they're both in the running as the best concluding sentence. On the other hand, notice that sentences A and D are only about cats. What's more, both are a bit off the focus of the paragraph: why cats are easier than dogs to have as pets. Eliminate A and D. That leaves B and C. Look at sentence B again. It flows logically from sentences 4 and 5, which also list drawbacks of owning dogs. But, does it tie together all the ideas in the paragraph? No. Sentence C does a much better job. Eliminate B and select C as the best choice.

Practice

Directions: Questions 1–10 are in the HSPT format. They are also useful for TACHS practice. Follow the directions for each question.

1. Choose the best word or words to join the thoughts together.

   I brush my teeth twice a day; _____, I floss at least once daily.

   A for example
   B besides
   C however
   D in addition

2. Choose the best word with which to begin the sentence.

   _____ the verdict of a jury, a trial judge has the authority to issue the final verdict in a court case.

   A Regarding
   B In addition to
   C Regardless of
   D Because of

3. Choose the group of words that best completes the sentence.

   In order to grow and thrive, _____.

   A the plants must be watered often
   B often the plants must be watered
   C watering the plants must be often
   D the plants being watered must often occur

4. Which of the following expresses the idea most clearly?

   A Nicotine, caffeine, and sugar have all been proven to be physically addictive.
   B The physical addictiveness of nicotine, of caffeine, and of sugar has been proven.
   C It's all been proven: Nicotine, caffeine, and sugar are physically addictive.
   D Nicotine, caffeine, and sugar are all physically addictive, a fact that's proven.

5. Choose the best word or words to join the thoughts together.

   Financial hardship is anything but alien to the American people; _____, more than 10% of the population fall below the poverty line.

   A nevertheless
   B therefore
   C in fact
   D also

6. Which topic is best suited for a one-paragraph essay?

   A The Origins of Christianity
   B Preventing Juvenile Crime
   C War in the 20th Century
   D none of the above

7. Choose the best sentence to insert between sentences 3 and 4 of the following paragraph.

   (1) Every person has something unique to offer, and so it is generally unwise to label other people. (2) For instance, standard I.Q. tests, which are designed to measure so-called "intelligence," only test "book smarts." (3) Test takers who are naturally "street smart" often perform poorly on this kind of test. (4) Therefore, it is foolish for companies to hire employees based largely on the results of such tests.

   A A person can get good grades in school but still not be very smart.
   B To succeed in most jobs, it helps to be street smart.
   C Some people are unfairly labeled as "dumb."
   D A good personality is just as important as intelligence.

8. Which of the following expresses the idea most clearly?

   A Many of the jobs of American workers are now being done by Indian, Pakistani, and Chinese workers.

   B Workers in India, Pakistan, and China are now doing many of the jobs that American workers once did.

   C In India, Pakistan, and China, workers are now doing the jobs that used to be done in America by workers.

   D Many of the jobs that American workers used to do are now in India, Pakistan, and China, done by the workers there.

9. Which sentence does *not* belong in the following paragraph?

   (1) Last year my class had a pet lizard named Ginger. (2) Ginger was quiet and liked to sleep on a rock in her cage for most of the day, so she made a good pet for our classroom. (3) She was a leopard gecko, a nocturnal lizard. (4) Nocturnal animals are most active at night and sleep in the daytime. (5) I sometimes sleep in the daytime. (6) My teacher said she would feed Ginger each evening before she left to go home.

   A sentence 1
   B sentence 2

   C sentence 4
   D sentence 5

10. Choose the pair of sentences that best fits under the following topic sentence.

    Artists perceive reality in ways that most other people are oblivious to.

    A No artist since Michelangelo has improved on his depiction of the human form in all its beauty. Nevertheless, nearly every serious art student since has tried.

    B When a true artist looks at a human form, she might first notice the interplay of light and shadow. For the artist, noses are sculptures, chiseled in flesh and bone.

    C During periods of great religious or political repression, artists are forced to explore "unacceptable" forms and subject matter in secret. During other eras, however, all art has been openly celebrated.

    D Some art scholars believe that only an artist can appreciate another artist's work. Others strongly disagree and claim that any human being with eyes to see can appreciate art on some level.

Directions: Questions 11–20 are in the COOP format. They are also useful for TACHS practice. Follow the directions for each question.

Read the following paragraph, and then answer questions 11 and 12.

Earthquakes, which are not uncommon in the Euphrates valley, can worsen the effects of the annual flooding, just as shaking any broad sheet of water would disrupt it. Typhoons can also exacerbate the flooding. If a hurricane from the southeast sweeps up the Persian Gulf at the height of an inundation of rain there, it can drive the Gulf's shallow waters up onto the valley's delta area, thereby damming back the outflow, perhaps for hundreds of miles upstream.

11. Choose the best topic sentence for the paragraph.

    A The entire delta area of the Euphrates valley experiences severe flooding each year.

    B Earthquakes and hurricanes cause even larger catastrophes in the Euphrates valley than the annual flooding there.

    C The inhabitants of the Euphrates valley must stay continually alert for floods, earthquakes, and hurricanes.

    D Other natural phenomena can intensify the annual flooding of the Euphrates valley.

12. Choose the best concluding sentence for the paragraph.

A Whirlwinds, which sweep up the powdery soil into dust clouds, are not uncommon in the valley.

B The end result can be catastrophic for the valley's entire delta region.

C The summer heat is intense, while in winter bitterly cold northern blasts sweep the valley.

D Small elevations and depressions here and there diversify the surface of the valley's alluvial region.

Here is a paragraph a student wrote about a popular tourist attraction. There are a few mistakes that need correcting. Read the paragraph, and then answer questions 13 and 14.

[1]Geysers are not the same things as a volcano. [2]A geyser spouts steam into the air. [3]The steam comes from boiling water beneath the ground. [4]The world's largest geyser is called Old Faithful. [5]It is located in Yellowstone National Park. [6]This park is in Southwestern Montana. [7]Yellowstone Park is a very popular tourist attraction.

13. Which is the best way to write sentence 1?

A Geysers are not the same as volcanoes.

B Geysers are not the same as a volcano.

C A geyser and a volcano are a different thing.

D best as is

14. Choose the best way to combine sentences 2 and 3.

A A geyser spouts steam into the air, coming from boiling water beneath the ground.

B A geyser spouts steam, which comes from boiling water beneath the ground, into the air.

C A geyser, spouting steam into the air, comes from boiling water beneath the ground.

D From boiling water beneath the ground spouts steam from a geyser into the air.

Here is a paragraph a student wrote about detecting lies. There are a few mistakes that need correcting. Read the paragraph, and then answer questions 15–17.

[1]Honesty is the best policy. [2]Sometimes I lie to my parents. [3]They know when I tell a lie. [4]Looking into my eyes is the best lie detector. [5]When I tell a lie my eyes give me away. [6]Sometimes my voice changes, too.

15. Which sentence does not belong in the paragraph?

A sentence 1

B sentence 4

C sentence 5

D sentence 6

16. Choose the best way to rewrite sentence 4.

A My eyes are the best lie detector.

B Looking into my eyes are the best lie detector.

C The best lie detector is looking into my eyes.

D best as is

17. Which is the best way to combine sentences 2 and 3?

A Sometimes when I lie to my parents they know when I lie.

B Sometimes I lie to my parents, who know when I tell a lie.

C Sometimes I lie to my parents, but they know when I do.

D I lie to my parents sometimes, they can tell that I am lying.

18. Choose the sentence that is written correctly.

A Organic buildings are often designed to be "green" as well.

B Organic buildings are often also designed as "green," too.

C Organic buildings are designed to often be "green" as well.

D Frequently, organic buildings are often designed to be "green."

19. Choose the sentence that is written correctly.

A Frank Lloyd Wright, among all modern architects, was more influential than them all.

B More influential than any modern architect was architect Frank Lloyd Wright.

C Frank Lloyd Wright was more influential than any other modern architect.

D More than any modern architect, architect Frank Lloyd Wright was influential.

20. Here are two related sentences:

Waka is a form of Japanese poetry.
Waka is used exclusively by women.

Which is the best way to combine these two sentences?

A *Waka* is a form of Japanese poetry, which is used exclusively by women.

B *Waka* is a form of Japanese poetry and it is used exclusively by women.

C *Waka* is used exclusively as a form of Japanese poetry by women.

D *Waka*, a form of Japanese poetry, is used exclusively by women.

Practice—Answers and Explanations

1. **D** The second thought continues in the same vein as the first—arguing that the speaker takes good care of her teeth. The phrase *in addition* works well here to signal a continuation of the same general idea. (Two other connectors that would work well here are *also* and *moreover.*)

2. **C** The first clause refers to the jury verdict, and then the second clause presents an opposing idea: that a judge can overrule that verdict. Beginning the sentence with the phrase *Regardless of* makes sense; it tells the reader that what follows the first clause will be an opposing idea. (Two other good ways to fill in the blank are the phrase *in spite of* and the word *despite.*)

3. **A** Because the first clause clearly refers to (or modifies) *the plants,* the second clause should begin with *the plants.* You can eliminate choices B and C. The phrase in choice D is wordy and awkward. That leaves the phrase in choice A, which helps convey the sentence's meaning clearly and gracefully.

4. **A** Sentence A is clear and effective. (The phrase *been proven to be* is idiomatic.) Sentence B suffers from two problems: the awkward word *addictiveness* (*addictive quality* would be better) and the unnecessary repetition of the word *of.* In sentence C, the opening clause (especially the use of the word *all*) is confusing and inappropriate. In sentence D, the final phrase—*a fact that's been proven*—is awkward and redundant.

5. **C** The sentence's second clause provides details to support the assertion in the first clause. The phrase *in fact* is an appropriate signal that such details are just ahead.

6. **D** Each of these three topics is quite complex. It would be impossible to cover any of them adequately in just one paragraph.

7. **B** The sentence in choice B helps complete the writer's line of reasoning, which is as follows: People with more "street smarts" than "book smarts" are just as valuable to employers than people with only book smarts, and therefore employers should not use I.Q. tests when making hiring decisions.

8. **B** Sentence B is clear and effective. Sentence A does not make clear that American workers no longer have their jobs. In choice C, the phrase *used to be done in America by workers* is awkward and confusing. In choice D, the second half of the sentence is constructed awkwardly; a more effective version would be: . . . *are now done by workers in India, Pakistan, and China.*

9. **D** The paragraph is about a nocturnal lizard, so sentence 5 is off topic.

10. **B** Discussion under the topic sentence should point out how artists differ from nonartists in how they see the world around them. Choice B tells us how the artist sees things in a unique way; this fits well under the topic.

11. **D** As a whole, the paragraph is about how earthquakes and hurricanes make the flooding of the Euphrates valley even worse than it would be from the annual inundation of rain alone. Choice D expresses this idea nicely.

12. **B** The rest of the paragraph discusses three natural phenomena that contribute to flooding. This discussion naturally leads to the concluding observation that the combined outcome can be disastrous.

13. **A** The original sentence compares the plural *geysers* to the singular *a volcano.* Both should be either singular or plural. Choice A fixes the problem, while omitting the word *thing,* which adds nothing to the meaning of the sentence.

14. B In choice B, the placement of the relative pronoun *which* immediately after its antecedent *steam* makes it clear that the clause between the commas refers to (describes) *steam*. Also, notice that you can remove the clause between the commas, and what's left makes perfect sense as a complete sentence.

15. A The paragraph is about how the writer's eyes, and sometimes voice, reveal that she is lying. Sentence 1 is slightly off this topic.

16. D Sentence 4 is clear in meaning and grammatically correct as it stands. The sentence in choice A wrongly implies that it is the writer's *eyes*—rather than *looking into* her eyes—that are lie detectors. The sentence in choice B incorrectly uses the plural verb form *are* to refer to the noun clause *Looking into my eyes,* which is considered singular. The sentence in choice C is grammatically correct, but it is awkward and confusing; its grammatical structure wrongly implies that the best lie detector is something apart from looking into the writer's eyes.

17. C A good way to combine the two sentences is with a comma followed by an appropriate connecting word. The connector *but* works well to convey the sentence's idea. The sentence in choice A is too wordy. Notice that it repeats the phrase *when I lie.* To improve it, you could replace *when I lie* at the end of the sentence with the single word *it.* The sentence in choice B is also too wordy. To improve it, you could replace *when I do* with *it.* Choice D supplies the needed comma, but a connecting word after the comma is missing. (The result is a "comma splice"—a clear grammatical error.)

18. A The sentence in choice A conveys the point clearly and without redundancy or grammatical error. The sentence in choice B contains a redundancy: The words *also* and *too* convey the same idea. In choice C, the word *often* is misplaced; the sentence implies that an organic building might sometimes be green while at other times *not* be green. The sentence in choice D suffers from a different redundancy: The words *frequently* and *often* convey the same idea.

19. C The best version of the sentence should make it clear that Wright was a modern architect and must compare Wright to *other* modern architects. Only choice C fits the bill.

20. D The sentence in choice D nicely combines two facts about *waka* into one clear, concise, and grammatically correct sentence. In choice A, the use of a comma followed by the word *which* wrongly implies that all Japanese poetry, not just *waka,* is used exclusively by women. The sentence in choice B should include a comma before the word *and*—to separate the two independent clauses. Or, you could create a more graceful and concise sentence by simply removing the word *it.* The sentence in choice C is confusing because it is awkwardly constructed.

Analogies

COOP | HSPT

Analogies test your ability to identify relationships between the meaning of different words or pictures, and to recognize similar relationships between other pairs of words or pictures. On the HSPT, the Verbal Skills subtest includes about 10 word analogy questions, mixed in with several other question types. On the COOP, the Analogies test contains nothing but picture analogy questions (20 altogether), while the Verbal Reasoning—Words test includes several word analogies, mixed in with other question types.

To handle analogy questions, follow this four-step approach:

Step 1: Determine how the first group of words (or pictures) are related, and make up a sentence that expresses that relationship.
Step 2: Try out your sentence with each answer choice, eliminating the choices that clearly don't work.
Step 3: If you're left with more than one answer, or no answer at all, go back and make your sentence fit better.
Step 4: Choose the best answer; if none of the choices fits exactly, choose the one that works best.

Next, you'll apply this approach to one HSPT example and two COOP examples. Then, you'll learn to recognize some common patterns in COOP and HSPT analogies.

HSPT Analogies—Step by Step

The HSPT Verbal Skills subtest includes about 10 word analogy questions. Here's a typical example:

Forest is to tree as library is to
  A school
  B book
  C librarian
  D aisle

Let's apply the four-step approach to this example:

Step 1: Here's a sentence that expresses the relationship between the first word pair: *A forest is a place where you see many trees.*

Step 2: Let's see which answer choices form a similar relationship. Is a library a place where you see many *schools*? No. Eliminate choice A. Is a library a place where you see many *books*? Yes. Is a library a place where you see many *librarians*? Maybe, depending on the size of the library. Is a library a place where you see many *aisles*? Probably, since most libraries are large enough to contain many aisles.

Step 3: The only choice we've eliminated so far is A. So, we'll need to refine our sentence from step 1. Let's try a sentence that expresses the relationship between *forest* and *tree* a bit more specifically: *Many trees together in one area make up a forest.*

Step 4: Among the three remaining answer choices, let's see which ones fit this sentence. Do many books together in one place make up a *library*? Yes. In fact, this is the definition of library. Choice B looks like a strong answer. But let's check the other two remaining choices anyway. First, choice C: Do many librarians together in one place make up a library? No; the sentence doesn't make much sense, does it? Finally, choice D: Do many, many aisles together make up a library? Yes, they can; but a group of aisles together might form many other things, such as a store, a sports arena, or a theater. So, the analogy between library-aisle and forest-tree isn't as strong as the analogy between library-book and forest-tree. Choice B is the correct answer.

COOP Picture Analogies—Step by Step

The COOP Analogies test consists of 20 questions based on picture analogies. Here are the directions for the COOP Analogies test:

Directions: For questions 1–20, the two upper pictures are related in some way. Select a picture that fills in the space so that the two lower pictures are related in the same way.

Here's a typical example of a COOP picture-analogy question:

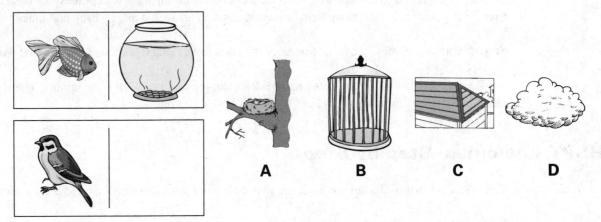

Let's tackle this question by applying the four steps we introduced at the beginning of this chapter.

Step 1: The first picture pair shows a goldfish and a goldfish bowl. Here's a sentence that expresses the relationship between the two: *A goldfish lives in a fishbowl.*

Step 2: The first picture of the second pair shows a bird. Let's see which of the four other pictures paired with a bird form a similar relationship to the one between a goldfish and a bowl.
Choice A: Does a bird live in a nest on a tree branch? Yes.
Choice B: Does a bird live in a birdcage? Yes.
Choice C: Does a bird live on a rooftop? Usually not, but possibly.
Choice D: Does a bird live in the clouds? No. Eliminate choice D.

Step 3: The only choice we've eliminated so far is D. So, we'll need to fine-tune our sentence from step 1. Let's try a sentence that expresses the relationship between a goldfish and a fishbowl a bit more specifically: *People often keep pet goldfish in a fishbowl.*

Step 4: Among the three remaining answer choices, let's see which ones fit this sentence.
Choice A: Do people often keep pet birds in tree nests? No; tree branches are where wild birds often build their nests. Eliminate A.
Choice B: Do people often keep pet birds in birdcages? Yes. Choice B looks like a strong answer.
Choice C: Do people often keep pet birds on rooftops? No. Rooftops are where wild birds often light briefly between flights. Eliminate C.

We've now homed in on the best answer choice: B. Here's the analogy again: *People often keep pet goldfish in fishbowls, just as people often keep their pet birds in birdcages.*

COOP Word Analogies—Step by Step

On the COOP, you'll find word analogies on the Verbal Reasoning—Words test, mixed in with other types of questions about words. Here are the directions for COOP word analogies:

Directions: In these questions, the words in the top line are related in some way. The words in the bottom line should be related in the same way. Find the word that completes the bottom row of words.

Here's a typical example of a COOP word analogy question:

book   shelf   aisle
_____

room   house   _____
  A street
  B block
  C driveway
  D family

As you can see, in COOP word analogies, the relationship involves *three* words, not just two. It's this feature that makes these questions a bit tricky. An additional step (step 2 below) is required to handle them.

Step 1: Determine how the first group of words (or pictures) are related, and make up a sentence that expresses that relationship.
Step 2: Try out your sentence with the two words in the bottom row; if the sentence doesn't work, revise it so that it does.
Step 3: Try out your sentence with each answer choice, eliminating the choices that clearly don't work.
Step 4: If you're left with more than one answer, or no answer at all, go back and make your sentence fit better.
Step 5: Choose the best answer; if none of the choices fits exactly, choose the one that works best.

Let's apply this five-step approach to our example:

Step 1: Here's a good sentence that captures the relationship between the three words in the top row: A *book* may be one of several located on a *shelf*, while a shelf may be one of several along an *aisle* (for example, in a library or bookstore).

Step 2: Let's first see if the relationship between the two words in the bottom row (*room* and *house*) are related in the same way as the first two words in the top row (*book* and *shelf*). Is a room one of several located in a house? Yes. It looks like the first part of the sentence from step 1 works well, so we can go to step 3.

Step 3: Let's try out the rest of our sentence with each of the four answer choices.
Choice A: Is a house often one of several on a *street*? Yes, very often. Choice A seems to work.
Choice B: Is a house often one of several on a *block*? Yes, very often. Choice B seems to work.
Choice C: Is a house often one of several on a *driveway*? Well, sometimes several houses can share a common driveway. But, this is not too common. So, let's eliminate choice C.
Choice D: Is a house often one of several on a *family*? No, this makes no sense. Eliminate choice D.

Step 4: We've narrowed down our choices to A and B. We need to fine-tune the relationship between *shelf* and *aisle* so that it's analogous to only one of those two choices. An aisle is a straight pathway, isn't it? So, a shelf is one of several that you might find along an aisle.

Step 5: A street is also a pathway, whereas a block is not. Aha! We have found the key to completing this analogy: A *shelf* (of *books*) may be one of several shelves along an *aisle,* just as a *house* (of *rooms*) may be one of several houses along a *street.* Select choice B as the one that best completes the analogy.

Know the Basic Relationship Types

Most HSPT and COOP analogies fall into one of several basic categories. Knowing these categories will help you identify the key relationship between the words (or pictures). Although not every analogy fits neatly into one of the following categories, many do. (Word examples are on the left; COOP picture examples are on the right.)

Function, purpose, or use. In this type of relationship, one word (or picture) identifies an instrument or tool whose use or function involves what another word (or picture) signifies.

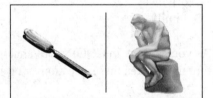

shovel : dig

finger : point

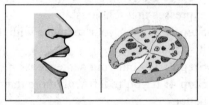

money : buy

compliment : flatter

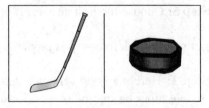

Preventing, correcting, reversing, or eliminating. In this type of relationship, one thing works against another thing in some way—by preventing, reversing, stopping, or eliminating it.

flood : dam

hunger : food

noise : muffler

accident : caution

Place or environment for. In this type of relationship, one thing is a place or environment where a certain event or condition occurs, or where a certain thing is often found.

wash : tub

compete : stadium

prosecute : court

mourn : funeral

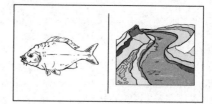

Condition for or ingredient of. In this type of relationship, one thing is an important condition or ingredient for another thing.

flour : cake

steel : skyscraper

cold : snowman

wind : sail

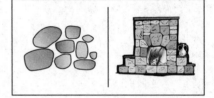

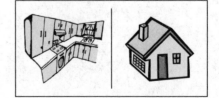

Part or element of. In this type of relationship, one thing is one of several different components, elements, or parts of another thing.

tire : bicycle

attic : house

keyboard : computer

chorus : song

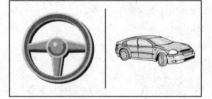

Process and product. In this type of relationship, one thing causes or produces another thing, or is a sign or symptom of another thing.

crime : trial

sauté : dinner

artist : painting

bored : yawn

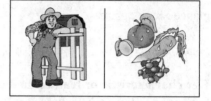

On the HSPT, look for the following additional types of word relationships.

Group-to-member. In this type of relationship, one word names a type of group, while the other word names a member of that group.

soldier : army

goose : gaggle

tomato : crop

mountain : range

Type, form, category, or example. In this type of relationship, one thing is a type, category, form, or example of another thing.

sparrow : bird

percussion : instrument

ounce : weight

mammal : species

Degree, quality, or extent. Here, the relationship between the two words is a difference in either *quantity* (number, duration, size, speed, loudness, etc.) or *quality* (neutral vs. negative, or positive vs. negative).

jog : sprint

drip : pour

critique : mock

like : adore

whisper : talk : shout

tap : hit : pound

glance : look : glare

pond : lake : ocean

Key characteristic or feature. In this type of relationship, one word (an adjective) defines another thing (a noun) or names a key characteristic of the other thing.

knife : sharp

cold : ice

stingy : miser

agile : acrobat

Contrary or opposed to. In this type of relationship, one thing might be essentially the opposite of another thing; or it might name a key feature that the other thing lacks.

money : broke

arc : straight

fool : prudent

novel : imitation

Other Analogy Strategies

The key to mastering an HSPT or COOP analogy is what you've just learned: to recognize the relationship between the words and formulate a good sentence that expresses that relationship. But, there are other strategies, which we'll look at now.

Some Analogies Work Better Backwards

Some analogies work better when you turn them around, so that the second word (picture) comes first in your sentence.

Example (COOP):

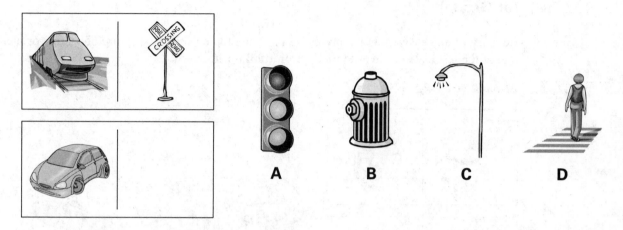

The correct answer is choice A. It's easier to formulate a useful sentence starting with the second picture: A railroad crossing signal (second picture) warns of a train (first picture) approaching and to wait to cross over the tracks. Similarly, a traffic light warns that other automobiles have the right of way and to wait before driving through an intersection.

Example (HSPT):
Illness is to pale as night is to
A day
B sleepy
C dark
D mysterious

The correct answer is choice C. It's easier to formulate a useful sentence starting with the second word: A *pale* complexion (second word) is a characteristic, or sign, of *illness* (first word). Similarly, *darkness* is a characteristic, or sign, of *night.*

Look Out for Answer Choices That Get It Backwards

If you're not thinking straight, it's easy to get the relationship between words or pictures turned around—so you think it's just the opposite of what it really is. The test makers often bait you with wrong answer choices that prey on this sort of confusion. Don't let them trap you!

Example (HSPT):
Separate is to combination as timid is to
A happiness
B shyness
C loneliness
D friendliness

The correct answer is choice D. *Combination* (from the verb *combine*) is opposed in meaning to *separate* (used as an adjective here). Among the four word choices, *friendliness* is the best opposite of *timid*. Notice that among the answer choices are not just one but *two* good synonyms of *timid:* shyness and loneliness. Both words mean just the opposite of what you should be looking for in the best choice.

Don't Be Fooled by Answer Choices That Are Too Much Like the First Pair (or Group)

Be wary of any answer choice involving the same topic as the first group of words (or pictures). This is one of the test makers' favorite tricks. Don't fall for it!

Example (COOP):

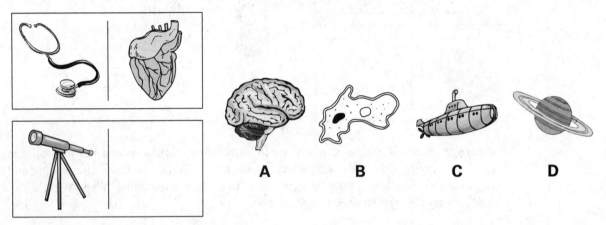

The correct answer is choice D. Notice that answer choice A, which shows a brain, is more closely related to the first pair of pictures (a stethoscope and a human heart) than any other answer choice. Does this mean that choice B is correct? Absolutely not! It's there to trick you; don't fall for it! Here's the correct analogy: You use a *stethoscope* to examine a *heart.* Similarly, you use a *telescope* to examine celestial bodies (planets, stars, and moons) such as the planet *Saturn* (pictured).

Don't Be Tempted by Off-the-Wall Answer Choices

Some answer choices simply won't make any sense when paired with the other word (or picture). Don't waste time puzzling over choices that seem "off-the-wall." They probably are, so eliminate them!

Example (COOP):

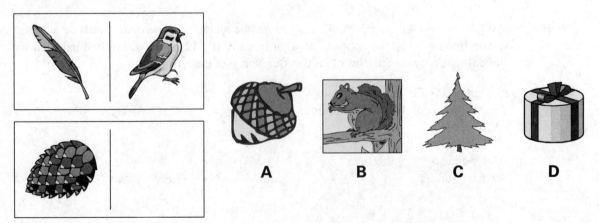

The correct answer is choice C. What's the connection between a pine cone and a gift-wrapped box, pictured in choice D? Well, Christmas trees are usually pine trees, and many people put presents under their Christmas tree. But that's a pretty weak connection, isn't it? Also, what's the relationship between a pine cone and a squirrel, pictured in choice B? Well, squirrels climb trees (including pine trees). But, otherwise, there's no connection. Don't be tempted by choices like B and D; they're designed to trap you! The best choice is C. Here's the analogy: A bird is covered with feathers, which the bird often sheds. Similarly, a pine tree is covered with pine cones, which the tree often sheds.

Analogies—Heads Up!

- Look for common relationship types, and make up a good sentence using the original pair.
- Some analogies work better when you turn them around, so that the second word (picture) comes first in your sentence.
- Eliminate any answer choice where there's no clear link between the two words (or pictures).
- Be wary of any answer choice involving the same topic as the original pair of words (or pictures).

Practice

Directions: Questions 1–6 are similar to COOP picture analogy questions. In each question, the two upper pictures are related in some way. Select a picture that fills in the space so that the two lower pictures are related in the same way.

1.

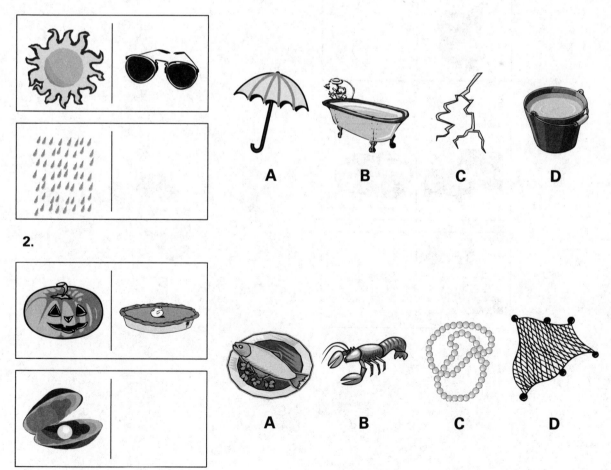

2.

3.

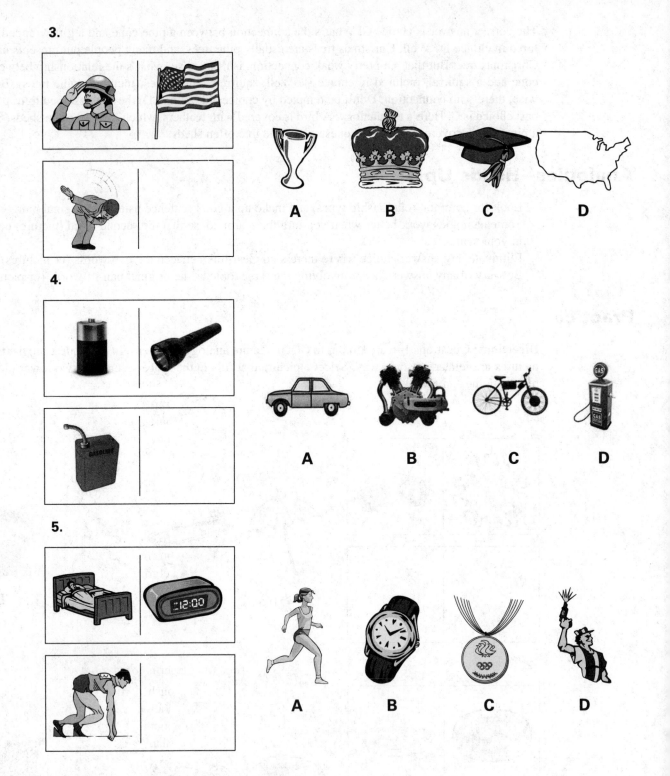

4.

5.

6.

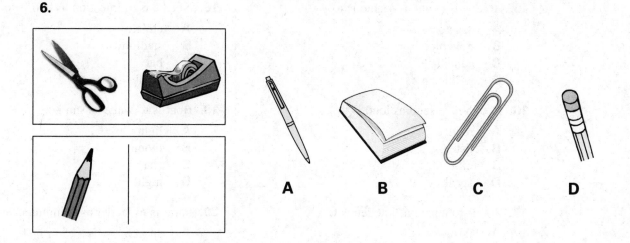

Directions: Questions 7–10 are similar to COOP word analogy questions. In each question, the words in the top line are related in some way. The words in the bottom line should be related in the same way. Find the word that completes the bottom row of words.

7. shirt   vest   coat
pit   fruit   _____

- A   rind
- B   vegetable
- C   salad
- D   juice

8. tub   shower   sink
oven   stove   _____

- A   refrigerator
- B   toaster
- C   kitchen
- D   dishwasher

9. shop   buy   wear
hunt   shoot   _____

- A   trap
- B   bury
- C   eat
- D   kill

10. touch   rub   pat
take   steal   _____

- A   lie
- B   give
- C   borrow
- D   return

Directions: Questions 11–20 are similar to HSPT word analogy questions. For each question, choose the best answer.

11. Convertible is to car as oak is to

- A   table
- B   wood
- C   maple
- D   truck

12. Graduation is to school as retirement is to

- A   leisure
- B   work
- C   home
- D   education

13. Simmer is to boil as tap is to

- A   push
- B   cool
- C   pound
- D   snap

14. Team is to coach as orchestra is to

- A   concert
- B   conductor
- C   violin
- D   music

15. Colony is to ant as senate is to

A senator
B governor
C candidate
D politician

16. Rough is to sand as loud is to

A reduce
B listen
C muzzle
D speak

17. Zoo is to jungle as kitchen is to

A farm
B pantry
C oven
D restaurant

18. Needle is to injection as ball is to

A athlete
B stadium
C bat
D game

19. Boat is to wake as sun is to

A light
B moon
C star
D night

20. Paint is to ladder as communicate is to

A speech
B advice
C letter
D ear

Practice—Answers and Explanations

1. A Sunglasses shield you from sunlight. Similarly, an umbrella shields you from rain.

2. C The insides of a pumpkin are used to make pumpkin pie. Similarly, what's inside an oyster—a pearl—is used to make a pearl necklace.

3. B Saluting is a show of respect for the U.S. flag, a symbol of a particular government. Similarly, bowing is a show of respect for the crown, a symbol of a monarchy (a particular form government).

4. A A battery powers a flashlight to make it work. Similarly, gasoline powers a car to make it go.

5. D The purpose of an alarm clock is to alert you to start the day's activities. Similarly, the purpose of a starter's pistol is to signal the start of a race.

6. D Scissors are used to cut apart, while tape is used for the opposite purpose: to join together. Similarly, the point of a pencil is used to write, while the pencil's eraser is used for the opposite purpose: to remove that writing.

7. A A *vest* is usually worn over a *shirt,* while a coat is worn over both a vest and a shirt. So the relationship involves layers. Similarly, in a piece of fruit, the *fruit* itself covers the *pit,* while the *rind* (which lies just beneath the skin or peel) covers both the fruit and the pit.

8. B A *tub, shower,* and *sink,* are all used for a similar purpose (washing) and usually in the same room (the bathroom). Similarly, an *oven, stove,* and *toaster* are all used for the same basic purpose (heating food) and are usually found in the same room (the kitchen).

9. C The words in the top line outline a series of events, in order from first to last: *shopping* for clothes, *buying* the clothes, and then using the clothes you bought—in other words, *wearing* them. Analogous to this series of events is the process of *hunting* an animal; then, once you've found it, *shooting* it; and then using the animal you shot—in other words, *eating* it.

10. C The words *rub* and *pat* each name a form of *touching.* However, a pat is far briefer than a rub, which may actually cause harm if it carries on. Similarly, to *borrow* is to *take* something only temporarily, whereas to *steal* is to take something permanently, often harming the victim.

11. **B** A convertible is one type of car. Similarly, an oak is one type of wood.

12. **B** Graduation occurs when you've finished school, much like retirement occurs when you've finished working.

13. **C** In order to simmer water, you apply low heat, whereas to boil water you apply greater heat; the relationship is one of degree. Similarly, to tap is to touch briefly and gently, whereas to pound is to touch briefly but hit hard.

14. **B** A coach directs or instructs a team. Similarly, a conductor directs an orchestra.

15. **A** A community of ants is called a colony, and so the relationship is group-to-member. Similarly, a senate is a group of senators.

16. **C** You reduce or eliminate roughness by sanding—a rough piece of wood, for example. Similarly, you reduce or eliminate loudness by muzzling—a barking dog, for example.

17. **A** A zoo is a civilized place where you might find an animal that came originally from a jungle. Similarly, a kitchen is a domestic place for food that might have come originally from a farm.

18. **D** A needle is an apparatus, or tool, commonly used for an injection (an activity). Similarly, a ball is an apparatus commonly used in a game (also an activity).

19. **A** A moving boat creates a wake (ripples in the water). Similarly, a sun creates light.

20. **C** A ladder is a tool often used for painting—in order to reach high places. Similarly, a letter is often used for communicating—with someone who is not nearby.

COOP | HSPT

Verbal logic questions test your ability to identify strong (good) and weak (poor) conclusions based on certain statements that you should assume are factual, or true. These statements are called *premises*. The COOP and HSPT both cover verbal logic.

- HSPT: The Verbal Skills subtest includes about 15 verbal logic questions, mixed in with several other question types.
- COOP: The Verbal Reasoning—Context test contains nothing but verbal logic questions, 20 altogether.

HSPT Verbal Logic Questions

In an HSPT verbal logic question, a series of two or three premises is followed by a conclusion. Your job is to figure out, based on the premises, whether the conclusion is (A) true, (B) false, or (C) uncertain. These are your three answer choices; *there's no fourth answer choice* (D). Here are the steps to handling an HSPT verbal logic question.

Step 1: Read the premises carefully. If they rank various people or things, draw a diagram to help organize the information.

Step 2: Read the conclusion carefully. Ask yourself if the conclusion *must* be true based on the premises. If the answer is "yes," select choice A. Otherwise, go to step 3.

Step 3: Ask yourself if the conclusion *must* be false based on the premises. If the answer is "yes," select choice B. Otherwise, select choice C: It is uncertain whether the conclusion is true or false.

Now look at a typical example:

Jan is taller than Ron. Melinda is the same height as Jan. Melinda is shorter than Ron. If the first two statements are true, the third is

  A true
  B false
  C uncertain

Let's apply the three-step approach to this example:

Step 1: In your test booklet, draw a simple diagram of the first statement, showing the relationship between J and R: (TALL)

                    J

                    R

               (SHORT)

Now add the information from the second statement to the diagram:

(TALL)

J = M

R

(SHORT)

Step 2: The third statement (the stated conclusion) is that Melinda (M) is shorter than Ron (R). Examining the diagram, you can see that Melinda (M) is *taller* than Ron (R). Eliminate choice A.

Step 3: According to the diagram, Melinda (M) is definitely taller (*not* shorter) than Ron (R). Therefore, the third statement must be false. The correct answer choice is B.

Now, let's apply the three-step approach to another example (this one's a bit more complicated):

Soda costs more than tea, and tea costs less than coffee. Juice costs less than soda but more than tea. Coffee costs less than juice. If the first two statements are true, the third is
   A   true
   B   false
   C   uncertain

Step 1: In your test booklet, draw a simple diagram of the first statement, showing the relationship between soda (S), tea (T), and coffee (C):

(MORE $)

S C

T

(LESS $)

This diagram shows that we don't know which costs more: soda (S) or coffee (C). Now, add the information from the second statement (you'll need to revise your previous diagram, but that's okay):

(MORE $)

S

J

    C

T ↑

(LESS $)

This diagram tells us is that all we know about coffee (C) is that it costs more than tea (T).

Step 2: The third statement (the stated conclusion) is that coffee (C) costs less than juice (J). Examining the diagram, you can see this conclusion is not necessarily true. Eliminate choice A.

Step 3: The diagram shows that all we know about coffee (C) is that it costs more than tea (T). We have no idea whether coffee's cost is more, less, or equal to the cost of juice (J) or soda (S). Therefore, the third statement might be either true or false (we simply do not know), and the correct answer choice is C.

HSPT Verbal Logic—Heads Up!

- Assume that all premises are factual.
- The answer choices are always the same, and there are only three of them.
- Draw diagrams for questions that rank people or things.
- Your job is to recognize what *must* be true. One—and only one—of the three conclusions will be a statement that must be true. There are no shades of gray!

COOP Verbal Logic Questions

On the COOP, verbal logic questions provide a series of two or three premises. Your job is to figure out, based on the premises, which of four conclusions is best. Here are the test directions:

Directions: For each question, find the statement that is most probably true according to the given information.

Here are the steps to handling these questions:

Step 1: Read the premises carefully. If they rank various people or things, draw a diagram to help organize the information.

Step 2: Ask yourself, "What else is probably true—either *very likely* or *certain*—based on the premises." If you think of an answer, jot it down.

Step 3: Scan the answer choices for a statement that closely matches your prediction from step 2. If you don't see a close match, go to step 4.

Step 4: Read the premises again. Then examine each answer choice in turn, asking yourself if the statement is *very likely to be true* based on the premises. One, and only one, of the four choices will fit the bill. When you figure out which it is, select that choice.

Here's a typical example:

Before going to sleep, Michael set his alarm clock for 7:00 in the morning. Michael went to sleep, and then woke up at 7:30 a.m.
  A Michael slept later than he wanted.
  B Michael was late for school.
  C Michael's alarm clock is broken.
  D Michael did not sleep well.

Let's apply the four-step approach to this example:

Step 1: The premises provide three facts: (1) Michael set his alarm for 7:00 a.m.; (2) he went to sleep after setting his alarm; and (3) he woke up at 7:30 a.m.

Step 2: What is a likely explanation for these facts; in other words, what can we confidently conclude from them? Common sense should tell you that Michael probably wanted to wake up at 7:00 but overslept.

Step 3: Scanning the answer choices for one that matches our explanation of the facts, choice A comes very close. At first glance, the facts don't support any of the other three choices, do they? If you're still not sure that statement A is more likely than any of the other three statements to be true, go to step 4.

Step 4: Think about the other three choices again. First, statement B: Nothing in the premises suggest that Michael was late for school—or that this was even a school day. So, we can safely eliminate choice B. As for statements C and D, the premises provide no clues as to why Michael overslept. Thus, both of these choices provide mere guesses, and we can safely eliminate them as well. The only statement that the premises strongly support is A. In other words, A is far more likely than any of the other three statements to be true. Select choice A.

Next, let's apply the four-step approach to another example (this one is quite unlike the previous one):

Soda costs more than tea, and tea costs less than coffee. Juice costs less than soda but more than tea.

  A Soda costs more than coffee.

  B Coffee costs less than juice.

  C Soda costs more than tea.

  D Tea costs less than milk.

Step 1: Since the premises rank various things, draw a simple diagram in your test booklet to organize the information. Here's a diagram of the first sentence, showing the relationship between soda (S), tea (T), and coffee (C):

(MORE $)

S C

T

(LESS $)

This diagram shows that we don't know which costs more: soda (S) or coffee (C). Now, add the information from the second sentence (you'll need to revise your previous diagram, but that's okay):

Step 2: This diagram tells us that soda costs more than juice, which costs more than tea, and so soda must cost more than tea. All we know about coffee (C) is that it costs more than tea (T); we don't know anything about its cost compared to the cost of either soda or juice. So, the only additional fact that we can confidently conclude from the premises is that soda costs more than tea. In fact, we're certain of it!

(MORE $)

S

J

T C

(LESS $)

Step 3: Scanning the answer choices, we see that choice C provides essentially what we predicted.

Step 4: Since we found a choice that, based on the premises, is not only likely to be true but indeed *must* be true, there's no need to go back and read the premises and answer choices again. Select choice C as correct.

COOP Verbal Logic—Heads Up!

- Assume that all premises are factual.
- Draw diagrams for questions that rank people or things.
- For most COOP questions, your job is to recognize which of the four conclusions is *most likely* to be true (rather than which *must* be true). Only the best answer choice will provide a statement that the premises strongly support.
- For some COOP questions, your task is to recognize what *must* be true. There are no shades of gray with these questions; one, and only one, of the four conclusions will be a statement that must be true.

Learn to Recognize Logical Fallacies

A *logical fallacy* is an argument whose premises do not support its conclusion—in other words, the argument makes no sense. On your exam, these fallacies will show up as incorrect answer choices.

Let's look at some basic forms of arguments, using letters as symbols to help you understand the pattern of reasoning. In each type of argument, notice that some conclusions are certain (they must be true) while other conclusions are uncertain (they're fallacies). To help you recognize these fallacies when you see them on your test, we've included examples to illustrate the various argument forms and fallacies.

Argument Form 1

Premise: If A, then B.
Certain conclusion: If not B, then not A.
Uncertain conclusion (fallacy): If B, then A.
Uncertain conclusion (fallacy): If not A, then not B.

Example (HSPT format):

Any student who has failed math class will not be allowed to graduate. Dan is not allowed to graduate. Dan has failed math class. If the first two statements are true, the third is
  A true
  B false
  C uncertain

The correct answer is C. The third statement (the conclusion) overlooks other possible reasons that Dan is not allowed to graduate.

Argument Form 2

Premise: All A are B.
Certain conclusion: All non-B are non-A. (No non-B is an A.)
Uncertain conclusion (fallacy): All B are A.
Uncertain conclusion (fallacy): No non-A is a B.

Example (COOP format):

All red gremlins are spotted. X is a spotted gremlin, and Y is a red gremlin.
  A X is a red gremlin.
  B All spotted gremlins are red.
  C Y is not spotted.
  D X and Y are both spotted.

The correct answer is choice D. The second premise states that X is spotted. Since all red gremlins are spotted and Y is a red gremlin, it must be true that Y is spotted.

Argument Form 3

Premise: All A are B.
Premise: All B are C.
Certain conclusion: All A are C.
Certain conclusion: No non-C is an A.
Uncertain conclusion (fallacy): No non-A is a C.
Uncertain conclusion (fallacy): All C are A.

Example (HSPT format):
All wool socks in the drawer are clean. All clean socks in the drawer are large. There is a small wool sock in the drawer. If the first two statements are true, the third is
  A true
  B false
  C uncertain

The correct answer is choice B. From the first two statements, you can deduce that all wool socks in the drawer are large. So, it is impossible for any wool sock in the drawer to be small, and the third statement must be false.

Argument Form 4

Premise: Some A are B.
Premise: All B are C.
Certain conclusion: Some B are A.
Certain conclusion: Some A are C.
Certain conclusion: Some C are A.
Uncertain conclusion (fallacy): All C are B.
Uncertain conclusion (fallacy): All C are A.

Example (COOP format):
Three menu items are vegetarian. No vegetarian items on the menu cost less than $5.
  A Some menu items cost less than $5.
  B Some menu items are non-vegetarian.
  C Some menu items costing $5 or more are vegetarian.
  D All menu items costing less than $5 are vegetarian.

The correct answer is choice C. The first premise tells us that some (at least three) menu items are vegetarian. The second premise tells us that all vegetarian menu items cost at least $5. From these two premises, it must be true that at least three of the menu items are vegetarian and cost at least $5.

Argument Form 5

Premise: Some A are B.
Premise: Some B are C.
Certain conclusion: Some B are A.
Certain conclusion: Some C are B.
Uncertain conclusion (fallacy): Some A are C.
Uncertain conclusion (fallacy): Some C are A.

Example (HSPT format):
Some of Nina's books were written by American authors. Some of Nina's books are novels. Some of Nina's novels were written by American authors. If the first two statements are true, the third is
  A true
  B false
  C uncertain

The correct answer is choice C. The third statement is not necessarily true. It's entirely possible that all of Nina's novels were written by non-American authors and that all of Nina's books written by American authors are of genres other than a novel.

More Strategies for COOP Verbal Logic

On the COOP, even the best answer choice might *not necessarily* be true based on the premises. But, it will be much more *probable* than any other answer choice. To zero in on the most probable conclusion (the best answer choice), apply the strategies you'll learn in the pages ahead.

Don't Jump to Conclusions

Be careful not to make up facts that aren't in the premise. Inventing facts may lead you to an uncertain conclusion and a wrong answer choice. This is the leading cause of incorrect answers in COOP logic questions. Here's an example:

Most children do not like to eat vegetables, even though they know that vegetables contribute to good health. Belinda likes to eat peas.
  A Belinda is concerned about her health.
  B Peas are Belinda's favorite vegetable.
  C Belinda is an unusual child.
  D Belinda likes certain vegetables.

Don't jump to the conclusion that Belinda eats peas because they're good for her health, and don't jump to the conclusion that Belinda is a child. Both are made-up facts that the premises do not support. Choice A is incorrect because Belinda may like to eat peas simply because she likes their taste. Choice B ignores the possibility that Belinda likes other vegetables just as much, or perhaps more, than peas. Choice C is incorrect because the premises do not tell us whether Belinda is a child. Choice D is the correct answer; Belinda likes to eat peas, which are vegetables. It's that simple.

Let's look at another example:

The candidate receiving the most votes won the election. Johnson received more votes than Weller.
  A Johnson won the election.
  B The election ballots were counted properly.
  C Weller was not a candidate for election.
  D Weller did not win the election.

If you're not paying close attention, you might assume that Johnson won the election and select choice A. After all, the premises don't mention any other candidates. But we don't know if there were any other candidates, do we? So, don't jump to that conclusion. Eliminate choice A. You can eliminate choices B and C because the premises provide absolutely no information allowing us to evaluate either statement. Either statement might be true, or it might not. Of the four conclusions, the only probable one is that Weller did not win—because he did not receive the most votes.

Play Sherlock Holmes

Many COOP logic questions are like little detective mysteries. Your job is to explain the events described in the premises, to figure out what probably caused them. Using common sense, try to predict what the best answer might look like, and these questions should be a cinch for you. Here's an example:

Last night a man climbed out of the house next door through a bedroom window. Today there is a police car in that house's driveway.
  A A police officer lives at the house.
  B The owner of the house is a burglary victim.
  C The house's bedroom window is broken.
  D The man who climbed through the window is a police officer.

What would Sherlock Holmes deduce from the facts? People do not normally climb through their own bedroom windows at night, do they? The most likely explanation for the sequence of events is that an intruder broke into the house. That's the most obvious explanation and the first one you'd think of, isn't it? You don't need to be Sherlock Homes to conjure up this theory. And this explanation is more than a mere guess; it's the most reasonable explanation for the sequence of events. Compare this explanation with those in choices A, C, and D. Notice that the weak ones amount to mere guesses, and that they're pretty unlikely. Common sense tells you that these are not convincing, but that choice B is. Good work, Sherlock!

Other Strategies for COOP Verbal Logic

- Thinking of a possible "best" answer before looking at the answer choices can help you zero in on the best answer choice. Just don't spend too much time in deep thought; if nothing occurs to you after a few seconds, read the answer choices.
- Read every answer choice before making a final selection. Unless you consider all four answer choices, you might choose a runner-up without even reading the best one!
- When in doubt, go with your initial hunch. Don't go against your instincts and common sense.
- Don't overlook the obvious by trying to make logic questions tougher than they are.

Practice

Directions: Questions 1–10 are in the HSPT format. For each question, select the best answer.

1. Bobbie is older than Trent. Suene is older than Bobbie. Trent is younger than Suene. If the first two statements are true, the third is

   A true
   B false
   C uncertain

2. The "large" soda at QuickMart costs less than the "jumbo" soda at Stop-n-Go. The "giant" soda at MaxMart is larger but costs less than the jumbo soda at Stop-n-Go. The large soda at QuickMart is smaller than the giant soda at MaxMart. If the first two statements are true, the third is

   A true
   B false
   C uncertain

3. All white cars at the auto show are convertibles. No convertible at the auto show is an import. Some imports at the auto show are white. If the first two statements are true, the third is

   A true
   B false
   C uncertain

4. Yolanda ate dinner later than Alex. Frank ate dinner at the same time as Yolanda. Frank ate dinner earlier than Alex. If the first two statements are true, the third is

   A true
   B false
   C uncertain

5. Short hair on men and boys is fashionable this year. Anthony's hair is short. Anthony's hair is fashionable. If the first two statements are true, the third is

   A true
   B false
   C uncertain

6. Diane goes to sleep earlier than Jessie and wakes up earlier than Chuck. Jessie wakes up earlier than Diane and goes to sleep later than Chuck. Diane get less sleep than Chuck. If the first two statements are true, the third is

   A true
   B false
   C uncertain

7. Mariah is a cheerleader. Some cheerleaders are popular and are good students. Mariah is popular. If the first two statements are true, the third is

A true
B false
C uncertain

8. Red marbles are larger than yellow marbles but smaller than blue marbles. Green marbles are smaller than orange marbles but larger than red marbles. Orange marbles are smaller than red marbles. If the first two statements are true, the third is

A true
B false
C uncertain

9. Peter is taller than Oliver, but Oliver is older than Peter. Gary is taller and older than Peter. Oliver is shorter and older than Gary. If the first two statements are true, the third is

A true
B false
C uncertain

10. Fricks can swim but not fly. Fracks can neither fly nor swim. Neither fricks nor fracks can fly. If the first two statements are true, the third is

A true
B false
C uncertain

Directions: Questions 11–20 are in the COOP format. For each question, find the statement that is most probably true according to the given information.

11. This month is January. Trent's 15th birthday is next week.

A Trent's birthday is on Valentine's Day.
B Trent was 14 years old 11 months ago.
C Trent's birthday is in January.
D Trent's birthday is in February.

12. Steven is a backgammon player, and his classmate Charlie is the best chess player in school.

A Steven does not play chess.
B Steven is better at backgammon than Charlie.
C Charlie is better at chess than Steven.
D Steven and Charlie are friends.

13. While seated at a table in a restaurant, Lisa said to her waiter, "Please bring me a glass of wine." The waiter left the table without replying, and then returned shortly with a glass of water for Lisa.

A The waiter misunderstood Lisa's request.
B Lisa had already had a glass of wine.
C Lisa had already paid for her meal.
D The restaurant did not have any wine.

14. This year, Lincoln High School's basketball team won the state championship. Susan was the highest scoring player on the team this year.

A Susan will be on the team next year.
B Susan is the tallest member of her team.
C The team was undefeated this year.
D Susan is a talented athlete.

15. It rained on Monday, but it was sunny all day Tuesday through Thursday. Friday evening, two umbrellas were sitting by the front door at a local restaurant.

A Friday was a rainy day.
B The restaurant's cashier owns two umbrellas.
C Rain had been predicted for Tuesday through Thursday.
D The restaurant sells umbrellas.

16. Nobody without a flag is allowed to march in the parade. Every band member wearing a uniform also has a flag.

   A Every person marching in the parade will be wearing a uniform.

   B Every person marching in the parade will have a flag.

   C Only band members are allowed to march in the parade.

   D Some band members do not have flags.

17. Jessica is a cheerleader but is a poor student in high school. Jessica is the most popular girl at her school.

   A Jessica dates the most popular boy in school.

   B Good students are unlikely to become cheerleaders.

   C Popular teenagers can also be poor students.

   D It is difficult to be a cheerleader and a good student.

18. Red marbles are larger than yellow marbles but smaller than blue marbles. Green marbles are smaller than orange marbles but larger than red marbles.

   A Yellow marbles are smaller than orange marbles.

   B Orange marbles are larger than red marbles.

   C Green marbles are smaller than yellow marbles.

   D Blue marbles are larger than orange marbles.

19. Nick knew that his friend Jared lived in one of three apartments—unit A, B, or C—in a building, but Nick did not know which one. While Jared was at home, Nick knocked on the door of unit A. One minute later, Nick went to unit B and knocked on that door.

   A Jared does not live in unit C.

   B Jared lives in unit C.

   C Jared lives in unit B.

   D Jared does not live in unit A.

20. On Monday, Joe wore a badly wrinkled white shirt to work. On Tuesday, Joe wore a neatly pressed blue shirt to work.

   A Joe only owns one white shirt.

   B White shirts wrinkle easier than blue shirts.

   C Joe did not wear a new shirt to work on Monday.

   D Joe ironed his blue shirt last night.

Practice—Answers and Explanations

1. A We know that Trent is younger than Bobbie, and that Bobbie is younger than Suene. Therefore, Trent must be younger than Suene.

2. C Neither of the first two statements provides any information about the size of QuickMart's large soda compared to MaxMart's giant soda—or any other soda, for that matter.

3. B Because no convertible is an import but all white cars are convertibles, no import can be white.

4. B Because Frank ate dinner at the same time as Yolanda, who ate later than Alex, Frank must have eaten *later* than Alex, and the third statement is false.

5. **A** Given that short hair is currently fashionable, Anthony's hair, which is short, must be fashionable.

6. **C** We know Diane wakes up earlier than Chuck. However, we do not know who goes to sleep earlier, Diane or Chuck. Thus, there is no way to know who gets more sleep, Diane or Chuck.

7. **C** We know that "some" cheerleaders are popular, but we do not know if Mariah is in that group.

8. **B** You can find the correct answer based just on the second statement. Given that orange marbles are larger than green ones, which in turn are larger than red ones, orange marbles must be *larger* than red marbles.

9. **C** We know that Gary is taller than Oliver, who is taller than Peter. Therefore, Oliver must be shorter than Gary. Although we know that Oliver and Gary are both older than Peter, we do not know who is older, Oliver or Gary.

10. **A** The first sentence tells us that fricks cannot fly. The second sentence tells us that fracks cannot fly. Therefore, it must be true that neither fricks nor fracks can fly.

11. **B** Because Trent is 14 years old now and his birthday is next week, Trent's previous birthday must have occurred more than 11 months ago. Choices C and D are incorrect because we don't know how late in January it is now.

12. **C** Given that Charlie is the best chess player in school, and that Steven and Charlie are classmates, Charlie must be better at chess than Steven.

13. **A** If the waiter could not comply with Lisa's request, he probably would have told her so immediately. Because he said nothing, choices B, C, and D do not provide a reasonable conclusion. Choice A makes much more sense,

especially considering that the word "wine" sounds a bit like "water."

14. **D** Because the team won the state championship, the team must be very good indeed. Because Susan is the highest scoring player on the team, it is reasonable to conclude that she is a very talented player. Choice B is incorrect because the tallest basketball player does not necessarily score the most points. Choice C is incorrect because winning a championship does not require winning every game during the season. Choice D is incorrect because it calls for a prediction and we don't know anything about Susan's plans. (For example, Susan might be graduating from high school this year.)

15. **A** Common experience tells us that, on a rainy day, restaurant customers often put their umbrellas near a restaurant's front door when they come in. The most likely explanation for umbrellas sitting by the restaurant's front door Friday evening is that it was rainy on Friday. Because four days have passed since the last rainy day, it is far less likely that the umbrellas had been sitting there since Monday.

16. **B** You can find the correct answer based on the premise's first sentence alone. Because nobody who does not have a flag will be allowed to march, the only people marching will be those who have flags. In other words, choice B says essentially the same thing as the premise's first sentence.

17. **C** Jessica is one example of a popular teenager (high school students are teenagers) who is a poor student. Therefore, the statement in choice C is true. We know nothing about Jessica's dating life, and so choice A is obviously incorrect. As for choices B and D, which provide essentially the same conclusion, one example of a cheerleader who is a poor student is hardly sufficient to conclude that good students are unlikely to be cheerleaders.

18. **B** You can find the correct answer based just on the second statement. Given that orange marbles are larger than green marbles, which in turn are larger than red ones, orange marbles must be larger than red marbles.

19. **D** Because Nick went to unit B after knocking on the door at unit A, it is reasonable to conclude that Jared was not at unit A and that Nick was still trying to determine where Jared lived.

20. **C** The first premise supports the conclusion that Joe had already worn his white shirt at least once before Monday. Otherwise, it probably would not have been wrinkled yet when he went to work that day.

Usage and Writing Mechanics

HSPT | TACHS

On both the HSPT and TACHS, the Language subtest includes questions that focus on word usage and writing mechanics (grammar, spelling, capitalization, and punctuation). This lesson focuses on how to handle these question types—step by step. The examples and practice questions in this lesson are in the HSPT format. However, TACHS students may also find these materials helpful.

Note: If you need to review the essential rules of grammar and writing mechanics, you should also read Chapter 11 ("Review of Grammar and Writing Mechanics").

Usage Questions—Step by Step

In usage questions, your job is to read three sentences, looking for any mistake in word choice, grammar, capitalization, or punctuation. No group of three sentences contains more than one mistake, and some groups won't contain any mistakes. Here are the directions for usage questions, along with a typical example.

Directions: For each question, choose the sentence that contains an error in punctuation, capitalization, or usage. If you find no mistakes, select choice D.

A I saw lots of monkeys at the zoo.
B Be sure to speak loudly.
C We're not suppose to touch the exhibits.
D No mistake.

Here are the steps for handing usage questions:

Step 1: Read all three sentences, looking for punctuation errors. If you think you spot one, earmark it.
Step 2: Read all three sentences again, looking for capitalization errors. If you spot one, earmark it.
Step 3: If you're certain you've found exactly one punctuation or capitalization mistake, select the sentence that contains the mistake as the correct answer choice. (Move ahead to the next question.) If you've found more than one possible mistake, choose one as your final selection. If you've found no mistakes yet, go to step 4.
Step 4: Read all three sentences again, looking for usage errors. If you spot one, select the sentence as the correct choice. If you find more than one, decide between them.

Let's apply these steps to our example.

Step 1: First, let's check end-of-sentence punctuation. Each sentence ends in a period. None of the sentences poses a question, and so there are no end-of-sentence punctuation mistakes. Now, let's check elsewhere for a punctuation mistake. None of the sentences needs any additional punctuation. Sentence C contains the contraction *we're,*—which is short for *we are.* This phrase makes sense in the context of the sentence, and so there's no contraction error. It looks like there are no punctuation mistakes among the three sentences.

Step 2: None of the three sentences contains any words that should be capitalized. There are no capitalization errors.

Step 3: We found no punctuation or capitalization errors in any of the three sentences. Let's go to step 4.

Step 4: For each sentence, examine every word carefully in the context of the entire sentence to see if they are all used properly. Sentence A looks fine. What about sentence B? Should the last word be *loud* (an adjective) instead of *loudly* (an adverb)? No. The word describes *speak,* which is a verb. The rule to apply here is that adverbs should be used to describe (modify) verbs. So, *loudly* is correct, and sentence B is fine. What about sentence C? The word *suppose* (a verb) is improper here and should be replaced with the adjective *supposed.* One missing letter made all the difference! Select C as the correct answer choice.

Let's try another example.

A Try to put yourself in my place.
B Did he just call you "stupid?"
C Waiting any longer is not worthwhile.
D No mistake.

Step 1: Neither sentence A nor sentence C contains any punctuation problems. Sentence B poses a question, and so a question mark at the end is correct. But should it come before or after the second quotation mark? Hmm . . . The speaker is asking a question, and quoting a single word that someone else said. So, it makes sense for the question mark to go *outside* the quotation marks, at the very end of the sentence. It looks like sentence B contains a punctuation mistake. Before selecting B as our final answer, let's check for other mistakes. If we don't find any, that tells us that we are probably right about the punctuation in sentence B.

Step 2: None of the three sentences contains any word that should be capitalized. There are no capitalization errors among the three sentences.

Step 3: We found what we think is one punctuation error, in sentence B, but no capitalization errors. We can stop here, and select B as the correct choice. Just to make sure we're right, let's check for usage mistakes (step 4).

Step 4: Are all three sentences correct in how they use words? The only word that looks suspicious is *worthwhile,* in sentence C. But the word *worthwhile* (which means "important or valuable") is correct here. The two-word phrase *worth while* would be incorrect. There are no usage errors in any of the three sentences. Select B as the correct answer choice.

Let's try one more example.

A Sandra means to call, but she forgot.
B I plan to contest my traffic ticket.
C Every U.S. citizen should read the Bill of Rights.
D No mistake.

Step 1: First, let's check end-of-sentence punctuation. Each sentence ends in a period. None of the sentences poses a question, and so there are no end-of-sentence punctuation mistakes. Now, let's check elsewhere for punctuation mistakes. In sentence A, each of the two clauses connected with a comma and the word *but* can stand on its own as a complete sentence (*Sandra means to call. She forgot.*). Using a comma (followed by a connecting word) is correct in this situation. Neither sentence B nor sentence C needs any additional punctuation. There are no punctuation mistakes among the three sentences.

Step 2: Sentences A and B contain no words that should be capitalized. In the third sentence, *U.S.* and *Bill of Rights* are proper nouns and therefore are correctly capitalized. (The word *of* is not capitalized, which is correct because it is a short preposition.) There are no capitalization errors in any of the three sentences.

Step 3: We found no punctuation or capitalization errors in any of the three sentences. Let's go to step 4.

Step 4: Sentence A shifts from the present time in the first clause (notice the present-tense verb form *means*) to the past in the second clause (notice the past-tense verb form *forgot*). This shift doesn't make sense, does it? One way to fix the problem is to replace *means* with the past-tense form *meant*. Of course, you don't need to fix the mistake; you just need to recognize that there is a mistake: the use of the word *means* together with *forgot*. Just to make sure that sentence A contains a usage mistake, let's check sentences B and C for any usage problems. Both sentences look entirely correct. Select A as the correct answer choice.

Spelling Questions—Step by Step

Spelling questions may look just like usage questions, except that the mistake (if any) among the three sentences is a spelling error. Here are the directions for spelling questions, along with a typical example.

Directions: For each question, choose the sentence that contains a spelling error. If you find no mistake, select choice D.

A The negative publicity bothered him.
B Persue your dream, and you will attain it.
C Please do not take me too seriously.
D No mistake.

Here are the steps for handing spelling questions:

Step 1: Carefully examine every word in sentence A. All you should look for is *one* spelling error. If you see a clear error, select choice A. If you see a word that you think might be spelled incorrectly, but you're not sure, circle it, and then go to step 2.
Step 2: Repeat step 1 for sentences B and C.
Step 3: If you're certain there's no error in spelling, select choice D. If you've earmarked one or more words as possibly incorrect, make a final selection based on your best hunch.

Let's apply these steps to our example.

Step 1: In sentence A, the word *negative* is the adjective form of the verb *negate*. The spelling matches, and so *negative* is probably correct. What about the word *publicity*? It's based on the root word *public*. The spelling matches, and so *publicity* is probably okay as well. Go to step 2.

Step 2: Sentence B contains two challenging words: *persue* and *attain.* If you pronounce these as they're spelled, they seem correct. But doesn't *persue* look a bit strange? Should the first letter *e* be *u* instead? Jot down this other spelling: *pursue.* Notice that this word contains the more common word *purse,* which is spelled correctly. So, it's a good bet that *pursue* is the correct spelling. Sentence C looks fine.

Step 3: We've only found one word that might be spelled incorrectly. Because *persue* looks wrong, let's go with our hunch, and select B.

Usage and Spelling—Heads Up!

- There can be *no more than one* mistake.
- Don't find mistakes where there aren't any. Remember: About one out of every four usage and spelling questions will contain *no* mistake.
- In a usage question, you might find any one of three types of errors: usage, capitalization, or punctuation. On the other hand, spelling questions contain *only* spelling errors.
- In usage questions, look carefully for contraction mistakes and for single words confused with two-word phrases. (You'll encounter some in the practice drill just ahead.) These mistakes are especially easy to overlook.
- In handling spelling questions, trust your instinct and your eye. Remember: If a word looks wrong, it probably is.

Practice

The practice questions in this lesson are in the HSPT format. However, the questions provide useful practice for the TACHS as well.

Directions: For questions 1–30, choose the sentence that contains an error in punctuation, capitalization, or usage. If you find no mistake, select choice D.

1.
- A I see the sun as well as the moon.
- B The design was overly ornate.
- C I'm Gary from Illinois.
- D No mistake.

2.
- A Melissa writes extremely neat.
- B How do you explain this mess?
- C Fluffy is the larger of the two cats.
- D No mistake.

3.
- A Liverpool is the name of an England city.
- B Remind me not to do that again.
- C Health-care access is becoming difficult.
- D No mistake.

4.
- A The computer program can debug itself.
- B Don't pay no attention to him.
- C Linda saw herself as overweight.
- D No mistake.

5.
- A It's as crowded as Grand Central Station in here.
- B Either parent can attend the open house.
- C One should never ignore one's health.
- D No mistake.

6.
- A It's not too late to go swimming.
- B Nicole overheard he and Rick talking.
- C The library is closed all day today.
- D No mistake.

7.

A A good soldier always salutes the flag.
B All this dust make my eyes hurt real bad.
C I ate too much and feel ill now.
D No mistake.

8.

A It's all right if you decide to stay home.
B There's nothing good on television.
C Tony is well-groomed but poorly dressed.
D No mistake.

9.

A He looked smarter than he actually was.
B Please deposit the money in the bank.
C Jim's tie—a Calvin Klein item—looks very sharp.
D No mistake.

10.

A Look up the word in the dictionary.
B This trail mix is nuts and berries.
C The dripping faucet kept me awake.
D No mistake.

11.

A Pour me a cold tall glass of water.
B Teresa and Hanna often help each other.
C I sympathize with your problem.
D No mistake.

12.

A That's not such a terrible thought.
B He himself was haunted by his past.
C The song ended abruptly.
D No mistake.

13.

A We're closed on Labor Day.
B You should not of stolen that book.
C Geoff plans to run for office next year.
D No mistake.

14.

A Peel me an orange, please.
B When unfolded, the sheet looks large enough.
C The window shattered to dozens of pieces.
D No mistake.

15.

A Can you spare some time?
B The teacher gave Kim a failing grade.
C Those are Frank's glasses over there.
D No mistake.

16.

A He swung, and hit the ball.
B I worry more than William does about you.
C She married at the age of twenty.
D No mistake.

17.

A The jury rendered a "not guilty" verdict.
B The yellow house is theirs.
C Beyond those trees is the farms.
D No mistake.

18.

A The host is responsible for serving lunch.
B Drawing blood does not hurt much.
C Washington was the first U.S. president.
D No mistake.

19.

A The walls are dark, blue in color.
B It's nine o'clock in the morning.
C Deep within the jungle flows the mighty Amazon.
D No mistake.

20.

A Writer's block plagues many a writer.
B Many people dislike to go to the dentist.
C Larry is good at conversation.
D No mistake.

21.

A Shandra was the first one of the guests to arrive.
B This class is for advanced students only.
C Unlike Rome, my tree house was built in a day.
D No mistake.

22.

A That is a fine piece of jewelry.
B Ted was born and raised in North Dakota.
C The artist hadn't drew a thing since July.
D No mistake.

23.

A This computer comes equipped with a monitor.
B Rich can jump farther than three meters.
C I can't think of anything else.
D No mistake.

24.

A Of the five senses sight is most crucial.
B Sharks will attack any metal object.
C Let's drive across the Golden Gate Bridge.
D No mistake.

25.

A I warned them don't go in there.
B Sam is without a doubt the best player.
C This poem is simply entitled "Why?"
D No mistake.

26.

A The natives were forced from their land.
B He died of lung cancer.
C The right of free speech is most precious.
D No mistake.

27.

A Scott looks forward to grow a beard.
B I'm here on behalf of Janice.
C He's created an original design.
D No mistake.

28.

A The truth is that she lied.
B A rose looks like neither a violet nor daisies.
C He shot an arrow from his bow.
D No mistake.

29.

A I read *The Great Gatsby* in seventh grade.
B Don't touch that until the paint dries.
C You must, however, clean your room first.
D No mistake.

30.

A Imagine what you'd do if you were invisible.
B Some folks are friendly, while others aren't.
C It isn't time to leave, at least, not yet.
D No mistake.

Directions: For questions 31–40, choose the sentence that contains a spelling error. If you find no mistake, select choice D.

31.

A I could not decipher her handwriting.
B He appealed to reason, not emotion.
C All compounds are made up of elements.
D No mistake.

32.

A Stalking is an invasion of privasy.
B This balmy weather is delightful.
C The situation was only temporary.
D No mistake.

33.

A The witness can verify these facts.
B The tornado left no building intact.
C It takes disipline to learn a language.
D No mistake.

34.

A The accused killer did not testify.
B What is the address on the envelope?
C Lion tamers put themselves in jeapordy.
D No mistake.

35.

    A Her rebellious son eventually matured.
    B Kathy is always a gratious host.
    C Use your credit card responsibly.
    D No mistake.

36.

    A Amy's explaination was confusing.
    B Some people are susceptible to fraud.
    C Toxic fumes polluted the atmosphere.
    D No mistake.

37.

    A The shortest route is a straight line.
    B He suffered only superficial wounds.
    C She could not be consoled in her grief.
    D No mistake.

38.

    A This home's underground garage is uneek.
    B Don't leave, or else you'll lose your place in line.
    C She's not at home, is she?
    D No mistake.

39.

    A The sound of ocean waves is pacifying.
    B His coin collection is impressive.
    C Are you lyeing or telling the truth?
    D No mistake.

40.

    A It's scary to go to the cemetary at night.
    B Bobbie is unbelievably good at math.
    C A total eclipse of the sun is very rare.
    D No mistake.

Practice—Answers and Explanations

1. **D** There are no mistakes.

2. **A** The adjective *neat* should be replaced by the adverb *neatly* because the word that is modified is a verb (*write*).

3. **A** The adjective form *English* is correct here because it modifies a noun (*city*).

4. **B** The sentence incorrectly uses a double negative; replace *no* with *any*.

5. **D** There are no mistakes.

6. **B** In the object case, the correct pronoun is *him*, not *he*. Also, *him* should come after (not before) the proper noun *Rick*. The sentence should read: *Nicole overheard Rick and him talking.*

7. **B** The phrase *real bad* modifies a verb (*hurt*), and so adverbs should be used in place of adjectives (*. . . my eyes hurt really badly.*)

8. **A** The two-word phrase *all right* is used incorrectly here and should be replaced with *alright*.

9. **D** There are no mistakes.

10. **B** The word *is* makes the sentence confusing. A good solution would be to replace *is* with *consists of* or *contains*.

11. **A** A comma is needed between the two adjectives *cold* and *tall*.

12. **B** The reflexive verb *himself* is inappropriate here because the sentence's subject is not the same as its object. The word should simply be omitted.

13. **B** The sentence contains no verb. The word *of* is incorrectly used here and should be replaced with *have*.

14. **C** The word *to* is not idiomatic here and should be replaced with *into*.

15. **D** There are no mistakes.

16. **A** The comma should be omitted.

17. **C** The plural *farms* should take the plural verb *are* instead of the singular *is*.

18. **D** There are no mistakes.

19. **A** No comma should appear between the two adjectives *dark* and *blue* because they serve together as a single descriptive feature.

20. **B** The phrase *dislike to go* is not idiomatic and should be replaced with *dislike going* or *do not like to go*.

21. **D** There are no mistakes.

22. **C** The correct past-perfect form of the verb *draw* is *drawn*.

23. **D** There are no mistakes.

24. **A** A comma is needed between *senses* and *sight*.

25. **A** The word *don't* should be replaced with *not to*. Another acceptable revision would transform part of the sentence into dialogue: *I warned them, "Don't go in there."*

26. **D** There are no mistakes.

27. **A** The word *grow* should be replaced with *growing*.

28. **B** The plural *daisies* is not grammatically parallel to the singular *A rose* and *a violet*; *a daisy* should be used instead.

29. **D** There are no mistakes.

30. **C** If you remove the parenthetical phrase *at least*, along with the commas that set it off, the sentence makes no sense. The second comma should be omitted.

31. **D** There are no spelling mistakes.

32. **A** The correct spelling is *privacy*.

33. **C** The correct spelling is *discipline*.

34. **D** There are no spelling mistakes.

35. **B** The correct spelling is *gracious*.

36. **A** The correct spelling is *explanation*.

37. **D** There are no spelling mistakes.

38. **A** The correct spelling is *unique*.

39. **C** The correct spelling is *lying*.

40. **B** The correct spelling is *cemetery*.

Review of Grammar and Writing Mechanics

COOP | HSPT | TACHS

The COOP, HSPT, and TACHS all test your ability to identify mistakes in grammar, sentence structure, punctuation, and capitalization. This review covers the rules and guidelines in these areas that the tests cover most often.

Rules of Grammar You Should Know

Here are the specific areas of grammar this section covers:

- Adjectives and adverbs
- Adjectives—comparison and superlative forms
- Subject-verb agreement
- Personal pronouns and case
- Relative pronouns
- Sentence fragments and run-on sentences

Adjectives and Adverbs

An **adjective** is a word that describes a noun. An **adverb** is a word that describes either a verb or an adjective (or possibly another adverb). To change most adjectives to adverbs, simply add *"ly"* to the end of the word.

Adjectives	*Adverbs*
He was caught up in the *swift* current.	He paddled *swiftly* through the current.
My clock shows the *correct* time.	I'm sure I set my clock *correctly*.
This *noisy* traffic is bothering me.	The traffic *noisily* made its way across town.
The gymnast's agility was *amazing*.	The gymnast was *amazingly* agile.

Most adverbs end with *-ly,* but some don't. In the next group of examples, notice that the adjective and adverb forms are the same.

Adjectives	*Adverbs*
The finished product looks *good*.	The finished product looks *good*.
This assignment is *hard* work.	I worked *hard* on my assignment.
Bob is a *fast* runner.	Bob can run *fast*.

Adjectives—Comparison and Superlative Forms

Use a **comparative** form of an adjective to compare two things. Use a **superlative** form to compare three or more things. For some adjectives, the comparative form ends in either "er" or "ier," and the superlative form ends in either "est" or "iest."

Comparative form (two things):
He sang much *better* than she did.
The sun is *brighter* than the moon.
You look *prettier* with long hair.

Superlative form (three or more things):
He was the *best* singer in the competition.
The sun is the *brightest* star in the sky.
You look your *prettiest* when you smile.

For longer adjectives, instead of adding a suffix to make a comparison, precede the adjective with a word such as *more* or *most.*

Comparative form (two things):
Math class is *more interesting* than I expected.
His new house is *less impressive* than his old one.

Superlative form (three or more things):
Christmas is the *most special* day of the year.
History is the *least demanding* subject in school.

For some adjectives, either form is correct. However, do not combine the two forms.

Wrong: My dog is *more furrier* than yours.
Correct: My dog is *furrier* than yours.
Correct: My dog is *more furry* than yours.

Subject–Verb Agreement

If a sentence's subject is *singular,* then the form of its verb should also be singular. Similarly, if a sentence's subject is *plural,* then the form of its verb should also be plural. In other words, there must be "agreement" between subject and verb.

Wrong: Beth are Tom's partner.
Correct: Beth is Tom's partner.
(The sentence's singular subject, *Beth,* should take the singular verb form *is.*)

Wrong: Beth and Tom is partners.
Correct: Beth and Tom are partners.
(The sentence's plural subject, *Beth and Tom,* should take the plural verb form *are.*)

In determining whether a verb form should be singular or plural, ignore words or phrases that come between the subject and verb.

Correct: The *play,* which consists of four acts, *is* very entertaining.
Correct: The *list* of chores *is* long.
Correct: The *students* in this class, but especially John, *need* to study harder.

The words *any, every, each, either,* and *neither* are considered singular. The words *all, some,* and *none* are plural.

Singular
Correct: *Every* person here *is* invited to the party.
Correct: *Neither* Dan nor Brad *has* a pen with *him.*
Correct: *Each* and *every* one of you *owes* me money.

Plural
Correct: *All* of you *are suspects* in the criminal investigation.
Correct: *None* of my teachers *are* well-liked.
Correct: *Some believe* that nothing ever happens accidentally.

Personal Pronouns and Case

A **personal pronoun** is a word that refers to a specific noun (person, place, or thing). A personal pronoun can either be singular (referring to one person, place, or thing) or plural (referring to two or more persons, places, or things). Personal pronouns take different forms ("cases") depending on how they're used in a sentence.

Subject-case pronouns: I, we, you, he, she, it, they

Example: **I** am going to the movies tonight.
Example: **He/She** is sitting in the front row of the theater.
Example: **We/They** were late for the movie.

Object–case pronouns: me, us, you, him, her, it, them

Example: Danita saw _____ at the restaurant.
Example: Danita will go with _____ to the restaurant.
(Any object-case pronoun would fill in the blank correctly.)

Object case-reflexive pronouns: myself, ourselves, yourself, yourselves, himself, herself, itself, themselves

Use a reflexive pronoun when describing an act performed upon the sentence's subject.
Example: I accidently cut *myself* while chopping vegetables.
Example: Hanna and Wendy should be ashamed of *themselves* for cheating on the test.
Example: If you don't behave *yourself (yourselves),* I'll report you to the school principal.

Possessive-case pronouns: my (mine), our (ours), your (yours), his, hers, its, their (theirs)

Use the possessive case to indicate ownership or possession.

Examples:
You just drove past *my (our/your/his/her/their)* house.
The second house on the left is *mine (ours/yours/his/hers/theirs).*

Be careful to apply pronoun cases properly to compound subjects and objects.

Wrong: Me and Bruce plan to meet her at the mall later today.
Correct: Bruce and I plan to meet her at the mall later today.
(*Bruce and I* is the sentence's compound subject.)

Wrong: Janet met Bruce and myself at the mall yesterday.
Correct: Janet met Bruce and me at the mall yesterday.
(*Bruce and me* is the sentence's compound object.)

Relative Pronouns

Relative pronouns include the words *which, who, that, whose, whichever, whoever,* and *whomever.* You should know certain rules about how to use these words. Use *which* when referring to things, but use *who* when referring to people.

Correct: Jim's bike, *which* was brand new, was stolen yesterday.
Correct: Hector, *who* is Jim's neighbor, might have stolen the bike.
Correct: The only neighbor *who* saw Hector yesterday was Kathy.

Use *who* (or *whoever*) when referring to the sentence's subject. Use *whom* (or *whomever*) when referring to a direct or indirect object.

Correct: The person *who* ate all the cookies should confess.
Correct: *Whoever* ate all the cookies should confess.
Correct: Laurie, *who* has a sweet tooth, ate all the cookies.
Correct: Laurie is the one *who* ate all the cookies.

Correct: Oliver, with *whom* I spoke yesterday, won the first match of the tournament.
Correct: I'll play the next match against *whomever* wins this one.

Verb Tenses

A verb's **tense** indicates the time (past, present, or future) of the events described in a sentence. For many verbs, you indicate past tense by adding *-ed* to the verb (for example, *folded* or *watched*). Many verbs, however, have peculiar past-tense forms, which you must memorize. If you don't know the correct verb forms, trust your ear as to whether a verb sounds correct. The following examples show which form of the verbs *to see* and *to run* you should use, depending on the time frame.

simple present	see	run
simple past	saw	ran
simple future	will see	will run
present perfect	has seen (have seen)	has run (have run)
past perfect	had seen	had run
future perfect	will have seen	will have run

In some cases, mixing different tenses in a sentence can be confusing.

Confusing: Valerie *passed* the test, but Jerome *fails* the test.
Clear: Valerie *passed* the test, but Jerome *failed* the test.

In other cases, however, shifting from one case to another in the same sentence is perfectly alright—if the sentence's events shift from one time frame to another.

Examples:
Hattie *failed* the test, but she *will take* the test again next month.
(This sentence shifts from past tense to future-perfect tense.)

Having failed the test, I *am* very discouraged.
(This sentence shifts from present-perfect tense to present tense.)

He *had failed* the test twice before he finally *passed* it.
(This sentence shifts from past-perfect tense to past tense.)

Sentence Fragments and Run-on Sentences

Every sentence must include a subject *and* a predicate. Otherwise, it is a **sentence fragment** (an incomplete sentence). A noun establishes a subject, while a verb establishes the predicate.

Wrong (Fragment): Strolling through the park without a care.
Correct: She strolled through the park without a care.
Correct: Strolling through the park at night can be dangerous.

A **main clause** is any clause that can stand alone as a complete sentence. Combining two main clauses into one sentence without properly connecting the two results in a **run-on sentence,** which is grammatically incorrect.

Wrong: Bill held the door open Nancy walked through the doorway.
Wrong: Bill held the door open, Nancy walked through the doorway.
Correct: Bill held the door open while Nancy walked through the doorway.
Correct: Bill held the door open, and Nancy walked through the doorway.
Correct: Bill held the door open; Nancy walked through the doorway.

Sentence Structure and Sense

Here are the specific topics this section covers:

- Parallelism
- Active and passive voices
- Placement of modifiers
- Redundancy (repetitiveness)
- Wordiness (unnecessary words)

Parallelism

If a sentence lists two or more things, they should be **parallel** (the same) in their grammatical structure.

Wrong: Gretchen bought eggs, milk, and bought meat at the store.
Correct: Gretchen bought eggs, milk, and meat at the store.

Wrong: The goose, hen, and the pig all lived happily ever after.
Correct: The goose, hen, and pig all lived happily ever after.
Correct: The goose, the hen, and the pig all lived happily ever after.

A parallel structure should be used when comparing two things.

Wrong: It's more fun to swim than running.
Correct: It's more fun to swim than to run.
Correct: It's more fun to swim than run.

The concept of parallelism also applies to **correlatives,** which are particular pairs of words used in special ways in sentences. The two most frequently used correlative word pairs are *either/or* and *neither/nor.* Whatever follows the first part of a correlative pair should be grammatically parallel to whatever follows the second part.

Wrong: You're *either* with me *or* you're against me.
Correct: You're *either* with me *or* against me.

Wrong: Either you're with me *or* against me.
Correct: Either you're with me *or* you're against me.

Active and Passive Voices

In the **active voice,** a sentence's subject is active, whereas in the **passive voice** the subject is acted upon. Using the passive voice often makes a sentence awkward and confusing, and so using the active voice is usually better.

Passive (Awkward): The sun's disappearance over the horizon was watched by us.
Active: We watched the sun disappear over the horizon.

In some cases, however, the passive voice sounds fine and actually helps get across the point of the sentence.

Examples:
The judge was appointed by President Clinton, not by Bush.
The defendant was tried and convicted by a jury of his peers.

Placement of Modifiers

A **modifier** is simply a word or phrase that describes or qualifies something else in the same sentence (usually the subject). Modifying phrases are often set off by commas. In general, you should place a modifier as close as possible to whatever it modifies; otherwise, the sentence might be confusing.

Confusing: This book is one of my favorites, written in 1990.
Clear: This book, written in 1990, is one of my favorites.
(The phrase *written in 1990* modifies *this book.*)

Confusing: Nearing the summit, the harsh wind began to take its toll on the mountain climbers.
Clear: The harsh wind began to take its toll on the mountain climbers as they neared the summit.
(The phrase *nearing the summit* modifies *the mountain climbers*.)

Confusing: Paula laughed at Janine as she left the room. (Who left the room: Paula or Jeanine?)
Clear: As she left the room, Paula laughed at Janine.
Clear: As Janine left the room, Paula laughed at her.

Redundancy (Repetitiveness)

Repeating the same essential idea is called **redundancy.** If a sentence contains a redundancy, often there's more than one way to correct the problem. (In the next examples, redundancies are italicized.)

Redundant: Gary is 20 years *old in age.*
Correct: Gary is 20 years old.
Correct: Gary's current age is 20 years.

Redundant: The *reason* I sat down is *because* I felt ill.
Correct: The reason I sat down is that I felt ill.
Correct: I sat down because I felt ill.

Redundant: I'm hungry, but I'm *also* tired, *too.*
Correct: I'm tired as well as hungry.
Correct: I'm tired, and I'm hungry, too.

Wordiness (Unnecessary Words)

Even if a sentence is free of grammatical errors, you might be able to improve it, especially if it uses too many words to get its point across. In general, briefer is better, as long as the sentence's meaning is clear. You might be able to improve a sentence by simply removing certain words because the sentence is more concise and graceful, yet still perfectly clear, without them.

Wordy: Danielle runs faster than Amy runs.
Concise: Danielle runs faster than Amy.

Wordy: I plan to arrive by the time of nine o'clock.
Concise: I plan to arrive by nine o'clock.

Wordy: This year it rained more than it ever rained before.
Concise: This year it rained more than ever before.

In other sentences, you might be able to replace wordy phrases with more concise, graceful ones.

Wordy: The view from the roof is better than the view from the first floor and the view from the second floor.
Concise: The view from the roof is better than from either the first or second floor.

Wordy: The band's guitarist, as well as the band's drummer, played too loudly.
Concise: The band's guitarist and drummer both played too loudly.

Wordy: I gave up for the reason that I was too tired to continue.
Concise: I gave up because I was too tired to continue.

Wordy: Ursula is a good student, but her sister is not a good student.
Concise: Ursula is a good student, but her sister is not.

Punctuation

This section covers the rules for using the following punctuation marks.

- Commas
- Colons, semicolons, and dashes
- Apostrophes—possessive nouns
- Apostrophes—contractions
- Quotation marks for dialogue
- Quotation marks and italics (or underlining) for titles

Commas

Use a comma followed by an appropriate connecting word (such as *and* or *but*) to connect two main clauses (which can stand alone as a complete sentence).

Wrong: Keith is a good swimmer and he is a good student as well.
Correct: Keith is a good swimmer, and he is a good student as well.

However, if the sentence contains only one main clause, do not use a comma to separate the main clause from the rest of the sentence.

Wrong: Keith is a good swimmer, and is a good student as well.
Correct: Keith is a good swimmer and is a good student as well.

Use commas when needed to make the logic and meaning of a sentence clear.

Confusing: An hour after you go call me.
Clear: An hour after you go, call me.

Use commas to separate three or more items in a list. Do not use a comma to separate only two list items.

Wrong: I plan to take algebra history and theater arts this year.
Correct: I plan to take algebra, history, and theater arts this year.

Wrong: I plan to take algebra, and history this year.
Correct: I plan to take algebra and history this year.

Use a pair of commas (not just one comma) as a substitute for a pair of parentheses—to set off a phrase that is not essential for the sentence to make sense and be grammatically correct.

Correct:
The tallest boy, whose name is Greg, is 12 years old.
Neil Armstrong, the first human to walk on the moon, is from Ohio.
The war, which occurred during the 1990s, resulted in many thousands of deaths.

Do not use commas to set off prepositional phrases in the middle or at the end of sentences.

Wrong: Beth loves to go to the beach, in the summer.
Wrong: Beth loves to go, to the beach, in the summer.
Correct: Beth loves to go to the beach in the summer.

Use a comma after a dependent clause (a clause that cannot stand alone as a complete sentence) at the beginning of a sentence to create a natural pause that helps the reader understand the sentence.

Correct: Upon arriving at the airport, Dru realized that he forgot his ticket at home.
Correct: During the summer, Beth loves to go to the beach.

Use a comma between two adjectives unless the first adjective is used to describe the second adjective—in which case you should not insert a comma.

Correct: It was a *hot, humid* day.
Correct: An *icy cold* beverage would be refreshing right now.

Colons, Semicolons, and Dashes

Use a **colon** (:) immediately preceding a list or a phrase that explains, paraphrases, or defines what came just before it. Do NOT use a colon if the sentence is grammatically correct without it.

Wrong: This summer I'm taking three classes, which include: geography, geometry, and art.
Wrong: The problem with my bike is: It has a flat tire.
Wrong: The only two ways to get to the island are: by boat and by small plane.

Correct: This summer I'm taking three classes: geography, geometry, and art.
Correct: There's a problem with my bike: It has a flat tire.
Correct: I know of two ways to get to the island: by boat and by small plane.

Use a **semicolon** (;) to combine two sentences whose ideas are very closely related. You do NOT need to use a connecting word (such as *and* or *but*) as well.

Correct: The middle school is very demanding; students must study hard to do well.
Correct: I ordered the hamburger; it was Gwen who ordered the hot dog.
Correct: I think I've sprained my ankle; could you please drive me home?

You can use a **dash** (—) instead of a comma just before a concluding phrase. You can also use a pair of dashes instead of commas or parentheses to set off a parenthetical phrase.

Correct: She looked straight ahead, as if she did not see him.
Correct: She looked straight ahead—as if she did not see him.

Wrong: The house across the street—the white one, is for sale.
Correct: The house across the street—the white one—is for sale.

Apostrophes—Possessive Nouns

Use an apostrophe to indicate possession or ownership.

Correct: Janice's book
Correct: my best friend's wedding
Correct: the women's choir

For plural nouns ending in the letter *s,* the apostrophe belongs after the *s.*

Correct: the four students' essays
Correct: the citizens' right to free speech

Possessive pronouns (for example, *his, hers, its*) do not take apostrophes.

Correct: The second car in the driveway is *ours.*
Correct: Among all the cars, *theirs* is the newest.

Apostrophes—Contractions

A **contraction** is a word made up of two or more words from which letters have been omitted. Insert an apostrophe where the letters have been omitted.

It's (It is) all up to you now.
If you'd (you would) like to go, just say so.
We've (we have) got three hours to finish this chore.
Why don't (do not) you like me?
There's (There is) nothing wrong with that.
My dog can't (cannot) do any tricks.
If they wouldn't (would not) have beat us, we'd (we would) have won first prize.

Be careful not to confuse contractions such as *they're* (they are), *who's* (who is), and *it's* (it is) with their homophones (words that sound the same).

I think *they're* (they are) traveling by plane.
I noticed that *their* luggage was missing.
I think I see the luggage over *there.*

If *it's* (it is) not too late, please don't eat the salmon.
The groundhog saw *its* shadow.

Who's (who is) up to bat next?
Whose bat is this?

Quotation Marks for Dialogue

Use quotation marks to begin and end written or spoken dialogue. An end-of-dialogue punctuation mark is part of the quotation (it should come *before* the second quotation mark). If the quotation comes at the end of a sentence, a comma should precede the quotation.

Wrong: Penny said "I like you."
Wrong: Penny exclaimed, "Of course I like him"!
Wrong: Penny asked me: Do you like her?

Correct: Penny said, "I like you."
Correct: Penny exclaimed, "Of course I like him!"
Correct: Penny asked me, "Do you like her?"

If the sentence continues after the quotation, punctuate the quotation. However, do not use a period.

Wrong: "We want a touchdown" said Jimmy.
Wrong: "We want a touchdown." said Jimmy.
Correct: "We want a touchdown," said Jimmy.

Correct: "We want a touchdown!" chanted Jimmy over and over.
Correct: After telling us, "Our team has no chance of winning," Jimmy got up and left.
Correct: "What are our chances of winning?" Jimmy asked.

Quotation Marks and Italics (or Underlining) for Titles

Use quotation marks for titles of poems, songs, speeches, and short stories. Use either italics or underlining for book titles and movie titles—whether or not you indicate the full title—as well as for names of specific ships and aircraft.

Correct:
The Beatles recorded "Hey Jude" in 1967.
Martin Luther King's "I Have a Dream" speech is familiar to most Americans.
The new book in the *Harry Potter* series arrived at bookstores this week.
Many movie critics rank *Citizen Kane* as the single best movie ever made.
The space shuttle *Discovery* is scheduled to launch again next month.

Capitalization

Capitalize all **proper nouns,** which are *specific* persons, places, events, and things. There are many categories of proper nouns, including:

- Names of specific persons and organizations
- Titles of specific persons (government and military officials)
- Titles of books, short stories, poems, songs, plays, and movies
- Geographic areas (streets, cities, states, regions, nations, continents)
- Special landmarks (parks, monuments, bridges, buildings, celestial bodies)

■ Days of the week, months, holidays, and other special events
■ Languages

Remember: You should NOT capitalize a noun unless it names a *specific* person, place, event, or thing. All of the following examples are correct.

Examples (official titles):
Who was the vice president of the United States in the year 2000?
Was Vice President Gore in office during the year 2000?
I wrote to Senator Smith about the proposed law.
You should write to your state senator about the proposed law.

Examples (places):
Mike lives on Madison Street in Brooklyn.
He was born in the state of New York, but he grew up in the Midwest.
I went to the Iowa State Fair last year, but I don't remember in which county the fair took place.
The continent of Africa is bordered by the Atlantic Ocean, the Indian Ocean, the Red Sea, and the Mediterranean Sea.

Examples (landmarks):
I've been to Yosemite National Park, but I've never been to Disneyland.
The Great Wall of China is visible from outer space but not from as far away as Mars.
It took us nearly half an hour to drive from the Empire State Building to the George Washington Bridge.

Example (various types):
At Appomattox Courthouse in Virginia, General Lee officially surrendered to General Grant and the Union Army. This event marked the end of the Civil War, a bloody era in American history, and the beginning of the period called Reconstruction.

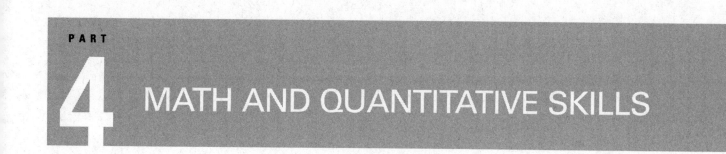

PART

4 MATH AND QUANTITATIVE SKILLS

Mathematics—
Concepts and Problem Solving

COOP | HSPT | TACHS

The COOP, HSPT, and TACHS Mathematics tests cover the same areas of math in the same format. All three tests consist of two basic kinds of questions:

Concept questions. These questions focus mainly on math concepts, not on calculations (although simple computations are sometimes required).
Problem-solving questions. In these questions, you work to a solution that matches one of the answer choices.

In this chapter, you'll learn a step-by-step approach to answering both kinds of questions. Then you'll learn some useful shortcuts and tips for handling problem-solving questions.

Math Concept Questions—Step by Step

Here are the steps to answering math concept questions:

Step 1: Read the question, and then ask yourself what math concepts and rules it covers. If the question involves a concept that is completely unfamiliar to you, skip it. Otherwise, go to step 2.
Step 2: Glance at the four answer choices; ask yourself what they have in common, and whether this makes sense to you, given the question. (If the way the answer choices look makes no sense at all to you, you might have misread the question; go back and read it more carefully.)
Step 3: Examine answer choice A to see if it answers the question. If it does, then stop right there, and select A as the correct choice. Otherwise, go to step 4.
Step 4: Examine each of the other three answer choices, in turn, until you find one that answers the question. When you find one, stop there, and select it as the correct choice.

Let's apply these steps to an example question:

Which of the following CANNOT be the lengths of a triangle's three sides?
A 4,6,3
B 3,10,7
C 13,2,14
D 3,5,6

Step 1: To answer the question, you need to know what's true about the three sides of *any* triangle. One of the properties of all triangles is that the combined length of any two sides must be greater than the length of the third side. (This makes sense if you think about it; unless two sides combined are longer than the third, you can't create a two-dimensional figure.) So you can add the two small sides and compare the sum to the longest side for a shortcut.

Step 2: The answer choices all list three numbers. Each group of three numbers is supposed to represent the lengths of a triangle's three sides. The way the answer choices look makes sense. The correct choice will describe what CANNOT possibly be a triangle. On the other hand, all the other choices will describe possible triangles.

Step 3: Starting with answer choice A, let's check to see whether it describes a triangle. If it does, then it's *not* the correct answer. If it doesn't, then it is. Choice A lists the lengths 4, 6, and 3. The sum of any two of these numbers is greater than the third number. For example, $3 + 4 > 6$. So, A cannot be the correct answer choice. Let's go to step 4.

Step 4: Let's try each other answer choice until we find one that CANNOT describe a triangle. First, choice B: Given lengths 3, 10, and 7, is the sum of any two numbers greater than the third number? No; $3 + 7$ is *not* greater than 10. The numbers in choice B cannot be the lengths of a triangle's three sides. You don't need to look at choices C and D. Select B as the correct answer choice.

Math Problem Solving—Step by Step

Here are the steps to answering problem-solving questions:

Step 1: Read the question, and then ask yourself what math concepts and rules it covers. If the question confuses you, skip it. Otherwise, go to step 2.
Step 2: Glance at the four answer choices for clues about how to handle the question. Pay special attention to what the answer choices have in common. This tells you what to aim for when solving the problem.
Step 3: Try to figure out the quickest way to identify the correct answer. Smart test takers will recognize shortcuts to the correct answer to many questions. (You'll learn the most useful shortcuts later in this chapter.) If there's a good shortcut, take it! If not, go to step 4.
Step 4: Set up and solve the problem. Two or three steps should be all that are needed. (For some questions, you may need to set up and solve an algebraic equation.)
Step 5: Scan the answer choices for your solution. If you don't see it, you did something wrong. Go back and check your work from step 4.

Let's apply these steps to a typical problem-solving question:

$$0.2 \times \frac{1}{3} =$$

A $\frac{1}{3}$

B $\frac{1}{30}$

C $\frac{1}{15}$

D $\frac{1}{6}$

Step 1: To solve this problem, you need to combine a decimal number and a fraction. You'll need to convert one number to the same form as the other.

Step 2: The answer choices are all fractions. What's more, in every fraction, the numerator is 1. This tells us that you should convert the decimal number (0.2) to a fraction before multiplying. Also, if the resulting fraction has a numerator larger than 1, you should reduce the fraction to lowest terms (so that the numerator is 1).

Step 3: Let's assume there's no shortcut to doing the math here. (Go to step 4).

Step 4: There are two steps to solving the problem:

1. Convert 0.2 to a fraction: $0.2 = \dfrac{2}{10}$. Reduce to lowest terms: $\dfrac{2}{10} = \dfrac{1}{5}$.

2. Combine numerators by multiplication, and combine denominators by multiplication: $\dfrac{1}{5} \times \dfrac{1}{3} = \dfrac{1}{15}$. Notice that the numerator is 1; this fraction is already in lowest terms.

Step 5: Scanning the answer choices, we see that our solution $\dfrac{1}{15}$ is among them. There's no need to go back and check our work. Select choice C.

Problem Solving—Strategies and Tips

Let's explore some useful strategies for helping you score your very best on the Mathematics portion of your exam.

Use Common Sense to Narrow Down the Choices

If the answer choices provide only numbers, first ask yourself what size number might make sense as a solution:

- a small fraction (between 0 and 1)?
- a negative number?
- an integer?
- an extremely large number?

With a good idea about the size of the number solution, you can probably eliminate at least one (and possibly two) of the four answer choices.

Example:
What is 40% of 40%?
A 1.6
B 0.16
C 0.8
D 0.2

40% is just under $\dfrac{1}{2}$, isn't it? And so, 40% of 40% must be a bit less than $\dfrac{1}{4}$. Since $\dfrac{1}{4}$ is .25, you can eliminate answer choices A and C because they are way off the mark. Just by applying common sense, you've increased your odds of choosing the correct answer by 50%. By the way, the correct answer choice is B: 40% of 40% = $0.4 \times 0.4 = 0.16$.

For Some Problems, It's Easier to Work Backward from the Answer Choices

You can answer any problem-solving question by working to a solution and then finding your solution among the answer choices. But it might be quicker and easier to solve some problems by testing each answer choice to see if it "fits the facts" of the problem.

Example:

$\sqrt{132}$ is between
A 13 and 14
B 12 and 13
C 11 and 12
D 10 and 11

One way to solve this problem is to compute the square root of 132. But it's probably easier to try squaring the numbers in the answer choices. Let's start somewhere in the middle. Since $12 \times 12 = 144$, you know that $\sqrt{132}$ is less than 12, and thus the correct answer must be either C or D. $11 \times 11 = 121$. Bingo! Since 132 is between 121 and 144, $\sqrt{132}$ must lie between 11 and 12. That's all you need to know. The correct answer is choice C.

Working backward from the answer choices can be especially useful when it comes to solving certain "story" problems, presented in a real-world setting.

Example:
Jan is 14 years younger than Thomas was 2 years ago. If Thomas is currently 23 years old, what is Jan's current age?
A 14
B 9
C 11
D 7

One way to solve this story problem is to set up and solve an algebraic equation. If you're not sure how to do that, you might find it easier to "try out" each answer choice, in turn, until you find one that works.

Start with choice A. Assume Jan is 14 years old. In 14 years, she will be 28. For this to be Thomas's age 2 years ago, he has to be 30 years old now. Since the problem tells us that Thomas is now 23, we know that A is not the right choice.

Next, choice B: Assume Jan is 9 years old. Her age (9) + 14 = Thomas's age 2 years ago: 23. If Thomas's age 2 years ago was 23, then he cannot be 23 years old now. So choice B doesn't fit the facts, either. Keep looking.

Next, choice C: Assume Jan is 11 years old. Her age (11) + 14 = Thomas's age 2 years ago: 25. If Thomas's age 2 years ago was 25, then he cannot be 23 years old now. So, choice C doesn't fit the facts, either. The correct answer must be choice D. But let's try it anyway, just to be sure.

Assume Jan is 7 years old. Her age (7) + 14 = Thomas's age 2 years ago: 21. If Thomas's age 2 years ago was 21, then he would be 23 years old now. Choice D fits the facts!

To Solve Some Problems, Estimates Are Good Enough

If a question asks for an approximate number value, it's telling you that precise calculations aren't necessary. Also, check the answer choices; if they're rounded off, you can round off your solution as well.

Example:
If you discount a $10 item by 15%, and then add a 15% tax based on the discounted price, then the item's final price, including tax, is nearest to
A $9.25
B $8.50
C $9.75
D $10

First, apply a dose of common sense to narrow down the choices: After the initial discount, the price (without tax) is $10–$1.50 = $8.50. Since the 15% tax is based on $8.50, the final price (with tax) must be greater than $8.50, so we can eliminate B. Since $8.50 is less than $10, we know that 15% of $8.50 is also less than 15% of $10. We subtract 15% of $10 and add 15% of $8.50, so the final price must be less than $10. Therefore, we can eliminate D. Choice C is the only one that works.

Plug in Easy Numbers for Variables

If the answer choices contain variables (like x and y), the question might be a good candidate for the "plug-in" strategy. Pick simple numbers (so the math is easy), and substitute them for the variables. You'll definitely need your pencil for this strategy.

Example:
Ken and Gary competed in a footrace. Ken finished the race in S seconds, and Gary finished the race T seconds behind Ken. Which of the following represents Gary's race time, in minutes?
A $60S + T$

B $\dfrac{S+T}{60}$

C $60(S - T)$

D $S + \dfrac{T}{60}$

One way to answer the question is to set up an algebraic equation. But if you're not sure how to do this, try using some simple numbers for S and T. Notice that the question asks for an expression in terms of *minutes*. So let's pick some values for S and T that can easily be converted into minutes. Let $S = 60$ and $T = 30$. Gary's race time was 60 seconds + 30 seconds, or $1\frac{1}{2}$ minutes. Now, for each answer choice, let's plug in 60 and 30 (for S and T). When we obtain the number 1.5, we've found the correct expression. First, choice A: $60S + T = 60(60) + (30) =$ a very large number (obviously, not 1.5). Let's try choice B:

$$\frac{S+T}{60} = \frac{S+T}{60} = \frac{60+30}{60} = \frac{90}{60} = \frac{3}{2}$$

Aha! $\frac{3}{2}$ (which equals $1\frac{1}{2}$) is the value we're looking for. While we know that B works, you should check C and D to ensure that you did not pick values of S and T that happen to be true for more than one answer. If that does happen, just go back and pick different values, and try the answers again.

Instead of Crunching Numbers, Look for a Shortcut

To answer most problem-solving questions, you'll need to make at least a few simple calculations. But if you find yourself doing a lot of pencil work, there's probably an easier route to the solution.

Example:
What's the difference between the sum of all integers from 1 to 20 and the sum of all integers from 26 to 45?
A 20
B 100
C 500
D 250

One way to answer the question is to do the addition. But that's a lot of number crunching! So, there must be an easier way. Think about it. The difference between 1 and 26 (the first number of each set) is 25. So is the difference between 2 and 27. See the pattern? For each of the 20 corresponding pairs of numbers in the two sets, the difference is 25. So, the difference between the two sums must be $25 \times 20 = 500$. That's easy math!

Solve Geometry Problems That Include Figures by Working the Numbers, Not by Visual Measurement

Some math problems include geometry figures. These figures are intended to help you understand the question. They may or may not be drawn precisely to scale. Don't try to solve these problems by making visual measurements of angles, lengths, and areas. Instead, use your knowledge of the rules of geometry to solve these problems.

Example:
In the figure below, $b = 30$. Find the value of a.

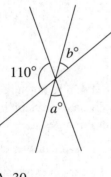

A 30
B 40
C 50
D 55

If you try to measure the size of angle a, you might conclude that it's $30°$ and select A as the correct answer choice. But you'd be wrong. Don't try to answer this question by visual estimation. Instead, let's apply the rules of geometry. Since $b = 30$, the angle that is vertical to b (directly across the vertex from b) must also measure $30°$. That angle, combined with the $110°$ angle and angle a, form a straight line, which measures $180°$. Thus, $a = 40$. The correct answer is choice B.

Beware of Answer Choices That Make the Problem Seem Too Easy

To answer most problem-solving questions, you'll need to make at least a few simple calculations. If you think you can choose an answer without doing any calculating at all, you've probably misunderstood something in the question.

Example:
The arithmetic mean (simple average) of 10, 20, and one other number is 30. What is the other number?
A 40
B 45
C 60
D 50

The numbers ascend in intervals of 10, from 10 to 20 to 30. It might be tempting to guess that the missing number is 40. But that guess would be wrong. There are two ways to solve this problem. One is by setting up and solving an algebraic equation:

$$\frac{10 + 20 + x}{3} = 30$$
$$10 + 20 + x = 90$$
$$30 + x = 90$$
$$x = 60$$

The other way is to work backward from the answer choices—another strategy you learned in this chapter.

Don't Assume You're Right Just Because Your Solution Is Among the Answer Choices

A certain wrong answer might seem correct to a test taker who solves the problem incorrectly. (That's how the test *makers* design math questions.) So even if the solution appears among the four choices, check your calculations to make sure you haven't fallen into the test makers' trap!

Example:
$$\frac{2}{5} + \frac{1}{5} \div \frac{2}{5} =$$

A $\dfrac{9}{10}$

B $\dfrac{3}{2}$

C $\dfrac{3}{10}$

D $\dfrac{6}{5}$

This problem focuses on the rules for the order of operations. The rule to apply here is that you perform division before addition:

$$\frac{2}{5}+\left(\frac{1}{5}\div\frac{2}{5}\right)=\frac{2}{5}+\left(\frac{1}{5}\times\frac{5}{2}\right)=\frac{2}{5}+\frac{5}{10}=\frac{4}{10}+\frac{5}{10}=\frac{9}{10}$$

The correct answer is choice A. Choices B and D are traps for the unwary test taker. Some test takers would *incorrectly* perform addition first:

$$\left(\frac{2}{5}+\frac{1}{5}\right)\div\frac{2}{5}=\frac{3}{5}\div\frac{2}{5}=\frac{3}{5}\times\frac{5}{2}=\frac{15}{10},\text{ or }\frac{3}{2}$$

The result would be to select choice B. Wrong! Other test takers would incorrectly divide the first term by the third term first:

$$\left(\frac{2}{5}\div\frac{2}{5}\right)+\frac{1}{5}=1+\frac{1}{5}=\frac{6}{5}$$

The result would be to select choice D. Wrong!

Math Questions—Heads Up!

- Always size up a question before taking pencil to paper. Ask yourself: What ballpark solution would make sense? Do I know how to solve this type of problem?
- Figure out what math concept is being tested. Review the rules in your mind before jumping into the problem.
- Always look for the quickest, easiest route to the correct answer. But remember: For most questions, there's no shortcut.
- Take time to check your calculations. Never assume that your solution is correct just because you see it among the answer choices.

Practice

This practice drill contains math concept and problem-solving questions. Apply the steps, strategies, and tips you learned in this chapter to these questions.

Directions: For each question, select the best answer choice.

1. If p is an integer and q is a non-integer, then it must be true that

    A $p-q$ is a non-integer
    B $p\times q$ is a non-integer
    C $p\div q$ is a non-integer
    D $p+q$ is an integer

2. $\dfrac{2}{3}+60\%+0.4=$

    A $\dfrac{8}{5}$
    B 1.8
    C 160%
    D $\dfrac{5}{3}$

3. If a printer prints 2 pages in 7 seconds, then it can print

A 1 page in 14 seconds
B 5 pages in 16.5 seconds
C 10 pages in 70 seconds
D 7 pages in 24.5 seconds

4. Paul has twice as many nickels as dimes, and he has four times as many dimes as quarters. If the value of these coins totals $3.15, then Paul has

A 12 dimes and 3 quarters
B 12 nickels and 4 quarters
C 10 dimes and 20 nickels
D 1 quarter and 16 nickels

5. A standard deck of 52 playing cards contains 13 cards of each of four suits: spades, hearts, diamonds, and clubs. What is the probability of randomly drawing a spade from the deck?

A $\dfrac{2}{5}$

B $\dfrac{1}{4}$

C $\dfrac{1}{13}$

D $\dfrac{1}{52}$

6. The figure below shows a parallelogram.

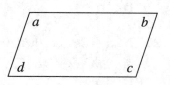

In the figure, angles a and b are

A complementary
B supplementary
C congruent
D none of the above

7. If $0 < n < 1$, then which of the following must be true?

A $0 < \sqrt{n} < n < 1$
B $0 < n < 1 < \sqrt{n}$
C $\sqrt{n} < 0 < n < 1$
D $0 < n < \sqrt{n} < 1$

8. Which of the following is equal to 0.025?

A $(0.05)^2$
B $0.05 + 0.02$
C $0.1 \div 4$
D 0.25×0.5

9. Real numbers X and Y are plotted on the number line as shown below:

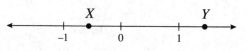

All of the following statements are true EXCEPT:

A $Y - X > 1$
B $X \times Y < 0$
C $X + Y < 0$
D $X \div Y > -1$

10. If an airplane travels M miles in T minutes, how many miles does it travel in $2T$ hours?

A $120M$

B $\dfrac{M}{30}$

C $2TM$

D $2M$

11. The graph below compares the number of truck sales to car sales during each of three different years.

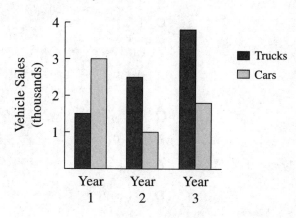

Approximately how many trucks were sold altogether during the three years shown?

A 13,400
B 6,600
C 5,600
D 7,800

12. What value does the digit 8 represent in the decimal number 35.9842?

   A $\dfrac{8}{100}$

   B $\dfrac{8}{10}$

   C $\dfrac{8}{1,000}$

   D $\dfrac{8}{10,000}$

13. Which of the following statements is true?

   A   The greatest prime factor of 18 is 9.
   B   The greatest prime factor of 21 is 3.
   C   The greatest prime factor of 4 is 2.
   D   The greatest prime factor of 34 is 11.

14. Which of the following is closest in value to $483{,}758 \div 2{,}429$?

   A   500
   B   200
   C   75
   D   1,250

15. For what value of P is it true that $\dfrac{2P+2}{3P-1}=2$?

   A $\dfrac{3}{2}$

   B   2
   C   1
   D -3

16. If $-1<x<-\dfrac{1}{2}$, then it must be true that

   A $\dfrac{x}{2}<-\dfrac{1}{2}$

   B $x>0$

   C $x^2<-\dfrac{1}{2}$

   D $-1>2x$

17. In the figure below, if $x=65$, what is the value of y?

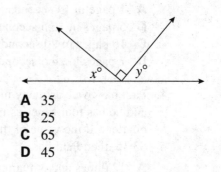

   A   35
   B   25
   C   65
   D   45

18. R = the set of all positive integers less than 100. S = the set of all multiples of 5. How many members does the set defined by $R \cap S$ contain?

   A   19
   B   99
   C   20
   D   25

19. $\dfrac{3^4}{6^4}=$

   A $\dfrac{1}{2}$

   B $\dfrac{1}{16}$

   C $\dfrac{1}{48}$

   D $\dfrac{1}{8}$

20. If $ab + 2c = c$, then $c =$

   A $2ab + c$
   B $4abc$
   C $3ab + 4c$
   D $c + 2ab$

Practice—Answers and Explanations

1. **A** When you combine any non-integer and any integer by either addition or subtraction, the result is always a *non*-integer.

2. **D** Look for the easiest way to combine the terms in the question. 60% = 0.6, and so the sum of the second and third terms is 1. This makes the problem easy to solve: $\frac{2}{3}+1=\frac{2}{3}+\frac{3}{3}=\frac{5}{3}$.

3. **D** The easiest way to solve this problem is to set it up as a proportion, or a set of two equal fractions. The first fraction is 2 pages over 7 seconds; use the answer choices to plug in values for the second fraction and eliminate any answer choices that make fractions that are not equal to $\frac{2}{7}$. Answer choice D gives you $\frac{2}{7}=\frac{7}{24.5}$, which is equal and therefore correct.

4. **A** Only choice A fits the facts: 12 dimes = $1.20, and 3 quarters = $0.75. The ratio of nickels to dimes is 2:1. Thus, in choice A, Paul has 24 nickels = $1.20. The total is $3.15.

5. **B** 13 of 52 cards are spades. Thus, the probability of drawing a spade is $\frac{13}{52}$, or $\frac{1}{4}$.

6. **B** You need to know the properties of parallelograms to answer this question. In a parallelogram, any two adjacent interior angles are supplementary, which means that their sum is 180°.

7. **D** When you multiply a fraction between 0 and 1 by itself, the product is less than the initial fraction but still greater than 0. If you're not sure, try plugging in some simple numbers—for example, $\frac{1}{2}\times\frac{1}{2}=\frac{1}{4}$.

8. **C** For choice C, calculating the number value is easier if you multiply instead of divide. Dividing a number by 4 is the same as multiplying by $\frac{1}{4}$, or 0.25. Thus, $0.1 \div 4 = 0.1 \times 0.25 = 0.025$. As you can see, C is the correct answer. Choice A is incorrect because $(0.05)^2 = (0.05)(0.05) = 0.0025$. Choice B is incorrect because $0.05 + 0.02 = 0.07$. Choice D is incorrect because $0.25 \times 0.5 = 0.125$.

9. **C** The figure shows that X is negative (less than 0) and Y is positive (greater than 0). The sum of a negative number and a positive number is always negative. Thus, statement C must be *false*. If you're not sure, try plugging in simple numbers for X and Y. For example, if $X=-\frac{1}{2}$ and $Y = 2$, then $X+Y+1\frac{1}{2}$, which is greater than 0.

10. **A** You can solve the problem by setting up an algebraic equation. Or, you can substitute simple numbers for M and T. Let's assume that $M = 1$ and $T = 1$. In 2 *minutes,* the airplane travels 2 miles. So, in 2 *hours,* it travels 60 times farther: 120 miles (because there are 60 minutes in an hour). If you substitute 1 for M in each answer choice, you see that choice A works—the number value is 120. Thus, choice A must be the correct answer.

11. **D** The answer choices are round numbers, and so you can estimate the number of truck sales. Truck sales totaled approximately 1,600 (year 1), 2,400 (year 2), and 3,800 (year 3). The grand total is 7,800.

12. **A** The digit 8 is located in the "hundredths" place.

13. **C** 2 is the only prime factor of 4. Choice A is incorrect because 9 is not a prime number. Choice B is incorrect because 7 is also a prime factor of 21. Choice D is incorrect because 11 is not a factor of 34.

14. **B** There's no need to perform long division here to calculate the quotient. Notice the relationship between the first two digits of each number: 48 is twice 24. Rounding off both numbers and expressing the quotient as the fraction $\dfrac{480,000}{2,400}$, you can see that the quotient is approximately 200.

15. **C** You solve the problem algebraically, by isolating P on one side of the equation. Or, you can test the answer choices, one at a time, substituting each number for P in the equation. Only choice C works:

$$\frac{2(1)+2}{3(1)-1}=2$$

16. **D** We know that x is less than $-\dfrac{1}{2}$ (to the left of $-\dfrac{1}{2}$ on the number line). Thus, $2x$ must be further to the left on the number line than -1. In other words, if you know that $x<-\dfrac{1}{2}$, then $2x<2\left(-\dfrac{1}{2}\right)$ or $2x<-1$.

17. **B** Don't try to answer the question by visual measurement. Instead, focus on the number information. Angles x, y, and a right ($90°$) angle combine to form a straight line, whose angle measure is $180°$; $x=65$, and so $y=25$. ($90+65+25=180$.)

18. **A** Look for a pattern that makes the problem easy to solve. The question asks for the *intersection* ($\cap$) of the two sets—how many numbers are in both sets. There are 20 multiples of 5 among all positive integers up to, and including, 100. ($5\times20=100$.) However, set R excludes the number 100, and so there are only 19 such integers in the set defined by $R\cap S$.

19. **B** Calculating the value of 3^4 and 6^4 and then dividing the two products involves far too much number crunching. There's an easy shortcut. Restate the denominator as $3^4\times2^4$, and then factor out 3^4 from the numerator and denominator. That leaves the fraction $\dfrac{1}{2^4}$, or $\dfrac{1}{16}$.

20. **C** There's no shortcut to the algebra here. In the equation given, substitute $ab+2c$ for c, then simplify:

$$c=ab+2(ab+2c)$$
$$c=ab+2ab+4c$$
$$c=3ab+4c$$

COOP | HSPT

One of the seven COOP tests is called Sequences. This subtest consists of 20 questions. Each question tests your ability to recognize a pattern in a series of numbers, letters, or pictures. You'll also find *number* sequences on the HSPT, in the Quantitative Reasoning subtest.

To handle sequence questions, follow these steps:

Step 1: Examine the series carefully. Ask yourself what rule, or pattern, explains how the numbers, letters, or pictures change from one to the next throughout the series.
Step 2: Predict what number, letter, or picture would continue the pattern. In your test booklet, draw or jot down your prediction of where the missing item would go.
Step 3: Scan the answer choices for the one that best fits your prediction.
Step 4: If your answer isn't listed, you probably missed the pattern. Examine the series again. When you've found a clear pattern and an answer choice that continues the pattern, circle that answer choice in your test booklet.

Next, you'll apply this approach to three examples. Then, you'll learn the common patterns to look for in COOP and HSPT sequences.

Number Sequences (COOP and HSPT)

One type of sequence question involves numbers in a series. Although these questions look a bit different on the HSPT than on the COOP, they're essentially the same. Look at the following example, and then read the step-by-step approach to handling it.

Example (HSPT style):
What is the next term in the following series: 2, 3, 5, 6, 8, . . . ?
A 9
B 11
C 7
D 10

Same example (COOP style):
2   3   5   6   8   __
A 9
B 11
C 7
D 10

Step 1: Examine the change from each number to the next. You add 1 to the first number (2) to obtain the second number (3), and you add 2 to the second number (3) to obtain the third number (5). So what's the pattern here? To find out, you need to examine the entire series:

$$2 \rightarrow (\text{add } 1) \rightarrow 3 \rightarrow (\text{add } 2) \rightarrow 5 \rightarrow (\text{add } 1) \rightarrow 6 \rightarrow (\text{add } 2) \rightarrow 8$$

Now the pattern is clear! To obtain each successive number, alternate between adding 1 and adding 2 to the previous number.

Step 2: Since the last operation was to add 2 to 6, the next operation is to add 1 to 8. Thus, the next number in the series should be 9.

Step 3: Scanning the answer choices, we see that the number 9 is indeed among them.

Step 4: Since our number prediction was among the four answer choices, we don't need to go back and examine the series again. Select choice A.

Number Sequences—Common Patterns

Most COOP and HSPT number sequences fit one of several basic patterns. To handle number sequences quickly and easily, be ready for the following patterns:

Repeat the same operation (add, subtract, multiply, or divide). To obtain each successive number in the series, repeat the same basic operation, using a constant number. This number might be an integer or a fraction, and it might be either positive or negative. Here are four examples—one for each operation.

12   17   22   27   32
(Add 5 to each number to obtain the next.)

4.5   2.0   −0.5   −3.0
(Subtract 2.5 from each number to obtain the next.)

$1 \quad \dfrac{3}{2} \quad \dfrac{9}{4} \quad \dfrac{27}{8}$

(Multiply each number by $\dfrac{3}{2}$ to obtain the next.)

$22 \quad 11 \quad \dfrac{11}{2} \quad \dfrac{11}{4}$
(Divide each number by 2 to obtain the next.)

Alternate (toggle) between two operations. This pattern is similar to the previous one, except that you alternate between two operations. Here are some examples:

4   8   11   15   18
(Alternate between adding 4 and adding 3.)

15 20 16 21 17
(Alternate between adding 5 and subtracting 4.)

3 12 8 32 28
(Alternate between multiplying by 4 and subtracting 4.)

30 15 18 9 12 6
(Alternate between dividing by 2 and adding 3.)

Operate with a larger (or smaller) number to obtain each successive term. This pattern is similar to the first type, except that you increase or decrease the number you use to add, subtract, multiply, or divide in order to obtain the next number. Here are some examples:

11 13 16 20 25
(Starting with 2, the number you add to obtain each successive term increases by 1.)

5 5 10 30 120
(Starting with 1, the multiplier used to obtain each successive term increases by 1.)

100 20 5 $\dfrac{5}{3}$ $\dfrac{5}{6}$
(Starting with 5, the number by which you divide to obtain each successive term decreases by 1.)

Combine short sequences into a longer sequence. In the next example, notice that each group of three numbers shows the same pattern: you add 3 to the first number to obtain the second, then subtract 1 from the second to obtain the third. But also notice that each successive group begins with the greatest number from the previous group.

2 5 4 | 5 8 7 | 8 11 10

Alternate sequences. Check to see if one particular number anchors the pattern. In the next example, 7 is the pivot, or anchor. Starting with 7, the sequence alternates between two operations: adding 2 and subtracting 1.

7 9 6 11 5 13 4

Apply the same exponent (power) or root repeatedly. In these sequences, the numbers can become much larger (or smaller) from one to the next. Here are two examples.

2 4 16 256
(Multiply each number by itself—"square" the number—to obtain the next.)

81 9 3 | 16 4 2 | 1 1 1
(In each group of three, you take the square root of a number to obtain the next.)

Letter Sequences (COOP)

Some of the questions on the COOP Sequences test involve alphabetical letters. Look at the following example, and then read the step-by-step approach to handling it.

a c d e g g ____
A h k
B i k
C j i
D f h

Step 1: Each of the three items in this series consists of two letters. Notice that, from one item to the next, the first letter in the pair skips two letters of the alphabet:

a → (skip b and c) → *d* → (skip e and f) → *g*

What about the second letter in each pair? Notice that, from one pair to the next, the second letter skips exactly *one* letter of the alphabet:

c → (skip d) → *e* → (skip f) → *g*

Step 2: Continuing these two patterns, the first letter of the fourth pair should be *j* (skipping h and i), and the second letter of the next pair should be *i* (skipping h).

Step 3: Scanning the answer choices, we see that choice C provides exactly what we predicted would be the next pair in the series: *j i.*

Step 4: Our prediction was among the four answer choices, and so we don't need to go back and examine the series again. Select choice C.

Letter Sequences—Common Patterns

Like number sequences, most COOP letter sequences fit one of several basic patterns. To handle letter sequences quickly and easily, be ready for any of the following patterns.

Alphabetical (or reverse alphabetical) order, no skipping. A straight alphabetical sequence is the easiest pattern to recognize:

f g h i j

To make things a bit trickier, the test might reverse the order and/or alternate (toggle) between upper-case and lower-case letters. Here's an example that shows both patterns:

P o N m L

Skipping the same number of letters from one item to the next. In this next example, look at the first letter of each pair. Notice that these letters are in reverse alphabetical order, skipping one letter of the alphabet from one item to the next: w-u-s-q.

w f u h s j q l

Now look at the second letter in each pair; they're in proper alphabetical order, but they also skip one letter of the alphabet between items: f-h-j-l. So, there are two patterns in the series.

Skipping more (or fewer) letters from one item to the next. In the first series below, notice that you skip one additional letter of the alphabet with each successive item. (The series starts by skipping one letter: d.) The second series below shows a similar pattern, except that the letters are in reverse alphabetical order, making the pattern tougher to recognize. (The series starts by not skipping any letters.)

c e h l q

Z Y W T P

Combining short sequences into a longer sequence. In the next example, notice that each group of three letters shows the same pattern: reverse alphabetical order (no skipping). But also notice that the four groups are shown in proper (not reverse) alphabetical order.

g f e | j i h | m l k | p o n

Keying off a "pivot" letter. Check to see if one particular letter anchors the pattern. In the next example, N is the pivot, or anchor. Notice that the sequence alternates between proper and reverse alphabetical order (N-O-P and N-M-L), returning to N before switching direction.

N O N M N P N L

Picture Sequences (COOP)

Some of the questions on the COOP Sequences test will involve a series of *pictures*. Look at the following example, and then read the step-by-step approach to handling it.

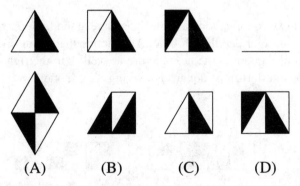

Step 1: Look at the three pictures in the series. Notice that the second picture simply adds a triangle to the first picture, and that the third picture simply darkens that triangle. What's the rule or pattern? From each picture to the next, exactly one feature, or detail, is added to the previous picture; otherwise, the previous picture is unchanged.

Step 2: The next picture in the series should add a detail to the third picture—perhaps by darkening the white triangle or by adding a fourth triangle. (Either addition would fit the pattern.)

Step 3: Scan the four answer choices for a picture that best matches your prediction. Figure D is the only one that fits this pattern; it adds one feature (another triangle) without making any other changes to the previous picture. What's wrong with the other three choices? Figures A and B each add a fourth triangle (which fits our pattern), but they also change the previous picture in some other way. Figure C doesn't add a feature; instead, it moves and removes shading from one of the three triangles in the previous picture.

Step 4: The type of picture we predicted was among the four answer choices, and so we don't need to go back and examine the series of pictures again. Select choice D.

Picture Sequences—Common Patterns

Most COOP picture sequences also fit one of several basic patterns. To handle picture sequences quickly and easily, be on the lookout for any of the following patterns.

Linear rotation (left-to-right or right-to-left). In the following example, each object moves to the right one position throughout the series of four pictures. Once an object reaches the far right, its next move is to jump to the far left.

Circular rotation (clockwise or counterclockwise). In the next example, look at how the positions of the balls change from picture to picture. With each successive picture, the left-hand object rotates clockwise 90 degrees, while the right-hand object rotates *counter*clockwise 90 degrees.

Adding (or removing) detail. In the next example, look at how the square at the far left evolves from picture to picture, adding an additional feature or detail each time. Also notice that whatever detail is added to this square is then added to the middle square in the next picture as well as to the right-most square in the following picture. In other words, the left-most square is serving as a model, which the other two squares imitate.

Movement along a path. In the next example, the black squares move in the same direction by two positions with each passing picture, while the black dot moves one position in the opposite direction. (When the dot reaches the end of the path, notice that it reverses course.)

Alternating, toggling, and flipping. From picture to picture, an object might alternate ("toggle") between large and small, black and white, round and square, or some other pair of characteristics. Or, an object might flip horizontally or vertically with each successive picture. For example, with each successive picture below, one more triangle flips from above the horizontal line to below it. In addition, all triangles toggle between black and white from one picture to the next.

Sequences—Heads Up!

- On your exam, look for the common patterns you learned in this lesson. But keep in mind that you might encounter other patterns as well.
- The key rule is that the pattern you're looking for in a sequence should apply to the entire sequence—not just part of it.
- On the HSPT, be ready for Roman numerals. You might run across them in a sequence question. Here are the Roman numerals you need to know: I = 1, V = 5, X = 10, L = 50, C = 100. (You'll try one in the practice drill just ahead.)
- Expect letter-number combinations on the COOP. Handle them just like any other sequence. (You'll try one in the practice drill just ahead.)
- For COOP letter sequences, learn the alphabet forwards *and* backwards. Also, when the timed Sequences test begins, quickly jot down the complete alphabet in your test booklet. Referring to it when you tackle letter-sequence questions will help you avoid careless mistakes.

Practice

Directions: Questions 1–5 are similar to questions appearing on the HSPT Quantitative Skills subtest. Select the best answer to each question.

1. What is the next number in the following series: 3, 7, 13, 21, 31, 43, . . . ?
   A 55
   B 49
   C 39
   D 57

2. What is the next number in the following series: 10.5, 9.2, 7.9, 6.6, 5.3, 4.0, . . . ?
   A 3.1
   B 2.7
   C 2.3
   D 2.5

3. What is the next number in the following series: $\dfrac{4}{9}$, $\dfrac{2}{3}$, 1, $\dfrac{3}{2}$, $\dfrac{9}{4}$, . . . ?
   A $\dfrac{27}{8}$
   B $\dfrac{9}{2}$
   C 3
   D $\dfrac{24}{5}$

4. What is the missing number in the following series: 17, 18, 9, 10, __, 6, 3 ?
   A 4
   B 5
   C 8
   D 7

5. What is the next number in the following series: XX, 19, XVII, 16, XIV, 13, . . . ?
   A XI
   B XVII
   C XX
   D XV

Directions: Questions 6–20 are similar to those appearing on the COOP Sequences test. For each question, select the answer that best continues or completes the series.

6. 9 8 7 12 11 10 15 14 __
   A 16
   B 14
   C 13
   D 12

7. 8 10 13 15 18 __
   A 17
   B 16
   C 20
   D 21

8. 16 18 9 | 8 10 5 | __ 14 7
   A 10
   B 12

   C 9
   D 11

9. 40 20 10 | 12 6 3 | 18 9 __
   A 4.5
   B 3
   C 6
   D 1

10. 3 27 81 | 1 1 1 | 2 8 __
   A 24
   B 32
   C 14
   D 16

11.

(A)   (B)   (C)   (D)

12.

(A)   (B)   (C)   (D)

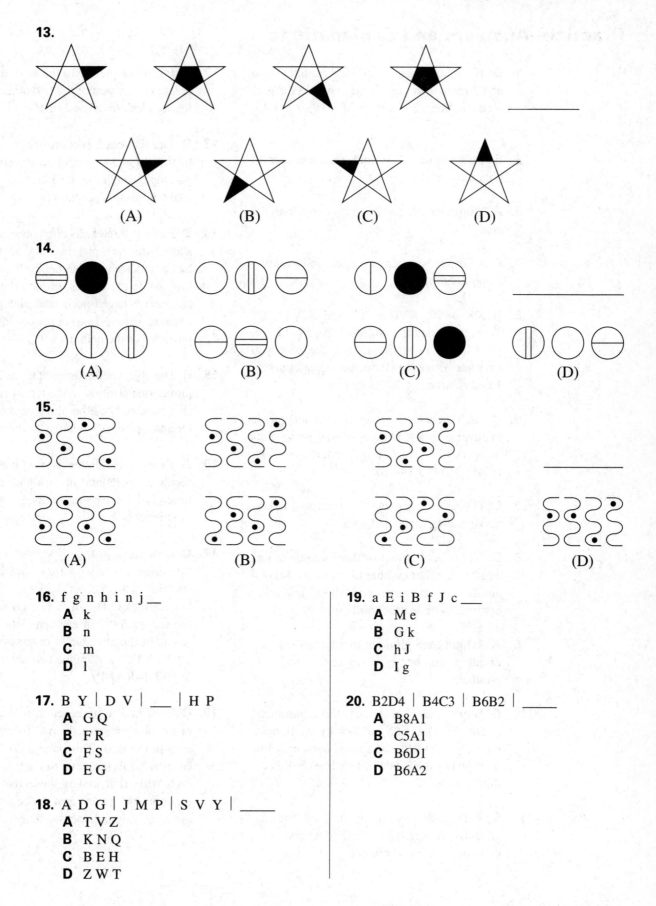

13.

(A)   (B)   (C)   (D)

14.

(A)   (B)   (C)   (D)

15.

(A)   (B)   (C)   (D)

16. f g n h i n j __
A k
B n
C m
D l

17. B Y │ D V │ __ │ H P
A G Q
B F R
C F S
D E G

18. A D G │ J M P │ S V Y │ ___
A T V Z
B K N Q
C B E H
D Z W T

19. a E i B f J c ___
A M e
B G k
C h J
D I g

20. B2D4 │ B4C3 │ B6B2 │ ___
A B8A1
B C5A1
C B6D1
D B6A2

Practice—Answers and Explanations

1. **D** To obtain each successive number, you add 2 more than you added to obtain the previous number: $21 + 10 = 31$; $31 + 12 = 43$; $43 + 14 = 57$.

2. **B** You subtract 1.3 from each number to obtain the next.

3. **A** Multiply each number by $\frac{3}{2}$ to obtain the next.

4. **B** Alternate between two operations: adding 1 and dividing by 2.

5. **A** XX = 20, XVII = 17, and XIV = 14. Thus, the series is as follows: 20, 19, 17, 16, 14, 13, ... From one term to the next, you alternate between two operations: subtracting 1 and subtracting 2. (XI = 11.)

6. **C** Each successive group of three integers is in reverse order. Otherwise, the series lists integers in ascending order: (9-8-7)-(12-11-10)-(15-14-13).

7. **C** The series alternates between two operations: adding 2 and adding 3.

8. **B** Within each group of three numbers, you add 2 to the first number to obtain the second number, and then you divide the second number by 2 to obtain the third number.

9. **A** Within each group of three numbers, you divide a number by 2 to obtain the next number.

10. **D** Within each group of three numbers, multiplying the first number by itself *twice* ("cubing" it) yields the second number, while multiplying it by itself *three* times yields the third number ($2 \times 2 \times 2 \times 2 = 16$).

11. **C** With each passing picture, all four U-shaped objects rotate 90 degrees in a counterclockwise direction.

12. **D** From one picture to the next, one circle is deleted from each of the two objects. All hollow circles are deleted first.

13. **B** The darkened portion of the star appears to travel clockwise around the star's points, passing through the star's center on its way to each successive point.

14. **D** Each of three balls alternates between two states from each picture to the next. The solid ball alternates between being shaded and hollow, while the stripes on the other two balls alternate between horizontal and vertical orientation. (There's no set pattern involving the positions of the balls.)

15. **B** The object to the far right in the first picture moves one position to the left in each successive picture. The other three objects remain in the same positions relative to one another.

16. **A** Every third letter is *n*. Otherwise, the series lists letters in straight alphabetical order (no letters are skipped). After *j*, the next letter is *k*.

17. **C** Looking at just the first letter in each pair, the series lists letters of the alphabet in order (starting with *B*), but skipping one letter in between (**B-C-D-E-F-G-H**). Looking at just the second letter in each pair, the series lists letters of the alphabet in reverse order (starting with *Y*), but skipping two letters (**Y-X-W-V-U-T-S-R-Q-P**).

18. **C** Each group of three letters is in alphabetical order, skipping exactly *two* letters from one item to the next. This pattern continues from each frame to the next. Since the third group ends with *Y*, it makes sense that the fourth group would start over at the beginning of the alphabet (skipping the two letters *Z* and *A*).

19. B Letters alternate between upper- and lower-case. You can eliminate choice C. Starting with the first letter in the series, *a,* if you skip two letters, the series continues alphabetically: *a-B-c.* You'll see the same pattern starting with the second letter, *E,* and the third letter, *i.* The first of the two final letters completes the sequence *E-f-G.* The last letter in the series completes the sequence *i-J-k.*

20. A Each group contains four elements. The first element is always "**B**." Otherwise, corresponding elements run in sequential order from one frame to the next: 2-4-6-**8** (second element), D-C-B-A (third element), and 4-3-2-**1** (fourth element).

COOP Quantitative Reasoning

On the COOP, the Quantitative Reasoning test contains 20 questions in various formats. Here are the three formats you're most likely to see on this test:

- Missing operations
- Geometric grids
- Scale balancing

In this lesson, you'll learn a step-by-step approach to each of these three unique question types.

Missing Operations

The best way to describe this question type is to read the directions and look at an example.

Directions: Find the operation (fill in the blank) that is applied to the first number in each of two pairs to obtain the second number. Then, apply the operation to find the missing number (?). Select the correct answer choice.

Example:
$4 \rightarrow \underline{} \rightarrow 8$
$3 \rightarrow \underline{} \rightarrow 7$
$7 \rightarrow \underline{} \rightarrow ?$

A 5
B 4
C 11
D 12

Here's a four-step approach for handling any missing-operation question:

Step 1: Look at the first pair of numbers (the top row). Answer the following two questions:

- What positive number do I add to (or subtract from) the first number to obtain the second number?
- What positive number do I multiply by (or divide from) the first number to obtain the second number?

Step 2: Apply the first operation that worked in step 1 to the second pair (middle row). If it works, go to step 3. If it doesn't work, apply the second operation that worked in step 1 to the second pair. (Only one operation will work for both pairs.)
Step 3: Apply the operation that worked for both pairs to the number in the bottom row. Jot down your answer.

Step 4: Scan the answer choices for your answer from step 3. If it's not among the four choices, you did something wrong. Go back and check your arithmetic from the first three steps.

Let's apply these four steps to our example:

Step 1: Find the two operations you apply to the number 4 to obtain the number 8:
4 (first number) + 4 (missing operation) = 8 (second number)
4 (first number) × 2 (missing operation) = 8 (second number)

Step 2: Apply the first operation from step 1 to the first number in the second pair:
Does 3 (first number) + 4 (missing operation) = 7 (second number)? *Yes.*
You know the missing operation that works for both pair of numbers: *add 4.*

Step 3: Apply the missing operation from step 2 to the number in the bottom row:
7 (first number) + 4 (missing operation) = 11 (missing number)
Jot down your result (11).

Step 4: Scanning the answer choices, we see the number 11 among them. There's no need to repeat our steps. The correct answer is choice C.

The missing operation will always be one of the four basic operations (addition, subtraction, multiplication, or division). Also, the missing operation will always involve a simple number, although the number won't necessarily be an integer. To see what we mean, apply our four steps to the next example, which is a bit tougher than the previous one:

Example:
24 → __ → 18
12 → __ → 9
28 → __ → ?

A 21
B 18
C 24
D 20

Step 1: Find the two operations you apply to the number 24 to obtain the number 18:
24 (first number) − 6 (missing operation) = 18 (second number)

24 (first number) $\times \dfrac{3}{4}$ (missing operation) = 18 (second number)

Step 2: Apply the first operation from step 1 to the number 12 (the first number in the second pair):
Does 12 (first number) − 6 (missing operation) = 9 (second number)? *No.*
Apply the second operation from step 1 to the number 12:

Does 12 (first number) $\times \dfrac{3}{4}$ (missing operation) = 9 (second number)? *Yes.*

You know the missing operation that works for both pair of numbers: *multiply by $\dfrac{3}{4}$.*

Step 3: Apply the missing operation that works for both pairs to the number in the bottom row:

$28 \times \dfrac{3}{4}$ (missing operation) = 21 (missing number)

Jot down your result (21).

Step 4: Scanning the answer choices, we see the number 21 among them. There's no need to repeat our steps. The correct answer is choice A.

Geometric Grids

Each geometric-grid question is based on a geometric figure divided into sections, some of which are darkened. Your job is to determine the fraction of the figure that is darkened. Here are the directions for these questions, along with a typical example:

Directions: Find the fraction of the grid that is darkened.

Example:

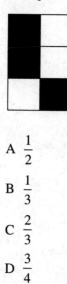

A $\frac{1}{2}$

B $\frac{1}{3}$

C $\frac{2}{3}$

D $\frac{3}{4}$

Here are the steps to handling a geometric-grid question:

Step 1: Count the total number of equally sized sections into which the figure is divided. (If two sections are merged into one, count them both.)

Step 2: Count the number of sections that are darkened. (If only half of a certain section is darkened, count it as $\frac{1}{2}$.)

Step 3: Express the number of darkened sections divided by the number of sections as a fraction. Reduce the fraction to lowest terms.

Step 4: Scan the answer choices for the fraction. If you don't see it, you did something wrong. Repeat steps 1–3.

Let's apply these four steps to our example:

Step 1: The figure is divided into 6 equal-sized rectangles (three rows of two sections each).

Step 2: 3 sections are darkened.

Step 3: The portion of the figure that is darkened is $\frac{3}{6}$. In lowest terms, the fraction is $\frac{1}{2}$.

Step 4: The fraction $\frac{1}{2}$ is among the four choices. The correct answer is choice A.

Now, let's step through a tougher example:

Example:

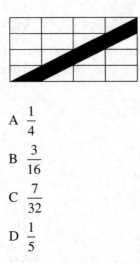

A $\dfrac{1}{4}$

B $\dfrac{3}{16}$

C $\dfrac{7}{32}$

D $\dfrac{1}{5}$

Step 1: The figure is divided into 16 equal-sized rectangles (four rows containing four rectangles each).

Step 2: None of the 16 rectangles is completely darkened. However, one half of each of 7 of the rectangles is darkened. So, $\dfrac{7}{2}$ rectangles are darkened.

Step 3: The portion of the figure that is darkened is $\dfrac{7}{2} \div 16$, or $\dfrac{7}{32}$.

Step 4: The fraction $\dfrac{7}{32}$ is among the four choices. The correct answer is choice C.

Scale Balancing

Each scale-balancing question is based on a picture of a scale with two kinds of objects (such as balls and cubes) placed on each side. Scale-balancing questions are essentially *ratio* problems. Here are the directions for these questions, along with a typical example:

Directions: Examine the balanced scale. Then, select another arrangement of objects that would also balance the scale.

Example:

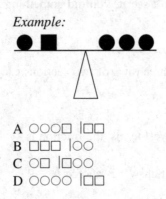

A ○○○○□ |□□
B □□□ |○○
C ○□ |□○○○
D ○○○○ |□□□

Here are the steps to handling a scale-balancing question:

Step 1: Look for any object on one side of the scale for which there's a matching object (a ball, for instance) on the other side. With your pencil, cross out every matching pair.

Step 2: After step 1, the left side of the scale should contain only one type of object, while the right side of the scale should contain only the other type of object. Count the number of objects on each side of the scale. (Don't count the objects you crossed out during step 1.)

Step 3: Jot down the ratio between the two totals you found in step 2. Cancel common factors, if any.

Step 4: For answer choice A, assign the ratio values to each corresponding object on the scale, and then add up the numbers on each side. If the two sums are equal, the arrangement balances, and the correct answer is choice A. If the two sums are different, go to step 5.

Step 5: Apply step 4 to the other answer choices until you find an answer in which the two sums are equal (the arrangement balances). This choice is the correct answer.

Let's apply these five steps to our example:

Step 1: One of the balls on the right side of the scale has a match on the left side. Cross out this matching pair of balls.

Step 2: After step 1, what remains on the scale is one cube on the left side and two balls on the right side.

Step 3: Here's an equation that expresses the cube-to-ball weight ratio: 1 cube = 2 balls. This 1:2 ratio is already in lowest terms. (There are no common factors to cancel out.)

Step 4: For answer choice A, assign a value of 2 to each cube and a value of 1 to each ball, and then add up the numbers on each side.
○○○□ |□□
$(1 + 1 + 1 + 2) = 5$ |$(2 + 2) = 4$

The sums are not equal (the arrangement does not balance), and so choice A is incorrect. Go to step 5.

Step 5: Apply step 4 to the other answer choices until you find the arrangement of objects that balances:

B □□□ |○○
$(2 + 2 + 2) = 6$ |$(1 + 1) = 2$
$6 \neq 2$, and so choice B is incorrect.

C ○□ |□○○
$(1 + 2) = 3$ |$(2 + 1 + 1) = 4$
$3 \neq 4$, and so choice C is incorrect.

D ○○○○ |□□
$(1 + 1 + 1 + 1) = 4$ |$(2 + 2) = 4$
$4 = 4$ (the arrangement balances), and so choice D is the correct choice.

COOP Quantitative Reasoning—Heads Up!

In missing-operation questions:

- The missing operation will always be one of the four basic operations: addition, subtraction, multiplication, or division.
- Don't worry: Only one operation will work for *both* pairs of numbers given.

In geometric-grid questions:

■ Figures are evenly divided (if grid sections look the same size and shape, they are).
■ If two (or more) grid sections are merged into one, count both sections in order to calculate the answer. (You'll see at least one question like this in the practice drill just ahead.)

In scale-balancing questions:

■ If the scale's left side contains the same number of objects as the right side, then so will the correct answer choice.
■ Cancel (cross out) any object that has a match on the scale's other side *before* checking the answer choices.

Practice

Directions: For questions 1–7, find the operation (fill in the blank) that is applied to the first number in each of two pairs to obtain the second number. Then, apply the operation to find the missing number (?). Select the correct answer choice.

1 $1 \to \_\_ \to 4$
$9 \to \_\_ \to 12$
$3 \to \_\_ \to ?$

A 8
B 7
C 6
D 10

2 $25 \to \_\_ \to 20$
$19 \to \_\_ \to 14$
$2 \to \_\_ \to ?$

A −3
B 7
C −7
D $\frac{1}{2}$

3 $\frac{1}{2} \to \_\_ \to \frac{1}{4}$

$1 \to \_\_ \to \frac{3}{4}$

$\frac{1}{4} \to \_\_ \to ?$

A $\frac{1}{2}$
B 0

C $\frac{1}{8}$

D $-\frac{1}{4}$

4 $3 \to \_\_ \to 24$
$8 \to \_\_ \to 64$
$7 \to \_\_ \to ?$

A 48
B 56
C 32
D 42

5 $42 \to \_\_ \to 21$
$14 \to \_\_ \to 7$
$10 \to \_\_ \to ?$

A 6
B $\frac{10}{3}$
C 3
D 5

6 $1.2 \to \_\_ \to 2.4$
$4.8 \to \_\_ \to 9.6$
$0.3 \to \_\_ \to ?$

A 3
B 1.3
C 0.15
D 0.6

7 $3 \rightarrow \_ \rightarrow \dfrac{3}{8}$

$4 \rightarrow \_ \rightarrow \dfrac{1}{2}$

$8 \rightarrow \_ \rightarrow ?$

A 1

B $\dfrac{2}{3}$

C $\dfrac{3}{4}$

D 2

Directions: For questions 8–13, find the fraction of the grid that is darkened.

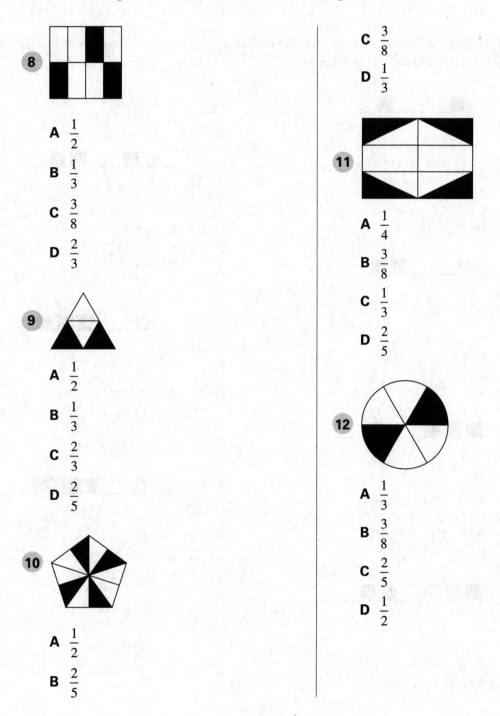

8

A $\dfrac{1}{2}$

B $\dfrac{1}{3}$

C $\dfrac{3}{8}$

D $\dfrac{2}{3}$

9

A $\dfrac{1}{2}$

B $\dfrac{1}{3}$

C $\dfrac{2}{3}$

D $\dfrac{2}{5}$

10

A $\dfrac{1}{2}$

B $\dfrac{2}{5}$

C $\dfrac{3}{8}$

D $\dfrac{1}{3}$

11

A $\dfrac{1}{4}$

B $\dfrac{3}{8}$

C $\dfrac{1}{3}$

D $\dfrac{2}{5}$

12

A $\dfrac{1}{3}$

B $\dfrac{3}{8}$

C $\dfrac{2}{5}$

D $\dfrac{1}{2}$

13

A $\dfrac{5}{9}$

B $\dfrac{1}{2}$

C $\dfrac{1}{3}$

D $\dfrac{4}{9}$

Directions: For questions 14–20, examine the balanced scale. Then, select another arrangement of objects that would also balance the scale.

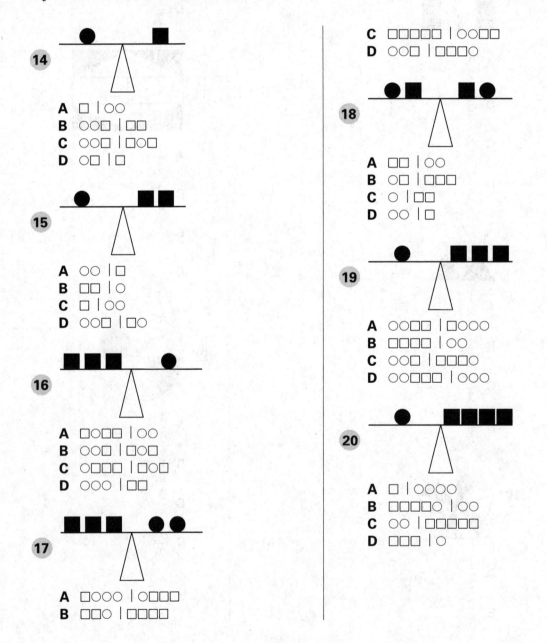

14

A □ | ○○
B ○○□ | □□
C ○○□ | □□□
D ○□ | □

15

A ○○ | □
B □□ | ○
C □ | ○○
D ○○□ | □○

16

A □○□□ | ○○
B ○○□ | □○□
C ○□□□ | □○□
D ○○○ | □□

17

A □○○○ | ○□□□
B □□○ | □□□□

18

C □□□□□ | ○○□□
D ○○□ | □□□□

A □□ | ○○
B ○□ | □□□
C ○ | □□
D ○○ | □

19

A ○○□□ | □○○○
B □□□□ | ○○
C ○○□ | □□□□
D ○○□□□ | □○○○

20

A □ | ○○○○
B □□□□○ | ○○
C ○○ | □□□□□
D □□□ | ○

Practice—Answers and Explanations

1. **C** You add 3 to the first number to obtain the second number: $3 + 3 = 6$.

2. **A** You subtract 5 from the first number to obtain the second: $2 - 5 = -3$.

3. **B** You subtract $\dfrac{1}{4}$ from the first number to obtain the second number: $\dfrac{1}{4} - \dfrac{1}{4} = 0$.

4. **B** You multiply the first number by 8 to obtain the second: $7 \times 8 = 56$.

5. **D** You divide the first number by 2 to obtain the second: $10 \div 2 = 5$.

6. **D** You multiply the first number by 2 to obtain the second number: $0.3 \times 2 = 0.6$.

7. **A** You divide the first number by 8 to obtain the second number: $8 \div 8 = 1$.

8. **C** The figure is divided into 8 congruent rectangles; 3 of these rectangles, which make up $\dfrac{3}{8}$ of the figure, are shaded.

9. **A** The figure is divided into 4 congruent triangles; 2 of these triangles, which make up $\dfrac{2}{4}$, or $\dfrac{1}{2}$, of the figure, are shaded.

10. **B** The figure, a regular pentagon, is divided into 10 congruent triangles; 4 of these triangles, which make up $\dfrac{4}{10}$, or $\dfrac{2}{5}$, of the figure, are shaded.

11. **C** The figure is divided into 6 congruent rectangles, 4 of which are each split into 2 congruent triangles. The figure's total area is 12 times the area of one of these small triangles; 4 triangles—the area equivalent of 2 of the 6 rectangles—are shaded. You can simplify the fraction $\dfrac{2}{6}$ to $\dfrac{1}{3}$.

12. **A** The circle is divided into 6 congruent segments; 2 of the segments, which make up $\dfrac{2}{6}$, or $\dfrac{1}{3}$, the area of the circle, are shaded.

13. **D** The figure is divided into 9 congruent rectangles. Together, the four shaded triangles have an area equal to the area of 2 squares. Thus, the figure's total shaded area is equivalent to 4 of the 9 congruent rectangles—or $\dfrac{4}{9}$ the area of the entire figure.

14. **C** □ and ○ are equal in weight (the □:○ ratio is 1:1). Thus, as long as the same total number of objects (of either type) appears on the left as on the right, as in choice C only, the weights balance. Otherwise, they won't.

15. **B** The scale shows that the ○:□ weight ratio is 1:2. Choice B provides the same arrangement as the original scale; the left and right sides are simply reversed. None of the other three arrangements balances.

16. **A** The scale shows that the □:○ weight ratio is 3:1. Assign a weight of 1 unit to □ and a weight of 3 units to ○. In choice A, the total on the left side equals the total on the right side: $(1 + 3 + 1 + 1) = (3 + 3)$.

17. **C** The scale shows that the ○:□ weight ratio is 2:3. Assign a weight of 2 units to □ and a weight of 3 units to ○. In choice C, the total on the left side equals the total on the right side: $(2 \times 5) = (3 + 3 + 2 + 2)$.

18. **A** □ and ○ are equal in weight (the □:○ ratio is 1:1). Thus, as long as the same total number of objects (of either type) appears on the left as on the right, as in choice A only, the weights balance. Otherwise, they won't.

19. D The scale shows that the ○:□ weight ratio is 1:3. Assign a weight of 3 units to ○ and a weight of 1 unit to □. In choice D, the total on the left side equals the total on the right side: $(3 + 3 + 1 + 1 + 1) = (3 + 3 + 3)$.

20. B The scale shows that the ○:□ weight ratio is 1:4. Choice B provides the same arrangement as the original scale; the left and right sides are simply reversed. None of the other three arrangements balance.

On the HSPT, the Quantitative Reasoning subtest covers many different skills involving numbers. Here are the four question formats you're most likely to see on this subtest:

- Number manipulation (verbal math)
- Geometric comparisons
- Non-geometric comparisons
- Number sequences

Chapter 10 covers number sequences. In this chapter, you'll explore the first three question types in this list.

Number-Manipulation (Verbal Math) Questions

In number-manipulation questions, your job is to perform a series of operations on different numbers. The operations you perform are usually the four basic ones: addition, subtraction, multiplication, and division. Here's an example:

When you subtract 5 from the product of $\frac{12}{5}$ and $\frac{5}{2}$ the result is

A 12
B 1
C 0
D 25

As you can see, number-manipulation questions are more than just math problems. You also need to translate words into the correct mathematical operations. (That's why we also call them "verbal math" questions.) To handle these questions, follow four steps:

Step 1: Read the question. Determine the operations you must perform—and in what order.
Step 2: Perform the first operation. (Simplify the result, if you can.)
Step 3: Using the result of step 2, perform the other operations in proper order. (Simplify the result, if you can.)
Step 4: Scan the answer choices for your final result. If you don't see it, you did something wrong. Go back and repeat the steps.

Let's apply these four steps to our example:

Step 1: The question asks you to subtract 5 from the product of two other numbers: $\frac{12}{5}$ and $\frac{5}{2}$. In math,

a *product* is the result of multiplying numbers together. Before you subtract, you must find the product (do the multiplication). That's the correct order.

Step 2: Perform the multiplication: $\frac{12}{5} \times \frac{5}{2} = \frac{60}{10} = 6$.

Step 3: With the result from step 2, perform the next operation: $6 - 5 = 1$.

Step 4: Your result (1) is among the answer choices. There's no need to repeat the steps. The correct answer is choice B.

For some number-manipulation questions, it helps to set up an algebraic equation, using a variable such as x to represent the final number you want to find. Here's an example, along with the four steps to handling it:

A certain number divided by three is four more than the difference between nine and three. What is the number?

A 24
B 12
C 6
D 30

Step 1: Translate the sentence into an equation containing numbers: $x \div 3 = 4 + 9 - 3$. Since we don't know the value of x, we obviously cannot perform division until we've combined the numbers on the right side of the equation. We can perform those two operations in either order.

Step 2: Combine the numbers on the right side of the equation:

$x \div 3 = 13 - 3$

$x \div 3 = 10$

Step 3: Isolate x by multiplying both side of the equation by 3:

$x \div 3 = 10$

$\quad x = 10 \times 3$

$\quad x = 30$

Our result (30) is among the answer choices, and so we don't need to go back and repeat the steps. The correct answer is choice D.

Geometric Comparisons

In a geometric-comparison question, your job is to rank different geometric figures based on certain quantifiable features. Here are the steps to handling these questions:

Step 1: Read the question, examine the figures, and then briefly scan the answer choices to determine what features you must compare.
Step 2: In figure (a), find the quantity that the question asks for. Jot down the number below figure (a).
Step 3: Repeat step 2 for figures (b) and (c).
Step 4: Scan the answer choices for an accurate comparison. If you don't see any, you did something wrong. Go back and repeat steps 2–4.

Some geometric-comparison questions ask you to compare the number of certain features in different displays. These questions test you on your ability to accurately count, record, and compare numbers. Let's apply our four-step approach (above) to an example of this question type:

Examine figures (a), (b), and (c), and then choose the correct statement.

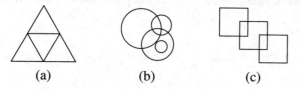

(a)   (b)   (c)

A The number of triangles in figure (a) is equal to the number of circles in figure (b).
B The number of circles in figure (b) is greater than the number of rectangles in figure (c).
C The number of rectangles in figure (c) is equal to the number of triangles in figure (a).
D The number of triangles in figure (a) is greater than the number of rectangles in figure (c).

Step 1: Figure (a) consists entirely of overlapping triangles. Figure (b) consists entirely of overlapping circles. Figure (c) consists entirely of overlapping squares. Scanning the answer choices tells you that your job is to count the number of triangles, circles, and rectangles, and then compare the totals.

Step 2: Count the number of triangles in figure (a). Notice that the large triangle consists of four smaller triangles. That's a total of 5 triangles. Jot down the number "5" below figure (a).

Step 3: Count the number of circles in figure (b). There are 3 partly overlapping circles; also notice the smaller circle completely inside one of the larger ones. That's a total of 4 circles. Jot down the number "4" below figure (b). Count the number of rectangles in figure (c). The figure contains 3 overlapping squares (a square is a type of rectangle), and the overlapping creates 2 additional, smaller rectangles. That's 5 rectangles altogether. Jot down the number "5" below figure (c).

Step 4: Examine each answer choice in turn until you find an accurate statement. First, choice A: Does the number of triangles in figure (a) equal the number of circles in figure (b)? Does 5 = 4? *No.* Choice A is incorrect. Next, choice B: Is the number of circles in figure (b) greater than the number of rectangles in figure (c)? Is 4 > 5? *No.* Choice B is incorrect. Next, choice C: Does the number of rectangles in figure (c) equal the number of triangles in figure (a)? Does 5 = 5? *Yes.* Choice C is correct. There's no need to look at choice D.

In another type of geometric-comparison question, your job is to figure out what fraction of each of three figures is shaded, and then compare those fractions. Here's a typical example, along with the steps to handling it:

Examine figures (a), (b), and (c), and then choose the correct statement.

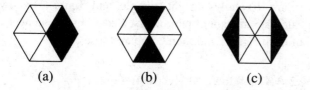

(a)   (b)   (c)

A The shaded area of figure (c) is less than the shaded area of figure (a).
B The shaded area of figure (a) is less than the shaded area of figure (b).
C The shaded area of figure (b) is greater than the shaded area of figure (c).
D The shaded area of figure (c) is equal to the shaded area of figure (a).

Step 1: All three figures show the same-sized hexagon, divided into 6 congruent segments. Scanning the answer choices tells us that our job is to determine what fraction of each figure is shaded, and then compare the fractions.

Step 2: In figure (a), 2 of 6 triangles are shaded; that's $\frac{2}{6}$ of the hexagon. Jot down the fraction "$\frac{2}{6}$" below figure (a).

Step 3: In figure (b), 2 of 6 triangles are shaded; that's $\frac{2}{6}$ of the hexagon. Jot down the fraction "$\frac{2}{6}$" below figure (a). In figure (c), half of each of 4 triangles is shaded; that's equivalent to 2 triangles, or $\frac{2}{6}$ of the hexagon. Jot down the fraction "$\frac{2}{6}$" below figure (a). Notice that all three quantities are equal.

Step 4: Since all three quantities are equal, the correct answer choice must state an equality. Scanning the four choices, you can see that only choice D fits the bill. All three other choices indicate that the shaded area of one figure is either less or greater than the shaded area of another figure. So, without even reading choices A, B, and C carefully, we can confidently conclude that choice D is the correct answer.

In yet another type of geometric-comparison question, you need to apply the properties and rules of geometry in order to rank features such as area, length, angle measure, or some other quantity. In the example below, notice that each answer choice compares all three quantities (rather than just two).

Examine figures (a), (b), and (c), and then choose the correct statement.

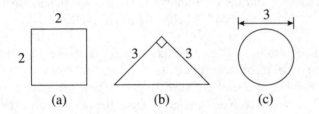

A   The area of figure (a) is less than the area of figure (b) but greater than the area of figure (c).
B   The area of figure (c) is equal to the area of figure (b) but greater than the area of figure (a).
C   The area of figure (b) is less than the area of figure (c) but greater than the area of figure (a).
D   The area of figure (a) is equal to the area of figure (b) but less than the area of figure (c).

Let's apply our four-step approach to this challenging question:

Step 1: Figure (a) shows a square, figure (b) shows a right triangle, and figure (c) shows a circle. The lengths that are given allow you to calculate areas and perimeters. Scanning the answer choices tells us that our job is to determine the area of each figure, and then compare those areas.

Step 2: The area of figure (a) $= 2 \times 2 = 4$. Jot down "4" below figure (a).

Step 3: To find the area of a right triangle, you multiply the length of its base by its height, and then multiply the product by $\frac{1}{2}$. So, the area of figure (b) $= (\frac{1}{2})(3)(3) = 4.5$. Next, figure (c): The area of a circle $= \pi r^2$ (where r is the circle's radius). Figure (c) shows that the circle's diameter is 3. Thus, its radius is 1.5. The value of π is approximately 3.14. We can approximate the value of $(1.5)^2$ as 2^+, and see that the area of figure (c) is greater than 6. Jot down "6^+" below figure (c). Rank the three areas: (a) < (b) < (c).

Step 4: Since no two quantities are equal, any answer choice that states an equality must be incorrect. Eliminate choices B and D. Next, read choice A carefully: Is the area of figure (a) less than the area of figure (b)? *Yes.* But is it greater than the area of figure (c)? *No*; it's less than the area of figure (c). Choice A is incorrect. You've eliminated every answer choice but C, and so C must be the correct choice. To make sure, read it carefully: Is the area of figure (b) less than the area of figure (c)? *Yes.* Is it greater than the area of figure (a)? *Yes.* Both parts of statement C are correct.

Note: On your test, if you encounter a geometric-comparison question with only *one* figure (instead of three), your job will be to compare three different features of the figure. You'll see a question like this in the practice drill just ahead.

Non-Geometric Comparisons

In these questions, your job is to calculate three or more quantities, and then compare them. Non-geometric comparisons cover many different math concepts, such as fractions, percents, decimal numbers, simple average, roots and exponents, factoring, and prime numbers. Use your knowledge of these areas to make the comparisons. Here's an example (as you can see, the basic format is the same as for geometric comparisons):

Examine (a), (b), and (c), and then choose the correct answer.
(a) $5 + 2 \times 4$
(b) $5 \times 2 + 4$
(c) $2 + 4 \times 5$

A (a) = (b) = (c)
B (b) = (c), and (b) > (a)
C (b) > (c) > (a)
D (a) < (b) < (c)

Here are the steps to handling non-geometric comparison questions:

Step 1: Examine the different expressions listed—usually labeled (a), (b), and (c). Ask yourself what they have in common, and what math concepts you need to understand to calculate the different number values.
Step 2: Applying your knowledge of the math concepts being tested, calculate the number value of each expression. (For some values, especially non-integers, approximations might be close enough.)
Step 3: Rank the number values you calculated in step 2. Jot down the comparison you're looking for among the answer choices.
Step 4: Scan the answer choices for a correct comparison. If you don't see one that's *completely* correct (not just partly correct), you did something wrong. Go back and repeat steps 1 and 2.

Let's apply these steps to our example:

Step 1: It looks like the three expressions—labeled (a), (b), and (c)—test on the rules for the order of performing operations. The basic rule is that you perform multiplication and division (in either order) *before* performing addition and subtraction.

Step 2: Calculate the number value of each expression, applying the rule stated above.
(a) Multiply first, and then add: $5 + (2 \times 4) = 5 + 8 = 13$
(b) Multiply first, and then add: $(5 \times 2) + 4 = 10 + 4 = 14$
(c) Multiply first, and then add: $2 + (4 \times 5) = 2 + 20 = 22$

Step 3: Rank the number values you calculated in step 2, in either order:

$$22 > 14 > 13 \; or \; 13 < 14 < 22$$

Jot down the comparison you're looking for among the answer choices. Here are two different ways to express the comparison:
(c) > (b) > (a)
(a) < (b) < (c)

Step 4: Scanning the answer choices, we see that choice D expresses the correct comparison. We don't need to go back and repeat steps 1 and 2.

In the previous example, all three quantities were different. But, that's not always the case. Also, all three expressions tested you on the same basic concept (order of operations). But, this isn't always the case. To show you what we mean, here's another example, along with the four steps to handling it:

Examine (a), (b), and (c), and then choose the correct answer.

(a) $\dfrac{7^6}{7^5}$

(b) $\sqrt{50}$

(c) $\left(\sqrt{7}\right)^2$

A (a) > (c) > (b)
B (a) = (c), and (b) > (a)
C (b) > (c) > (a)
D (a) = (b), and (b) = (c)

Step 1: Expression (a) tests on the rules for canceling exponents. Expressions (b) and (c) test on square roots. Notice that (a) and (c) both involve the integer "7"; that's a good clue that the number 7 will be key in making the comparisons.

Step 2: Calculate the number value of each expression.
(a) Since the base number in the numerator (7) is the same as in the denominator, you can apply the general
    rule $\dfrac{a^x}{a^y} = a^{(x-y)}$ as follows: $\dfrac{7^6}{7^5} = 7^{(6-5)} = 7^1 = 7$. Jot down the number "7" next to expression (a).

(b) We know that $\sqrt{49} = 7$. Thus, $\sqrt{50}$ must be just over 7. Jot down "7^+" next to expression (b).

(c) $\left(\sqrt{7}\right)^2 = \sqrt{7} \times \sqrt{7} = 7$. Jot down "7" next to expression (c).

Step 3: Here are the number values you calculated in step 2:
(a) = 7
(b) = 7^+
(c) = 7

Here's a good way to express the comparison (write it down in your test booklet):
(a) = (c) < (b)

Step 4: Scanning the answer choices, we don't see *exactly* what we jotted down during step 3. But choice B expresses the same comparison, doesn't it? Since we found an accurate comparison among the four choices, we don't need to go back and repeat steps 1 and 2.

HSPT Quantitative Reasoning—Heads Up!

When handling number-manipulation (verbal math) questions:

- There's usually one correct order to perform the operations.
- You might need to set up and solve an algebraic equation.

When making geometric comparisons:

- Careful counting is crucial! When counting polygons, look for different sizes and shapes.
- Always jot down the quantity you've calculated below the figure. Don't rely on your memory.
- Read the answer choices *very* carefully; otherwise, it's easy to get an inequality (*greater than* or *less than*) backward.
- When comparing areas, lengths, or angles, don't try to estimate by eye. Instead, apply your knowledge of the rules and properties of geometry.

When making non-geometric comparisons:

- Scan the answer choices for any equalities ("=" signs). If you see at least one, then it's possible that at least two of the quantities are equal. (Otherwise, you know that all of the quantities are different.)
- Always jot down the quantities you've calculated next to the expressions. Don't rely on your memory.
- Read the answer choices *very* carefully; otherwise, it's easy to get inequalities (">" and "<") backward.
- Don't do more calculating than necessary to make the comparison. Sometimes, approximate values are close enough to make the comparisons.

Practice

1. Twelve one-hundredths multiplied by three thousand five equals

   A 36.6
   B 306.06
   C 3,060
   D 360.6

2. When you divide 4 by $\frac{4}{3}$, and multiply the quotient by $\frac{3}{4}$, the result is

   A 3
   B $\frac{4}{9}$
   C 12
   D $\frac{9}{4}$

3. When you subtract a certain number from the sum of 8 and −7, the result is 8. What is the number?

   A −7
   B 8
   C −1
   D 7

4. What number added to 5 is 2 less than 30% of 20?

   A −3

   B 3

   C −1

   D 2

5. Four-thirds of a certain number is eight-thirds. What is the number?

   A 3

   B 2

   C $\dfrac{4}{3}$

   D $\dfrac{1}{2}$

6. Subtracting 12 from a certain number results in four times the product of −3 and −5. What is the number?

   A 44

   B 72

   C −36

   D 60

7. Five hundred percent divided by what percent yields a quotient of fifty?

   A 1

   B 5

   C 10

   D 50

8. Examine figures (a), (b), and (c) and then choose the correct statement.

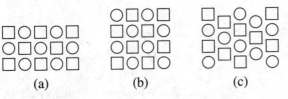

   (a)   (b)   (c)

   A The number of circles in figure (b) is greater than the number of circles in figure (a).

   B The number of circles in figure (b) is less than the number of circles in figure (a).

   C The number of squares in figure (a) is equal to the number of circles in figure (c).

   D The number of squares in figure (c) is equal to the number of circles in figure (b).

9. Examine figures (a), (b), and (c) and then choose the correct statement.

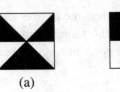

   (a)   (b)   (c)

   A The shaded area of figure (a) is less than the shaded area of figure (b).

   B The shaded area of figure (b) is greater than the shaded area of figure (c).

   C The shaded area of figure (c) is equal to the shaded area of figure (a).

   D The shaded area of figure (b) is less than the shaded area of figure (a).

10. Examine figures (a), (b), and (c) and then choose the correct statement.

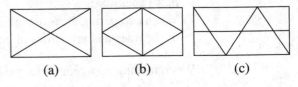

   (a)   (b)   (c)

   A Figure (c) contains more triangles than figure (a).

   B Figure (b) contains fewer triangles than figure (a).

   C Figure (c) contains the same number of triangles as figure (b).

   D Figure (a) contains the same number of triangles as figure (b).

11. Examine the figure below and then choose the correct statement.

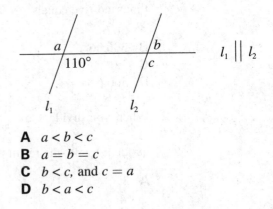

   A $a < b < c$

   B $a = b = c$

   C $b < c$, and $c = a$

   D $b < a < c$

12. Examine figures (a), (b), and (c) and then choose the correct statement.

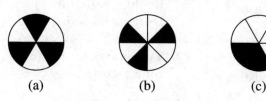

(a)   (b)   (c)

A The shaded area of figure (b) is less than the shaded area of figure (a) but greater than the shaded area of figure (c).

B The shaded area of figure (a) is less than the shaded area of figure (b) but greater than the shaded area of figure (c).

C The shaded area of figure (c) is equal to the shaded area of figure (b) but greater than the shaded area of figure (a).

D The shaded area of figure (b) is equal to the shaded area of figure (a) but less than the shaded area of figure (c).

13. Examine figures (a), (b), and (c) and then choose the correct statement.

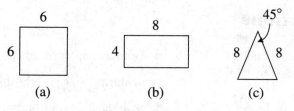

(a)   (b)   (c)

A The perimeter of figure (a) is equal to the perimeter of figure (b) and to the perimeter of figure (c).

B The perimeter of figure (b) is equal to the perimeter of figure (a) but greater than the perimeter of figure (c).

C The perimeter of figure (c) is equal to the perimeter of figure (a) but less than the perimeter of figure (b).

D The perimeter of figure (a) is less than the perimeter of figure (b) but greater than the perimeter of figure (c).

14. Examine (a), (b), and (c) and then choose the correct answer.

(a) 500% of 7
(b) 700% of 5
(c) 500% of 700%

A (a) = (b), and (a) < (c)
B (b) = (c), and (c) < (a)
C (b) > (c) > (a)
D (a) = (b) = (c)

15. Examine (a), (b), and (c) and then choose the correct answer.

(a) $\dfrac{1}{3} + \dfrac{1}{2}$

(b) $\dfrac{3}{4} \times \dfrac{4}{3}$

(c) $\dfrac{2}{3} \div \dfrac{1}{2}$

A (b) < (c) < (a)
B (c) > (a) > (b)
C (a) < (b) < (c)
D (b) > (c) > (a)

16. Examine (a), (b), and (c) and then choose the correct answer.

(a) The greatest prime factor of 11
(b) The greatest prime factor of 21
(c) The greatest prime factor of 34

A (a) < (c) < (b)
B (b) > (a) > (c)
C (b) < (c) < (a)
D (c) > (a) > (b)

17. Examine (a), (b), and (c) and then choose the correct answer.

(a) 2.2 × 0.02
(b) 44 × 0.001
(c) 0.11 × 0.04

A (b) = (c), and (a) > (c)
B (c) < (a), and (a) = (b)
C (a) = (b), and (b) = (c)
D (b) > (c), and (c) = (a)

18. Examine (a), (b), and (c) and then choose the correct answer.

    (a) The arithmetic mean (simple average) of 2, 4, and 7

    (b) The arithmetic mean (simple average) of 3, 4, and 5

    (c) The arithmetic mean (simple average) of 2, 5, and 6

    A (a) = (c), and (a) > (b)
    B (a) = (b), and (b) = (c)
    C (b) > (c), and (c) > (a)
    D (a) > (b), and (b) = (c)

19. Examine (a), (b), and (c) and then choose the correct answer.

    (a) $\left(-\dfrac{1}{2}\right)^2$

    (b) $\left(-\dfrac{1}{2}\right)^3$

    (c) $\left(-\dfrac{1}{2}\right)^4$

A (a) < (c) < (b)
B (b) > (a) > (c)
C (b) < (c) < (a)
D (c) > (a) > (b)

20. Examine (a), (b), and (c) and then choose the correct answer.

    (a) $\sqrt{2} + \sqrt{2}$

    (b) $\sqrt{2} \times \sqrt{2}$

    (c) $\sqrt{2}$

    A (c) < (b) < (a)
    B (b) < (a) < (c)
    C (a) < (b) < (c)
    D (b) < (c) < (a)

Practice—Answers and Explanations

1. **D** Convert the verbal expression to numbers, and then solve: $0.12 \times 3{,}005 = 360.6$.

2. **D** First, perform division: $4 \div \dfrac{4}{3} = 4 \times \dfrac{3}{4} = \dfrac{12}{4}$, or 3. Next, multiply: $3 \times \dfrac{3}{4} = \dfrac{9}{4}$.

3. **A** First, perform addition: $-7 + 8 = 1$. With this sum, set up and solve an equation: $1 - x = 8$; $x = -7$.

4. **C** To find 30% of 20, multiply: $20 \times 0.3 = 6$. With this result, set up and solve an equation:

   $$x + 5 + 2 = 6$$
   $$x + 7 = 6$$
   $$x = -1$$

5. **B** Translate the verbal fractions into numbers: "four-thirds" $= \dfrac{4}{3}$; "eight-thirds" $= \dfrac{8}{3}$. With these numbers, set up and solve an equation:

   $$\frac{4}{3} \times x = \frac{8}{3}$$
   $$x = \frac{8}{3} \times \frac{3}{4}$$
   $$x = 2$$

6. **B** First, tackle the two operations in the last part of the sentence:

   "Four times the product of -3 and -5" $= 4 \times (-3) \times (-5) = 4 \times 15 = 60$.

   Thus, subtracting 12 from a certain number results in 60. To find the number, set up and solve this verbal equation: $x - 12 = 60$; $x = 72$.

7. C First, set up an equation, translating words into numbers:

$$500\% \div x = 50$$

Convert the percentage to a decimal number, and then solve for x:

$$5 \div x = 50$$

$$\frac{1}{x} = \frac{50}{5}$$

$$\frac{1}{x} = 10$$

$$x = \frac{1}{10}$$

The question asks "what percent . . . ?" Since $\frac{1}{10} = 10\%$, the answer is 10.

8. A Figure (a) contains 8 squares and 7 circles. Figure (b) contains 8 squares and 8 circles. Figure (a) contains 9 squares and 9 circles.

9. C In all three figures, the shaded area accounts for exactly $\frac{1}{2}$ of the total area.

10. B Figure (a) contains 8 triangles—4 right triangles, each one-half the area of the rectangle, and 4 smaller, isosceles triangles, each one-fourth the area of the rectangle. Figure (b) contains 6 triangles. Figure (c) contains 4 pairs of similar triangles—8 triangles altogether.

11. C Given $l_1 \parallel l_2$, the cluster of four angles to the left is identical to the cluster to the right. Angles a and c both measure $110°$, while angle b, which is supplementary to angle c, measures $70°$.

12. A In figure (a), 3 of 6 congruent sectors are shaded; $\frac{1}{2}$ of the circle is shaded. In figure (b), 3 of 8 congruent sectors are shaded; $\frac{3}{8}$ of the circle is shaded. In figure (c), 2 congruent sectors are shaded; $\frac{2}{6}$, or $\frac{1}{3}$, of the circle is shaded. $\frac{1}{2} > \frac{3}{8} > \frac{1}{3}$.

13. B Figure (a) shows a square with perimeter $6 \times 4 = 24$. Figure (b) shows a rectangle with perimeter $4 + 4 + 8 + 8 = 24$. Figure (c) shows an isosceles triangle (two sides are congruent). If the top angle were $60°$, the triangle would be equilateral, the length of each side would be 8, and the perimeter would be 24—the same as the perimeter of figure (a) and figure (b). However, since the top angle is smaller than $60°$, the length of the triangle's base must be *less* than 8 units. Accordingly, the triangle's perimeter must be less than 24 units.

14. D
(a) 500% of $7 = 5 \times 7 = 35$
(b) 700% of $5 = 7 \times 5 = 35$
(c) 500% of $700\% = 5 \times 7 = 35$

15. C
(a) $\frac{1}{3} + \frac{1}{2} = \frac{2}{6} + \frac{3}{6} = \frac{5}{6}$

(b) $\frac{3}{4} \times \frac{4}{3} = 1$

(c) $\frac{2}{3} \div \frac{1}{2} = \frac{2}{3} \times \frac{2}{1} = \frac{4}{3}$

16. D Determine the prime factors of each number:
(a) 11 is a prime number.
(b) The prime factors of 21 are 3 and 7.
(c) The prime factors of 34 are 2 and 17.

17. B
(a) $2.2 \times 0.02 = 0.044$
(b) $44 \times 0.001 = 0.044$
(c) $0.11 \times 0.04 = 0.0044$

18. A To find arithmetic mean (average), divide the sum of the terms by the number of terms:
(a) $(2 + 4 + 7) \div 3 = \frac{13}{3}$

(b) $(3 + 4 + 5) \div 3 = \frac{12}{3}$

(c) $(2 + 5 + 6) \div 3 = \frac{13}{3}$

19. C The key to making the comparison is that a negative number raised to an *even*-numbered power is *positive*, while a negative number raised to an *odd*-numbered power is *negative:*

(a) $\left(-\dfrac{1}{2}\right)^2 = \dfrac{1}{4}$

(b) $\left(-\dfrac{1}{2}\right)^3 = -\left(\dfrac{1}{8}\right)$

(c) $\left(-\dfrac{1}{2}\right)^4 = \dfrac{1}{16}$

20. A

(a) $\sqrt{2} + \sqrt{2} = 2\sqrt{2} \approx 2 \times 1.4 = 2.8$

(b) $\sqrt{2} \times \sqrt{2} = 2$

(c) $\sqrt{2} \approx 1.4$

Review of Mathematics

COOP | HSPT | TACHS

This math review covers the terminology and concepts you need to know for the Mathematics portions of the COOP, HSPT, and TACHS, as well as for COOP and HSPT Quantitative Reasoning. This review is organized into five sections:

- Number theory
- Number forms
- Sets, statistical measurements, and probability
- Elementary algebra
- Basic plane geometry and coordinate geometry

Number Theory

In this section, you'll review basic "number theory," which includes the following concepts:

- The real-number line and absolute value
- Operations on signed numbers
- Integers and the number zero (0)
- Factors, multiples, and divisibility
- Prime numbers
- Factoring and prime factorization
- Commutative, associative, and distributive laws of number operations
- Order of operations

The Real-Number Line and Absolute Value

On the real-number line (shown below), all numbers to the left of zero (0) are negative numbers, and all numbers to the right of zero (0) are positive numbers.

$$\longleftarrow \overset{|}{\underset{-4}{}} \quad \overset{|}{\underset{-3}{}} \quad \overset{|}{\underset{-2}{}} \quad \overset{|}{\underset{-1}{}} \quad \overset{|}{\underset{0}{}} \quad \overset{|}{\underset{1}{}} \quad \overset{|}{\underset{2}{}} \quad \overset{|}{\underset{3}{}} \quad \overset{|}{\underset{4}{}} \longrightarrow$$

A real number's **absolute value** is the number's distance from zero (0) on the number line. The absolute value of real number x is written as $|x|$. Absolute value is never negative.

Examples:

$\lvert 3 \rvert = 3$	$\lvert 4 - 6 \rvert = \lvert -2 \rvert = 2$
$\lvert -5 \rvert = 5$	$-\lvert 8 \rvert = -8$
$\lvert 0 \rvert = 0$	$-\lvert -3 - 4 \rvert = -\lvert -7 \rvert = -7$

Operations on Signed Numbers

Any real number's *sign* is either positive (+) or negative (−), except for the number zero (0), which is neither positive nor negative. Positive numbers are greater than zero (0), and negative numbers are less than zero (0).

When you combine two numbers using one of the four basic operations (addition, subtraction, multiplication, or division), the sign of the resulting number depends on the signs of the two numbers you combine. Here are the rules you should know (a "?" indicates that the sign depends on which number is greater):

Addition	Subtraction	Multiplication	Division
$(+) + (+) = +$	$(+) - (-) = (+)$	$(+) \times (+) = +$	$(+) \div (+) = +$
$(-) + (-) = -$	$(-) - (+) = (-)$	$(+) \times (-) = -$	$(+) \div (-) = -$
$(+) + (-) = ?$	$(+) - (+) = ?$	$(-) \times (-) = +$	$(-) \div (+) = -$
$(-) + (+) = ?$	$(-) - (-) = ?$		$(-) \div (-) = +$

As the table above indicates, when you multiply (or divide) one negative number by another negative number, the resulting number is always positive. Thus, when you combine four negative numbers by multiplication (or division), the result is always positive. The same rule is true whenever you combine any *even* number of negative terms by multiplication (or division).

Examples:

Combine two negative numbers: $(-2) \times (-3) = 6$ (a positive number)
Combine two negative numbers: $(-4) \div (-2) = 2$ (a positive number)
Combine four negative numbers: $(-4) \times (-3) \times (-2) \times (-2) = 48$ (a positive number)
Combine four negative numbers: $(-4) \div (-4) \times (-6) \div (-2) = 3$ (a positive number)
Combine six negative numbers: $(-3) \times (-5) \div (-3) \times (-4) \div (-4) \times (-2) = 10$ (a positive number)

On the other hand, when the number of negative terms you combine by multiplication (or division) is *odd*, the result is always a negative number.

Examples:

Combine three negative numbers: $(-3) \times (-1) \times (-3) = -9$ (a negative number)

Combine three negative numbers: $(-4) \div (-4) \div (-2) = -\dfrac{1}{2}$ (a negative number)

Combine five negative numbers: $(-3) \times (-8) \div (-2) \times (-4) \div (-2) = -24$ (a negative number)

Integers and the Number Zero (0)

A real number is an **integer** if it is a member of the following set: $\{\ldots -3, -2, -1, 0, 1, 2, 3, \ldots\}$. As you can see, an integer can be either positive or negative. An integer is *even* if it is a member of the following set: $\{\ldots -6, -4, -2, 2, 4, 6, \ldots\}$. An integer is *odd* if it is a member the following set: $\{\ldots -5, -3, -1, 1, 3, 5, \ldots\}$. The number zero (0) is an integer but is neither even nor odd.

Adding or subtracting with integers. When you combine two integers by either addition or subtraction, the result is always an integer. However, whether the result is odd, even, or zero (0) depends on the particular integers you combine:

(integer) $\pm$ (integer) = integer
(even integer) $\pm$ (even integer) = even integer
(even integer) $\pm$ (odd integer) = odd integer
(odd integer) $\pm$ (odd integer) = even integer

Multiplying or dividing with integers. When you combine two integers by either multiplication or division, the result might be an even integer, odd integer, or non-integer—depending on the particular integers you combine.

Multiplication:
(integer) $\times$ (integer) = integer
(odd integer) $\times$ (odd integer) = odd integer
(even integer) $\times$ (non-zero integer) = even integer

Division:
(integer) $\div$ (non-zero integer) = integer, but only if the integer is a multiple of the non-integer
(even integer) $\div$ (2) = integer
(odd integer) $\div$ (2) = non-integer

Special properties of the number zero (0). The number zero (0) is an integer but is neither odd nor even.

(zero) $\times$ (any real number) = zero
(zero) $\div$ (any non-zero real number) = zero

You CANNOT divide a real number by zero (0). In other words, no fraction can have a denominator of zero (0).

Factors, Multiples, and Divisibility

The terms *factor, multiple,* and *divisibility* are closely related to one another. When you divide one integer (x) by another integer (y), if the resulting quotient (z) is also an integer, then:

y is a **factor** of x, and z is a **factor** of x
x is **divisible** by y (and by z)
x is a **multiple** of y (and of z)

If the quotient is NOT an integer, then y and z are NOT factors of x, and x is NOT a multiple of (and is NOT divisible by) either y or z. (You'll end up with a *remainder* after dividing.)

Example:
4 is a factor of 12 because $12 \div 4 = 3$ (an integer).
3 is also a factor of 12.
12 is divisible by 4 and by 3.
12 is a multiple of both 4 and 3.

Example:
5 is not a factor of 12 (because $12 \div 5 = \dfrac{12}{5}$, a non-integer).

12 is not divisible by 5.
12 is not a multiple of 5.

Example:
There are five multiples of 7 that are less than 40: 7, 14, 21, 28, and 35.
7 is a factor of all five of these multiples.
14 is a factor of two of these multiples: 14 and 28.

Prime Numbers

A **prime number** is a positive integer that has only two positive factors: 1 and the number itself. You should memorize the list of all prime numbers less than 50:

2, 3, 5, 7
11, 13, 17, 19
23, 29
31, 37
41, 43, 47

The smallest prime number is 2. (1 is not a prime number.)

Factoring and Prime Factorization

When listing all factors of an integer, remember the following basic rules about factors:

1. Any integer is a factor of itself.
2. 1 and −1 are factors of all integers (except 0).
3. The integer zero (0) has no factors and is not a factor of any integer.
4. A positive integer's largest factor (other than itself) cannot be greater than half the value of the integer.

A large integer does not necessarily have more factors than a smaller integer.

Examples:
The integer 12 has a total of 6 positive factors: 1, 2, 3, 4, 6, and 12.
The integer 27 has a total of 4 positive factors: 1, 3, 9, and 27.
The integer 40 has a total of 7 positive factors: 1, 2, 4, 5, 8, 10, 20, and 40.
The integer 62 has a total of 4 positive factors: 1, 2, 31, and 62.

To find all factors of a large integer, use a method called **prime factorization.** Try to divide the integer by prime numbers, starting with 2 and working your way up (2, 3, 5, 7, 11 . . .). As you find a quotient that is an integer, list it as a factor. Try to find factors of each quotient as well, using the same method. Test prime numbers up to the point where your quotient is no greater than the largest factor you've already found.

Example:
Find all positive factors and prime factors of 156:

$156 \div 2 = 78$	$156 \div 3 = 52$	$156 \div 5 = $ non-integer
$78 \div 2 = 39$	$52 \div 2 = 26$	$156 \div 7 = $ non-integer
$39 \div 3 = 13$	$26 \div 2 = 13$	$156 \div 11 = $ non-integer
Stop. (13 is a prime number.)	Stop. (13 is a prime number.)	$156 \div 13$ (already covered)

Here's the set of all positive factors of 156: {1, 2, 3, 13, 26, 39, 52, 78, 156}. Here's the set of all prime factors of 156: {2, 3, 13}.

Commutative Laws of Multiplication and Addition

The commutative laws of multiplication and addition state that for any two numbers a and b:

$$a \times b = b \times a$$
$$a + b = b + a$$

Examples:
$2 \times 3 = 6$, and $3 \times 2 = 6$
$2 + 3 = 5$, and $3 + 2 = 5$

The commutative law does NOT apply to either subtraction or division.

Examples:
Does $(8 - 2)$ equal $(2 - 8)$? No! $8 - 2 = 6$, but $2 - 8 = -6$.
Does $(8 \div 2)$ equal $(2 \div 8)$? No! $8 \div 2 = 4$, but $2 \div 8 = \dfrac{1}{4}$.

Associative Laws of Multiplication and Addition

The associative law of multiplication states that for any three numbers a, b, and c:

$$(a \times b) \times c = a \times (b \times c)$$

Example:
$(2 \times 3) \times 4 = 6 \times 4 = 24$
$2 \times (3 \times 4) = 2 \times 12 = 24$

The associative law of addition states that for any three numbers a, b, and c:

$$(a + b) + c = a + (b + c)$$

Example:
$(6 + 5) + 1 = 11 + 1 = 12$
$6 + (5 + 1) = 6 + 6 = 12$

The associative law does NOT apply to either subtraction or division.

Example:
Does $(8 - 2) - 3$ equal $8 - (2 - 3)$?
No! $6 - 3 = 3$, but $8 - (-1) = 9$.

Example:
Does $(8 \div 4) \div 2 = 8 \div (4 \div 2)$?
No! $2 \div 2 = 1$, but $8 \div 2 = 4$.

Distributive Law of Multiplication

The distributive law of multiplication states that for any three numbers a, b, and c:

$a(b + c) = ab + ac$
$a(b - c) = ab - ac$

Example:
$5(2 + 4) = 5 \times 6 = 30$
$5(2 + 4) = (5)(2) + (5)(4) = 10 + 20 = 30$

Example:
$3(6 - 1) = 3 \times 5 = 15$
$3(6 - 1) = (3)(6) - (3)(1) = 18 - 3 = 15$

You can also distribute a minus sign $(-)$ immediately preceding a parenthesized expression to all terms inside the parentheses, reversing the sign of each term.

$a - (b + c - d) = a - b - c + d$

Example:
Combining parenthesized terms first: $10 - (4 - 2 + 8) = 10 - 10 = 0$
Distributing minus sign to terms first: $10 - (4 - 2 + 8) = 10 - 4 + 2 - 8 = 0$

Order of Operations

When performing multiple operations, always perform operations within parentheses first.

Examples:
$(2 + 3) \times 5 = 5 \times 5 = 25$
$10 \div (3 - 5) = 10 \div (-2) = -5$

Absent parentheses to indicate the order of operations, follow these rules:

- You can multiply and divide in either order.
- You can add and subtract in either order.
- Always perform multiplication and division *before* addition and subtraction.

Example (multiplication and division):
Calculate $4 \times 6 \div 2$ in three different ways.
First, multiply: $4 \times 6 = 24$. Next, divide: $24 \div 2 = 12$.
First, divide: $6 \div 2 = 3$. Next, multiply: $3 \times 4 = 12$.
First, divide: $4 \div 2 = 2$. Next, multiply: $2 \times 6 = 12$.

Example (addition and subtraction):
Calculate $3 + 5 - 1$ in three different ways.
First, add: $3 + 5 = 8$. Then, subtract: $8 - 1 = 7$.
First, subtract: $5 - 1 = 4$. Next, add: $4 + 3 = 7$.
First, subtract: $3 - 1 = 2$. Next, add: $2 + 5 = 7$.

Example (three different operations):
Calculate $4 \times 6 - 8 \div 2$.
Perform multiplication and division first: $(4 \times 6) - (8 \div 2) = 24 - 4 = 20$.

Example (three different operations):
Calculate $3 + 10 \div 5 - 8$.
First, perform division: $3 + (10 \div 5) - 8 = 3 + 2 - 8$.
Then, add and subtract (in either order): $3 + 2 - 8 = -3$.

Number Forms

This section covers the basic rules for expressing and combining numbers in three different forms: fractions, percents, and decimal numbers. Here are the specific topics covered:

- Fractions and mixed numbers
- Combining fractions by addition, subtraction, multiplication, and division
- Decimal numbers and place value
- Multiplying and dividing decimal numbers
- Rounding off decimal numbers
- Converting between decimal numbers and percents
- Converting between fractions and percents
- Scientific notation

Fractions and Mixed Numbers

Any **fraction** contains a numerator "over" a denominator. In a **proper fraction,** the numerator is less than the denominator, and the fraction's absolute value is greater than 0 but less than 1. In an **improper fraction,** the fraction's numerator is greater than its denominator, and the fraction's absolute value is greater than 1.

Examples (proper fractions):

$$\frac{2}{5}$$

$$\frac{1}{100}$$

$$\frac{75}{76}$$

Examples (improper fractions):

$$\frac{7}{3}$$

$$\frac{98}{23}$$

$$\frac{9}{4}$$

A **mixed number** contains two elements: an integer and a proper fraction—for example, $2\frac{1}{3}$. To convert a mixed number to an improper fraction, add the product of the fraction's denominator and the integer to the fraction's numerator. The result is the numerator of the improper fraction. The fraction's denominator remains unchanged.

Examples:

$$2\frac{1}{3} = \frac{(3 \times 2) + 1}{3} = \frac{7}{3}$$

$$6\frac{3}{5} = \frac{(5 \times 6) + 3}{5} = \frac{33}{5}$$

To convert an improper fraction to a mixed number, divide the numerator by the denominator. The quotient is the mixed number's integer, and the remainder (if any) is the fraction's numerator.

Examples:

$$\frac{11}{3} = 3\frac{2}{3} \text{ (3 goes into 11 } \textit{3} \text{ times, with a remainder of } \textit{2}\text{)}$$

$$\frac{5}{2} = 2\frac{1}{2} \text{ (2 goes into 5 } \textit{2} \text{ times, with a remainder of } \textit{1}\text{)}$$

Fractions—Addition and Subtraction

To add or subtract fractions, the denominator of the fractions *must* be the same. If they are, you can simply add or subtract the numerators. The denominator remains the same.

Examples:

$$\frac{3}{7} + \frac{2}{7} = \frac{3+2}{7} = \frac{5}{7}$$

$$\frac{1}{4} + \frac{3}{4} - \frac{5}{4} = \frac{1+3-5}{4} = \frac{-1}{4}, \text{ or } -\frac{1}{4}$$

If the denominators are not the same, you *cannot* add or subtract fractions. You must first find a common denominator, and then convert fractions so that all denominators are the same. One way to find a common denominator is to multiply all different denominators together. In each fraction, the numerator and denominator must be multiplied by the same number, so that the fraction's value remains the same.

Example:

$$\frac{4}{5}+\frac{1}{2}=\frac{4\times2}{5\times2}+\frac{1\times5}{2\times5}=\frac{8}{10}+\frac{5}{10}=\frac{13}{10}, \text{ or } 1\frac{3}{10}$$

To simplify the process, use the **least common denominator (LCD)** of all fractions. To determine the LCD, find successive multiples of the greatest denominator. The lowest multiple that is also a multiple of all other denominators is the LCD.

Example:

To calculate $\frac{2}{3}+\frac{1}{4}+\frac{1}{2}$, find successive multiples of 4 (the greatest denominator). 4 is not a multiple of 3, and so 4 cannot be the LCD. The next multiple of 4 is 8, which is not a multiple of 3 and thus is not the LCD. The next multiple of 4 is 12, which is a multiple of both 3 and 2. Thus, 12 is the LCD. Using 12 as the denominator of all three fractions, you can now combine them:

$$\frac{2}{3}+\frac{1}{4}+\frac{1}{2}=\frac{8}{12}+\frac{3}{12}+\frac{6}{12}=\frac{8+3+6}{12}=\frac{17}{12}, \text{ or } 1\frac{5}{12}$$

Fractions—Multiplication and Division

To find the product of two or more fractions, combine numerators by multiplication, and combine denominators by multiplication. The denominators do not need to be the same.

Examples:

$$\frac{2}{3}\times\frac{5}{7}=\frac{2\times5}{3\times7}=\frac{10}{21}$$

$$\frac{3}{2}\times\frac{4}{5}\times\frac{4}{3}=\frac{3\times4\times4}{2\times5\times3}=\frac{48}{30}=\frac{8}{5}, \text{ or } 1\frac{3}{5}$$

To simplify the calculations, cancel common factors across fractions before multiplying.

Examples:

$$\frac{5}{4}\times\frac{3}{10}=\frac{1}{4}\times\frac{3}{2}=\frac{1\times3}{4\times2}=\frac{3}{8}$$

(The common factor 5 is cancelled before fractions are combined.)

$$\frac{1}{4}\times\frac{4}{3}\times\frac{6}{7}=\frac{1}{1}\times\frac{1}{1}\times\frac{2}{7}=\frac{1\times1\times2}{1\times1\times7}=\frac{2}{7}$$

(The common factors 4 and 3 are cancelled before fractions are combined.)

To divide fractions, first invert the divisor (the number after the division sign) by switching its numerator and denominator. Then combine by multiplying. To simplify the multiplication or division, cancel factors common to a numerator and a denominator before combining fractions. It's okay to cancel across fractions.

Example:

$$\frac{5}{6} \div \frac{3}{4} = \frac{5}{6} \times \frac{4}{3} = \frac{5}{3} \times \frac{2}{3} = \frac{10}{9}$$

(The common factor 2 is cancelled before fractions are combined.)

If a division problem includes mixed numbers, first convert the mixed numbers to improper fractions.

Example:

$$3\frac{2}{3} \div 2\frac{3}{4} = \frac{11}{3} \div \frac{11}{4} = \frac{11}{3} \times \frac{4}{11} = \frac{1}{3} \times \frac{4}{1} = \frac{4}{3}$$

Decimal Numbers—Place Value

A **decimal number** is a number that contains a decimal point. In any decimal number, every digit represents a different value. Any digit to the left of a decimal point has a whole number place value. Any digit to the right of a decimal point has a fractional place value less than 1.

Example:
The number 3,481.952 consists of 7 digits.
The digit 3 is in the "thousands" place. Its place value is 3,000.
The digit 4 is in the "hundreds" place. Its place value is 400.
The digit 8 is in the "tens" place. Its place value is 80.
The digit 1 is in the "ones" place. Its place value is 1.

The digit 9 is in the "tenths" place. Its place value is $\frac{9}{10}$.

The digit 5 is in the "hundredths" place. Its place value is $\frac{5}{100}$.

The digit 2 is in the "thousandths" place. Its place value is $\frac{2}{1,000}$.

Any decimal number can be expressed as the sum of its digits' place values.

Example:

$$3,481.952 = 3,000 + 400 + 80 + 1 + \frac{9}{10} + \frac{5}{100} + \frac{2}{1,000}.$$

Example:

Express the sum of $\frac{3}{1,000}$, $\frac{4}{100}$, and $\frac{9}{100}$ as a decimal number:

$\frac{3}{1,000} = 0.003$. $\frac{4}{100} + \frac{9}{100} = 0.13$. Thus, the sum of the three fractions is 0.133.

Decimal Numbers—Multiplication and Division

To multiply one decimal number by another without using a calculator, follow these three steps:

1. Ignoring the decimal points, find the product of the numbers.
2. Count the total number of decimal places (digits to the right of the decimal point) in the original numbers.
3. Add a decimal point to the number you calculated in step 1. In your product, the number of decimal places should be the same as the number you calculated in step 2.

Examples:
$(7)(0.3) = 2.1$ (1 decimal place)
$(0.1)(0.2) = 0.02$ (2 decimal places altogether)
$(0.4)(0.06) = 0.024$ (3 decimal places altogether)
$(0.02)(0.03) = 0.0006$ (4 decimal places altogether)
$(1.1)(0.1)(0.001) = 0.00011$ (5 decimal places altogether)
$(0.04)(0.02)(0.02) = 0.000016$ (6 decimal places altogether)

To divide one decimal number by another without using a calculator:

1. Convert to the form of a fraction.
2. Remove decimals by shifting decimal points in the numerator and denominator to the right by the same number of places.
3. Simplify the resulting fraction.

Examples:

$$6 \div 0.3 = \frac{6}{0.3} = \frac{60}{3} = 20 \text{ (Decimal point moved to the right by 1 place)}$$

$$0.12 \div 0.2 = \frac{0.12}{0.2} = \frac{12}{20} = \frac{3}{5}, \text{ or } 0.6 \text{ (Decimal point moved to the right by 2 places)}$$

Rounding Off Decimal Numbers

To round off a decimal number, round any digit less than 5 down to 0, and round any digit 5 or greater up to 0 (increasing the next digit to the left by 1).

Examples:
Round off the 7-digit decimal number 3,481.752
to the nearest *hundredth:* 3,481.75
to the nearest *tenth:* 3,481.7 or 3,481.8
to the nearest *whole number:* 3,482
to the nearest *ten:* 3,480
to the nearest *hundred:* 3,500
to the nearest *thousand:* 3,000

To avoid complex calculations when combining two long decimal numbers by multiplication or division, round off both numbers *before* combining them. Combining rounded numbers will yield an approximate value. Try rounding to numbers that are easy to combine. When multiplying, try to round the two numbers in *opposite* directions.

Example:
Find the product of 337 and 614, rounded to the nearest ten thousand.
The number 337 is 13 less than 350. The number 614 is 14 more than 600. Rounding both numbers to the nearest 50 will make the calculation easier and yield a close approximate product: $337 \times 614 \approx 350 \times 600 = 210{,}000$.

When dividing one decimal number by another, try to round the two numbers in the same direction.

Example:
Find the value of $4.42 \div 894$, rounded to the nearest thousandth.
The number 4.42 is greater than 4.4 and less than 4.5. The number 894 is greater than 890 and less than 900. Since 4.5 is easily divisible by 900, rounding to these numbers will make the calculation easy and yield a close approximate quotient: $4.42 \div 894 \approx 4.5 \div 900 = 0.005$.

Decimal-Percent Conversions

You can convert any decimal number to a **percent** by shifting the decimal point two places to the *right* and adding a percent sign (%). To convert a percent to a decimal number, move the decimal point two places to the *left* (and drop the percent sign). Decimal numbers greater than 1 convert to percents greater than 100.

Examples (decimal → percent):
$0.78 = 78\%$
$0.614 = 61.4\%$
$0.003 = 0.3\%$
$8.21 = 821\%$

Examples (percent → decimal):
$23\% = 0.23$
$7.5\% = 0.075$
$0.9\% = 0.009$
$167\% = 1.67$

Percent-Fraction Conversions

To convert a percent to a fraction, *divide* by 100 (and drop the percent sign). To convert a fraction to a percent, *multiply* by 100 (and add the percent sign). Percents greater than 100 convert to numbers greater than 1.

Examples (percent → fraction):

$$36\% = \frac{36}{100} = \frac{9}{25}$$

$$440\% = \frac{440}{100} = \frac{22}{5}, \text{ or } 4\frac{2}{5}$$

Examples (fraction → percent):

$$\frac{3}{4} = \frac{300}{4}\% = \frac{150}{2}\% = 75\%$$

$$\frac{6}{5} = \frac{600}{5}\% = \frac{120}{1}\% = 120\%$$

You should memorize the following fraction-percent-decimal equivalents. In the right-hand column, decimal numbers are rounded to the nearest one-thousandth (the third decimal place):

$$\frac{1}{10} = 10\% = 0.1 \qquad \frac{1}{8} = 12\frac{1}{2}\% = 0.125 \qquad \frac{1}{6} = 16\frac{2}{3}\% \approx 0.167$$

$$\frac{2}{10} = \frac{1}{5} = 20\% = 0.2 \qquad \frac{2}{8} = \frac{1}{4} = 25\% = 0.25 \qquad \frac{2}{6} = \frac{1}{3} = 33\frac{1}{3}\% \approx 0.333$$

$$\frac{3}{10} = 30\% = 0.3 \qquad \frac{3}{8} = 37\frac{1}{2}\% = 0.375 \qquad \frac{3}{6} = \frac{1}{2} = 50\% = 0.5$$

$$\frac{4}{10} = \frac{2}{5} = 40\% = 0.4 \qquad \frac{4}{8} = \frac{1}{2} = 50\% = 0.5 \qquad \frac{4}{6} = \frac{2}{3} = 66\frac{2}{3}\% \approx 0.667$$

$$\frac{5}{10} = \frac{1}{2} = 50\% = 0.5 \qquad \frac{5}{8} = 62\frac{1}{2}\% = 0.625 \qquad \frac{5}{6} = 83\frac{1}{3}\% \approx 0.833$$

$$\frac{6}{10} = \frac{3}{5} = 60\% = 0.6 \qquad \frac{6}{8} = \frac{3}{4} = 75\% = 0.75$$

$$\frac{7}{10} = 70\% = 0.7 \qquad \frac{7}{8} = 87\frac{1}{2}\% = 0.875$$

$$\frac{8}{10} = \frac{4}{5} = 80\% = 0.8$$

$$\frac{9}{10} = 90\% = 0.9$$

Scientific Notation

You can express any decimal number in **scientific notation** by positioning the decimal point after the number's first digit and multiplying that number by 10 raised to the number (power) of places you shifted the decimal point. Use a negative exponent for fractional numbers between 0 and 1. The left-hand column below shows values of 10 raised to different powers. The right-hand column shows how to apply each of these values in scientific notation.

Power of 10:
$10^4 = 10,000$
$10^3 = 1,000$
$10^2 = 100$
$10^1 = 10$
$10^0 = 1$
$10^{-1} = 0.1$
$10^{-2} = 0.01$
$10^{-3} = 0.001$
$10^{-4} = 0.0001$

Scientific Notation Examples:
$45,200 = 4.52 \times 10^4$ (decimal point is shifted 4 places to the left)
$4,520 = 4.52 \times 10^3$ (decimal point is shifted 3 places to the left)
$452 = 4.52 \times 10^2$ (decimal point is shifted 2 places to the left)
$45.2 = 4.52 \times 10^1$ (decimal point is shifted 1 place to the left)
$4.52 = 4.52 \times 10^0$ (decimal point is unchanged)
$0.452 = 4.52 \times 10^{-1}$ (decimal point is shifted 1 place to the right)
$0.0452 = 4.52 \times 10^{-2}$ (decimal point is shifted 2 places to the right)
$0.00452 = 4.52 \times 10^{-3}$ (decimal point is shifted 3 places to the right)
$0.000452 = 4.52 \times 10^{-4}$ (decimal point is shifted 4 places to the right)

To express a fraction or percent using scientific notation, first convert the fraction or percent to a decimal number.

Examples:

$$\frac{30,000}{2} = 15,000 = 1.5 \times 10^4$$

$$5.8\% = 0.058 = 5.8 \times 10^{-2}$$

$$\frac{2}{10,000} = 0.0002 = 2 \times 10^{-4}$$

Sets, Statistical Measurements, and Probability

In this section, you'll review the basics of an area that mathematicians call "descriptive statistics." Here are the specific concepts covered:

- Sets
- Arithmetic mean (simple average)
- Median
- Mode
- Arithmetic series
- Probability

Sets

A **set** is a group of numbers or variables, called the set's **terms** or **members.**
The **union** of two sets, P and Q, is symbolized by $P \cup Q$ and includes all members of either set P or set Q (or both).
The **intersection** of two sets, P and Q, is symbolized by $P \cap Q$ and includes all members that the two sets share in common.

Example:
Set P: {2,3,5,7,8}
Set Q: {all positive even integers less than 10}
$P \cup Q = \{2,3,4,5,6,7,8\}$
$P \cap Q = \{2,8\}$

Arithmetic Mean (Simple Average)

The **arithmetic mean,** or **simple average,** of a set of terms is the sum of the terms divided by the number of terms in the set.

Example:
Calculate the arithmetic mean of 3, −2, 5, and 4:

$$AM = \frac{(3-2+5+4)}{4} = \frac{10}{4}, \text{ or } \frac{5}{2}$$

Apply the same formula to find an unknown term when the average is given.

Example:
Given that the arithmetic mean of three numbers—13, 6, and one other number—is 8, find the third number:

$$8 = \frac{(13 + 6 + x)}{3}$$

$$24 = 19 + x$$

$$5 = x$$

Solve arithmetic-mean problems that involve variables (letters) in the same way.

Example:
Given that M is the arithmetic mean of S and one other number, to express the missing number in terms of M and S, let $x =$ the missing number. Solve for x by the arithmetic-mean formula:

$$M = \frac{S + x}{2}$$

$$2M = S + x$$

$$2M - S = x$$

Median and Mode

The **median** value of a set of terms is the set's middle term in value if the set contains an odd number of terms, or the arithmetic mean (simple average) of the two middle terms if the set contains an even number of terms.

Examples:
In set $P\{3,6,1,9,8\}$, the median is 6. (Two terms are lower in value, and two terms are higher in value.)
In set $Q\{2,1,4,7\}$, the median is 3 (the arithmetic mean of the two middle terms, 2 and 4).

The **mode** of a set is the term appearing most often in the set.

Example:
In set $P\{6, -1, 8, 6\}$, the mode is 6.

Arithmetic Series

An **arithmetic series** is a set of numbers in which the difference between any two successive numbers is constant (unchanging). Any series of successive integers, odd integers, or even integers would be an example of an arithmetic series.

The concept of arithmetic series is closely related to arithmetic mean (simple average). The average of the numbers in an arithmetic series is half the sum of the least and greatest numbers. The sum of the numbers is the product of the average and the number of terms in the series.

Example:

Let set P = the set of positive integers 10 through 24.

The arithmetic mean of all members of set $P = \dfrac{10 + 24}{2} = \dfrac{34}{2}$, or 17.

The sum of all members of set $P = 17 \times 15 = 255$.

Probability

Probability refers to the statistical chances of a particular event occurring. A probability is never less than 0 (zero) nor greater than 1. You can express a probability as a decimal number, a percent, or a fraction.

$$\text{Probability} = \frac{\text{number of ways the event can occur}}{\text{total number of possible occurrences}}$$

Example:

A jar contains 10 marbles altogether. Three marbles are blue, and four marbles are red. The probability of randomly selecting a marble that is neither blue nor red is $\dfrac{3}{10}$ (or 30%, or 0.3).

Elementary Algebra

In this section, you'll review the basic tools for working with algebraic expressions and solving algebraic equations and inequalities. Then, you'll apply those tools to the various types of word problems. Here are the specific topics covered:

- Solving algebraic equations
- Solving algebraic inequalities
- Solving algebraic equations
- Functions
- Exponents and roots
- Solving algebra story problems

Solving Algebraic Equations

To solve an equation containing one variable (a letter such as x), isolate the variable on one side of the equation with one or more of these tools:

- Add or subtract the same term from both sides.
- Multiply or divide the same term from both sides.
- Clear fractions by cross-multiplication.

Example:

In the equation $x + 5 = 6$, solve for x by subtracting 5 from both sides of the equation:

$$x + 5 - 5 = 6 - 5$$
$$x = 1$$

Example:
To solve for x in the equation $3x = 2 - x$, first place both x-terms on one side of the equation by adding x to both sides:

$$3x = 2 - x$$

$$3x + x = 2 - x + x$$

$$4x = 2$$

Then, divide both sides of the equation by 4:

$$\frac{4x}{4} = \frac{2}{4}$$

$$x = \frac{1}{2}$$

Example:

To solve for x in the equation $\dfrac{x+3}{2} = \dfrac{5x}{4}$, first clear the fractions by cross-multiplication. Multiply the numerator of each fraction by the denominator of the other fraction, and equate the two products:

$$(4)(x + 3) = (2)(5x)$$

Next, combine terms on each side of the equation (on the left side, distribute 4 to both x and 3):

$$(4)(x) + (4)(3) = (2)(5x)$$

$$4x + 12 = 10x$$

Finally, isolate x on one side of the equation (this requires two steps):

$$4x - 4x + 12 = 10x - 4x$$

$$12 = 6x$$

$$2 = x$$

Unlike linear equations in *one* variable, a linear equation in *two* (or more) variables has no unique solution.

Example:
Consider the equation $x = 2y$. There are an infinite number of (x,y) value pairs that satisfy the equation. Here are just three examples:

$$x = 2 \text{ and } y = 1$$

$$x = 4 \text{ and } y = 2$$

$$x = -6 \text{ and } y = -3$$

However, you can express either variable *in terms of* the other using the three tools you just reviewed.

Example:
In the equation $2x + y = 10$, express the value of x in terms of y:

$$2x = 10 - y$$

$$x = \frac{10}{2} - \frac{y}{2}$$

$$x = 5 - \frac{y}{2}$$

In the same equation, expressing the value of y in terms of x is easier:

$$y = 10 - 2x$$

Solving Algebraic Inequalities

Solve algebraic inequalities like you solve equations. However, when you multiply or divide by a *negative* number, you must reverse the inequality symbol.

Example:
Solve for a in the inequality $2 - a > 4$:

$$-a > 4 - 2$$

$$-a > 2$$

To isolate a, divide both sides by -1, which reverses the inequality: $a < -2$.

Example:
In the inequality $y < 3 - \dfrac{x}{3}$, to express x in terms of y, first subtract 3 from both sides (this operation does not change the inequality):

$$y - 3 < -\frac{x}{3}$$

To isolate x, multiply both sides by -3, which reverses the inequality:

$$-3(y - 3) > x$$

Functions

A **function** is an equation in which the value of one variable depends upon the value of another variable. If you know the value of one variable, you can find the value of the other variable by plugging the value you know into the equation.

Example:

Consider the equation $y = 2x + 3$. Find x when $y = 4$:

$$4 = 2x + 3$$

$$4 - 3 = 2x$$

$$1 = 2x$$

$$\frac{1}{2} = x$$

In the same equation, find y when $x = 4$:

$$y = 2(4) + 3$$

$$y = 8 + 3$$

$$y = 11$$

Exponents

An **exponent** refers to the number of times a given number, called the **base number,** is to be multiplied by itself. In the term a^x, the base number is a, and the exponent is x. Another way of referring to the value of a^x is to say that "a is raised to the power of x."

Examples:
$3^2 = 3 \times 3 = 9$
$4^3 = 4 \times 4 \times 4 = 64$
$2^4 = 2 \times 2 \times 2 \times 2 = 16$
$1^5 = 1 \times 1 \times 1 \times 1 \times 1 = 1$

A non-zero number (a) raised to a negative power ($-x$) equals 1 divided by the exponential number a^x. That is, $a^{-x} = \dfrac{1}{a^x}$. The number zero (0) raised to any power is zero (0). Any non-zero number raised to the power of zero (0) = 1.

Examples:

$$3^{-2} = \frac{1}{3^2} = \frac{1}{9}$$

$$0^3 = 0 \times 0 \times 0 = 0$$

$$3^0 = 1$$

Exponents—Addition and Subtraction

When you add or subtract exponential numbers, you CANNOT combine base numbers, nor can you combine exponents:

$$a^x + b^x \neq (a + b)^x \qquad\qquad a^x + a^y \neq a^{(x+y)}$$

Examples:

Does $3^2 + 4^2 = (3 + 4)^2$? No. $9 + 16 \neq 7 \times 7$.

Does $2^3 + 2^4 = 2^{(3+4)}$? No. $2^3 + 2^4 = 8 + 16 = 24$, but $2^{(3+4)} = 2^7 = 128$.

Exponents—Multiplication and Division

When you multiply or divide exponential numbers, you can combine base numbers first, but ONLY if the exponents are the same:

$$a^x \times b^x = (ab)^x \qquad\qquad \frac{a^x}{b^x} = \left(\frac{a}{b}\right)^x$$

Example:

$$4^2 \times 3^2 = 16 \times 9 = 144$$

$$(4 \times 3)^2 = 12^2 = 144$$

Example:

$$\frac{6^2}{3^2} = \frac{36}{9} = 4$$

$$\left(\frac{6}{3}\right)^2 = 2^2 = 4$$

Similarly, you can combine exponents first, but ONLY if the base numbers are the same:

$$a^x \times a^y = a^{(x+y)} \qquad\qquad \frac{a^x}{a^y} = a^{(x-y)}$$

Example:

$$2^2 \times 2^3 = 4 \times 8 = 32$$

$$2^{(2+3)} = 2^5 = 32$$

Example:

$$\frac{3^3}{3^2} = \frac{27}{9} = 3$$

$$3^{(3-2)} = 3^1 = 3$$

When the same base number (or term) appears in both the numerator and denominator of a fraction, you can factor out, or cancel, the number of powers common to both.

Example:

$$\frac{2^6}{2^9} = \frac{2^0}{2^3} = \frac{1}{8}$$

When raising an exponential number to a power, multiply exponents:

$$(a^x)^y = a^{xy}$$

Example:

$$(2^3)^2 = 8^2 = 64$$

$$2^{(3 \times 2)} = 2^6 = 64$$

Roots

The **square root** of a number x, written as $\sqrt{x}$, is the number you "square" (raise to the second power) to obtain x. Thus, $\sqrt{x} \times \sqrt{x} = x$. Similarly, the **cube root** of a number x, written as $\sqrt[3]{x}$, is the number you "cube" (raise to the third power) to obtain x. Thus, $\sqrt[3]{x} \times \sqrt[3]{x} \times \sqrt[3]{x} = x$. The symbol $\sqrt{}$ is called a **radical** sign.

Examples (square root):
$2 \times 2 = 4$. Thus, $\sqrt{4} = 2$.

$\frac{1}{2} \times \frac{1}{2} = \frac{1}{4}$. Thus, $\sqrt{\frac{1}{4}} = \frac{1}{2}$.

Examples (cube root):
$2 \times 2 \times 2 = 8$. Thus, $\sqrt[3]{8} = 2$.

$\frac{1}{2} \times \frac{1}{2} \times \frac{1}{2} = \frac{1}{8}$. Thus, $\sqrt[3]{\frac{1}{8}} = \frac{1}{2}$.

A number whose square root is an integer is called a **perfect square,** and a number whose cube root is an integer is called a **perfect cube.** You should memorize the following examples of perfect squares and cubes:

Perfect Squares

$\sqrt{4} = 2$

$\sqrt{9} = 3$

$\sqrt{16} = 4$

$\sqrt{25} = 5$

$\sqrt{36} = 6$

$\sqrt{49} = 7$

$\sqrt{64} = 8$

$\sqrt{81} = 9$

$\sqrt{100} = 10$

$\sqrt{121} = 11$

$\sqrt{144} = 12$

Perfect Cubes

$\sqrt[3]{8} = 2$

$\sqrt[3]{27} = 3$

$\sqrt[3]{64} = 4$

$\sqrt[3]{125} = 5$

$\sqrt[3]{1,000} = 10$

Simplifying Radical Expressions

You can remove any perfect square from inside a square-root radical and change it to its square-root value. In some cases, you need to factor a term inside a radical to reveal a perfect square. The same applies to perfect cubes.

Examples (radical expressions containing perfect-square factors):

$$\sqrt{a^2 b} = a\sqrt{b}$$

$$\sqrt{16x^2} = 4x$$

$$\sqrt{28} = \sqrt{(4)(7)} = 2\sqrt{7}$$

$$\sqrt{12a^3} = \sqrt{(4)(3)a^2 a} = 2a\sqrt{3a}$$

Examples (radical expressions containing perfect-cube factors):

$$\sqrt[3]{a^3 b^2} = a\sqrt[3]{b^2}$$

$$\sqrt[3]{8x^5} = \sqrt[3]{8x^3 x^2} = 2x\sqrt[3]{x^2}$$

$$\sqrt[3]{54} = \sqrt[3]{(27)(2)} = 3\sqrt[3]{2}$$

$$\sqrt[3]{16a^4} = \sqrt[3]{(8)(2)a^3 a} = 2a\sqrt[3]{2a}$$

Operations on Radical Expressions

You can add or subtract radical expressions ONLY if they're the same:

Examples:

$$\sqrt{a} + \sqrt{a} = 2\sqrt{a}$$

$$\sqrt{a} + \sqrt{b} \neq \sqrt{a+b}$$

$$\sqrt{a} - \sqrt{b} \neq \sqrt{a-b}$$

Examples:

$$\sqrt{3} + 2\sqrt{3} = 3\sqrt{3}$$

$$5\sqrt{5} - 3\sqrt{5} = 2\sqrt{5}$$

$$\sqrt{2} + \frac{\sqrt{2}}{2} = \frac{2\sqrt{2}}{2} + \frac{\sqrt{2}}{2} = \frac{3\sqrt{2}}{2}$$

On the other hand, you can multiply or divide radical expressions, even if the terms inside the radicals differ:

Examples:

$$\sqrt{a} \times \sqrt{b} = \sqrt{ab}$$

$$\frac{\sqrt{a}}{\sqrt{b}} = \sqrt{\frac{a}{b}}$$

Examples:

$$\sqrt{2} \times \sqrt{\frac{1}{4}} = \sqrt{2 \times \frac{1}{4}} = \sqrt{\frac{1}{2}}$$

$$\sqrt{3} \times \sqrt{6} = \sqrt{(3)(6)} = \sqrt{18} = \sqrt{(2)(9)} = 3\sqrt{2}$$

$$\frac{\sqrt{6}}{\sqrt{3}} = \sqrt{\frac{6}{3}} = \sqrt{2}$$

Solving Algebra Story Problems

Some of the algebra problems on the COOP, HSPT, and TACHS are stories about made-up situations. In this section, you'll review the following types of story problems, which are the ones you're most likely to see on your exam:

- Ratio and proportion
- Interest on investment
- Profit and discount

- Rate of travel (speed) or production
- Weighted average
- Currency (coins and bills)
- Mixtures
- Comparing ages
- Converting units of measurement

Ratio and Proportion

You express the comparative size of two numbers as their **ratio.** Given two numbers x and y, the ratio of x to y is $x:y$. You can also express this ratio as a fraction: $\dfrac{x}{y}$.

Example:
A bag contains 7 blue marbles and 3 red marbles. Therefore:

The ratio of blue marbles to red marbles is 7 to 3, or 7:3, or $\dfrac{7}{3}$.

The ratio of red marbles to blue marbles is 3 to 7, or 3:7, or $\dfrac{3}{7}$.

You can reduce ratios to lowest terms by cancelling common factors.

Example:
In a carton of one dozen eggs, 4 eggs are white, 2 eggs are brown, and the rest are spotted. Therefore:
The ratio of white eggs to brown eggs is 4:2, or 2:1, or 2.

The ratio of brown eggs to white eggs is 2:4, or 1:2, or $\dfrac{1}{2}$.

The ratio of brown eggs to spotted eggs is 2:6, or 1:3, or $\dfrac{1}{3}$.

Because you can express any ratio as a fraction. You can set up an equation between two equivalent ratios. If one of the four terms is missing from the equation, you can solve for the missing term using algebra.

Example:
In history class, the ratio of boys to girls is 3:2. If there are 24 boys in the class, calculate the number of girls in the class:

$$\frac{3}{2} = \frac{24}{x}$$

$$3x = (2)(24)$$

$$3x = 48$$

$$x = 16$$

There are 16 girls in the history class.

Solve proportion problems involving variables (letters instead of numbers) the same way.

Example:
If one brick weighs 5 pounds, how many ounces do *B* bricks weigh in terms of *B*? [1 pound = 16 ounces]

To answer the question, set up an equation, letting *x* equal the weight of *B* bricks. Because the question asks for the weight in *ounces,* convert 1 pound to 16 ounces. Solve for *x:*

$$\frac{1 \text{ brick}}{5 \times 16 \text{ ounces}} = \frac{B \text{ bricks}}{x}$$

$$\frac{1}{80} = \frac{B}{x}$$

$$x = 80B$$

The weight of *B* bricks is $80B$ ounces.

Interest on Investment

Investment problems involve interest earned at a certain percentage rate on money over a certain time period, usually one year. To calculate interest earned, multiply the original amount of money by the interest rate:

(amount of money) × (interest rate) = (amount of interest)

Example:
Given $100 earning interest at an annual rate of 5%, calculate the interest earned after one year: $100 × 0.05 = $5.

You apply the same basic formula to calculate the interest rate, where the amount invested and the interest earned are given.

Example:
After one year, a $7,500 savings deposit has earned $300 in interest. Calculate the interest rate earned on this investment:

$$(7,500)(x) = 300$$

$$x = \frac{300}{7,500}$$

$$x = \frac{4}{100}, \text{ or } 4\%$$

You also apply the same basic formula to calculate the original amount of money invested, where the interest rate and amount of interest earned are given.

Example:
A certain amount of money is invested at an annual rate of 15%. After one year, the interest earned totals $45. Calculate the amount of money invested:

$$(x)(0.15) = 45$$

$$x = \frac{45}{0.15}$$

$$x = \frac{4500}{15}, \text{ or } 300$$

(The amount invested was $300.)

Profit and Discount

Profit is the difference between cost and selling price. Given any two of these three values, you can find the third value.

Example:
A merchant earns a 15% profit on an item that costs the merchant $20. Calculate the selling price: $20 + (0.15)($20) = $20 + $3 = $23.

Example:
A merchant sells an item for $44 and earns a 10% profit on the sale. Calculate the amount of the profit:

First, find the cost:
$$(1.10)\,(C) = \$44$$

$$C = \frac{44}{1.1} = 40$$

The cost was $40. Thus, the amount of profit = $4.

Profit can be expressed as either an amount or a percent *over cost*. In other words, percent profit is always calculated based on cost, not on selling price.

Example:
A merchant paying $36 for a certain product resells the product for $48. Find the merchant's percent profit:
The amount of profit = $48 − $36 = $12.

The percent profit $= \dfrac{\$12}{\$36} = 33\dfrac{1}{3}\%$.

Solve problems involving discount in the same way. Always calculate percent discount based on the original price before the discount.

Example:
After a 25% discount, a certain product sells for $15. Find the item's price before the discount:

Calculate the discount based on the original price, before the discount. The discounted price ($15) is 75% of the original price (*P*). Express as an equation, and then solve for *P*:

$$P \times 0.75 = 15$$
$$P = \frac{15}{0.75}$$
$$P = 20$$

The original price (before discount) was $20.

Rate of Travel (Speed) or Production

To calculate speed (rate of travel), divide the distance traveled by the time to travel that distance:

$$\text{rate of travel} = \frac{\text{distance}}{\text{time}}$$

If you know any two of the three terms in this equation, you can find the third term.

Example:
Rachel drives 86 miles in 2 hours. If she drives at the same rate, how far will she drive in 5 hours?

$$\text{Rate} = \frac{86}{2} = 43 \text{ miles per hour}$$

In 5 hours, Rachel will drive $43 \times 5 = 215$ miles.

Example:
At a rate of 24 miles per hour, calculate the number of minutes it would take for a car to travel 40 miles:

$$24 = \frac{40}{t}$$
$$24t = 40$$
$$t = \frac{40}{24}, \text{ or } \frac{5}{3} \text{ hours}$$

To convert to minutes, multiply by 60: $\frac{5}{3} \times 60 = 100$.

It would take the car 100 minutes to travel 40 miles.

Example:

A train departing from station A at 1:00 p.m. travels at an average speed of 46 miles per hour, arriving at station B at 5:30 p.m. Calculate the number of miles the train has traveled:

Time $= 4\dfrac{1}{2}$ hours, or $\dfrac{9}{2}$ hours

$$46 = \dfrac{d}{\dfrac{9}{2}}$$

$$46 = d \times \dfrac{2}{9}$$

$$46 = \dfrac{2d}{9}$$

$$2d = 414$$

$$d = 207 \text{ miles}$$

You solve problems involving rate of production similarly. Here's the general formula:

$$\text{rate of production} = \dfrac{\text{number of units produced}}{\text{time}}$$

Example:

A candy-making machine produces candies at a rate of 240 per hour. Calculate the number of candies the machine can produce in 210 minutes:

A rate of 240 per hour is equivalent to a rate of 240 per 60 minutes.

$$\dfrac{240}{60} = \dfrac{c}{210}$$

$$\dfrac{4}{1} = \dfrac{c}{210}$$

$$(210)(4) = c$$

$$840 = c$$

In 210 minutes, the machine can produce 840 candies.

Weighted Average

The term **weighted average** means that some of the numbers being averaged are given more "weight" than others. To solve a weighted average problem, apply the arithmetic mean formula, but adjust the numbers that are given more weight.

Example:
Soda and tea each cost $1.25 per bottle. Juice costs $2.75 per bottle. Wendy has bought two bottles of tea, three bottles of soda, and one bottle of juice. Calculate Wendy's average cost (*AC*) per bottle:

$$AC = \frac{(2)(1.25) + (3)(1.25) + (1)(2.75)}{6} = \frac{2.50 + 3.75 + 2.75}{6} = \frac{9.00}{6} = 1.50$$

The average cost of Wendy's six beverages is $1.50.

Another type of weighted-average problem involves the averaging of percents (or fractions). The next example shows how to solve this type of problem.

Example:
In a math class, the final exam is worth 60% of a student's final grade, and the midterm exam is worth 40% of a student's final grade. Dan's midterm exam score was 75, and his final grade was 90. Calculate Dan's final-exam score.

$$90 = (0.4)(75) + (0.6)(f)$$

$$90 = 30 + 0.6f$$

$$60 = 0.6f$$

$$100 = f$$

Dan's final-exam score was 100.

Currency (Coins and Bills)

Every type of coin or bill (for example, a dime, a quarter, or a one-dollar bill) has a unique "weight": its monetary value. To solve a currency-counting problem, formulate an algebraic expression that indicates the *number* of each type of currency and that weights that number according to its monetary value.

Example:
Darla has $7.00 in dimes and quarters. She has the same number of dimes as quarters. Calculate the number of quarters:

Letting Q equal the number of quarters and D equal the number of dimes, you can set up the following simple equation:

$$(0.25)Q + (0.10)D = 7.00$$

To make your calculations easier, multiply all terms by 100 to remove decimal places:

$$25Q + 10D = 700$$

Since Darla has the same number of quarters and dimes, substitute Q for D, and then solve for Q:

$$25Q + 10D = 700$$

$$35Q = 700$$

$$Q = \frac{700}{35}$$

$$Q = 20$$

Darla has 20 quarters (and 20 dimes).

Example:
John has seven fewer dimes than nickels, and a total of \$4.25 in nickels and dimes. Calculate how much money John has in nickels:

Letting N equal the number of nickels and D equal the number of dimes, you can set up the following equation:

$$(0.05)N + (0.10)D = 4.25$$

To make your calculations easier, multiply all terms by 100 to remove decimal places:

$$(5)N + (10)D = 425$$

Since John has seven fewer dimes than nickels, substitute $(N - 7)$ for D, and then solve for N:

$$5N + 10(N - 7) = 425$$

$$5N + 10N - 70 = 425$$

$$15N = 495$$

$$N = 33$$

John has 33 nickels (and 26 dimes).

Mixtures
In mixture problems, you combine two or more different substances to create a mixture, which consists of a certain amount of each substance. You can solve a mixture problem by setting up and solving an algebraic equation.

Example:
A granola recipe calls for 4:1 ratio of nuts to raisins by weight. Find how many pounds of raisins are needed to create 15 pounds of granola.

Let R equal the pound weight of raisins and N equal the pound weight of nuts. The sum of the two weights is 15 pounds: $R + N = 15$. Given a 4:1 nut-to-raisin ratio, you can substitute $4R$ for N in this equation and then solve for R:

$$R + 4R = 15$$

$$5R = 15$$

$$R = 3$$

3 pounds of raisins are needed to create 15 pounds of granola.

Example:
A 20-ounce water-syrup mixture contains 20% syrup. Calculate the amount of syrup that must be added to create a mixture that contains 50% syrup.

The mixture originally contained 4 ounces of syrup. Letting S equal the additional syrup added, the amount of syrup after adding more syrup is $(4 + S)$. This amount equals 50% of $(20 + S)$. Set up an equation, and then solve for S:

$$4 + S = (0.5)(20 + S)$$

$$4 + S = 10 + 0.5S$$

$$0.5S = 6$$

$$S = \frac{6}{0.5}, \text{ or } \frac{60}{5}$$

$$S = 12$$

12 ounces of syrup were added to obtain a mixture containing 50% syrup.

Comparing Ages

A word problem might ask you to compare one person's age—either current or past—with another's age. To solve an age problem, you can set up and solve an algebraic equation. An age problem might focus on the *difference* in age between two people, which always remains constant. For instance, someone 3 years older than you will always be 3 years older than you.

Example:
Pam is currently 12 years older than Quincy was 8 years ago. If Quincy's current age is 21 years, find Pam's current age:

Subtract 12 from Pam's current age to find Quincy's age 8 years ago. Here's the equation: $P - 12 = Q - 8$. Solve for P:

$$P - 12 = 21 - 8$$

$$P - 12 = 13$$

$$P = 25$$

Pam is currently 25 years old.

An age problem might instead focus on the *ratio* of one person's age to another's. This ratio changes from each year to the next.

Example:
P's age is twice Q's age, and R's age is 50 percent greater than Q's age. If Q's current age is 40 years, calculate the age difference between P and R:

Based on the given information, you can write two equations:

$$P = 2Q$$

$$R = \frac{3}{2}Q$$

Given $Q = 40$, you can find P and R and, in turn, the difference between P and R:

$$P = (2)(40) = 80$$

$$R = \left(\frac{3}{2}\right)(40) = 60$$

The age difference between P and R is 20.

Converting Units of Measurement

In solving some word problems, you'll need to convert one unit of measurement to another.

Example:
Find the number of feet in 80% of one yard.

This problem is essentially asking, "3 feet is to 1 yard as how many feet are to 0.8 yards?" To solve the problem, equate two ratios, each of which you can express as a fraction. Use the *cross-product method* (multiplying numerator by denominator across the equality sign), and then solve for the missing value (x):

$$\frac{3}{1} = \frac{x}{0.8}$$

$$(1)(x) = (3)(0.8)$$

$$x = 2.4$$

If you need to convert between a U.S. system and a metric system, the test will provide the conversion rate you need to solve the problem.

Example:
At the rate of 5 miles in 3 minutes, find the number of minutes it would take a plane to travel 4 kilometers. [1 mile = 1.6 kilometers]

This problem is essentially asking, "5 miles is to 3 minutes as 4 kilometers is to how many minutes?" To solve the problem, equate two ratios, each of which you can express as a fraction: $\frac{5m}{3} = \frac{4k}{x}$. Next, convert miles to kilometers by multiplying the numerator in the left-hand fraction by 1.6. Then, use the cross-product method to quickly solve for the missing value (x):

$$\frac{5m}{3} = \frac{4k}{x}$$

$$\frac{(5)(1.6)k}{3} = \frac{4k}{x}$$

$$\frac{8k}{3} = \frac{4k}{x}$$

$$x = 1.5$$

It would take the plane 1.5 minutes to travel 4 kilometers.

Don't count on the exam providing the conversion rate you need to solve the problem. To be safe, memorize the following conversion rates:

Fluid ounces
8 ounces = 1 cup
2 cups = 1 pint
2 pints = 1 quart

4 quarts = 1 gallon

Pound weight
16 ounces = 1 pound
2,000 pounds = 1 ton

Metric weight
1000 milligrams = 1 gram
1000 grams = 1 kilogram

Foot lengths
12 inches = 1 foot
3 feet = 1 yard
5,280 feet = 1 mile

Metric lengths
10 millimeters = 1 centimeter
100 centimeters = 1 meter
1000 meters = 1 kilometer

Basic Geometry and Coordinate Geometry

In this section, you'll review the basics of plane and coordinate geometry:

- Angles formed by intersecting lines
- Polygons
- Triangles (including isosceles, equilateral, and right triangles)
- Quadrilaterals (including squares and other rectangles, parallelograms, and trapezoids)
- Circles
- Rectangular solids
- Right cylinders
- Coordinate geometry (defining and plotting points and lines on the standard *xy*-coordinate plane)

Angles and Intersecting Lines

You should know the following terms and symbols relating to angles, which are created by intersecting lines:

vertex: the point where two lines intersect, forming two or more angles
degree: the unit of measurement for the size of angles (shown by the symbol °)
complementary angles: two or more angles whose degree measures total 90°
supplementary angles: two or more angles whose degree measures total 180°
vertical angles: angles across the vertex from each other and formed by the same two lines
congruent angles: angles whose degree measures are equal (congruency is shown by the symbol $\cong$)

Here are the basic properties of angles formed by intersecting lines:

- Vertical angles are congruent (the same size).
- Where angles combine to form a straight line, the sum of their measures is 180°.
- Two intersecting lines create four angles. The sum of the measures of the four angles is 360°.

Example:

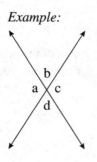

In the figure above:

- $\angle a$ and $\angle b$ are supplementary (m$\angle a$ + m$\angle b$ = 180°)
- $\angle b$ and $\angle c$ are also supplementary (m$\angle b$ + m$\angle c$ = 180°)
- $\angle c$ and $\angle d$ are also supplementary (m$\angle c$ + m$\angle d$ = 180°)
- $\angle a$ and $\angle d$ are also supplementary (m$\angle a$ + m$\angle d$ = 180°)
- $\angle b$ is vertical to $\angle d$, and so $\angle b \cong \angle d$
- $\angle a$ is vertical to $\angle c$, and so $\angle a \cong \angle c$
- m$\angle a$ + m$\angle b$ + m$\angle c$ + m$\angle d$ = 360°
- If you know the measure of any of the four angles, you can find the measures of the other three angles. For example, if m$\angle a$ = 100°, then m$\angle b$ = 80°, m$\angle c$ = 100°, and m$\angle d$ = 80°.

You should also know the following additional terms and symbols:

right angle: a 90° angle (often indicated by a square box at the angle's vertex)
perpendicular lines: two lines that intersect at 90° angles (shown by the symbol $\perp$)
parallel lines: two lines that do not intersect (shown by the symbol $\parallel$)
acute angle: an angle measuring less than 90°
obtuse angle: an angle measuring greater than 90° but less than 180°

Here are the features of angles formed by the intersection of parallel and perpendicular lines:

- The intersection of two perpendicular lines creates four right angles.
- The two vertexes formed by a line intersecting two parallel lines are identical (all corresponding angles are congruent).

Examples:

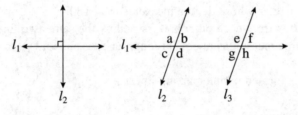

The left-hand figure shows a right angle. Thus, $l_1 \perp l_2$, and all four angles at the vertex are congruent—they each measure 90°. In the right-hand figure, given $l_2 \parallel l_3$:

- $m\angle a = m\angle d = m\angle e = m\angle h$
- $m\angle b = m\angle c = m\angle f = m\angle g$
- If you know the measure of any of the eight angles, you can find the measures of the other seven angles.
- If one angle is a right angle, then all eight angles must be right angles. Otherwise, four of the angles must be acute, while the other four must be obtuse.

Polygons

A **polygon** is a 2-dimensional figure (on a plane) formed only by straight lines. Here are some common types of polygons:

triangle: 3-sided polygon
quadrilateral: 4-sided polygon
pentagon: 5-sided polygon
hexagon: 6-sided polygon
heptagon: 7-sided polygon
octagon: 8-sided polygon

In a **regular polygon,** all sides are congruent (equal in length), and all angles are congruent (equal in size). Here are the angle measures of certain regular polygons:

Regular triangle (3 sides): each angle = 60° (total = 180°)
Regular quadrilateral (a square): each angle = 90° (total = 360°)
Regular pentagon (5 sides): each angle = 108° (total = 540°)
Regular hexagon (6 sides): each angle = 120° (total = 720°)
Regular octagon (8 sides): each angle = 135° (total = 1,080°)

Triangles

All triangles share the following properties:

- The sum of the lengths of any two sides is greater than the length of the third side.
- The combined measure of the three interior angles is 180°.
- Interior angles rank in size according to the lengths of the sides opposite the angles.
- Area $= \frac{1}{2} \times$ base $\times$ height. (You can use any side as the base to calculate area. The height is not necessarily the length of any side.)

Example:

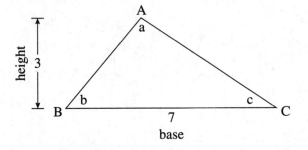

In the figure above:

- $AB + AC > BC$, $AB + BC > AC$, and $AC + BC > AB$
- $m\angle a + m\angle b + m\angle c = 180°$
- If you know the measure of any two interior angles, you can find the measure of the third. For example, if $m\angle b = 50°$ and $m\angle c = 35°$, then $m\angle a = 95°$.
- If $AB < AC < BC$ (as the figure appears to show), then $m\angle c < m\angle b < m\angle a$.
- Area $= \frac{1}{2} \times 7 \times 3 = 10\frac{1}{2}$ square units

You should also be familiar with the following four specific types of triangles:

isosceles triangle: Two sides are congruent (and the two angles opposite those sides are congruent).
equilateral triangle: All three sides are congruent (and all three angles are congruent).
right triangle: One of the interior angles is a right angle.
right isosceles triangle: A right triangle in which the two sides forming the right angle are congruent.

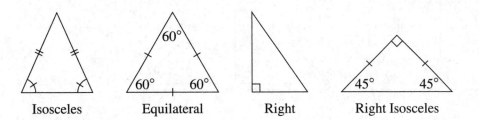

| Isosceles | Equilateral | Right | Right Isosceles |

Given the measures of two interior angles, you can determine whether a triangle is isosceles, equilateral, or right.

Examples:

If two of a triangle's interior angles measure 80° and 50°, then the third angle must measure 50°, and the triangle is *isosceles.*

If two of a triangle's interior angles both measure 60°, then the third angle must also measure 60°, and the triangle is *equilateral.*

If two of a triangle's interior angles measure 65° and 25°, then the third angle must measure 90°, and the triangle is *right.*

If two of a triangle's interior angles measure 45° and 45°, then the third angle must measure 90°, and the triangle is *right* and *isosceles.*

The two sides forming the 90° angle of a right triangle are the triangle's base and height. Thus, given the lengths of these two sides, you can easily find the triangle's area.

Examples:

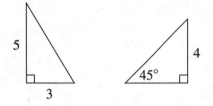

Find the area of the left-hand triangle above:

$$Area = \frac{1}{2} \times 5 \times 3 = 7\frac{1}{2} \text{ square units.}$$

Find the area of the right-hand triangle above:

Given two interior angles 90° and 45°, the third angle must measure 45°, and the two sides forming the 90° angle are congruent (base = 4; height = 4). $Area = \frac{1}{2} \times 4 \times 4 = 8$ square units.

A line bisecting any angle divides an equilateral triangle into two right triangles (each one half the area of the large triangle). Similarly, a line bisecting the 90° angle of a right isosceles triangle divides that triangle into two right isosceles triangles (each one half the area of the large triangle).

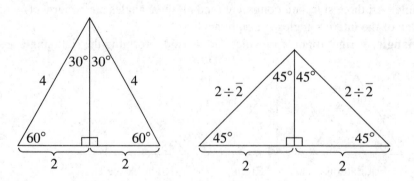

Quadrilaterals

Quadrilaterals are four-sided figures. You should be especially familiar with the following types of quadrilaterals:

parallelogram: Opposite sides are congruent and parallel; opposite angles are congruent.
rectangle: Opposite sides are congruent and parallel; all interior angles measure 90°.
square: All four sides are congruent; all interior angles measure 90°.
trapezoid: Two sides are parallel (the other two sides are not parallel).

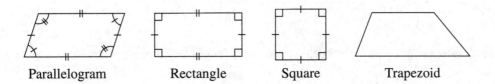

Parallelogram   Rectangle   Square   Trapezoid

A square is actually a specific type of rectangle, which is a specific type of parallelogram. In all four types, the combined measure of all four interior angles is 360°.

You should know how to find the **perimeter** (the combined length of all sides) and *area* of each of these three types of quadrilaterals. In the figures below, l = length and w = width:

Rectangle
Perimeter = $2l + 2w$
Area = $l \times w$

Square
Perimeter = $4s$ [s = side]
Area = s^2

Parallelogram
Perimeter = $2l + 2w$
Area = base (b) × height (h)

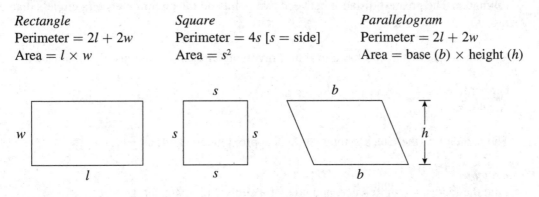

Example:
A rectangle has a length of 8 feet and a width of 4 feet. Find the perimeter and area:
Perimeter = $2l + 2w$ = (2)(8) + (2)(4) = 16 + 8 = 24 feet. Area = 8 × 4 = 32 square feet.

Example:
A square has an area of 8 square inches. Find the length of each side:
The length of each side = $\sqrt{8} = 2\sqrt{2}$ inches.

Example:
One interior angle of a parallelogram measures 60°. Find the other three angles:
The opposite angle also measures 60°. The two other angles (which are opposite each other) measure 120°.

Example:
The length of a rectangle with a perimeter of 20 centimeters is one centimeter longer than the rectangle's width. Find the rectangle's length and width:

Substitute $(w + 1)$ for l in the perimeter formula, then solve for w:

$$2(w + 1) + 2w = 20$$

$$2w + 2 + 2w = 20$$

$$4w = 18$$

$$w = 4.5$$

The rectangle's width = 4.5 centimeters, and so its length = 5.5 centimeters.

Circles

You should be familiar with the following terms relating to circles:

circumference: The set of all points equidistant from a circle's center (the circle's "perimeter").
radius: The distance from a circle's center to any point along its circumference.
diameter: The greatest distance between two points on the circumference (a circle's diameter is twice its radius).

You should know the two basic formulas involving circles (r = radius, d = diameter):

Circumference = $2\pi r$, or πd
Area = πr^2

The value of π (the Greek symbol "pi") is approximately 3.14, or $\dfrac{22}{7}$.

Example:
Find the radius, circumference, and area of a circle with diameter 4.

Radius = 2
Circumference = $2\pi(2) = 4\pi$
Area = $\pi(2)^2 = 4\pi$

Example:
Find the circumference of a circle with area 36π.
First, find the radius:

Area $(36\pi) = \pi r^2$

$$\frac{36\pi}{\pi} = r^2$$

$$36 = r^2$$

$$\sqrt{36} = r$$

Now you can find the circumference: $2\pi r = 2\pi(6) = 12\pi$.

Rectangular Solids

A **rectangular solid** is essentially a three-dimensional box in which all angles measure 90°. You should know how to find the **surface area** (the combined area of all 6 faces) and **volume** (amount of cubic space) of any rectangular solid. In the following two formulas, l = length, w = width, and h = height:

Surface area = $2lw + 2hw + 2hl = 2(lw + hw + hl)$
Volume = $l \times w \times h$

Example:
Find the volume of a rectangular solid with dimensions 3, 7, and 5 inches.

Volume = $l \times w \times h = 3 \times 7 \times 5 = 105$ cubic inches.

Example:
Find the height of a rectangular solid with volume 20, length 2, and width 4.

Volume (20) = $2 \times 4 \times h$
$20 = 8h$
$2.5 = h$

Example:
A rectangular solid has a volume of 16 cubic feet. Its height is twice its length, and its length is the same as its width. Find the total surface area of the solid.
In the volume formula, substitute w for l and $2w$ for h, and then solve for w:

Volume (16) = $l \times w \times h = w \times w \times 2w = 2w^3$
$16 = 2w^3$
$8 = w^3$
$2 = w$

Thus, $l = 2$ and $h = 4$. Now you can calculate the surface area: $2(4 + 8 + 8) = 40$ square feet.

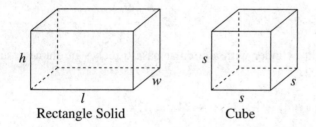

Rectangle Solid   Cube

A **cube** is a special type of rectangular solid in which all three dimensions are the same: length = width = height. Each face of a cube is a square. To find a cube's surface area and volume, apply these formulas (s = the length of any edge of the cube):

Surface Area = $6s^2$
Volume = s^3

Example:
A cube's volume is 32 cubic feet. Find the length of each side.
Volume $= s^3$, it follows that $s = \sqrt[3]{\text{Volume}} = \sqrt[3]{32} = 2\sqrt[3]{4}$.

Example:
One face of a cube has a surface area of 8 square inches. Find the cube's volume.
First, find the length of any side 9(*s*): $s = \sqrt{8}$. Now you can find the volume: $V = s^3 = \left(\sqrt{8}\right)^3 = 8\sqrt{8} = 16\sqrt{2}$.

Right Cylinders

A **right cylinder** is a three-dimensional tube (see the figure below). The total surface area of a right cylinder is the combined area of its circular base, its circular top, and the rectangular surface around the cylinder's vertical face. (Visualize a rectangular label wrapped around a soup can.)

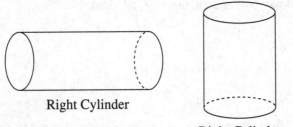

Right Cylinder

Right Cylinder

In other words, surface area is the sum of two circles and one rectangle. Here's the formula (*r* = radius and *h* = height):

Surface Area $(SA) = \pi r^2 + \pi r^2 + (2\pi r)(h)$

To find the volume of a right cylinder, multiply the area of its circular base by its height:

Volume $= \pi r^2 h$

Example:
Find the total surface area of a right cylinder with a circular base 6 inches in diameter and a height of 4 inches.

Surface Area $= \pi(3)^2 + \pi(3)^2 + 2\pi(3)(4) = 9\pi + 9\pi + 24\pi = 42\pi$.

Example:
Find the volume of a right cylinder with a circular base 4 inches in diameter and a height of 5 inches.

Volume $= \pi r^2 h = \pi(2)^2(5) = 20\pi$ cubic inches.

The xy-Coordinate Plane

The figure below shows the standard *xy*-**coordinate plane.** The horizontal axis, or *x*-**axis,** shows the horizontal location of any point on the plane. The vertical axis, or **y-axis,** shows the vertical location of any point on the plane. You can define any point on the plane by its unique pair of *x* and *y* coordinates (*x,y*). The figure below shows the coordinate signs (positive or negative) of points in the four different quadrants of the plane.

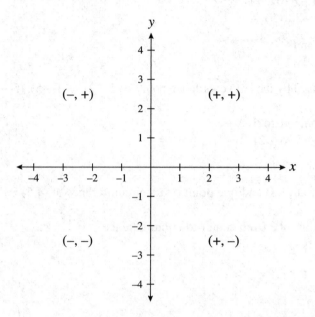

The next figure shows various points plotted on the *xy*-coordinate plane. Any point along the *x*-axis has a *y*-coordinate of zero (0), while any point along the *y*-axis has an *x*-coordinate of zero (0). At the center of the coordinate plane is the **origin,** where both coordinates are zero: (*x,y*) = (0,0).

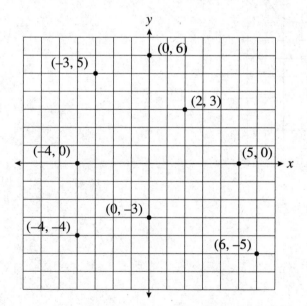

You can easily find the length of any horizontal or vertical line on the plane: Simply count the units from one point to the other. Using this method, you can easily determine the characteristics of right triangles, rectangles, and circles plotted neatly on the plane.

Examples:

Find the area of a triangle defined by the (*x,y*) coordinate points (−2,2), (−5,−5), and (−2,−5).

Base = 3 (horizontal distance from −5 to −2)
Height = 7 (vertical distance from −2 to 5)
Area = $\frac{1}{2} \times 3 \times 7 = 10\frac{1}{2}$ square units

Find the perimeter of a rectangle defined by the (*x,y*) coordinate points (−1,−2), (−1,−5), (5,−2), and (5,−5).

Length = 6 (horizontal distance from −1 to 5)
Height = 3 (vertical distance from −5 to −2)
Perimeter = 2(6) + (2)3 = 18

Find the area of a circle with center at (4,3) and one point on its circumference at (4,5).

Radius = 2 (horizontal or vertical distance from center to circumference)
Area = $\pi r^2 = \pi 2^2 = 4\pi$ square units

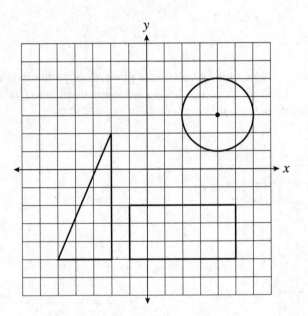

PART

5 PRACTICE TESTS

COOP PRACTICE TEST 1

Answer Sheet

Directions: For each answer that you select, blacken the corresponding oval on this sheet.

Sequences

1. Ⓐ Ⓑ Ⓒ Ⓓ
2. Ⓕ Ⓖ Ⓗ Ⓙ
3. Ⓐ Ⓑ Ⓒ Ⓓ
4. Ⓕ Ⓖ Ⓗ Ⓙ
5. Ⓐ Ⓑ Ⓒ Ⓓ
6. Ⓕ Ⓖ Ⓗ Ⓙ
7. Ⓐ Ⓑ Ⓒ Ⓓ
8. Ⓕ Ⓖ Ⓗ Ⓙ
9. Ⓐ Ⓑ Ⓒ Ⓓ
10. Ⓕ Ⓖ Ⓗ Ⓙ
11. Ⓐ Ⓑ Ⓒ Ⓓ
12. Ⓕ Ⓖ Ⓗ Ⓙ
13. Ⓐ Ⓑ Ⓒ Ⓓ
14. Ⓕ Ⓖ Ⓗ Ⓙ
15. Ⓐ Ⓑ Ⓒ Ⓓ
16. Ⓕ Ⓖ Ⓗ Ⓙ
17. Ⓐ Ⓑ Ⓒ Ⓓ
18. Ⓕ Ⓖ Ⓗ Ⓙ
19. Ⓐ Ⓑ Ⓒ Ⓓ
20. Ⓕ Ⓖ Ⓗ Ⓙ

Quantitative Reasoning

1. Ⓐ Ⓑ Ⓒ Ⓓ
2. Ⓕ Ⓖ Ⓗ Ⓙ
3. Ⓐ Ⓑ Ⓒ Ⓓ
4. Ⓕ Ⓖ Ⓗ Ⓙ
5. Ⓐ Ⓑ Ⓒ Ⓓ
6. Ⓕ Ⓖ Ⓗ Ⓙ
7. Ⓐ Ⓑ Ⓒ Ⓓ
8. Ⓕ Ⓖ Ⓗ Ⓙ
9. Ⓐ Ⓑ Ⓒ Ⓓ
10. Ⓕ Ⓖ Ⓗ Ⓙ
11. Ⓐ Ⓑ Ⓒ Ⓓ
12. Ⓕ Ⓖ Ⓗ Ⓙ
13. Ⓐ Ⓑ Ⓒ Ⓓ
14. Ⓕ Ⓖ Ⓗ Ⓙ
15. Ⓐ Ⓑ Ⓒ Ⓓ
16. Ⓕ Ⓖ Ⓗ Ⓙ
17. Ⓐ Ⓑ Ⓒ Ⓓ
18. Ⓕ Ⓖ Ⓗ Ⓙ
19. Ⓐ Ⓑ Ⓒ Ⓓ
20. Ⓕ Ⓖ Ⓗ Ⓙ

Verbal Reasoning—Context

1. Ⓐ Ⓑ Ⓒ Ⓓ
2. Ⓕ Ⓖ Ⓗ Ⓙ
3. Ⓐ Ⓑ Ⓒ Ⓓ
4. Ⓕ Ⓖ Ⓗ Ⓙ
5. Ⓐ Ⓑ Ⓒ Ⓓ
6. Ⓕ Ⓖ Ⓗ Ⓙ
7. Ⓐ Ⓑ Ⓒ Ⓓ
8. Ⓕ Ⓖ Ⓗ Ⓙ
9. Ⓐ Ⓑ Ⓒ Ⓓ
10. Ⓕ Ⓖ Ⓗ Ⓙ
11. Ⓐ Ⓑ Ⓒ Ⓓ
12. Ⓕ Ⓖ Ⓗ Ⓙ
13. Ⓐ Ⓑ Ⓒ Ⓓ
14. Ⓕ Ⓖ Ⓗ Ⓙ
15. Ⓐ Ⓑ Ⓒ Ⓓ
16. Ⓕ Ⓖ Ⓗ Ⓙ
17. Ⓐ Ⓑ Ⓒ Ⓓ
18. Ⓕ Ⓖ Ⓗ Ⓙ
19. Ⓐ Ⓑ Ⓒ Ⓓ
20. Ⓕ Ⓖ Ⓗ Ⓙ

Analogies

1. Ⓐ Ⓑ Ⓒ Ⓓ
2. Ⓕ Ⓖ Ⓗ Ⓙ
3. Ⓐ Ⓑ Ⓒ Ⓓ
4. Ⓕ Ⓖ Ⓗ Ⓙ
5. Ⓐ Ⓑ Ⓒ Ⓓ
6. Ⓕ Ⓖ Ⓗ Ⓙ
7. Ⓐ Ⓑ Ⓒ Ⓓ
8. Ⓕ Ⓖ Ⓗ Ⓙ
9. Ⓐ Ⓑ Ⓒ Ⓓ
10. Ⓕ Ⓖ Ⓗ Ⓙ
11. Ⓐ Ⓑ Ⓒ Ⓓ
12. Ⓕ Ⓖ Ⓗ Ⓙ
13. Ⓐ Ⓑ Ⓒ Ⓓ
14. Ⓕ Ⓖ Ⓗ Ⓙ
15. Ⓐ Ⓑ Ⓒ Ⓓ
16. Ⓕ Ⓖ Ⓗ Ⓙ
17. Ⓐ Ⓑ Ⓒ Ⓓ
18. Ⓕ Ⓖ Ⓗ Ⓙ
19. Ⓐ Ⓑ Ⓒ Ⓓ
20. Ⓕ Ⓖ Ⓗ Ⓙ

Verbal Reasoning—Words

1. Ⓐ Ⓑ Ⓒ Ⓓ
2. Ⓕ Ⓖ Ⓗ Ⓙ
3. Ⓐ Ⓑ Ⓒ Ⓓ
4. Ⓕ Ⓖ Ⓗ Ⓙ
5. Ⓐ Ⓑ Ⓒ Ⓓ
6. Ⓕ Ⓖ Ⓗ Ⓙ
7. Ⓐ Ⓑ Ⓒ Ⓓ
8. Ⓕ Ⓖ Ⓗ Ⓙ
9. Ⓐ Ⓑ Ⓒ Ⓓ
10. Ⓕ Ⓖ Ⓗ Ⓙ
11. Ⓐ Ⓑ Ⓒ Ⓓ
12. Ⓕ Ⓖ Ⓗ Ⓙ
13. Ⓐ Ⓑ Ⓒ Ⓓ
14. Ⓕ Ⓖ Ⓗ Ⓙ
15. Ⓐ Ⓑ Ⓒ Ⓓ
16. Ⓕ Ⓖ Ⓗ Ⓙ
17. Ⓐ Ⓑ Ⓒ Ⓓ
18. Ⓕ Ⓖ Ⓗ Ⓙ
19. Ⓐ Ⓑ Ⓒ Ⓓ
20. Ⓕ Ⓖ Ⓗ Ⓙ

Reading and Language Arts

1. Ⓐ Ⓑ Ⓒ Ⓓ
2. Ⓕ Ⓖ Ⓗ Ⓙ
3. Ⓐ Ⓑ Ⓒ Ⓓ
4. Ⓕ Ⓖ Ⓗ Ⓙ
5. Ⓐ Ⓑ Ⓒ Ⓓ
6. Ⓕ Ⓖ Ⓗ Ⓙ
7. Ⓐ Ⓑ Ⓒ Ⓓ
8. Ⓕ Ⓖ Ⓗ Ⓙ
9. Ⓐ Ⓑ Ⓒ Ⓓ
10. Ⓕ Ⓖ Ⓗ Ⓙ
11. Ⓐ Ⓑ Ⓒ Ⓓ
12. Ⓕ Ⓖ Ⓗ Ⓙ
13. Ⓐ Ⓑ Ⓒ Ⓓ
14. Ⓕ Ⓖ Ⓗ Ⓙ
15. Ⓐ Ⓑ Ⓒ Ⓓ
16. Ⓕ Ⓖ Ⓗ Ⓙ
17. Ⓐ Ⓑ Ⓒ Ⓓ
18. Ⓕ Ⓖ Ⓗ Ⓙ
19. Ⓐ Ⓑ Ⓒ Ⓓ
20. Ⓕ Ⓖ Ⓗ Ⓙ

COOP PRACTICE TEST 1

Answer Sheet *(continued)*

21.	Ⓐ Ⓑ Ⓒ Ⓓ			21.	Ⓐ Ⓑ Ⓒ Ⓓ			
22.	Ⓕ Ⓖ Ⓗ Ⓙ			22.	Ⓕ Ⓖ Ⓗ Ⓙ			
23.	Ⓐ Ⓑ Ⓒ Ⓓ			23.	Ⓐ Ⓑ Ⓒ Ⓓ			
24.	Ⓕ Ⓖ Ⓗ Ⓙ			24.	Ⓕ Ⓖ Ⓗ Ⓙ			
25.	Ⓐ Ⓑ Ⓒ Ⓓ			25.	Ⓐ Ⓑ Ⓒ Ⓓ			
26.	Ⓕ Ⓖ Ⓗ Ⓙ			26.	Ⓕ Ⓖ Ⓗ Ⓙ			
27.	Ⓐ Ⓑ Ⓒ Ⓓ			27.	Ⓐ Ⓑ Ⓒ Ⓓ			
28.	Ⓕ Ⓖ Ⓗ Ⓙ			28.	Ⓕ Ⓖ Ⓗ Ⓙ			
29.	Ⓐ Ⓑ Ⓒ Ⓓ			29.	Ⓐ Ⓑ Ⓒ Ⓓ			
30.	Ⓕ Ⓖ Ⓗ Ⓙ			30.	Ⓕ Ⓖ Ⓗ Ⓙ			
31.	Ⓐ Ⓑ Ⓒ Ⓓ			31.	Ⓐ Ⓑ Ⓒ Ⓓ			
32.	Ⓕ Ⓖ Ⓗ Ⓙ			32.	Ⓕ Ⓖ Ⓗ Ⓙ			
33.	Ⓐ Ⓑ Ⓒ Ⓓ			33.	Ⓐ Ⓑ Ⓒ Ⓓ			
34.	Ⓕ Ⓖ Ⓗ Ⓙ			34.	Ⓕ Ⓖ Ⓗ Ⓙ			
35.	Ⓐ Ⓑ Ⓒ Ⓓ			35.	Ⓐ Ⓑ Ⓒ Ⓓ			
36.	Ⓕ Ⓖ Ⓗ Ⓙ			36.	Ⓕ Ⓖ Ⓗ Ⓙ			
37.	Ⓐ Ⓑ Ⓒ Ⓓ			37.	Ⓐ Ⓑ Ⓒ Ⓓ			
38.	Ⓕ Ⓖ Ⓗ Ⓙ			38.	Ⓕ Ⓖ Ⓗ Ⓙ			
39.	Ⓐ Ⓑ Ⓒ Ⓓ			39.	Ⓐ Ⓑ Ⓒ Ⓓ			
40.	Ⓕ Ⓖ Ⓗ Ⓙ			40.	Ⓕ Ⓖ Ⓗ Ⓙ			

Mathematics

1. Ⓐ Ⓑ Ⓒ Ⓓ
2. Ⓕ Ⓖ Ⓗ Ⓙ
3. Ⓐ Ⓑ Ⓒ Ⓓ
4. Ⓕ Ⓖ Ⓗ Ⓙ
5. Ⓐ Ⓑ Ⓒ Ⓓ
6. Ⓕ Ⓖ Ⓗ Ⓙ
7. Ⓐ Ⓑ Ⓒ Ⓓ
8. Ⓕ Ⓖ Ⓗ Ⓙ
9. Ⓐ Ⓑ Ⓒ Ⓓ
10. Ⓕ Ⓖ Ⓗ Ⓙ
11. Ⓐ Ⓑ Ⓒ Ⓓ
12. Ⓕ Ⓖ Ⓗ Ⓙ
13. Ⓐ Ⓑ Ⓒ Ⓓ
14. Ⓕ Ⓖ Ⓗ Ⓙ
15. Ⓐ Ⓑ Ⓒ Ⓓ
16. Ⓕ Ⓖ Ⓗ Ⓙ
17. Ⓐ Ⓑ Ⓒ Ⓓ
18. Ⓕ Ⓖ Ⓗ Ⓙ
19. Ⓐ Ⓑ Ⓒ Ⓓ
20. Ⓕ Ⓖ Ⓗ Ⓙ

COOP PRACTICE TEST 1

Sequences (20 Questions, 15 Minutes)

Directions: Choose the answer that will best continue or complete the sequence or pattern.

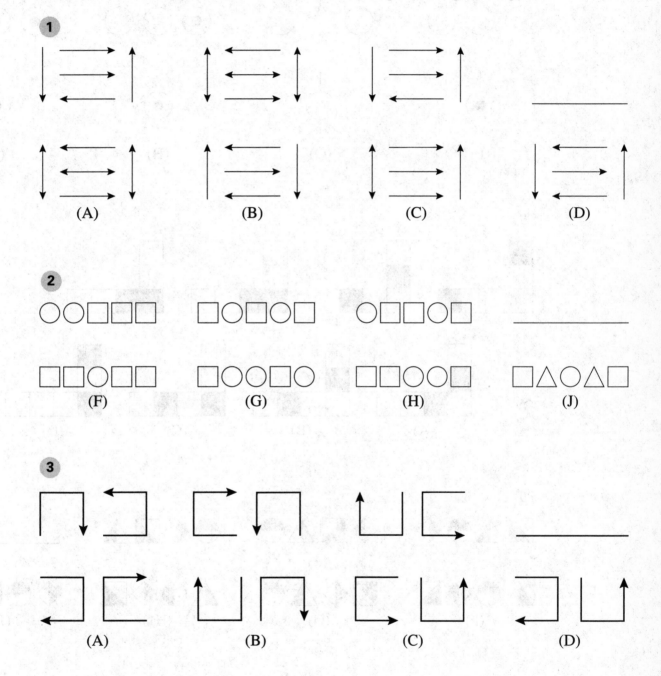

Sequences *(continued)*

4

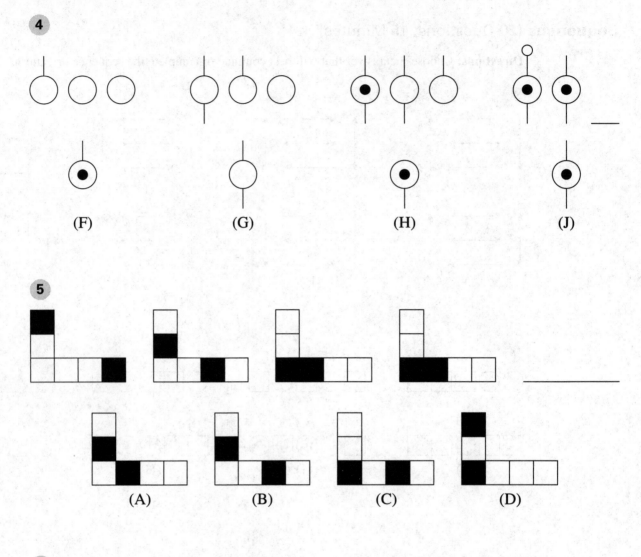

5

6

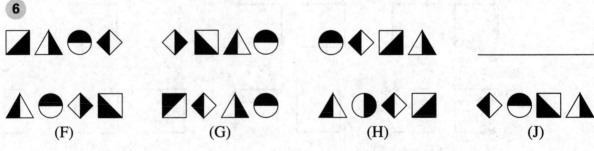

Sequences (continued)

7 c e g i k __

- **A** j
- **B** l
- **C** m
- **D** h

8 f h g i __ i k

- **F** h k
- **G** h j
- **H** j h
- **J** g h

9 A B D | D E G | G H K | ____

- **A** L M N
- **B** K M N
- **C** I L M
- **D** K L N

10 Z Y A | X W B | V U C | ____

- **F** T S R
- **G** R T F
- **H** S T D
- **J** T S D

11 g f h | j i k | ____ | p o q

- **A** l m n
- **B** m l n
- **C** l n m
- **D** m o n

12 B C C | D C E | F C G | ____

- **F** H C I
- **G** C I F
- **H** H I J
- **J** E C H

13 $A_1 2$ | $B_2 2$ | $C_3 2$ | ____

- **A** $C_2 2$
- **B** $D_4 4$
- **C** $D_4 2$
- **D** $D_5 2$

14 $8B^3G$ | $6D^5E$ | ____ | $2H^9A$

- **F** $5F^7B$
- **G** $4FC^4$
- **H** $4G^6D$
- **J** $4F^7C$

15 1 2 4 5 7 8 ____

- **A** 9 10
- **B** 10 11
- **C** 11 12
- **D** 9 11

16 24 12 6 3 __

- **F** $\frac{3}{2}$
- **G** 1
- **H** 2
- **J** $\frac{2}{3}$

17 9 6 3 | 8 5 2 | __ 4 1

- **A** 3
- **B** 5
- **C** 9
- **D** 7

18 3 9 81 | 2 4 16 | 1 1 __

- **F** 4
- **G** 3
- **H** 2
- **J** 1

19 64 16 4 | 16 4 1 | 48 12 __

- **A** 3
- **B** 2
- **C** 6
- **D** 4

20 1.5 6 2 | 6 24 8 | 9 __ 12

- **F** 16
- **G** 30
- **H** 36
- **J** 24

STOP!
If you finish before time runs out, check your work on this section only.

Analogies (20 Questions, 7 Minutes)

Directions: For questions 1–20, the two upper pictures are related in some way. Select a picture that fills in the space so that the two lower pictures are related in the same way.

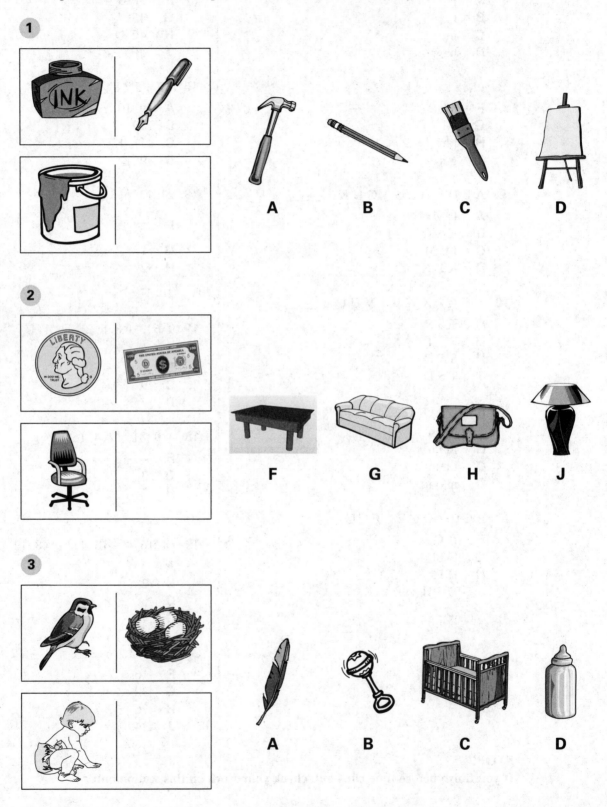

Analogies *(continued)*

4

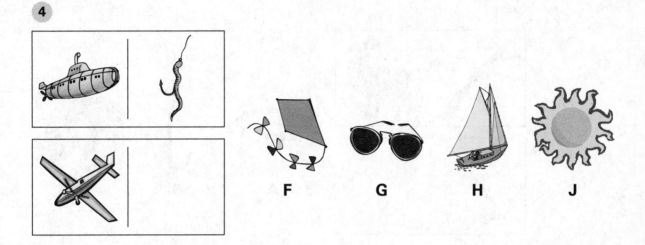

5

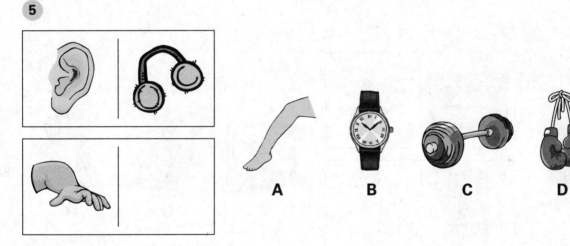

6

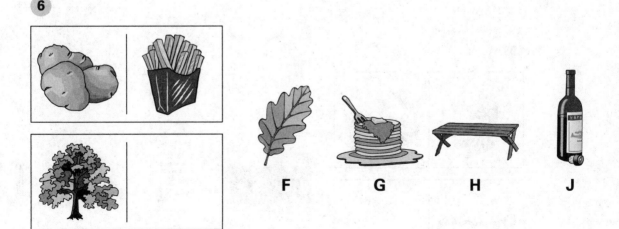

Analogies *(continued)*

7

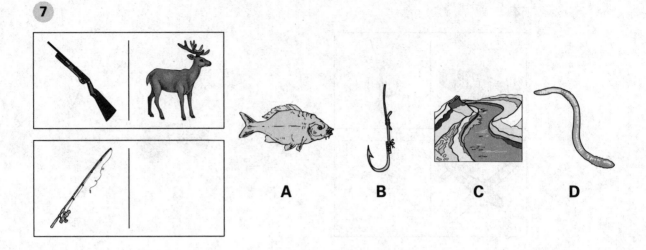

A   **B**   **C**   **D**

8

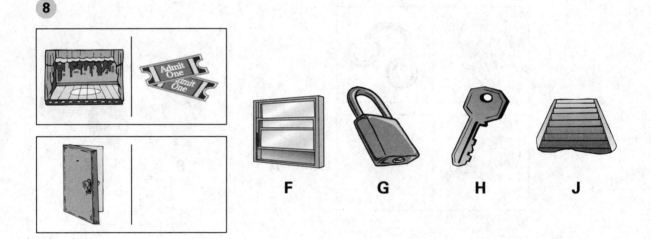

F   **G**   **H**   **J**

9

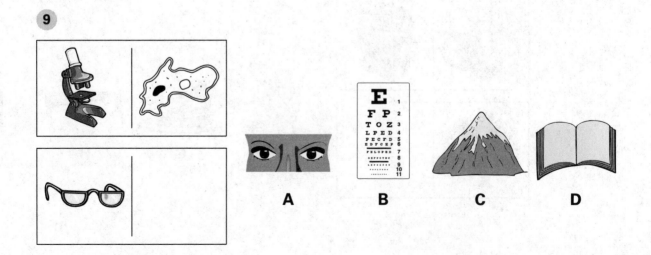

A   **B**   **C**   **D**

Analogies *(continued)*

10

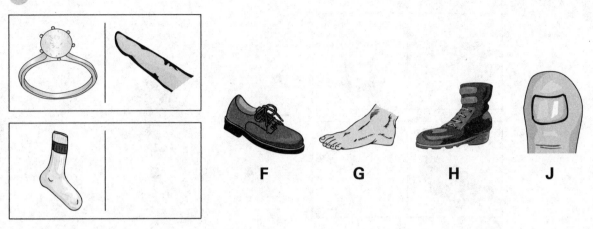

    F   **G**   **H**   **J**

11

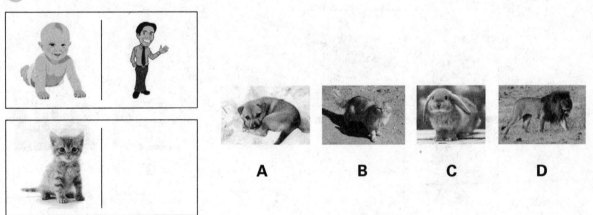

    A   **B**   **C**   **D**

12

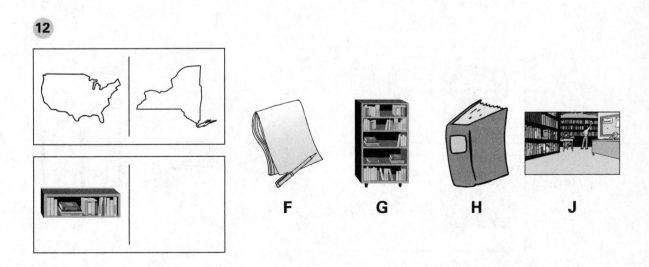

    F   **G**   **H**   **J**

Analogies *(continued)*

13

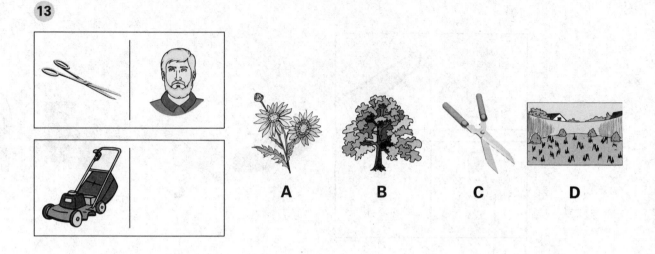

A   B   C   D

14

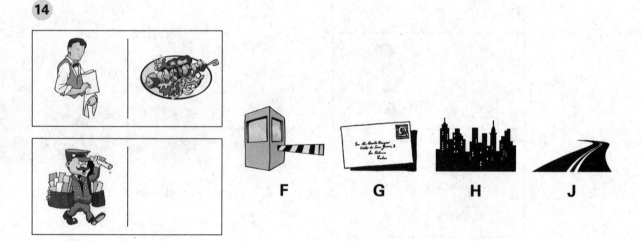

F   G   H   J

15

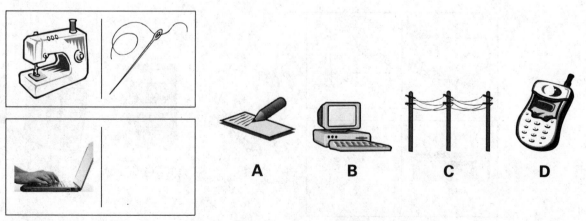

A   B   C   D

Analogies (continued)

16

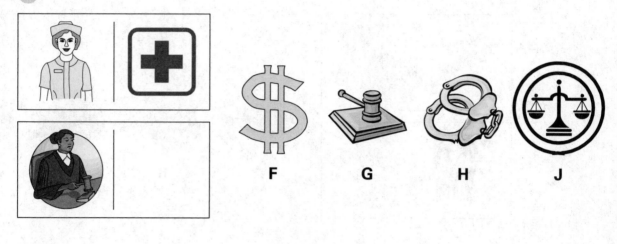

F   G   H   J

17

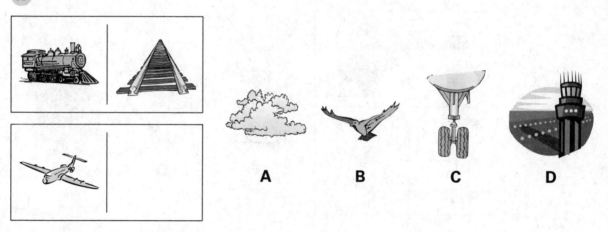

A   B   C   D

18

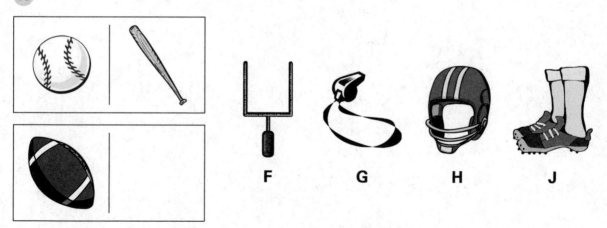

F   G   H   J

Analogies *(continued)*

19

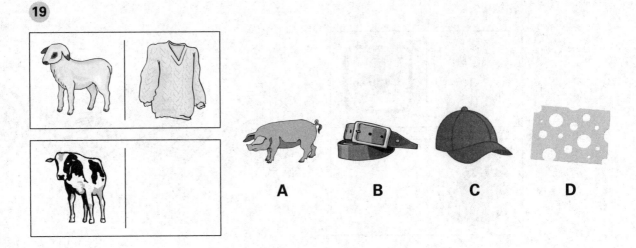

20

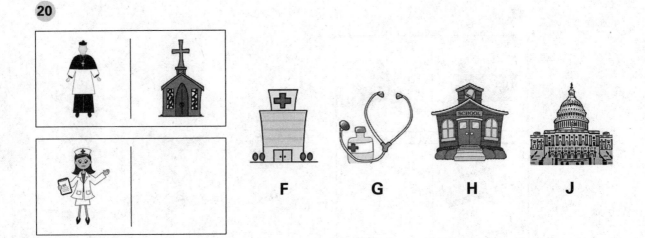

STOP!
If you finish before time runs out, check your work on this section only.

Quantitative Reasoning (20 Questions, 15 Minutes)

Directions: For questions 1–7, find the operation (fill in the blank) that is applied to the first number in each of two pairs to obtain the second number. Then, apply the operation to find the missing number. Select the correct answer choice.

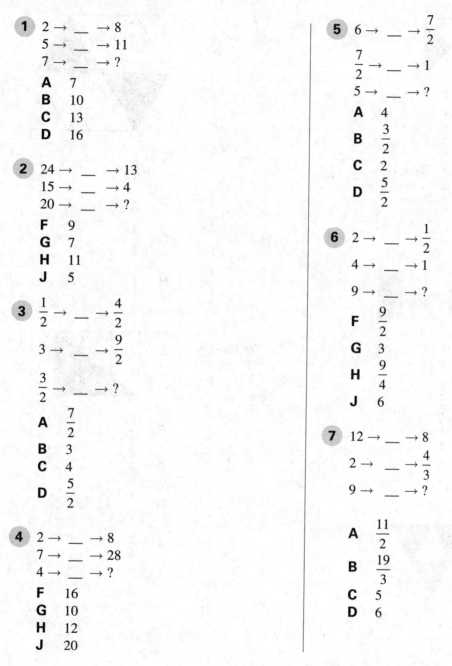

1 $2 \rightarrow \underline{\ \ } \rightarrow 8$
$5 \rightarrow \underline{\ \ } \rightarrow 11$
$7 \rightarrow \underline{\ \ } \rightarrow ?$

A 7
B 10
C 13
D 16

2 $24 \rightarrow \underline{\ \ } \rightarrow 13$
$15 \rightarrow \underline{\ \ } \rightarrow 4$
$20 \rightarrow \underline{\ \ } \rightarrow ?$

F 9
G 7
H 11
J 5

3 $\frac{1}{2} \rightarrow \underline{\ \ } \rightarrow \frac{4}{2}$
$3 \rightarrow \underline{\ \ } \rightarrow \frac{9}{2}$
$\frac{3}{2} \rightarrow \underline{\ \ } \rightarrow ?$

A $\frac{7}{2}$
B 3
C 4
D $\frac{5}{2}$

4 $2 \rightarrow \underline{\ \ } \rightarrow 8$
$7 \rightarrow \underline{\ \ } \rightarrow 28$
$4 \rightarrow \underline{\ \ } \rightarrow ?$

F 16
G 10
H 12
J 20

5 $6 \rightarrow \underline{\ \ } \rightarrow \frac{7}{2}$
$\frac{7}{2} \rightarrow \underline{\ \ } \rightarrow 1$
$5 \rightarrow \underline{\ \ } \rightarrow ?$

A 4
B $\frac{3}{2}$
C 2
D $\frac{5}{2}$

6 $2 \rightarrow \underline{\ \ } \rightarrow \frac{1}{2}$
$4 \rightarrow \underline{\ \ } \rightarrow 1$
$9 \rightarrow \underline{\ \ } \rightarrow ?$

F $\frac{9}{2}$
G 3
H $\frac{9}{4}$
J 6

7 $12 \rightarrow \underline{\ \ } \rightarrow 8$
$2 \rightarrow \underline{\ \ } \rightarrow \frac{4}{3}$
$9 \rightarrow \underline{\ \ } \rightarrow ?$

A $\frac{11}{2}$
B $\frac{19}{3}$
C 5
D 6

Quantitative Reasoning *(continued)*

Directions: For questions 8–14, find the fraction of the grid that is darkened.

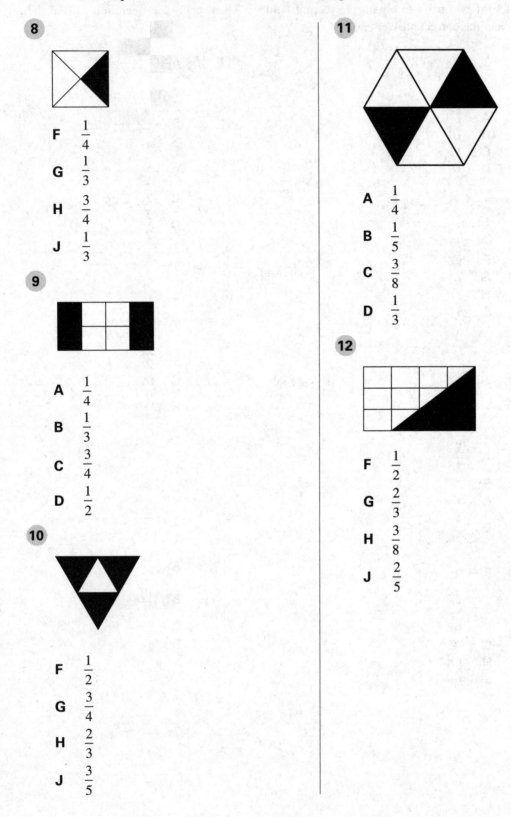

8

F $\dfrac{1}{4}$

G $\dfrac{1}{3}$

H $\dfrac{3}{4}$

J $\dfrac{1}{3}$

9

A $\dfrac{1}{4}$

B $\dfrac{1}{3}$

C $\dfrac{3}{4}$

D $\dfrac{1}{2}$

10

F $\dfrac{1}{2}$

G $\dfrac{3}{4}$

H $\dfrac{2}{3}$

J $\dfrac{3}{5}$

11

A $\dfrac{1}{4}$

B $\dfrac{1}{5}$

C $\dfrac{3}{8}$

D $\dfrac{1}{3}$

12

F $\dfrac{1}{2}$

G $\dfrac{2}{3}$

H $\dfrac{3}{8}$

J $\dfrac{2}{5}$

Quantitative Reasoning *(continued)*

13

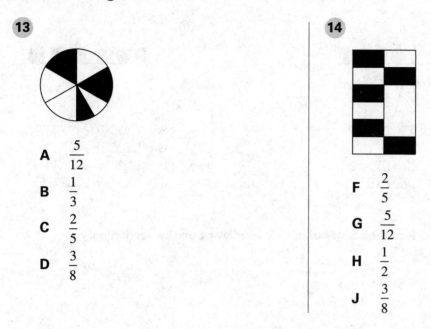

A $\dfrac{5}{12}$

B $\dfrac{1}{3}$

C $\dfrac{2}{5}$

D $\dfrac{3}{8}$

14

F $\dfrac{2}{5}$

G $\dfrac{5}{12}$

H $\dfrac{1}{2}$

J $\dfrac{3}{8}$

Directions: For questions 15–20, examine the balanced scale. Then, select another arrangement of objects that would also balance the scale.

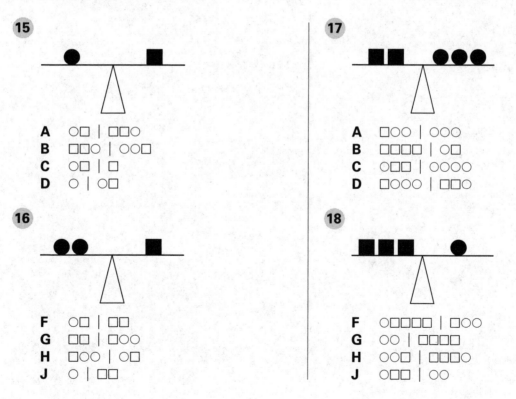

15

A ○□ | □□○
B □□○ | ○○○
C ○□ | □
D ○ | □□

16

F ○□ | □□
G □□ | □○○
H □○○ | ○□
J ○ | □□

17

A □○○ | ○○○
B □□□□ | ○□
C ○□□ | ○○○○
D □○○○ | □□○

18

F ○□□□□ | □○○
G ○○ | □□□□
H ○○□ | □□□○
J ○□□ | ○○

Quantitative Reasoning *(continued)*

19

A ○ | □□□□
B ○○○○○ | □
C ○○□□ | □○○○○
D ○○○○□ | □□

20

F □□□□ | ○□□□□
G □□□□ | ○□□
H □□○ | ○○○○
J ○○□ | □□□□□

STOP!
If you finish before time runs out, check your work on this section only.

Verbal Reasoning—Words (20 Questions, 15 Minutes)

Directions: For questions 1–6, find the word that names a necessary element of the underlined word.

1 fire
- **A** smoke
- **B** flame
- **C** ashes
- **D** oven

2 umpire
- **F** fight
- **G** play
- **H** win
- **J** decide

3 street
- **A** pathway
- **B** automobile
- **C** concrete
- **D** sidewalk

4 professional
- **F** enjoyment
- **G** fascination
- **H** experience
- **J** complexity

5 door
- **A** lock
- **B** opening
- **C** hinge
- **D** doorknob

6 customer
- **F** product
- **G** purchase
- **H** store
- **J** service

Directions: In questions 7–10, the words in the top line are related in some way. The words in the bottom line should be related in the same way. Find the word that completes the bottom row of words.

7 slumber sleep nap
stare look _____
- **A** glance
- **B** ignore
- **C** leer
- **D** squint

8 foot toe sock
wheel spoke _____
- **F** brake
- **G** tire
- **H** peddle
- **J** bicycle

9 rut valley canyon
saucer bowl _____
- **A** plate
- **B** pan
- **C** spoon
- **D** pitcher

10 dip swim plunge
nibble eat _____
- **F** drink
- **G** smell
- **H** devour
- **J** chew

Verbal Reasoning—Words *(continued)*

Directions: For questions 11–15, find the word that does not belong with the others.

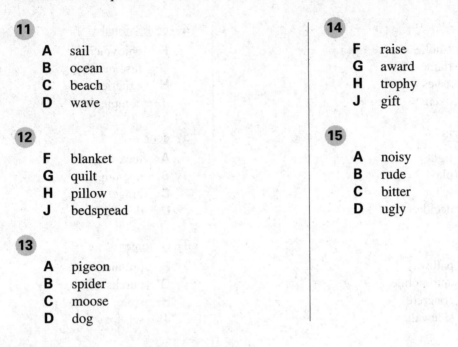

11
- A sail
- B ocean
- C beach
- D wave

12
- F blanket
- G quilt
- H pillow
- J bedspread

13
- A pigeon
- B spider
- C moose
- D dog

14
- F raise
- G award
- H trophy
- J gift

15
- A noisy
- B rude
- C bitter
- D ugly

Directions: For questions 16–20, find the word that is most like the underlined words.

16 basketball volleyball football
- F bowling
- G golf
- H boxing
- J soccer

17 region area territory
- A border
- B plot
- C zone
- D map

18 youngster preteen juvenile
- F child
- G infant
- H baby
- J son

19 jest kid clown
- A joke
- B laugh
- C riddle
- D smile

20 terse short concise
- F simple
- G light
- H brief
- J plain

STOP!
If you finish before time runs out, check your work on this section only.

Verbal Reasoning—Context (20 Questions, 15 Minutes)

Directions: For questions 1–20, find the statement that is most probably true according to the given information.

1 Artists prefer a peaceful environment when they paint. Kim prefers quiet places over noisy places.

  A Kim enjoys the company of artists.
  B Kim is an artist.
  C Kim likes the same places that artists do.
  D Kim likes to paint scenes of peaceful places.

2 Briana ate cereal for breakfast this morning, but Briana did not have either eggs or toast for breakfast.

  F Briana prefers cereal to toast.
  G Briana is allergic to eggs.
  H Briana's toaster is broken.
  J Briana ate breakfast today.

3 If I throw a baseball at the window, the window will break. The window is not broken.

  A I missed the window when I threw a baseball at it.
  B I threw something smaller than a baseball at the window.
  C I have not thrown a baseball at the window.
  D The window is too strong to break with a baseball.

4 If Gwen does not leave her house by 12:00, she will be late for work. Gwen is usually late for work when she stops for lunch on the way. Gwen was late for work today.

  F Gwen stopped for lunch on her way to work today.
  G Gwen ate lunch after 12:00 today.
  H Gwen left for work before 12:00 today but stopped for lunch on the way.
  J Gwen was hungry when she left for work today.

5 Whenever Serena's cat sees a mouse, she chases it. Serena's house is full of mice.

  A Serena owns many cats.
  B Serena's cat is a poor mouse catcher.
  C Serena feeds her cat too much.
  D Serena is afraid of mice.

6 Girls enjoy reading fashion magazines more than boys do. Ann reads the same magazine that her brother Bruce reads.

  F Bruce does not read magazines.
  G Ann reads more than one type of magazine.
  H Girls do not enjoy reading sports magazines.
  J Ann enjoys reading fashion magazines.

7 Javier is taller than Samantha but shorter than Carl. Victoria is shorter than Javier.

  A Carl is taller than Victoria.
  B Victoria is taller than Samantha.
  C Samantha is taller than Victoria.
  D Carl is shorter than Samantha.

8 At a grocery store, Elizabeth went to checkout stand #1 with 11 items. The cashier said to Elizabeth, "This is an express lane only; you must go to another line."

  F Checkout stand #1 was closed.
  G The cashier miscounted the number of items Elizabeth wanted to buy.
  H Stand #1 does not allow more than 10 items per customer.
  J Elizabeth was not willing to wait in a long line.

Verbal Reasoning—Context *(continued)*

9. No house lights on this side of the street are on. At every house across the street, at least one light is on.

A Residents on this side of the street are trying to save energy.

B Residents across the street have not turned off their lights.

C It is the middle of the night.

D The power company has turned off electricity on this side of the street.

10. A new movie now playing in theaters is based on an old television series. Rick Spencer appears in the movie but did not appear in the television show.

F Rick Spencer is the star of the movie.

G The television show is popular today.

H The television show was cancelled.

J The movie is about the history of television.

11. Long hair is not currently fashionable for men and boys. Anthony is keeping his hair long.

A Anthony cannot afford a haircut.

B Anthony's hair is not fashionable.

C Anthony is a member of a rock band.

D It has been a long time since Anthony's last haircut.

12. All new books are on the store's main floor. The store carries both new and used computer books.

F Some books on the store's main floor are computer books.

G Not all of the store's computer books are located on the main floor.

H All books on the store's main floor are new.

J None of the store's used books are located on the main floor.

13. Rude people are not well-liked but are often successful in business. Treating customers politely is good for business.

A A polite person is unlikely to succeed in business.

B A well-liked person also likes other people.

C Polite people are often well-liked.

D Success in business does not depend on politeness.

14. Twenty-five (25) students took the test. Keith received a score of 99 out of 100 possible points on the test. Petra was the only student that scored higher than Keith on the test.

F Petra received a score of 100 on the test.

G Petra and Keith studied for the test together.

H Petra cheated on the test.

J Keith's teacher is a fair grader.

15. On her way to work today, Wendy paid one dollar more to fill her car's gas tank than she paid one week ago to fill the same tank.

A Wendy's car is leaking gasoline.

B The price of gasoline has gone down.

C Wendy needs her car for transportation.

D Wendy took a trip out of town this week.

16. Disneyland is in California, but Disney World is in Florida. Thomas has visited Disneyland but not Disney World.

F Thomas lives closer to Disneyland than to Disney World.

G Disneyland is more popular than Disney World.

H Thomas has not been to Florida.

J Thomas has been to California.

Verbal Reasoning—Context *(continued)*

17 Every ninth-grade student at Elm School is required to take an algebra class. All eighth- and ninth-graders at Elm School must enroll in a math class. Paula is in the eighth grade at Elm School.

  A Paula is not learning algebra.
  B Paula is enrolled in a math class.
  C Paula is good at math.
  D Paula is taking an algebra class.

18 The city of Seaside has more seafood restaurants than any other type of restaurant. Tourists flock to Seaside, primarily during the summer.

  F Tourists who visit Seaside are people who enjoy seafood.
  G Seaside's seafood restaurants serve mainly lobster.
  H Seaside's restaurants are closed during the winter.
  J Most Seaside residents work in the restaurant business.

19 Marc and Jeanine both used the same sunscreen lotion before going to the beach today. Marc's skin was burned while they were at the beach, but Jeanine's skin was not burned.

  A It was foggy at the beach today.
  B Jeanine sat under an umbrella at the beach.
  C Marc wore a hat to the beach.
  D Jeanine read a book while at the beach.

20 Tracy and her family begin eating dinner at 6:00 every evening. It is now 8:00 in the evening.

  F Tracy is late for dinner.
  G Tracy has already eaten dessert.
  H Tracy is eating dinner later than usual today.
  J Tracy has eaten dinner today.

STOP!
If you finish before time runs out, check your work on this section only.

Reading and Language Arts (40 Questions, 40 Minutes)

Directions: Questions 1–40 are based on reading passages, brief essays, and sentences. For each question, select the best answer.

Questions 1–5 are based on the following passage:

Until the twentieth century, American art—especially painting—was dominated by what is called "romanticism." The goal of the romanticist painter was to capture the ideal world on canvas. This type of art reached its peak during the nineteenth century with a famous group of painters in New York. Referred to as the Hudson River Valley school, these painters turned for their inspiration almost entirely to the beauty of nature—the wilderness, mountains, and sea.

After these romanticists came the impressionist painters, such as Inness, Blakelock, and Ryder. Like the Hudson River Valley painters before them, the impressionists were interested in depicting ideal beauty and the ideal life. What was different about the impressionists was that sometimes they would paint scenes of cities. But even in portraying city life, they tried to idealize it, focusing only on swanky, upper-class neighborhoods such as New York City's upper east side.

Then, during the first decade of the twentieth century, a group of artists known as the "progressives" revolted against romanticism. The progressives believed that paintings should focus less on the ideal and more on real life. Led by artist Robert Henri, the progressives tried to capture the architectural and industrial ugliness that America's urban landscapes were becoming in the industrial age. The ultimate goal of the progressives, however, was to show through their art the real, and often negative, impact of the new industrial age on human beings.

Initially, the political and art establishments in America refused to accept the art of the progressives, who were viewed as radical liberals. But the progressives started to gain wide acceptance in the art world during New York City's Armory Show in 1913. At this show, their paintings, along with those of the European painters Picasso, Matisse, and Gauguin, who were already widely known in Europe, launched the modernist era of art.

1 Which of the following was NOT an American impressionist painter?

   A Ryder
   B Hudson
   C Inness
   D Blakelock

2 The author implies that Inness

   F rebelled against the art establishment
   G was a member of the Hudson Valley River school
   H was the most famous American painter of the nineteenth century
   J lived and worked in the United States

3 It would be accurate to describe Robert Henri as

   A a romanticist
   B an impressionist
   C a realist
   D a minimalist

4 Paintings created by the progressives

   F appeared in the Armory Show of 1913
   G appealed to the art establishment
   H were unlike those of Robert Henri
   J focused more on scenery than people

5 The passage is mainly about the

   A American impressionist painters
   B art of the Hudson Valley River school
   C influence of Robert Henri
   D rise of modern American art

Reading and Language Arts *(continued)*

Read the following paragraph, which is related to the previous passage. Then answer questions 6 and 7.

Shortly thereafter, Edward Hopper, a student of Henri, began to elevate the city itself to a level equal in importance to that of his painting's human actors. Hopper's works reveal the uncompromising truth about the everyday world. His paintings reveal the seamy underside—the architectural disorder and ugliness—of the wealth and energy of modern industry, as well as how the industrial age can alienate ordinary people. Perhaps no other artist created as unforgettable a depiction of life in the modern industrial age as Hopper.

6 The best place in the passage to add this paragraph is

F between the passage's first and second paragraphs

G between the passage's second and third paragraphs

H between the passage's third and fourth paragraphs

J after the passage's fourth paragraph

7 Which sentence would NOT belong in this paragraph?

A Hopper's paintings portray not just urban America but other modern cities as well, especially Paris.

B Hopper's most famous work, *American Diner,* captures the loneliness of urban existence in the modern era.

C Hopper showed a keen interest in drawing and painting as young as age five.

D Hopper eventually became more famous than his teacher, Robert Henri.

Questions 8–12 are based on the following passage:

Marco launched the canoe into the swiftest part of the current, desperate not to go home without his cap. It would have guaranteed his detection and a double punishment. Recovering the cap, Marco went to shore, his conscience now reproaching him for his wrong, and set out for home, crossing the threshold just before noon.

His cousin Forester came in shortly thereafter but said nothing. Marco's wet clothes were woolen and dark in color, and the sun and air had been warm that morning. Though satisfied that his truancy would escape detection, he felt ill at ease. So he stayed outside and out of sight until dinnertime, and then was reluctant to go in, for fear that his uncle might have noticed his absence and ask him about it.

At dinnertime, Marco was usually interested in talking with Forester about the next day's plans; but now he felt guilty and afraid, and he was disinclined to look his uncle or his cousin in the face, or to speak a word. Yet, it was not punishment that Marco was afraid of. There were few boys who could bear punishment of any kind with more fortitude than he, or to whom the idea of punishment gave less concern. It was the detection itself, rather than what was to come after it, that he feared. There is something in the very act of being detected and exposed in guilt, which the heart instinctively shrinks from; and many a boy would willingly bear in secret twice the pain that the punishment for an offense would bring, rather than have his commission of the offense discovered and made known.

8 Marco was concerned about being punished for

F losing his cap

G being late for dinner

H coming home in wet clothes

J disobeying his uncle

9 Marco's main fear was that his

A uncle would punish him

B cousin would betray him to Marco's uncle

C canoe would be damaged beyond repair

D uncle would learn of his morning activities

Reading and Language Arts *(continued)*

10 At dinnertime, Marco was feeling

   F relieved
   G anxious
   H desperate
   J confused

11 As used in the passage, the word <u>truancy</u> is best defined as

   A falsehood
   B unexcused absence
   C mischievous deed
   D true motive

12 Why did Marco decide to stay outdoors all afternoon?

   F so that his clothes would finish drying
   G because the weather was sunny and warm
   H to avoid his cousin and his uncle
   J to help his cousin with chores

Questions 13–17 are based on the following passage:

Nearly all of us have known people who are convinced that their pet dog, cat, or other animal possesses extraordinary intelligence for its species. The proud pet owner will brag on and on about his pet animal's ability to speak (in the pet owner's own language, of course), or perhaps to perform arithmetic (but never beyond the pet owner's own facility with numbers, of course), or perhaps to perform some other intellectual feat that we humans generally assume is reserved for ourselves.

These pet owners can learn a lesson from the story of Hans the horse, whose owner had convinced not just himself but many other people as well that Hans could add and subtract numbers, multiply them, and even calculate square roots to the nearest integer. Hans would signal his answers to arithmetic questions by repeatedly stomping his hoof. What's amazing is that Hans even had the scientists fooled . . . except one. It occurred to this one bright researcher to try recruiting questioners who were very bad at arithmetic—so that they themselves did not know the answers to the math questions they were asking Hans. The results: Hans consistently gave *wrong* answers to these questioners!

As it turns out, Hans *was* intelligent . . . very intelligent. But could he perform arithmetic? Of course not. Hans had become an expert at reading body language! When Hans reached the correct number, every questioner who knew the correct answer responded with a subtle, involuntary change in posture, head position, or breathing. Hans had learned to pay close attention, no doubt largely because his owner rewarded him with a treat whenever he gave a correct answer.

13 This article is most likely to appear in a magazine catering to

   A veterinarians
   B pet owners
   C horse trainers
   D zookeepers

14 Hans's owner believed he had trained Hans to

   F accept treats from strangers who asked him to perform arithmetic
   G observe the body language of a person asking him for an answer to an arithmetic problem
   H perform simple arithmetic such as addition and subtraction
   J stomp his hoof upon the owner's command to do so

Reading and Language Arts *(continued)*

15 The article's author seems skeptical about the

A honesty of people who brag about the intelligence of their pets

B intelligence of scientists who study animals

C claim that only humans can develop high-level language skills

D ability of animals to converse using human language

16 Which of the following is probably NOT a reason that Hans learned to respond correctly to arithmetic questions?

F Hans was extremely intelligent.

G Hans was punished for giving wrong answers.

H Hans was very observant of the humans around him.

J Hans was rewarded for his behavior.

17 The article strongly supports the claim that animals

A pay close attention to their owners' behavior

B are more intelligent than most people think

C can be trained to do almost anything

D mimic the behavior of their owners

Here is a paragraph a student wrote about training pet animals. There are a few mistakes that need correcting. Read the paragraph, and then answer questions 18–20.

[1]Training a dog is easier than cats. [2]Each time your dog does what you want, reward him with food. [3]Some dogs can be trained without rewarding them with food. [4]I trained my dog to sit just by saying good boy. [5]I cannot teach my cat to do tricks. [6]My cat has a mind of her own.

18 Which is the best way to write sentence 1?

F Training dogs is easier than cats.

G It's easier to train a dog than a cat.

H Training dogs are easier than training cats.

J best as is

19 Which is the best way to combine sentences 5 and 6?

A I cannot teach my cat, who has a mind of her own, to do tricks.

B I cannot teach my cat to do tricks, she has a mind of her own.

C With a mind of her own, my cat cannot be taught tricks.

D My cat has a mind of her own because I cannot teach her to do tricks.

20 Choose the best way to rewrite sentence 4.

F I trained my dog to sit, just by saying good boy.

G I trained my dog to sit just by saying: good boy.

H I trained my dog to sit just by saying, "Good boy."

J best as is

Reading and Language Arts *(continued)*

Questions 21–25 are based on the following passage:

What type of person are you? Chances are, you've taken at least one or two tests that try to label you according to your attitudes and overall personality. Popular magazines for teens and young adults often publish "quizzes" of these sorts. But don't get the wrong idea—systematic attempts to pigeonhole all of us are far from new.

If you lived in ancient India, you would be classified under one of three body-mind types: *pitta* (intense and bold), *kapha* (relaxed and affectionate), or *vata* (moody and unpredictable). The ancient Greeks identified four basic personality types—choleric (energetic and volatile), sanguine (cheerful and vivacious), phlegmatic (dependable and easy-going), and melancholic (brooding and meditative)—based on four bodily "humours," or liquids.

In the early twentieth century, German psychologist Carl Jung devised a personality grid to account for human tendencies of various sorts—for example, whether people tend to be introverted or extroverted, and whether they tend to make decisions based on thoughts or on feelings. Jung even analyzed Sigmund Freud—Jung's contemporary and another influential twentieth-century psychologist—according to this system. Jung concluded that Freud's theories about human personality actually stemmed from Freud's own tendency toward introversion.

Jung never intended that his theories be interpreted to typecast people—to label them or put them in "boxes." Nevertheless, his work has spawned dozens of classification systems that attempt to do just that. Perhaps most influential among these tests is the Myers-Briggs Type Indicator, developed during the 1940s, which to this day is the most widely used of any personality test. Psychologists, career counselors, and even business managers all use the Myers-Briggs Type Indicator to help them in their work. So, don't be surprised if someday, perhaps soon, you find yourself taking this test.

21 The passage discusses ancient attempts to classify people based mainly on their

  A physical size
  B intelligence
  C personality
  D wealth

22 A phlegmatic person tends to be

  F steady
  G optimistic
  H irritable
  J sociable

23 Carl Jung developed a classification system based on

  A humours
  B race and ethnic origin
  C attitudes
  D personal tastes

24 According to the passage, Carl Jung and Sigmund Freud

  F both attended the same university in Germany
  G disagreed about whether Freud was an introvert
  H both developed a body-mind classification system
  J both influenced twentieth-century popular psychology

25 The Myers-Briggs Type Indicator

  A was based on Freud's work
  B popularized Jung's work
  C influenced Jung and Freud
  D is not widely used today

Reading and Language Arts *(continued)*

Here is a brief essay a student wrote about intelligence tests (I.Q. tests). There are a few mistakes that need correcting. Read the essay, and then answer questions 26–28.

¹It is wrong to label other people. ²Every body is different and one of a kind. ³Standard I.Q. tests only test on "book smarts." ⁴However, "street smart" people like Donald Trump might do bad on this kind of test. ⁵So, big Companies should not hire people based on these tests.

26 Choose the best way to write sentence 2.

   F Everybody is different and one of a kind.

   G Every body are different and one of a kind.

   H Everyone of us are different and one of a kind.

   J best as is

27 Which sentence contains a capitalization error?

   A sentence 1

   B sentence 3

   C sentence 4

   D sentence 5

28 Which is the best sentence to insert between sentences 4 and 5?

   F I get good grades in school, but I don't think I am very smart.

   G To succeed in most jobs, it helps to be street smart.

   H Some people are unfairly labeled as "dumb."

   J A good personality is just as important as intelligence.

Questions 29–32 are based on the following passage:

Upon the mention of Afghanistan, most Westerners today think of a <u>forbidding</u> and severe wasteland at the western edge of the Himalayas, devastated by wave upon wave of strife and suffering. The 1979 Russian invasion and the U.S. bombings more than twenty years later are just two recent afflictions the Afghans have suffered in their long and bloody history.

Should the rest of the world give up on this mostly agricultural nation, which is largely in ruins, and simply abandon it? True, invading countries have left its agricultural lands barren, farm animals wiped out, and water and electricity systems destroyed. True, generations must pass before the deep-seated distrust its people must surely feel toward younger, mightier nations subsides. But sweep away the land mines, gaze through the fog of war, and look deeply into the eyes of the Afghan people. You will see a colorful assortment of clans almost too numerous to count, and a proud, strong-willed people with a long and varied heritage far too valuable to see wither from neglect.

29 As used in the selection, the word <u>forbidding</u> is best defined as

   A prohibited

   B unfriendly

   C unpredictable

   D mountainous

30 The selection can best be described as

   F an explanation

   G a plea

   H a debate

   J a complaint

Reading and Language Arts *(continued)*

31 The author would strongly agree that, as a people, Afghans are

A   pitiful
B   ambitious
C   optimistic
D   determined

32 Among the following, the selection would most likely be an excerpt from

F   a speech made at an antiwar rally
G   an academic lecture on current world events
H   a chapter from a textbook on modern world history
J   an article at a famine-relief organization's website

33 Here are two sentences related to the previous passage:

There are millions of land mines buried in Afghanistan.

It will takes several decades to find and remove them all.

Choose the best way to combine the two sentences.

A   Of the millions of land mines buried in Afghanistan, in several decades they all can be found and removed.
B   Millions of land mines are buried in Afghanistan, and it will take several decades to find and remove them all.
C   There are millions of land mines buried in Afghanistan, which it will take several decades to find and remove.
D   It will take several decades to find and remove all the land mines, millions of which are buried in Afghanistan.

34 Which sentence is written correctly?

F   Afghanistan's barren deserts are dotted with an occasional green oasis.
G   Afghanistan's barren deserts they are dotted with an occasional green oasis.
H   Afghanistan's deserts are barren and dotted occasionally with green oases.
J   Afghanistan's barren deserts dotted with occasional green oases.

Questions 35–39 are based on the following passage:

Scientific work involving particles no greater than 100 nanometers in length is called *nanotechnology*. A *nanometer* is one 100 billionth of a meter in length, or about ten times the length of a hydrogen atom.

Nanotechnology may be about very *small* things, but it is often called the "Next *Big* Thing" that will make the Internet revolution <u>pale</u> in significance. Research companies specializing in this new technology are springing up everywhere today. Any high-tech company whose name starts with *Nano* is probably involved in nanotechnology.

Nanotechnology is already used to make a variety of new-and-improved consumer products, from televisions and computer monitors to wrinkle cream and sunblock. Scientists working with nano-sized particles are developing super-fast and energy-efficient computer chips, ultra-strong fabrics and building materials, and, more crucially, faster-acting medicines for the treatment of diseases.

When it comes to human health, however, nanotechnology might prove more hazardous than helpful. Studies with laboratory animals suggest that contact with nano-sized particles, which are by definition considered toxic due to their small size, can cause various forms of cancer. Particles so small easily enter a person's bloodstream and central nervous system.

Reading and Language Arts *(continued)*

35 A hydrogen atom is

    A about one nanometer in length

    B longer than a nanometer

    C shorter than a nanometer

    D larger than a nano-sized particle

36 As used in the passage, the word <u>pale</u> most nearly means

    F shrink

    G boast

    H faster

    J continue

37 According to the passage, nanotechnology is used to develop

    A cosmetics

    B genetically modified grains

    C alcoholic beverages

    D household cleaning products

38 The author seems worried about

    F the safety of scientists who work with nano-sized particles

    G the long-term impact of nanotechnology on human health

    H government putting a stop to nanotechnology research

    J the use of nanotechnology to make weapons of mass destruction

39 Choose the best concluding sentence for the passage.

    A Nanotechnology will no doubt make the Internet seem old-fashioned someday.

    B Nobody will benefit from nanotechnology in the long run.

    C It seems that nanotechnology's benefits might not come without human cost.

    D The future of nanotechnology depends on financial support from the government.

40 Which sentence is written correctly?

    F "Nanotubes" four nanometers wide are being used to improve computer processors.

    G "Nanotubes" four nanometers wide is being used to improve computer processors.

    H "Nanotubes," four nanometers wide, being used to improve computer processors.

    J "Nanotubes" four nanometers wide, used now to improve computer processors.

STOP!
If you finish before time runs out, check your work on this section only.

Mathematics (40 Questions, 35 Minutes)

Directions: Choose the best answer to each question.

1 $-(4-5)(5-4) =$

A -1
B 0
C 1
D -2

2 Which of the following is less than $\dfrac{13}{40}$?

F $\dfrac{1}{3}$
G $\dfrac{7}{20}$
H $\dfrac{2}{5}$
J $\dfrac{3}{10}$

3 $11.1 + 1.11 + 0.111 =$

A 12.321
B 13.21
C 12.211
D 12.11

4 Which of the three triangles in the figure below MUST be equilateral?

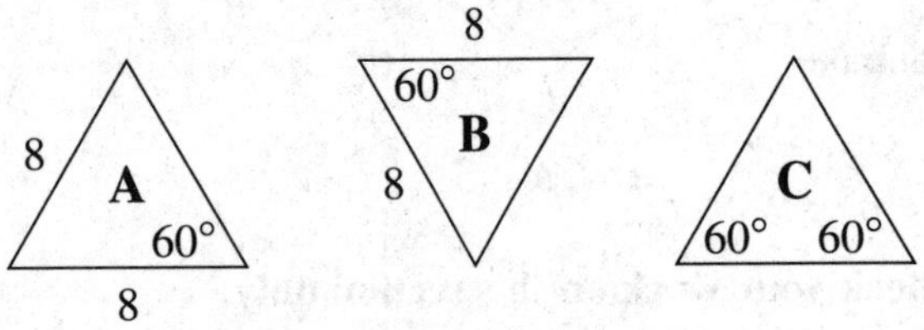

F Triangles A and C only
G Triangle C only
H Triangles B and C only
J Triangles A, B, and C

5 What value does the digit 4 represent in the number 534,792?

A 40,000
B 400
C 40
D 4,000

6 In a class of 40 students, the ratio of boys to girls is 3:5. How many girls are in the class?

F 20
G 25
H 24
J 15

7 $\dfrac{8}{9} \div \dfrac{4}{3} =$

A $\dfrac{2}{3}$
B $\dfrac{1}{3}$
C $\dfrac{3}{4}$
D $\dfrac{3}{2}$

8 For what value of x is it true that $x = 3(x + 2)$?

F 2
G -3
H -2
J 3

9 Children are admitted to the movie theater at half the adult admission price. If one adult accompanies three children to the theater, paying $18.75 for all four tickets, what was the price of admission for each child?

A $4.50
B $4.00
C $3.75
D $7.50

10 What is the length of a rectangle whose area is 8 and whose width is half its length?

F 6
G 4
H 2
J 3

Mathematics *(continued)*

11 If you add two ounces of water to a 16-ounce mixture consisting of equal amounts of milk and water, what portion of the resulting mixture is water?

A $\dfrac{3}{5}$

B $\dfrac{5}{9}$

C $\dfrac{5}{8}$

D $\dfrac{4}{9}$

12 Which of the following is closest to the product of 825 and 775?

F 640,000

G 65,000

H 560,000

J 5,900,000

13 $x(y + x + z) =$

A $x^2 + xy + xz$

B $xy + xz + yz$

C $(x + y)(x + z)$

D $2x + xy + xz$

14 One prime number divided by another prime number is always

F a fraction between 0 and 1

G an integer

H a positive non-integer

J a prime number

15 If a triangle contains one right angle, then the other two angles could measure

A 70° and 20°

B 35° and 60°

C 20° and 90°

D 45° and 40°

16 $4^3 \times 4^3 =$

F $4 \times 3 \times 4 \times 3$

G 196

H 4^9

J $16 \times 16 \times 16$

17 The graph below compares the daily production of Ultra Corporation's Divisions A, B, and C.

▨ = Division A

☐ = Division B

▦ = Division C

55%

25%

If the total production of the three divisions is 7,500 units, how many units does Division A produce per day?

A 1,875

B 1,250

C 1,500

D 1,050

18 A train left Station A at 12:30 p.m. and arrived at Station B at 3:00 p.m. If the train's average speed was 40 miles per hour, how many miles did the train travel?

F 120

G 80

H 90

J 100

19 If p packs of gum cost d dollars, then you can express the cost of one pack of gum as

A $\dfrac{p}{d}$

B dp

C $\dfrac{d}{p}$

D $p + d$

20 $5 + 4 \times 3 \div 2 =$

F $\dfrac{11}{2}$

G 4

H $\dfrac{3}{2}$

J 11

Mathematics *(continued)*

21 What is the difference between the sum of all even integers between 0 and 101 and the sum of all odd integers between 0 and 100?

- **A** 50
- **B** 0
- **C** 100
- **D** 1

22 What are the (x,y) coordinates of point A on the coordinate plane below?

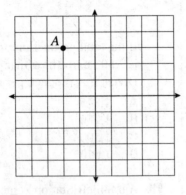

- **F** $(2,-3)$
- **G** $(-2,3)$
- **H** $(-3,2)$
- **J** $(3,-2)$

23 For which of the following values of x is the inequality $2x < x$ true?

- **A** $\dfrac{1}{2}$
- **B** $-\dfrac{1}{2}$
- **C** 0
- **D** 2

24 The number 2,000,000 is equivalent to

- **F** 2×10^6
- **G** 10×2^7
- **H** 2×10^7
- **J** $(2 \times 10)^6$

25 If $x < \dfrac{11}{2}$ and $x > -\dfrac{10}{2}$, and if x is a non-zero integer, the total number of possible values of x is

- **A** 10
- **B** 13
- **C** 9
- **D** 18

26 At a 12% annual interest rate, how much interest is earned on $500 in one year?

- **F** $60.00
- **G** $12.00
- **H** $4.00
- **J** $9.00

27 Point O lies at the center of the circle shown below.

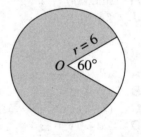

What is the area of the shaded region?

- **A** 36
- **B** 24π
- **C** 24
- **D** 30π

28 The set $\{4,5,6\}$ represents

- **F** $\{0,2,4,6,8\} \cap \{1,3,5,7,9\}$
- **G** $\{2,3,4,5,6\} \cap \{3,4,5,6,7\}$
- **H** $\{3,4,5,6,7\} \cap \{2,3,4,5,6\}$
- **J** $\{4,5,6,7,8\} \cap \{2,3,4,5,6\}$

29 Including a 5% sales tax, what is the total cost of a sweater whose price is $55 without tax?

- **A** $57.50
- **B** $60.00
- **C** $57.75
- **D** $62.50

Mathematics *(continued)*

30 Karen's average score for two tests is 90. What score must Karen earn on a third test to raise her average to 92?

F 96
G 93
H 95
J 94

31 If 1 mile is equivalent to 1.6 kilometers, then 10 kilometers is equivalent to

A 9.2 miles
B 16 miles
C 1.6 miles
D 6.25 miles

Questions 32 and 33 are based on the following information:

The graph below shows the number of visitors to Woodlands State Park during each of six months.

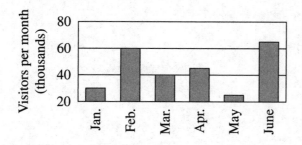

32 The greatest *increase* in the number of park visitors from one month to the next occurred

F from January through February
G from February through March
H from March through April
J from May through June

33 Approximately how many visitors did the park receive altogether during the six months shown?

A 190,000
B 265,000
C 240,000
D 225,000

34 If $x = \sqrt{3}$ and $y = 81$, then $x^4 + \sqrt[4]{y} =$

F 9
G 12
H 27
J 15

35 There are 12 balls in a bag; 4 are red, 2 are blue, and the rest are green. The probability of randomly selecting a green marble from the bag is

A $\dfrac{1}{3}$

B $\dfrac{2}{3}$

C $\dfrac{3}{4}$

D $\dfrac{1}{2}$

36 Which of the following is equivalent to *thirty thousand twenty-four?*

F 30,204
G 30,024
H 324,000
J 30,000.24

37 What is the total unit area of the figure below?

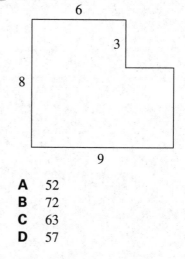

A 52
B 72
C 63
D 57

Mathematics (continued)

38 If a soda costs S cents and a burger costs B dollars, which of the following represents the cost of one burger and one soda, in cents?

F $B + 100S$
G $100(S + B)$
H $100B + S$
J $S + B$

39 What is the measure of one interior angle of a pentagon whose sides are all equal in length?

A 136°
B 96°
C 120°
D 108°

40 Choose the closest approximation of $\sqrt{40} + \sqrt{60}$.

F 14
G 12
H 10
J 13

STOP!
If you finish before time runs out, check your work on this section only.

COOP PRACTICE TEST 1

Answer Key

Sequences

1.	A	11.	B
2.	H	12.	F
3.	D	13.	C
4.	G	14.	J
5.	B	15.	B
6.	F	16.	F
7.	C	17.	D
8.	G	18.	J
9.	D	19.	A
10.	J	20.	H

Analogies

1.	C	11.	B
2.	G	12.	H
3.	C	13.	D
4.	F	14.	G
5.	D	15.	A
6.	H	16.	J
7.	A	17.	A
8.	H	18.	J
9.	D	19.	B
10.	G	20.	F

Quantitative Reasoning

1.	C	11.	D
2.	F	12.	H
3.	B	13.	A
4.	F	14.	G
5.	D	15.	B
6.	H	16.	G
7.	D	17.	C
8.	F	18.	F
9.	D	19.	D
10.	G	20.	F

Verbal Reasoning—Words

1.	B	11.	A
2.	J	12.	H
3.	A	13.	A
4.	H	14.	J
5.	B	15.	B
6.	G	16.	J
7.	A	17.	C
8.	G	18.	F
9.	D	19.	A
10.	H	20.	H

Verbal Reasoning—Context

1.	C	11.	B
2.	J	12.	F
3.	C	13.	D
4.	F	14.	F
5.	B	15.	C
6.	J	16.	J
7.	A	17.	B
8.	H	18.	F
9.	B	19.	B
10.	H	20.	J

Reading and Language Arts

1.	B	11.	B
2.	J	12.	H
3.	C	13.	B
4.	F	14.	H
5.	D	15.	D
6.	J	16.	G
7.	C	17.	A
8.	F	18.	G
9.	D	19.	A
10.	G	20.	H

COOP PRACTICE TEST 1

Answer Key *(continued)*

Reading and Language Arts

21.	C	31.	D
22.	F	32.	J
23.	C	33.	B
24.	J	34.	F
25.	B	35.	C
26.	F	36.	J
27.	D	37.	A
28.	G	38.	G
29.	B	39.	C
30.	G	40.	F

Mathematics

1.	C	21.	A
2.	J	22.	G
3.	A	23.	B
4.	J	24.	F
5.	D	25.	C
6.	G	26.	F
7.	A	27.	D
8.	G	28.	J
9.	C	29.	C
10.	G	30.	F
11.	B	31.	D
12.	F	32.	J
13.	A	33.	B
14.	H	34.	G
15.	A	35.	D
16.	J	36.	G
17.	C	37.	C
18.	J	38.	H
19.	C	39.	D
20.	J	40.	F

COOP PRACTICE TEST 1

Answers and Explanations

Sequences

1. **A** With each passing group, each horizontal arrow switches direction, while each vertical arrow switches back and forth between two-way and one-way.

2. **H** Each group presents a random arrangement of two circles and three squares. (There's no sequential pattern from one group to the next.)

3. **D** From one group to the next, both U-shaped arrows rotate 90 degrees counterclockwise.

4. **G** Beginning in the second group, one feature is added to the first icon and to the second icon. The specific feature added to the second is the same added to the first icon in the previous group. Beginning in the third group, whatever feature was added to the second icon in the previous group is added to the *third* icon.

5. **B** From one group to the next, the two shaded boxes move in opposite directions, passing each as they move from the third to the fourth group.

6. **F** In each successive group, each object moves one position to the right (the object furthest to the right jumps to the far left) *and* flips to its horizontal mirror image.

7. **C** Beginning with the letter *c*, the series lists the letters of the alphabet in order, skipping every other letter.

8. **G** In each pair, you skip one letter of the alphabet to determine the second letter. Also, from each pair to the next, corresponding letters are in alphabetical order: f-g-*h*-i (first letter) and h-i-*j*-k (second letter). As you can see, the pair *hj* completes the series.

9. **D** Each group lists two successive letters of the alphabet, then skips one letter. Each successive group begins with the third letter of the previous group.

10. **J** Looking at just the first two letters in each group, from one group to the next the series lists letters of the alphabet in reverse order (starting with *Z*). Looking at just the third letter in each group, the series lists letters of the alphabet in order (starting with *A*).

11. **B** Alphabetically, in each group the first letter lies immediately between the second and third. Each successive group contains the three letters of the alphabet that come immediately after the three letters in the previous group.

12. **F** In each group, the second letter is *C*. Looking at just the first and third letters in the groups, the series lists letters of the alphabet in order (starting with *B*).

13. **C** Each group contains three elements. The third element is constant (2). Otherwise, corresponding elements run in sequential order from one group to the next: A-B-C-*D* (first element) and subscript 1-2-3-*4* (second element).

14. **J** Each group contains four elements. From one group to the next, corresponding elements run in sequential order, skipping every other letter or number: 8-6-4-2 (first element), B-D-F-H (second element), superscript 3-5-7-9 (third element), and G-E-C-A (fourth element).

15. **B** The series lists integers in ascending order, skipping every multiple of 3.

16. **F** Divide each number by 2 to obtain the next one.

Answers and Explanations *(continued)*

17. **D** Within each group, subtracting 3 from a number yields the next number. Accordingly, since the third group's second number is 4, that group's first number should be 7.

18. **J** Within each group, squaring a number (multiplying it by itself) yields the next number.

19. **A** Within each group, dividing a number by 4 yields the next number.

20. **H** Within each group, multiplying the first number by 4 yields the second number, and dividing the second number by 3 yields the third number ($9 \times 4 = 36$; $36 \div 3 = 12$).

Analogies

1. **C** To draw ink from an inkwell, you dip a fountain pen into it. Similarly, to draw paint from a paint can, you dip a brush into it.

2. **G** Coins and bills serve the same purpose: they're used as money. Similarly, chairs and sofas are used for the same purpose: they're used for sitting.

3. **C** A bird's nest is the place where a bird can rest safely, just as a crib is where a baby rests safely.

4. **F** A submarine and a fish hook are both things that people launch into a body of water and that go beneath the water's surface. Similarly, an airplane and a kite are both things that people launch into the air.

5. **D** You wear earmuffs over your ears to protect them (from the cold). Similarly, you wear boxing gloves on your hands to protect them (from injury caused by hitting another boxer).

6. **H** Potatoes are the raw materials used to make french fries. Similarly, wood from trees is the raw material used to make wooden furniture such as tables.

7. **A** A rifle is a tool used to hunt deer. Similarly, a fishing rod is a tool used to fish. Choices B and D are incorrect because a hook and bait are analogous to a rifle's bullet, not to the rifle itself.

8. **H** You gain admission to a theater with an admission ticket. Similarly, you gain access through a locked door with the key that unlocks it.

9. **D** You use a microscope to obtain a good view of an amoeba. Similarly, you use reading glasses to obtain a good view of the pages of a book.

10. **G** A ring is worn on the finger. Similarly, a sock is worn on the foot.

11. **B** A baby grows up to be an adult human. Similarly, a kitten grows up to be an adult cat.

12. **H** New York is one of many states that together form the United States. Similarly, a single book is just one of several books that form a row of books on a shelf. Choice J is incorrect because a library building is made up of much more than just books.

13. **D** A pair of scissors is a tool for trimming a beard and mustache. Similarly, a lawn mower is a tool for trimming a yard of grass.

14. **G** A waiter delivers your plate of food to you in a restaurant. Similarly, a mail carrier delivers your mail to you.

15. **A** A sewing machine performs the same function as a needle and thread but does so using a more advanced technology. Similarly, writing by hand and typing on a computer are both means of writing, but typing uses a more advanced technology.

Answers and Explanations *(continued)*

16. **J** The first-aid symbol represents the services of a nurse (among other health care providers). Similarly, the scales of justice is a symbol that represents the services of a judge.

17. **A** A train travels along tracks, its pathway, that take it to its ultimate destination. Similarly, a plane travels through the sky, its pathway, in order to reach its destination. As for choice D, a plane uses a runway, or tarmac, only to reach the pathway (the sky) that takes it to its destination.

18. **J** You hit a baseball with a bat. Similarly, you kick a football with your foot.

19. **B** A sheep is covered with wool, which you can use to make a sweater. Similarly, a cow is covered in hide, which you can use to make a leather belt.

20. **F** This one may be easier to work backwards. A church is a building where a priest works. Similarly, a hospital is a building where a doctor works.

Quantitative Reasoning

1. **C** You add 6 to the first number to obtain the second number: $7 + 6 = 13$.

2. **F** You subtract 11 from the first number to obtain the second one: $20 - 11 = 9$.

3. **B** You add $\frac{3}{2}$ to the first number to obtain the second one: $\frac{3}{2} + \frac{3}{2} = \frac{6}{2}$, or 3.

4. **F** You multiply the first number by 4 to obtain the second one: $4 \times 4 = 16$.

5. **D** You subtract $\frac{5}{2}$ from the first number to obtain the second one: $5 - \frac{5}{2} = \frac{5}{2}$.

6. **H** You divide the first number by 4 to obtain the second one: $9 \div 4 = \frac{9}{4}$.

7. **D** You multiply the first number by $\frac{2}{3}$ to obtain the second one: $9 \times \frac{2}{3} = 6$.

8. **F** The figure is divided into 4 congruent triangles. One triangle, or $\frac{1}{4}$ of the figure, is shaded.

9. **D** The figure is divided into 8 congruent rectangles; 4 of the rectangles, which make up $\frac{4}{8}$, or $\frac{1}{2}$ of the figure, are shaded.

10. **G** The figure is divided into 4 congruent triangles; 3 of these triangles, which make up $\frac{3}{4}$ of the figure, are shaded.

11. **D** The figure, a regular hexagon, is divided into 6 congruent triangles; 2 of these triangles, which make up $\frac{2}{6}$, or $\frac{1}{3}$, of the figure, are shaded.

12. **H** The figure is divided into 12 congruent rectangles, 3 of which are each split into 2 congruent triangles. The figure's total area is 24 times the area of one of these small triangles. Three (3) triangles are shaded, and 3 rectangles—the equivalent of 6 triangles—are shaded. Thus, an area equal to that of 9 of 24 triangles is shaded. You can simplify the fraction $\frac{9}{24}$ to $\frac{3}{8}$.

13. **A** The circle is divided into 6 congruent segments; 2 of these segments are shaded and account for $\frac{2}{6}$ of the circle. One of the other four segments is divided into 2 congruent segments, each one accounting for $\frac{1}{12}$ of the circle. One of these segments is shaded. Altogether, the shaded segments account for $\frac{5}{12}$ of the circle: $\frac{2}{6} + \frac{1}{12} = \frac{4}{12} + \frac{1}{12} = \frac{5}{12}$.

Answers and Explanations *(continued)*

14. **G** The figure is divided into 12 congruent rectangles, although 3 of the rectangles in the right-hand column are merged into one larger rectangle. Five of the original 12 congruent rectangles are shaded. These shaded rectangles account for $\frac{5}{12}$ of the figure.

15. **B** □ and ○ are equal in weight (the □:○ ratio is 1:1). Thus, as long as the same total number of total objects (of either type) appears on the left as on the right, as in choice (B) only, the weights balance. Otherwise, they won't.

16. **G** The scale shows that the □:○ weight ratio is 2:1. Assign a weight of 2 units to □ and a weight of 1 unit to ○. In choice G, the total on the left side equals the total on the right side: $(2 + 2) = (2 + 1 + 1)$.

17. **C** The scale shows that the □:○ weight ratio is 3:2. Assign a weight of 3 units to □ and a weight of 2 units to ○. In choice C, the total on the left side equals the total on the right side: $(2 + 3 + 3) = (2 \times 4)$.

18. **F** The scale shows that the □:○ weight ratio is 1:3. Assign a weight of 1 unit to □ and a weight of 3 units to ○. In choice F, the total on the left side equals the total on the right side: $(3 + 1 + 1 + 1 + 1) = (1 + 3 + 3)$.

19. **D** The scale shows that the □:○ weight ratio is 4:1. Assign a weight of 4 units to □ and a weight of 1 unit to ○. In choice D, the total on the left side equals the total on the right side: $(4 \times 1) + 4 = (4 + 4)$.

20. **F** The scale shows that the □:○ weight ratio is 2:3. Assign a weight of 2 units to □ and a weight of 3 units to ○. In choice F, the total on the left side equals the total on the right side: $(2 + 3 + 3 + 3) = (3 + 2 + 2 + 2 + 2)$.

Verbal Reasoning—Words

1. **B** A *flame* is an inherent feature of any fire. A fire does not necessarily produce either smoke or ash, and an oven is only one possible place where a fire might occur.

2. **J** In any game or sport, an umpire's job is to make decisions or calls (to *decide*)—for example, whether a ball is in or out, whether a foul has been committed, and so forth—by applying the rules of the game.

3. **A** The purpose of any street is to provide a route, or *pathway,* for going from one place (or condition) to another.

4. **H** A professional is someone who has developed a high level of skill at a job, sport, or other activity through extensive *experience.* The activity might, but need not, be complex, enjoyable, or fascinating.

5. **B** The inherent function of a door is to provide an *opening.* A door may or may not have a lock, hinge, or knob.

6. **G** A customer is someone who buys, or *purchases,* either a product or a service. The purchase may or may not take place in a store.

7. **A** A *slumber* is a deep, long *sleep;* at the other extreme, a *nap* is a brief, fleeting sleep. Similarly, a *stare* is an intense, long *look* while, at the other extreme, a *glance* is a brief, fleeting look.

8. **G** Several *toes* together are one component of a *foot,* which is covered and protected by a *sock.* Similarly, several *spokes* together are one component of a *wheel,* which is covered and protected by a *tire.*

Answers and Explanations *(continued)*

9. **D** The three words in the top line all describe concave land features; the distinction is in degree. A *rut* is a small, shallow hole; a *valley* is much larger and has gently sloping sides; a *canyon* is also much larger but is deep with steep sides. A *saucer* is small and shallow; a *bowl* is larger and has gently sloping sides, whereas a *pitcher* is deep with steep sides.

10. **H** In the top row, the neutral word *swim* is flanked by two contrasting forms of swimming. When you take a *dip,* you test the water briefly to get a feel for it; in contrast, when you *plunge,* you dive in with no reluctance whatsoever. In the bottom row, the neutral word *eat* should also be flanked by two contrasting words. To *nibble* is to taste just a bit of food; in contrast, to *devour* is to eat ravenously without reluctance.

11. **A** A *sail* is part of a boat, whereas an *ocean,* a *beach,* and a *wave* are all features of nature.

12. **H** A *blanket,* a *quilt,* and a *bedspread* are all bed covers. Although a *pillow* might sit atop a bed, it is not a bed covering.

13. **A** Among the four types of animals listed, the *pigeon* is the only one that flies.

14. **J** A *raise,* an *award,* and a *trophy* are usually earned through some accomplishment, whereas a *gift* is not.

15. **B** Each of the incorrect choices is a word associated primarily with a sensory experience—you hear something *noisy,* taste something *bitter,* and see something *ugly.* However, something *rude* is not clearly experienced through one particular sense (sight, hearing, smell, taste, or touch).

16. **J** Each of the underlined words refers to a sport where two opposing teams play the same ball. Of the four sports listed among the answer choices, only *soccer* matches the same description.

17. **C** The word *zone* and the three underlined words can each be used to refer to a specific geographical or spatial section or patch—of land, for instance.

18. **F** The word *child* and the three underlined words are each used to refer to a young person who is older than an infant (baby) but younger than a teenager.

19. **A** The word *joke,* like any of the underlined words, is used in describing the behavior of a person who is not being serious. Rather than saying that someone is not being serious, we might say that he is "just kidding," "clowning around," "joking," or saying something "in jest."

20. **H** The word *brief* and all the underlined words can be used interchangeably to describe writing or speech that is compact (as opposed to lengthy or wordy) in its use of words.

Verbal Reasoning—Context

1. **C** A quiet place makes for a peaceful environment; thus, Kim likes the same sorts of places that artists do. However, just because Kim might enjoy the same kinds of places that artists do, you cannot infer that Kim is an artist or that Kim likes being around artists.

2. **J** Choice J provides a certain conclusion. Choice G provides a reason why Briana did not eat eggs, but does not tell us why Briana did not eat toast. Choices F and H tell us why Briana did not eat toast, but they do not explain why Briana did not eat eggs.

3. **C** Given that both premises are factual, the speaker could not have thrown a baseball at the window; otherwise, the window would be broken. Choices A and D contradict the first premise, and choice B provides only one possible conclusion.

Answers and Explanations *(continued)*

4. **F** Given the second premise, a likely reason Gwen was late today is that she stopped for lunch. Choice G fails to consider the possibility that Gwen ate lunch *after* arriving at work. Choice H provides a weaker conclusion than choice F because Gwen would be less likely to be late for work if she leaves her house before 12:00. The conclusion in choice J depends on the assumption that Gwen stops for lunch whenever she leaves for work hungry.

5. **B** If Serena's cat were a good mouse catcher, Serena's house would probably not be full of mice.

6. **J** Based on the first statement, you know that girls like reading fashion magazines—at least to some extent. Therefore, Ann, a girl who reads fashion magazines, probably enjoys reading them. Statement F contradicts the second premise. Statements G and H are poor conclusions because Ann might read more than one type of magazine.

7. **A** Given that Victoria is shorter than Javier, who in turn is shorter than Carl, Carl must be taller than Victoria.

8. **H** Nothing in the premises suggests that the cashier miscounted the number of items Elizabeth wanted to buy. The best conclusion is that 11 items is over the limit for an express lane.

9. **B** The premises do not tell us why the lights are off on only one side of the street, and so choices A and D are mere guesses. However, we know for certain that lights are on across the street and, therefore, that the residents there have not turned those lights off. Choice C is easy to eliminate as nonsense; if it were the middle of the night, lights would be off on both sides of the street.

10. **H** The two premises together strongly imply that the television show is no longer running.

11. **B** Given that long hair is not fashionable, Anthony's long hair must not be fashionable. Choices A and C are incorrect because the premises provide absolutely no information as to why Anthony has decided to keep his hair long. Choice D is incorrect because it is possible that Anthony's hair has been even longer recently and that he recently had it trimmed to its current length.

12. **F** The store carries new computer books, and all new books are on the main floor. Therefore, some of the books on that floor must be computer books.

13. **D** Together, the two premises suggest that rude and polite people alike can do well in business. Choice A runs contrary to what the premises tell us. Choices B and C may or may not be true in real life, but the premises do not support them.

14. **F** The only score higher than 99 is 100. Given that Keith received a score of 99 and that Petra received a higher score than Keith, Petra must have received a score of 100. Choices G and H are easy to eliminate because the premises provide no information to suggest that Keith and Petra studied together or that Petra could not have scored so high without cheating. Choice J is incorrect because we have no way of knowing whether the test was fair.

15. **C** The premises do not tell us why Wendy paid more to fill the tank this time than the previous time. Perhaps the price of gas has increased, or perhaps the car's tank was emptier this time. What is far more certain is that Wendy needs her car to commute to work—because she was on her way to work today and because she's filled the tank at least twice within the last week.

16. **J** Because Thomas has visited Disneyland, which is in California, he must have been to California.

Answers and Explanations (continued)

17. **B** Because Paula is an eighth-grader at Elm School, Paula must be taking a math class—because all eighth-graders at the school are required to do so.

18. **F** It makes sense that restaurants at a popular tourist destination such as Seaside would cater to the tastes of tourists. Thus, choice F provides a reasonable conclusion. The conclusion in choice G is completely unsupported by the premises. Choice H is incorrect because, for all we know, Seaside's restaurants might cater to local residents year round. As for choice J, it's entirely possible that Seaside's residents work in many different industries; nothing in the premises suggest otherwise.

19. **B** Because Marc and Jeanine both used sunscreen lotion, we would expect that either both or neither would burn (depending on how effective the lotion is). A good reason why Marc might have burned while Jeanine did not is that Jeanine was less exposed to the sun. Although sitting under an umbrella is not the only way to avoid the sun while at the beach, this conclusion is the best of the four listed.

20. **J** Because dinner is at 6:00, Tracy and her family are probably done eating by 8:00. Choices F and H are incorrect because nothing in the premises suggests that Tracy might not have eaten dinner yet. As for choice G, we are not told whether Tracy's family usually eats dessert after dinner.

Reading and Language Arts

1. **B** In the second paragraph, the author lists Inness, Blakelock, and Ryder all as American impressionists. In the passage, the word *Hudson* refers to the Hudson River Valley, which is a place, not a person.

2. **J** The author makes it clear in the passage's first sentence that the topic at hand is "American art." Also, in the second paragraph the author tells us that when the impressionists (including Inness) did paint city scenes, their subjects were settings such as the upscale neighborhoods of New York City. In all likelihood, then, Inness lived and worked in the United States.

3. **C** According to the passage, Henri and the progressives revolted against the romanticism and impressionism that had dominated the American art scene, determined to portray what the American landscape was truly becoming. Accordingly, it would be accurate to describe Henri as a "realist."

4. **F** In the third paragraph, the author informs us that the progressives gained a foothold into mainstream art at the Armory Show of 1913, where their paintings helped launch a new era in art.

5. **D** In the passage, the author talks about how the progressive movement emerged as a reaction to established art of the time, and then how it gained prominence in the art world—through Henri and the 1913 Armory Show.

6. **J** The passage traces the chronological development—from earlier events to later ones—of America's progressive and modern art movements. The additional paragraph describes Hopper's contribution to American art, which occurred after the 1913 Armory Show. Therefore, the best place to add this paragraph is at the end of the passage.

Answers and Explanations *(continued)*

7. **C** As a whole, the paragraph is about how Hopper's paintings took the ideas of Henri and the progressives a step further. Details about Hopper's childhood, even those related to his artistic development, are off the topic at hand.

8. **F** In the first paragraph, the narrator tells us that Marco was desperate to retrieve his cap to avoid "double punishment." We can infer that Marco would be punished partly for losing the cap.

9. **D** Marco fears that a missing cap, wet clothes, or his absence during the morning might betray him—in other words, that his uncle would figure out that Marco had been canoeing that morning.

10. **G** The narrator tells us that at dinner Marco felt "guilty and afraid." Together, these feeling are likely to produce anxiety.

11. **B** Later in the second paragraph, the narrator tells us that Marco feared that his uncle might have noticed his absence, probably because his uncle would not have approved of Marco's morning canoe trip without first obtaining his permission. In this context, substituting the phrase *unexcused absence* for *truancy* makes perfect sense.

12. **H** We know that Marco went outside for the afternoon because he felt "ill at ease." We also know that he tried to stay "out of sight" and that he dreaded talking to, or even seeing, his cousin and uncle. Thus, the best explanation for Marco's staying outside all afternoon was that he wanted to avoid both of them as long as possible.

13. **B** In the second paragraph, the author states that pet owners can learn a lesson from Hans the horse. This statement strongly suggests that the article is directed to pet owners.

14. **H** The author tells us that Hans had fooled his owner (as well as other people) into thinking that Hans could perform arithmetic.

15. **D** In the first paragraph, the author refers to people who claim that their pets can speak in human languages. Then, in the second paragraph, the author tells us that these people can learn a lesson from Hans, who, as we learn in the third paragraph, does not possess the sort of high-level, human-like intellectual ability that he appeared to demonstrate. The lesson, then, is that we should be highly skeptical about claims of animal intelligence that seems too human-like.

16. **G** Nothing in the article suggests that Hans was ever punished for giving wrong answers to arithmetic questions, or for any other reason.

17. **A** In all probability, Hans learned to stomp his hoof the appropriate number of times by watching his owner's body language very closely.

18. **G** The problem with the original sentence lies in the faulty parallelism between the phrase *Training a dog* and the single word *cats*. There are several ways to fix this problem. One way would be to replace *cats* with *training a cat*. However, this solution is not among the answer choices. The sentence in choice G offers another solution; notice the proper parallelism between the two phrases *a dog* and *a cat*.

Answers and Explanations *(continued)*

19. **A** The sentence in choice A is grammatically correct, and the way it is constructed neatly conveys the idea that it is because the cat has a mind of her own that she cannot be trained. Choice B connects two complete sentences with only a comma. The result is not only grammatically incorrect (an example of a "comma splice") but also ineffective in conveying that the cat's independence is the reason she cannot be trained. The sentence in choice C contains no grammatical errors. However, like the sentence in choice B, it fails to convey the writer's point. The sentence in choice D is grammatically correct, but it gets the logic backwards. It's not because the writer cannot teach her cat tricks that the cat has a mind of her own. Instead, it's the other way around.

20. **H** The phrase *good boy* is dialogue (spoken words) within a narration and therefore should be set off by quotation marks.

21. **C** The ancients classified people based on personality types.

22. **F** According to the passage, a *phlegmatic* person is dependable and easy-going—in other words, *steady*.

23. **C** Jung's personality grid accounted for a person's attitudes toward other people and toward decision making.

24. **J** The author tells us that Freud was Jung's "contemporary," which means that these two psychologists lived and worked during the same time period: the early twentieth century. The author also tells us that both Jung and Freud were influential.

25. **B** The author tells us that Jung's work inspired others to develop various personality classification systems, and that the Myers-Briggs Type Indicator became the "most widely used"—in other words, the most popular—among these systems.

26. **F** In the original sentence, the two words *Every body* should be replaced with the single word *Everybody*, which means "everyone or every person." The word *everybody* is considered singular, and so it calls for the singular verb form *is*.

27. **D** The word *companies* is not a proper noun, and so it should not be capitalized.

28. **G** The sentence in choice G helps complete the writer's line of reasoning, which is as follows: People with more "street smarts" than "book smarts" are just as valuable to employers than people with only book smarts, and therefore employers should not use I.Q. tests when making hiring decisions.

29. **B** In this sentence, the author is attempting to impress upon the reader how harsh the environment is throughout Afghanistan. The word *unfriendly* is often used to describe such an environment, and so substituting this word for *forbidding* makes perfect sense.

30. **G** In the selection, the author marvels at the rich traditions and pride of the Afghan people and wonders how the rest of the world can possibly allow this civilization to wither away. Implicitly, the author is appealing to those who are listening to help save Afghanistan and its people—a *plea* for help on their behalf.

31. **D** At the end of the passage, the author refers to the Afghan people as "proud" and "strong-willed." These adjectives, along with the fact they have faced so much hardship, strongly suggest that they very *determined* to survive as a people.

32. **J** The author's point of view is that of a person concerned mainly with human welfare and speaking as an advocate for the alleviation of widespread hunger and suffering.

Answers and Explanations *(continued)*

33. **B** The sentence in choice B is clear and grammatically correct. Simply using the word *and* to connect the two ideas works well here. Each of the other three choices is awkward and confusing.

34. **F** The sentence in choice F is clear and grammatically correct. In choice G, the word *they* should be omitted. Although the sentence in choice H is grammatically correct, it doesn't make much sense; the word *but* should be used instead of *and* to make the meaning of the sentence clear. Also, the use of the adjective *occasionally* implies that the deserts are dotted with oases only some of the time—which makes no sense, of course. Choice J provides a mere sentence fragment (an incomplete sentence).

35. **C** The author informs us that the length of a nanometer is about 10 times that of a hydrogen atom. Thus, a hydrogen atom is shorter than a nanometer.

36. **J** The sentence's point is that the potential of nanotechnology is so great and far-reaching that we might soon look back on the Internet as comparatively insignificant—in other words, its importance will seem to *shrink*.

37. **A** Wrinkle cream and sunblock are two types of cosmetics.

38. **G** The author devotes the entire third paragraph to expressing concern about the nanotechnology's potential threat to public health.

39. **C** In the passage, the author first lists the benefits of nanotechnology. Then the author points out its potential human costs (cancers and other health problems). Choice C sums up the passage nicely.

40. **F** The sentence in choice F is clear and grammatically correct. The sentence in choice G contains a subject-verb agreement error; the plural subject *Nanotubes* does not match the singular verb form *is*. Each of the other two choices, H and J, provides a mere sentence fragment (an incomplete sentence).

Mathematics

1. **C** First, combine terms in each parenthesized expression: $-(-1)(1) = 1$. (A negative number multiplied by a negative number is a positive number.)

2. **J** To compare with $\dfrac{13}{40}$, convert the denominators in choices G, H, and J to 40:

   Choice G: $\dfrac{7}{20} \times \dfrac{2}{2} = \dfrac{14}{40} > \dfrac{13}{40}$

   Choice H: $\dfrac{2}{5} \times \dfrac{8}{8} = \dfrac{16}{40} > \dfrac{13}{40}$

   Choice J: $\dfrac{3}{10} \times \dfrac{4}{4} = \dfrac{12}{40} < \dfrac{13}{40}$

   For choice F, you can compare this way:

   Choice F: $\dfrac{1}{3} \times \dfrac{13}{13} = \dfrac{13}{39} > \dfrac{13}{40}$

3. **A** To add, align the three numbers vertically at the decimal point.

4. **J** In an equilateral triangle, all sides are congruent (equal in length) and all angles are congruent (60° each). In any triangle, angles opposite congruent sides are congruent, and vice versa. Also, in any triangle, the sum of the degree measures of the interior angles is 180°. Apply these properties to each triangle:

   Triangle A: Because one angle opposite a side of length 8 measures 60°, the angle opposite the other side of length 8 must also measure 60° and, therefore, so must the third angle. The triangle is equilateral.

Answers and Explanations *(continued)*

Triangle B: The two angles other than the indicated 60° angle must be congruent, and therefore they must measure 60° each. The triangle is equilateral.

Triangle C: Because two angles measure 60°, the third angle must also measure 60°. The triangle is equilateral.

5. **D** The digit 4 is in the "thousands" place.

6. **G** $\frac{5}{8}$ of the 40 students are girls:

$$\frac{5}{8} \times 40 = 25.$$

7. **A** To divide, multiply the numerator fraction $\frac{8}{9}$ by the reciprocal of the denominator fraction $\frac{4}{3}$, simplifying by cancelling common factors before combining: $\frac{8}{9} \times \frac{3}{4} = \frac{2}{3} \times \frac{1}{1} = \frac{2}{3}.$

8. **G** To answer the question, you can try plugging in each answer choice in turn. (With the correct number, the equation will hold true.) Or you can solve for x using algebra:

$$x = 3(x + 2)$$
$$x = 3x + 6$$
$$-2x = 6$$
$$x = -3$$

9. **C** Letting the price of a child's ticket equal C, the price of an adult ticket equals $2C$. Set up an algebraic equation, then solve for C:

$$C + C + C + 2C = \$18.75$$
$$5C = \$18.75$$
$$C = \$3.75$$

10. **G** Using the plug-in method, you can try substituting each answer choice for l in the following formula: $Area = lw$. Or, you can substitute $\frac{l}{2}$ for w in the formula, then solve for l:

$$8 = (l)\left(\frac{l}{2}\right)$$
$$16 = l^2$$
$$4 = l$$

11. **B** The new, 18-ounce mixture contains 10 ounces of water. Thus, water accounts for $\frac{10}{18}$, or $\frac{5}{9}$, of the new mixture.

12. **F** Notice that 825 is greater than 800 by 25, and that 775 is less than 800 by 25. Thus, to estimate their product, you can round off both numbers to 800, then multiply: 800 × 800 = 640,000. Choice F provides this approximation.

13. **A** Distribute x to (multiply x by) each term inside the parentheses.

14. **H** Only positive integers can be prime numbers, and a fraction whose numerator and denominator are two different prime numbers cannot be simplified and therefore must be a positive non-integer.

15. **A** In any triangle, the sum of the three interior angle measures is 180°. Since a right angle measures 90°, the sum of the other two angle measures must be 90°. Only choice A provides a pair of numbers that totals 90.

16. **J** $4^3 = 4 \times 4 \times 4$. Thus, $4^3 \times 4^3 = (4 \times 4) \times (4 \times 4) \times (4 \times 4) = 16 \times 16 \times 16$.

17. **C** Division A accounts for 20% (100% − 55% − 25%) of the total production (7,500). To find Division A's daily production, multiply: 0.2 × 7,500 = 1,500.

Answers and Explanations *(continued)*

18. **J** The total trip time was 2.5 hours. Apply the *rate × time = distance* formula: 40 (m.p.h.) × 2.5 (hours) = 100 (miles).

19. **C** Try plugging in simple numbers for p and q. For example, if one pack of gum (p) costs 2 dollars (d), then the cost of one pack of gum $= \dfrac{2}{1} = \dfrac{d}{p}$.

20. **J** Perform multiplication and division (in either order) before addition: $5 + 4 \times 3 \div 2 = 5 + 12 \div 2 = 5 + 6 = 11$.

21. **A** Each of the two series contains exactly 50 terms. Each term in the series of even integers is greater than the corresponding term in the series of odd integers by *exactly 1*. Thus, the difference between the sums is 50.

22. **G** Left of the y-axis (vertical axis), the x-coordinate (first coordinate in the pair) is negative. Above the x-axis (horizontal axis), the y-coordinate (second coordinate in the pair) is positive.

23. **B** $(2)\left(-\dfrac{1}{2}\right) = -1$, which is less than $-\dfrac{1}{2}$.

24. **F** $10^6 = 10 \times 10 \times 10 \times 10 \times 10 \times 10 = 1{,}000{,}000$. Thus, $2 \times 10^6 = 2{,}000{,}000$.

25. **C** Given that a non-zero integer x is greater than -5 but less that $5\dfrac{1}{2}\left(\dfrac{11}{2}\right)$, the possible values of x are: $-4, -3, -2, -1, 1, 2, 3, 4, 5$.

26. **F** To find 12% of $500, multiply: $0.12 \times \$500 = \$60$.

27. **D** A circle contains $360°$. The segment defined by the $60°$ angle accounts for $\dfrac{60}{360}$, or $\dfrac{1}{6}$, the circle's total area. Given a radius of 6, the circle has an area of $6^2\pi = 36\pi$. The shaded area is $\dfrac{5}{6}$ of 36π, or 30π.

28. **J** The two sets in choice J have in common the numbers 4, 5, and 6.

29. **C** The tax $= \$55 \times 0.05 = \$2.75$. Add this tax to the sweater's price: $\$55 + \$2.75 = \$57.75$.

30. **F** The sum of the three scores must equal three times the average score. Set up an equation, letting x equal the third score, and then solve for x:

$$90 + 90 + x = 92 \times 3$$
$$180 + x = 276$$
$$x = 96$$

31. **D** You can determine the correct answer choice by making a commonsense estimate: Based on a mile-to-kilometer ratio of 1:1.6, 10 kilometers is significantly less than 10 miles but a bit more than 5 miles. Or, to compute the precise answer, divide 10 by 1.6. Try converting 1.6 to the fraction $\dfrac{8}{5}$, then multiply 10 by its reciprocal:

$$10 \div \dfrac{8}{5} = 10 \times \dfrac{5}{8} = \dfrac{50}{8} = 6.25$$

$$\dfrac{1}{1.6} = \dfrac{x}{10}$$
$$1.6x = 10$$
$$x = \dfrac{10}{1.6}$$

32. **J** The number of visitors during May was approximately 25,000. The number of visitors during June was approximately 65,000—an increase of 40,000.

33. **B** The approximate number of visitors during each of the six months are as follows:

January: 30,000
February: 60,000
March: 40,000
April: 45,000
May: 25,000
June: 65,000

The sum of these six numbers is 265,000.

Answers and Explanations *(continued)*

34. **G** $\left(\sqrt{3}\right)^4 = \sqrt{3} \times \sqrt{3} \times \sqrt{3} \times \sqrt{3} = 9.$

    Because $3^4 = 81$, $\sqrt[4]{81} = 3$.

35. **D** 6 of the 12 marbles are green. The probability of selecting a green marble is $\frac{6}{12}$, or $\frac{1}{2}$.

36. **G** *Thirty thousand* is equivalent to 30,000; *twenty-four* is equivalent to 24. The verbal expression adds one amount to the other.

37. **C** Divide the figure into two rectangles, as shown below.

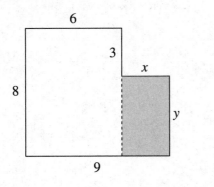

    Then, find x and y in the figure. $x = 9 - 6 = 3$, and $y = 8 - 3 = 5$. The area of the shaded rectangle $= x \times y = 3 \times 5 = 15$. The area of the larger (unshaded) rectangle is $6 \times 8 = 48$. The total area of the figure is $15 + 48 = 63$.

38. **H** One burger costs B dollars. There are 100 cents to a dollar. Thus, the cost of a burger in *cents* is 100B. The question asks for the *cent* cost of one burger (100B) *and* one soda (S).

39. **D** All five interior angles are congruent (the same size). The total measure of the interior angles of a pentagon is 540°. Thus, each interior angle measures $\frac{1}{5}$ of 540°, or 108°.

40. **F** $\sqrt{40}$ is between 6 and 7, but nearer to 6.

    $\sqrt{60}$ is between 7 and 8, but nearer to 8. Thus, their sum is approximately 14.

COOP PRACTICE TEST 2

Answer Sheet

Directions: For each answer that you select, blacken the corresponding oval on this sheet.

Sequences

1. Ⓐ Ⓑ Ⓒ Ⓓ
2. Ⓕ Ⓖ Ⓗ Ⓙ
3. Ⓐ Ⓑ Ⓒ Ⓓ
4. Ⓕ Ⓖ Ⓗ Ⓙ
5. Ⓐ Ⓑ Ⓒ Ⓓ
6. Ⓕ Ⓖ Ⓗ Ⓙ
7. Ⓐ Ⓑ Ⓒ Ⓓ
8. Ⓕ Ⓖ Ⓗ Ⓙ
9. Ⓐ Ⓑ Ⓒ Ⓓ
10. Ⓕ Ⓖ Ⓗ Ⓙ
11. Ⓐ Ⓑ Ⓒ Ⓓ
12. Ⓕ Ⓖ Ⓗ Ⓙ
13. Ⓐ Ⓑ Ⓒ Ⓓ
14. Ⓕ Ⓖ Ⓗ Ⓙ
15. Ⓐ Ⓑ Ⓒ Ⓓ
16. Ⓕ Ⓖ Ⓗ Ⓙ
17. Ⓐ Ⓑ Ⓒ Ⓓ
18. Ⓕ Ⓖ Ⓗ Ⓙ
19. Ⓐ Ⓑ Ⓒ Ⓓ
20. Ⓕ Ⓖ Ⓗ Ⓙ

Quantitative Reasoning

1. Ⓐ Ⓑ Ⓒ Ⓓ
2. Ⓕ Ⓖ Ⓗ Ⓙ
3. Ⓐ Ⓑ Ⓒ Ⓓ
4. Ⓕ Ⓖ Ⓗ Ⓙ
5. Ⓐ Ⓑ Ⓒ Ⓓ
6. Ⓕ Ⓖ Ⓗ Ⓙ
7. Ⓐ Ⓑ Ⓒ Ⓓ
8. Ⓕ Ⓖ Ⓗ Ⓙ
9. Ⓐ Ⓑ Ⓒ Ⓓ
10. Ⓕ Ⓖ Ⓗ Ⓙ
11. Ⓐ Ⓑ Ⓒ Ⓓ
12. Ⓕ Ⓖ Ⓗ Ⓙ
13. Ⓐ Ⓑ Ⓒ Ⓓ
14. Ⓕ Ⓖ Ⓗ Ⓙ
15. Ⓐ Ⓑ Ⓒ Ⓓ
16. Ⓕ Ⓖ Ⓗ Ⓙ
17. Ⓐ Ⓑ Ⓒ Ⓓ
18. Ⓕ Ⓖ Ⓗ Ⓙ
19. Ⓐ Ⓑ Ⓒ Ⓓ
20. Ⓕ Ⓖ Ⓗ Ⓙ

Verbal Reasoning—Context

1. Ⓐ Ⓑ Ⓒ Ⓓ
2. Ⓕ Ⓖ Ⓗ Ⓙ
3. Ⓐ Ⓑ Ⓒ Ⓓ
4. Ⓕ Ⓖ Ⓗ Ⓙ
5. Ⓐ Ⓑ Ⓒ Ⓓ
6. Ⓕ Ⓖ Ⓗ Ⓙ
7. Ⓐ Ⓑ Ⓒ Ⓓ
8. Ⓕ Ⓖ Ⓗ Ⓙ
9. Ⓐ Ⓑ Ⓒ Ⓓ
10. Ⓕ Ⓖ Ⓗ Ⓙ
11. Ⓐ Ⓑ Ⓒ Ⓓ
12. Ⓕ Ⓖ Ⓗ Ⓙ
13. Ⓐ Ⓑ Ⓒ Ⓓ
14. Ⓕ Ⓖ Ⓗ Ⓙ
15. Ⓐ Ⓑ Ⓒ Ⓓ
16. Ⓕ Ⓖ Ⓗ Ⓙ
17. Ⓐ Ⓑ Ⓒ Ⓓ
18. Ⓕ Ⓖ Ⓗ Ⓙ
19. Ⓐ Ⓑ Ⓒ Ⓓ
20. Ⓕ Ⓖ Ⓗ Ⓙ

Analogies

1. Ⓐ Ⓑ Ⓒ Ⓓ
2. Ⓕ Ⓖ Ⓗ Ⓙ
3. Ⓐ Ⓑ Ⓒ Ⓓ
4. Ⓕ Ⓖ Ⓗ Ⓙ
5. Ⓐ Ⓑ Ⓒ Ⓓ
6. Ⓕ Ⓖ Ⓗ Ⓙ
7. Ⓐ Ⓑ Ⓒ Ⓓ
8. Ⓕ Ⓖ Ⓗ Ⓙ
9. Ⓐ Ⓑ Ⓒ Ⓓ
10. Ⓕ Ⓖ Ⓗ Ⓙ
11. Ⓐ Ⓑ Ⓒ Ⓓ
12. Ⓕ Ⓖ Ⓗ Ⓙ
13. Ⓐ Ⓑ Ⓒ Ⓓ
14. Ⓕ Ⓖ Ⓗ Ⓙ
15. Ⓐ Ⓑ Ⓒ Ⓓ
16. Ⓕ Ⓖ Ⓗ Ⓙ
17. Ⓐ Ⓑ Ⓒ Ⓓ
18. Ⓕ Ⓖ Ⓗ Ⓙ
19. Ⓐ Ⓑ Ⓒ Ⓓ
20. Ⓕ Ⓖ Ⓗ Ⓙ

Verbal Reasoning—Words

1. Ⓐ Ⓑ Ⓒ Ⓓ
2. Ⓕ Ⓖ Ⓗ Ⓙ
3. Ⓐ Ⓑ Ⓒ Ⓓ
4. Ⓕ Ⓖ Ⓗ Ⓙ
5. Ⓐ Ⓑ Ⓒ Ⓓ
6. Ⓕ Ⓖ Ⓗ Ⓙ
7. Ⓐ Ⓑ Ⓒ Ⓓ
8. Ⓕ Ⓖ Ⓗ Ⓙ
9. Ⓐ Ⓑ Ⓒ Ⓓ
10. Ⓕ Ⓖ Ⓗ Ⓙ
11. Ⓐ Ⓑ Ⓒ Ⓓ
12. Ⓕ Ⓖ Ⓗ Ⓙ
13. Ⓐ Ⓑ Ⓒ Ⓓ
14. Ⓕ Ⓖ Ⓗ Ⓙ
15. Ⓐ Ⓑ Ⓒ Ⓓ
16. Ⓕ Ⓖ Ⓗ Ⓙ
17. Ⓐ Ⓑ Ⓒ Ⓓ
18. Ⓕ Ⓖ Ⓗ Ⓙ
19. Ⓐ Ⓑ Ⓒ Ⓓ
20. Ⓕ Ⓖ Ⓗ Ⓙ

Reading and Language Arts

1. Ⓐ Ⓑ Ⓒ Ⓓ
2. Ⓕ Ⓖ Ⓗ Ⓙ
3. Ⓐ Ⓑ Ⓒ Ⓓ
4. Ⓕ Ⓖ Ⓗ Ⓙ
5. Ⓐ Ⓑ Ⓒ Ⓓ
6. Ⓕ Ⓖ Ⓗ Ⓙ
7. Ⓐ Ⓑ Ⓒ Ⓓ
8. Ⓕ Ⓖ Ⓗ Ⓙ
9. Ⓐ Ⓑ Ⓒ Ⓓ
10. Ⓕ Ⓖ Ⓗ Ⓙ
11. Ⓐ Ⓑ Ⓒ Ⓓ
12. Ⓕ Ⓖ Ⓗ Ⓙ
13. Ⓐ Ⓑ Ⓒ Ⓓ
14. Ⓕ Ⓖ Ⓗ Ⓙ
15. Ⓐ Ⓑ Ⓒ Ⓓ
16. Ⓕ Ⓖ Ⓗ Ⓙ
17. Ⓐ Ⓑ Ⓒ Ⓓ
18. Ⓕ Ⓖ Ⓗ Ⓙ
19. Ⓐ Ⓑ Ⓒ Ⓓ
20. Ⓕ Ⓖ Ⓗ Ⓙ

COOP PRACTICE TEST 2

Answer Sheet (continued)

21.	Ⓐ	Ⓑ	Ⓒ	Ⓓ		21.	Ⓐ	Ⓑ	Ⓒ	Ⓓ
22.	Ⓕ	Ⓖ	Ⓗ	Ⓙ		22.	Ⓕ	Ⓖ	Ⓗ	Ⓙ
23.	Ⓐ	Ⓑ	Ⓒ	Ⓓ		23.	Ⓐ	Ⓑ	Ⓒ	Ⓓ
24.	Ⓕ	Ⓖ	Ⓗ	Ⓙ		24.	Ⓕ	Ⓖ	Ⓗ	Ⓙ
25.	Ⓐ	Ⓑ	Ⓒ	Ⓓ		25.	Ⓐ	Ⓑ	Ⓒ	Ⓓ
26.	Ⓕ	Ⓖ	Ⓗ	Ⓙ		26.	Ⓕ	Ⓖ	Ⓗ	Ⓙ
27.	Ⓐ	Ⓑ	Ⓒ	Ⓓ		27.	Ⓐ	Ⓑ	Ⓒ	Ⓓ
28.	Ⓕ	Ⓖ	Ⓗ	Ⓙ		28.	Ⓕ	Ⓖ	Ⓗ	Ⓙ
29.	Ⓐ	Ⓑ	Ⓒ	Ⓓ		29.	Ⓐ	Ⓑ	Ⓒ	Ⓓ
30.	Ⓕ	Ⓖ	Ⓗ	Ⓙ		30.	Ⓕ	Ⓖ	Ⓗ	Ⓙ
31.	Ⓐ	Ⓑ	Ⓒ	Ⓓ		31.	Ⓐ	Ⓑ	Ⓒ	Ⓓ
32.	Ⓕ	Ⓖ	Ⓗ	Ⓙ		32.	Ⓕ	Ⓖ	Ⓗ	Ⓙ
33.	Ⓐ	Ⓑ	Ⓒ	Ⓓ		33.	Ⓐ	Ⓑ	Ⓒ	Ⓓ
34.	Ⓕ	Ⓖ	Ⓗ	Ⓙ		34.	Ⓕ	Ⓖ	Ⓗ	Ⓙ
35.	Ⓐ	Ⓑ	Ⓒ	Ⓓ		35.	Ⓐ	Ⓑ	Ⓒ	Ⓓ
36.	Ⓕ	Ⓖ	Ⓗ	Ⓙ		36.	Ⓕ	Ⓖ	Ⓗ	Ⓙ
37.	Ⓐ	Ⓑ	Ⓒ	Ⓓ		37.	Ⓐ	Ⓑ	Ⓒ	Ⓓ
38.	Ⓕ	Ⓖ	Ⓗ	Ⓙ		38.	Ⓕ	Ⓖ	Ⓗ	Ⓙ
39.	Ⓐ	Ⓑ	Ⓒ	Ⓓ		39.	Ⓐ	Ⓑ	Ⓒ	Ⓓ
40.	Ⓕ	Ⓖ	Ⓗ	Ⓙ		40.	Ⓕ	Ⓖ	Ⓗ	Ⓙ

Mathematics

1.	Ⓐ	Ⓑ	Ⓒ	Ⓓ
2.	Ⓕ	Ⓖ	Ⓗ	Ⓙ
3.	Ⓐ	Ⓑ	Ⓒ	Ⓓ
4.	Ⓕ	Ⓖ	Ⓗ	Ⓙ
5.	Ⓐ	Ⓑ	Ⓒ	Ⓓ
6.	Ⓕ	Ⓖ	Ⓗ	Ⓙ
7.	Ⓐ	Ⓑ	Ⓒ	Ⓓ
8.	Ⓕ	Ⓖ	Ⓗ	Ⓙ
9.	Ⓐ	Ⓑ	Ⓒ	Ⓓ
10.	Ⓕ	Ⓖ	Ⓗ	Ⓙ
11.	Ⓐ	Ⓑ	Ⓒ	Ⓓ
12.	Ⓕ	Ⓖ	Ⓗ	Ⓙ
13.	Ⓐ	Ⓑ	Ⓒ	Ⓓ
14.	Ⓕ	Ⓖ	Ⓗ	Ⓙ
15.	Ⓐ	Ⓑ	Ⓒ	Ⓓ
16.	Ⓕ	Ⓖ	Ⓗ	Ⓙ
17.	Ⓐ	Ⓑ	Ⓒ	Ⓓ
18.	Ⓕ	Ⓖ	Ⓗ	Ⓙ
19.	Ⓐ	Ⓑ	Ⓒ	Ⓓ
20.	Ⓕ	Ⓖ	Ⓗ	Ⓙ

COOP PRACTICE TEST 2

Sequences (20 Questions, 15 Minutes)

Directions: Choose the answer that will best continue or complete the sequence or pattern.

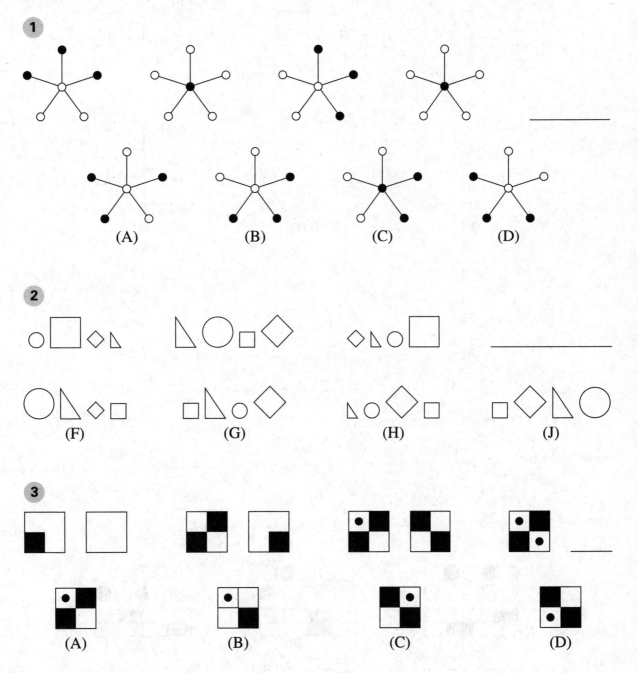

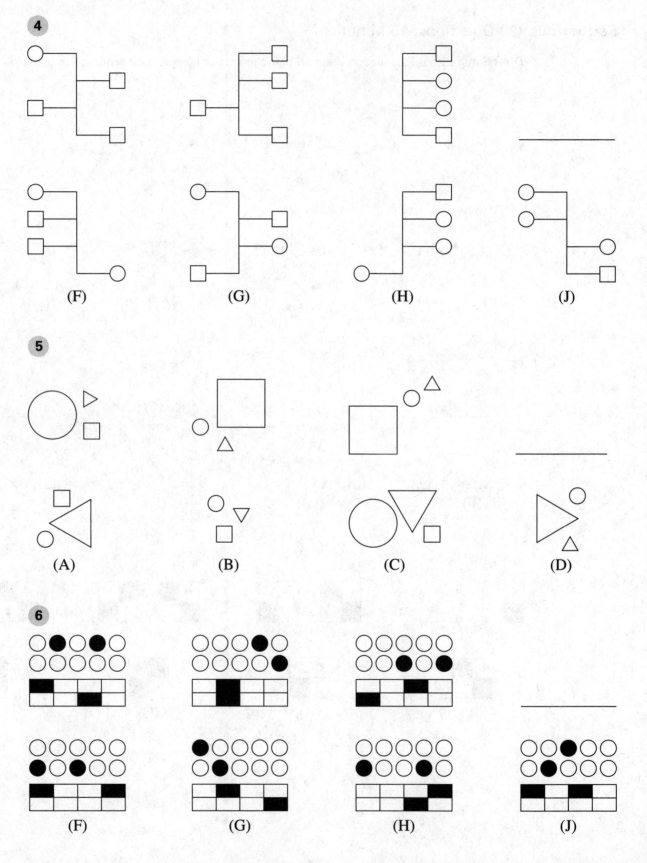

Sequences (continued)

7 D G J M P __

- A Q
- B S
- C R
- D N

8 Z A Y C __ W G

- F E F
- G X W
- H F G
- J X E

9 C P J | D Q K | E R L | ____

- A M N O
- B F G H
- C G M P
- D F S M

10 e g f | h j i | ____ | n p o

- F l n m
- G j l m
- H k m l
- J k l m

11 w U s | q O m | k I g | ____

- A f E b
- B e C a
- C d C b
- D e c A

12 k l m | j l n | i l o | ____

- F h l p
- G g l q
- H h m p
- J k n q

13 A_1BC | B_2BC | ____ | D_4BC

- A C_3BC
- B A_3CB
- C B_3BC
- D C_3CA

14 DA^5D | CB^4C | BC^3B | ____

- F BD^6A
- G ADC^2
- H CB^2B
- J AD^2A

15 10 14 18 __ 26

- A 20
- B 22
- C 24
- D 26

16 24 23 21 18 14 __

- F 10
- G 11
- H 9
- J 8

17 9 3 1 | 18 6 2 | 36 __ 4

- A 18
- B 12
- C 9
- D 6

18 3 9 27 | 2 4 8 | 4 16 __

- F 30
- G 36
- H 48
- J 64

19 13 5 9 | 10 2 6 | 19 __ 15

- A 7
- B 11
- C 13
- D 9

20 10 20 15 | 20 40 30 | 5 10 __

- F 7.5
- G 15
- H 2.5
- J 12.5

STOP!
If you finish before time runs out, check your work on this section only.

Analogies (20 Questions, 7 Minutes)

Directions: For questions 1–20, the two upper pictures are related in some way. Select a picture that fills in the space so that the two lower pictures are related in the same way.

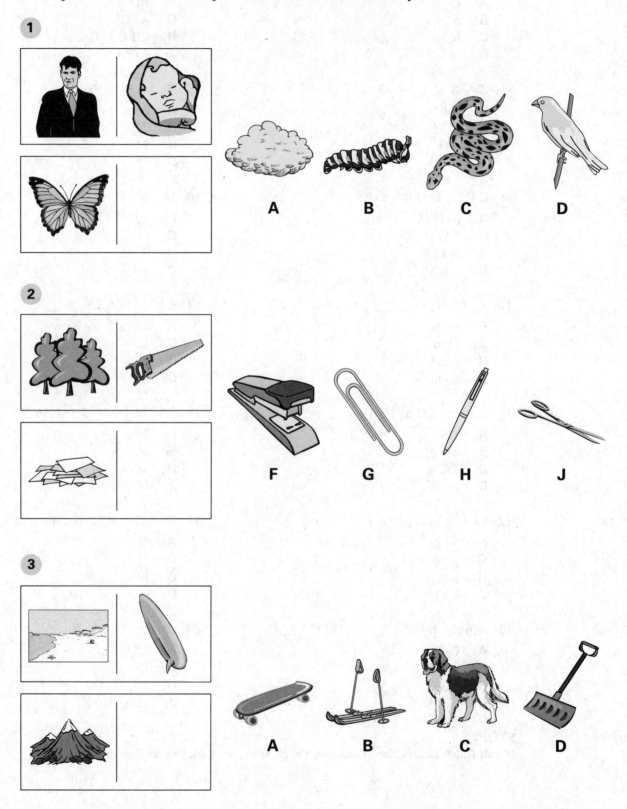

Analogies (continued)

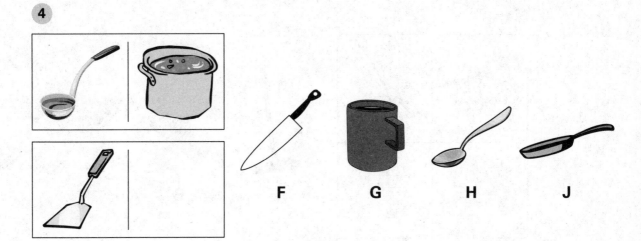

4

F   G   H   J

5

A   B   C   D

6

F   G   H   J

Analogies *(continued)*

7

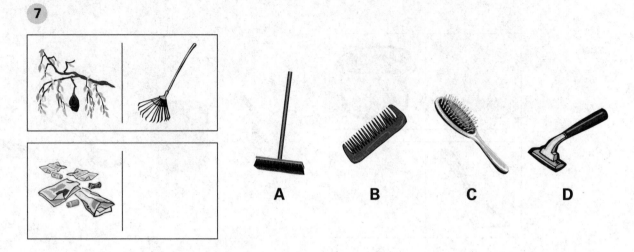

8

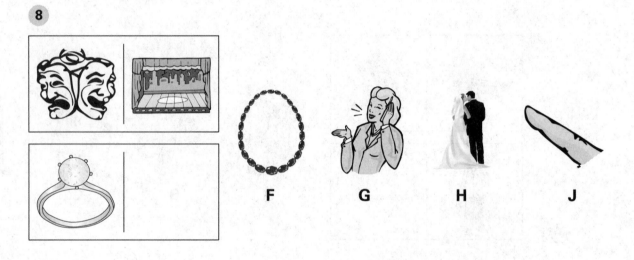

9

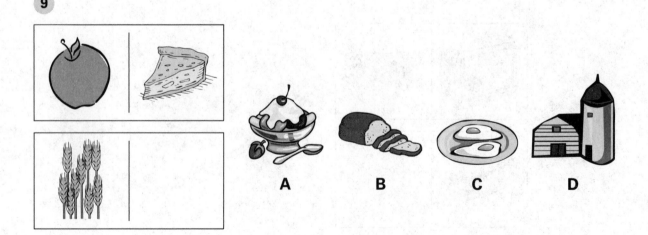

Analogies *(continued)*

10

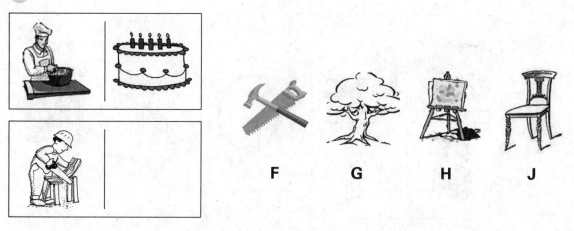

11

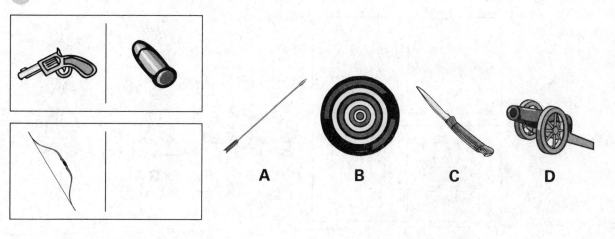

12

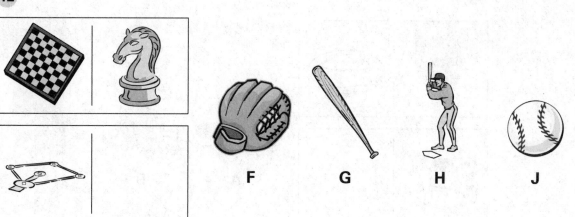

Analogies *(continued)*

13

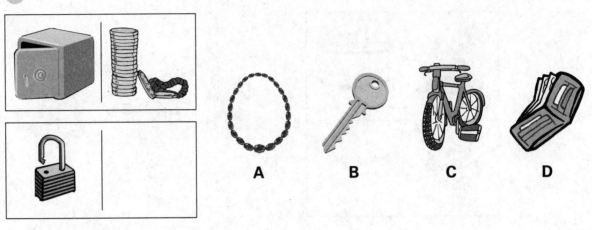

14

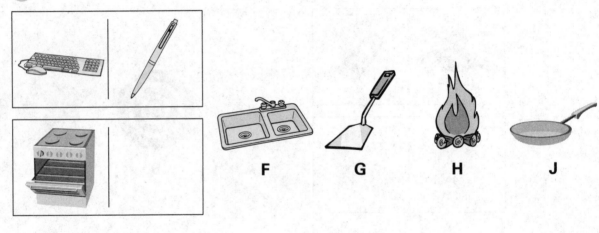

15

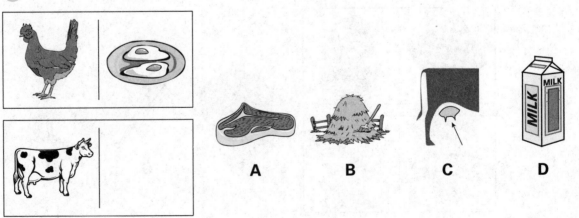

Analogies (continued)

16

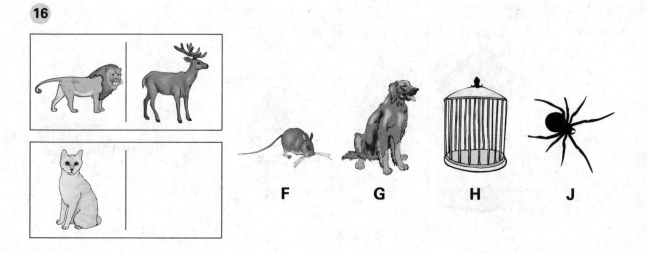

17

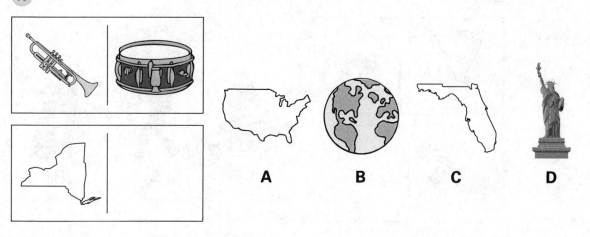

18

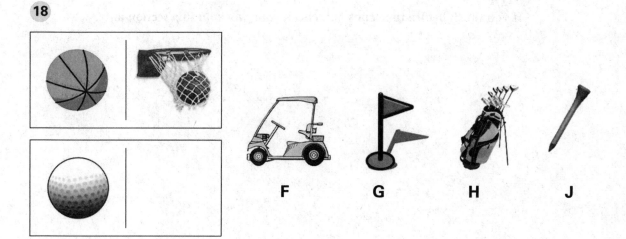

Analogies *(continued)*

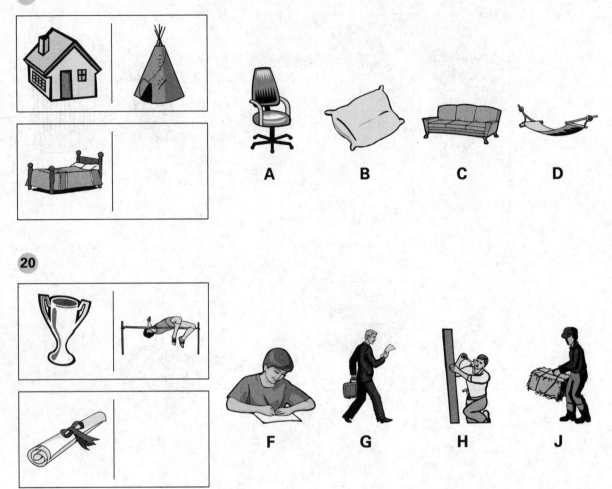

19

A B C D

20

F G H J

STOP!
If you finish before time runs out, check your work on this section only.

Quantitative Reasoning (20 Questions, 15 Minutes)

Directions: For questions 1–7, find the operation (fill in the blank) that is applied to the first number in each of two pairs to obtain the second number. Then, apply the operation to find the missing number. Select the correct answer choice.

1 $12 \to \underline{} \to 21$
$8 \to \underline{} \to 17$
$1 \to \underline{} \to ?$
- **A** 15
- **B** 10
- **C** 13
- **D** 9

2 $9 \to \underline{} \to 3$
$18 \to \underline{} \to 12$
$8 \to \underline{} \to ?$
- **F** 1
- **G** 4
- **H** 6
- **J** 2

3 $\dfrac{3}{2} \to \underline{} \to \dfrac{7}{2}$
$1 \to \underline{} \to 3$
$\dfrac{4}{3} \to \underline{} \to ?$
- **A** $\dfrac{8}{3}$
- **B** 4
- **C** $\dfrac{10}{3}$
- **D** 5

4 $3 \to \underline{} \to 2$
$\dfrac{3}{2} \to \underline{} \to \dfrac{1}{2}$
$\dfrac{2}{3} \to \underline{} \to ?$
- **F** 1
- **G** $-\dfrac{1}{3}$
- **H** $\dfrac{1}{3}$
- **J** $\dfrac{3}{2}$

5 $18 \to \underline{} \to 9$
$8 \to \underline{} \to 4$
$11 \to \underline{} \to ?$
- **A** 7
- **B** $\dfrac{11}{3}$
- **C** 5
- **D** $\dfrac{11}{2}$

6 $7 \to \underline{} \to 35$
$5 \to \underline{} \to 25$
$4 \to \underline{} \to ?$
- **F** 20
- **G** 30
- **H** 15
- **J** 16

7 $\dfrac{5}{2} \to \underline{} \to \dfrac{1}{2}$
$\dfrac{15}{2} \to \underline{} \to \dfrac{3}{2}$
$5 \to \underline{} \to ?$
- **A** $-\dfrac{3}{2}$
- **B** $\dfrac{5}{2}$
- **C** 1
- **D** 2

Quantitative Reasoning *(continued)*

Directions: For questions 8–14, find the fraction of the grid that is darkened.

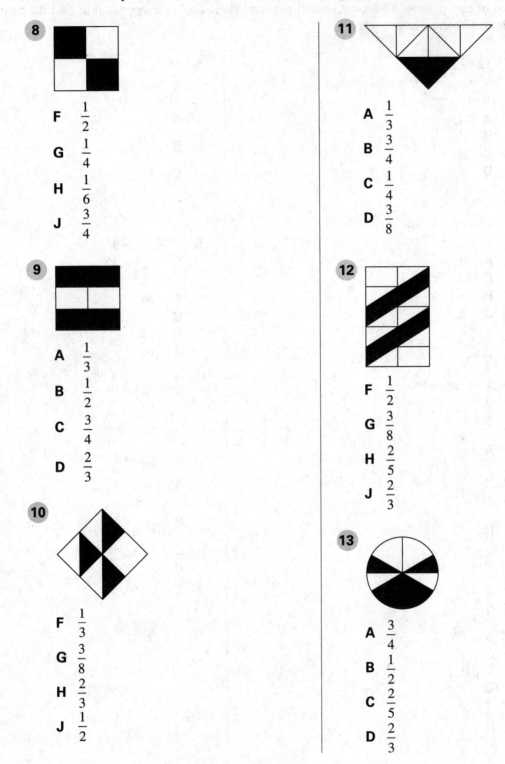

8

F $\dfrac{1}{2}$

G $\dfrac{1}{4}$

H $\dfrac{1}{6}$

J $\dfrac{3}{4}$

9

A $\dfrac{1}{3}$

B $\dfrac{1}{2}$

C $\dfrac{3}{4}$

D $\dfrac{2}{3}$

10

F $\dfrac{1}{3}$

G $\dfrac{3}{8}$

H $\dfrac{2}{3}$

J $\dfrac{1}{2}$

11

A $\dfrac{1}{3}$

B $\dfrac{3}{4}$

C $\dfrac{1}{4}$

D $\dfrac{3}{8}$

12

F $\dfrac{1}{2}$

G $\dfrac{3}{8}$

H $\dfrac{2}{5}$

J $\dfrac{2}{3}$

13

A $\dfrac{3}{4}$

B $\dfrac{1}{2}$

C $\dfrac{2}{5}$

D $\dfrac{2}{3}$

Quantitative Reasoning *(continued)*

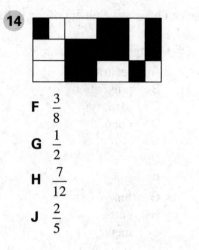

14

F $\frac{3}{8}$

G $\frac{1}{2}$

H $\frac{7}{12}$

J $\frac{2}{5}$

Directions: For questions 15–20, examine the balanced scale. Then, select another arrangement of objects that would also balance the scale.

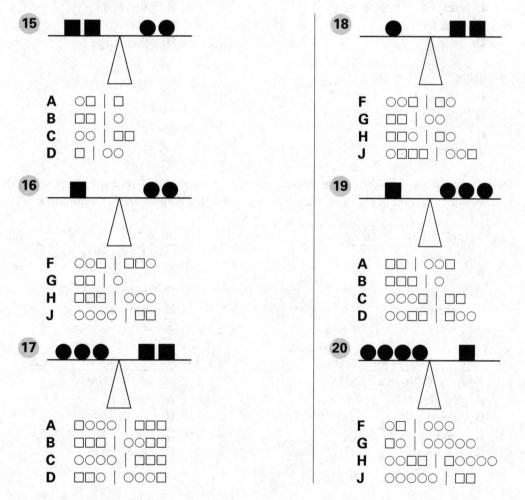

15

A ○□ | □
B □□ | ○
C ○○ | □□
D □ | ○○

16

F ○○□ | □□○
G □□ | ○
H □□□ | ○○○
J ○○○○ | □□

17

A □○○○ | □□□
B □□□ | ○○□□
C ○○○○ | □□□
D □□○ | ○○○□

18

F ○○□ | □○
G □□ | ○○
H □□○ | □○
J ○□□□ | ○○□

19

A □□ | ○○□
B □□□ | ○
C ○○○□ | □□
D ○○□□ | □○○

20

F ○□ | ○○○
G □○ | ○○○○○
H ○○□□ | □○○○○
J ○○○○○ | □□

STOP!
If you finish before time runs out, check your work on this section only.

Verbal Reasoning—Words (20 Questions, 15 Minutes)

Directions: For questions 1–7, find the word that names a necessary element of the underlined word.

1 <u>fan</u>

    A blade
    B air
    C heat
    D switch

2 <u>orchestra</u>

    F instrument
    G concert
    H audience
    J violin

3 <u>weapon</u>

    A harm
    B fear
    C crime
    D gun

4 <u>debate</u>

    F blame
    G resolve
    H win
    J disagree

5 <u>badge</u>

    A security
    B prevention
    C identity
    D honor

6 <u>chain</u>

    F rope
    G link
    H cuff
    J metal

7 <u>destination</u>

    A predicting
    B succeeding
    C hoping
    D planning

Directions: In questions 8–11, the words in the top line are related in some way. The words in the bottom line should be related in the same way. Find the word that completes the bottom row of words.

8 <u>scream   talk   whisper</u>
    sever cut _____

    F slice
    G scratch
    H chop
    J stab

9 <u>crime   trial   conviction</u>
    song concert _____

    A band
    B music
    C applause
    D audience

10 <u>clock   watch   sun</u>
    calculator slide-rule _____

    F pencil
    G battery
    H arithmetic
    J sum

11 <u>song   melody   note</u>
    essay sentence _____

    A author
    B word
    C page
    D paragraph

Verbal Reasoning—Words *(continued)*

Directions: For questions 12–15, find the word that does not belong with the others.

12
F peel
G shell
H husk
J pit

13
A hammer
B bat
C whip
D drill

14
F erase
G replace
H forget
J delete

15
A experience
B education
C talent
D knowledge

Directions: For questions 16–20, find the word that is most like the underlined words.

16 carrot squash spinach
F apple
G cabbage
H cheese
J rice

17 torch flashlight lamp
A bulb
B cord
C switch
D lantern

18 post column pole
F pillar
G bar
H beam
J row

19 jot scribble notate
A draw
B erase
C outline
D write

20 bright alert witty
F crisp
G wise
H sharp
J edgy

STOP!
If you finish before time runs out, check your work on this section only.

Verbal Reasoning—Context (20 Questions, 15 Minutes)

Directions: For questions 1–20, find the statement that is most probably true according to the given information.

1 Lynn ate an entire chocolate bar this afternoon. Lynn did not eat dinner tonight, and her stomach hurts now.

A Lynn ate too much chocolate.
B Lynn is not feeling well.
C Lynn is trying to lose weight.
D Lynn is hungry.

2 On average, women bear 2–3 children during their lifetime. Laura has given birth to only one child.

F Laura has fewer children than most women her age.
G Laura does not want more than one child.
H Laura is too old to have more children.
J Laura will have at least one more child.

3 All gremlins are cute. All male gremlins have black fur.

A All cute gremlins are female.
B Female gremlins are cuter than male gremlins.
C All furry gremlins are cute.
D All gremlins with black fur are male.

4 Josh, a baseball fan, recently moved from Atlanta to Detroit. A team called the Braves plays professional baseball in Atlanta, while the Tigers play professional baseball in Detroit.

F Josh is a fan of the Detroit Tigers.
G The Braves play in a city where Josh used to live.
H Josh has seen the Detroit Tigers play in Detroit.
J Josh is no longer a Braves fan.

5 More members of the school orchestra play flute than any other instrument. Fewer members of the school orchestra play tuba than any other instrument.

A The school's flute players are more talented than its tuba players.
B The orchestra's flute section is louder than its tuba section.
C There are more flutes than tubas in the orchestra.
D It is more difficult to pass the orchestra's flute audition than its tuba audition.

6 My dog Sparky barks whenever he is riding in my car. Sparky also barks whenever he sees our mail carrier.

F Sparky is afraid of other cars.
G Sparky barks when he sees his owner.
H The mail carrier is a man.
J Sparky makes a good guard dog.

7 In the Miss Hartford County pageant, Teresa won the talent competition, but Karen won the swimsuit competition.

A Teresa and Karen were both judged on their talent.
B Either Teresa or Karen won the pageant.
C Teresa is a good public speaker.
D Teresa is a talented singer.

8 Lauren yelled to Mandie, "Look out for the car!" Mandie turned to see a car coming at her. Mandie was not hurt.

F Lauren was trying to frighten Mandie.
G Mandie was not driving.
H Lauren warned Mandie in time.
J The car's driver tried to hit Mandie.

Verbal Reasoning—Context *(continued)*

9 During February, Jill sold more houses than any other real estate sales agent in the city.

- **A** House prices were low in February.
- **B** Jill is an effective sales agent.
- **C** Jill sold fewer houses in January than in February.
- **D** The weather was unusually mild in February.

10 Cocoa is more expensive than tea. Soda is more expensive than cocoa. Coffee is the same price as tea.

- **F** Tea is more expensive than soda.
- **G** Tea and cocoa are the same price.
- **H** Coffee and cocoa are the same price.
- **J** Coffee is less expensive than soda.

11 At the local theater, movie previews start 10 minutes before the main feature. The line at the theater's snack bar is longest during movie previews.

- **A** The theater's snack bar is operated by inexperienced employees.
- **B** Having snacks for the main feature is important to the moviegoers.
- **C** Many of the moviegoers are too impatient to stand in long lines.
- **D** The theater often runs out of popcorn before the main feature begins.

12 Wumpies can swim. Fripples cannot fly. Fripples can swim.

- **F** Wumpies and fripples can swim.
- **G** Wumpies can fly.
- **H** Neither wumpies nor fripples can fly.
- **J** Fripples can run.

13 All white cars at the auto show are convertibles, but no convertible at the auto show is an import.

- **A** None of the imports at the auto show are white.
- **B** All cars at the auto show are white.
- **C** All convertibles at the auto show are white.
- **D** All cars at the auto show are convertibles.

14 A parcel delivery service left a package addressed to John Smith on the front doorstep of Becky Smith's house. Within a few minutes, Becky opened the door and took the package inside the house.

- **F** John and Becky live in the same house.
- **G** The package was delivered to the wrong address.
- **H** Becky thought the package was for her.
- **J** John is not expecting the package.

15 This box contains red candies and black candies. Real licorice candy is always black in color.

- **A** The box contains real licorice candy.
- **B** Some candies in the box are not real licorice.
- **C** Licorice candy comes in two colors.
- **D** The word "licorice" does not appear on the box.

16 The chimney of Gary's house is made of stones. There are many similar stones on the land around Gary's house.

- **F** Gary's neighbors like his chimney.
- **G** Gary's house is fireproof.
- **H** The chimney blends with the surrounding land.
- **J** Gary built the chimney himself.

17 Pamela goes to a movie every Friday evening, and she attends a ballet class every Tuesday and Thursday evening. On Monday and Wednesday evenings, Pamela stays at home and does homework.

- **A** Pamela wants to be a professional ballet dancer.
- **B** Pamela gets good grades in school.
- **C** Pamela has a lot of free time on weekends.
- **D** Pamela is busy every weeknight.

Verbal Reasoning—Context *(continued)*

18 During the spring, Jim mows his lawn twice per week. During the summer, Jim mows his lawn once per week.

F Jim's lawn grows faster in the summer than in the spring.

G Jim bought a new lawn mower just before summer.

H It is important to Jim to keep his lawn trimmed.

J Jim's lawn has a lot of weeds that need to be removed.

19 Only high school graduates can attend Wheeler College. David is a high school student. Bill is not a high school student.

A David is not a Wheeler College student.

B David is a Wheeler College student.

C Bill is not a Wheeler College student.

D Bill is a Wheeler College student.

20 For the last five years, the minimum hourly wage that businesses must pay workers has been 10 dollars. Monica makes 12 dollars per hour at her job, and Cathy makes 10 dollars per hour at her job. Monica and Cathy both started their jobs last year.

F Cathy has a different job than Monica.

G Monica is a better worker than Cathy.

H Monica has received a pay raise.

J Cathy has not received a pay raise.

STOP!
If you finish before time runs out, check your work on this section only.

Reading and Language Arts (40 Questions, 40 Minutes)

Directions: Questions 1–40 are based on reading passages, brief essays, and sentences. For each question, select the best answer.

Questions 1–5 are based on the following passage:

The last known case of the smallpox virus was in 1978. But, the world is not necessarily rid of the virus forever; it lives on in science laboratories, and the threat of bioterrorism today has caused new concerns about a smallpox epidemic.

Smallpox originated in Africa. The virus traveled to Europe from Arabia via Egypt, while the first outbreak in the U.S. occurred shortly after new slaves arrived from Africa. The first English-language description of the disease is in an Anglo-Saxon manuscript written during the tenth century. However, it was not until the sixteenth century that the name "smallpox" was given to the disease, in order to distinguish it from chickenpox and from the Great Pox, also called syphilis. Both of those diseases had already spread across Europe, due mainly to crowded and unsanitary conditions in the cities.

Like syphilis, smallpox bacteria could be carried through the air for considerable distances and could cling for long periods to clothes, books, furniture, and so forth. Europeans came to accept an attack as certain. In fact, by the eighteenth century, so many faces were permanently pitted from severe smallpox that any woman who had no smallpox marks was instantly considered beautiful!

At the end of the eighteenth century, smallpox accounted for more than 200 in every 1,000 deaths on the European continent, while in Russia two million persons perished from smallpox in just one year. With these statistics in mind, it's no wonder that our public-health officials today are so worried.

1 Smallpox first came to the United States from

   A Africa

   B Continental Europe

   C Russia

   D England

2 Smallpox was

   F easily preventable

   G rarely fatal

   H primarily a women's disease

   J transmitted through the air

3 The name "smallpox" was given to that virus

   A in an Anglo-Saxon manuscript

   B to distinguish it from syphilis

   C before chickenpox became a problem

   D because it afflicted children

4 The smallpox virus

   F does not exist anymore

   G can still be found in some laboratories

   H originated in the sixteenth century

   J is named after the scientist who cured it

5 Which of the following questions does the passage best answer?

   A How many people altogether have died from smallpox?

   B Why did chickenpox spread throughout Europe?

   C Why is smallpox no longer a commonplace disease?

   D How did smallpox spread to Russia?

Reading and Language Arts (continued)

Read the following paragraph, which is related to the previous passage. Then answer questions 6 and 7.

Smallpox could be prevented through inoculation (getting a "shot"). By going through a mild attack of the disease, an inoculated person became immune to its more serious natural form. However, inoculated persons were infectious and sometimes introduced smallpox into towns that had been free from the natural disease. As a result, even at the height of a smallpox epidemic in 1900, public opinion was strongly against the practice of inoculation. Europe needed a better idea if it was to rid itself of the virus completely.

6 Choose the sentence that might also belong in the paragraph.

   F Europe had also faced epidemics of anthrax, rabies, plague, and typhoid fever.

   G Today's world is a much safer place to live, thanks to smallpox inoculation.

   H During the nineteenth century, smallpox was responsible for one in every 10 deaths.

   J The practice of inoculation greatly reduced the number of deaths due to smallpox.

7 You might expect the next paragraph to provide information about the

   A discovery of a cure for smallpox

   B number of deaths resulting from smallpox

   C practice of intentional smallpox inoculation

   D smallpox disease from 1800 to 1900

Questions 8–12 are based on the following passage:

When I was young, I used to think that middle-aged people recalled their youth as something seen through a haze. I know better now. The last years that I spent in my native land and my first years in America come back to me with the distinctness of yesterday.

One of my pastimes was to imagine a host of tiny soldiers each the size of my little finger, but alive and real. These I would drill as I saw officers do their men in front of the barracks not far from our home. Or else I would march up and down the room with mother's rolling-pin for a rifle, grunting, ferociously, in Russian: "Left one! Left one! Left one!" in the double capacity of a Russian soldier and of David fighting Goliath.

During my ninth and tenth years, my greatest sport was to play buttons. These we would flip around on some patch of unpaved ground with a little pit for a billiard pocket. My own pockets were usually full of these buttons. As the game was restricted to brass ones from the uniforms of soldiers, my mother had plenty to do to keep those pockets of mine in good repair.

I would spend hours in some secluded spot developing skill for the sport. I gambled passionately and was continually counting my treasure, or running around the big courtyard, jingling it self-consciously. But one day I suddenly wearied of it all and traded my entire hoard for a pocket-knife and some trinkets.

"Don't you care for buttons any more?" Mother inquired.

"I can't bear the sight of them," I replied. She shrugged her shoulders smilingly.

8 The passage's narrator

   F immigrated to America from Russia

   G grew up in a wealthy family

   H had few if any friends as a child

   J was a poor student as a youngster

9 As a young boy, the narrator liked to

   A listen to his mother tell stories

   B shop for toys and trinkets

   C daydream about being in the military

   D play stickball in the courtyard

Reading and Language Arts *(continued)*

10 As a youngster, the narrator was very proud of his

   F trinkets

   G brass buttons

   H pocket knife

   J toy soldiers

11 As a youngster, the narrator probably

   A played buttons on the floor of his house

   B became a skilled button player without practice

   C wagered his buttons when playing against others

   D played buttons against his mother's wishes

12 During the narrator's childhood, his mother was

   F lonely

   G patient

   H anxious

   J happy

Questions 13–17 are based on the following passage:

The illegal selling of human body parts is commonplace among the poor in India, Brazil, and many other countries. Kidneys are an especially hot commodity, since we're born with two but only need one. However, <u>donors</u> typically learn after the fact that, if they weren't cheated completely, what little money they did receive for their organ is less than the wages they lost by missing work while recovering from surgery.

Human organs are in short supply in the United States; more than 100 thousand people are on waiting lists for human organs. Most of these people desperately need a new organ in order to live. Some U.S. lawmakers have proposed a law that would simply make it legal in the U.S. to sell human organs. Other proposed laws would legalize this activity only in certain circumstances. For example, one such law would allow death-row prisoners to avoid execution by donating bone marrow or a kidney.

Supporters of these laws often base their support on what they believe is a basic right to choose when it comes to decisions about one's own body. Many opponents of these laws are concerned, however, that making it legal to sell human body parts would result in just one more way for the rich to exploit the poor. Others who oppose legalization argue that selling human body parts is morally wrong because it reduces humans to mere commodities—like any other product sold on Ebay to the highest bidder.

13 In the United States, the supply of human organs

   A increases with each passing year

   B cannot keep up with the demand

   C is less than the supply in Brazil

   D decreases from year to year

14 The most frequently sold human body part is the

   F liver

   G bone marrow

   H kidney

   J heart

15 As it is used in the passage, the word <u>donors</u> most nearly means

   A suppliers

   B buyers

   C brokers

   D recipients

Reading and Language Arts *(continued)*

16 In the passage, the author

F argues that a certain illegal activity should be legal

G criticizes U.S. lawmakers for outlawing a certain activity

H proposes a law that would help the U.S. economy

J identifies arguments for and against a proposed law

17 Which of the following questions does the passage best answer?

A Does the practice of selling human organs victimize poor people?

B Is it morally wrong to sell one's own body parts?

C Does the selling of human organs pose a public-health danger?

D Would legalizing the selling of human organs help people live longer?

Here is a paragraph a student wrote about donating blood. There are a few mistakes that need correcting. Read the paragraph, and then answer questions 18–20.

¹Blood donations is easy to do. ²Most people have never donated blood. ³Many are afraid to give blood. ⁴Donating blood is usually safe. ⁵The blood type of the donor and recipient must match. ⁶The human body can replace a pint of blood in less that a week.

18 Which sentence does not belong in the paragraph?

F sentence 1

G sentence 2

H sentence 5

J sentence 6

19 Which is the best way to write sentence 1?

A Blood donation is easily done.

B Blood donations are easy to do.

C Donating blood is easy.

D best as is

20 Choose the best way to combine sentences 2 and 3.

F Many are afraid to give blood; donating blood is usually safe.

G Though many are afraid to give blood, donating blood is usually safe.

H Many are afraid to give blood, and donating blood is usually safe.

J Many people are afraid to give blood, so donating blood is usually safe.

Questions 21–25 are based on the following passage:

Every serious student of world history knows how the armies of Rome conquered the nations of the ancient world. But far fewer students know the story of Latin's conquest of the ancient world's languages. If asked how it came about, most people would probably guess that the worldwide supremacy of Latin was a natural result of the worldwide supremacy of the Roman legions or of Roman law. But in making this guess, one would be shutting one's eyes to modern history.

Conquered people do not always accept their conqueror's tongue. For example, at the turn of the twentieth century the country of India had been subjected to British rule for more than 150 years. However, in 1900 only one percent of the population of India could read and write English. Another example involves Algeria, where the French language has never threatened to replace Arabic.

Of course, unlike the regions subdued by Rome, India and Algeria had their own large bodies of literature, which strengthened their resistance to other tongues. Even so, the extent of Latin's supremacy throughout the ancient world is remarkable. From its narrow confines within an area initially covering less than 100 square miles, Latin spread through Italy and the islands of the Mediterranean, through France, Spain, England, northern Africa, and the Danubian provinces. The Latin language triumphed over all other tongues in those regions more completely than Roman arms triumphed over the peoples who spoke those tongues.

Reading and Language Arts *(continued)*

21 Throughout the passage, the author uses the word *tongue* to mean

- **A** mouth
- **B** words
- **C** education
- **D** language

22 In describing Latin as a conqueror, the author means that Latin

- **F** became India's official language
- **G** is a difficult language to learn
- **H** replaced many other languages
- **J** was the only language spoken in Rome

23 The author's main point in the passage is that

- **A** the Latin language eventually died because the Roman Empire fell
- **B** many people misunderstand why Latin became so widely spoken
- **C** people adopt a new language only when it is forced upon them
- **D** most people in India and Algeria cannot read or write Latin

24 To the author, the fact that Latin spread so widely is

- **F** surprising
- **G** understandable
- **H** encouraging
- **J** tragic

25 The author would probably agree that

- **A** all languages evolved from Latin
- **B** all languages, like all roads, once led to Rome
- **C** a language can be mightier than an army
- **D** the language of war is the same as that of peace

Here is a brief essay a student wrote about learning a new language. There are a few mistakes that need correcting. Read the essay, and then answer questions 26–29.

[1]They say that the Latin Language is dead. [2]It's true. [3]Latin is no longer spoken. [4]When I decided to take a Latin class, my friends all laughed. [5]They asked, "Why don't you learn a language you can use?" [6]My friends, they have a point. [7]Maybe I'll take German or French or Spanish instead.

26 Choose the best way to combine sentences 2 and 3.

- **F** It's true Latin is no longer spoken.
- **G** True Latin is no longer spoken.
- **H** It's true, that Latin is no longer spoken.
- **J** It's true; Latin is no longer spoken.

27 Which sentence contains a capitalization error?

- **A** sentence 1
- **B** sentence 3
- **C** sentence 5
- **D** sentence 7

28 Which is the best way to rewrite sentence 6?

- **F** My friends have a point.
- **G** They, my friends, have a point.
- **H** Do they have a point?
- **J** best as is

29 Choose the best way to write sentence 7.

- **A** Instead maybe I'll take German or French or Spanish.
- **B** Maybe I'll take German, French, or Spanish instead.
- **C** Maybe I'll instead take German, French, or Spanish.
- **D** best as is

Reading and Language Arts (continued)

Questions 30–33 are based on the following passage:

The game of chess is perhaps the most intellectually challenging of any game ever invented. It may also be the most scientific, while at the same time more entertaining than any pure science could ever be. Yet many chess players never stop to think about how this game—with all its various playing pieces, rules, and strategies—was invented in the first place.

With the possible exception of the simpler game of draughts, from which the modern game of checkers evolved, chess is the most ancient of games. Oriental manuscripts, Eastern fables, and works of the early poets all attest to its antiquity. Although there is some disagreement concerning the origin of chess, most historians believe that the game originated in ancient India, then reached Persia from India in the first half of the sixth century, and then from there eventually reached Europe and, subsequently, America.

Though chess has never been honored throughout its long life by any continuous written history or record, its traditions from time immemorial have been of the most noble and even royal character. In fact, for many ages Europeans have referred to chess as "The Royal Game." Perhaps by coincidence, though hardly surprising, is that the key piece on a chessboard is the king, and that chess takes its modern-day name from the Persian word *Schach*, or *Shah*, which in that language signifies "King." Interestingly, combining the Persian word *Matt*, meaning "dead," with *Schach* results in a two-word phrase meaning "the King is dead." It is from this phrase that the term *checkmate*, which English-speaking chess players now use, originated.

So, the next time you're about to make your final, winning move in a good game of chess, take your opponent by surprise by saying, "Schach Matt!"

30 Chess probably originated in

- **F** China
- **G** Persia
- **H** Europe
- **J** India

31 Why is it *hardly surprising* to the author that the key chess piece is the king?

- **A** Chess has always been popular among royalty.
- **B** The king is the largest piece on the chessboard.
- **C** The Persian name for the game means "king."
- **D** The player who captures the opponent's king wins the game.

32 The author would probably agree that checkers

- **F** was invented before chess
- **G** originated in ancient India
- **H** is known in Europe as "The Royal Game"
- **J** is more popular today than chess

33 A good title for the selection would be

- **A** "Chess and Checkers in Ancient Times"
- **B** "A Brief History of the Game of Chess"
- **C** "Why Chess is the World's Most Popular Game"
- **D** "How the Game of Chess Changed Through the Ages"

34 Here are two sentences related to the previous passage:

Chess is a game of strategy.
A beginner rarely defeats an experienced player.

Which is the best way to combine these two sentences?

- **F** Chess is a game of strategy, and a beginner rarely defeats an experienced player.
- **G** Chess, a game of strategy, a beginner rarely defeats an experienced player.
- **H** A game of strategy, a chess beginner rarely defeats an experienced player.
- **J** Because chess is a game of strategy, a beginner rarely defeats an experienced player.

Reading and Language Arts *(continued)*

35 Choose the sentence that is written correctly.

A Before the nineteenth century, few books on chess strategy have been written.

B Before the nineteenth century, few books on chess strategy were wrote.

C Before the nineteenth century, few books on chess strategy had been wrote.

D Before the nineteenth century, few books on chess strategy had been written.

Questions 36–39 are based on the following passage:

Humanity has not finished its conquest of nature; on the contrary, it has barely begun. We have, not centuries or even thousands of years before us, but, as astronomy assures us, in all probability millions of years of earthly destiny to realize.

Barely 3,000 years of scientific research have brought the ends of the earth, and even the solar system, to our doorstep. Just 300 years of research have made us masters where we were slaves—of distance, of the air and oceans, of space, and of many of the most dreaded aspects of disease and suffering. Isn't it odd that life today would seem inconceivable without X-ray machines, which didn't exist 100 years ago? Or without airplanes, which were practically unheard of a century ago? Or without space travel, which was impossible only 50 years ago? Not to mention personal computers, which didn't exist even 30 years ago!

What will the millions of years ahead bring to humankind? Things too vast to grasp, no doubt. Things that would make the imaginings of today's most brilliant scientists and even science-fiction novelists seem ordinary by comparison. The future will bring us amazing control over things that seem to us almost sacred—over life and death and over the development of thought itself. Although this prospect might seem disturbing, through all that may happen to humankind, we can be sure that we will remain human, and so we can face the future confident that it will be better than the present.

36 The author's overall attitude toward science is

F fearful

G critical

H enthusiastic

J skeptical

37 The author seems to believe that science-fiction writers

A are less imaginative than many scientists

B will help science to advance in the future

C are out of touch with real science

D underestimate future advances in science

38 In the passage, the author does NOT

F pose a question, and then answer that question

G describe the impact of certain historical events

H evaluate conflicting predictions for the future

J ask a question that does not require a response

Reading and Language Arts *(continued)*

39 Which of the following is the best title for the passage?

A "Scientific Advancements of the Last 3,000 Years"

B "The Past and Future of Scientific Research"

C "Why Society Must Encourage Scientific Progress"

D "A Bleak Past but a Bright Future for Humankind"

40 Choose the sentence that is written correctly.

F Society should encourage the advancement of science.

G The advancement of science society should encourage.

H Encouraging science advancement is something society should do.

J Advancing science should be encouraged by society.

STOP!
If you finish before time runs out, check your work on this section only.

Mathematics (40 Questions, 40 Minutes)

Directions: Choose the best answer to each question.

1 $3.8 - 0.38 =$

A 3.42
B 3.5
C 3.58
D 3.3

2 $\dfrac{26 \times 48}{24 \times 52} =$

F 7
G 13
H 2
J 1

3 A salad costs $3.75, a beverage costs $1.50, and a bagel costs $2.25. Kevin, who has $5.50 to spend, can buy any of the following EXCEPT:

A three beverages
B two beverages and a bagel
C a salad and beverage
D a salad and bagel

4 Find the value of y in the figure below.

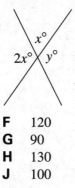

F 120
G 90
H 130
J 100

5 Each of 24 candies in a box is either chewy or hard. If 9 candies are chewy, how many hard candies alone must be removed from the box in order for it to contain the same number of hard candies and chewy candies?

A 9
B 12
C 6
D 15

6 Which of the following operations yields the greatest sum?

F $2.1 + \dfrac{3}{5}$

G $0.8 + \dfrac{8}{4}$

H $2.0 + \dfrac{3}{4}$

J $0.1 + \dfrac{5}{2}$

7 If the lengths of two sides of a triangle are 5 and 9, the length of the third side could be

A 9
B 14
C 4
D 15

8 $\dfrac{4}{5} + 0.2 + 5\% =$

F $\dfrac{5}{4}$

G $\dfrac{21}{20}$

H $\dfrac{6}{5}$

J $\dfrac{11}{10}$

9 Find the value of the expression $\dfrac{3x}{z} - 4y^z$ when $x = 4$, $y = 3$, and $z = 2$.

A 12
B −6
C 42
D −30

Mathematics *(continued)*

10 Which of the three figures below has the largest area?

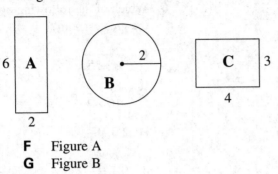

- **F** Figure A
- **G** Figure B
- **H** Figure C
- **J** All three figures are equal in area.

11 If $0 < x < y < 1$, then it must be true that

- **A** $xy > 1$
- **B** $\dfrac{x}{y} > 1$
- **C** $x + y > 1$
- **D** $\dfrac{y}{x} > 1$

12 A team played 25 games in the season, losing 8 more games than it won. Three (3) of the games resulted in ties. How many games did the team win?

- **F** 15
- **G** 12
- **H** 7
- **J** 10

13 $298.67 + 1.33 =$

- **A** 301
- **B** 299.90
- **C** 300.01
- **D** 300

14 Which of the following is the set of common factors of 60 and 36?

- **F** (2,3,6,12,18)
- **G** (2,3,4,6,12)
- **H** (2,3,4,6,8,12)
- **J** (2,3,6,12)

15 The number 500,000 is equivalent to

- **A** 5×10^5
- **B** 10×5^6
- **C** 5×10^6
- **D** 10×5^5

16 The table below shows distances (in miles) between five cities—labeled A, B, C, D, and E.

	A	B	C	D	E
A		24	63	15	32
B	24		12	40	6
C	63	12		20	27
D	15	40	20		52
E	32	6	27	52	

Which of the following trips, each involving two legs, is longest in distance?

- **F** From D to E, and then to C
- **G** From C to A, and then to D
- **H** From A to E, and then to B
- **J** From D to B, and then to C

17 Fill in the blank to complete the following equation:

$11 - 10 \div (\_ \times 3) + 3 = 4$

- **A** $-\dfrac{1}{3}$
- **B** 4
- **C** -4
- **D** $\dfrac{1}{3}$

18 Which of the following integers has the greatest number of factors?

- **F** 18
- **G** 42
- **H** 36
- **J** 50

Mathematics *(continued)*

19 $\frac{5}{3}$ is most nearly equal to

A   3.5
B   170%
C   1.6
D   230%

20 Four points appear on the (x,y) coordinate plane below.

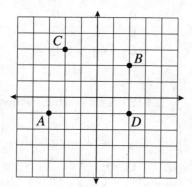

For which of the four points is the product of the point's x and y coordinates least in value?

F   Point A
G   Point B
H   Point C
J   Point D

21 If 30 ounces of coffee beans are removed from a 5-pound bag of coffee beans, the new weight of the bag of coffee beans is

A   50 ounces
B   20 ounces
C   40 ounces
D   60 ounces

22 $c(a + b) + bc =$

F $ca + ba + bc$
G $b(2c + a)$
H $c(a + 2b)$
J $2c(a + 2b)$

23 If Stacy drinks 25% of a 1-pint carton of milk, and then later drinks 25% of the remaining milk, how many ounces of milk are left? (1 pint = 16 ounces.)

A   11
B   9
C   8
D   10

24 In the figure below, if the area of triangle ABC is 15 square feet, what is the length of BC?

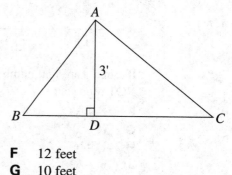

F   12 feet
G   10 feet
H   12.5 feet
J   7.5 feet

25 Of 27 animals at the zoo, 15 are monkeys. Which of the following fractions expresses the ratio of monkeys to all other animals at the zoo?

A   5:4
B   5:9
C   4:5
D   4:3

26 If one of the angles of an isosceles triangle measures 100°, one of the other angles must measure

F   80°
G   100°
H   40°
J   60°

Mathematics (continued)

27 Ashley earns \$15 per hour and receives a 5% commission on all of her sales. How much did Ashley earn during an 8-hour day during which Ashley's sales totaled \$400?

   A   \$160
   B   \$175
   C   \$150
   D   \$140

28 Point *A* appears on the number line as shown below:

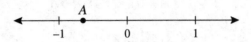

If *x* and *y* are real numbers, point *A* CAN-NOT represent

   F $x^2 - y^2$
   G $x^3 + y^3$
   H $x^2 + y^2$
   J $x^3 - y^3$

29 On a cold winter day, the low temperature was $-6°$ and the high temperature was $11°$. Based on these two statistics, what was the average temperature for the day?

   A   2.5°
   B   0.5°
   C   1.5°
   D $-0.5°$

30 $2\sqrt{5} + 2\sqrt{125} =$

   F $4\sqrt{10}$

   G $10\sqrt{5}$

   H $8\sqrt{12}$

   J $12\sqrt{5}$

31 Which of the following represents $\{3,5,8,2,4\} \cap \{2,4,6,8,10\}$?

   A   {2,3,4,5,6,8,10}
   B   {2,4,8}
   C   {3,5,10}
   D   {1,7,9}

32 A rectangular plot of land with length 150 feet has an area of 12,000 square feet. The width of the plot is

   F   80 feet
   G   100 feet
   H   65 feet
   J   135 feet

33 If $x < -1$ and $y > 1$, then it must be true that

   A $x + y < 0$
   B $xy < -1$
   C $x + y > 0$
   D $xy > 1$

34 25 cents is what fraction of 100 dollars?

   F $\dfrac{1}{250}$

   G $\dfrac{1}{500}$

   H $\dfrac{1}{400}$

   J $\dfrac{25}{1,000}$

Questions 35 and 36 are based on the following information:

At Hill Farm, the daily production of chicken eggs in four separate coops is closely monitored. The table below shows the results during one particular week.

	Su	M	T	W	Th	F	S
Coop A	0	1	2	3	1	0	0
Coop B	4	0	0	1	0	1	2
Coop C	0	1	2	2	1	2	0
Coop D	1	1	2	0	0	3	1

35 Which of the following is nearest to the average weekly production per coop?

   A   7 eggs
   B   6 eggs
   C   5 eggs
   D   8 eggs

Mathematics *(continued)*

36 Which of the following pairs of days accounted for the greatest number of eggs produced?

F   Saturday and Sunday
G   Thursday and Friday
H   Monday and Tuesday
J   Tuesday and Friday

37 It took Matt twice the time to drive from home to work as it took him to drive back home from work by the same route. If Matt averaged 30 miles per hour (mph) on his drive to work, his average speed for the entire round trip was

A   30 mph
B   25 mph
C   40 mph
D   15 mph

38 If you increase the perimeter of a square by 50%, you increase its area by

F   200%
G   50%
H   100%
J   125%

39 If Kira randomly selects an integer from 1 to 50, the probability that she will select a multiple of 3 is

A $\dfrac{1}{6}$

B $\dfrac{3}{10}$

C $\dfrac{8}{25}$

D $\dfrac{1}{5}$

40 Four times what number is two less than three-fourths of eight?

F $\dfrac{7}{2}$

G   1

H   3

J   2

STOP!
If you finish before time runs out, check your work on this section only.

COOP PRACTICE TEST 2

Answer Key

Sequences

1.	B	11.	B
2.	J	12.	F
3.	C	13.	A
4.	H	14.	J
5.	A	15.	B
6.	F	16.	H
7.	B	17.	B
8.	J	18.	J
9.	D	19.	B
10.	H	20.	F

Analogies

1.	B	11.	A
2.	J	12.	H
3.	B	13.	C
4.	J	14.	H
5.	A	15.	D
6.	G	16.	F
7.	A	17.	C
8.	H	18.	G
9.	B	19.	D
10.	J	20.	F

Quantitative Reasoning

1.	B	11.	C
2.	J	12.	H
3.	C	13.	B
4.	G	14.	G
5.	D	15.	C
6.	F	16.	J
7.	C	17.	A
8.	F	18.	J
9.	D	19.	C
10.	G	20.	G

Verbal Reasoning—Words

1.	B	11.	B
2.	F	12.	J
3.	A	13.	D
4.	J	14.	H
5.	C	15.	C
6.	G	16.	G
7.	D	17.	D
8.	G	18.	F
9.	C	19.	D
10.	F	20.	H

Verbal Reasoning—Context

1.	B	11.	B
2.	J	12.	F
3.	C	13.	A
4.	G	14.	F
5.	C	15.	B
6.	J	16.	H
7.	A	17.	D
8.	H	18.	H
9.	B	19.	A
10.	J	20.	J

Reading and Language Arts

1.	A	21.	D
2.	J	22.	H
3.	B	23.	B
4.	G	24.	F
5.	A	25.	C
6.	J	26.	J
7.	A	27.	A
8.	F	28.	F
9.	C	29.	B
10.	G	30.	J
11.	C	31.	C
12.	G	32.	F
13.	B	33.	B
14.	H	34.	J
15.	A	35.	D
16.	J	36.	H
17.	A	37.	D
18.	H	38.	H
19.	C	39.	B
20.	G	40.	F

COOP PRACTICE TEST 2

Answer Key *(continued)*

Mathematics

1.	A	21.	A
2.	J	22.	H
3.	D	23.	B
4.	F	24.	G
5.	C	25.	A
6.	G	26.	H
7.	A	27.	D
8.	G	28.	H
9.	D	29.	A
10.	G	30.	J
11.	D	31.	B
12.	H	32.	F
13.	D	33.	B
14.	G	34.	H
15.	A	35.	D
16.	F	36.	J
17.	D	37.	C
18.	H	38.	J
19.	B	39.	C
20.	H	40.	G

COOP PRACTICE TEST 2

Answers and Explanations

Sequences

1. **B** From group to group, the three shaded circles around the perimeter converge at the center circle, then move back out to the perimeter, but to the next position in a clockwise direction.

2. **J** From one group to the next, each object moves one position to the right (the object furthest to the right jumps to the far left) *and* alternates between two sizes.

3. **C** In each group, the two objects are mirror images of each other. Beginning with the second group, one additional feature is added to each of the two objects. The feature added to the right-hand object is the one that was added to the left-hand object in the previous group.

4. **H** In each successive group, one of the tree's four horizontal "branches" flips horizontally to the other side of the vertical "trunk." When a branch flips, its "leaf" changes shape (from circular to square, or vice versa).

5. **A** From group to group, a triangle, a square, and a circle are repositioned in a random fashion. In each group, one of the three objects is larger than the other two.

6. **F** In the top figure, the shaded circles move clockwise around the "track," skipping every other circle. In the bottom figure, the two shaded squares move clockwise around the "track," without skipping any squares.

7. **B** The series lists letters of the alphabet in order, skipping *two* letters from one to the next.

8. **J** Looking at just the first letter of each pair, the series lists letters of the alphabet in reverse order (Z-Y-X-W). Looking at just the second letter of each pair, the series lists letters of the alphabet in order, skipping every other letter (A-C-E-G). As you can see, the pair *XE* completes the series.

9. **D** Look at the three groups' corresponding letters. Notice that the first letters (*C-D-E*) are consecutive, as are the second letters (*P-Q-R*) and the third letters (*J-K-L*). Accordingly, the first, second, and third letters in the fourth group should be *F, S,* and *M*—in that order.

10. **H** Each group lists consecutive letters of the alphabet, except that the second and third letters are reversed. Otherwise, from group to group the letters are presented in alphabetical order (from *e* to *p*). No letters are skipped.

11. **B** In every group, the second letter is uppercase, while the other two letters are lowercase. All letters are in reverse alphabetical order (beginning with *w*), skipping one letter of the alphabet between each pair of consecutive letters.

12. **F** In every group, the second letter is *l.* Looking at just the first letter in each group, the letters are in reverse alphabetical order (k-j-i-*h*). Looking at just the third letter in each group, the letters are in alphabetical order (m-n-o-*p*).

13. **A** Each group contains four elements. The third and fourth elements are constant (BC). The first and second elements each run in sequential order from one group to the next: A-B-*C*-D (first element) and subscript 1-2-*3*-4 (second element).

Answers and Explanations *(continued)*

14. **J** Each group contains four elements. Corresponding elements run in a clear sequential order from one group to the next: D-C-B-*A* (first element), A-B-C-*D* (second element), superscript 5-4-3-*2* (third element), and D-C-B-*A* (fourth element).

15. **B** Adding 4 to any number in the series yields the next number.

16. **H** The number you subtract from a term to obtain the next one increases by 1 from each term to the next: $24 - 1 = 23$; $23 - 2 = 21$; $21 - 3 = 18$; $18 - 4 = 14$; $14 - 5 = 9$.

17. **B** Within each group, dividing a number by 3 yields the next number.

18. **J** Within each group, multiplying the first number by the second number yields the third number.

19. **B** Within each group, subtracting 4 from the first number or adding 4 to the second number yields the third number.

20. **F** Within each group, multiplying the first number by 2 yields the second number, while multiplying it by 1.5 yields the third number ($5 \times 1.5 = 7.5$).

Analogies

1. **B** A baby grows up to become an adult. Similarly, a caterpillar grows up to become a butterfly.

2. **J** A saw is a tool used to cut trees. Similarly, a pair of scissors is a tool used to cut paper.

3. **B** A beach is the place where you're most likely to see people using surfboards. Similarly, a snow-covered mountain is where you're most likely to see people using snow skis.

4. **J** You usually use a ladle with a deep pot. Similarly, you usually use a spatula with a skillet.

5. **A** A motorboat moves through water by the action of its propeller. Similarly, people transport, or "propel," themselves with their own feet and legs.

6. **G** You experience television with your sense of vision. Similarly, you experience a hot dog with your sense of taste.

7. **A** A rake is often used to clear away fallen leaves. Similarly, a broom is often used to clear away litter.

8. **H** The two muses (comedy and tragedy) symbolize the theater arts. Similarly, a diamond ring symbolizes the engagement or marriage of two people.

9. **B** Apples can be baked into an apple pie. Wheat can be baked into a loaf of bread.

10. **J** A baker produces baked goods, such as a cake. A carpenter produces things made of wood, such as a chair.

11. **A** Bullets are ammunition you use with a gun. Similarly, arrows are ammunition you use with a bow.

12. **H** A knight is one of the playing pieces on a chess board. Similarly, a batter is one of the players on a baseball field.

13. **C** A safe is used to protect valuable items such as jewels and collectibles from theft. Similarly, a padlock is used to protect a bicycle from theft.

Answers and Explanations *(continued)*

14. **H** A computer keyboard serves the same purpose as a pen—to write—but is a more modern technology. Similarly, a kitchen oven serves the same purpose as an open fire—to cook—but is a more modern technology.

15. **D** A chicken produces eggs, which we eat. Similarly, a cow produces milk, which we drink.

16. **F** A lion is a predator, and a deer is its prey. Similarly, a cat is a predator, and a mouse is its prey.

17. **C** A trumpet and snare drum are two of many instruments that together form an orchestra (or band). Similarly, New York and Florida are two of many states that make up the continental United States.

18. **B** A basketball is thrown through a hoop in order to score in a game of basketball. A golf ball is putted into a hole in order to score in a game of golf.

19. **D** A house and a teepee are both dwellings, but a teepee is more primitive. Similarly, a bed and a hammock are both for sleeping on, but a hammock is more primitive.

20. **F** A trophy symbolizes an athletic accomplishment. Similarly, a diploma symbolizes an academic accomplishment.

Quantitative Reasoning

1. **B** You add 9 to the first number to obtain the second one: $1 + 9 = 10$.

2. **J** You subtract 6 from the first number to obtain the second one: $8 - 6 = 2$.

3. **C** You add 2 to the first number to obtain the second: $\dfrac{4}{3} + \dfrac{6}{3} = \dfrac{10}{3}$.

4. **G** You subtract 1 from the first number to obtain the second one: $\dfrac{2}{3} - 1 = -\dfrac{1}{3}$.

5. **D** You divide the first number by 2 to obtain the second one: $11 \div 2 = \dfrac{11}{2}$.

6. **F** You multiply the first number by 5 to obtain the second one: $4 \times 5 = 20$.

7. **C** You divide the first number by 5 to obtain the second one: $5 \div 5 = 1$.

8. **F** The figure is divided into 4 congruent squares. Two (2) of the 4 squares, which make up $\dfrac{1}{2}$ of the figure, are shaded.

9. **D** The figure is divided into 6 congruent rectangles; 4 of the rectangles, which make up $\dfrac{4}{6}$, or $\dfrac{2}{3}$, of the figure, are shaded.

10. **G** The figure is divided into 8 congruent triangles, but two of the triangles (on the right) are merged into one diamond. Three (3) of the 8 original triangles, which make up $\dfrac{3}{8}$ of the figure, are shaded.

11. **C** The figure is divided into 8 congruent triangles; 2 of these triangles, which make up $\dfrac{2}{6}$, or $\dfrac{1}{3}$, of the figure, are shaded.

12. **H** The figure is divided into 10 congruent rectangles. Each of the small shaded triangles is $\dfrac{1}{2}$ the area of any of the 10 rectangles. There are 8 small shaded triangles, or the area equivalent of 4 of the figure's 10 congruent rectangles. You can simplify the fraction $\dfrac{4}{10}$ to $\dfrac{2}{5}$.

13. **B** The circle is divided into 8 congruent segments; 4 of the segments, which make up $\dfrac{4}{6}$, or $\dfrac{2}{3}$, of the figure, are shaded.

Answers and Explanations *(continued)*

14. **G** The figure is first divided into a grid of 3 rows and 4 columns—12 congruent rectangles. The shaded area in the middle two columns accounts for four of these 12 congruent rectangles, or $\frac{4}{12}$ of the figure. The column furthest to the right has been divided into two columns. Thus, the shaded rectangle in the upper right corner accounts for $\frac{1}{12}$ of the figure area. The two smallest rectangles together account for $\frac{1}{12}$ of the figure. The total shaded area accounts for $\frac{1}{2}$ of the figure:
$$\frac{4}{12}+\frac{1}{12}+\frac{1}{12}=\frac{6}{12}, \text{ or } \frac{1}{2}.$$

15. **C** □ and ○ are equal in weight (the □:○ ratio is 1:1). Thus, as long as the same number of objects (of either type) appears on the left as on the right, as in choice C only, the weights balance. Otherwise, they won't.

16. **J** The scale shows that the □:○ weight ratio is 2:1. Assign a weight of 2 units to □ and a weight of 1 unit to ○. In choice J, the total on the left side equals the total on the right side: $(1 + 1 + 1 + 1) = (2 + 2)$.

17. **A** The scale shows that the □:○ weight ratio is 3:2. Assign a weight of 3 units to □ and a weight of 2 units to ○. In choice A, the total on the left side equals the total on the right side: $(3 + 2 + 2 + 2) = (3 + 3 + 3)$.

18. **J** The scale shows that the □:○ weight ratio is 1:2. Assign a weight of 1 unit to □ and a weight of 2 units to ○. In choice J, the total on the left side equals the total on the right side: $(2 + 1 + 1 + 1) = (2 + 2 + 1)$.

19. **C** The scale shows that the □:○ weight ratio is 3:1. Assign a weight of 3 units to □ and a weight of 1 unit to ○. In choice C, the total on the left side equals the total on the right side: $(1 + 1 + 1 + 3) = (3 + 3)$.

20. **G** The scale shows that the □:○ weight ratio is 4:1. Assign a weight of 4 units to □ and a weight of 1 unit to ○. In choice G, the total on the left side equals the total on the right side: $(4 + 1) = (1 \times 5)$.

Verbal Reasoning—Words

1. **B** To serve its inherent purpose, a fan requires the movement of *air*. A fan might be used to heat or to cool, and a fan may or may not have a blade or switch.

2. **F** An orchestra is an assemblage of *instruments,* which together create something—usually a piece of music. Without instruments, there can be no orchestra.

3. **A** By definition, a weapon has the potential to *harm* someone or something.

4. **J** A debate inherently involves *disagreement* over an issue.

5. **C** The purpose of a badge is to *identify* the person wearing it—either by name, title, or association.

6. **G** By definition, a chain is created by connecting, or *linking,* together a series of parts in loops. The parts can be made of rope, metal, or other material.

7. **D** A *destination* is a specific place where a person intends to travel to. Although a specific timetable or route is not required, having a destination inherently requires an intent or *plan*—not just a mere hope.

8. **G** The word *talk* is neutral. To *scream* is to talk very loudly, while to *whisper* is to talk very quietly; the relationship is one of degree, with *scream* and *whisper* at opposite extremes. The word *cut* is neutral. To *sever* is to cut through completely. At the other extreme, to *scratch* is to barely cut at all.

Answers and Explanations *(continued)*

9. **C** The three words in the top row name a series of related events in time sequence. After a *crime* is committed, a *trial* for the crime might occur, possibly followed by a *conviction* (by a judge or jury), which is an outcome of the trial. Similarly, after a *song* is written, it might be performed at a *concert,* one possible outcome of which is *applause* (by the audience).

10. **F** You can consult a *clock,* a *watch,* and even the *sun* to determine the time of day. Similarly, you can use a *calculator,* a *slide-rule,* or even a *pencil* to perform arithmetic.

11. **B** A *note* is combined with other notes to create a *melody,* which in turn is a building block for creating an entire *song.* Similarly, *words* are combined to form *sentences,* which in turn are combined to create an entire *essay.*

12. **J** A *peel,* a *shell,* and a *husk* are outer layers (skins) of certain fruits, vegetables, and nuts. A *pit,* however, is not an outer layer; it's found inside, usually at the center, of certain fruits.

13. **D** To use a *hammer, bat,* or *whip,* you swing the tool and it strikes its object. Using a *drill,* however, does not involve a swinging motion, nor does a drill strike or hit its object.

14. **H** The words *erase, replace,* and *delete* each involve an act of removing something—for example, written words on paper. The word *forget* does not convey this idea at all.

15. **C** *Talent* is an innate, or inborn, trait. On the other hand, *experience, education,* and *knowledge* are all acquired during life.

16. **G** The underlined words are all vegetables; *cabbage* is also a vegetable.

17. **D** The word *lantern* and the three underlined words each refers to a distinct kind of lighting device.

18. **F** The word *pillar* and the three underlined words all name some type of architectural structure that is long and thin, and that is placed on its end when in use.

19. **D** The word *write* describes generally what someone is doing when he either jots, scribbles, or notates.

20. **H** The word *sharp,* like each of the underlined words, is often used to describe an intelligent person—especially someone with a quick and agile mind.

Verbal Reasoning—Context

1. **B** Based on the premises, we know for certain that Lynn has a stomachache—in other words, she is not feeling well. However, the real cause of the stomachache is unknown. (The cause might have been eating the chocolate, or the fact that Lynn skipped dinner, or perhaps some other cause.)

2. **J** Based on the statistic given in the premises, Laura is likely to have at least one more child. You can rule out the other three choices because the premises provide no information about Laura's age or why she currently has one and only one child.

3. **C** The first premise tells us that *all* gremlins are cute; no exceptions are given. This premise alone is sufficient to conclude that furry gremlins are cute.

4. **G** Josh used to live in Atlanta, which is where the Braves play.

5. **C** The two premises together tells us that there are more flute players than tuba players in the orchestra.

6. **J** Regardless of why Sparky barks at the mail carrier, this behavior makes Sparky a good guard dog because he alerts his owner when people are near the house.

Answers and Explanations *(continued)*

7. **A** The premises tell us that Teresa and Karen both participated in the pageant. It is reasonable to conclude that both competed in all of the various competitions during the pageant.

8. **H** The sequence of events makes it clear that what Lauren yelled at Mandie served as a genuine warning and, because Mandie was not hurt, the warning might have helped Mandie avoid injury.

9. **B** Because Jill made more sales than anyone else in the entire city, Jill's performance was probably due to more than luck; in all likelihood, Jill is an effective sales agent. The problem with choices A and D is that neither one accounts for Jill's strong performance *compared to* other realtors. Choice C is easy to rule out because the premises provide absolutely no information about Jill's sales in January.

10. **J** Given that soda is more expensive than cocoa, which is more expensive than tea, soda must be more expensive than tea. Because tea and coffee are the same price, soda is also more expensive than coffee.

11. **B** The willingness of many moviegoers to stand in a long line before the main feature shows that having snacks for the feature is important to them. The problem with choice A is that the premises give no information as to why the long lines form during previews. Choice C contradicts what the premises suggest—that moviegoers are patient enough to stand in a long line. As for choice D, we have no idea how much popcorn is available, or whether it is enough for everyone who wants to buy some.

12. **F** The first sentence tells us that wumpies can swim. The third sentence tells us that fripples can swim.

13. **A** Because no convertible is an import but all white cars are convertibles, no import can be white.

14. **F** The one reasonable explanation for someone other than John Smith taking the package inside is that the person is accepting it for John, who also lives there. Because John and Becky have the same last name, this explanation is especially convincing.

15. **B** Because real licorice is always black, the red candies in the box cannot be real licorice.

16. **H** The chimney is made from the same type of stones found lying on the land around the property. Obviously, the chimney blends nicely with its natural environment.

17. **D** The premises tell us that Pamela is engaged in activities every Monday, Tuesday, Wednesday, Thursday, and Friday evening. In other words, she is busy every weeknight.

18. **H** All we know from the premises is that Jim is conscientious about taking care of his lawn. Choice F runs contrary to the premises, which tell us that Jim mows the lawn more often in the spring than in the summer. As for choices G and J, the premises provide absolutely no information to support either statement.

19. **A** Since Bill is not a high school student, it is *possible* (though not certain) that Bill is a student at Wheeler College. On the other hand, because David is still in high school, he cannot be a student at Wheeler College.

20. **J** Given that the least possible hourly wage is 10 dollars, it is impossible that Cathy has received a raise for her current job. Otherwise, her current wage would be more than 10 dollars.

Answers and Explanations *(continued)*

Reading and Language Arts

1. **A** In the second paragraph, the author tells us that "the first outbreak in the United States occurred shortly after new slaves arrived from Africa."

2. **J** According to the passage, smallpox bacteria could be carried through the air for considerable distances.

3. **B** In the second paragraph, the author tells us that the name "was given to the disease . . . to distinguish it from . . . the Great Pox, or syphilis. . . ."

4. **G** In the first paragraph, the author mentions that the smallpox virus "lives on today" in science laboratories.

5. **A** In the second paragraph, the author tells us that chickenpox spread across Europe due mainly to crowded and unsanitary conditions in the cities.

6. **J** If you insert this sentence between the paragraph's second and third sentences (immediately before *However*), you'll see that this additional sentence makes perfect sense there.

7. **A** At the end of the paragraph, the author tells us that Europe needed a better idea for eliminating smallpox than intentional inoculation. A cure for the disease would be just such an idea, and therefore just the topic you might expect for the next paragraph.

8. **F** At the beginning of the passage, the narrator mentions his "native land" and his "first years in America." Later, he mentions ordering his imaginary toy soldiers about in Russian. Clearly, the narrator immigrated to America from Russia.

9. **C** The narrator tells us that one of his favorite pastimes was to imagine that he had toy soldiers, and then bark out commands to them as if he were their leader.

10. **G** The narrator talks about continually "counting his treasure" (his buttons) and "jingling it self-consciously." Obviously, his button collection was very important to him and he was no doubt quite proud of it.

11. **C** In recounting the sport of buttons, the narrator tells us that he "gambled passionately" and would continually count his "treasure" (his buttons). From this account, we can infer that, in a game of buttons, the winner's prize was the opponent's buttons themselves.

12. **G** The narrator kept his mother busy mending his pockets, which probably would tear open frequently from the weight of his button collection. When he suddenly lost interest in the buttons altogether, rather than expressing frustration or anger that she had spent so much time mending his pockets because of the buttons, his mother simply smiled. Clearly, then, the narrator's mother was very *patient* with her son.

13. **B** According to the passage, currently there is a long waiting list for organ donations. Therefore, the supply of organs must not be keeping up with demand.

14. **H** In the first paragraph, the author tells us that "kidneys are an especially hot commodity," meaning that they are probably sold more frequently than any other human body part.

15. **A** For the sentence to make sense, the word *donors* must refer to the people who undergo surgery to have organs removed for the purpose of selling them—in other words, donors must be the organ *suppliers*.

Answers and Explanations *(continued)*

16. **J** In the second paragraph, the author provides one reason that proponents of the laws sometimes cite for their support, followed by two reasons that those who are against the proposed laws give for their opposition.

17. **A** In the first paragraph, the author explains how people in other countries are often victimized by others who promise to pay them for their organs but never follow through on their promise.

18. **H** Sentence 5 explains why donated blood might not be safe for the *recipient*. However, the rest of the paragraph is about blood donating from the viewpoint of the *donor*.

19. **C** In the original sentence, the plural subject (*donations*) does not agree in number with the singular verb (*is*). However, simply replacing *donations* with *donation*—or replacing *is* with *are*—isn't enough because what is easy is the act of *donating,* not the donation. Choice C fixes both problems with a clear and concise alternative.

20. **G** In sentences 2 and 3, the writer no doubt wants to make the point that people who are afraid to give blood have nothing to fear. Transforming sentence 2 into a subordinate clause that starts with the word *Though* gets the point across nicely. Linking the two sentences with only a comma, or with a comma followed by either *and* or *so,* fails to communicate this idea. Thus, none of the other three choices is as effective as choice G.

21. **D** The topic of the entire passage is how the Latin *language* spread throughout much the ancient world, and so substituting the word *language* for *tongue* throughout the passage makes perfect sense.

22. **H** In the third paragraph, the author describes how Latin spread throughout Europe and northern Africa, "triumphing over" (in other words, conquering) "all the other tongues of those regions," meaning that Latin replaced those tongues as the primary language spoken in those regions.

23. **B** In the first paragraph, the author asserts this point. Then, in the second and third paragraphs, the author explains the misunderstanding.

24. **F** In the third paragraph, the author tells us that it is "remarkable"—in other words, *surprising*—that the language used throughout such a small geographical area spread so widely throughout other regions.

25. **C** In the passage's final sentence, the author points out that Latin triumphed over the languages of the regions that Rome conquered more completely than Roman arms triumphed over the peoples using those languages. In other words, ultimately the Latin language was mightier than the Roman military.

26. **J** A semicolon works well here because we are combining two closely related ideas into one sentence.

27. **A** Although the word *Latin* should be capitalized (like the name of any other language), the word *language* should not be capitalized (because it is not a proper noun).

28. **F** In the original sentence, the use of both *they* and *My friends* is redundant. One or the other, but not both, suffices. Choice F corrects the redundancy by omitting *they.* Choice G does not fix the problem. As for choice H, it makes no sense to ask this question at this point in the paragraph, especially since the following sentence does not answer it.

Answers and Explanations *(continued)*

29. **B** The original sentence is grammatically correct. However, using the word *or* twice between the list of languages is repetitive and overly wordy. Choice B fixes the problem. Although choice C also corrects the problem, the phrase *Maybe I'll instead* is awkward. (Nothing should come between *I'll* and *take*.)

30. **J** In the second paragraph, the author tells us that chess probably originated in ancient India.

31. **C** Given that the game's name literally means "King," it makes sense—and therefore is not surprising—that a chess piece designated as the king would play a key role in the game.

32. **F** In the third paragraph, the author tells us that except for draughts (an early form of checkers), chess is probably the world's oldest game, inferring that checkers predates chess.

33. **B** Aside from the first paragraph, which introduces the topic, the passage as a whole is concerned with the history of the game of chess. Choice D is probably the second-best one. However, since the author does not discuss how the game changed over time, choice D does not provide as fitting a title as choice B.

34. **J** The first sentence explains *why* beginners rarely defeat experienced players. By using the word *Because,* choice J conveys the link in logic between the two sentences.

35. **D** The sentence should use the past-perfect verb form *had been written* because it describes past events that occurred earlier than other past events.

36. **H** The passage's author is very optimistic about the future of science and how it will benefit humankind. Of the four choices, the word *enthusiastic* best describes such optimism.

37. **D** In the second paragraph, the author asserts that the most imaginative ideas that today's science-fiction writers dream up about the future of science will turn out "ordinary" compared to what the future will actually hold.

38. **H** In the third paragraph, the author poses, and then answers, a question. Hence, choice F is incorrect. Throughout the first two paragraphs, the author tells us that scientific developments in the last 300 years have made life without anesthetics inconceivable today; hence, choice G is incorrect. In the last sentence of the second paragraph, the author asks a question that does not call for a response, or answer. (The question itself is intended to make the author's point.) Hence, choice J is incorrect. Nowhere in the passage, however, does the author evaluate any predictions for the future.

39. **B** The author's main idea in the passage is that the great, and unexpected, scientific advancements in the past give us reason to believe that more such advancements will occur in what's sure to be a long future for humankind. Choice B supplies a title that captures the gist of the passage nicely.

40. **F** The sentence in choice F is clear, concise, and grammatically correct. The sentence in choice G is constructed in a very confusing way. The sentence in choice H, though grammatically correct, is wordy and awkward. There are two problems with choice J. One is the awkward use of the passive voice; the other is the improper use of *advancing* (instead of *advancement*) as the object of the verb *encouraged.*

Answers and Explanations *(continued)*

Mathematics

1. **A** Align the two numbers vertically at the decimal point, and then subtract corresponding digits, borrowing a 1 from the "tenths" position for the "hundredths" position.

2. **J** You can cancel the common factors 24 and 26 from the numerator and denominator, leaving $\frac{2}{2}$, or 1.

3. **D** A salad and bagel would cost \$3.75 + \$2.25, or a total of \$6.00, which is more money than Kevin has.

4. **F** The angles that $x°$ and $2x°$ represent are supplementary—their sum is 180°. Thus, $x = 60$, and $2x = 120$. The angle that $y°$ represents is vertical to a 120° angle; thus, $y = 120$.

5. **C** Fifteen (15) of the 24 candies are hard. Eating 6 of the 15 hard candies leaves 9 of each type (hard and chewy).

6. **G** Convert fractions to decimal numbers, then add:

   (F) $2.1 + \frac{3}{5} = 2.1 + 0.6 = 2.7$

   (G) $0.8 + \frac{8}{4} = 0.8 + 2 = 2.8$

   (H) $2.0 + \frac{3}{4} = 2.0 + 0.75 = 2.75$

   (J) $0.1 + \frac{5}{2} = 0.1 + 2.5 = 2.6$

7. **A** In any triangle, the sum of the two shortest sides must be longer than the longest side. Only choice A meets this requirement.

8. **G** Because the answers are expressed in fractions, convert 0.2 and 5% to fractions, find the lowest common denominator, and then combine: $\frac{4}{5} + 0.2 + 5\% = \frac{4}{5} + \frac{2}{10} + \frac{5}{100} = \frac{16}{20} + \frac{4}{20} + \frac{1}{20} = \frac{21}{20}$.

9. **D** In the expression, substitute the three values given, then simplify: $\frac{3x}{z} + 4y^z = \frac{(3)(4)}{2} - 4(3)^2 = \frac{12}{2} - (4)(9) = 6 - 36 = -30$.

10. **G** The area of Figure A $= 6 \times 2 = 12$. The area of Figure C $= 3 \times 4 = 12$. The area of Figure B $= \pi 2^2 = 4\pi \approx (4)(3.1) > 12$.

11. **D** In any fraction where the numerator and denominator are both positive and the numerator is larger than the denominator, the fraction's value is greater than 1.

12. **H** Twenty-two (22) games were either won or lost. You can find the number of games won by trying each answer choice in turn. Choice H works: $7 + 8 = 15$, and $15 + 7 = 22$. Or, you can solve the problem using algebra (let x equal the number of games won):

    $$x + (x + 8) = 22$$
    $$2x = 14$$
    $$x = 7$$

13. **D** Align the two numbers vertically at the decimal point. As you add columns from right to left, you carry a 1 from each column to the next.

14. **G** This set includes the complete and accurate list of numbers that are factors of both 36 and 60. Neither 18 nor 8 is a factor of 60, and so choices F and H are incorrect. Choice J omits 4, a factor of both 36 and 60.

15. **A** $5 \times 10^5 = 5 \times 10 \times 10 \times 10 \times 10 \times 10 = 5 \times 100,000 = 500,000$.

16. **F** The distances for the four trips are as follows:

    (F) $42 + 27 = 79$
    (G) $63 + 15 = 78$
    (H) $32 + 6 = 38$
    (J) $40 + 12 = 52$

Answers and Explanations *(continued)*

17. **D** You can use the plug-in method, trying each answer choice in turn. Or, you can solve the problem using algebra, isolating the missing term on one side of the equation:
$$11 - 10 \div (\_ \times 3) + 3 = 4$$
$$-10 \div (\_ \times 3) = -10$$
$$-10 = -10(\_ \times 3)$$
$$1 = (\_ \times 3)$$
$$\frac{1}{3} = \_$$

18. **H** Of the four numbers, 36 has the greatest number of factors. Here's a list of positive factors for each number (excluding 1 and the number itself):
24: {2,3,4,6,12}
42: {2,3,6,7,21}
36: {2,3,4,6,9,12,18}
50: {2,5,10,25}

19. **B** The fraction $\frac{5}{3}$ is equal to $1\frac{2}{3}$, which is 100% plus approximately 66%, or 166%. Choice B provides the closest approximation.

20. **H** Here are the four coordinate pairs and their *xy*-products:
Point *A* is at $(-3,-1)$; $xy = 3$.
Point *B* is at $(2,2)$; $xy = 4$.
Point *C* is at $(-2,3)$; $xy = -6$.
Point *D* is at $(2,-1)$; $xy = -2$.

21. **A** There are 16 ounces in a pound and, accordingly, 80 ounces in 5 pounds. Removing 30 ounces from 80 ounces leaves 50 ounces.

22. **H** First, apply the distributive law of multiplication:
$$c(a + b) + bc = ca + cb + bc$$
The commutative properties of addition and multiplication allow you to reverse the order of variables in any term and to rearrange the terms:
$$ca + (cb + bc) = ac + 2bc$$
Finally, you can factor out *c* from both terms:
$$ac + 2bc = c(a + 2b)$$

23. **B** After Stacy drinks 25% of 16 ounces (which is 4 ounces), 12 ounces remain. After Stacy drinks 25% of 12 ounces (which is 3 ounces), 9 ounces remain.

24. **G** The area of a triangle equals half the product of its base and height $\left(A = \frac{1}{2}bh\right)$. Applying this formula, solve for *b*:
$$15 = \left(\frac{3}{2}\right)b$$
$$\left(\frac{2}{3}\right)(15) = b$$
$$10 = b$$

25. **A** Because 15 of 27 animals are monkeys, 12 are *not* monkeys. The ratio of monkeys to other animals is 15:12, or 5:4. You can express this ratio as the fraction $\frac{5}{4}$.

26. **H** In any isosceles triangle, two sides are congruent (the same length) and, accordingly, the two angles opposite those sides are congruent (the same degree measure). In any triangle, the sum of the measures of the three angles is 180°. Thus, if one angle of an isosceles triangle measures 100°, the other two angles must each measure 40°.

27. **D** At $15 per hour, Ashley earns $120 in wages during an 8-hour shift. Her 5% commission on $400 in sales is $20. Ashley's total earnings were $140 ($120 + $20).

28. **H** Any number squared is a positive number. Therefore, for any real numbers *x* and *y*, $x^2 + y^2 > 0$. On the number line shown, however, point *A* is a negative number.

29. **A** To find the average temperature, add the high and low, and then divide the sum by 2:
$$\frac{(-6+11)}{2} = \frac{5}{2}, \text{ or } 2.5°.$$

Answers and Explanations *(continued)*

30. **J** First, simplify the second term by removing the perfect square from inside the radical:

$$2\sqrt{5} + 2\sqrt{125} = 2\sqrt{5} + 2\sqrt{5^2 5} =$$

$$2\sqrt{5} + 2 \times 5\sqrt{5} = 2\sqrt{5} + 10\sqrt{5}$$

Then, combine terms:

$$2\sqrt{5} + 10\sqrt{5} = 12\sqrt{5}$$

31. **B** Three members are common to the two sets: 2, 4, and 8.

32. **F** A rectangular plot's area equals the product of its length and width ($A = lw$). Apply this equation, solving for *w:*

$$12,000 = 150w$$

$$\frac{12,000}{150} = w$$

$$80 = w$$

33. **B** Because *x* is negative and *y* is positive, their product must be a negative number. In addition, because the absolute value (distance from the origin on the number line) of both *x* and *y* is greater than 1, their product must be less than -1.

34. **H** Twenty-five (25) cents is $\frac{1}{4}$ of a dollar. Because one dollar is $\frac{1}{100}$ of $100, 25 cents is $\frac{1}{4} \times \frac{1}{100}$, or $\frac{1}{400}$, of $100.

35. **D** The total number of eggs produced during the week is 31. To find the average per coop, divide by 4: $31 \div 4 \approx 8$.

36. **J** To find daily totals, add the numbers in each column. Here are the totals for each pair of days listed in the question:
    Choice F: Saturday and Sunday: $3 + 5 = 8$
    Choice G: Thursday and Friday: $2 + 6 = 8$
    Choice H: Monday and Tuesday: $3 + 6 = 9$
    Choice J: Tuesday and Friday: $6 + 6 = 12$

37. **C** Matt drove twice as fast, on average, coming home as going to work. Thus, his average speed during the drive home must have been 60 miles per hour. Since the route to and from work is the same distance, we can give it any value, for instance 60 miles. This means that the trip to work was $\frac{60 \ miles}{30 \ mph} = 2$ hours.

    The trip back home took $\frac{60 \ miles}{60 \ mph} = 1$ hour. To find the overall rate, we need to divide the overall distance by the overall time: $\frac{120 \ miles}{3 \ hours} = 40$ miles per hour.

38. **J** Assume each side of a certain square is 2 units in length. The area of this square is $2 \times 2 = 4$. Now, increase the length of each side by 50%—to 3 units. The square's new area is $3 \times 3 = 9$. An increase from 4 to 9 is a 125% increase.

39. **C** Because $3 \times 16 = 48$, from 1 to 50 there are 16 multiples of 3. Accordingly, the probability that Kira will select a multiple of 3 is $\frac{16}{50}$, or $\frac{8}{25}$.

40. **G** Convert the verbal equation to an equation with numbers, and then solve for the missing number (*x*):

$$4x + 2 = \frac{3}{4} \times 8$$

$$4x = 6 - 2$$

$$4x = 4$$

$$x = 1$$

HSPT PRACTICE TEST 1

Answer Sheet

Directions: For each answer that you select, blacken the corresponding oval on this sheet.

Verbal Skills

1. Ⓐ Ⓑ Ⓒ Ⓓ
2. Ⓐ Ⓑ Ⓒ Ⓓ
3. Ⓐ Ⓑ Ⓒ Ⓓ
4. Ⓐ Ⓑ Ⓒ Ⓓ
5. Ⓐ Ⓑ Ⓒ Ⓓ
6. Ⓐ Ⓑ Ⓒ Ⓓ
7. Ⓐ Ⓑ Ⓒ Ⓓ
8. Ⓐ Ⓑ Ⓒ Ⓓ
9. Ⓐ Ⓑ Ⓒ Ⓓ
10. Ⓐ Ⓑ Ⓒ Ⓓ
11. Ⓐ Ⓑ Ⓒ Ⓓ
12. Ⓐ Ⓑ Ⓒ Ⓓ
13. Ⓐ Ⓑ Ⓒ Ⓓ
14. Ⓐ Ⓑ Ⓒ Ⓓ
15. Ⓐ Ⓑ Ⓒ Ⓓ
16. Ⓐ Ⓑ Ⓒ Ⓓ
17. Ⓐ Ⓑ Ⓒ Ⓓ
18. Ⓐ Ⓑ Ⓒ Ⓓ
19. Ⓐ Ⓑ Ⓒ Ⓓ
20. Ⓐ Ⓑ Ⓒ Ⓓ
21. Ⓐ Ⓑ Ⓒ Ⓓ
22. Ⓐ Ⓑ Ⓒ Ⓓ
23. Ⓐ Ⓑ Ⓒ Ⓓ
24. Ⓐ Ⓑ Ⓒ Ⓓ
25. Ⓐ Ⓑ Ⓒ Ⓓ
26. Ⓐ Ⓑ Ⓒ Ⓓ
27. Ⓐ Ⓑ Ⓒ Ⓓ
28. Ⓐ Ⓑ Ⓒ Ⓓ
29. Ⓐ Ⓑ Ⓒ Ⓓ
30. Ⓐ Ⓑ Ⓒ Ⓓ
31. Ⓐ Ⓑ Ⓒ Ⓓ
32. Ⓐ Ⓑ Ⓒ Ⓓ
33. Ⓐ Ⓑ Ⓒ Ⓓ
34. Ⓐ Ⓑ Ⓒ Ⓓ
35. Ⓐ Ⓑ Ⓒ Ⓓ
36. Ⓐ Ⓑ Ⓒ Ⓓ
37. Ⓐ Ⓑ Ⓒ Ⓓ
38. Ⓐ Ⓑ Ⓒ Ⓓ
39. Ⓐ Ⓑ Ⓒ Ⓓ
40. Ⓐ Ⓑ Ⓒ Ⓓ
41. Ⓐ Ⓑ Ⓒ Ⓓ
42. Ⓐ Ⓑ Ⓒ Ⓓ
43. Ⓐ Ⓑ Ⓒ Ⓓ
44. Ⓐ Ⓑ Ⓒ Ⓓ
45. Ⓐ Ⓑ Ⓒ Ⓓ
46. Ⓐ Ⓑ Ⓒ Ⓓ
47. Ⓐ Ⓑ Ⓒ Ⓓ

48. Ⓐ Ⓑ Ⓒ Ⓓ
49. Ⓐ Ⓑ Ⓒ Ⓓ
50. Ⓐ Ⓑ Ⓒ Ⓓ
51. Ⓐ Ⓑ Ⓒ Ⓓ
52. Ⓐ Ⓑ Ⓒ Ⓓ
53. Ⓐ Ⓑ Ⓒ Ⓓ
54. Ⓐ Ⓑ Ⓒ Ⓓ
55. Ⓐ Ⓑ Ⓒ Ⓓ
56. Ⓐ Ⓑ Ⓒ Ⓓ
57. Ⓐ Ⓑ Ⓒ Ⓓ
58. Ⓐ Ⓑ Ⓒ Ⓓ
59. Ⓐ Ⓑ Ⓒ Ⓓ
60. Ⓐ Ⓑ Ⓒ Ⓓ

Quantitative Skills

61. Ⓐ Ⓑ Ⓒ Ⓓ
62. Ⓐ Ⓑ Ⓒ Ⓓ
63. Ⓐ Ⓑ Ⓒ Ⓓ
64. Ⓐ Ⓑ Ⓒ Ⓓ
65. Ⓐ Ⓑ Ⓒ Ⓓ
66. Ⓐ Ⓑ Ⓒ Ⓓ
67. Ⓐ Ⓑ Ⓒ Ⓓ
68. Ⓐ Ⓑ Ⓒ Ⓓ
69. Ⓐ Ⓑ Ⓒ Ⓓ
70. Ⓐ Ⓑ Ⓒ Ⓓ
71. Ⓐ Ⓑ Ⓒ Ⓓ
72. Ⓐ Ⓑ Ⓒ Ⓓ
73. Ⓐ Ⓑ Ⓒ Ⓓ
74. Ⓐ Ⓑ Ⓒ Ⓓ
75. Ⓐ Ⓑ Ⓒ Ⓓ
76. Ⓐ Ⓑ Ⓒ Ⓓ
77. Ⓐ Ⓑ Ⓒ Ⓓ
78. Ⓐ Ⓑ Ⓒ Ⓓ
79. Ⓐ Ⓑ Ⓒ Ⓓ
80. Ⓐ Ⓑ Ⓒ Ⓓ
81. Ⓐ Ⓑ Ⓒ Ⓓ
82. Ⓐ Ⓑ Ⓒ Ⓓ
83. Ⓐ Ⓑ Ⓒ Ⓓ
84. Ⓐ Ⓑ Ⓒ Ⓓ
85. Ⓐ Ⓑ Ⓒ Ⓓ
86. Ⓐ Ⓑ Ⓒ Ⓓ
87. Ⓐ Ⓑ Ⓒ Ⓓ
88. Ⓐ Ⓑ Ⓒ Ⓓ
89. Ⓐ Ⓑ Ⓒ Ⓓ
90. Ⓐ Ⓑ Ⓒ Ⓓ
91. Ⓐ Ⓑ Ⓒ Ⓓ
92. Ⓐ Ⓑ Ⓒ Ⓓ

93. Ⓐ Ⓑ Ⓒ Ⓓ
94. Ⓐ Ⓑ Ⓒ Ⓓ
95. Ⓐ Ⓑ Ⓒ Ⓓ
96. Ⓐ Ⓑ Ⓒ Ⓓ
97. Ⓐ Ⓑ Ⓒ Ⓓ
98. Ⓐ Ⓑ Ⓒ Ⓓ
99. Ⓐ Ⓑ Ⓒ Ⓓ
100. Ⓐ Ⓑ Ⓒ Ⓓ
101. Ⓐ Ⓑ Ⓒ Ⓓ
102. Ⓐ Ⓑ Ⓒ Ⓓ
103. Ⓐ Ⓑ Ⓒ Ⓓ
104. Ⓐ Ⓑ Ⓒ Ⓓ
105. Ⓐ Ⓑ Ⓒ Ⓓ
106. Ⓐ Ⓑ Ⓒ Ⓓ
107. Ⓐ Ⓑ Ⓒ Ⓓ
108. Ⓐ Ⓑ Ⓒ Ⓓ
109. Ⓐ Ⓑ Ⓒ Ⓓ
110. Ⓐ Ⓑ Ⓒ Ⓓ
111. Ⓐ Ⓑ Ⓒ Ⓓ
112. Ⓐ Ⓑ Ⓒ Ⓓ

Reading

113. Ⓐ Ⓑ Ⓒ Ⓓ
114. Ⓐ Ⓑ Ⓒ Ⓓ
115. Ⓐ Ⓑ Ⓒ Ⓓ
116. Ⓐ Ⓑ Ⓒ Ⓓ
117. Ⓐ Ⓑ Ⓒ Ⓓ
118. Ⓐ Ⓑ Ⓒ Ⓓ
119. Ⓐ Ⓑ Ⓒ Ⓓ
120. Ⓐ Ⓑ Ⓒ Ⓓ
121. Ⓐ Ⓑ Ⓒ Ⓓ
122. Ⓐ Ⓑ Ⓒ Ⓓ
123. Ⓐ Ⓑ Ⓒ Ⓓ
124. Ⓐ Ⓑ Ⓒ Ⓓ
125. Ⓐ Ⓑ Ⓒ Ⓓ
126. Ⓐ Ⓑ Ⓒ Ⓓ
127. Ⓐ Ⓑ Ⓒ Ⓓ
128. Ⓐ Ⓑ Ⓒ Ⓓ
129. Ⓐ Ⓑ Ⓒ Ⓓ
130. Ⓐ Ⓑ Ⓒ Ⓓ
131. Ⓐ Ⓑ Ⓒ Ⓓ
132. Ⓐ Ⓑ Ⓒ Ⓓ
133. Ⓐ Ⓑ Ⓒ Ⓓ
134. Ⓐ Ⓑ Ⓒ Ⓓ
135. Ⓐ Ⓑ Ⓒ Ⓓ
136. Ⓐ Ⓑ Ⓒ Ⓓ
137. Ⓐ Ⓑ Ⓒ Ⓓ

HSPT PRACTICE TEST 1

Answer Sheet (continued)

138. Ⓐ Ⓑ Ⓒ Ⓓ	186. Ⓐ Ⓑ Ⓒ Ⓓ	236. Ⓐ Ⓑ Ⓒ Ⓓ
139. Ⓐ Ⓑ Ⓒ Ⓓ	187. Ⓐ Ⓑ Ⓒ Ⓓ	237. Ⓐ Ⓑ Ⓒ Ⓓ
140. Ⓐ Ⓑ Ⓒ Ⓓ	188. Ⓐ Ⓑ Ⓒ Ⓓ	238. Ⓐ Ⓑ Ⓒ Ⓓ
141. Ⓐ Ⓑ Ⓒ Ⓓ	189. Ⓐ Ⓑ Ⓒ Ⓓ	
142. Ⓐ Ⓑ Ⓒ Ⓓ	190. Ⓐ Ⓑ Ⓒ Ⓓ	**Language**
143. Ⓐ Ⓑ Ⓒ Ⓓ	191. Ⓐ Ⓑ Ⓒ Ⓓ	239. Ⓐ Ⓑ Ⓒ Ⓓ
144. Ⓐ Ⓑ Ⓒ Ⓓ	192. Ⓐ Ⓑ Ⓒ Ⓓ	240. Ⓐ Ⓑ Ⓒ Ⓓ
145. Ⓐ Ⓑ Ⓒ Ⓓ	193. Ⓐ Ⓑ Ⓒ Ⓓ	241. Ⓐ Ⓑ Ⓒ Ⓓ
146. Ⓐ Ⓑ Ⓒ Ⓓ	194. Ⓐ Ⓑ Ⓒ Ⓓ	242. Ⓐ Ⓑ Ⓒ Ⓓ
147. Ⓐ Ⓑ Ⓒ Ⓓ	195. Ⓐ Ⓑ Ⓒ Ⓓ	243. Ⓐ Ⓑ Ⓒ Ⓓ
148. Ⓐ Ⓑ Ⓒ Ⓓ	196. Ⓐ Ⓑ Ⓒ Ⓓ	244. Ⓐ Ⓑ Ⓒ Ⓓ
149. Ⓐ Ⓑ Ⓒ Ⓓ	197. Ⓐ Ⓑ Ⓒ Ⓓ	245. Ⓐ Ⓑ Ⓒ Ⓓ
150. Ⓐ Ⓑ Ⓒ Ⓓ	198. Ⓐ Ⓑ Ⓒ Ⓓ	246. Ⓐ Ⓑ Ⓒ Ⓓ
151. Ⓐ Ⓑ Ⓒ Ⓓ	199. Ⓐ Ⓑ Ⓒ Ⓓ	247. Ⓐ Ⓑ Ⓒ Ⓓ
152. Ⓐ Ⓑ Ⓒ Ⓓ	200. Ⓐ Ⓑ Ⓒ Ⓓ	248. Ⓐ Ⓑ Ⓒ Ⓓ
153. Ⓐ Ⓑ Ⓒ Ⓓ	201. Ⓐ Ⓑ Ⓒ Ⓓ	249. Ⓐ Ⓑ Ⓒ Ⓓ
154. Ⓐ Ⓑ Ⓒ Ⓓ	202. Ⓐ Ⓑ Ⓒ Ⓓ	250. Ⓐ Ⓑ Ⓒ Ⓓ
155. Ⓐ Ⓑ Ⓒ Ⓓ	203. Ⓐ Ⓑ Ⓒ Ⓓ	251. Ⓐ Ⓑ Ⓒ Ⓓ
156. Ⓐ Ⓑ Ⓒ Ⓓ	204. Ⓐ Ⓑ Ⓒ Ⓓ	252. Ⓐ Ⓑ Ⓒ Ⓓ
157. Ⓐ Ⓑ Ⓒ Ⓓ	205. Ⓐ Ⓑ Ⓒ Ⓓ	253. Ⓐ Ⓑ Ⓒ Ⓓ
158. Ⓐ Ⓑ Ⓒ Ⓓ	206. Ⓐ Ⓑ Ⓒ Ⓓ	254. Ⓐ Ⓑ Ⓒ Ⓓ
159. Ⓐ Ⓑ Ⓒ Ⓓ	207. Ⓐ Ⓑ Ⓒ Ⓓ	255. Ⓐ Ⓑ Ⓒ Ⓓ
160. Ⓐ Ⓑ Ⓒ Ⓓ	208. Ⓐ Ⓑ Ⓒ Ⓓ	256. Ⓐ Ⓑ Ⓒ Ⓓ
161. Ⓐ Ⓑ Ⓒ Ⓓ	209. Ⓐ Ⓑ Ⓒ Ⓓ	257. Ⓐ Ⓑ Ⓒ Ⓓ
162. Ⓐ Ⓑ Ⓒ Ⓓ	210. Ⓐ Ⓑ Ⓒ Ⓓ	258. Ⓐ Ⓑ Ⓒ Ⓓ
163. Ⓐ Ⓑ Ⓒ Ⓓ	211. Ⓐ Ⓑ Ⓒ Ⓓ	259. Ⓐ Ⓑ Ⓒ Ⓓ
164. Ⓐ Ⓑ Ⓒ Ⓓ	212. Ⓐ Ⓑ Ⓒ Ⓓ	260. Ⓐ Ⓑ Ⓒ Ⓓ
165. Ⓐ Ⓑ Ⓒ Ⓓ	213. Ⓐ Ⓑ Ⓒ Ⓓ	261. Ⓐ Ⓑ Ⓒ Ⓓ
166. Ⓐ Ⓑ Ⓒ Ⓓ	214. Ⓐ Ⓑ Ⓒ Ⓓ	262. Ⓐ Ⓑ Ⓒ Ⓓ
167. Ⓐ Ⓑ Ⓒ Ⓓ	215. Ⓐ Ⓑ Ⓒ Ⓓ	263. Ⓐ Ⓑ Ⓒ Ⓓ
168. Ⓐ Ⓑ Ⓒ Ⓓ	216. Ⓐ Ⓑ Ⓒ Ⓓ	264. Ⓐ Ⓑ Ⓒ Ⓓ
169. Ⓐ Ⓑ Ⓒ Ⓓ	217. Ⓐ Ⓑ Ⓒ Ⓓ	265. Ⓐ Ⓑ Ⓒ Ⓓ
170. Ⓐ Ⓑ Ⓒ Ⓓ	218. Ⓐ Ⓑ Ⓒ Ⓓ	266. Ⓐ Ⓑ Ⓒ Ⓓ
171. Ⓐ Ⓑ Ⓒ Ⓓ	219. Ⓐ Ⓑ Ⓒ Ⓓ	267. Ⓐ Ⓑ Ⓒ Ⓓ
172. Ⓐ Ⓑ Ⓒ Ⓓ	220. Ⓐ Ⓑ Ⓒ Ⓓ	268. Ⓐ Ⓑ Ⓒ Ⓓ
173. Ⓐ Ⓑ Ⓒ Ⓓ	221. Ⓐ Ⓑ Ⓒ Ⓓ	269. Ⓐ Ⓑ Ⓒ Ⓓ
174. Ⓐ Ⓑ Ⓒ Ⓓ	222. Ⓐ Ⓑ Ⓒ Ⓓ	270. Ⓐ Ⓑ Ⓒ Ⓓ
	223. Ⓐ Ⓑ Ⓒ Ⓓ	271. Ⓐ Ⓑ Ⓒ Ⓓ
Mathematics	224. Ⓐ Ⓑ Ⓒ Ⓓ	272. Ⓐ Ⓑ Ⓒ Ⓓ
175. Ⓐ Ⓑ Ⓒ Ⓓ	225. Ⓐ Ⓑ Ⓒ Ⓓ	273. Ⓐ Ⓑ Ⓒ Ⓓ
176. Ⓐ Ⓑ Ⓒ Ⓓ	226. Ⓐ Ⓑ Ⓒ Ⓓ	274. Ⓐ Ⓑ Ⓒ Ⓓ
177. Ⓐ Ⓑ Ⓒ Ⓓ	227. Ⓐ Ⓑ Ⓒ Ⓓ	275. Ⓐ Ⓑ Ⓒ Ⓓ
178. Ⓐ Ⓑ Ⓒ Ⓓ	228. Ⓐ Ⓑ Ⓒ Ⓓ	276. Ⓐ Ⓑ Ⓒ Ⓓ
179. Ⓐ Ⓑ Ⓒ Ⓓ	229. Ⓐ Ⓑ Ⓒ Ⓓ	277. Ⓐ Ⓑ Ⓒ Ⓓ
180. Ⓐ Ⓑ Ⓒ Ⓓ	230. Ⓐ Ⓑ Ⓒ Ⓓ	278. Ⓐ Ⓑ Ⓒ Ⓓ
181. Ⓐ Ⓑ Ⓒ Ⓓ	231. Ⓐ Ⓑ Ⓒ Ⓓ	279. Ⓐ Ⓑ Ⓒ Ⓓ
182. Ⓐ Ⓑ Ⓒ Ⓓ	232. Ⓐ Ⓑ Ⓒ Ⓓ	280. Ⓐ Ⓑ Ⓒ Ⓓ
183. Ⓐ Ⓑ Ⓒ Ⓓ	233. Ⓐ Ⓑ Ⓒ Ⓓ	281. Ⓐ Ⓑ Ⓒ Ⓓ
184. Ⓐ Ⓑ Ⓒ Ⓓ	234. Ⓐ Ⓑ Ⓒ Ⓓ	282. Ⓐ Ⓑ Ⓒ Ⓓ
185. Ⓐ Ⓑ Ⓒ Ⓓ	235. Ⓐ Ⓑ Ⓒ Ⓓ	283. Ⓐ Ⓑ Ⓒ Ⓓ

HSPT PRACTICE TEST 1

Answer Sheet *(continued)*

284. Ⓐ Ⓑ Ⓒ Ⓓ
285. Ⓐ Ⓑ Ⓒ Ⓓ
286. Ⓐ Ⓑ Ⓒ Ⓓ
287. Ⓐ Ⓑ Ⓒ Ⓓ
288. Ⓐ Ⓑ Ⓒ Ⓓ
289. Ⓐ Ⓑ Ⓒ Ⓓ
290. Ⓐ Ⓑ Ⓒ Ⓓ
291. Ⓐ Ⓑ Ⓒ Ⓓ
292. Ⓐ Ⓑ Ⓒ Ⓓ
293. Ⓐ Ⓑ Ⓒ Ⓓ
294. Ⓐ Ⓑ Ⓒ Ⓓ
295. Ⓐ Ⓑ Ⓒ Ⓓ
296. Ⓐ Ⓑ Ⓒ Ⓓ
297. Ⓐ Ⓑ Ⓒ Ⓓ
298. Ⓐ Ⓑ Ⓒ Ⓓ

HSPT PRACTICE TEST 1

Verbal Skills (60 questions) (16 minutes)

Directions: For questions 1–60, choose the best answer.

1. Ascend most nearly means
   A face
   B climb
   C forgive
   D weaken

2. Which word does *not* belong with the others?
   A custom
   B behavior
   C ritual
   D habit

3. Cake is to flour as bench is to
   A varnish
   B leg
   C table
   D wood

4. Affable most nearly means
   A laughable
   B tiny
   C agreeable
   D cheap

5. There are more restaurants in Seaside than in Valley View. There are fewer restaurants in Seaside than in Appleton. There are fewer restaurants in Appleton than in Valley View. If the first two statements are true, the third is
   A true
   B false
   C uncertain

6. Ratify most nearly means
   A magnify
   B lie
   C punch
   D confirm

7. Bull is to horn as deer is to
   A doe
   B nose
   C antler
   D ear

8. Obsess means the *opposite* of
   A glance
   B ignore
   C heal
   D straighten

9. Which word does *not* belong with the others?
   A smoke
   B heat
   C ash
   D oven

10. Painters like a peaceful environment when they paint. Kim likes peaceful environments. Kim is a painter. If the first two statements are true, the third is
    A true
    B false
    C uncertain

11. Which word does *not* belong with the others?
    A sail
    B ocean
    C beach
    D wave

12. Rebecca ate breakfast before Carlos but after Ted. James ate breakfast after Ted but before Carlos. Rebecca ate breakfast before James. If the first two statements are true, the third is
    A true
    B false
    C uncertain

Verbal Skills *(continued)*

13. Which word does *not* belong with the others?

    A   quarrel
    B   play
    C   spar
    D   fight

14. Which word does *not* belong with the others?

    A   blanket
    B   quilt
    C   bedspread
    D   pillow

15. Deed most nearly means

    A   illness
    B   hike
    C   act
    D   failure

16. Store is to closet as perform is to

    A   school
    B   concert
    C   theater
    D   library

17. Javier is taller than Samantha but shorter than Carl. Victoria is shorter than Javier. Carl is taller than Victoria. If the first two statements are true, the third is

    A   true
    B   false
    C   uncertain

18. Digress most nearly means

    A   play
    B   annoy
    C   consume
    D   stray

19. Which word does *not* belong with the others?

    A   pigeon
    B   spider
    C   moose
    D   dog

20. If I throw a baseball at the window, the window will break; the window is not broken. I have not thrown a baseball at the window. If the first two statements are true, the third is

    A   true
    B   false
    C   uncertain

21. Static means the *opposite* of

    A   brittle
    B   clean
    C   active
    D   wet

22. Saga most nearly means

    A   wagon
    B   brush
    C   tale
    D   plea

23. Which word does *not* belong with the others?

    A   raise
    B   award
    C   trophy
    D   gift

24. Which word does *not* belong with the others?

    A   track
    B   route
    C   hurdle
    D   course

25. Eyeglasses is to vision as food is to

    A   vegetable
    B   hunger
    C   energy
    D   stomach

26. Verbose means the *opposite* of

    A   plentiful
    B   incomplete
    C   aged
    D   concise

Verbal Skills *(continued)*

27. Which word does *not* belong with the others?

A noisy
B slow
C bitter
D ugly

28. Malice most nearly means

A cooperation
B hostility
C quiet
D variety

29. If Gwen does not leave her house by 12:00, she will be late for work. Gwen stopped for lunch on the way to work today. Gwen was late for work today. If the first two statements are true, the third is

A true
B false
C uncertain

30. Food is to spoil as metal is to

A rust
B mine
C strengthen
D mold

31. Abyss means the *opposite* of

A noise
B peak
C exit
D beginning

32. Palatial most nearly means

A kind
B sad
C tasty
D grand

33. Computer B is slower than computer A, but computer A is older than computer B. Computer C is older than computer A. Computer C is slower than computer A. Computer B is newer than computer C. If the first three statements are true, the fourth is

A true
B false
C uncertain

34. Which word does *not* belong with the others?

A rookie
B novice
C veteran
D amateur

35. Army is to soldier as shirt is to

A skin
B thread
C sweater
D collar

36. Epitome most nearly means

A model
B note
C center
D proverb

37. Which word does *not* belong with the others?

A infant
B youngster
C preteen
D juvenile

38. Vein is to blood as river is to

A flood
B lake
C canoe
D water

Verbal Skills *(continued)*

39. Wavering means the *opposite* of

A playful
B discouraging
C eager
D mournful

40. Which word does *not* belong with the others?

A jest
B kid
C joke
D laugh

41. Respite most nearly means

A illusion
B rest
C choice
D hatred

42. Lax most nearly means

A careless
B ordinary
C empty
D quick

43. Johnson received more votes than Weller. Lauter received fewer votes than Johnson. Weller received fewer votes than Lauter. If the first two statements are true, the third is

A true
B false
C uncertain

44. Which word does *not* belong with the others?

A simple
B terse
C short
D brief

45. Patient is to doctor as customer is to

A service
B business
C cashier
D product

46. Pacify means the *opposite* of

A trust
B irritate
C promote
D dispose

47. Epidemic most nearly means

A skinny
B deadly
C widespread
D shallow

48. Anita is faster and lighter than Brent. Sheila is heavier but faster than Anita. Brent is faster but heavier than Sheila. If the first two statements are true, the third is

A true
B false
C uncertain

49. Review is to movie as score is to

A exam
B symphony
C rehearsal
D preview

50. Reciprocate most nearly means

A drink
B trade
C elect
D sweat

51. Remorse most nearly means

A regret
B mow
C smooth
D refresh

52. Robust means the *opposite* of

A honest
B strong
C graceful
D sickly

Verbal Skills *(continued)*

53. Deplete means the *opposite* of

A replenish
B compliment
C unfold
D starve

54. Jim mows his lawn twice per month. Andy mows his lawn once per week. Jim mows his lawn more often than Andy. If the first two statements are true, the third is

A true
B false
C uncertain

55. Mistake is to correction as problem is to

A puzzle
B failure
C riddle
D solution

56. Which word does *not* belong with the others?

A region
B territory
C border
D zone

57. Candid means the *opposite* of

A secretive
B bland
C open
D hopeful

58. Only high school graduates can attend Wheeler College. David is a high school student. David attends Wheeler College. If the first two statements are true, the third is

A true
B false
C uncertain

59. Which word does *not* belong with the others?

A lock
B secure
C beware
D fasten

60. Innovation means the *opposite* of

A explanation
B exiting
C maturity
D imitation

STOP!
If you finish before time runs out, check your work on this section only.

Quantitative Skills (52 questions), (30 minutes)

Directions: Choose the best answer to each question.

61. What number added to 9 leaves 11 more than $\frac{2}{3}$ of 27?

  A   31
  B   22
  C   29
  D   20

62. What is the next number in the following series: 11, 12, 14, 17, 21, 26, . . . ?

  A   32
  B   30
  C   27
  D   29

63. Two-thirds of a certain number is $\frac{1}{2}$. What is the number?

  A $\frac{3}{4}$

  B $\frac{3}{2}$

  C $\frac{5}{6}$

  D   1

64. Examine (a), (b), and (c) and then choose the correct answer.

  (a) $12 + 4(11 - 13)$
  (b) $4 - 12(13 - 11)$
  (c) $11 - 4(12 - 13)$

  A   (c) < (b) < (a)
  B   (b) < (a) < (c)
  C   (a) < (b) < (c)
  D   (b) < (c) < (a)

65. What is the next number in the following series: 9, 6, 3, 8, 5, 2, 7, . . . ?

  A   3
  B   5
  C   4
  D   10

66. What is the next number in the following series: 1, 2, 7, 8, 13, 14, . . . ?

  A   19
  B   18
  C   15
  D   20

67. Subtracting −1 from a certain number results in twice the product of −1 and −1. What is the number?

  A   1
  B   0
  C   2
  D   −1

68. Examine the circle, whose center is (O), and select the best answer.

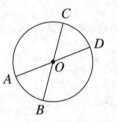

  A $BC - BO = OD$
  B $AD < BC$
  C $AO + DO = OC$
  D $2 \times BO < AD$

69. Examine (a), (b), and (c) and then choose the correct answer.

  (a) $24 \times \frac{8}{3}$

  (b) $14 \times \frac{30}{7}$

  (c) $35 \times \frac{9}{5}$

  A   (c) > (a) > (b)
  B   (a) < (b) < (a)
  C   (a) > (b) > (c)
  D   (b) < (c) < (a)

Quantitative Skills (continued)

70. Examine figures (a), (b), and (c) and then choose the correct statement.

(a)　　　　　　(b)

(c)

A The number of circles in figure (a) is equal to the number of circles in figure (c).

B The number of triangles in figure (b) is equal to the number of circles in figure (c).

C The number of triangles in figure (a) is less than the number of circles in figure (c).

D The number of circles in figure (b) is greater than the number of triangles in figure (c).

71. Two hundred percent divided by what percent yields a quotient of two hundred fifty percent?

A 60
B 80
C 120
D 75

72. Examine (a), (b), and (c) and then choose the best answer.

(a) 0.4%

(b) $\dfrac{1}{40}$

(c) 0.04

A (b) is greater than (a) and less than (c)
B (a) is greater than (b) and less than (c)
C (b) is greater than (c) and less than (a)
D (c) is greater than (a) and less than (b)

73. What is the next number in the following series: 2, 4, 8, 16, 32, . . . ?

A 48
B 40
C 56
D 64

74. $\dfrac{2}{3}$ of 27 is equal to what fraction of 30?

A $\dfrac{3}{4}$

B $\dfrac{3}{5}$

C $\dfrac{4}{5}$

D $\dfrac{5}{8}$

75. What is the next number in the following series: $\dfrac{3}{4}, \dfrac{4}{3}, \dfrac{2}{3}, \dfrac{3}{2}, \dfrac{1}{2}, \ldots$?

A 1
B 2
C 0
D $\dfrac{1}{4}$

Quantitative Skills *(continued)*

76. Examine (a), (b), and (c) and then choose the best answer.

(a) 1.5×10^4

(b) 30×10^3

(c) 450×10^2

A (b) is greater than (c) and less than (a)

B (c) is greater than (a) and less than (b)

C (b) is greater than (a) and less than (c)

D (a) is greater than (b) and less than (c)

77. What is the missing number in the following series: 57, 52, 54, 49, __, 46, 48 ?

A 47

B 50

C 51

D 53

78. Examine (a), (b), (c), and (d) and then choose the correct answer.

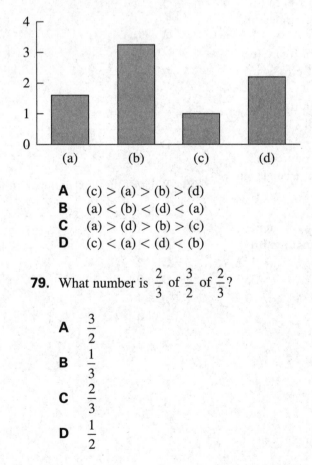

A (c) > (a) > (b) > (d)

B (a) < (b) < (d) < (a)

C (a) > (d) > (b) > (c)

D (c) < (a) < (d) < (b)

79. What number is $\frac{2}{3}$ of $\frac{3}{2}$ of $\frac{2}{3}$?

A $\frac{3}{2}$

B $\frac{1}{3}$

C $\frac{2}{3}$

D $\frac{1}{2}$

80. What is the next number in the following series: 0.5, 1.5, 4.5, 13.5, . . . ?

A 32

B 27.5

C 22.5

D 40.5

81. Examine (a), (b), and (c) and then choose the best answer.

(a) $(-2)^4$

(b) $(-3)^3$

(c) 4^2

A (b) is less than (a) and greater than (c)

B (a) is equal to (c) and greater than (b)

C (a) is greater than (b) and less than (c)

D (a) is equal to (c) and less than (b)

82. 25 percent of what number is equal to 75 percent of 20?

A 50

B 80

C 100

D 60

83. What is the next number in the following series: −1, 3, 7, 11, . . . ?

A 15

B −1

C 4

D 6

84. Examine figures (a), (b), and (c) and then choose the correct statement.

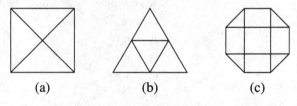

(a)   (b)   (c)

A Figure (b) contains more triangles than figure (a).

B Figure (a) contains twice the number of triangles as figure (c).

C Figure (c) contains the same number of triangles as figure (a).

D Figure (b) contains fewer triangles than figure (c).

Quantitative Skills *(continued)*

85. What are the next two numbers in the following series: 0, 2, 0, 2, 4, 0, 2, 0, 2, . . . ?

A 0, 2
B 0, 4
C 4, 2
D 4, 0

86. $\frac{1}{2}$ subtracted from a certain number is $-\frac{1}{4}$. What is the number?

A 0.4
B 0.5
C 0.25
D 0.05

87. What is the next number in the following series: 256, 64, 16, 4, . . . ?

A 1
B $\frac{1}{4}$
C 2
D $\frac{1}{2}$

88. Examine (a), (b), (c), and (d) and then choose the correct answer.

(a) The greatest prime factor of 10
(b) The greatest prime factor of 11
(c) The greatest prime factor of 12
(d) The greatest prime factor of 13

A (c) < (a) < (b) < (d)
B (a) < (d) < (c) < (b)
C (a) < (b) < (d) < (c)
D (b) < (c) < (a) < (d)

89. What number is 8 less than $\frac{3}{2}$ of 30?

A 42
B 18
C 37
D 32

90. In the figure below, *ADEC* is a rectangle, and triangle *ABC* is equilateral.

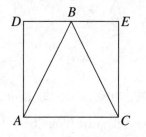

Which of the following statements CANNOT be true?

A $BD = BE$
B $AC = AB$
C $AD > BE$
D $AB < DE$

91. What are the next two numbers in the following series: 3, 4, 5, 4, 3, 4, 5, 4, . . . ?

A 4, 5
B 3, 4
C 5, 6
D 5, 3

92. Examine (a), (b), and (c) and then choose the correct answer.

(a) $\frac{4}{7}$
(b) $\frac{3}{5}$
(c) $\frac{2}{3}$

A (c) < (a) < (b)
B (a) < (c) < (b)
C (a) < (b) < (c)
D (b) < (c) < (a)

93. $\frac{6}{5}$ of what number is twice the product of $\frac{3}{2}$ and 8?

A 10
B 28
C 14
D 20

Quantitative Skills (continued)

94. What is the next letter in the following series: h, g, f, k, j, i, n, m, l, . . . ?

   A p
   B o
   C q
   D m

95. 30% of the quotient of 30 and 6 is $\frac{3}{2}$ less than what number?

   A 40
   B 3
   C 9/2
   D 2.1

96. What is the missing number in the following series: 29, 12, 28, __, 27, 8, 26, 6?

   A 11
   B 9
   C 10
   D 14

97. Examine (a), (b), and (c) and then choose the correct answer.

  (a) $3 + \sqrt{4}$
  (b) $\sqrt{3} + 4$
  (c) $\sqrt{4} + \sqrt{4}$

   A (a) is less than (b) and greater than (c)
   B (c) is greater than (a) and less than (b)
   C (b) is equal to (a) and less than (c)
   D (a) is equal to (b) and greater than (c)

98. $\frac{1}{2}$ cubed is equal to three-fourths of what number?

   A $\frac{1}{2}$
   B $\frac{1}{4}$
   C $\frac{3}{2}$
   D $\frac{1}{6}$

99. What is the next number in the following series: $5, \frac{21}{4}, \frac{11}{2}, \frac{23}{4}, \ldots$?

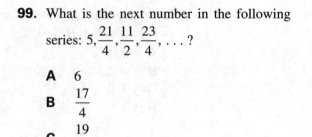

   A 6
   B $\frac{17}{4}$
   C $\frac{19}{2}$
   D 5

100. Examine figures (a), (b), and (c) and then choose the correct statement.

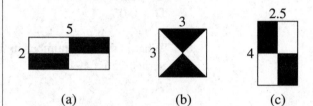

   (a)   (b)   (c)

   A The shaded area of figure (c) is equal to the shaded area of figure (a).
   B The shaded area of figure (a) is less than the shaded area of figure (b).
   C The shaded area of figure (b) is equal to the shaded area of figure (c).
   D The shaded area of figure (c) is greater than the shaded area of figure (a).

101. What is the next term in the following series: 13n, p20, 28r, t37, 47v, . . . ?

   A 60x
   B w56
   C x58
   D 57u

102. Five more than what number is equal to six times seven-fourths?

   A 16
   B $\frac{11}{2}$
   C 3
   D 18

Quantitative Skills *(continued)*

103. The average of −3, 2, and another number is 2. What is the number?

A 7
B 1
C 3
D 5

104. Examine (a), (b), and (c) and then choose the correct answer.

(a) The average of all integers between −50 and 50

(b) The average of all integers between −51 and 51

(c) The average of all integers between −50 and 51

A (c) is less than (a) but greater than (b)
B (a) is less than (c) but greater than (b)
C (b) is equal to (a) but is less than (c)
D (a) is equal to (b), and b is equal to (c)

105. When you multiply both the numerator and the denominator of $\frac{2}{3}$ by ___, you obtain $\frac{4}{6}$.

A 2
B 5
C 4
D 9

106. What is the next number in the following series: 160, CXXV, 90, LV, ... ?

A 20
B 10
C 25
D 15

107. 6 times what number is the square root of 64?

A $\frac{8}{3}$
B 2
C $\frac{4}{3}$
D $\frac{2}{3}$

108. What are the next two numbers in the following series of three integer patterns: 1, 0, 1, 2, 1, 1, 3, 2, 1, 4, 3, ... ?

A 2, 5
B 3, 2
C 2, 1
D 1, 5

109. Examine figures (a), (b), and (c) and then choose the correct statement.

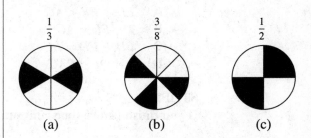

(a)   (b)   (c)

A The shaded area of figure (b) is less than the shaded area of figure (a).
B The shaded area of figure (c) is equal to the shaded area of figure (b).
C The shaded area of figure (a) is equal to the shaded area of figure (b).
D The shaded area of figure (c) is greater than the shaded area of figure (b).

110. What is the missing number in the following series: 4, 5, 8, __, 12, 13, 16, ... ?

A 11
B 10
C 9
D 12

Quantitative Skills *(continued)*

111. In the figure below, *ABCD* is a rectangle, $AE = EC$, and $EF \| CD$. Examine the figure and select the best answer.

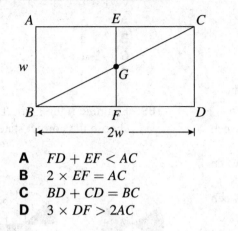

A $FD + EF < AC$
B $2 \times EF = AC$
C $BD + CD = BC$
D $3 \times DF > 2AC$

112. What number multiplied by 25 is the square of the sum of 4 and 6?

A 4
B $\dfrac{6}{5}$
C 1
D $\dfrac{1}{2}$

STOP!
If you finish before time runs out, check your work on this section only.

Reading (62 questions) (25 minutes)

Comprehension

Directions: Questions 113–152 are based on reading passages. Read the passages and answer the questions.

Questions 113–118 are based on the following passage:

The story of how the Roman armies conquered the nations of the ancient world is well known. But the story of Latin's conquest of the ancient world's languages is less known. Most people would guess that the worldwide supremacy of Latin was a natural result of the worldwide supremacy of the Roman <u>legions</u> or of Roman law. But this guess ignores modern history.

Conquered people do not always accept their conqueror's tongue. At the turn of the twentieth century, after 150 years of British rule, only one percent of the population of India could read and write English. Also, the French language has never threatened to replace Arabic in Algeria.

Of course, unlike the regions subdued by Rome, India and Algeria had their own large bodies of literature, which strengthened their resistance to other tongues. Even so, the extent of Latin's supremacy throughout the ancient world is remarkable. From its narrow confines within an area initially covering less than 100 square miles, Latin spread through Italy and the islands of the Mediterranean, through France, Spain, England, northern Africa, and the Danubian provinces. The Latin language triumphed over all other tongues in those regions more completely than Roman arms triumphed over the peoples who spoke those tongues.

113. Throughout the passage, the author uses the word *tongue* to mean

  A mouth
  B words
  C education
  D language

114. The author's main point in the passage is that

  A the Latin language eventually died because the Roman Empire fell
  B many people misunderstand why Latin became so widely spoken
  C people adopt a new language only when it is forced upon them
  D most people in India and Algeria cannot read or write Latin

115. In describing Latin as a conqueror, the author means that Latin

  A replaced many other languages
  B is a difficult language to learn
  C became India's official language
  D was the only language spoken in Rome

116. To the author, the fact that Latin spread so widely is

  A surprising
  B understandable
  C encouraging
  D tragic

117. As used in the passage, the word <u>legions</u> most nearly means

  A diseases
  B armies
  C civilizations
  D leaders

118. The author would probably agree that

  A all languages evolved from Latin
  B all languages, like all roads, once led to Rome
  C a language can be mightier than an army
  D the language of war is the same as that of peace

Reading *(continued)*

Questions 119–125 are based on the following passage:

The illegal selling of human body parts is commonplace among the poor in India, Brazil, and many other countries. Kidneys are an especially hot commodity, since we're born with two but only need one. However, <u>donors</u> typically learn after the fact that, if they weren't cheated completely, what little money they did receive for their organ is less than the wages they lost by missing work while recovering from surgery.

Human organs are in short supply in the United States; the waiting list exceeds 100,000 potential donees. Some U.S. lawmakers propose legalizing the selling of human organs. One proposed law would allow death-row prisoners to avoid execution by donating bone marrow or a kidney. Supporters of these laws often <u>invoke</u> what they believe is a fundamental right to choose when it comes to decisions about one's own body. Many opponents are concerned, however, that legalization would result in just one more way for the rich to exploit the poor, while others argue that selling human body parts is morally wrong because it reduces humans to saleable commodities.

119. The author implies that the selling of human organs is

  A illegal only in the United States
  B legal only in India and Brazil
  C common only in Brazil and India
  D illegal in India and Brazil

120. As it is used in the passage, the word <u>invoke</u> is best defined as

  A believe in
  B oppose
  C point out
  D legalize

121. In the United States, the supply of human organs

  A increases with each passing year
  B cannot keep up with the demand
  C is less than the supply in Brazil
  D decreases from year to year

122. The most frequently sold human body part is the

  A liver
  B bone marrow
  C kidney
  D heart

123. As it is used in the passage, the word <u>donors</u> most nearly means

  A suppliers
  B buyers
  C brokers
  D recipients

124. In the passage, the author

  A advocates legalization of the selling of human organs
  B criticizes U.S. lawmakers for outlawing sales of human organs
  C proposes a law to help the supply of human organs meet demand
  D identifies arguments for and against a proposed law

125. Which of the following questions does the passage best answer?

  A Does the practice of selling human organs victimize poor people?
  B Is it morally wrong to sell one's own body parts?
  C Does the selling of human organs pose a public-health danger?
  D Would legalizing the selling of human organs help people live longer?

Reading *(continued)*

Questions 126–131 are based on the following passage:

We've all known people who are convinced that their pet dog or cat possesses extraordinary intelligence for its species, as demonstrated by an ability to speak (in the pet owner's own language, of course), or to perform arithmetic (but never beyond the pet owner's own facility with numbers, of course) or some other intellectual feat that we humans generally assume is reserved for ourselves.

These people can learn a lesson from the story of Hans the horse, whose owner had convinced not just himself but many other people as well that Hans could add and subtract numbers and even multiply them. Hans would signal his answers by repeatedly stomping his hoof. Hans even fooled the scientists . . . except one, who tried recruiting questioners who were bad at math and didn't know the answers to their own questions. The results: Hans consistently gave *wrong* answers for these questioners!

As it turns out, Hans *was* intelligent . . . very intelligent. But could he perform arithmetic? Of course not. Hans had become an expert at reading body language! When Hans reached the correct number, every questioner who knew the correct answer responded with a subtle, involuntary change in posture, head position, or breathing. Hans had learned to pay close attention, no doubt largely because his owner rewarded him with a treat whenever he gave a correct answer.

126. This article is mainly about

- **A** a pet owner
- **B** a dog
- **C** a horse
- **D** an animal psychologist

127. Hans's owner believed he had trained Hans to

- **A** accept treats from strangers who asked him to perform arithmetic
- **B** observe the body language of a person asking him for an answer to an arithmetic problem
- **C** perform simple arithmetic such as addition and subtraction
- **D** stomp his hoof upon the owner's command to do so

128. Which of the following is probably NOT a reason that Hans learned to respond correctly to arithmetic questions?

- **A** Hans was extremely intelligent.
- **B** Hans was punished for giving wrong answers.
- **C** Hans was very observant of the humans around him.
- **D** Hans was rewarded for his behavior.

129. The article's author seems skeptical about the

- **A** honesty of people who brag about the intelligence of their pets
- **B** intelligence of scientists who study animals
- **C** claim that only humans can develop high-level language skills
- **D** ability of animals to converse using human language

130. The article strongly supports the claim that animals

- **A** pay close attention to their owners' behavior
- **B** are more intelligent than most people think
- **C** can be trained to do almost anything
- **D** mimic the behavior of their owners

131. This article is most likely to appear in a magazine catering to

- **A** veterinarians
- **B** pet owners
- **C** horse trainers
- **D** zookeepers

Reading (continued)

Questions 132–139 are based on the following passage:

Chess is the most intellectual, entertaining, and scientific of games, while at the same time more pleasingly absorbing than any pure science. With the possible exception of the simpler game of draughts, from which the modern game of checkers evolved, chess is also the most ancient of games. Oriental manuscripts, Eastern fables, and works of the early poets all <u>attest to</u> its antiquity. Although there is some disagreement concerning the origin of chess, most historians believe that the game originated in ancient India, then reached Persia from India in the first half of the sixth century, and then from there eventually reached Europe and, subsequently, America.

Though chess has never been honored throughout its long life by any continuous written history or record, its traditions from time immemorial have been of the most noble and even royal character. In fact, for many ages Europeans have referred to chess as "The Royal Game." Perhaps by coincidence, though hardly surprising, is that the key piece on a chessboard is the king, and that chess takes its modern-day name from the Persian word *Schach,* or *Shah,* which in that language signifies "King." Interestingly, combining the Persian word *Matt,* meaning "dead," with *Schach* results in a two-word phrase meaning "the King is dead." It is from this phrase that the term *checkmate,* which English-speaking chess players now use, originated.

132. The author would probably agree that chess is

   A too difficult for most people to master

   B more popular in America than in Europe

   C more challenging than any other game

   D more of a science than a game

133. Chess probably originated in

   A India

   B Persia

   C Europe

   D China

134. As proof that chess is an ancient game, the author mentions all of the following EXCEPT:

   A manuscripts from the Orient

   B ancient poems

   C fables from the East

   D ancient bone sculptures

135. As used in the passage, the phrase <u>attest to</u> means

   A mention

   B prove

   C dispute

   D include

136. Chess is also known as

   A Draughts

   B Matt

   C The Royal Game

   D Dead King

137. Why is it *hardly surprising* to the author that the key chess piece is the king?

   A Chess has always been popular among royalty.

   B The king is the largest piece on the chessboard.

   C The player who captures the opponent's king wins the game.

   D The Persian name for the game means "king."

Reading *(continued)*

138. The author would probably agree that checkers

   A was invented before chess
   B originated in ancient India
   C is known in Europe as "The Royal Game"
   D is more popular today than chess

139. A good title for the selection would be

   A "Chess and Checkers in Ancient Times"
   B "A Brief History of the Game of Chess"
   C "Why Chess is the World's Most Popular Game"
   D "How the Game of Chess Changed Through the Ages"

Questions 140–145 are based on the following passage:

What type of person are you? If you lived in ancient India, you would be classified under one of three body-mind types: *pitta* (intense and bold), *kapha* (relaxed and affectionate), or *vata* (moody and unpredictable). The ancient Greeks identified four basic personality types—choleric (energetic and volatile), sanguine (cheerful and vivacious), phlegmatic (dependable and easy-going), and melancholic (brooding and meditative)—based on four bodily "humours," or liquids.

In the early twentieth century, German psychologist Carl Jung devised a personality grid to account for human tendencies of various sorts—for example, whether people tend to be introverted or extroverted, and whether they tend to make decisions based on thoughts or on feelings. Jung even analyzed Sigmund Freud—Jung's contemporary and another influential twentieth-century psychologist—according to this system. Jung concluded that Freud's theories about human personality actually stemmed from Freud's own tendency toward introversion.

Jung never intended that his theories be interpreted to typecast people—to label them or put them in "boxes." Nevertheless, his work has <u>spawned</u> dozens of classification systems that attempt to do just that. Perhaps most influential among them is the Myers-Briggs Type Indicator, developed during the 1940s, which to this day is the most widely used of any personality test.

140. The passage discusses ancient attempts to classify people based on their

   A physical size
   B intelligence
   C personality
   D wealth

141. A phlegmatic person tends to be

   A steady
   B optimistic
   C irritable
   D sociable

142. Carl Jung developed a classification system based on

   A humours
   B race and ethnic origin
   C attitudes
   D personal tastes

143. As it is used in the passage, the word <u>spawned</u> most nearly means

   A contradicted
   B generated
   C favored
   D evaluated

Reading *(continued)*

144. According to the passage, Carl Jung and Sigmund Freud

  A both attended the same university in Germany

  B disagreed about whether Freud was an introvert

  C both developed a body-mind classification system

  D both influenced twentieth-century popular psychology

145. The Myers-Briggs Type Indicator

  A was based on Freud's work

  B popularized Jung's work

  C influenced Jung and Freud

  D is not widely used today

Questions 146–152 are based on the following passage:

Humanity has only just begun its conquest of nature. As astronomy assures us, in all probability we have, not centuries or even thousands of years, but millions of years of earthly destiny to realize.

Barely 3,000 years of scientific research have brought the ends of the earth, and even the solar system, to our doorstep. Just 300 years of research have made us masters where we were slaves—of distance, of the air and oceans, of space, and of many of the most dreaded aspects of disease and suffering. Isn't it odd that life today would seem inconceivable without airplanes, which were practically unheard of a century ago?

What will the future bring humankind? Things too vast to grasp today. Things that would make the imaginings of today's most <u>eminent</u> scientists and even science-fiction novelists seem ordinary by comparison. The future will bring us amazing control over things that seem to us almost sacred—over life and death and development and thought itself. Although this prospect might seem disturbing, through all that may happen to humankind, we can be sure that we will remain human, and so we can face the future confident that it will be better than the present.

146. The author's overall attitude toward science is

  A fearful

  B critical

  C enthusiastic

  D skeptical

147. The author believes that science-fiction writers

  A are less imaginative than many scientists

  B will help science to advance in the future

  C are out of touch with real science

  D underestimate future advances in science

148. As used in the selection, the word <u>eminent</u> is best defined as

  A unusual

  B accomplished

  C ethical

  D wealthy

149. According to the selection, science of the future will

  A give us control over human thought

  B enable us to travel through time

  C become more important than religion

  D find cures for every human disease

Reading *(continued)*

150. The author would agree that it is human nature to

A improve our own lives

B dwell too much on the past

C believe we are smarter than we really are

D ignore scientific evidence

151. In the selection, the author does NOT

A ask a question, and then answer that question

B describe the impact of certain historical events

C ask a question that does not require a response

D evaluate conflicting predictions for the future

152. Which of the following is the best title for the selection?

A "Scientific Advancements of the Last 3,000 Years"

B "The Past and Future of Scientific Research"

C "Why Society Must Encourage Scientific Progress"

D "A Bleak Past but a Bright Future for Humankind"

Vocabulary

Directions: For questions 153–174, choose the word that is nearest in meaning to the underlined word.

153. an astute comment

A rude

B perceptive

C humorous

D timely

154. to mimic another person

A respect

B imitate

C tease

D follow

155. a solemn oath

A occasion

B mood

C meal

D promise

156. to attain a goal

A set

B change

C achieve

D score

157. a somber occasion

A unique

B cheerful

C special

D gloomy

158. a minor skirmish

A illness

B battle

C injury

D error

159. a plausible story

A believable

B short

C interesting

D sad

160. to cultivate good manners

A display

B observe

C develop

D communicate

Reading *(continued)*

161. an <u>unwarranted</u> penalty
   A minor
   B insufficient
   C illegal
   D undeserved

162. to <u>stow</u> gear
   A buy
   B break
   C steal
   D pack

163. an oily <u>residue</u>
   A slick
   B remainder
   C politician
   D scalp

164. a <u>temperate</u> climate
   A mild
   B unpredictable
   C hot
   D rainy

165. A sudden <u>whim</u>
   A urge
   B breeze
   C disaster
   D noise

166. an <u>abundant</u> supply
   A plentiful
   B bundled
   C hidden
   D annual

167. to <u>recuperate</u> from surgery
   A die
   B recover
   C collapse
   D return

168. <u>pliable</u> material
   A raw
   B flammable
   C flexible
   D strong

169. to <u>persevere</u> in a task
   A improve
   B slacken
   C faint
   D continue

170. an <u>affluent</u> professional
   A influential
   B wealthy
   C well-spoken
   D trained

171. to <u>waft</u> out a window
   A drift
   B view
   C climb
   D fall

172. <u>petrified</u> wood
   A knotty
   B split
   C waterlogged
   D hard

173. an impressive <u>array</u>
   A performance
   B example
   C display
   D costume

174. an <u>amiable</u> fellow
   A hard-working
   B handsome
   C pleasant
   D strong

STOP!
If you finish before time runs out, check your work on this section only.

Mathematics (64 questions, 45 minutes)

Directions: Choose the best answer to each question.

Concepts

175. Which of the following is less than $\frac{13}{40}$?

   A $\frac{1}{3}$

   B $\frac{7}{20}$

   C $\frac{2}{5}$

   D $\frac{3}{10}$

176. One prime number divided by another prime number is always

   A   a fraction between 0 and 1
   B   an integer
   C   a positive non-integer
   D   a prime number

177. If a triangle contains one right angle, then the other two angles could measure

   A   70° and 20°
   B   35° and 60°
   C   20° and 90°
   D   45° and 40°

178. What value does the digit 4 represent in the number 534,792?

   A   40,000
   B   400
   C   40
   D   4,000

179. What are the (x, y) coordinates of point A on the coordinate plane below?

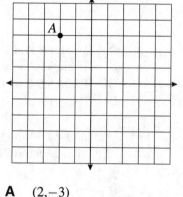

   A $(2, -3)$
   B $(-2, 3)$
   C $(-3, 2)$
   D $(3, -2)$

180. $x(y + x + z) =$

   A $x^2 + xy + xz$
   B $xy + xz + yz$
   C $(x + y)(x + z)$
   D $2x + xy + xz$

181. If a soda costs S cents and a burger costs B dollars, which of the following represents the cost of one burger and one soda, in cents?

   A $B + 100S$
   B $100(S + B)$
   C $100B + S$
   D $S + B$

182. $a^4 + a^4 =$

   A a^{16}
   B $2a^8$
   C a^8
   D $2a^4$

Mathematics *(continued)*

183. Determine which of the three triangles in the figure below MUST be equilateral.

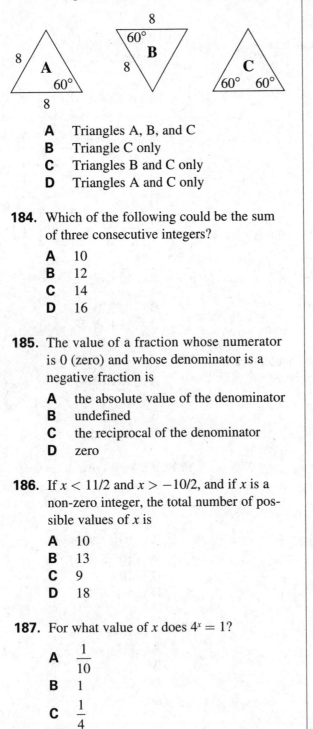

- **A**   Triangles A, B, and C
- **B**   Triangle C only
- **C**   Triangles B and C only
- **D**   Triangles A and C only

184. Which of the following could be the sum of three consecutive integers?

- **A**   10
- **B**   12
- **C**   14
- **D**   16

185. The value of a fraction whose numerator is 0 (zero) and whose denominator is a negative fraction is

- **A**   the absolute value of the denominator
- **B**   undefined
- **C**   the reciprocal of the denominator
- **D**   zero

186. If $x < 11/2$ and $x > -10/2$, and if x is a non-zero integer, the total number of possible values of x is

- **A**   10
- **B**   13
- **C**   9
- **D**   18

187. For what value of x does $4^x = 1$?

- **A** $\dfrac{1}{10}$
- **B**   1
- **C** $\dfrac{1}{4}$
- **D**   0

188. The figure below shows a square and a circle.

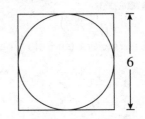

Which of the following statements is true?

- **A**   The radius of the circle is 6.
- **B**   The perimeter of the square is 24.
- **C**   The circle's circumference is 9.
- **D**   The area of the square is 32.

189. Which of the following integers has the greatest number of factors?

- **A**   24
- **B**   42
- **C**   36
- **D**   50

190. When you multiply the product of four consecutive negative integers by the product of four consecutive positive integers, the product is

- **A**   a positive odd integer
- **B**   a negative odd integer
- **C**   a positive even integer
- **D**   a negative even integer

191. $xy + zx =$

- **A** $x^2 + zy$
- **B** $x(y + z)$
- **C** $2x + yz$
- **D** $2x + y + z$

192. What is the measure of one interior angle of a pentagon in which all sides are congruent?

- **A**   136°
- **B**   96°
- **C**   120°
- **D**   108°

Mathematics (continued)

193. Examine the following three sets of numbers.

Set A: {20,41,60}
Set B: {5,15,10}
Set C: {30,9,20}

In which set is the arithmetic mean (simple average) closest in value to the median?

A Set A
B Set B
C Set C
D The median and mean are equally close in all three sets.

194. P = the set of all two-digit positive multiples of 4. Q = the set of all even integers. How many members does the set defined by P $\cap$ Q contain?

A 22
B 33
C 44
D 16

195. If you increase the perimeter of a square by 50%, you increase its area by

A 125%
B 50%
C 100%
D 200%

196. For which of the following values of x is the inequality $2x < x$ true?

A $\dfrac{1}{2}$

B $-\dfrac{1}{2}$

C 0

D 2

197. The number 2,000,000 is equivalent to

A 2×10^6
B 10×2^7
C 2×10^7
D $(2 \times 10)^6$

198. The set {4,5,6} represents

A {0,2,4,6,8} $\cap$ {1,3,5,7,9}
B {2,3,4,5,6} $\cap$ {3,4,5,6,7}
C {3,4,5,6,7} $\cap$ {2,3,4,5,6}
D {4,5,6,7,8} $\cap$ {2,3,4,5,6}

Problem Solving

199. $0.2 \times \dfrac{1}{3} =$

A $\dfrac{1}{3}$

B $\dfrac{1}{30}$

C $\dfrac{1}{15}$

D $\dfrac{1}{6}$

200. $11.1 + 1.11 + 0.111 =$

A 12.321
B 13.21
C 12.211
D 12.11

201. $|-2| + |3| =$

A -1
B -5
C 5
D 1

202. In one year, how much interest is earned on $500 in savings at a 12% annual interest rate?

A $60.00
B $12.00
C $4.00
D $9.00

Mathematics *(continued)*

203. In the figure below, what is the value of *x*?

B

125°
A

x°
C

- **A** 35
- **B** 30
- **C** 40
- **D** 45

204. A burger costs $2.75 and a bag of french fries cost $1.50. What is the greatest number of burger-fries combination meals you can buy with $25?

- **A** 7
- **B** 4
- **C** 5
- **D** 6

205. Samir is 8 years older than Renata but 4 years younger than Mark. How many years older is Mark than Renata?

- **A** 8
- **B** 12
- **C** 4
- **D** 0

206. In an election among three candidates—A, B, and C—candidate A received 20% of the votes, while candidate B received exactly three times as many votes as candidate C. What percent of the votes did candidate C receive?

- **A** 20%
- **B** 15%
- **C** 60%
- **D** 25%

207. If the diameter of a circle is 5, then its circumference is

- **A** 10π
- **B** 25
- **C** 10
- **D** 5π

208. $4^3 \times 4^3 =$

- **A** $4 \times 3 \times 4 \times 3$
- **B** 196
- **C** 4^9
- **D** $16 \times 16 \times 16$

209. The graph below compares the daily production of Ultra Corporation's divisions A, B, and C.

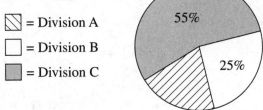

= Division A
= Division B
= Division C

55%

25%

If the total production of the three divisions is 7,500 units, how many units does division A produce per day?

- **A** 1,875
- **B** 1,250
- **C** 1,500
- **D** 1,050

210. Children are admitted to the movie theater at half the adult admission price. If one adult accompanies three children to the theater, paying $18.75 for all four tickets, what was the price of admission for each child?

- **A** $4.50
- **B** $4.00
- **C** $3.75
- **D** $7.50

Mathematics *(continued)*

211. Which of the following is closest to the product of 825 and 775?

A 640,000
B 63,000
C 560,000
D 5,800,000

212. Including a 5% sales tax, what is the total cost of a sweater whose price is $55 without tax?

A $57.50
B $60.00
C $57.75
D $62.50

213. $\dfrac{8}{9} \div \dfrac{4}{3} =$

A $\dfrac{2}{3}$
B $\dfrac{1}{3}$
C $\dfrac{3}{4}$
D $\dfrac{3}{2}$

214. A train left Station A at 12:30 p.m. and arrived at Station B at 3:00 p.m. If the train's average speed was 40 miles per hour, how many miles did the train travel?

A 120
B 80
C 90
D 100

215. If 1 mile is equivalent to 1.6 kilometers, then 10 kilometers is equivalent to

A 9.2 miles
B 16 miles
C 1.6 miles
D 6.25 miles

216. $-(4 - 5)(5 - 4) =$

A -1
B 0
C 1
D -2

217. In the figure below, $b = 30$. Find the value of a.

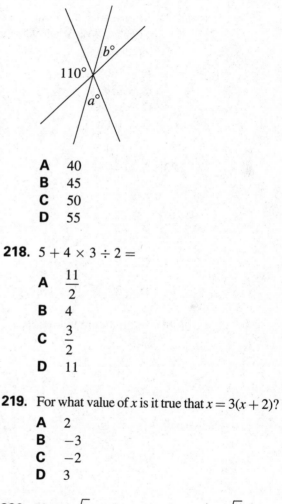

A 40
B 45
C 50
D 55

218. $5 + 4 \times 3 \div 2 =$

A $\dfrac{11}{2}$
B 4
C $\dfrac{3}{2}$
D 11

219. For what value of x is it true that $x = 3(x + 2)$?

A 2
B -3
C -2
D 3

220. If $x = \sqrt{3}$ and $y = 81$, then $x^4 + \sqrt[4]{y} =$

A 9
B 12
C 27
D 15

Mathematics *(continued)*

221. The circular base of a right cylinder has a diameter of 4 meters (m). If the cylinder's height is 5m, what is the cylinder's volume?

A   40m³
B   20πm³
C   30m³
D   40πm³

222. After a 10% discount, the price of a computer is $540. What was the price before the discount?

A $608
B $592
C $486
D $600

223. $\dfrac{2^{10} \times 3^{10}}{3^{9} \times 2^{11}} =$

A   1
B $\dfrac{3}{2}$
C $\dfrac{2}{3}$
D   2

224. In the figure below, $l_1 \parallel l_2$.

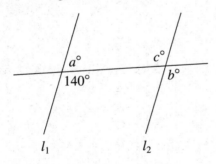

Find the sum of *a*, *b*, and *c*.

A   360
B   320
C   300
D   280

225. What is $66\dfrac{2}{3}\%$ of 120?

A   82
B   80
C   72
D   84

226. In a class of 40 students, the ratio of boys to girls is 3:5. How many girls are in the class?

A   20
B   25
C   24
D   15

227. A rectangular field is 140 feet long and 60 feet wide. What is the minimum linear feet of fencing needed to divide the field into four rectangular enclosures of equal size?

A   200
B   160
C   180
D   240

228. Karen's average score for two tests is 90. What score must Karen earn on a third test to raise her average to 92?

A   96
B   93
C   95
D   94

229. $\sqrt{300} =$

A $10 + \sqrt{3}$
B $3 + \sqrt{10}$
C $10\sqrt{3}$
D $5\sqrt{10}$

Mathematics *(continued)*

230. Point *O* lies at the center of the circle shown below.

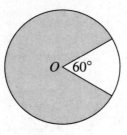

If the circle's radius is 6, what is the area of the shaded region?

A 36

B 24π

C 24

D 30π

231. There are 12 balls in a bag; 4 are red, 2 are blue, and the rest are green. The probability of randomly selecting a green marble from the bag is

A $\dfrac{1}{3}$

B $\dfrac{2}{3}$

C $\dfrac{3}{4}$

D $\dfrac{1}{2}$

232. If 100 ounces of sugar are available to be packed into one-pound bags, how much sugar will be left unpacked?

A 4 ounces

B 0 ounces

C 12 ounces

D 9 ounces

233. What is the length of a rectangle whose area is 8 and whose width is half its length?

A 6

B 4

C 2

D 3

Mathematics *(continued)*

Questions 234 and 235 are based on the following information:

At Hill Farm, the daily production of chicken eggs in four separate coops is closely monitored. The table below shows the results during one particular week.

	Su	M	T	W	Th	F	S
Coop A	0	1	2	3	1	0	0
Coop B	4	0	0	1	0	1	2
Coop C	0	1	2	2	1	2	0
Coop D	1	1	2	0	0	3	1

234. Which is nearest to the average weekly production per coop?

A   7 eggs
B   6 eggs
C   5 eggs
D   8 eggs

235. Which of the following pairs of days accounted for the greatest number of eggs produced?

A   Saturday and Sunday
B   Thursday and Friday
C   Monday and Tuesday
D   Tuesday and Friday

236. If you add two ounces of water to a 16-ounce mixture consisting of equal amounts of milk and water, what portion of the resulting mixture is water?

A $\dfrac{3}{5}$

B $\dfrac{5}{9}$

C $\dfrac{5}{8}$

D $\dfrac{4}{9}$

237. A triangle is plotted on the *xy*-coordinate plane as shown below.

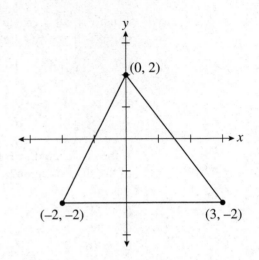

What is the area of the triangle, in square units?

A   12
B   15
C   8
D   10

238. Choose the closest approximation of $\sqrt{40} + \sqrt{60}$.

A   14
B   12
C   10
D   13

STOP!
If you finish before time runs out, check your work on this section only.

Language (60 questions, 25 minutes)

Usage

Directions: For questions 239–278, choose the sentence that contains an error in punctuation, capitalization, or usage. If you find no mistakes, select choice D.

239.
A When crossing the street, walk don't run.
B Most flowers bloom in Spring.
C He is often mistaken for his twin.
D No mistake.

240.
A The fire spread very quickly.
B Etta lost ten pounds while on that diet.
C You should brush your teeth everyday.
D No mistake.

241.
A You'll find my number in the phone book.
B The price increased over last year's price.
C More importantly, the economy is slowing.
D No mistake.

242.
A Billy failed in spite of his efforts.
B Fido sits when I tell him to, "Sit."
C Ellis is not as young as he once was.
D No mistake.

243.
A The corpse is too gory to even look at.
B Swimming can cause an ear infection.
C This house dates back to a previous century.
D No mistake.

244.
A Few dictators are loved by his people.
B Sam and Kari are the best of friends.
C I believe in honesty as the best policy.
D No mistake.

245.
A The property line runs south along the road.
B I, on the other hand, am not interested.
C Neither Josie or Maureen knew the answer.
D No mistake.

246.
A He accomplished a great deal before retiring.
B Don't leave until you've cleaned up.
C The White House is on Pennsylvania avenue.
D No mistake.

247.
A Were it not for the lifeguard, I'd have drowned.
B When in Paris, you must visit the Eiffel Tower.
C Oil can't easily be combined together with water.
D No mistake.

248.
A We are on the same side as them.
B I met Jamie's sister, Ariana, only yesterday.
C April's rainy, but May's sunny.
D No mistake.

249.
A That house belongs to the Smiths.
B Dan scored only one goal all year.
C Robert has joined the Marine corps.
D No mistake.

Language *(continued)*

250.
- **A** The facts don't support your conclusion.
- **B** Its hard to see without my glasses.
- **C** Amy left for college yesterday.
- **D** No mistake.

251.
- **A** His life was very different from her.
- **B** You should apologize for being rude.
- **C** Christine was horrified at the kidnapping.
- **D** No mistake.

252.
- **A** I've seen every Star Trek movie at least twice.
- **B** It's just you and I from now on.
- **C** Fix your car here, and then drive it home.
- **D** No mistake.

253.
- **A** This box weighs at least five pounds.
- **B** As a show of respect, he bowed before the prince.
- **C** How do you pronounce "entrepreneur"?
- **D** No mistake.

254.
- **A** I can't hardly wait until school's over.
- **B** Gorran's report turned out excellent.
- **C** What is the name of Mr. Runyon's dog?
- **D** No mistake.

255.
- **A** Bread is made of flour, water, and yeast.
- **B** The solution therefore is to lower taxes.
- **C** Karina took her time; I, on the other hand, did not.
- **D** No mistake.

256.
- **A** Steve took first prize in the contest.
- **B** I have nothing to show for my time.
- **C** Paul stutters some times.
- **D** No mistake.

257.
- **A** A rising tide lifts all boats.
- **B** Who is the team's sponsor?
- **C** I'll miss my friends when I'm gone.
- **D** No mistake.

258.
- **A** Tom, tell me what to do now.
- **B** I was mistaken to think she cheated.
- **C** With who else did you speak?
- **D** No mistake.

259.
- **A** Whether or not I go, she will.
- **B** Besides: you don't have a thing to lose.
- **C** Rita bought a new dress for the occasion.
- **D** No mistake.

260.
- **A** The book portrays President Nixon as a likeable man.
- **B** Isn't it a shame that so many people died?
- **C** She hardly lifted a finger to help.
- **D** No mistake.

261.
- **A** To whom is the letter addressed?
- **B** "What for?" asked Andrew.
- **C** He already left when I had arrived.
- **D** No mistake.

262.
- **A** Show your rifle to Sergeant Baker.
- **B** Rich took the car without asking.
- **C** Shauna is more friendlier than Latifa.
- **D** No mistake.

263.
- **A** With such looks, you should be a model.
- **B** The epic poem "Beowulf" is a literary classic.
- **C** Stay with me for a while longer.
- **D** No mistake.

Language (continued)

264.
A Douse the flames in order to put them out.
B Aaron was born on August the 13th.
C He was being as honest as he could.
D No mistake.

265.
A George is widely known for his music.
B They say that nothing lasts for ever.
C Is skateboarding allowed here?
D No mistake.

266.
A Just when he left, it started to rain.
B They went to the movie by themselves.
C "Oh," exclaimed Janice, "I didn't know that."
D No mistake.

267.
A Drive past three streets: Main, Broad, and 1st.
B She writes children's books for a living.
C Michael, Luke, and I are all 15 years old.
D No mistake.

268.
A I now see what you meant.
B He selected Louis and I for the job.
C Her personal opinions don't matter.
D No mistake.

269.
A I don't like none of your friends.
B I believe you're correct.
C The Cougars beat the Panthers in today's game.
D No mistake.

270.
A It's a dirty job but I'll do it.
B She used to wear a hat to church.
C The third song—a ballad—put me to sleep.
D No mistake.

271.
A Please pay closer attention.
B Mark was fired for incompetence.
C She hinted that something was wrong.
D No mistake.

272.
A How much do you want to spend.
B Lunch is at 12:00, and dinner is at 6:00.
C Alex forgot to remind me in time.
D No mistake.

273.
A The flood resulted from too much rain.
B Movie stars are often vain.
C He kept his personal life secretive.
D No mistake.

274.
A This charity is a worthy one.
B My prediction is rain tomorrow.
C I think Congress will pass the bill.
D No mistake.

275.
A Jack can't spell very good.
B She and her mom went together.
C Anything worth doing takes time.
D No mistake.

276.
A Broken rubber bands are worthless.
B Amanda is brilliant but arrogant.
C Her statement was a half-truth.
D No mistake.

277.
A Believe it or not, Sue and Pablo are related.
B Of the two shirts, the blue one is best.
C Vanessa yelled, "Wait for me!"
D No mistake.

278.
A The Sahara Desert is in Africa.
B A car with no gas won't run.
C To play soccer is a fun sport.
D No mistake.

Language (continued)

Spelling

Directions: For questions 279–288, choose the sentence that contains a spelling error. If you find no spelling errors, select choice D.

279.
A His performance was superb.
B Can I borrow your pencil?
C The old man has a poor memery.
D No mistake.

280.
A What was her ultimate legacy?
B I am available for consultation.
C The patient suffered severe symtoms.
D No mistake.

281.
A I subscribe to this magazine.
B Jason's father is forty years old.
C Smoking is strictly prohibited here.
D No mistake.

282.
A I need time to ascess the damage.
B She always dresses elegantly.
C The inaugural gala is next week.
D No mistake.

283.
A Greg recieved a score of 92 on the exam.
B The novel I am reading is fascinating.
C The attorneys chose the jury members.
D No mistake.

284.
A I foresee a problem ahead.
B Can you deliver the parsel early?
C Anita missed the professor's lecture.
D No mistake.

285.
A Indigestion can cause a stomach ache.
B The line at the theater was too long.
C A sensitive person is easily offended.
D No mistake.

286.
A Pam's sister is a sophomore in college.
B The admission price is affordable.
C Teresa indulged in a manicure.
D No mistake.

287.
A This meal is delicious.
B Humid weather makes me sweat.
C The trophie symbolized her victory.
D No mistake.

288.
A Several students are absent today.
B The car narrowly averted an accident.
C Laghter is the best medicine.
D No mistake.

Language *(continued)*

Composition

Directions: For questions 289–298, follow the directions for each question.

289. Choose the best word to join the thoughts together.

It's safe to cross the street; _____ be sure to look both ways first.

A but
B also
C and
D to

290. Choose the group of words that best completes the sentence.

Unlike roulette and other games of pure chance, _____.

A playing poker involves strategy and cunning.
B poker involves the use of strategy and cunning.
C to play poker you use strategy and cunning.
D the game of poker is strategic and cunning.

291. Which of the following expresses the idea most clearly?

A She reads both of the city's major newspapers each morning.
B Each morning, both of the city's major newspapers are read by her.
C Both of the city's major newspapers are read each morning by her.
D She reads both major newspapers of the city each morning.

292. Choose the best word or words with which to begin the sentence.

_____ he never held a public office, Benjamin Franklin was such an important figure in U.S. history that he ended up gracing the face of our nation's currency.

A The fact that
B Surprisingly,
C Because
D Even though

293. Choose the best word to join the thoughts together.

Shakespeare portrayed Richard III as a murderous monster, _____ there's little historical evidence of the crimes he supposedly committed while King of England.

A unless
B yet
C and
D once

294. Which topic is best suited for a one-paragraph essay?

A How to Repair Computers
B Modern American Architecture
C Why Salmon Swim Upstream
D none of the above

Language (continued)

295. Which sentence in the following paragraph is unnecessary?

(1) They say that the Latin language is dead, and it's true; Latin is no longer spoken. (2) So when I decided to take a Latin class, my friends all laughed. (3) They asked, "Why don't you learn a language you can use?" (4) My friends might have a point. (5) So perhaps I'll take German, French, or Spanish instead.

    A   sentence 1
    B   sentence 2
    C   sentence 4
    D   All five sentences are necessary.

296. Which of the following expresses the idea most clearly?

    A   Gold will always have great intrinsic value. This is because of its unsurpassed beauty, and it's also very rare.
    B   Because gold's beauty is unsurpassed and gold is very rare, its value will always be great intrinsically.
    C   Gold will always have great intrinsic value because it's very rare and its beauty is unsurpassed.
    D   Unsurpassed in beauty and very rare, for these reasons gold will always have great intrinsic value.

297. Choose the best topic sentence for the following paragraph.

There's been more change in the past four generations (one generation is 25 years) than in the previous 796 combined. Eight hundred generations ago, nearly all humans lived in caves, and not all that much changed until 1900. In the 20th century, however, we went from a race of hunters and gatherers (ranches and farms) to a race capable of destroying the entire world as we know it.

    A   The human race is experiencing change as never before.
    B   The human race has come a long way in 20,000 years.
    C   The future of humankind is as bright as its past.
    D   Human progress is in danger of coming to an end soon.

298. Which is the best place to insert the sentence "Today, people all over the world use the Library of Congress for research" in the following paragraph?

(1) The Library of Congress in Washington, D.C. is by far the world's largest library. (2) The Library did not always serve the general public, however. (3) Originally, the Library was available only to members of Congress. (4) It wasn't until the 1860s, several decades after the Library's inception, that it was opened to the general public.

    A   before sentence 1
    B   between sentences 1 and 2
    C   between sentences 3 and 4
    D   after sentence 4

STOP!
If you finish before time runs out, check your work on this section only.

HSPT PRACTICE TEST 1

Answer Key

Verbal Skills

1. **B**	31. **B**	87. **A**	100. **A**
2. **B**	32. **D**	88. **A**	101. **C**
3. **D**	33. **A**	89. **C**	102. **B**
4. **C**	34. **C**	90. **D**	103. **A**
5. **B**	35. **B**	91. **B**	104. **C**
6. **D**	36. **A**	92. **C**	105. **A**
7. **C**	37. **A**	93. **D**	106. **A**
8. **B**	38. **D**	94. **C**	107. **C**
9. **D**	39. **C**	95. **B**	108. **D**
10. **C**	40. **D**	96. **C**	109. **D**
11. **A**	41. **B**	97. **A**	110. **C**
12. **C**	42. **A**	98. **D**	111. **B**
13. **B**	43. **C**	99. **A**	112. **A**
14. **D**	44. **A**		
15. **C**	45. **B**	**Reading**	
16. **C**	46. **B**	113. **D**	144. **D**
17. **A**	47. **C**	114. **B**	145. **B**
18. **D**	48. **B**	115. **A**	146. **C**
19. **A**	49. **A**	116. **A**	147. **D**
20. **A**	50. **B**	117. **B**	148. **B**
21. **C**	51. **A**	118. **C**	149. **A**
22. **C**	52. **D**	119. **D**	150. **A**
23. **D**	53. **A**	120. **C**	151. **D**
24. **C**	54. **B**	121. **B**	152. **B**
25. **C**	55. **D**	122. **C**	153. **B**
26. **D**	56. **C**	123. **A**	154. **B**
27. **B**	57. **A**	124. **D**	155. **D**
28. **B**	58. **B**	125. **A**	156. **C**
29. **C**	59. **C**	126. **C**	157. **D**
30. **A**	60. **D**	127. **C**	158. **B**
		128. **B**	159. **A**
		129. **D**	160. **C**
Quantitative Skills		130. **A**	161. **D**
61. **D**	74. **B**	131. **B**	162. **D**
62. **A**	75. **B**	132. **C**	163. **B**
63. **A**	76. **C**	133. **A**	164. **A**
64. **B**	77. **C**	134. **D**	165. **A**
65. **C**	78. **D**	135. **B**	166. **A**
66. **A**	79. **C**	136. **C**	167. **B**
67. **A**	80. **D**	137. **D**	168. **C**
68. **A**	81. **B**	138. **A**	169. **D**
69. **D**	82. **D**	139. **B**	170. **B**
70. **C**	83. **A**	140. **C**	171. **A**
71. **B**	84. **B**	141. **A**	172. **D**
72. **A**	85. **D**	142. **C**	173. **C**
73. **D**	86. **C**	143. **B**	174. **C**

HSPT PRACTICE TEST 1

Answer Key (continued)

Mathematics				**Language**			
175.	D	207.	D	239.	A	269.	A
176.	C	208.	D	240.	C	270.	A
177.	A	209.	C	241.	B	271.	D
178.	D	210.	C	242.	B	272.	A
179.	B	211.	A	243.	D	273.	C
180.	A	212.	C	244.	A	274.	B
181.	C	213.	A	245.	C	275.	A
182.	D	214.	D	246.	C	276.	D
183.	A	215.	D	247.	C	277.	B
184.	B	216.	C	248.	D	278.	C
185.	D	217.	A	249.	C	279.	C
186.	C	218.	D	250.	B	280.	C
187.	D	219.	B	251.	A	281.	D
188.	B	220.	B	252.	A	282.	A
189.	C	221.	B	253.	D	283.	A
190.	C	222.	D	254.	A	284.	B
191.	B	223.	B	255.	B	285.	A
192.	D	224.	B	256.	C	286.	D
193.	B	225.	B	257.	D	287.	A
194.	A	226.	B	258.	C	288.	C
195.	A	227.	C	259.	B	289.	A
196.	B	228.	A	260.	D	290.	B
197.	A	229.	C	261.	C	291.	A
198.	D	230.	D	262.	C	292.	D
199.	C	231.	D	263.	D	293.	B
200.	A	232.	A	264.	B	294.	C
201.	C	233.	B	265.	B	295.	D
202.	A	234.	A	266.	D	296.	A
203.	A	235.	D	267.	D	297.	A
204.	C	236.	B	268.	B	298.	B
205.	B	237.	D				
206.	A	238.	A				

HSPT PRACTICE TEST 1

Answers and Explanations

Verbal Skills

1. **B** To *ascend* is to climb.

2. **B** The words *custom, ritual,* and *habit* all refer to *behavior* that is repeated frequently and on a regular basis. The word *behavior* does not belong because it is not as specific in meaning as the other three words.

3. **D** The main ingredient, or raw material, used to make a cake is usually flour, much like the basic material often used to make a bench is wood.

4. **C** *Affable* means "easygoing or agreeable."

5. **B** Appleton has more restaurants than Seaside, which in turn has more restaurants than Valley View. Therefore, Appleton must have *more* restaurants than Valley View.

6. **D** To *ratify* is to approve, confirm, or endorse.

7. **C** A horn and an antler are both long, sharp protrusions on an animal's head used for fighting as well as to signify the animal's gender and age.

8. **B** To *obsess* is to be continually troubled about, in one's mind. To *ignore* is to put out of one's mind.

9. **D** *Smoke, heat,* and *ash* are all signs of fire; an *oven* is not.

10. **C** Just because Kim likes the same kind of environment as painters, we cannot conclude that Kim must be a painter (although she might be).

11. **A** A *sail* is part of a boat, whereas an *ocean,* a *beach,* and a *wave* are all features of nature.

12. **C** We know that Rebecca and James both ate breakfast after Ted but before Carlos. However, we do not know who ate breakfast earlier—Rebecca or James.

13. **B** The words *quarrel, spar,* and *fight* are all used to describe a conflict, usually between two people. The word *play* need not involve conflict, nor need it involve more than one person.

14. **D** A *blanket,* a *quilt,* and a *bedspread* are all bed covers. Although a *pillow* might sit atop a bed, it is not a bed covering.

15. **C** A *deed* is an act—as in performing a "great deed."

16. **C** A closet is a place where you store things, just as a theater is a place where you perform—a concert or play, for instance.

17. **A** Given that Victoria is shorter than Javier, who in turn is shorter than Carl, Carl must be taller than Victoria.

18. **D** To *digress* is to deviate, wander, or stray—as from a path or from a topic under discussion.

19. **A** Among the four types of animals listed, the *pigeon* is the only one that flies.

20. **A** Given the first two statements, the speaker could not have thrown a baseball at the window; otherwise, the window would be broken.

21. **C** *Static* means "unchanging or motionless," just the opposite of *active.*

22. **C** A *saga* is a long story or tale.

Answers and Explanations *(continued)*

23. **D** A *raise,* an *award,* and a *trophy* are usually earned through some accomplishment, whereas a *gift* is not.

24. **C** The words *track, route,* and *course* are all used to refer to a path, or way, for getting from one place (or condition) to another. A *hurdle* is an obstacle one might encounter along the way.

25. **C** The function of eyeglasses is to improve vision, much like the function of food is to provide energy.

26. **D** *Verbose* means "overly wordy in speech or writing." The word *concise* means just the opposite: brief and to the point.

27. **B** Each of the incorrect choices is a word associated primarily with a sensory experience—you hear something *noisy,* taste something *bitter,* and see something *ugly.* However, something *slow* is not clearly experienced through one particular sense (sight, hearing, smell, taste, or touch).

28. **B** *Malice* means "viciousness, hatred, or ill will toward another."

29. **C** We do not know whether Gwen left her house by 12:00 today. Therefore, we do not know whether she was late for work.

30. **A** When food ages it might go bad by spoiling. Similarly, metal exposed to air for a long time eventually deteriorates by rusting.

31. **B** An *abyss* is a place of great depth—a deep pit. A *peak* is a high point.

32. **D** *Palatial* means "luxurious, opulent, stately, or grand," as in a "palatial estate."

33. **A** We know that computer B is newer than computer A, which in turn is newer than computer C. Therefore, computer B must be newer than computer C.

34. **C** A *rookie* or *novice* is a beginner. The word *veteran* means just the opposite: someone with experience. The word *amateur* belongs more with *rookie* and *novice* than with *veteran,* because an amateur is someone who typically lacks the experience or ability of a professional.

35. **B** Many soldiers can be organized to form an army. Similarly, many threads can be combined to make a shirt.

36. **A** An *epitome* is an ideal, model, or prototype.

37. **A** The other three words are each used to refer to a young person who is older than an infant (baby).

38. **D** A vein is a pathway through which blood flows, just as a river is pathway through which water flows.

39. **C** *Wavering* means "unwilling or hesitant," just the opposite of *eager.*

40. **D** The words *jest, kid,* and *joke* are each used in describing the behavior of a person who is not being serious. Rather than saying that someone is not being serious, we might say that he is "just kidding," "joking," or saying something "in jest." The word *laugh* does not fit the pattern.

41. **B** A *respite* is a brief pause, break, or rest.

42. **A** *Lax* means "careless, negligent, or remiss." A person might be said to be *lax* in failing to enforce a law or other rule.

43. **C** We know that Johnson received more votes than either Weller or Lauter. However, we do not know who received more votes— Weller or Lauter.

Answers and Explanations *(continued)*

44. **A** The words *terse, short,* and *brief* can be used interchangeably to describe writing or speech that is compact (as opposed to lengthy or wordy) in its use of words. However, *simple* writing or speech is not necessarily brief.

45. **B** A doctor's function is to help serve a patient's needs. Similarly, the function of a business is to help serve the needs of its customers, by providing either a product or a service.

46. **B** To *pacify* is to soothe or calm, the opposite of *irritate*.

47. **C** *Epidemic* means "widespread." For example, an epidemic disease is one that has spread throughout a large geographical area.

48. **B** We know that Sheila is faster than Anita, who in turn is faster than Brent. Therefore, Brent must be *slower* than Sheila, and at least part of the third statement is false.

49. **A** After seeing a movie, a critic might review (evaluate) it. Similarly, after administering an exam, an instructor might score (evaluate) it.

50. **B** To *reciprocate* is to return or exchange something of equal kind or value. For example, one is said to reciprocate when returning a favor. The word *trade* is a good synonym.

51. **A** *Remorse* means "regret," a feeling of sorrow or being sorry about something in the past.

52. **D** *Robust* means "vigorous or healthy," just the opposite of *sickly*.

53. **A** To *deplete* is to use up or drain—for example, to deplete one's energy. To *replenish* is to restore or refill, the opposite of *deplete*.

54. **B** The second statement tells us that Andy mows his lawn once per week, which means that he mows it four times in one month— more often than Jim, who mows his lawn only twice each month.

55. **D** A correction reverses or eliminates a mistake. Similarly, a solution reverses or eliminates a problem.

56. **C** The other three words are each used to refer to a spatial area or section. A border, however, is what surrounds that area.

57. **A** *Candid* means "sincere or forthright," just the opposite of *secretive*.

58. **B** Because David is still in high school, he cannot be a student at Wheeler College.

59. **C** The words *lock, secure,* and *fasten* all refer to means of protection against harm or loss. However, *beware* means "take care or be careful."

60. **D** An *innovation* is new and unique invention or design. An *imitation* is a copy of something else.

Quantitative Skills

61. **D** $\frac{2}{3}$ of $27 = \frac{2}{3} \times 27 = 18$. Express the question as an equation, and then solve for the answer (x): $x + 9 = 11 + 18$; $x = 20$.

62. **A** You add *1* to the first term (11) to obtain the second term (12). Then, you add *2* to 12 to obtain the third term (14). To obtain each successive number, the number you add to the previous number increases by 1.

63. **A** Let x equal the missing number: $\left(\frac{2}{3}\right)(x) = \frac{1}{2}$; $x = \left(\frac{1}{2}\right)\left(\frac{3}{2}\right)$; $x = \frac{3}{4}$.

Answers and Explanations *(continued)*

64. **B** (a) = 4; (b) = −20; (c) = 15.

65. **C** In each successive group of three terms, subtract 3 to obtain the next number. Begin the next group (of three) by subtracting 1 from the previous group's first term.

66. **A** Alternate between two operations: adding 1 and adding 5.

67. **A** Express the statement as an algebraic equation, and then solve for the answer (x): $x - (-1) = 2(-1)(-1)$; $x + 1 = 2$; $x = 1$.

68. **A** Both AD and BC pass through the circle's center (O). Thus, AD = BD = the circle's diameter. Accordingly, $AO = DO = BO = CO$.

69. **D** (a) = 64; (b) = 60; (c) = 63.

70. **C** Figure (a) contains 10 triangles and 12 circles. Figure (b) contains 12 triangles and 10 circles. Figure (c) contains 11 triangles and 11 circles.

71. **B** First, convert percents: 200% = 2; 250% = 2.5, or 5/2. Letting x equal the missing number, solve for x: $2/x = 5/2$; $5x = 4$; $x = 4/5$, or 80%.

72. **A** (a) = 0.004; (b) = 0.025; (c) = 0.04.

73. **D** Multiply each number by 2 to obtain the next number.

74. **B** $\frac{2}{3} \times 27 = 18$. Set up an equation, solving for the missing fraction (x): $30x = 18$; $x = \frac{18}{30}$, or $\frac{3}{5}$.

75. **B** Each successive number pair are reciprocal fractions. In subsequent pairs, the numerators and denominators decrease by 1. The reciprocal of $\frac{1}{2}$ is $\frac{2}{1}$, or 2.

76. **C** (a) = 15,000; (b) = 30,000; (c) = 45,000.

77. **C** Alternate between two operations: subtracting 5 and adding 2.

78. **D** The four bars compare in height as follows (from shortest to tallest): (c), (a), (d), (b).

79. **C** $\frac{2}{3} \times \frac{3}{2} \times \frac{2}{3} = \frac{2}{3}$.

80. **D** Multiply each number by 3 to obtain the next number.

81. **B** (a) = 16; (b) = −27; (c) = 16.

82. **D** 75% of $20 = \frac{3}{4} \times 20 = 15$. Thus, solve for the answer (x) in the following equation: $0.25x = 15$; $\left(\frac{1}{4}\right)(x) = 15$; $x = 15 \times 4$; $x = 60$.

83. **A** Add 4 to each number to obtain the next one.

84. **B** Figure (a) contains 8 triangles together— 4 right triangles, each one-half the area of the square, and 4 right triangles, each one one-fourth the area of the square. Figure (b) contains 5 triangles and figure (c) contains 4 triangles.

85. **D** The sequential pair 0, 2 alternates with the sequential group of three numbers 0, 2, 4.

86. **C** Solve for x: $x - \frac{1}{2} = -\frac{1}{4}$; $x = -\frac{1}{4} + \frac{1}{2}$; $x = \frac{1}{4}$, or 0.25.

87. **A** Divide each number by 4 to obtain the next number.

88. **A** (a) = 5; (b) = 11; (c) = 3; (d) = 13.

89. **C** Multiply first, then subtract: $\left(\frac{3}{2} \times 30\right) - 8 = 45 - 8 = 37$.

Answers and Explanations *(continued)*

90. **D** Since *ADEC* is a square, $AC = DE$, and therefore $AB = DE$; statement D cannot be true.

91. **B** The four-term series 3-4-5-4 simply repeats itself.

92. **C** Compare (a) to (b) by restating with common denominator 35: $\frac{4}{7} = \frac{20}{35}$, and $\frac{3}{5} = \frac{21}{35}$. Thus, (a) < (b). Compare (b) to (c) by restating with common denominator 15: $\frac{3}{5} = \frac{9}{15}$, and $\frac{2}{3} = \frac{10}{15}$. Thus, (b) < (c).

93. **D** $\frac{3}{2} \times 8 = 12$, and $12 \times 2 = 24$. Express the question as an equation, and then solve for the answer (*x*): $\frac{6x}{5} = 24$; $\frac{x}{5} = 4$; $x = 20$.

94. **C** In each successive group of three letters, the letters are in reverse alphabetical sequence.

95. **B** The quotient of 30 and 6 is $30 \div 6 = 5$, and 30% of 5 = 1.5, or $\frac{3}{2}$—which is $\frac{3}{2}$ less than $\frac{6}{2}$, or 3.

96. **C** Beginning with the first term (29), subtract 1 to obtain alternate successive terms: 29-28-27-26. Beginning with the second term (12), subtract 2 to obtain alternate successive terms: 12-*10*-8-6.

97. **A** $\sqrt{4} = 2$, and $\sqrt{3} \approx 1.7$. Thus, (a) = 5; (b) ≈ 5.7; (c) = 4.

98. **D** Express the statement as an algebraic equation, and then solve for the answer (*x*): $\left(\frac{1}{2}\right)^3 = \frac{3}{4}x$; $\frac{1}{8} = \frac{3}{4}x$; $x = \frac{4}{24}$, or $\frac{1}{6}$.

99. **A** Add $\frac{1}{4}$ to each number to obtain the next one: $\frac{23}{4} + \frac{1}{4} = \frac{24}{4} = 6$.

100. **A** Exactly one-half of each of the three figures is shaded. Therefore, you need only compare areas. The area of figure (a) = 2 × 5 = 10; the area of figure (b) = 3 × 3 = 9; the area of figure (c) = 2.5 × 4 = 10.

101. **C** With each successive number, the amount you add to obtain the next number increases by 1. Letters progress in alphabetical order, skipping a letter from one term to the next. Also, the number-letter order reverses from one term to the next.

102. **B** Express the statement as an algebraic equation, and then solve for the answer (*x*): $x + 5 = 6 \times \frac{7}{4}$; $x + 5 = \frac{21}{2}$; $x = \frac{11}{2}$.

103. **A** The average (2) equals the sum of the three terms divided by 3: $2 = \frac{(-3 + 2 + x)}{3}$; $2 = -1 + x$; $3 = x$.

104. **C** Both (a) and (b) describe sets of consecutive integers whose largest and smallest terms are equidistant from zero (they have the same absolute value). Thus, (a) = 0 and (b) = 0. However, (c) describes a set where the absolute value of the largest integer (51) is greater than the absolute value of the smallest integer (−50). Thus, (c) < 0.

105. **A** $\frac{(2 \times 2)}{(3 \times 2)} = \frac{4}{6}$.

106. **A** Subtract 35 from each number to obtain the next number. (CXXV = 125; LV = 55.)

107. **C** The square root of 64 = 8, which is $\frac{8}{6}$ or $\frac{4}{3}$, of 6.

Answers and Explanations (continued)

108. **D** In each successive group of three numbers, subtract 1 from the first number to obtain the second number. The third number is always 1. Begin each successive group one integer higher than the first number of the previous group.

109. **D** $\frac{2}{6}$, or $\frac{1}{3}$, of figure (a) is shaded; $\frac{3}{8}$ of figure (b) is shaded; $\frac{2}{4}$, or $\frac{1}{2}$, of figure (c) is shaded. $\frac{1}{3} < \frac{3}{8} < \frac{1}{2}$.

110. **C** To progress from each term to the next, alternate between two operations: adding 1 and adding 3. ($8 + 1 = 9$; $9 + 3 = 12$.)

111. **B** Rectangle *ABDC* contains two congruent squares: *ABFE* and *ECDF*. $AE = EC = EF$, and therefore $2 \times EF = AC$.

112. **A** $4 + 6 = 10$. $10^2 = 100$. Express the question as an equation, and then solve for the answer (*x*): $25x = 100$; $x = 4$.

Reading

113. **D** The topic of the entire passage is how the Latin *language* spread throughout much of the ancient world, and so substituting the word *language* for *tongue* throughout the passage makes perfect sense.

114. **B** In the first paragraph, the author asserts this point. Then, in the second and third paragraphs, the author explains the misunderstanding.

115. **A** In the third paragraph, the author describes how Latin spread throughout Europe and northern Africa, "triumphing over" (in other words, conquering) "all the other tongues of those regions," meaning that Latin replaced those tongues as the primary language spoken in those regions.

116. **A** In the third paragraph, the author tells us that it is "remarkable"—in other words, *surprising*—that the language used throughout such a small geographical area spread so widely throughout other regions.

117. **B** As the author points out in the first paragraph, most people would assume that Latin spread throughout the Roman Empire because the Roman armies imposed the language (through military force and Roman law) on the people they conquered. Hence, it would make sense to substitute *armies* for *legions* in this paragraph.

118. **C** In the passage's final sentence, the author points out that Latin triumphed over the languages of the regions that Rome conquered more completely than Roman arms triumphed over the peoples using those languages. In other words, ultimately the Latin language was mightier than the Roman military.

119. **D** In the first sentence, the author indicates that the *illegal* selling of human organs is common in India and Brazil.

120. **C** A person who supports legalization of the selling of human organs might very well *point out*, or call our attention to, what they think is our basic right to choose what we do with our own bodies.

121. **B** According to the passage, currently there is a long waiting list for organ donations. Therefore, the supply of organs must not be keeping up with demand.

122. **C** In the first paragraph, the author tells us that "kidneys are an especially hot commodity," meaning that they are probably sold more frequently than any other human body part.

Answers and Explanations *(continued)*

123. **A** For the sentence to make sense, the word *donors* must refer to the people who undergo surgery to have organs removed for the purpose of selling them—in other words, donors must be the organ *suppliers*.

124. **D** In the second paragraph, the author provides one reason that proponents of the laws sometimes cite for their support, followed by two reasons that those who are against the proposed laws give for their opposition.

125. **A** In the first paragraph, the author explains how people in other countries are often victimized by others who promise to pay them for their organs but never follow through on their promise.

126. **C** The main subject of the article is Hans the horse. The author refers only briefly to Hans's owner and to the researchers who studied Hans.

127. **C** The author tells us that Hans had fooled his owner (as well as other people) into thinking that Hans could perform arithmetic.

128. **B** Nothing in the article suggests that Hans was ever punished for giving wrong answers to arithmetic questions, or for any other reason.

129. **D** In the first paragraph, the author refers to people who claim that their pets can speak in human languages. Then, in the second paragraph, the author tells us that these people can learn a lesson from Hans who, as we learn in the third paragraph, does not possess the sort of high-level, human-like intellectual ability that he appeared to demonstrate. The lesson, then, is that we should be highly skeptical about claims of animal intelligence that seems too human-like.

130. **A** In all probability, Hans learned to stomp his hoof the appropriate number of times by watching his owner's body language very closely.

131. **B** In the second paragraph, the author states that pet owners can learn a lesson from Hans the horse. This statement strongly suggests that the article is directed to pet owners.

132. **C** The first sentence of the passage states explicitly that chess is probably the most challenging of games.

133. **A** In the first paragraph, the author tells us that chess probably originated in ancient India.

134. **D** In the second paragraph, the author mentions the artifacts listed in choices A, B, and C each as attesting to the antiquity of chess. Nowhere in the passage does the author mention bone sculptures in any context.

135. **B** In the preceding sentence, the author tells us that chess is probably the world's second-oldest game. It makes sense that the three types of artifacts the author mentions in the next sentence would help "prove" the antiquity of chess, in other words, that chess is an ancient game.

136. **C** In Europe, chess has also been known for many ages as "The Royal Game."

137. **D** Given that the game's name literally means "King," it makes sense, and therefore is not surprising, that a chess piece designated as the king would play a key role in the game.

138. **A** In the first paragraph, the author tells us that except for draughts (an early form of checkers), chess is probably the world's oldest game, inferring that checkers predates chess.

Answers and Explanations (continued)

139. **B** Aside from the first few sentences, which introduce the topic, the passage as a whole is concerned with the history of the game of chess. Choice D is probably the second-best one; however, because the author does not discuss how the game changed over time, choice D does not provide as fitting a title as choice B.

140. **C** The ancients classified people based on personality.

141. **A** According to the passage, a *phlegmatic* person is dependable and easygoing, in other words, *steady*.

142. **C** Jung's personality grid accounted for a person's attitudes toward other people and toward decision making.

143. **B** Jung's work gave others the idea of categorizing people according to personality type. In other words, his work *generated* other classification systems.

144. **D** The author tells us that Freud was Jung's "contemporary," which means that these two psychologists lived and worked during the same time period: the early twentieth century. The author also tells us that Jung and Freud were both influential.

145. **B** The author tells us that Jung's work inspired others to develop various personality classification systems, and that the Myers-Briggs Type Indicator became the "most widely used," in other words, the most popular, among these systems.

146. **C** The passage's author is very optimistic about the future of science and how it will benefit humankind. Of the four choices, the word *enthusiastic* best describes such optimism.

147. **D** In the second paragraph, the author asserts that the most imaginative ideas that today's science-fiction writers dream up about the future of science will turn out "ordinary" compared to what the future will actually hold.

148. **B** The author's point here is that even our most distinguished and talented—in other words, *accomplished*—scientists and science-fiction writers couldn't dream up what the future of science will actually hold.

149. **A** In the final paragraph, the author asserts that, in the future, science will give us "amazing control over . . . the development of thought itself."

150. **A** In the final sentence, the author expresses confidence that, thanks to science, the condition of humankind will be better in the future than it is today.

151. **D** In the third paragraph, the author poses, and then answers, a question. Hence, choice A is incorrect. In the first two paragraphs, the author tells us that scientific developments in the last 300 years have made life without anesthetics inconceivable today; hence, choice B is incorrect. In the last sentence of the second paragraph, the author asks a question that does not call for a response, or answer. (The question itself is intended to make the author's point.) Hence, choice C is incorrect. Nowhere in the passage, however, does the author evaluate any predictions for the future.

152. **B** The passage's main idea is that the great, and unexpected, scientific advancements in the past give us reason to believe that more great advancements will occur in what's sure to be a long future for humankind. Choice B supplies a title that captures the gist of the passage nicely.

Answers and Explanations *(continued)*

153. **B** *Astute* means "discerning, keen, or perceptive."

154. **B** To *mimic* is to imitate or parrot.

155. **D** An *oath* is a promise or pledge to be truthful or accountable.

156. **C** To *attain* is to acquire or achieve.

157. **D** *Somber* means "dismal, dreary, or gloomy."

158. **B** A *skirmish* is a fight, conflict, or scuffle.

159. **A** *Plausible* means "convincing, probable, or believable."

160. **C** To *cultivate* is to grow or develop.

161. **D** *Unwarranted* means "groundless, uncalled for, or unfounded."

162. **D** To *stow* is to put away, store, or pack.

163. **B** A *residue* means "remains, remnant, or remainder"—in other words, what's left over.

164. **A** *Temperate* means "mild, calm, or pleasant."

165. **A** A *whim* is an urge, impulse, or spur-of-the-moment thought.

166. **A** *Abundant* means "plentiful or abounding."

167. **B** To *recuperate* is to recover, improve, or rally—usually after illness or other setback involving one's health.

168. **C** *Pliable* means "flexible, supple, or limber."

169. **D** To *persevere* is to persist, carry on, or endure.

170. **B** *Affluent* means "prosperous, moneyed, or wealthy."

171. **A** To *waft* is to float or drift, usually in the wind—as a scent might waft in a gentle breeze.

172. **D** *Petrified* means "stony or hard."

173. **C** An *array* is a display or arrangement of things.

174. **C** *Amiable* means "likeable, good-natured, or friendly."

Mathematics

175. **D** To compare with 13/40, convert the denominators in choices B, C, and D to 40:

$$\frac{7}{20} \times \frac{2}{2} = \frac{14}{40} > \frac{13}{40}$$

$$\frac{2}{5} \times \frac{8}{8} = \frac{16}{40} > \frac{13}{40}$$

$$\frac{3}{10} \times \frac{4}{4} = \frac{12}{40} < \frac{13}{40}$$

For choice A, you can compare this way:

$$\frac{1}{3} \times \frac{13}{13} = \frac{13}{39} > \frac{13}{40}$$

176. **C** Only positive integers can be prime numbers, and a fraction whose numerator and denominator are two different prime numbers cannot be simplified and therefore must be a positive non-integer.

177. **A** In any triangle, the sum of the three interior angle measures is 180°. Because a right angle measures 90°, the sum of the other two angle measures must be 90°. Only choice A provides a pair of numbers that totals 90.

178. **D** The digit 4 is in the "thousands" place.

Answers and Explanations *(continued)*

179. **B** Left of the *y*-axis (vertical axis), the *x*-coordinate (first coordinate in the pair) is negative. Above the *x*-axis (horizontal axis), the *y*-coordinate (second coordinate in the pair) is positive.

180. **A** Distribute *x* to (multiply *x* by) each term inside the parentheses.

181. **C** One burger costs *B* dollars. There are 100 cents to a dollar. Thus, the cost of a burger in *cents* is 100*B*. The question asks for the *cent* cost of one burger (100*B*) **and** one soda (*S*).

182. **D** The coefficient of each term in the binomial is 1. Since the two terms share the same exponential variable (a^4), you can combine terms simply by adding coefficients (1 + 1 = 2).

183. **A** In an equilateral triangle, all sides are congruent (equal in length) and all angles are congruent (60° each). In any triangle, angles opposite congruent sides are congruent, and vice versa. Also, in any triangle, the sum of the degree measures of the interior angles is 180°. Apply these properties to each triangle:

    Triangle A: Because one angle opposite a side of length 8 measures 60°, the angle opposite the other side of length 8 must also measure 60° and, therefore, so must the third angle. The triangle is equilateral.

    Triangle B: The two angles other than the indicated 60° angle must be congruent, and therefore they must measure 60° each. The triangle is equilateral.

    Triangle C: Because two angles measure 60°, the third angle must also measure 60°. The triangle is equilateral.

184. **B** 3 + 4 + 5 = 12.

185. **D** The value of any fraction whose numerator is zero (0) and whose denominator is any non-zero number is 0 (zero).

186. **C** Given that a non-zero integer *x* is greater than −5 but less that $5\frac{1}{2}\left(\frac{11}{2}\right)$, the possible values of *x* are: −4, −3, −2, −1, 1, 2, 3, 4, 5.

187. **D** Any non-zero number raised to the power of zero (0) equals 1.

188. **B** The perimeter of any square is four times the length of each side: 4 × 6 = 24. (The circle's radius is 3, and its circumference is 6π; the square's area is 36.)

189. **C** Of the four numbers, 36 has the greatest number of factors. Here's a list of positive factors for each number (excluding 1 and the number itself):

    24: {2,3,4,6,12}
    42: {2,3,6,7,21}
    36: {2,3,4,6,9,12,18}
    50: {2,5,10,25}

190. **C** The product of four consecutive negative integers is always a *positive even* integer. Similarly, the product of four consecutive positive integers is always a *positive even* integer. The product of two positive even integers is another positive even integer.

191. **B** In the original binomial expression, *x* is distributed to both terms of the binomial.

192. **D** All five interior angles are congruent (the same size). The total measure of the interior angles of a pentagon is 540°. Thus, each interior angle measures $\frac{1}{5}$ of 540°, or 108°.

Answers and Explanations *(continued)*

193. **B** In set B, the mean and median are both 15. In each of the other two sets, notice that the middle value is *not* equidistant from the other two numbers on the number line, which means that the median does *not* equal the mean.

194. **A** $4 \times 25 = 100$. The integers 4, 8, and 100 are the only three multiples in this range that are *not* 2-digit numbers. Thus, P contains 22 members. All of these members are also members of Q.

195. **A** Assume each side of a certain square is 2 units in length. The area of this square is $2 \times 2 = 4$. Now, increase the length of each side by 50%—to 3 units. The square's new area is $3 \times 3 = 9$. An increase from 4 to 9 is a 125% increase.

196. **B** $(2)\left(-\dfrac{1}{2}\right) = -1$, which is less than $-\dfrac{1}{2}$.

197. **A** $10^6 = 10 \times 10 \times 10 \times 10 \times 10 \times 10 = 1{,}000{,}000$. Thus, $2 \times 10^6 = 2{,}000{,}000$.

198. **D** The two sets in choice D have in common the numbers 4, 5, and 6.

199. **C** The decimal number 0.2 is equivalent to the fraction $\dfrac{2}{10}$, or $\dfrac{1}{5}$. To combine, multiply numerators, and multiply denominators: $\dfrac{1}{5} \times \dfrac{1}{3} = \dfrac{1}{15}$.

200. **A** To add, align the three numbers vertically at the decimal point.

201. **C** $|-2| + |3| = 2 + 3 = 5$.

202. **A** To find 12% of $500, multiply: $0.12 \times \$500 = \$60$.

203. **A** Interior angle *BAC* is supplementary to a 125° angle and therefore must measure 55°. Interior angle *ABC* is a right angle and therefore measures 90°. The total measure of the triangle's three interior angles is 180°. Thus, $x = 35$.

204. **C** One burger-and-fries meal costs $4.25. Five of these meals costs $21.25, while six of these meals costs $25.50 (more than $25).

205. **B** Mark is 4 years older than Samir, who in turn is 8 years older than Renata. Thus, Mark is 12 years older than Renata.

206. **A** Together, candidates B and C received 80% of the votes (100% − 20%). Candidate C received 1/4 of that 80%, or 20% of the total number of votes. (Candidate B received 3 times as many votes: 3/4 of 80%, or 60%.)

207. **D** A circle's circumference equals the product of its diameter and π: $C = \pi d$.

208. **D** $4^3 = 4 \times 4 \times 4$. Thus, $4^3 \times 4^3 = (4 \times 4) \times (4 \times 4) \times (4 \times 4) = 16 \times 16 \times 16$.

209. **C** Division A accounts for 20% (100% − 55% − 25%) of the total production (7,500). To find Division A's daily production, multiply: $0.2 \times 7{,}500 = 1{,}500$.

210. **C** Letting the price of a child's ticket equal *C*, the price of an adult ticket equals 2*C*. Set up an algebraic equation, then solve for *C*:

$$C + C + C + 2C = \$18.75$$

$$5C = \$18.75$$

$$C = \$3.75$$

Answers and Explanations *(continued)*

211. **A** Notice that 825 is greater than 800 by 25, and that 775 is less than 800 by 25. Thus, to estimate their product, you can round off both numbers to 800, then multiply: 800 × 800 = 640,000. Choice A provides the closest approximation.

212. **C** The tax = $55 × 0.05 = $2.75. Add this tax to the sweater's price: $55 + $2.75 = $57.75.

213. **A** To divide, multiply the numerator fraction $\frac{8}{9}$ by the reciprocal of the denominator fraction $\frac{4}{3}$, simplifying by cancelling common factors before combining: $\frac{8}{9} \times \frac{3}{4} = \frac{2}{3} \times \frac{1}{1} = \frac{2}{3}$.

214. **D** The total trip time was 2.5 hours. Apply the *rate* × *time* = *distance* formula: 40 (m.p.h.) × 2.5 (hours) = 100 (miles).

215. **D** You can determine the correct answer choice by making a common-sense estimate: Based on a mile-to-kilometer ratio of 1:1.6, 10 kilometers is significantly less than 10 miles, but a bit more than 5 miles. Or, to compute the precise answer, divide 10 by 1.6. Try converting 1.6 to the fraction $\frac{8}{5}$, then multiply 10 by its reciprocal:

$$10 \div \frac{8}{5} = 10 \times \frac{5}{8} = \frac{50}{8} = 6.25$$

$$\frac{1}{1.6} = \frac{x}{10}$$

$$1.6x = 10$$

$$x = \frac{10}{1.6}$$

216. **C** First, combine terms in each parenthesized expression: $-(-1)(1) = 1$. (A negative number multiplied by a negative number is a positive number.)

217. **A** Because $b = 30$, the angle that is vertical to b (directly across the vertex from b) must also measure 30°. That angle, combined with the 110° angle and angle a, form a straight line, which measures 180°. Thus, $a = 40$.

218. **D** Perform multiplication and division (in either order) before addition: $5 + 4 \times 3 \div 2 = 5 + 12 \div 2 = 5 + 6 = 11$.

219. **B** To answer the question, you can try plugging in each answer choice in turn. (With the correct number, the equation will hold true.) Or, you can solve for x using algebra:

$$x = 3(x + 2)$$

$$x = 3x + 6$$

$$-2x = 6$$

$$x = -3$$

220. **B** $\left(\sqrt{3}\right)^4 = \sqrt{3} \times \sqrt{3} \times \sqrt{3} \times \sqrt{3} = 9$. Since $3^4 = 81$, $\sqrt[4]{81} = 3$.

221. **B** The formula for the volume of a right cylinder is: *Volume* $= \pi r^2 h$. Letting $r = 2$ and $h = 5$, solve for *V*: $V = \pi 2^2 5 = 20\pi$.

222. **D** $540 is 90%, or 9/10, of the original price. Letting x equal the original price: $(9/10)x = 540; $x = $540(10/9) = 600.

223. **B** Factoring out (cancelling) 3^9 and 2^{10} from both the numerator and the denominator leaves $\frac{3^1}{2^1} = \frac{3}{2}$.

224. **B** Angle a is supplementary to a 140° angle and therefore measures 40°. Since $l_1 \parallel l_2$, angles c and b each measure 140°. Thus, $a + b + c = 40 + 140 + 140 = 320$.

225. **B** $66\frac{2}{3}\%$ is equivalent to 2/3. Since $120 \div 3 = 40$, $\frac{2}{3}$ of 120 = 2 × 40 = 80.

Answers and Explanations *(continued)*

226. **B** $\frac{5}{8}$ of the 40 students are girls: $\frac{5}{8} \times 40 = 25$.

227. **C** To minimize the fencing used, it should run across the 60-foot width of the field. Three 60-foot sections (180 linear feet altogether) are needed to divide the field into four rectangles.

228. **A** The sum of the three scores must equal three times the average score. Set up an equation, letting x equal the third score, and then solve for x:

$$90 + 90 + x = 92 \times 3$$

$$180 + x = 276$$

$$x = 96$$

229. **C** First, find the prime factors of the term inside the radical: $300 = 2 \times 2 \times 3 \times 5 \times 5$. Then, identify perfect squares and remove them from inside the radical: $\sqrt{300} = \sqrt{2^2 \times 3 \times 5^2} = 2 \times 5\sqrt{3} = 10\sqrt{3}$.

230. **D** A circle contains 360°. The segment defined by the 60° angle accounts for $\frac{60}{360}$, or $\frac{1}{6}$ the circle's total area. Given a radius of 6, the circle has an area of $\pi 6^2 = 36\pi$. The shaded area is $\frac{5}{6}$ of 36π, or 30π.

231. **D** Six (6) of the 12 marbles are green. The probability of selecting a green marble is $\frac{6}{12}$, or $\frac{1}{2}$.

232. **A** There are 16 ounces in a pound; 16 ounces of sugar $\times$ 6 bags $= 96$ ounces, with 4 ounces left over.

233. **B** Using the plug-in method, you can try substituting each answer choice for l in the following formula: *Area = lw*. Or, you can substitute $\frac{l}{2}$ for w in the formula, then solve for l:

$$8 = (l)\left(\frac{l}{2}\right)$$

$$16 = l^2$$

$$4 = l$$

234. **A** The total number of eggs produced during the week is 29. To find the average per coop, divide by 4: $29 \div 4 \approx 7$.

235. **D** To find daily totals, add the numbers in each column. Here are the totals for each pair of days listed in the question:

(A) Saturday and Sunday: $3 + 5 = 8$
(B) Thursday and Friday: $2 + 5 = 7$
(C) Monday and Tuesday: $3 + 4 = 7$
(D) Tuesday and Friday: $4 + 5 = 9$

236. **B** The new, 18-ounce mixture contains 10 ounces of water. Thus, water accounts for $\frac{10}{18}$, or $\frac{5}{9}$, of the new mixture.

237. **D** The triangle's height is 4, and its base is 5. $A = \frac{1}{2}bh = \frac{1}{2}(5)(4) = 10$.

238. **A** $\sqrt{40}$ is between 6 and 7, but nearer to 6. $\sqrt{60}$ is between 7 and 8, but nearer to 8. Thus, their sum is approximately 14.

Answers and Explanations *(continued)*

Language

239. **A** To signify a separation of ideas, a punctuation mark such as a period, semicolon, or comma should be inserted between *walk* and *don't*.

240. **C** The two-word phrase *every day* (meaning "each day") is proper in this context. (The word *everyday* is an adjective meaning "ordinary.")

241. **B** It is not idiomatic to say that a price increased *over* another price. One solution is to replace *over* with *beyond*.

242. **B** Either the word *to* should be omitted or the dialogue should be omitted (. . . *tell him to sit*).

243. **D** There are no mistakes.

244. **A** The plural subject *dictators* calls for the plural pronoun *their* instead of the singular form *his*.

245. **C** The proper correlative pair is *neither . . . nor*. (Replace *or* with *nor*.)

246. **C** The capitalized word *Avenue* is correct here because it is part of a proper noun (a street name).

247. **C** The phrase *combined together* is redundant. One solution is to simply delete the word *together*.

248. **D** There are no mistakes.

249. **C** The capitalized word *Corps* should be used here because it is part of a proper noun.

250. **B** The contraction *It's* (or *it is*) should replace *Its*.

251. **A** To make a proper comparison (between lives), the word *her* should be replaced with either *her life* or *hers*.

252. **A** The sentence refers to a movie title, which should be either italicized or underlined.

253. **D** There are no mistakes.

254. **A** It is idiomatic to say either *can't wait* or *can hardly wait*. However, *can't hardly* is not idiomatic.

255. **B** The word *therefore* is parenthetical and should be set off by commas (one before the word and one after it).

256. **C** The two-word phrase *some times* is not idiomatic here. One way to fix the problem is to use the single word *sometimes* (meaning "occasionally") instead. Another way to correct the problem is to replace *some* with *at*.

257. **D** There are no mistakes.

258. **C** The subject-case *who* is incorrect because the word is used here as an indirect object. The object-case *whom* should be used instead.

259. **B** The colon is improper here because it is not followed by either a list or definition of what precedes it. A comma should be used in its place.

260. **D** There are no mistakes.

261. **C** The past-perfect tense is appropriate throughout this sentence. The past-perfect verb form *had left* should replace the simple-past form *left*.

262. **C** The comparative form of *friendly* can either be *friendlier* or *more friendly*—but not *more friendlier*.

263. **D** There are no mistakes.

264. **B** The word *the* should be omitted.

Answers and Explanations (continued)

265. **B** The two-word phrase *for ever* makes no sense and should be replaced with the single word *forever*.

266. **D** There are no mistakes.

267. **D** There are no mistakes.

268. **B** The subject-case pronoun *I* should be replaced with object-case pronoun *me*.

269. **A** The sentence incorrectly uses a double negative; replace *none* with *any*.

270. **A** A comma should be inserted between *job* and *but* because *It's a dirty job* and *I'll do it* are independent clauses, each of which can stand alone as a complete sentence.

271. **D** There are no mistakes.

272. **A** This sentence poses a question, and so it should end with a question mark.

273. **C** The proper choice of words in this context is *secret*.

274. **B** The prediction should not be rain but rather *for* rain or *that it will* rain.

275. **A** The word *good* is slang in this context and should be replaced with *well*.

276. **D** There are no mistakes.

277. **B** The sentence compares exactly two things, so the word *better* should be used instead of *best*.

278. **C** The grammatical structure equates *to play soccer* with *a fun sport*. This makes no sense; it is *soccer* that is a fun sport. A good solution is to simply omit *To play*.

279. **C** The correct spelling is *memory*.

280. **C** The correct spelling is *symptoms*.

281. **D** There are no spelling mistakes.

282. **A** The correct spelling is *assess*.

283. **A** The correct spelling is *received*.

284. **B** The correct spelling is *parcel*.

285. **A** The correct spelling is *stomachache*.

286. **D** There are no spelling mistakes.

287. **A** The correct spelling is *trophy*.

288. **C** The correct spelling is *laughter*.

289. **A** The second thought *qualifies* the first one; in other words, it presents a somewhat contrary idea—that it might not be completely safe to cross the street. The word *but* works perfectly for this purpose.

290. **B** The sentence's opening words (*Unlike roulette*) tell you that the second clause (after the comma) should begin by identifying a game that is somehow different from roulette. Choices B and D both fit the bill, but choices A and C do not. (They refer to *playing* poker rather than to poker itself.) The problem with the phrase in choice D is that it results in a grammatical comparison between the game of poker itself and *strategic and cunning*. This comparison is illogical, and so you can eliminate choice D. That leaves choice B, the best of the four completions.

291. **A** Sentence A is clear and effective. Sentences B and C make awkward use of the passive voice. Sentence D is awkward and confusing.

292. **D** After the first clause, the sentence reverses direction and presents a contrary idea. Beginning the sentence with *Even though* provides an appropriate clue that contrary or opposing ideas lie ahead.

Answers and Explanations *(continued)*

293. **B** The sentence's second clause presents an idea that opposes, or runs contrary to, the idea in the first clause. The word *yet* signals an opposing idea. (Two other good connecting words here would be *although* and *but*.)

294. **C** In one paragraph of reasonable length, it is quite possible to explain why salmon swim upstream. The other two topics are too complex, however.

295. **D** Sentence 2, which begins with *So,* is clearly a continuation of the thought started in sentence 1. Similarly, in starting with *They asked,* sentence 3 continues that same train of thought. Without sentence 4, the transition from sentence 3 to 5 is too rough, while sentence 5 only make sense as a continuation of sentence 4. Thus, it's impossible to simply omit one and only one of the five sentences without interrupting and undermining the flow of ideas in the paragraph.

296. **A** Version C is clear and effective. In sentence A, the final clause appears to be an afterthought tacked awkwardly onto the end of the sentence. In version B, the first clause is awkward and confusing. Here's a better opening clause for sentence B: *Because of gold's rarity and unsurpassed beauty, . . .*) Also, *great intrinsically* is awkward and confusing. (The two words should be reversed.) In choice D, the first clause should be positioned closer to its intended antecedent, *gold.* (An easy solution would be to simply omit *for these reasons.*)

297. **A** As a whole, the paragraph explains how the pace of change for the human race accelerated dramatically beginning about 100 years ago. Choice A provides a sentence that expresses this essential idea.

298. **B** The key to the sentence's best placement is the word *however* at the end of sentence 3. It makes sense that what immediately precedes sentence 3 should convey the idea that the Library is used widely by the general public today.

HSPT PRACTICE TEST 2

Answer Sheet

Directions: For each answer that you select, blacken the corresponding oval on this sheet.

Verbal Skills

1. Ⓐ Ⓑ Ⓒ Ⓓ
2. Ⓐ Ⓑ Ⓒ Ⓓ
3. Ⓐ Ⓑ Ⓒ Ⓓ
4. Ⓐ Ⓑ Ⓒ Ⓓ
5. Ⓐ Ⓑ Ⓒ Ⓓ
6. Ⓐ Ⓑ Ⓒ Ⓓ
7. Ⓐ Ⓑ Ⓒ Ⓓ
8. Ⓐ Ⓑ Ⓒ Ⓓ
9. Ⓐ Ⓑ Ⓒ Ⓓ
10. Ⓐ Ⓑ Ⓒ Ⓓ
11. Ⓐ Ⓑ Ⓒ Ⓓ
12. Ⓐ Ⓑ Ⓒ Ⓓ
13. Ⓐ Ⓑ Ⓒ Ⓓ
14. Ⓐ Ⓑ Ⓒ Ⓓ
15. Ⓐ Ⓑ Ⓒ Ⓓ
16. Ⓐ Ⓑ Ⓒ Ⓓ
17. Ⓐ Ⓑ Ⓒ Ⓓ
18. Ⓐ Ⓑ Ⓒ Ⓓ
19. Ⓐ Ⓑ Ⓒ Ⓓ
20. Ⓐ Ⓑ Ⓒ Ⓓ
21. Ⓐ Ⓑ Ⓒ Ⓓ
22. Ⓐ Ⓑ Ⓒ Ⓓ
23. Ⓐ Ⓑ Ⓒ Ⓓ
24. Ⓐ Ⓑ Ⓒ Ⓓ
25. Ⓐ Ⓑ Ⓒ Ⓓ
26. Ⓐ Ⓑ Ⓒ Ⓓ
27. Ⓐ Ⓑ Ⓒ Ⓓ
28. Ⓐ Ⓑ Ⓒ Ⓓ
29. Ⓐ Ⓑ Ⓒ Ⓓ
30. Ⓐ Ⓑ Ⓒ Ⓓ
31. Ⓐ Ⓑ Ⓒ Ⓓ
32. Ⓐ Ⓑ Ⓒ Ⓓ
33. Ⓐ Ⓑ Ⓒ Ⓓ
34. Ⓐ Ⓑ Ⓒ Ⓓ
35. Ⓐ Ⓑ Ⓒ Ⓓ
36. Ⓐ Ⓑ Ⓒ Ⓓ
37. Ⓐ Ⓑ Ⓒ Ⓓ
38. Ⓐ Ⓑ Ⓒ Ⓓ
39. Ⓐ Ⓑ Ⓒ Ⓓ
40. Ⓐ Ⓑ Ⓒ Ⓓ
41. Ⓐ Ⓑ Ⓒ Ⓓ
42. Ⓐ Ⓑ Ⓒ Ⓓ
43. Ⓐ Ⓑ Ⓒ Ⓓ
44. Ⓐ Ⓑ Ⓒ Ⓓ
45. Ⓐ Ⓑ Ⓒ Ⓓ
46. Ⓐ Ⓑ Ⓒ Ⓓ
47. Ⓐ Ⓑ Ⓒ Ⓓ

48. Ⓐ Ⓑ Ⓒ Ⓓ
49. Ⓐ Ⓑ Ⓒ Ⓓ
50. Ⓐ Ⓑ Ⓒ Ⓓ
51. Ⓐ Ⓑ Ⓒ Ⓓ
52. Ⓐ Ⓑ Ⓒ Ⓓ
53. Ⓐ Ⓑ Ⓒ Ⓓ
54. Ⓐ Ⓑ Ⓒ Ⓓ
55. Ⓐ Ⓑ Ⓒ Ⓓ
56. Ⓐ Ⓑ Ⓒ Ⓓ
57. Ⓐ Ⓑ Ⓒ Ⓓ
58. Ⓐ Ⓑ Ⓒ Ⓓ
59. Ⓐ Ⓑ Ⓒ Ⓓ
60. Ⓐ Ⓑ Ⓒ Ⓓ

Quantitative Skills

61. Ⓐ Ⓑ Ⓒ Ⓓ
62. Ⓐ Ⓑ Ⓒ Ⓓ
63. Ⓐ Ⓑ Ⓒ Ⓓ
64. Ⓐ Ⓑ Ⓒ Ⓓ
65. Ⓐ Ⓑ Ⓒ Ⓓ
66. Ⓐ Ⓑ Ⓒ Ⓓ
67. Ⓐ Ⓑ Ⓒ Ⓓ
68. Ⓐ Ⓑ Ⓒ Ⓓ
69. Ⓐ Ⓑ Ⓒ Ⓓ
70. Ⓐ Ⓑ Ⓒ Ⓓ
71. Ⓐ Ⓑ Ⓒ Ⓓ
72. Ⓐ Ⓑ Ⓒ Ⓓ
73. Ⓐ Ⓑ Ⓒ Ⓓ
74. Ⓐ Ⓑ Ⓒ Ⓓ
75. Ⓐ Ⓑ Ⓒ Ⓓ
76. Ⓐ Ⓑ Ⓒ Ⓓ
77. Ⓐ Ⓑ Ⓒ Ⓓ
78. Ⓐ Ⓑ Ⓒ Ⓓ
79. Ⓐ Ⓑ Ⓒ Ⓓ
80. Ⓐ Ⓑ Ⓒ Ⓓ
81. Ⓐ Ⓑ Ⓒ Ⓓ
82. Ⓐ Ⓑ Ⓒ Ⓓ
83. Ⓐ Ⓑ Ⓒ Ⓓ
84. Ⓐ Ⓑ Ⓒ Ⓓ
85. Ⓐ Ⓑ Ⓒ Ⓓ
86. Ⓐ Ⓑ Ⓒ Ⓓ
87. Ⓐ Ⓑ Ⓒ Ⓓ
88. Ⓐ Ⓑ Ⓒ Ⓓ
89. Ⓐ Ⓑ Ⓒ Ⓓ
90. Ⓐ Ⓑ Ⓒ Ⓓ
91. Ⓐ Ⓑ Ⓒ Ⓓ
92. Ⓐ Ⓑ Ⓒ Ⓓ

93. Ⓐ Ⓑ Ⓒ Ⓓ
94. Ⓐ Ⓑ Ⓒ Ⓓ
95. Ⓐ Ⓑ Ⓒ Ⓓ
96. Ⓐ Ⓑ Ⓒ Ⓓ
97. Ⓐ Ⓑ Ⓒ Ⓓ
98. Ⓐ Ⓑ Ⓒ Ⓓ
99. Ⓐ Ⓑ Ⓒ Ⓓ
100. Ⓐ Ⓑ Ⓒ Ⓓ
101. Ⓐ Ⓑ Ⓒ Ⓓ
102. Ⓐ Ⓑ Ⓒ Ⓓ
103. Ⓐ Ⓑ Ⓒ Ⓓ
104. Ⓐ Ⓑ Ⓒ Ⓓ
105. Ⓐ Ⓑ Ⓒ Ⓓ
106. Ⓐ Ⓑ Ⓒ Ⓓ
107. Ⓐ Ⓑ Ⓒ Ⓓ
108. Ⓐ Ⓑ Ⓒ Ⓓ
109. Ⓐ Ⓑ Ⓒ Ⓓ
110. Ⓐ Ⓑ Ⓒ Ⓓ
111. Ⓐ Ⓑ Ⓒ Ⓓ
112. Ⓐ Ⓑ Ⓒ Ⓓ

Reading

113. Ⓐ Ⓑ Ⓒ Ⓓ
114. Ⓐ Ⓑ Ⓒ Ⓓ
115. Ⓐ Ⓑ Ⓒ Ⓓ
116. Ⓐ Ⓑ Ⓒ Ⓓ
117. Ⓐ Ⓑ Ⓒ Ⓓ
118. Ⓐ Ⓑ Ⓒ Ⓓ
119. Ⓐ Ⓑ Ⓒ Ⓓ
120. Ⓐ Ⓑ Ⓒ Ⓓ
121. Ⓐ Ⓑ Ⓒ Ⓓ
122. Ⓐ Ⓑ Ⓒ Ⓓ
123. Ⓐ Ⓑ Ⓒ Ⓓ
124. Ⓐ Ⓑ Ⓒ Ⓓ
125. Ⓐ Ⓑ Ⓒ Ⓓ
126. Ⓐ Ⓑ Ⓒ Ⓓ
127. Ⓐ Ⓑ Ⓒ Ⓓ
128. Ⓐ Ⓑ Ⓒ Ⓓ
129. Ⓐ Ⓑ Ⓒ Ⓓ
130. Ⓐ Ⓑ Ⓒ Ⓓ
131. Ⓐ Ⓑ Ⓒ Ⓓ
132. Ⓐ Ⓑ Ⓒ Ⓓ
133. Ⓐ Ⓑ Ⓒ Ⓓ
134. Ⓐ Ⓑ Ⓒ Ⓓ
135. Ⓐ Ⓑ Ⓒ Ⓓ
136. Ⓐ Ⓑ Ⓒ Ⓓ
137. Ⓐ Ⓑ Ⓒ Ⓓ

HSPT PRACTICE TEST 2

Answer Sheet *(continued)*

138. Ⓐ Ⓑ Ⓒ Ⓓ
139. Ⓐ Ⓑ Ⓒ Ⓓ
140. Ⓐ Ⓑ Ⓒ Ⓓ
141. Ⓐ Ⓑ Ⓒ Ⓓ
142. Ⓐ Ⓑ Ⓒ Ⓓ
143. Ⓐ Ⓑ Ⓒ Ⓓ
144. Ⓐ Ⓑ Ⓒ Ⓓ
145. Ⓐ Ⓑ Ⓒ Ⓓ
146. Ⓐ Ⓑ Ⓒ Ⓓ
147. Ⓐ Ⓑ Ⓒ Ⓓ
148. Ⓐ Ⓑ Ⓒ Ⓓ
149. Ⓐ Ⓑ Ⓒ Ⓓ
150. Ⓐ Ⓑ Ⓒ Ⓓ
151. Ⓐ Ⓑ Ⓒ Ⓓ
152. Ⓐ Ⓑ Ⓒ Ⓓ
153. Ⓐ Ⓑ Ⓒ Ⓓ
154. Ⓐ Ⓑ Ⓒ Ⓓ
155. Ⓐ Ⓑ Ⓒ Ⓓ
156. Ⓐ Ⓑ Ⓒ Ⓓ
157. Ⓐ Ⓑ Ⓒ Ⓓ
158. Ⓐ Ⓑ Ⓒ Ⓓ
159. Ⓐ Ⓑ Ⓒ Ⓓ
160. Ⓐ Ⓑ Ⓒ Ⓓ
161. Ⓐ Ⓑ Ⓒ Ⓓ
162. Ⓐ Ⓑ Ⓒ Ⓓ
163. Ⓐ Ⓑ Ⓒ Ⓓ
164. Ⓐ Ⓑ Ⓒ Ⓓ
165. Ⓐ Ⓑ Ⓒ Ⓓ
166. Ⓐ Ⓑ Ⓒ Ⓓ
167. Ⓐ Ⓑ Ⓒ Ⓓ
168. Ⓐ Ⓑ Ⓒ Ⓓ
169. Ⓐ Ⓑ Ⓒ Ⓓ
170. Ⓐ Ⓑ Ⓒ Ⓓ
171. Ⓐ Ⓑ Ⓒ Ⓓ
172. Ⓐ Ⓑ Ⓒ Ⓓ
173. Ⓐ Ⓑ Ⓒ Ⓓ
174. Ⓐ Ⓑ Ⓒ Ⓓ

Mathematics

175. Ⓐ Ⓑ Ⓒ Ⓓ
176. Ⓐ Ⓑ Ⓒ Ⓓ
177. Ⓐ Ⓑ Ⓒ Ⓓ
178. Ⓐ Ⓑ Ⓒ Ⓓ
179. Ⓐ Ⓑ Ⓒ Ⓓ
180. Ⓐ Ⓑ Ⓒ Ⓓ

181. Ⓐ Ⓑ Ⓒ Ⓓ
182. Ⓐ Ⓑ Ⓒ Ⓓ
183. Ⓐ Ⓑ Ⓒ Ⓓ
184. Ⓐ Ⓑ Ⓒ Ⓓ
185. Ⓐ Ⓑ Ⓒ Ⓓ
186. Ⓐ Ⓑ Ⓒ Ⓓ
187. Ⓐ Ⓑ Ⓒ Ⓓ
188. Ⓐ Ⓑ Ⓒ Ⓓ
189. Ⓐ Ⓑ Ⓒ Ⓓ
190. Ⓐ Ⓑ Ⓒ Ⓓ
191. Ⓐ Ⓑ Ⓒ Ⓓ
192. Ⓐ Ⓑ Ⓒ Ⓓ
193. Ⓐ Ⓑ Ⓒ Ⓓ
194. Ⓐ Ⓑ Ⓒ Ⓓ
195. Ⓐ Ⓑ Ⓒ Ⓓ
196. Ⓐ Ⓑ Ⓒ Ⓓ
197. Ⓐ Ⓑ Ⓒ Ⓓ
198. Ⓐ Ⓑ Ⓒ Ⓓ
199. Ⓐ Ⓑ Ⓒ Ⓓ
200. Ⓐ Ⓑ Ⓒ Ⓓ
201. Ⓐ Ⓑ Ⓒ Ⓓ
202. Ⓐ Ⓑ Ⓒ Ⓓ
203. Ⓐ Ⓑ Ⓒ Ⓓ
204. Ⓐ Ⓑ Ⓒ Ⓓ
205. Ⓐ Ⓑ Ⓒ Ⓓ
206. Ⓐ Ⓑ Ⓒ Ⓓ
207. Ⓐ Ⓑ Ⓒ Ⓓ
208. Ⓐ Ⓑ Ⓒ Ⓓ
209. Ⓐ Ⓑ Ⓒ Ⓓ
210. Ⓐ Ⓑ Ⓒ Ⓓ
211. Ⓐ Ⓑ Ⓒ Ⓓ
212. Ⓐ Ⓑ Ⓒ Ⓓ
213. Ⓐ Ⓑ Ⓒ Ⓓ
214. Ⓐ Ⓑ Ⓒ Ⓓ
215. Ⓐ Ⓑ Ⓒ Ⓓ
216. Ⓐ Ⓑ Ⓒ Ⓓ
217. Ⓐ Ⓑ Ⓒ Ⓓ
218. Ⓐ Ⓑ Ⓒ Ⓓ
219. Ⓐ Ⓑ Ⓒ Ⓓ
220. Ⓐ Ⓑ Ⓒ Ⓓ
221. Ⓐ Ⓑ Ⓒ Ⓓ
222. Ⓐ Ⓑ Ⓒ Ⓓ
223. Ⓐ Ⓑ Ⓒ Ⓓ
224. Ⓐ Ⓑ Ⓒ Ⓓ
225. Ⓐ Ⓑ Ⓒ Ⓓ

226. Ⓐ Ⓑ Ⓒ Ⓓ
227. Ⓐ Ⓑ Ⓒ Ⓓ
228. Ⓐ Ⓑ Ⓒ Ⓓ
229. Ⓐ Ⓑ Ⓒ Ⓓ
230. Ⓐ Ⓑ Ⓒ Ⓓ
231. Ⓐ Ⓑ Ⓒ Ⓓ
232. Ⓐ Ⓑ Ⓒ Ⓓ
233. Ⓐ Ⓑ Ⓒ Ⓓ
234. Ⓐ Ⓑ Ⓒ Ⓓ
235. Ⓐ Ⓑ Ⓒ Ⓓ
236. Ⓐ Ⓑ Ⓒ Ⓓ
237. Ⓐ Ⓑ Ⓒ Ⓓ
238. Ⓐ Ⓑ Ⓒ Ⓓ

Language

239. Ⓐ Ⓑ Ⓒ Ⓓ
240. Ⓐ Ⓑ Ⓒ Ⓓ
241. Ⓐ Ⓑ Ⓒ Ⓓ
242. Ⓐ Ⓑ Ⓒ Ⓓ
243. Ⓐ Ⓑ Ⓒ Ⓓ
244. Ⓐ Ⓑ Ⓒ Ⓓ
245. Ⓐ Ⓑ Ⓒ Ⓓ
246. Ⓐ Ⓑ Ⓒ Ⓓ
247. Ⓐ Ⓑ Ⓒ Ⓓ
248. Ⓐ Ⓑ Ⓒ Ⓓ
249. Ⓐ Ⓑ Ⓒ Ⓓ
250. Ⓐ Ⓑ Ⓒ Ⓓ
251. Ⓐ Ⓑ Ⓒ Ⓓ
252. Ⓐ Ⓑ Ⓒ Ⓓ
253. Ⓐ Ⓑ Ⓒ Ⓓ
254. Ⓐ Ⓑ Ⓒ Ⓓ
255. Ⓐ Ⓑ Ⓒ Ⓓ
256. Ⓐ Ⓑ Ⓒ Ⓓ
257. Ⓐ Ⓑ Ⓒ Ⓓ
258. Ⓐ Ⓑ Ⓒ Ⓓ
259. Ⓐ Ⓑ Ⓒ Ⓓ
260. Ⓐ Ⓑ Ⓒ Ⓓ
261. Ⓐ Ⓑ Ⓒ Ⓓ
262. Ⓐ Ⓑ Ⓒ Ⓓ
263. Ⓐ Ⓑ Ⓒ Ⓓ
264. Ⓐ Ⓑ Ⓒ Ⓓ
265. Ⓐ Ⓑ Ⓒ Ⓓ
266. Ⓐ Ⓑ Ⓒ Ⓓ
267. Ⓐ Ⓑ Ⓒ Ⓓ
268. Ⓐ Ⓑ Ⓒ Ⓓ

HSPT PRACTICE TEST 2

Answer Sheet *(continued)*

269. Ⓐ Ⓑ Ⓒ Ⓓ	279. Ⓐ Ⓑ Ⓒ Ⓓ	289. Ⓐ Ⓑ Ⓒ Ⓓ
270. Ⓐ Ⓑ Ⓒ Ⓓ	280. Ⓐ Ⓑ Ⓒ Ⓓ	290. Ⓐ Ⓑ Ⓒ Ⓓ
271. Ⓐ Ⓑ Ⓒ Ⓓ	281. Ⓐ Ⓑ Ⓒ Ⓓ	291. Ⓐ Ⓑ Ⓒ Ⓓ
272. Ⓐ Ⓑ Ⓒ Ⓓ	282. Ⓐ Ⓑ Ⓒ Ⓓ	292. Ⓐ Ⓑ Ⓒ Ⓓ
273. Ⓐ Ⓑ Ⓒ Ⓓ	283. Ⓐ Ⓑ Ⓒ Ⓓ	293. Ⓐ Ⓑ Ⓒ Ⓓ
274. Ⓐ Ⓑ Ⓒ Ⓓ	284. Ⓐ Ⓑ Ⓒ Ⓓ	294. Ⓐ Ⓑ Ⓒ Ⓓ
275. Ⓐ Ⓑ Ⓒ Ⓓ	285. Ⓐ Ⓑ Ⓒ Ⓓ	295. Ⓐ Ⓑ Ⓒ Ⓓ
276. Ⓐ Ⓑ Ⓒ Ⓓ	286. Ⓐ Ⓑ Ⓒ Ⓓ	296. Ⓐ Ⓑ Ⓒ Ⓓ
277. Ⓐ Ⓑ Ⓒ Ⓓ	287. Ⓐ Ⓑ Ⓒ Ⓓ	297. Ⓐ Ⓑ Ⓒ Ⓓ
278. Ⓐ Ⓑ Ⓒ Ⓓ	288. Ⓐ Ⓑ Ⓒ Ⓓ	298. Ⓐ Ⓑ Ⓒ Ⓓ

HSPT PRACTICE TEST 2

Verbal Skills (60 Questions) (16 Minutes)

Directions: For questions 1–60, choose the best answer.

1. Which word does *not* belong with the others?
   A   compute
   B   calculate
   C   figure
   D   guess

2. Host is to party as judge is to
   A   jury
   B   trial
   C   lawyer
   D   courtroom

3. Lucrative most nearly means
   A   profitable
   B   slippery
   C   flowery
   D   fresh

4. Which word does *not* belong with the others?
   A   director
   B   guide
   C   inventor
   D   conductor

5. Susan scored more points in the game than Rose. Rose scored more points in the game than Bill. Bill scored more points in the game than Randy. If the first two statements are true, the third is
   A   true
   B   false
   C   uncertain

6. Guitar is to string as piano is to
   A   key
   B   musician
   C   bench
   D   drum

7. Reclined means the *opposite* of
   A   willing
   B   upright
   C   recycled
   D   wealthy

8. Which word does *not* belong with the others?
   A   warrior
   B   rogue
   C   outlaw
   D   villain

9. Refute means the *opposite* of
   A   prove
   B   shrink
   C   reveal
   D   win

10. In the parade, X marched behind Y but ahead of Z. In the same parade, W marched behind X but ahead of Z. Y marched behind W in the parade. If the first two statements are true, the third is
    A   true
    B   false
    C   uncertain

11. Which word does *not* belong with the others?
    A   blame
    B   accuse
    C   indict
    D   dispute

12. Show is to flaunt as drink is to
    A   gulp
    B   spit
    C   gargle
    D   sip

Verbal Skills *(continued)*

13. Confer most nearly means

    A delay
    B discuss
    C forget
    D bury

14. Duress most nearly means

    A cover
    B harmony
    C enthusiasm
    D pressure

15. Every ninth-grade student takes algebra. Paula is in the ninth grade. Paula takes algebra. If the first two statements are true, the third is

    A true
    B false
    C uncertain

16. Vociferous means the *opposite* of

    A evil
    B humble
    C helpful
    D quiet

17. Dam is to flood as medicine is to

    A vitamin
    B pill
    C health
    D illness

18. Which word does *not* belong with the others?

    A emblem
    B badge
    C insignia
    D medal

19. More orchestra members play flute than violin. Fewer orchestra members play tuba than any other instrument. More orchestra members play violin than tuba. If the first two statements are true, the third is

    A true
    B false
    C uncertain

20. Evade most nearly means

    A answer
    B avoid
    C convict
    D ask

21. Which word does *not* belong with the others?

    A hinge
    B yoke
    C marry
    D sever

22. Omit means the *opposite* of

    A include
    B fix
    C undo
    D climb

23. Contemporary most nearly means

    A disliked
    B angry
    C current
    D proper

24. Poke is to finger as inflate is to

    A tire
    B price
    C bubble
    D pump

25. This week, Wendy paid more for gas per gallon than she did last week. Last week, Wendy paid less for gas per gallon than she did two weeks ago. This week, Wendy paid less for gas per gallon than she did two weeks ago. If the first two statements are true, the third is

    A true
    B false
    C uncertain

26. Which word does *not* belong with the others?

    A destiny
    B end
    C fate
    D prophecy

Verbal Skills *(continued)*

27. Which word does *not* belong with the others?

    A peel
    B shell
    C husk
    D pit

28. All gremlins are cute. All male gremlins have black fur. All furry gremlins are cute. If the first two statements are true, the third is

    A true
    B false
    C uncertain

29. Book is to chapter as newspaper is to

    A article
    B press
    C headline
    D magazine

30. Anarchy most nearly means

    A government
    B bottom
    C bridge
    D disorder

31. Emulate most nearly means

    A steal
    B protect
    C liquefy
    D imitate

32. Exemplary means the *opposite* of

    A widespread
    B gloomy
    C faulty
    D uncertain

33. Cocoa is more expensive than tea. Soda is more expensive than cocoa. Coffee is the same price as tea. Coffee is less expensive than soda. If the first three statements are true, the fourth is

    A true
    B false
    C uncertain

34. Which word does *not* belong with the others?

    A hammer
    B bat
    C drill
    D whip

35. Cavity is to brush as cheating is to

    A steal
    B monitor
    C fail
    D punish

36. Retaliation most nearly means

    A revenge
    B gift
    C patriotism
    D greed

37. Crude means the *opposite* of

    A rude
    B satisfied
    C refined
    D liquid

38. Which word does *not* belong with the others?

    A erase
    B eradicate
    C forget
    D delete

39. Malady most nearly means

    A song
    B disease
    C peacemaker
    D supervisor

40. All new books are on the store's main floor. The store carries used books as well as new books. Some of the store's used books are on the main floor. If the first two statements are true, the third is

    A true
    B false
    C uncertain

Verbal Skills (continued)

41. Impair means the *opposite* of

    A retreat
    B explode
    C join
    D improve

42. Agriculture is to food as rescue is to

    A danger
    B victim
    C safety
    D emergency

43. Which word does *not* belong with the others?

    A experience
    B education
    C talent
    D knowledge

44. Which word does *not* belong with the others?

    A carrot
    B apple
    C squash
    D spinach

45. Inept most nearly means

    A fancy
    B hidden
    C insane
    D awkward

46. Renovate means the *opposite* of

    A copy
    B ruin
    C enter
    D approach

47. Louise's house is larger and more expensive than Suzie's house. Suzie's house is more expensive but smaller than Howard's house. Howard's house is larger and more expensive than Louise's house. If the first two statements are true, the third is

    A true
    B false
    C uncertain

48. Savor most nearly means

    A enjoy
    B injure
    C rescue
    D sleep

49. Tree is to shade as bandage is to

    A bleed
    B scrape
    C wrap
    D remove

50. Which word does *not* belong with the others?

    A flashlight
    B lamp
    C bulb
    D lantern

51. Gullible most nearly means

    A tasty
    B trusting
    C seasick
    D thirsty

52. Girls enjoy reading fashion magazines. Boys enjoy reading sports magazines. Girls do not enjoy reading sports magazines. If the first two statements are true, the third is

    A true
    B false
    C uncertain

53. Which word does *not* belong with the others?

    A beam
    B post
    C column
    D pillar

54. Subdue means the *opposite* of

    A borrow
    B empower
    C highlight
    D disrupt

Verbal Skills (continued)

55. Provoke most nearly means

- **A** protect
- **B** assist
- **C** anger
- **D** sweep

56. Blush is to embarrassment as wince is to

- **A** wisdom
- **B** bravery
- **C** flattery
- **D** pain

57. Which word does *not* belong with the others?

- **A** jot
- **B** draw
- **C** scribble
- **D** note

58. Sweetie is fluffier than Boots, but Sweetie sheds less than Tiger. Boots is not as fluffy as Tiger, but Boots sheds more than Tiger. Sweetie sheds more than Boots. If the first two statements are true, the third is

- **A** true
- **B** false
- **C** uncertain

59. Recur most nearly means

- **A** shake
- **B** repeat
- **C** free
- **D** add

60. Disparity means the *opposite* of

- **A** approval
- **B** excitement
- **C** contentment
- **D** similarity

STOP!
If you finish before time runs out, check your work on this section only.

Quantitative Skills (52 Questions) (30 Minutes)

Directions: Choose the best answer to each question.

61. What is the next number in the following series: 12, 24, 36, 48, . . . ?

- **A** 60
- **B** 56
- **C** 72
- **D** 64

62. 2 percent of a number is equal to 2 times 0.2 percent. What is the number?

- **A** 4
- **B** 2
- **C** 0.4
- **D** 0.2

63. Examine (a), (b), and (c) and then choose the correct answer.

- (a) the arithmetic mean (simple average) of 9 and −10
- (b) the arithmetic mean (simple average) of 10 and −9
- (c) the arithmetic mean (simple average) of 2 and −2

- **A** (b) is greater than (c) and less than (a)
- **B** (c) is less than (b) and greater than (a)
- **C** (a) is greater than (c) and less than (b)
- **D** (a) is equal to (b), and (b) is equal to (c)

64. What is the next number in the following series: $-2, -\dfrac{3}{2}, -1, -\dfrac{1}{2}, \ldots$?

- **A** 0
- **B** 1
- **C** $\dfrac{1}{2}$
- **D** −1

65. $\dfrac{5}{4}$ of $\dfrac{4}{5}$ is what fraction of $\dfrac{5}{4}$?

- **A** $\dfrac{5}{4}$
- **B** $\dfrac{15}{16}$
- **C** $\dfrac{4}{5}$
- **D** $\dfrac{1}{2}$

66. What is the missing number in the following series: −4, 5, __, 7, −8, 9, . . . ?

- **A** 6
- **B** −7
- **C** −6
- **D** −5

67. Examine figures (a), (b), and (c) and then choose the correct statement.

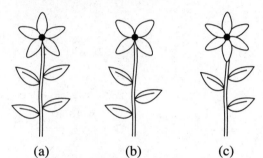

(a)   (b)   (c)

- **A** The number of petals in figure (b) is greater than the number of leaves in figure (a).
- **B** The number of leaves in figure (c) is less than the number of petals in figure (b).
- **C** The number of leaves in figure (b) is equal to the number of petals in figure (a).
- **D** The number of petals in figure (a) is equal to the number of petals in figure (c).

68. What are the next two numbers in the following series: 3, 7, 2, 3, 7, 2, 3, . . . ?

- **A** 2, 3
- **B** 7, 2
- **C** 4, 7
- **D** 7, 3

69. One-third is one-third of what number?

- **A** 1
- **B** $\dfrac{1}{9}$
- **C** $\dfrac{1}{6}$
- **D** $\dfrac{1}{3}$

Quantitative Skills *(continued)*

70. What number is three-fourths added to one-half?

- **A** 1.1
- **B** 1.2
- **C** 1.25
- **D** 0.25

71. Examine (a), (b), and (c) and then choose the best answer.

- (a) 225% of 8
- (b) 75% of 12
- (c) 5% of 20

- **A** (a) × (c) = (b)
- **B** 2(b) × (c) = (a)
- **C** (c) = 4(a) + (b)
- **D** (a) = (b) + (c)

72. What integer is less than eleven-fourths but greater than eleven-tenths?

- **A** 1
- **B** 4
- **C** 3
- **D** 2

73. What is the next number in the following series: 2.4, 2.1, 1.8, 1.5, 1.2, . . . ?

- **A** 0.09
- **B** 1.1
- **C** 0.9
- **D** 1.0

74. What is the missing number in the following series: 9, 3, 1, 18, __, 2, 36, 12, 4?

- **A** 4
- **B** 9
- **C** 6
- **D** 8

75. 40 percent of what number is equal to 10 percent of 40?

- **A** 16
- **B** 10
- **C** 4
- **D** 20

76. Examine the cube and select the best answer.

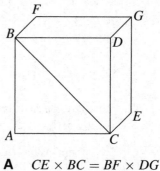

- **A** $CE \times BC = BF \times DG$
- **B** $BF + DC = 3 \times GE$
- **C** $AB + BC > 2 \times CE$
- **D** $DG + AC = BC$

77. What is the next number in the following series: 3, 9, 7, 13, 11, 17, 15, . . . ?

- **A** 19
- **B** 20
- **C** 23
- **D** 21

78. Examine (a), (b), and (c) and then choose the best answer.

- (a) $32 \div \frac{1}{3}(10 - 4)$
- (b) $4(2 \times 3) - 8 \div 2$
- (c) $48 \div \frac{3}{2}(15 - 7)$

- **A** (c) + (a) = (b)
- **B** (b) = 2(c) + (a)
- **C** (a) − (c) = (b)
- **D** (a) = (c) − (b)

79. What is the next letter in the following series: a, b, d, g, k, . . . ?

- **A** o
- **B** n
- **C** q
- **D** p

80. What number is 20% of the average of 20%, 60%, and 70%?

- **A** 10%
- **B** 15%
- **C** 20%
- **D** 12.5%

Quantitative Skills *(continued)*

81. What is the next number in the following series: 13, 12, 14, 11, 15, 10, 16, . . . ?

    A   13
    B   17
    C   9
    D   11

82. What are the next two numbers in the following series: 2, 5, 5, 1, 2, 5, 5, 1, . . . ?

    A   2, 2
    B   5, 1
    C   1, 2
    D   2, 5

83. Examine figures (a), (b), and (c), and then choose the correct statement.

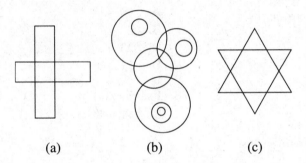

    (a)   (b)   (c)

    A   The number of triangles in figure (c) is greater than the number of circles in figure (b).
    B   The number of triangles in figure (c) equals the number of rectangles in figure (a).
    C   The number of rectangles in figure (a) is less than the number of triangles in figure (c).
    D   The number of circles in figure (b) equals the number of triangles in figure (c).

84. What is the next number in the following series: 15, 30, 10, 40, 8, . . . ?

    A   48
    B   60
    C   25
    D   36

85. What number's square root is the square of 3?

    A   9
    B   27
    C   81
    D   36

86. Four times what number is two less than three-fourths of eight?

    A $\dfrac{7}{2}$
    B   1
    C   3
    D   2

87. Examine (a), (b), and (c) and then choose the best answer.

    (a)   0.2 × 0.2
    (b)   20 × .002
    (c)   0.02 × 2

    A   (b) > (c) > (a)
    B   (c) = (a), and (b) < (a)
    C   (a) = (b) = (c)
    D   (a) = (b), and (c) > (b)

88. What is the next number in the following series: IV, 8, XVI, 32, LXIV, . . . ?

    A   128
    B   156
    C   96
    D   72

89. Which of the three figures below has the largest area?

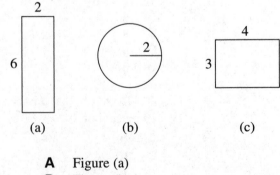

    (a)   (b)   (c)

    A   Figure (a)
    B   Figure (b)
    C   Figure (c)
    D   All three figures are equal in area.

Quantitative Skills *(continued)*

90. Examine (a), (b), and (c) and then choose the correct answer.

(a) $\dfrac{2}{5} - \dfrac{1}{2} + \dfrac{3}{10}$

(b) $\dfrac{5}{6} - \dfrac{4}{3} + \dfrac{7}{12}$

(c) $\dfrac{1}{2} - \dfrac{3}{4} + \dfrac{3}{8}$

A (b) is greater than (c) and less than (a)
B (c) is less than (a) and greater than (b)
C (a) is greater than (c) and less than (b)
D (a) is less than (c) and greater than (b)

91. Examine figures (a), (b), and (c), which show grids of equal size and proportion, and then choose the correct statement.

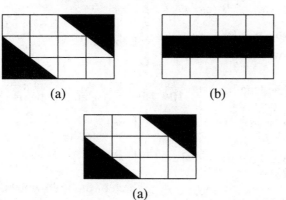

(a)　　　　　(b)

(a)

A The shaded area of figure (a) is less than the shaded area of figure (c).
B The shaded area of figure (b) is less than the shaded area of figure (a).
C The shaded area of figure (a) is equal to the shaded area of figure (c).
D The shaded area of figure (c) is equal to the shaded area of figure (b).

92. What number must you add to both the numerator and denominator of $\dfrac{1}{3}$ to obtain $\dfrac{3}{4}$?

A 7
B 3
C 5
D 9

93. What is the next number in the following series: $\dfrac{16}{2}, \dfrac{30}{4}, \dfrac{24}{3}, 7\dfrac{1}{2}, \dfrac{48}{6}, \dfrac{15}{2}, \ldots$?

A $\dfrac{11}{4}$
B 8
C $\dfrac{12}{5}$
D $\dfrac{30}{4}$

94. Examine (a), (b), and (c).

(a) the reciprocal of $\dfrac{1}{2}$

(b) the reciprocal of $\dfrac{3}{4}$

(c) the reciprocal of $\dfrac{3}{2}$

All of the following are true EXCEPT:

A (a) × (c) = (b)
B (b) + (c) = (a)
C (b) − (c) = (a) ÷ 3
D (a) ÷ 2 = (b) × (c)

95. What is the next number in the following series: $\dfrac{34}{5}, 6\dfrac{1}{5}, \dfrac{28}{5}, 5, 4\dfrac{2}{5}, \ldots$?

A $3\dfrac{4}{5}$
B $\dfrac{23}{5}$
C $3\dfrac{3}{5}$
D $\dfrac{21}{5}$

96. One-fourth of four less than a number is equal to six more than eleven. What is the number?

A $9\dfrac{1}{2}$
B 72
C 6
D 16

Quantitative Skills *(continued)*

97. What number is 150 percent of 350 percent?

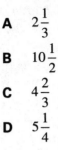

   A $2\dfrac{1}{3}$

   B $10\dfrac{1}{2}$

   C $4\dfrac{2}{3}$

   D $5\dfrac{1}{4}$

98. The figure below shows a square and a circle.

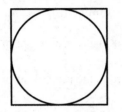

Which of the following statements is true?
   A   The square's perimeter is twice the circle's diameter.
   B   The circle's radius equals the length of a side of the square.
   C   The circle's circumference is less than the square's perimeter.
   D   The area of the square is equal to the area of the circle.

99. Three-fourths is four-fifths of what number?

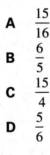

   A $\dfrac{15}{16}$

   B $\dfrac{6}{5}$

   C $\dfrac{15}{4}$

   D $\dfrac{5}{6}$

100. What is the missing number in the following series: 37, 35, 36, 34, __, 33, 34, 32?
   A   34
   B   33
   C   35
   D   32

101. What positive integer multiplied by itself twice is most nearly equal to 100?
   A   4
   B   10
   C   33
   D   5

102. What is the next term in the following series: 14EH, 12GG, 10IF, 8KE, 6MD, ... ?
   A   5OC
   B   4NB
   C   2MK
   D   4OC

103. 13 more than two-thirds of a number is equal to 35. What is the number?
   A   33
   B   17
   C   29
   D   24

104. In (a), (b), and (c) below, $p < 0$ and $q < 0$.
   (a) $|p| + |q|$
   (b) $p + |q|$
   (c) $p - |q|$

Which of the following statements is true?
   A   (a) < (c) < (b)
   B   (b) < (a) < (c)
   C   (c) < (b) < (a)
   D   (a) < (b) < (c)

Quantitative Skills *(continued)*

105. Examine figures (a), (b), and (c), and then choose the correct statement.

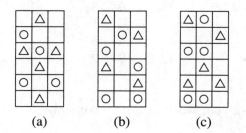

   (a)   (b)   (c)

A   The number of circles in figure (a) equals the number of triangles in figure (c).

B   The number of triangles in figure (a) equals the number of triangles in figure (b).

C   The number of circles in figure (c) equals the number of triangles in figure (a).

D   The number of triangles in figure (b) is greater than the number of circles in figure (b).

106. Examine (a), (b), and (c) and then choose the correct answer.

(a) $\sqrt{81}$

(b) 2^3

(c) 3^2

A   (a) $<$ (b)

B   (c) $>$ (a)

C   (b) $=$ (c)

D   (a) $=$ (c)

107. What number subtracted from -1 is one greater than the sum of -1 and -1?

A   1

B   0

C   2

D -1

108. Assume that $x > 1$, $y > 1$, and $z > 1$ and that x, y, and z are integers. Examine (a), (b), and (c) and then choose the best answer.

(a) $x(y + z)$

(b) $xz + xy$

(c) $x + y + z$

A   (a) is equal to (b) and less than (c)

B   (a) is equal to (b) and to (c)

C   (a) is equal to (c) and greater than (b)

D   (b) is less than (c) and greater than (a)

109. What is the next number in the following series: 100, 50, 25, 12.5, 6.25, . . . ?

A   3.125

B   3.025

C   2.50

D   1.75

110. Examine figures (a), (b), and (c), and then choose the correct statement.

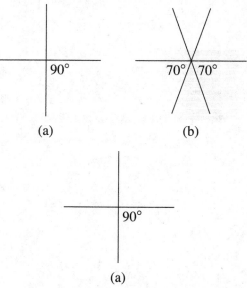

A   Figure (a) contains more right angles than figure (c).

B   Figure (b) contains the same number of 20° angles as figure (c).

C   Figure (c) contains the same number of 70° angles as figure (b).

D   Figure (b) contains more acute angles than figure (c).

Quantitative Skills *(continued)*

111. What are the next two numbers in the following series: 2, 4, 3, 4, 4, 4, 5, 4, . . . ?

- **A**   4, 3
- **B**   3, 4
- **C**   4, 5
- **D**   6, 4

112. What number is 64 divided by the cube root of 64?

- **A**   8
- **B**   16
- **C**   4
- **D**   2

STOP!

If you finish before time runs out, check your work on this section only.

Reading (62 Questions) (25 Minutes)

Comprehension

Directions: Questions 113–152 are based on reading passages. Read the passages and answer the questions.

Questions 113–119 are based on the following passage:

Science involving particles no greater than 100 nanometers in length is called *nanotechnology*. A *nanometer* is one 100 billionth of a meter in length, or about ten times the length of a hydrogen atom.

Nanotechnology is often referred to as the "Next Big Thing" that will make the Internet revolution <u>pale</u> in significance. Nanotechnology is already used to make a variety of new-and-improved consumer products, from televisions and computer monitors to wrinkle cream and sunblock. Scientists working with nano-sized particles are developing super-fast and energy-efficient computer chips, ultra-strong fabrics and building materials, and, more crucially, faster-acting medicines for the treatment of diseases.

When it comes to human health, however, nanotechnology might prove more hazardous than helpful. Studies with laboratory animals suggest that contact with nano-sized particles, which are by definition considered toxic due to their small size, can cause various forms of cancer. Particles so small easily enter a person's bloodstream and central nervous system. Only time and further medical research will tell whether the full potential of nanotechnology will be realized.

113. A hydrogen atom is

   A   about one nanometer in length

   B   longer than a nanometer

   C   shorter than a nanometer

   D   larger than a nano-sized particle

114. As used in the passage, the word <u>pale</u> most nearly means

   A   shrink

   B   boast

   C   faster

   D   continue

115. The author implies that nanotechnology plays its most important role in the

   A   development of consumer products

   B   exploration of outer space

   C   development of faster computer processors

   D   treatment of medical problems

116. According to the passage, nanotechnology is used to develop

   A   cosmetics

   B   genetically modified grains

   C   alcoholic beverages

   D   household cleaning products

117. The author seems worried about

   A   the safety of scientists who work with nano-sized particles

   B   the long-term impact of nanotechnology on human health

   C   government putting a stop to nanotechnology research

   D   the use of nanotechnology to make weapons of mass destruction

118. The author implies that skin contact with nano-sized particles

   A   might cause cancer

   B   lightens the skin

   C   must be avoided at all costs

   D   is less risky than breathing in the particles

119. The main idea of the passage is that

   A   nanotechnology will make the Internet obsolete someday

   B   nobody will benefit from nanotechnology in the long run

   C   nanotechnology's benefits will not come without human cost

   D   the future of nanotechnology depends on government support

Reading *(continued)*

Questions 120–126 are based on the following passage:

Until the twentieth century, art in America was dominated by romanticists. In the nineteenth century, the Hudson River Valley school of painters turned for their inspiration almost entirely to the beauty of nature—the wilderness, mountains, and sea. After the romanticists came the American impressionists, including Inness, Blakelock, and Ryder, who continued in much the same way. Whenever they did paint city scenes, the impressionists focused only on upper-class neighborhoods such as New York City's upper east side.

During the first decade of the twentieth century, a group of artists known as the progressives revolted against this too-narrow focus on the idyllic. Led by Robert Henri, the progressives tried to capture the architectural and industrial ugliness that America's urban landscapes were truly becoming in the industrial age.

But it was the impact of this new age on human beings that the progressives were most interested in portraying. Initially, the political and art establishments refused to accept the progressives, who were part of the bohemian culture of New York's Greenwich Village. But the progressives finally gained acceptance in the art world during the New York City's Armory Show in 1913. It was at this show that their paintings, along with those of the European painters Picasso, Matisse, and Gauguin, who were already widely known in Europe, launched the modernist era of art.

120. Which of the following was NOT an American impressionist painter?

A Hudson
B Ryder
C Inness
D Blakelock

121. The author's attitude toward the progressives is

A realistic
B sympathetic
C critical
D passionate

122. It would be accurate to describe Robert Henri as

A a romantic
B an impressionist
C a realist
D a minimalist

123. A progressive painter of the early twentieth century was most likely to paint

A a seascape
B a character study
C an abstract work
D a work portraying a religious figure

124. As used in the passage, the word idyllic most nearly means

A idealized
B brilliant
C spiritual
D thoughtful

125. Paintings created by the progressives

A appeared in the Armory Show of 1913
B appealed to the art establishment
C were unlike those of Robert Henri
D focused more on scenery than people

126. The passage is mainly about the

A American impressionist painters
B art of the Hudson Valley River school
C influence of Robert Henri
D rise of modern American art

Reading *(continued)*

Questions 127–132 are based on the following selection:

Upon the mention of Afghanistan, most Westerners today think of a <u>forbidding</u> and severe wasteland at the western edge of the Himalayas, devastated by wave upon wave of strife and suffering. The 1979 Russian invasion and the U.S. bombings more than twenty years later are just two recent afflictions the Afghan people have endured in their long and bloody history.

Should the rest of the world give up on this mostly agricultural nation, which is largely in ruins, and simply abandon it? True, invaders have left its agricultural lands barren, farm animals wiped out, and electricity and water systems destroyed. True, generations must pass before the deep-seated distrust its people must surely feel toward younger, mightier nations subsides. But sweep away the land mines, gaze through the fog of war, and look deeply into the eyes of the Afghan people. You will see a colorful <u>pastiche</u> of clans almost too numerous to count, and a proud and strong-willed people with a long and varied heritage far too valuable to see wither from neglect.

127. As used in the selection, the word <u>forbidding</u> is best defined as

A prohibited
B unfriendly
C unpredictable
D mountainous

128. In the selection, the speaker implies that in current-day Afghanistan

A no government exists
B the number of clans is decreasing
C people cannot defend themselves
D producing food is difficult

129. The selection can best be described as

A an explanation
B a debate
C a plea
D a complaint

130. As used in the selection, the word <u>pastiche</u> most nearly means

A village
B assortment
C generation
D population

131. The speaker would strongly agree that the Afghan people are

A pitiful
B ambitious
C optimistic
D determined

132. Among the following, the selection would most likely be an excerpt from

A a speech made at an antiwar rally
B an academic lecture on current world events
C a chapter from a textbook on modern world history
D an article at a famine-relief organization's website

Reading *(continued)*

Questions 133–138 are based on the following passage:

When I was young I used to think that middle-aged people recalled their youth as something seen through a haze. I know better now. The last years that I spent in my native land and my first years in America come back to me with the distinctness of yesterday.

One of my pastimes was to imagine a host of tiny soldiers each the size of my little finger, but alive and real. These I would drill as I saw officers do their men in front of the barracks not far from our home. Or else I would march up and down the room with mother's rolling-pin for a rifle, grunting, ferociously, in Russian: "Left one! Left one! Left one!" in the double capacity of a Russian soldier and of David fighting Goliath.

During my ninth and tenth years, my greatest sport was to play buttons. These we would flip around on some patch of unpaved ground with a little pit for a billiard pocket. My own pockets were usually full of these buttons. As the game was restricted to brass ones from the uniforms of soldiers, my mother had plenty to do to keep those pockets of mine in good repair.

I would spend hours in some secluded spot developing skill for the sport. I gambled passionately and was continually counting my treasure, or running around the big courtyard, jingling it self-consciously. But one day I suddenly wearied of it all and traded my entire hoard for a pocket-knife and some trinkets.

"Don't you care for buttons any more?" mother inquired.

"I can't bear the sight of them," I replied. She shrugged her shoulders smilingly.

133. The passage's narrator

   A   immigrated to America from Russia
   B   grew up in a wealthy family
   C   had few if any friends as a child
   D   was a poor student as a youngster

134. As a child, the narrator probably lived

   A   in a rural area
   B   in a large city
   C   near a factory
   D   near a military base

135. As a young boy, the narrator liked to

   A   listen to his mother tell stories
   B   shop for toys and trinkets
   C   daydream about being in the military
   D   play stickball in the courtyard

136. As a youngster, the narrator was very proud of his

   A   trinkets
   B   brass buttons
   C   pocket knife
   D   toy soldiers

137. As a youngster, the narrator probably

   A   played buttons on the floor of his house
   B   became a skilled button player without practice
   C   wagered his buttons when playing against others
   D   played buttons against his mother's wishes

138. During the narrator's childhood, his mother was

   A   lonely
   B   patient
   C   anxious
   D   happy

Reading *(continued)*

Questions 139–146 are based on the following passage:

The last known case of the smallpox virus was in 1978. But the world is not necessarily rid of the virus forever; it lives on in science laboratories, and the threat of bioterrorism today has caused new concerns about a smallpox epidemic.

Smallpox originated in Africa. The virus traveled to Europe from Arabia via Egypt, while the first outbreak in the U.S. occurred shortly after a new batch of slaves arrived from Africa. The first English-language description of the disease is in an Anglo-Saxon manuscript written during the tenth century. The name "smallpox" was given to the disease in the sixteenth century to distinguish it from chickenpox and from the Great Pox, also called syphilis, both of which had already spread across Europe due mainly to crowded and unsanitary conditions in the cities.

Like syphilis, smallpox bacteria could be carried through the air for considerable distances and could cling for long periods to clothes, books, furniture, and so forth. Europeans came to accept an attack as <u>inevitable</u>. Even in Russia, two million persons died from smallpox in one year. At the end of the eighteenth century, so many faces were permanently pitted from severe smallpox that any woman who had no smallpox marks was considered beautiful. It's no wonder that our public-health officials today are so worried.

139. Smallpox first came to the United States from

  A Africa
  B Continental Europe
  C Russia
  D England

140. Smallpox was

  A easily preventable
  B rarely fatal
  C primarily a women's disease
  D transmitted through the air

141. The smallpox virus

  A does not exist anymore
  B originated in the sixteenth century
  C can still be found in some laboratories
  D is named after the scientist who cured it

142. As used in the passage, the word <u>inevitable</u> most nearly means

  A painful
  B powerful
  C certain
  D widespread

143. According to the passage, one of the symptoms of smallpox was

  A extreme fatigue
  B breathing difficulties
  C hair loss
  D facial scarring

144. Which of the following questions does the passage best answer?

  A How many people altogether have died from smallpox?
  B Why did chickenpox spread throughout Europe?
  C Why is smallpox no longer a commonplace disease?
  D How did smallpox spread to Russia?

145. The name "smallpox" was given to that virus

  A in an Anglo-Saxon manuscript
  B to distinguish it from syphilis
  C before chickenpox became a problem
  D because it afflicted children

146. In the passage, the author's underlying purpose is to

  A caution
  B summarize
  C predict
  D amuse

Reading (continued)

Questions 147–152 are based on the following passage:

The main function of a building is to provide a safe shelter and living space. Beyond this function, however, what should be the goal of architecture? To impress people? To glorify the architect or owner? To create something new for its own sake? An increasing number of architects today—myself included—believe that the <u>overriding</u> goal should be to elevate the human spirit. Architecture designed with this goal in mind is known as *organic* architecture. While the "organic" label is new, the principle is centuries old. The current revival of organic architecture actually began in the middle of the twentieth century with the work of architects such as Frank Lloyd Wright and Spain's Antonio Gaudi.

Organic architecture should not be confused with *green* architecture, in which the primary design concern is with a structure's environmental cost in terms of the natural resources used to build and maintain it. Also, unlike *feng shui* design, which dictates that a building should conform to certain rules of proportion and direction, there's no objective test for whether a building is organic. If people feel more alive in and around it, or even just looking at pictures of it, then it passes as organic.

147. In the passage, the author's primary concern is to

  A compare various forms of architecture
  B explain the meaning of "organic architecture"
  C describe a typical organic building
  D criticize green architecture

148. Which of the following would the author agree should be the most important factor in designing a building?

  A its effect on a person's mood
  B its energy efficiency
  C its overall appearance
  D how much it costs to build

149. As it is used in the passage, the word <u>overriding</u> is best defined as

  A strongest
  B accidental
  C quickest
  D primary

150. A building designed to use energy only from the sun is an example of

  A organic architecture
  B green architecture
  C natural architecture
  D elemental architecture

151. Frank Lloyd Wright

  A helped revive the concept of organic architecture
  B incorporated *feng shui* principles into his designs
  C was a strong advocate of green architecture
  D worked with architect Antonio Gaudi in designing houses

152. Which of the following would probably be most important to an architect applying *feng shui* to a building's design?

  A how to heat and cool the inside of the building
  B whether the building looks like nearby structures
  C a room's ceiling height compared to its length and width
  D the personal tastes and preferences of the building's owner

Reading *(continued)*

Vocabulary

Directions: For questions 153–174, choose the word that is nearest in meaning to the underlined word.

153. an <u>agile</u> athlete

- **A** determined
- **B** strong
- **C** young
- **D** nimble

154. to <u>intimidate</u> an opponent

- **A** battle
- **B** scare
- **C** analyze
- **D** defeat

155. to <u>hoist</u> a crate

- **A** measure
- **B** drop
- **C** lift
- **D** weigh

156. a <u>naive</u> youngster

- **A** spirited
- **B** innocent
- **C** optimistic
- **D** dishonest

157. an <u>arid</u> climate

- **A** dry
- **B** windy
- **C** friendly
- **D** flat

158. to <u>aspire</u> to greatness

- **A** succeed
- **B** envy
- **C** admire
- **D** strive

159. a <u>reclusive</u> celebrity

- **A** conceited
- **B** rich
- **C** famous
- **D** antisocial

160. to <u>construe</u> a sentence

- **A** explain
- **B** change
- **C** write
- **D** spell

161. a helpful <u>mentor</u>

- **A** outline
- **B** guide
- **C** decision
- **D** worker

162. a <u>vital</u> function

- **A** social
- **B** formal
- **C** essential
- **D** boring

163. to <u>replenish</u> a drink

- **A** share
- **B** refuse
- **C** enjoy
- **D** refill

164. a <u>tactful</u> answer

- **A** diplomatic
- **B** correct
- **C** stupid
- **D** complicated

165. a crazy <u>notion</u>

- **A** madman
- **B** sport
- **C** idea
- **D** fact

166. <u>sparse</u> vegetation

- **A** thin
- **B** low
- **C** thick
- **D** dead

Reading *(continued)*

167. to <u>affix</u> a note

   A correct

   B read

   C scribble

   D attach

168. an ugly <u>grimace</u>

   A scene

   B smell

   C face

   D argument

169. an <u>apparent</u> suicide

   A assisted

   B likely

   C unfortunate

   D violent

170. a safe <u>refuge</u>

   A harbor

   B vehicle

   C investment

   D move

171. a <u>devious</u> maneuver

   A delayed

   B sly

   C sudden

   D brilliant

172. to <u>repeal</u> a law

   A vote

   B enact

   C cancel

   D oppose

173. to <u>forage</u> for food

   A work

   B search

   C fight

   D diet

174. a <u>domineering</u> mother

   A pushy

   B loving

   C unmarried

   D patient

STOP!
If you finish before time runs out, check your work on this section only.

Mathematics (64 Questions) (45 Minutes)

Directions: Choose the best answer to each question.

Concepts

175. What value does the digit 4 represent in the decimal number 35.9842?

A $\dfrac{4}{1,000}$

B $\dfrac{4}{10}$

C $\dfrac{4}{100}$

D $\dfrac{4}{10,000}$

176. How many integers are greater than 10 but less than 100?

A 90
B 88
C 91
D 89

177. Which of the following is a quadrilateral?

A hexagon
B triangle
C pentagon
D trapezoid

178. If $a + 2b = b$, then $b =$

A $2ab + b$
B $4ab$
C $3a + 4b$
D $b + 2a$

179. What is the difference between the sum of all even integers between 0 and 101 and the sum of all odd integers between 0 and 100?

A 50
B 0
C 100
D 1

180. In the figure below, $\angle BEC$ is a right angle.

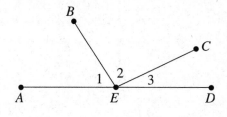

Which of the following statements must be true?

A $m\angle 1 = m\angle 3$
B $m\angle 1 + m\angle 3 = m\angle 2$
C $m\angle 1 + m\angle 2 + m\angle 3 = 360°$
D $m\angle 1 + m\angle 2 = 180°$

181. The number 500,000 is equivalent to

A 5×10^5
B 10×5^6
C 5×10^6
D 10×5^5

182. $x + 2x + 3x =$

A $5x^3$
B $6x$
C $5 + 3x$
D $6x^3$

183. Which of the following represents $\{3,5,8,2,4\} \cap \{2,4,6,8,10\}$?

A $\{2,3,4,5,6,8,10\}$
B $\{1,7,9\}$
C $\{3,5,10\}$
D $\{2,4,8\}$

Mathematics *(continued)*

184. Point *A* appears on the real number line as shown below:

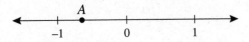

If *x* and *y* are real numbers, point *A* below CANNOT represent

A $x^2 - y^2$
B $x^3 + y^3$
C $x^2 + y^2$
D $x^3 - y^3$

185. Which of the following is a complete and accurate list of the prime factors of 48?

A 2,3
B 2,3,4
C 2,3,6
D 2,3,13

186. If the lengths of two sides of a triangle are 5 and 9, the length of the third side could be

A 9
B 14
C 4
D 15

187. If $\dfrac{P}{2+Q} = R$, then which of the following equals 2*R*?

A $\dfrac{P}{4+2Q}$

B $\dfrac{P}{1+\dfrac{Q}{2}}$

C $\dfrac{2P}{4+Q}$

D $\dfrac{P}{2+\dfrac{2}{Q}}$

188. The population of a certain city is 2,355,002. Rounded to the nearest ten thousand, what is the city's population?

A 2,400,000
B 2,450,000
C 2,356,000
D 2,360,000

189. If one of the angles of an isosceles triangle measures 100°, one of the other angles must measure

A 80°
B 100°
C 40°
D 60°

190. If $x < -1$ and $y > 1$, then it must be true that

A $x + y < 0$
B $xy < -1$
C $x + y > 0$
D $\dfrac{x}{y} > 1$

191. In the figure below, $l_1 \parallel l_2$.

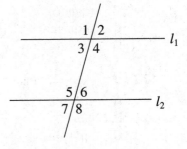

All of the following statements are true EXCEPT:

A $m\angle 2 + m\angle 8 = m\angle 5 + m\angle 3$
B $m\angle 3 + m\angle 7 = m\angle 6 + m\angle 2$
C $m\angle 1 + 180 = m\angle 5 + m\angle 8$
D $m\angle 4 = 180 - m\angle 7$

Mathematics *(continued)*

192. Which of the following is a prime number?

- **A** 69
- **B** 73
- **C** 87
- **D** 55

193. Twenty-five (25) cents is what fraction of 100 dollars?

- **A** $\dfrac{1}{250}$
- **B** $\dfrac{1}{500}$
- **C** $\dfrac{1}{400}$
- **D** $\dfrac{25}{1,000}$

194. If *a*, *b*, and *c* are consecutive integers such that $0 < a < b < c$, which of the following could be an integer?

- **A** $\dfrac{a}{b}$
- **B** $\dfrac{b}{c}$
- **C** $\dfrac{c}{b}$
- **D** $\dfrac{b}{a}$

195. When you increase a cube's height by 100%, you increase its volume by

- **A** 600%
- **B** 400%
- **C** 700%
- **D** 200%

196. Which of the following is the set of common factors of 60 and 36?

- **A** (2,3,6,12,18)
- **B** (2,3,6,12)
- **C** (2,3,4,6,8,12)
- **D** (2,3,4,6,12)

197. The figure below shows a parallelogram.

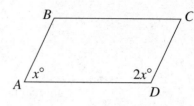

Which of the following statements is true?

- **A** Interior angle *BCD* measures *x°*.
- **B** *AB* is perpendicular to *AD*.
- **C** $x > 90$
- **D** Interior angle *ABC* is an acute angle.

198. If Kira randomly selects an integer from 1 to 50, the probability that she will select a multiple of 3 is

- **A** $\dfrac{1}{6}$
- **B** $\dfrac{3}{10}$
- **C** $\dfrac{8}{25}$
- **D** $\dfrac{1}{5}$

Problem Solving

199. $-1 - (-2) - (-3) =$

- **A** −6
- **B** 4
- **C** 0
- **D** 3

200. A salad costs $3.75, a beverage costs $1.50, and a bagel costs $2.25. Kevin, who has $5.50 to spend, can buy any of the following EXCEPT:

- **A** three beverages
- **B** two beverages and a bagel
- **C** a salad and beverage
- **D** a bagel and salad

Mathematics (continued)

201. Find the value of *y* in the figure below.

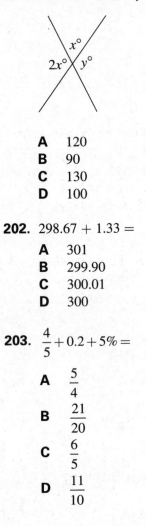

A 120
B 90
C 130
D 100

202. $298.67 + 1.33 =$

A 301
B 299.90
C 300.01
D 300

203. $\frac{4}{5} + 0.2 + 5\% =$

A $\frac{5}{4}$

B $\frac{21}{20}$

C $\frac{6}{5}$

D $\frac{11}{10}$

204. On a cold winter day, the low temperature was $-6°$ and the high temperature was $11°$. Based on these two statistics, what was the average temperature for the day?

A 2.5°
B 0.5°
C 1.5°
D $-0.5°$

205. In the figure below, if the area of triangle *ABC* is 15 square feet, what is the length of *BC*?

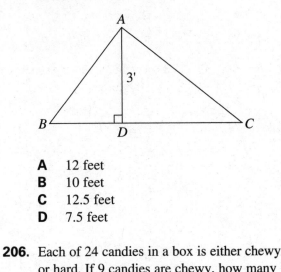

A 12 feet
B 10 feet
C 12.5 feet
D 7.5 feet

206. Each of 24 candies in a box is either chewy or hard. If 9 candies are chewy, how many hard candies must you remove in order for the box to contain the same number of hard candies and chewy candies?

A 9
B 12
C 6
D 15

207. Which of the following is most nearly equal to $\frac{5}{3}$?

A 3.5
B 170%
C 1.6
D 230%

208. For what value of *x* does $\frac{x}{2} = \frac{1}{2}(2 - x)$?

A 1
B 0
C 2
D $\frac{1}{2}$

Mathematics *(continued)*

209. $\dfrac{3^4}{6^4} =$

A $\dfrac{1}{4}$

B $\dfrac{1}{16}$

C $\dfrac{3}{32}$

D $\dfrac{1}{20}$

210. If 30 ounces of coffee beans are removed from a 5-pound bag of coffee beans, the new weight of the bag of coffee beans is

A 50 ounces
B 20 ounces
C 40 ounces
D 60 ounces

211. A circle is divided into four sectors around a central vertex, forming central angles measuring 68°, 82°, and 120°. What is the size of the fourth central angle?

A 70°
B 110°
C 60°
D 90°

212. A team played 25 games in the season, losing 8 more games than it won. Three (3) of the games resulted in ties. How many games did the team win?

A 15
B 12
C 7
D 10

213. Which of the following operations yields the greatest sum?

A $2.1 + \dfrac{3}{5}$

B $0.8 + \dfrac{8}{4}$

C $2.0 + \dfrac{3}{4}$

D $0.1 + \dfrac{5}{2}$

214. The table below shows distances (in miles) between five cities.

	A	B	C	D	E
A		24	63	15	32
B	24		12	40	6
C	63	12		20	27
D	15	40	20		52
E	32	6	27	52	

Which of the following trips, each involving two legs, is longest in distance?

A From D to E, and then to C
B From C to A, and then to D
C From A to E, and then to B
D From D to B, and then to C

215. Fill in the blank to complete the following equation:

$11 - 10 \div (\underline{\quad} \times 3) + 3 = 4$

A $-\dfrac{1}{3}$

B 4

C -4

D $\dfrac{1}{3}$

216. If Stacy drinks 25% of a 16-ounce carton of milk, and then later drinks 25% of the remaining milk, how many ounces of milk are left?

A 11
B 9
C 8
D 10

217. A rectangular plot of land with a length of 150 feet has an area of 12,000 square feet. The width of the plot is

A 80 feet
B 100 feet
C 65 feet
D 135 feet

Mathematics *(continued)*

218. 3.8 − 0.38 =

A 3.42

B 3.5

C 3.58

D 3.3

219. Currently, Pam's age is greater than Terry's age by 15 years. Two years ago, Pam's age was twice Terry's age. What is Pam's current age?

A 28

B 32

C 40

D 36

220. Four points appear on the (x,y) coordinate plane below.

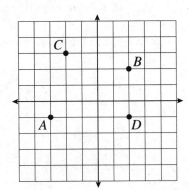

For which of the four points is the product of the point's x and y coordinates least in value?

A Point A

B Point B

C Point C

D Point D

221. After one year, a $700 deposit in a savings account earning simple interest is worth $735. What annual rate of interest did the deposit earn?

A 3.5%

B 2%

C 17.5%

D 5%

222. It took Matt twice the time to drive from home to work as it took him to drive back home from work. If Matt averaged 20 miles per hour (mph) on his drive to work, his average speed for the entire round trip was

A 15.75 mph

B 20 mph

C 26.67 mph

D 30 mph

223. $|-6| - |-6| =$

A −12

B −6

C 0

D 12

224. $\dfrac{26 \times 48}{24 \times 52} =$

A 7

B 13

C 1

D 2

225. A box has sides 4 inches, 5 inches, and 8 inches. All faces of the box are rectangles. How many 1-inch cubes can you pack into the box?

A 200

B 90

C 120

D 160

226. Carrie skates only forward in straight lines. If she skates 10 feet, then turns 90° to the right and skates 6 feet, then turns 180° and skates 10 feet, which of the following series of instructions must Carrie follow in order to return to the spot where she started?

A Turn 90° to the right and skate 10 feet; then turn 180° and skate 4 feet.

B Turn 180° and skate 6 feet; then turn 90° to the right and skate 10 feet.

C Turn 180° and skate 4 feet; then turn 90° to the right and skate 10 feet.

D Turn 90° to the left and skate 10 feet; then turn 90° to the left and skate 6 feet.

Mathematics *(continued)*

227. How many centimeters is equivalent to one fourth of one meter?

A 250
B 40
C 25
D 4

228. Of 27 animals at the zoo, 15 are monkeys. Which of the following fractions expresses the ratio of monkeys to all other animals at the zoo?

A 5:4
B 5:9
C 4:5
D 4:3

229. $2\sqrt{5} + 2\sqrt{125} =$

A $4\sqrt{10}$
B $10\sqrt{5}$
C $8\sqrt{12}$
D $12\sqrt{5}$

Questions 230 and 231 are based on the following information:

The graph below shows the number of visitors to Seaside State Park during each of six months.

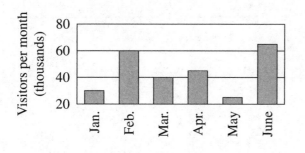

230. The greatest *increase* in the number of park visitors from one month to the next occurred

A from January through February
B from February through March
C from March through April
D from May through June

231. Approximately how many visitors did the park receive altogether during the six months shown?

A 190,000
B 265,000
C 240,000
D 225,000

232. Find the value of the expression $\dfrac{3x}{z} - 4y^z$ when $x = 4$, $y = 3$, and $z = 2$.

A −30
B −6
C 42
D 12

233. $(-3)^3 + (-2)^2 =$

A −23
B 31
C 14
D −5

234. The central angle of one sector of a circle measures 80°. What is the area of the sector as a portion of the circle?

A $\dfrac{1}{5}$
B $\dfrac{2}{5}$
C $\dfrac{3}{8}$
D $\dfrac{2}{9}$

235. Ashley earns $15 per hour and receives a 5% commission on all of her sales. How much did Ashley earn during an 8-hour day during which Ashley's sales totaled $400?

A $160
B $175
C $150
D $140

Mathematics *(continued)*

236. What is the total unit area of the figure below?

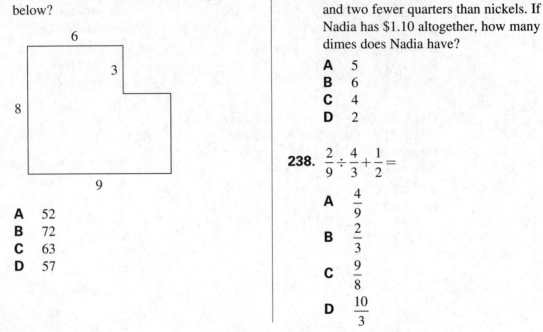

A   52
B   72
C   63
D   57

237. Nadia has two more dimes than quarters, and two fewer quarters than nickels. If Nadia has $1.10 altogether, how many dimes does Nadia have?

A   5
B   6
C   4
D   2

238. $\dfrac{2}{9} \div \dfrac{4}{3} + \dfrac{1}{2} =$

A $\dfrac{4}{9}$

B $\dfrac{2}{3}$

C $\dfrac{9}{8}$

D $\dfrac{10}{3}$

STOP!
If you finish before time runs out, check your work on this section only.

Language (60 Questions) (25 Minutes)

Usage

Directions: For questions 239–278, choose the sentence that contains an error in punctuation, capitalization, or usage. If you find no mistakes, select choice D.

239.
A   I've never seen such a lovely scenery.
B   This conversation is nonsense.
C   Phil suffered a heart attack.
D   No mistake.

240.
A   The new teacher is popular with students.
B   How bad do you want to win?
C   She'd do better if she'd try harder.
D   No mistake.

241.
A   The faster I spin, the dizzier I become.
B   Has Frank been paid yet?
C   He voted against the proposal.
D   No mistake.

242.
A   Have you ever seen *My fair Lady,* starring Audrey Hepburn?
B   The post office sells stamps.
C   He was punished for his disobedience.
D   No mistake.

243.
A   Allison's hair is darker than Angela's.
B   For every dollar won, two were lost.
C   I think your bluffing.
D   No mistake.

244.
A   This blender is the best on the market.
B   Eve mistook my compliment for an insult.
C   The entire meal was homemade.
D   No mistake.

245.
A   No one suspected him.
B   She attends Iowa State university.
C   This heat is more than I can endure.
D   No mistake.

246.
A   I don't believe the witness' story.
B   "Hurry up" she shouted!
C   I live simply—from one day to the next.
D   No mistake.

247.
A   The store is closed up to tomorrow.
B   You must act now to qualify.
C   The team narrowly avoided defeat.
D   No mistake.

248.
A   He didn't understand her point.
B   The pizza was divided into six pieces.
C   The struggle for womens' rights never ends.
D   No mistake.

249.
A   You may choose whomever you want.
B   He tripped on the cord and fell.
C   She was in good spirits.
D   No mistake.

250.
A   Be proud—like an Olympic champion.
B   Let's replay the game over.
C   Nicholas and I are both good students.
D   No mistake.

Language (continued)

251.

A You should not of stolen that book.
B We're closed on Labor Day.
C Adam plans to run for office next year.
D No mistake.

252.

A On the contrary, I do agree.
B My pen just ran out of ink.
C She looked as if she seen a ghost.
D No mistake.

253.

A I prefer raw carrots to cooking them.
B Ronald strongly supports the arts.
C To lose weight, eat less.
D No mistake.

254.

A The tide is at its lowest now.
B She auditioned not just once but twice.
C Sunlight can cause skin cancer.
D No mistake.

255.

A Higher prices lead to a lower savings rate.
B Joan lives near to the airport.
C The company's president resigned.
D No mistake.

256.

A Music needn't be loud to be good.
B The hike exhausted me.
C The sign said Welcome Home!
D No mistake.

257.

A Not one of the hostages was hurt.
B Frankly, I don't agree with you.
C I love gazing to the moon.
D No mistake.

258.

A Now is the time for action.
B You don't believe me, do you.
C Sarah scored high on the exam.
D No mistake.

259.

A He bought a brand new car.
B The sweltering heat drove them inside.
C Millions mourned pope John Paul's death.
D No mistake.

260.

A Wave if you see me approaching.
B She was born in April of 1990.
C Michelle visited her grandmother in Canada.
D No mistake.

261.

A Eric is handsome, compared to Dave.
B Taxes hurt mainly the middle class.
C Jobs are scarce in this city.
D No mistake.

262.

A Railroad ties can be used as steps.
B The drummer's tempo was to fast.
C I found the movie boring.
D No mistake.

263.

A She used to be more talkative.
B The Grand Canyon is in Arizona.
C My strategy is to be defensive.
D No mistake.

264.

A Nika learned to read at an early age.
B That idea makes good sense.
C We rehearse on Thursdays.
D No mistake.

Language (continued)

265.
- **A** I got to leave right now.
- **B** The pie was awfully good.
- **C** She seems quite earnest.
- **D** No mistake.

266.
- **A** According to my watch, I'm early.
- **B** Who has the right of way at this inter-section?
- **C** He armed himself with a gun.
- **D** No mistake.

267.
- **A** Long hair is in fashion.
- **B** He slows if seeing a light ahead.
- **C** His greed outweighs his fear.
- **D** No mistake.

268.
- **A** I cannot wait any longer.
- **B** Karen has only begun to fight.
- **C** That dress fits you nicely.
- **D** No mistake.

269.
- **A** Leland lacks self-confidence.
- **B** My dog has a lot of fleas.
- **C** The chimes ring once in every day.
- **D** No mistake.

270.
- **A** She's feeling healthier and stronger.
- **B** The officer yelled, "freeze, or I'll shoot!"
- **C** Their reunion was an emotional one.
- **D** No mistake.

271.
- **A** I have more to do than you.
- **B** Sequoias are the largest of all trees.
- **C** The prices range from $26 to $42.
- **D** No mistake.

272.
- **A** The integer 3 immediately follows 2.
- **B** A lake is merely a large pond.
- **C** Words are used to makeup sentences.
- **D** No mistake.

273.
- **A** Stuart finished first; just ahead of Arthur.
- **B** By the way, that phone is broken.
- **C** In which month is his birthday: June, July, or August?
- **D** No mistake.

274.
- **A** There are 12 inches in one foot.
- **B** He left without saying nothing.
- **C** I regret having never married.
- **D** No mistake.

275.
- **A** Either you tell him or I will.
- **B** I make no exceptions to my rules.
- **C** Yuki and Jonathan are both trying out for the part.
- **D** No mistake.

276.
- **A** Do you know what sushi tastes like?
- **B** Either Carl or Keith cooked dinner.
- **C** The medicine had no affect on me.
- **D** No mistake.

277.
- **A** Math doesn't interest me much.
- **B** Lisa and me are in the same class.
- **C** I regret having never married.
- **D** No mistake.

278.
- **A** The stoplight had turned red already.
- **B** It's amazingly easy to stub your toe.
- **C** In general, wisdom requires experience.
- **D** No mistake.

Language *(continued)*

Spelling

Directions: For questions 279–288, choose the sentence that contains a spelling error. If you find no spelling errors, select choice D.

279.
  A Do what is politically correct.
  B He feared a conspiracy among his peers.
  C Patience is a virtue.
  D No mistake.

280.
  A Will you acept my invitation?
  B Every problem has a solution.
  C It was your fault; so don't blame me.
  D No mistake.

281.
  A We are staunch supporters of the mayor.
  B Victor drove across the country in four days.
  C Take the elevater to the hotel lobby.
  D No mistake.

282.
  A Leave a message on my answering machine.
  B The orchestra played beautifully.
  C Try to avoid excess coffee consumption.
  D No mistake.

283.
  A Mr. Renfrow committed a serious error.
  B The fog resulted in poor visability.
  C Oscar strode confidently across the room.
  D No mistake.

284.
  A Pat is competing in the big tournament.
  B Next Monday is a federal holiday.
  C You'll sleep easier if you relax.
  D No mistake.

285.
  A The vote was unanimous.
  B Please do not interrupt me.
  C Nadia and Justin own a house jointly.
  D No mistake.

286.
  A The temperature plummeted to ten degrees.
  B Neil is attending Simon's graduation.
  C A farm tractor is easy to operate.
  D No mistake.

287.
  A I would like a receipt for my purchase.
  B Let your conscience be your guide.
  C This homework assignment is challenging.
  D No mistake.

288.
  A I appreciate the importance of this election.
  B Those two teams are arch rivals.
  C The editorial contained many false acusations.
  D No mistake.

Language (continued)

Composition

Directions: For questions 289–298, follow the directions for each question.

289. Choose the best word or words to join the thoughts together.

Your baby boy gets bigger every day, _____ you probably buy new clothes for him quite often.

A otherwise
B since
C and so
D or else

290. Which of the following expresses the idea most clearly?

A Greatness, which seems to be most young geniuses' destiny, is rarely achieved.
B Most young geniuses that seem destined for greatness never achieve it.
C The greatness that young geniuses seem destined for, in most cases, is never achieved.
D Achieving greatness is never achieved by most young geniuses that seem destined for it.

291. Choose the group of words that best completes the sentence.

Because of the noise, _____.

A my concentration was impossible.
B to concentrate was impossible for me.
C it was impossible for me to concentrate.
D to concentrate was an impossibility for me.

292. Choose the best word with which to begin the sentence.

_____, the British forces arrived at the battle scene after the massacre of their American allies had already occurred.

A Undoubtedly
B Consequently
C Historically
D Unfortunately

293. Choose the best word or words to join the thoughts together.

As a natural resource, water is becoming increasingly scarce; _____, large corporations see the profit potential of water and are now battling for control over it.

A as a result
B moreover
C in contrast
D specifically

294. Which is the best place to insert the sentence "A geyser is much different than a volcano" in the following paragraph?

(1) Geysers spout steam into the air. (2) This steam comes from boiling water beneath the ground. (3) Volcanoes, on the other hand, spew gas and ash formed by burning molten lava. (4) Also, lava can seep through a volcano's cracks and through its open crater.

A before sentence 1
B between sentences 2 and 3
C between sentences 3 and 4
D after sentence 4

Language (continued)

295. Which topic is best for a one-paragraph theme?

   A How Movies are Made
   B The Death of Abraham Lincoln
   C The Fall of the Roman Empire
   D none of the above

296. Which of the following expresses the idea most clearly?

   A The process of gerrymandering, which is the redrawing of boundaries of voting districts, is sometimes used by lawmakers for partisan political purposes.
   B The process of gerrymandering is redrawing boundaries of voting districts. It's used by lawmakers for partisan political purposes sometimes.
   C Gerrymandering, a process by which boundaries of voting districts are redrawn, is sometimes used by lawmakers for partisan political purposes.
   D Lawmakers sometimes use gerrymandering for partisan political purposes, which involves redrawing the boundaries of voting districts.

297. Which sentence does *not* belong in the following paragraph?

   (1) Most people have never donated blood, even though it's easy to do. (2) Many people are afraid to give blood; however, donating blood is usually safe. (3) The blood type of the donor and recipient must match. (4) The human body can replace a pint of blood in less that a week.

   A sentence 1
   B sentence 2
   C sentence 3
   D sentence 4

298. Which of the following sentences best fits the topic "The Warning Signs of Global Warming"?

   A Today's fuel-efficient hybrid cars are helping to reduce carbon dioxide emissions that contribute to global warming.
   B Large industrial companies have little incentive to voluntarily reduce the amount of harmful pollutants they emit into the atmosphere.
   C The entire world looks to the U.S. for leadership in helping to prevent global warming.
   D The number of cases of skin cancer from exposure to unfiltered sunlight is increasing at an alarming rate.

STOP!
If you finish before time runs out, check your work on this section only.

HSPT PRACTICE TEST 2

Answer Key

Verbal Skills				Quantitative Skills			
1.	D	31.	D	61.	A	87.	C
2.	B	32.	C	62.	D	88.	A
3.	A	33.	A	63.	B	89.	B
4.	C	34.	C	64.	A	90.	B
5.	C	35.	B	65.	C	91.	A
6.	A	36.	A	66.	C	92.	C
7.	B	37.	C	67.	B	93.	B
8.	A	38.	C	68.	B	94.	D
9.	A	39.	B	69.	A	95.	A
10.	B	40.	C	70.	C	96.	B
11.	D	41.	D	71.	B	97.	D
12.	A	42.	C	72.	D	98.	C
13.	B	43.	C	73.	C	99.	A
14.	D	44.	B	74.	C	100.	C
15.	A	45.	D	75.	B	101.	D
16.	D	46.	B	76.	C	102.	D
17.	D	47.	B	77.	D	103.	A
18.	D	48.	A	78.	A	104.	C
19.	A	49.	C	79.	D	105.	C
20.	B	50.	C	80.	A	106.	D
21.	D	51.	B	81.	C	107.	B
22.	A	52.	C	82.	D	108.	A
23.	C	53.	A	83.	D	109.	A
24.	D	54.	B	84.	A	110.	D
25.	C	55.	C	85.	C	111.	D
26.	D	56.	D	86.	B	112.	B
27.	D	57.	B				
28.	A	58.	B				
29.	A	59.	B				
30.	D	60.	D				

HSPT PRACTICE TEST 2

Answer Key *(continued)*

Reading				Mathematics			
113.	C	144.	A	175.	A	207.	B
114.	A	145.	B	176.	D	208.	A
115.	D	146.	A	177.	D	209.	B
116.	A	147.	B	178.	C	210.	A
117.	B	148.	A	179.	A	211.	D
118.	A	149.	D	180.	B	212.	C
119.	C	150.	B	181.	A	213.	B
120.	A	151.	A	182.	B	214.	A
121.	B	152.	C	183.	D	215.	D
122.	C	153.	D	184.	C	216.	B
123.	B	154.	B	185.	A	217.	A
124.	A	155.	C	186.	A	218.	A
125.	C	156.	B	187.	B	219.	B
126.	D	157.	A	188.	D	220.	C
127.	B	158.	D	189.	C	221.	D
128.	D	159.	D	190.	B	222.	A
129.	C	160.	A	191.	C	223.	C
130.	B	161.	B	192.	B	224.	C
131.	D	162.	C	193.	C	225.	D
132.	D	163.	D	194.	D	226.	C
133.	A	164.	A	195.	C	227.	C
134.	D	165.	C	196.	D	228.	A
135.	C	166.	A	197.	A	229.	D
136.	B	167.	D	198.	C	230.	D
137.	C	168.	C	199.	B	231.	B
138.	B	169.	B	200.	D	232.	A
139.	A	170.	A	201.	A	233.	A
140.	D	171.	B	202.	D	234.	D
141.	C	172.	C	203.	B	235.	D
142.	C	173.	B	204.	A	236.	C
143.	D	174.	A	205.	B	237.	C
				206.	C	238.	B

HSPT PRACTICE TEST 2

Answer Key *(continued)*

Language

239.	**A**	269.	**C**
240.	**B**	270.	**B**
241.	**B**	271.	**D**
242.	**A**	272.	**C**
243.	**C**	273.	**A**
244.	**D**	274.	**B**
245.	**B**	275.	**B**
246.	**B**	276.	**C**
247.	**A**	277.	**B**
248.	**C**	278.	**D**
249.	**D**	279.	**D**
250.	**B**	280.	**A**
251.	**A**	281.	**C**
252.	**C**	282.	**D**
253.	**A**	283.	**B**
254.	**D**	284.	**A**
255.	**B**	285.	**B**
256.	**C**	286.	**C**
257.	**C**	287.	**D**
258.	**B**	288.	**C**
259.	**C**	289.	**C**
260.	**D**	290.	**B**
261.	**A**	291.	**C**
262.	**B**	292.	**D**
263.	**D**	293.	**A**
264.	**D**	294.	**A**
265.	**A**	295.	**B**
266.	**D**	296.	**C**
267.	**B**	297.	**C**
268.	**D**	298.	**D**

HSPT PRACTICE TEST 2

Answers and Explanations

Verbal Skills

1. **D** The words *compute, figure,* and *reckon* are all used to refer to the act of calculating—quite the opposite of making a *guess.*

2. **B** A host is the person in charge of a party, like a judge is the person in charge of a trial.

3. **A** *Lucrative* means "profitable or fruitful," as in a lucrative business deal.

4. **C** A *director, conductor,* or *guide* is someone who leads others. The word *inventor* does not fit this definition at all.

5. **C** Neither of the first two statements provides any information about Randy. Therefore, it is impossible to know whether Bill scored more points than Randy.

6. **A** You pluck the string of a guitar in order for the guitar to make a musical sound. Similarly, you strike a key of a piano in order for the piano to make a musical sound.

7. **B** *Reclined* (an adjective here) means "leaned back or relaxed." Upright means "erect or vertical."

8. **A** The words *rogue, outlaw,* and *villain* all refer to a person who commits evil, dastardly, or unlawful acts. The word *warrior,* which refers to someone who goes to war, does not fit this definition.

9. **A** To *refute* is to disprove, the opposite of *prove.*

10. **B** We know that W marched behind X, who in turn marched behind Y. Therefore, W must have marched behind Y, and the statement is false.

11. **D** The words *blame, accuse,* and *indict* are all synonyms that mean "to assign fault or guilt to someone." The verb *dispute,* which means "disagree with," does not fit this definition.

12. **A** To flaunt is to show in an obvious and boastful way. So, flaunting is an extreme manner of showing. Similarly, gulping—drinking eagerly and audibly—is an extreme manner of drinking.

13. **B** To *confer* is to discuss or consult.

14. **D** *Duress* means "coercion or threat." For example, a confession made under undue pressure is said to be made under duress.

15. **A** We know that all ninth-graders take algebra. Since Paula is in the ninth grade, she must take algebra.

16. **D** *Vociferous* means "noisy or clamorous," just the opposite of *quiet.*

17. **D** A dam can either prevent or stop flooding, just as medicine can either prevent or cure an illness.

18. **D** A *badge,* a *symbol,* and an *insignia* all serve as symbols or signs representing a person or institution. Although a *medal* is a type of symbol, it usually represents a victory or other accomplishment.

19. **A** Because fewer members play the tuba than any other instrument, there must be fewer tuba players than violin players. (You don't need the first sentence to conclude that the third sentence is true.)

20. **B** To *evade* is to elude, dodge, or avoid.

Answers and Explanations *(continued)*

21. **D** *Hinge, yoke,* and *marry* all mean to connect or to join other things. The word *sever* means just the opposite: to cut apart or away from.

22. **A** To *omit* is to exclude or leave out, the opposite of *climb.*

23. **C** One meaning of *contemporary* is "present-day." For example, literature written during the present time is referred to as "contemporary literature." The word *current* is a good synonym.

24. **D** A finger is commonly used to poke, just as a pump is commonly used to inflate (a tire or balloon, for example).

25. **C** All we know is that Wendy paid a higher price for gas last week than she did either this week or two weeks ago.

26. **D** The words *destiny, hope,* and *fate* all refer to the future itself, whereas a *prophecy* is a prediction or foretelling of the future.

27. **D** A *peel,* a *shell,* and a *husk* are outer layers (skins) of certain fruits, vegetables, and nuts. A *pit,* however, is not an outer layer; it's found inside, usually at the center, of certain fruits.

28. **A** The first statement tells us that *all* gremlins are cute; no exceptions are given. This statement alone is sufficient to conclude that furry gremlins are cute.

29. **A** A book is a whole that is usually made up of many parts called chapters. Similarly, a newspaper is a whole that is made up of many articles.

30. **D** *Anarchy* means "lawlessness,"—in other words, the absence of any government or civil order.

31. **D** To *emulate* is to pattern after or imitate. For example, a person might try be like, or emulate, a hero or role model.

32. **C** Exemplary means "flawless or ideal," quite contrary to something that is *faulty.*

33. **A** Given that soda is more expensive than cocoa, which is more expensive than tea, soda must be more expensive than tea. Since tea and coffee are the same price, soda is also *more* expensive than coffee.

34. **C** To use a *hammer, bat,* or *whip,* you swing the tool and it strikes its object. Using a *drill,* however, does not involve a swinging motion, nor does a drill strike or hit its object.

35. **B** You might help prevent a cavity by brushing your teeth. Similarly, you might prevent cheating during a test by monitoring (watching closely) the test takers during the exam.

36. **A** *Retaliation* means "vengeance, revenge, or getting even."

37. **C** *Crude* means "rugged, coarse, or raw," just the opposite of *refined,* which means "polished, purified, or distilled."

38. **C** The words *erase, eradicate,* and *delete* each involve an act of removing something— for example, written words on paper. The word *forget* does not convey this idea at all.

39. **B** A *malady* is an affliction or illness.

40. **C** All we know for certain about that main floor is that we can find new books there.

41. **D** To *impair* is to lessen, damage, or worsen, the opposite of *improve.*

Answers and Explanations *(continued)*

42. **C** Food is the intentional result of agriculture, which is the process of growing crops. Similarly, safety is the intentional result of a rescue, which is the act of saving someone or something from danger.

43. **C** *Talent* is an innate, or inborn, trait. On the other hand, *experience, education,* and *knowledge* are all acquired during life.

44. **B** Each word except for *apple* names a vegetable.

45. **D** *Inept* means "ill-suited or awkward."

46. **B** To *renovate* is to "renew, remake, or restore," just the opposite of *ruin,* which means "demolish, wreck, or destroy."

47. **B** We know that Louise's house is more expensive than Suzie's house, which in turn is more expensive than Howard's house. Therefore, Howard's house must be *less* expensive than Louise's house—and at least part of the third statement is false.

48. **A** One meaning of the word savor is "enjoy, appreciate, or relish." For example, a gourmet meal is something that you might *savor.*

49. **C** One possible function or use of a tree is to shade—a lawn, for example. Similarly, one possible way to use a bandage is to wrap—an arm or finger, for example.

50. **C** The words *flashlight, lamp,* and *lantern* each refer to a distinct kind of lighting device. A *bulb* is what you insert into any of these three devices.

51. **B** A *gullible* person is someone who is naive, innocent, or trusting.

52. **C** Just because girls enjoy reading one type of magazine, we cannot conclude that they do not enjoy reading another type of magazine as well.

53. **A** Each of the four words names a structural element used in buildings. However, a *beam* is horizontally oriented, while the other three elements are vertically oriented.

54. **B** To *subdue* is to defeat, conquer, or overcome. To *empower* is to "strengthen or fortify."

55. **C** To *provoke* is to annoy, anger, or vex.

56. **D** Blushing is an outward sign of embarrassment, just as wincing is an outward sign of pain.

57. **B** The words *jot, scribble,* and *note* all describe an informal style of writing, which is obviously quite distinct from *drawing.*

58. **B** We know that Tiger sheds more than Sweetie, and that Boots sheds more than Tiger. Therefore, Boots must shed more than Sweetie, and the third statement is false.

59. **B** To *recur* is to happen or occur again. The word *repeat* is a close synonym.

60. **D** *Disparity* means "difference, disproportion, or dissimilarity," contrary to *similarity,* which means "resemblance."

Quantitative Skills

61. **A** Add 12 to each number to obtain the next.

62. **D** Express the statement as an algebraic equation (convert percents to decimal numbers), and then solve for the answer (x): $0.02x = 2 \times 0.002$; $0.02x = 0.004$, $20x = 4$; $x = \dfrac{1}{5}$, or 0.2.

63. **B** To make the comparisons, you need only determine the sign of each arithmetic mean: (a) < 0; (b) > 0; (c) = 0.

Answers and Explanations *(continued)*

64. **A** Add $\frac{1}{2}$ to each number to obtain the next one: $-\frac{1}{2} + \frac{1}{2} = 0$.

65. **C** $\frac{5}{4} \times \frac{4}{5} = 1$.

66. **C** The series lists consecutive integers, except that the signs alternate (between positive and negative).

67. **B** Figure (a) contains 4 leaves and 5 petals. Figure (b) contains 3 leaves and 4 petals. Figure (c) contains 3 leaves and 6 petals.

68. **B** The three-term series 3-7-2 simply repeats itself.

69. **A** Let x equal the missing number: $\left(\frac{1}{3}\right)(x) = \frac{1}{3}$; $x = 1$.

70. **C** $\frac{3}{4} + \frac{1}{2} = \frac{3}{4} + \frac{2}{4} = \frac{5}{4}$, or 1.25.

71. **B** (a) = 18; (b) = 9; (c) = 1.

72. **D** Convert to fractions: $\frac{11}{10} = 1\frac{1}{10}$, and $\frac{11}{4} = 2\frac{3}{4}$. The only integer between these two numbers is 2.

73. **C** Subtract 0.3 from each term to obtain the next one.

74. **C** In each consecutive group of three terms, you divide by 3 to obtain the next number. The number 18 begins the second group of three terms.

75. **B** Express the statement as an algebraic equation (convert percents to decimals or fractions), and then solve for the answer (x): $\left(\frac{4}{10}\right)(x) = \left(\frac{1}{10}\right)(40)$; $\left(\frac{4}{10}\right)(x) = 4$; $x = 10$.

76. **C** Because the figure shows a cube, all sides are congruent (equal in length). The length of diagonal *BC* must be greater than the length of any single side, but less than twice the length of any side.

77. **D** To determine successive numbers, alternate between two operations: adding 6 and subtracting 2.

78. **A** (a) = 16; (b) = 20; (c) = 4.

79. **D** After skipping one letter of the alphabet, the series skips two letters, then skips three letters, and so on. After k, the series should skip past four letters—l, m, n, and o—to p.

80. **A** To find the average, add terms and divide by 3: $\frac{(20\% + 60\% + 70\%)}{3} = \frac{150\%}{3} = 50\%$. Next, multiply: 20% of 50% = $0.2 \times 0.5 = 0.1$, or 10%.

81. **C** Beginning with the first term (13), each alternate term is an increase of 1: 13-14-15-16. Beginning with the second term (12), each alternate term is a decrease of 1: 12-11-10-9.

82. **D** The four-term series 2-5-5-1 simply repeats itself.

83. **D** Figure (a) contains 11 rectangles; figure (b) contains 8 circles; figure (c) contains 8 triangles.

84. **A** You *multiply* the first term (15) by *2* to obtain the second (30). You *divide* the second term (30) by *3* to obtain the third term (10). The pattern here is that, to obtain successive terms, you alternative multiplication with division, using consecutive integers.

85. **C** The square of 3 is 9, and the square of 9 is 81.

Answers and Explanations *(continued)*

86. **B** Convert the verbal equation to an equation with numbers, and then solve for the missing number (x):

$$4x + 2 = \frac{3}{4} \times 8$$

$$4x = 6 - 2$$

$$4x = 4$$

$$x = 1$$

87. **C** (a) = 0.04; (b) = 0.04; (c) = 0.04.

88. **A** Multiply each number by 2 to obtain the next number. (IV = 4; XVI = 16; LXIV = 64.)

89. **B** The area of figure (a) = $6 \times 2 = 12$. The area of figure (c) = $3 \times 4 = 12$. The area of figure (b) = $\pi 2^2 = 4\pi \approx (4)(3.1) > 12$.

90. **B** (a) = $\frac{1}{5}$; (b) = $\frac{1}{12}$; (c) = $\frac{1}{8}$.

91. **A** Each figure is divided into a grid of 12 congruent squares. The shaded area in figure (a) includes 2 squares and half of each of 4 squares—the equivalent of 4 squares altogether. The shaded area in figure (b) accounts for 4 squares. The shaded area in figure (c) is the equivalent of $4\frac{1}{2}$ squares (half of each of 9 squares). Therefore, the amount of shaded area is the same in all three figures.

92. **C** $\frac{(1+5)}{(3+5)} = \frac{6}{8}$, or $\frac{3}{4}$.

93. **B** The terms in the series alternate between two values—8 and $7\frac{1}{2}$.
$$\left(\frac{16}{2} = \frac{24}{3} = \frac{48}{6} = 8 \right)$$

94. **D** The product of a number and its reciprocal is 1. Thus, (a) = 2, (b) = $\frac{4}{3}$, and (c) = $\frac{2}{3}$.
Choices A, B, and C provide accurate statements. However, the statement in choice D is false: $2 \div 2 \neq \frac{4}{3} \times \frac{2}{3}$.

95. **A** Subtract $\frac{3}{5}$ from each number to obtain the next one: $4\frac{2}{5} - \frac{3}{5} = \frac{22}{5} - \frac{3}{5} = \frac{19}{5}$ or $3\frac{4}{5}$.

96. **B** Express the statement as an algebraic equation, and then solve for the answer (x):
$\frac{1}{4}(x-4) = 6 + 11$; $\frac{x}{4} - 1 = 17$; $\frac{x}{4} = 18$; $x = 72$.

97. **D** Convert to fractions, then multiply:
$150\% \times 350\% = \frac{3}{2} \times \frac{7}{2} = \frac{21}{4}$, or $5\frac{1}{4}$.

98. **C** The perimeter of a square is four times the length of any side S: $4 \times S$. The circle's diameter equals the length of any side of the square (S). The circle's circumference is $\pi \times S$; Since $\pi < 4$, the circle's circumference is less than the square's perimeter, and statement C must be true.

99. **A** Let x equal the missing number:
$\left(\frac{4}{5}\right)(x) = \frac{3}{4}$; $x = \left(\frac{3}{4}\right)\left(\frac{5}{4}\right)$; $x = \frac{15}{16}$.

100. **C** Alternate between two operations: subtracting 2 and adding 1.

101. **D** $5 \times 5 \times 5 = 125$. ($4 \times 4 \times 4 = 64$, which is not as close to 100.)

Answers and Explanations *(continued)*

102. **D** In successive terms, numbers decrease by 2 (14-12-10-8-6-4). The letters in the second position progress alphabetically, skipping one letter: E-G-I-K-M-*O*. The letters in the third position progress in reverse alphabetical order: H-G-F-E-D-*C*.

103. **A** Express the statement as an algebraic equation, and then solve for the answer (*x*):
$$13 + \frac{2}{3}x = 35; \frac{2}{3}x = 22; x = 22 \times \frac{3}{2} = 33.$$

104. **C** The absolute value of any negative number (such as *p* and *q*) is positive (greater than 0). Thus, (a) must be greater than either (b) or (c), and (c) must be less than (b).

105. **C** Figure (a) contains 5 triangles; figure (c) contains 5 circles.

106. **D** (a) = 9; (b) = 8; (c) = 9.

107. **B** Express the statement as an algebraic equation, and then solve for the answer (*x*):
$-1 - x - 1 = -1 + (-1); -2 - x = -2;$
$-x = 0; x = 0.$

108. **A** The expression in (b) simply restates the expression in (a), distributing *x* to both *y* and *z*. Thus, (a) = (b). Because (a), (b), and (c) are all integers greater than 1, (c) must be less than (a) and (b).

109. **A** Divide each number by 2 to obtain the next one.

110. **D** An acute angle measures between 0° and 90°. Figure (b) contains six acute angles, while figure (c) contains only four acute angles. Thus, statement D is correct. Figures (a) and (c) each contains four right (90°) angles. Figure (b) contains four 70° angles and two 40° angles (but no 20° angles). Figure (c) contains two 70° angles (formed by the same two lines) and two 20° angles (formed by the same two lines).

111. **D** Successive terms alternate between the number 4 and a series of consecutive integers: 2-3-4-5-6.

112. **B** The cube root of 64 = 4. (4 × 4 × 4 = 64.)
$64 \div 4 = 16.$

Reading

113. **C** In the first paragraph, the author informs us that the length of a nanometer is about 10 times that of a hydrogen atom. Thus, a hydrogen atom is shorter than a nanometer.

114. **A** The sentence's point is that the potential of nanotechnology is so great and far-reaching that we might soon look back on the Internet as comparatively insignificant—in other words, its importance will seem to *shrink*.

115. **D** The author characterizes the development of fast-acting medicines for treating diseases as "more crucial"—in other words, more important—than other developments.

116. **A** Wrinkle cream and sunblock are two types of cosmetics.

117. **B** The author devotes the entire third paragraph to expressing concern about the nanotechnology's potential threat to public health.

118. **A** Skin products made with nano-sized particles might seep into the bloodstream, which the author strongly implies causes cancer in laboratory animals and might cause cancer in humans as well.

119. **C** In the second paragraph, the author lists the benefits of nanotechnology. Then, in the third paragraph, the author points out its potential human costs (cancer and other health problems). The passage's final sentence, which choice C essentially paraphrases, sums up the author's main point nicely.

Answers and Explanations *(continued)*

120. **A** In the first paragraph, the author lists Inness, Blakelock, and Ryder all as American impressionists. In the passage, the word *Hudson* refers to the Hudson River Valley, which is a place, not a person.

121. **B** In the first sentence of the second paragraph, the author refers to the focus of American art prior to the progressive movement as too narrow. As this seems to be the author's personal opinion, she probably would have been sympathetic to (supportive of) the progressive movement.

122. **C** According to the passage, Henri and the progressives revolted against the romanticism and impressionism that had dominated the American art scene, determining to portray what the American landscape was truly becoming. Accordingly, it would be accurate to describe Henri as a "realist."

123. **B** In the third paragraph, the author explains that Henri and the progressives were primarily interested in showing the impact of the industrial age on human beings. We can infer that the progressives intended their paintings primarily as character studies.

124. **A** The progressives revolted against the romanticists and impressionists, who chose to paint an idealized picture of the world, in which all appeared perfect, ignoring life's ugly and unpleasant aspects.

125. **C** In the third paragraph, the author tells us that the progressives gained a foothold into mainstream art at the Armory Show of 1913, where their paintings helped launch a new era in art.

126. **D** In the passage, the author talks about how the progressive movement emerged as a reaction to established art of the time, and then how it gained prominence in the art world. Choice D sums it all up nicely.

127. **B** In this sentence, the author is attempting to impress the reader of how harsh the environment is throughout Afghanistan. The word *unfriendly* is often used to describe such an environment, and so substituting this word for *forbidding* makes perfect sense.

128. **D** The speaker tells us that Afghanistan's farm lands and farm animals have been destroyed. Accordingly, it must be difficult for the nation, which is almost entirely agricultural, to produce food.

129. **C** In the selection, the speaker marvels at the rich traditions and pride of the Afghan people and wonders how the rest of the world can possibly allow this civilization to wither away. Implicitly, the speaker is appealing to those who are listening to help save Afghanistan and its people, a *plea* for help on their behalf.

130. **B** In the sentence, the speaker refers to the Afghan people as many, many different clans, each with its own distinct features and heritage. Also, in the next sentence the speaker refers to their "varied" heritage. The word *assortment* would fit nicely in place of *pastiche,* which means "medley or potpourri (variety or assortment)."

131. **D** At the end of the passage, the speaker refers to the Afghan people as "proud" and "strong-willed." These adjectives, along with the fact they have faced so much hardship, strongly suggest that they very *determined* to survive as a people.

132. **D** The speaker's point of view is that of a person concerned mainly with human welfare and speaking as an advocate for the alleviation of widespread hunger and suffering.

133. **A** At the beginning of the passage, the narrator mentions his "native land" and his "first years in America." Later, he mentions ordering his imaginary toy soldiers about in Russian. Clearly, the narrator immigrated to America from Russia.

Answers and Explanations *(continued)*

134. **D** The narrator talks about using brass buttons from soldiers' uniforms for the sport of buttons. He also mentions seeing soldiers going through their drills in front of their barracks, not far from his house. Obviously, he lived near a military base.

135. **C** The narrator tells us that one of his favorite pastimes was to imagine that he had toy soldiers, and then bark out commands to them as if he were their leader.

136. **B** The narrator talks about continually "counting his treasure" (his buttons) and "jingling it self-consciously." Obviously, his button collection was very important to him and he was no doubt quite proud of it.

137. **C** In recounting the sport of buttons, the narrator tells us that he "gambled passionately" and would continually count his "treasure" (his buttons). From this account, we can infer that, in a game of buttons, the winner's prize was the opponent's buttons themselves.

138. **B** The narrator kept his mother busy mending his pockets, which probably would tear open frequently from the weight of his button collection. When he suddenly lost interest in the buttons altogether, rather than expressing frustration or anger that she had spent so much time mending his pockets because of the buttons, his mother simply smiled. Clearly, then, the narrator's mother was very *patient* with her son.

139. **A** In the second paragraph, the author tells us that "the first outbreak in the U.S. occurred shortly after a new batch of slaves arrived from Africa."

140. **D** According to the passage, smallpox bacteria could be carried through the air for considerable distances.

141. **C** In the first paragraph, the author mentions that the smallpox virus "lives on today" in some science laboratories.

142. **C** The main gist of the last two paragraphs is that almost no person could be sure to escape smallpox, which seemed to spread everywhere and affect nearly everybody. Within this context, it makes perfect sense that Europeans accepted a smallpox attack as *certain,* or as the passage states, *inevitable.*

143. **D** In the third paragraph, the author mentions the disfigured, pitted faces of smallpox victims.

144. **A** In the second paragraph, the author tells us that chickenpox spread across Europe due mainly to crowded and unsanitary conditions in the cities.

145. **B** In the second paragraph, the author tells us that the name "was given to the disease . . . to distinguish it from . . . the Great Pox, or syphilis. . . ."

146. **A** The author devotes most of the passage to discussing the history of smallpox. Nevertheless, the first paragraph and the closing sentence together give us the clear impression that the author's larger purpose in this passage, rather than to simply recount historical events, is to alert, or *caution,* us about renewed dangers.

147. **B** In the first paragraph, the author provides a basic definition of the term "organic architecture." Then, in the second paragraph, the author distinguishes organic architecture from green architecture and *feng shui* to help the reader understand what organic architecture is, and what it is not.

148. **A** In the first paragraph, the author informs us that she is an architect who, like a growing number of architects today, believes that one of the chief goals of architecture is to elevate the human spirit. Accordingly, the author would probably agree that how a building affect's a person's mood is very important.

Answers and Explanations *(continued)*

149. **D** Choice D provides the only word that makes sense in the context of the sentence as well as the passage as a whole.

150. **B** The goal of green architecture is to design a building in a way that helps conserve natural resources. Using solar energy would be consistent with that goal.

151. **A** According to the passage, Wright was at least partially responsible for the renewed interest in organic architecture in the twentieth century.

152. **C** The author tells us that one of the principles of *feng shui* has to do with a building's proportions. The height of a room's ceiling compared to its other dimensions is a good example of proportion.

153. **D** Agile means "quick or nimble."

154. **B** To *intimidate* is to frighten, scare, or alarm.

155. **C** To *hoist* is to lift, elevate, or heave.

156. **B** *Naive* means "innocent, untaught, or believing." A person with little experience or guidance in a certain endeavor would be considered *naive*.

157. **A** *Arid* means "dry or desert."

158. **D** To *aspire* is to strive, desire, or yearn.

159. **D** *Reclusive* means "antisocial or solitary." A reclusive person avoids other people and being in public.

160. **A** To *construe* is to define, explain, or interpret.

161. **B** A *mentor* is a teacher, guide, or counselor.

162. **C** *Vital* means "necessary, essential, or critically important."

163. **D** To *replenish* is to fill up or make full.

164. **A** *Tactful* means "discreet, judicious, or diplomatic," especially in what one says (or does not say) to other people.

165. **C** A *notion* is an idea or opinion.

166. **A** *Sparse* means "meager, insufficient, or scattered."

167. **D** One common meaning of *affix* is "attach, stick on, or fasten."

168. **C** A *grimace* is a smirk, sneer, or similar facial expression.

169. **B** One common meaning of *apparent* is "probable, evident, or likely."

170. **A** A *refuge* is a shelter, retreat, sanctuary, or other place of safety (such as a harbor).

171. **B** *Devious* means "crafty, sly, underhanded, or dishonest."

172. **C** To *repeal* is to revoke, reverse, or invalidate—in other words, to cancel.

173. **B** To *forage* is to search, scavenge, scrounge, or hunt, usually for food.

174. **A** *Domineering* means "aggressive, overly assertive, or pushy."

Mathematics

175. **A** The digit 4 is located in the "thousandths" place.

176. **D** Among the integers 1 through 100, if you exclude 1–10 and 100—which account for 11 of the 100 integers—you're left with 89 integers (11–99).

Answers and Explanations *(continued)*

177. **D** A quadrilateral is any four-sided polygon. A trapezoid is a quadrilateral in which one (and only one) pair of opposite sides are parallel to each other.

178. **C** In the equation given, substitute $a + 2b$ for b, then simplify:

$$b = a + 2(a + 2b)$$

$$b = a + 2a + 4b$$

$$b = 3a + 4b$$

179. **A** Each of the two series contains exactly 50 terms. Each term in the series of even integers is greater than the corresponding term in the series of odd integers by *exactly 1*. Thus, the difference between the sums is 50.

180. **B** $m\angle 1 + m\angle 2 + m\angle 3 = 180°$. (The three angles combine to form a straight line.) Because $m\angle 2$ is $90°$, the sum of $m\angle 1$ and $m\angle 3$ must also be $90°$.

181. **A** $5 \times 10^5 = 5 \times 10 \times 10 \times 10 \times 10 \times 10 = 5 \times 100,000 = 500,000$.

182. **B** Since all three terms share the same variable (x), you can combine terms by simply adding coefficients $(1 + 2 + 3)$.

183. **D** Three members are common to the two sets: 2, 4, and 8.

184. **C** Any number squared is a positive number. Therefore, for any real numbers x and y, $x^2 + y^2 > 0$. On the number line shown, however, point A is a negative number.

185. **A** The prime factorization of 48 is as follows: $48 = 2^4 \times 3$. (4 and 6 are not prime numbers, and 13 is not a factor of 48.)

186. **A** In any triangle, the two shortest sides must be longer than the longest side. Only choice A meets this requirement.

187. **B** To double the value of a fraction, you can either multiply the numerator by 2 or divide the denominator by 2, as in choice B.

188. **D** You need consider only the right-most five digits. The number 55,002 is closer to 60,000 than to 50,000.

189. **C** In any isosceles triangle, two sides are congruent (the same length) and, accordingly, the two angles opposite those sides are congruent (the same degree measure). In any triangle, the sum of the measures of the three angles is $180°$. Thus, if one angle of an isosceles triangle measures $100°$, the other two angles must each measure $40°$.

190. **B** Because x is negative and y is positive, their product must be a negative number. In addition, since the absolute value (distance from the origin on the number line) of both x and y is greater than 1, their product must be less than -1.

191. **C** Because $l_1 \parallel l_2$, corresponding angles created by the two vertices are congruent. Thus, $m\angle 1 + 180 = m\angle 5 + m\angle 7 + m\angle 8$—and statement C is false.

192. **B** The number 73 is not divisible by any integer other than 1 and itself. $69 = 3 \times 23$. $87 = 3 \times 29$. $55 = 5 \times 11$.

193. **C** Twenty-five (25) cents is $\frac{1}{4}$ of a dollar.

Because one dollar is $\frac{1}{100}$ of \$100, 25 cents is $\frac{1}{4} \times \frac{1}{100}$, or $\frac{1}{400}$, of \$100.

Answers and Explanations *(continued)*

194. **D** Among three consecutive positive integers, only a larger number divided by a smaller number can possibly be an integer. Eliminate choices A and B. In addition, dividing one of the three numbers by another yields an integer only in three cases: If $\{a,b,c\} = \{1,2,3\}$, then $\dfrac{b}{a}$ and $\dfrac{c}{a}$ are both integers, or, if $\{a,b,c\} = \{2,3,4\}$, then $\dfrac{c}{a}$ is an integer.

195. **C** The volume of a cube is s^3, where s is the length of any side (including its height). For example, if $s = 1$, then $V = 1^3 = 1$. If you increase the height of this cube by 100%, the length of each side (s) is now 2, and $V = 2^3 = 8$. The percent increase from 1 to 8 is 700%.

196. **D** Set D includes all numbers that are factors of both 36 and 60. Neither 18 nor 8 is a factor of 60, and so choices A and C are incorrect. Choice B omits 4, a factor of both 36 and 60.

197. **A** In any parallelogram, opposite angles are congruent (the same size).

198. **C** Because $3 \times 16 = 48$, from 1 to 50 there are 16 multiples of 3. Accordingly, the probability that Kira will select a multiple of 3 is $\dfrac{16}{50}$, or $\dfrac{8}{25}$.

199. **B** Subtracting a negative number is equivalent to adding a positive number. Thus, $-1 - (-2) - (-3) = -1 + 2 + 3 = 4$.

200. **D** A salad and bagel would cost $3.75 + $2.25, or a total of $6.00, which is more money than Kevin has.

201. **A** The angles that $x°$ and $2x°$ represent are supplementary—their sum is 1,800°. Thus, $x = 60$, and $2x = 120$. The angle that $y°$ represents is vertical to a 120° angles; thus, $y = 120$.

202. **D** Align the two numbers vertically at the decimal point. As you add columns from right to left, you carry a 1 from each column to the next.

203. **B** Since the answers are expressed in fractions, convert 0.2 and 5% to fractions, find the lowest common denominator, and then combine: $\dfrac{4}{5} + 0.2 + 5\% = \dfrac{4}{5} + \dfrac{2}{10} + \dfrac{5}{100} = \dfrac{16}{20} + \dfrac{4}{20} + \dfrac{1}{20} = \dfrac{21}{20}$.

204. **A** To find the average temperature, add the high and low, and then divide the sum by 2: $\dfrac{(-6 + 11)}{2} = \dfrac{5}{2}$, or 2.5°.

205. **B** The area of a triangle equals half the product of its base and height ($A = \dfrac{1}{2} bh$). Applying this formula, solve for b:

$$15 = \left(\dfrac{3}{2}\right)b$$

$$\left(\dfrac{2}{3}\right)(15) = b$$

$$10 = b$$

206. **C** Fifteen (15) of the 24 candies are hard. Eating 6 of the 15 hard candies leaves 9 of each type (hard and chewy).

207. **B** The fraction $\dfrac{5}{3}$ is equal to $1\dfrac{2}{3}$, which is 100% plus approximately 66%, or 166%. Choice B provides the closest approximation.

Answers and Explanations *(continued)*

208. **A** To answer the question, you can try plugging in each answer choice in turn. (With the correct number, the equation will hold true.) Or, you can solve for x using algebra:

$$\frac{x}{2} = \frac{1}{2}(2-x)$$

$$\frac{x}{2} = 1 - \frac{x}{2}$$

$$x = 2 - x$$

$$2x = 2$$

$$x = 1$$

209. **B** To solve quickly, first factor 6^4, then cancel and simplify:

$$\frac{3^4}{6^4} = \frac{3^4}{2^4 3^4} = \frac{1}{2^4} = \frac{1}{16}.$$

210. **A** There are 16 ounces in a pound and, accordingly, 80 ounces in 5 pounds. Removing 30 ounces from 80 ounces leaves 50 ounces.

211. **D** A circle contains 360°. Three of the sectors combined account for 270°. Thus, the remaining angle must measure 90° (360° − 270°).

212. **C** Twenty-two (22) games were either won or lost. You can find the number of games won by trying each answer choice in turn. Choice C works: $7 + 8 = 15$, and $15 + 7 = 22$. Or, you can solve the problem using algebra (let x equal the number of games won):

$$x + (x+8) = 22$$

$$2x = 14$$

$$x = 7$$

213. **B** Convert fractions to decimal numbers, then add:

Choice A: $2.1 + \frac{3}{5} = 2.1 + 0.6 = 2.7$

Choice B: $0.8 + \frac{8}{4} = 0.8 + 2 = 2.8$

Choice C: $2.0 + \frac{3}{4} = 2.0 + 0.75 = 2.75$

Choice D: $0.1 + \frac{5}{2} = 0.1 + 2.5 = 2.6$

214. **A** The distances for the four trips are as follows:

Choice A: $42 + 27 = 79$

Choice B: $63 + 15 = 78$

Choice C: $32 + 6 = 38$

Choice D: $40 + 12 = 52$

215. **D** You can use the plug-in method, trying each answer choice in turn. Or, you can solve the problem using algebra, isolating the missing term on one side of the equation:

$$11 - 10 \div (\underline{\quad} \times 3) + 3 = 4$$

$$-10 \div (\underline{\quad} \times 3) = -10$$

$$-10 = -10(\underline{\quad} \times 3)$$

$$1 = (\underline{\quad} \times 3)$$

$$\frac{1}{3} = \underline{\quad}$$

216. **B** After Stacy drinks 25% of 16 ounces (which is 4 ounces), 12 ounces remain. After Stacy drinks 25% of 12 ounces (which is 3 ounces), 9 ounces remain.

217. **A** A rectangle's area equals the product of its length and width ($A = lw$). Apply this equation, solving for w:

$$12,000 = 150w$$

$$\frac{12,000}{150} = w$$

$$80 = w$$

Answers and Explanations *(continued)*

218. **A** Align the two numbers vertically at the decimal point, and then subtract corresponding digits, borrowing a 1 from the "tenths" position for the "hundredths" position.

219. **B** You can use the plug-in method, trying each answer choice in turn. Here's how you'd use this method for choice B: Assume Pam's age is 32; Pam's age minus 15 equals 17 (Terry's age); two years ago, Pam was 30 and Terry was 15, which is exactly half of 30; these numbers fit the facts in the question, and so choice B is the correct one. Or, you can solve the problem formally, setting up and solving algebraic equations. First, set up two equations:

    $T = P - 15$

    $P - 2 = 2(T - 2)$

    Next, substitute the value of T from the first equation into the second, then solve for P:

    $P - 2 = 2(P - 15) - 4$

    $P - 2 = 2P - 30 - 4$

    $-P = -32$

    $P = 32$

220. **C** Here are the four coordinate pairs and their xy-products:

    Point A is at $(-3, -1)$; $xy = 3$.

    Point B is at $(2, 2)$; $xy = 4$.

    Point C is at $(-2, 3)$; $xy = -6$.

    Point D is at $(2, -1)$; $xy = -2$.

221. **D** You need to answer the question, "$700 multiplied by what percent gives you $35"? Letting x equal the interest rate, set up and solve an equation:

    $700x = 35$

    $x = \dfrac{35}{700}$

    $x = 0.05$, or 5%

222. **C** Matt drove twice as fast, on average, coming home as going to work. Thus, his average speed during the drive home must have been 40 miles per hour. If x is the time to drive home, then $2x$ is the time to drive to work, and the time for the round trip is $3x$. Because distance = rate × time, the distance from work to home is $40x$, and the round trip distance is $80x$. Average speed is the total distance divided by the total time = $80x \div 3x = 80/3 = 26.67$ miles per hour.

223. **C** $|-6| = 6$. Thus, $|-6| - |-6| = 6 - 6 = 0$.

224. **C** You can cancel the common factors 24 and 26 from the numerator and denominator, leaving $\dfrac{2}{2}$, or 1.

225. **D** The number of 1-inch cubes contained in the box is the same as the box's volume (in inches): $4 \times 5 \times 8 = 160$.

226. **C** Following these instructions, Carrie will retrace her path to her starting spot.

227. **C** There are 100 centimeters in 1 meter. Thus, there are 25 centimeters in $\dfrac{1}{4}$ meter.

228. **A** Because 15 of 27 animals are monkeys, 12 are not monkeys. The ratio of monkeys to other animals is 15:12, or 5:4. You can express this ratio as the fraction $\dfrac{5}{4}$.

229. **D** First, simplify the second term by removing the perfect square from inside the radical:

    $2\sqrt{5} + 2\sqrt{125} = 2\sqrt{5} + 2\sqrt{5^2 5} =$

    $2\sqrt{5} + 2 \times 5\sqrt{5} = 2\sqrt{5} + 10\sqrt{5}$

    Then, combine terms:

    $2\sqrt{5} + 10\sqrt{5} = 12\sqrt{5}$

Answers and Explanations *(continued)*

230. **D** The number of visitors during May was approximately 25,000. The number of visitors during June was approximately 65,000—an increase of 40,000.

231. **B** The approximate number of visitors during each of the six months are as follows:

    January: 30,000

    February: 60,000

    March: 40,000

    April: 45,000

    May: 25,000

    June: 65,000

    The sum of these six numbers is 265,000.

232. **A** In the expression, substitute the three values given, then simplify:

    $$\frac{3x}{z} + 4y^z = \frac{(3)(4)}{2} - 4(3)^2$$

    $$= \frac{12}{2} - (4)(9) = 6 - 36 = -30$$

233. **A** A negative number raised to an even power is positive, but a negative number raised to an odd power is negative: $(-3)^3 + (-2)^2 = (-3)(-3)(-3) + (-2)(-2) = -27 + 4 = -23$

234. **D** A circle contains 360°. The sector defined by the 80° angle accounts for $\frac{80}{360}$, or $\frac{2}{9}$, of the circle's total area.

235. **D** At \$15 per hour, Ashley earns \$120 in wages during an 8-hour shift. Her 5% commission on \$400 in sales is \$20. Ashley's total earnings were \$140 (\$120 + \$20).

236. **C** Divide the figure into two rectangles, as shown below.

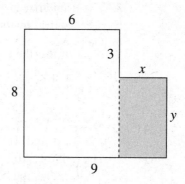

    Then, find *x* and *y* in the figure: $x = 9 - 6 = 3$, and $y = 8 - 3 = 5$. The area of the shaded rectangle $= x \times y = 3 \times 5 = 15$. The area of the larger (unshaded) rectangle is $6 \times 8 = 48$. The total area of the figure is $15 + 48 = 63$.

237. **C** Use the plug-in method, trying each answer choice in turn. Assuming Nadia has 4 dimes (40 cents), then she has the same number of nickels (20 cents) and 2 quarters (50 cents), for a total of \$1.10.

238. **B** Perform division before addition. To divide $\frac{2}{9}$ by $\frac{4}{3}$, multiply $\frac{2}{9}$ by the reciprocal of $\frac{4}{3}$ (cancel common factors): $\frac{2}{9} \times \frac{3}{4} = \frac{1}{3} \times \frac{1}{2} = \frac{1}{6}$. Next, add: $\frac{1}{6} + \frac{1}{2} = \frac{1}{6} + \frac{3}{6} = \frac{4}{6}$, or $\frac{2}{3}$.

Language

239. **A** As a modifier of the word *scenery* (as opposed to *scene*), the article *a* is not idiomatic and should simply be omitted.

240. **B** The adverb *badly* should replace the adjective *bad* because the word that is modified is a verb (*win*).

Answers and Explanations *(continued)*

241. **B** There are no mistakes.

242. **A** The capitalized word *Fair* should be used because in this sentence it is part of a movie title.

243. **C** The contraction *you're* (or *you are*) would be correct here.

244. **D** There are no mistakes.

245. **B** The capitalized word *University* should be used because it is part of a proper noun here.

246. **B** The exclamation mark should be part of the quotation: *"Hurry Up!" she shouted.*

247. **A** The phrase *up to* is not idiomatic in this context and should be replaced with *until*.

248. **C** The correct possessive form of *women* is *women's*.

249. **D** There are no mistakes.

250. **B** The words *replay* and *over* are redundant. Either replace *replay* with *play* or omit *over*.

251. **A** The present-perfect tense form of steal is *have* stolen (not *of* stolen).

252. **C** The past-perfect form of the verb *see* is *had seen*, as in *she had seen a ghost* or *she'd seen a ghost.*

253. **A** The sentence makes an illogical comparison between *raw carrots* and *cooking them*. One solution is to replace *cooking them* with *cooked carrots.*

254. **D** There are no mistakes.

255. **B** The phrase *near to* is not idiomatic in this context. The word *to* should be omitted.

256. **C** The sentence is quoting the sign, and so the phrase "Welcome Home!" should appear in quotation marks.

257. **C** The word *to* is not idiomatic in this context and should be replaced with *at*.

258. **B** This sentence poses a question, and so the correct punctuation at the end is a question mark.

259. **C** The capitalized word *Pope* is correct here because it is part of a proper noun.

260. **D** There are no mistakes.

261. **A** The comma should be omitted.

262. **B** The word *too* should replace *to*.

263. **D** There are no mistakes.

264. **D** There are no mistakes.

265. **A** The word *got* is used as slang here and should be replaced with *need*.

266. **D** There are no mistakes.

267. **B** The word *if* is not idiomatic here; the word *when* is better.

268. **D** There are no mistakes.

269. **C** The phrase *in every day* is not idiomatic. The word *in* should be omitted.

270. **B** The capitalized word *Freeze* should be used here because it begins a quoted sentence.

271. **D** There are no mistakes.

272. **C** The word *makeup* (facial cosmetics) is improper here and should be replaced by either *make* or *make up*.

Answers and Explanations *(continued)*

273. **A** A semicolon is improper here because the clause that follows it is not an independent clause (it cannot stand alone as a complete sentence). Either a comma or a dash should be used instead.

274. **B** In this context, the word *nothing* is incorrect and should be replaced with *anything*.

275. **B** There are no mistakes.

276. **C** The word *affect* (a verb) should be replaced with the noun *effect*.

277. **B** The subject-case pronoun *I* should be used instead of the object-case *me*.

278. **D** There are no mistakes.

279. **D** There are no spelling mistakes.

280. **A** The correct spelling is *accept*.

281. **C** The correct spelling is *elevator*.

282. **D** There are no spelling mistakes.

283. **B** The correct spelling is *visibility*.

284. **A** The correct spelling is *tournament*.

285. **B** The correct spelling is *interrupt*.

286. **C** The correct spelling is *temperature*.

287. **D** There are no spelling mistakes.

288. **C** The correct spelling is *accusations*.

289. **C** The second thought is a *conclusion* based on the first thought. The words *and so*—which mean "and therefore" here—provide a good bridge in this line of reasoning.

290. **B** Sentence B is clear and effective. There are several problems with version A: the awkward possessive from *geniuses'*; the awkward use of the passive voice (*is rarely achieved*); and the sentence's overall construction, which distorts the intended idea that greatness is rarely achieved *specifically* by people who were young geniuses. Choices C and D are confusing, due to their awkward structure and use of the passive voice.

291. **C** The phrase in choice C is clear, graceful, and idiomatic. None of the other versions are idiomatic. (Another good version would be: *concentrating was impossible for me.* However, this version is not among the four choices.)

292. **D** Because the Americans were allies of the British forces—meaning that they fought together against a common enemy—it makes perfect sense that their arrival after the Americans had been massacred was *unfortunate*.

293. **A** The sentence's second clause presents a consequence of the idea in the first clause. The phrase *as a result* signals that a consequence is described just ahead. (Two other good connecting words here would be *so* and *hence*.)

294. **A** The additional sentence would make a good topic sentence for the paragraph and would fit best at the beginning.

295. **B** In one reasonably brief paragraph, it is possible to describe the sequence of events involving Lincoln's assassination. The other two topics are too complex, however.

Answers and Explanations (continued)

296. **C** Of the four choices, sentence B is the clearest and most effective. In sentence (A), the second clause (set off by commas) is wordy and awkward. (Notice especially that the word *of* is repeated unnecessarily.) There are two problems with choice C. First, the opening phrase *the process of* would be more appropriate immediately before a description of the process rather than after its name—as in version B. The way sentence D is constructed suggests that the description following the comma refers to *partisan political purposes.* This "misplaced modifier" should be positioned closer to *gerrymandering,* the noun the phrase is intended to modify, as in version B.

297. **C** Sentence 3 explains why donated blood might not be safe for the *recipient.* However, the rest of the paragraph is about blood donating from the viewpoint of the *donor.*

298. **D** The given topic calls for a writer to point out and examine evidence that global warming exists. The sentence in choice D is the only one that is directly on point.

TACHS PRACTICE TEST 1

Answer Sheet

Directions: For each answer that you select, blacken the corresponding oval on this sheet.

Reading, Part 1

1. Ⓐ Ⓑ Ⓒ Ⓓ
2. Ⓙ Ⓚ Ⓛ Ⓜ
3. Ⓐ Ⓑ Ⓒ Ⓓ
4. Ⓙ Ⓚ Ⓛ Ⓜ
5. Ⓐ Ⓑ Ⓒ Ⓓ
6. Ⓙ Ⓚ Ⓛ Ⓜ
7. Ⓐ Ⓑ Ⓒ Ⓓ
8. Ⓙ Ⓚ Ⓛ Ⓜ
9. Ⓐ Ⓑ Ⓒ Ⓓ
10. Ⓙ Ⓚ Ⓛ Ⓜ
11. Ⓐ Ⓑ Ⓒ Ⓓ
12. Ⓙ Ⓚ Ⓛ Ⓜ
13. Ⓐ Ⓑ Ⓒ Ⓓ
14. Ⓙ Ⓚ Ⓛ Ⓜ
15. Ⓐ Ⓑ Ⓒ Ⓓ
16. Ⓙ Ⓚ Ⓛ Ⓜ
17. Ⓐ Ⓑ Ⓒ Ⓓ
18. Ⓙ Ⓚ Ⓛ Ⓜ
19. Ⓐ Ⓑ Ⓒ Ⓓ
20. Ⓙ Ⓚ Ⓛ Ⓜ

Reading, Part 2

21. Ⓐ Ⓑ Ⓒ Ⓓ
22. Ⓙ Ⓚ Ⓛ Ⓜ
23. Ⓐ Ⓑ Ⓒ Ⓓ
24. Ⓙ Ⓚ Ⓛ Ⓜ
25. Ⓐ Ⓑ Ⓒ Ⓓ
26. Ⓙ Ⓚ Ⓛ Ⓜ
27. Ⓐ Ⓑ Ⓒ Ⓓ
28. Ⓙ Ⓚ Ⓛ Ⓜ
29. Ⓐ Ⓑ Ⓒ Ⓓ
30. Ⓙ Ⓚ Ⓛ Ⓜ
31. Ⓐ Ⓑ Ⓒ Ⓓ
32. Ⓙ Ⓚ Ⓛ Ⓜ
33. Ⓐ Ⓑ Ⓒ Ⓓ
34. Ⓙ Ⓚ Ⓛ Ⓜ
35. Ⓐ Ⓑ Ⓒ Ⓓ
36. Ⓙ Ⓚ Ⓛ Ⓜ
37. Ⓐ Ⓑ Ⓒ Ⓓ
38. Ⓙ Ⓚ Ⓛ Ⓜ
39. Ⓐ Ⓑ Ⓒ Ⓓ
40. Ⓙ Ⓚ Ⓛ Ⓜ
41. Ⓐ Ⓑ Ⓒ Ⓓ

42. Ⓙ Ⓚ Ⓛ Ⓜ
43. Ⓐ Ⓑ Ⓒ Ⓓ
44. Ⓙ Ⓚ Ⓛ Ⓜ
45. Ⓐ Ⓑ Ⓒ Ⓓ
46. Ⓙ Ⓚ Ⓛ Ⓜ
47. Ⓐ Ⓑ Ⓒ Ⓓ
48. Ⓙ Ⓚ Ⓛ Ⓜ
49. Ⓐ Ⓑ Ⓒ Ⓓ
50. Ⓙ Ⓚ Ⓛ Ⓜ

Written Expression, Part 1

1. Ⓐ Ⓑ Ⓒ Ⓓ
2. Ⓙ Ⓚ Ⓛ Ⓜ
3. Ⓐ Ⓑ Ⓒ Ⓓ
4. Ⓙ Ⓚ Ⓛ Ⓜ
5. Ⓐ Ⓑ Ⓒ Ⓓ
6. Ⓙ Ⓚ Ⓛ Ⓜ
7. Ⓐ Ⓑ Ⓒ Ⓓ
8. Ⓙ Ⓚ Ⓛ Ⓜ
9. Ⓐ Ⓑ Ⓒ Ⓓ
10. Ⓙ Ⓚ Ⓛ Ⓜ
11. Ⓐ Ⓑ Ⓒ Ⓓ
12. Ⓙ Ⓚ Ⓛ Ⓜ
13. Ⓐ Ⓑ Ⓒ Ⓓ
14. Ⓙ Ⓚ Ⓛ Ⓜ
15. Ⓐ Ⓑ Ⓒ Ⓓ
16. Ⓙ Ⓚ Ⓛ Ⓜ
17. Ⓐ Ⓑ Ⓒ Ⓓ
18. Ⓙ Ⓚ Ⓛ Ⓜ
19. Ⓐ Ⓑ Ⓒ Ⓓ
20. Ⓙ Ⓚ Ⓛ Ⓜ
21. Ⓐ Ⓑ Ⓒ Ⓓ
22. Ⓙ Ⓚ Ⓛ Ⓜ
23. Ⓐ Ⓑ Ⓒ Ⓓ
24. Ⓙ Ⓚ Ⓛ Ⓜ
25. Ⓐ Ⓑ Ⓒ Ⓓ
26. Ⓙ Ⓚ Ⓛ Ⓜ
27. Ⓐ Ⓑ Ⓒ Ⓓ
28. Ⓙ Ⓚ Ⓛ Ⓜ
29. Ⓐ Ⓑ Ⓒ Ⓓ
30. Ⓙ Ⓚ Ⓛ Ⓜ
31. Ⓐ Ⓑ Ⓒ Ⓓ
32. Ⓙ Ⓚ Ⓛ Ⓜ
33. Ⓐ Ⓑ Ⓒ Ⓓ

34. Ⓙ Ⓚ Ⓛ Ⓜ
35. Ⓐ Ⓑ Ⓒ Ⓓ
36. Ⓙ Ⓚ Ⓛ Ⓜ
37. Ⓐ Ⓑ Ⓒ Ⓓ
38. Ⓙ Ⓚ Ⓛ Ⓜ
39. Ⓐ Ⓑ Ⓒ Ⓓ
40. Ⓙ Ⓚ Ⓛ Ⓜ

Written Expression, Part 2

41. Ⓐ Ⓑ Ⓒ Ⓓ
42. Ⓙ Ⓚ Ⓛ Ⓜ
43. Ⓐ Ⓑ Ⓒ Ⓓ
44. Ⓙ Ⓚ Ⓛ Ⓜ
45. Ⓐ Ⓑ Ⓒ Ⓓ
46. Ⓙ Ⓚ Ⓛ Ⓜ
47. Ⓐ Ⓑ Ⓒ Ⓓ
48. Ⓙ Ⓚ Ⓛ Ⓜ
49. Ⓐ Ⓑ Ⓒ Ⓓ
50. Ⓙ Ⓚ Ⓛ Ⓜ

Mathematics, Part 1

1. Ⓐ Ⓑ Ⓒ Ⓓ
2. Ⓙ Ⓚ Ⓛ Ⓜ
3. Ⓐ Ⓑ Ⓒ Ⓓ
4. Ⓙ Ⓚ Ⓛ Ⓜ
5. Ⓐ Ⓑ Ⓒ Ⓓ
6. Ⓙ Ⓚ Ⓛ Ⓜ
7. Ⓐ Ⓑ Ⓒ Ⓓ
8. Ⓙ Ⓚ Ⓛ Ⓜ
9. Ⓐ Ⓑ Ⓒ Ⓓ
10. Ⓙ Ⓚ Ⓛ Ⓜ
11. Ⓐ Ⓑ Ⓒ Ⓓ
12. Ⓙ Ⓚ Ⓛ Ⓜ
13. Ⓐ Ⓑ Ⓒ Ⓓ
14. Ⓙ Ⓚ Ⓛ Ⓜ
15. Ⓐ Ⓑ Ⓒ Ⓓ
16. Ⓙ Ⓚ Ⓛ Ⓜ
17. Ⓐ Ⓑ Ⓒ Ⓓ
18. Ⓙ Ⓚ Ⓛ Ⓜ
19. Ⓐ Ⓑ Ⓒ Ⓓ
30. Ⓙ Ⓚ Ⓛ Ⓜ
31. Ⓐ Ⓑ Ⓒ Ⓓ
32. Ⓙ Ⓚ Ⓛ Ⓜ

Answer Sheet *(continued)*

Mathematics, Part 2

33. Ⓐ Ⓑ Ⓒ Ⓓ
34. Ⓙ Ⓚ Ⓛ Ⓜ
35. Ⓐ Ⓑ Ⓒ Ⓓ
36. Ⓙ Ⓚ Ⓛ Ⓜ
37. Ⓐ Ⓑ Ⓒ Ⓓ
38. Ⓙ Ⓚ Ⓛ Ⓜ
39. Ⓐ Ⓑ Ⓒ Ⓓ
40. Ⓙ Ⓚ Ⓛ Ⓜ
41. Ⓐ Ⓑ Ⓒ Ⓓ
42. Ⓙ Ⓚ Ⓛ Ⓜ
43. Ⓐ Ⓑ Ⓒ Ⓓ
44. Ⓙ Ⓚ Ⓛ Ⓜ
45. Ⓐ Ⓑ Ⓒ Ⓓ
46. Ⓙ Ⓚ Ⓛ Ⓜ
47. Ⓐ Ⓑ Ⓒ Ⓓ
48. Ⓙ Ⓚ Ⓛ Ⓜ
49. Ⓐ Ⓑ Ⓒ Ⓓ
50. Ⓙ Ⓚ Ⓛ Ⓜ

Ability, Part 1

1. Ⓐ Ⓑ Ⓒ Ⓓ Ⓔ
2. Ⓙ Ⓚ Ⓛ Ⓜ Ⓝ
3. Ⓐ Ⓑ Ⓒ Ⓓ Ⓔ
4. Ⓙ Ⓚ Ⓛ Ⓜ Ⓝ
5. Ⓐ Ⓑ Ⓒ Ⓓ Ⓔ
6. Ⓙ Ⓚ Ⓛ Ⓜ Ⓝ
7. Ⓐ Ⓑ Ⓒ Ⓓ Ⓔ
8. Ⓙ Ⓚ Ⓛ Ⓜ Ⓝ
9. Ⓐ Ⓑ Ⓒ Ⓓ Ⓔ
10. Ⓙ Ⓚ Ⓛ Ⓜ Ⓝ
11. Ⓐ Ⓑ Ⓒ Ⓓ Ⓔ
12. Ⓙ Ⓚ Ⓛ Ⓜ Ⓝ
13. Ⓐ Ⓑ Ⓒ Ⓓ Ⓔ
14. Ⓙ Ⓚ Ⓛ Ⓜ Ⓝ
15. Ⓐ Ⓑ Ⓒ Ⓓ Ⓔ
16. Ⓙ Ⓚ Ⓛ Ⓜ Ⓝ

17. Ⓐ Ⓑ Ⓒ Ⓓ Ⓔ
18. Ⓙ Ⓚ Ⓛ Ⓜ Ⓝ
19. Ⓐ Ⓑ Ⓒ Ⓓ Ⓔ
20. Ⓙ Ⓚ Ⓛ Ⓜ Ⓝ
21. Ⓐ Ⓑ Ⓒ Ⓓ Ⓔ
22. Ⓙ Ⓚ Ⓛ Ⓜ Ⓝ
23. Ⓐ Ⓑ Ⓒ Ⓓ Ⓔ
24. Ⓙ Ⓚ Ⓛ Ⓜ Ⓝ
25. Ⓐ Ⓑ Ⓒ Ⓓ Ⓔ
26. Ⓙ Ⓚ Ⓛ Ⓜ Ⓝ
27. Ⓐ Ⓑ Ⓒ Ⓓ Ⓔ
28. Ⓙ Ⓚ Ⓛ Ⓜ Ⓝ
29. Ⓐ Ⓑ Ⓒ Ⓓ Ⓔ
30. Ⓙ Ⓚ Ⓛ Ⓜ Ⓝ
31. Ⓐ Ⓑ Ⓒ Ⓓ Ⓔ
32. Ⓙ Ⓚ Ⓛ Ⓜ Ⓝ
33. Ⓐ Ⓑ Ⓒ Ⓓ Ⓔ
34. Ⓙ Ⓚ Ⓛ Ⓜ Ⓝ
35. Ⓐ Ⓑ Ⓒ Ⓓ Ⓔ
36. Ⓙ Ⓚ Ⓛ Ⓜ Ⓝ
37. Ⓐ Ⓑ Ⓒ Ⓓ Ⓔ
38. Ⓙ Ⓚ Ⓛ Ⓜ Ⓝ
39. Ⓐ Ⓑ Ⓒ Ⓓ Ⓔ
40. Ⓙ Ⓚ Ⓛ Ⓜ Ⓝ

Ability, Part 2

41. Ⓐ Ⓑ Ⓒ Ⓓ Ⓔ
42. Ⓙ Ⓚ Ⓛ Ⓜ Ⓝ
43. Ⓐ Ⓑ Ⓒ Ⓓ Ⓔ
44. Ⓙ Ⓚ Ⓛ Ⓜ Ⓝ
45. Ⓐ Ⓑ Ⓒ Ⓓ Ⓔ
46. Ⓙ Ⓚ Ⓛ Ⓜ Ⓝ
47. Ⓐ Ⓑ Ⓒ Ⓓ Ⓔ
48. Ⓙ Ⓚ Ⓛ Ⓜ Ⓝ
49. Ⓐ Ⓑ Ⓒ Ⓓ Ⓔ
50. Ⓙ Ⓚ Ⓛ Ⓜ Ⓝ

Reading, Part 1 *(20 Questions, 10 minutes)*

Directions: For questions 1–20, decide which of the four answer choices is closest in meaning to the underlined word(s). Choose the best answer.

1 To <u>burgeon</u>
- A flourish
- B take a trip
- C write in a diary
- D build a city

2 A <u>cryptic</u> message
- J welcoming
- K coded
- L grave
- M urgent

3 A <u>decadent</u> feast
- A joyful
- B effortless
- C occurring once every ten years
- D luxurious

4 An <u>eclectic</u> collection
- J diverse
- K valuable
- L thrilling
- M antique

5 To <u>forgo</u> payment
- A reduce
- B refuse
- C accept
- D offer

6 A primitive <u>ideology</u>
- J system of belief
- K technology
- L science
- M way of working

7 An <u>illicit</u> plan
- A illegal
- B scandalous
- C unauthorized
- D hidden

8 An <u>infamous</u> politician
- J dishonest
- K principled
- L unknown
- M notorious

9 To <u>mediate</u> a conflict
- A referee
- B worsen
- C resolve
- D delay

10 To <u>mollify</u> someone
- J calm down
- K soothe
- L pacify
- M all of the above

11 Receiving <u>partisan</u> support
- A unbiased
- B unanimous
- C one-sided
- D financial

12 A <u>pensive</u> feeling
- J brooding
- K celebratory
- L apologetic
- M serene

13 To <u>renounce</u> a belief
- A return to
- B solidify
- C abandon
- D repeat

14 A <u>sanguine</u> mood
- J content
- K dispirited
- L wrathful
- M overjoyed

Reading, Part 1 *(continued)*

15 To <u>spawn</u> criticism
   A   reject
   B   generate
   C   agree with
   D   ignore

16 A <u>terse</u> statement
   J   strained
   K   prepared
   L   concise
   M   off-the-cuff

17 A <u>venal</u> official
   A   corrupt
   B   judicial
   C   moral
   D   all of the above

18 Choose a <u>vocation</u>
   J   holiday
   K   career
   L   partner
   M   diversion

19 An <u>ironic</u> situation
   A   difficult
   B   bitter
   C   paradoxical
   D   promising

20 To be <u>compliant</u>
   J   disagreeable
   K   calm
   L   contrary
   M   obedient

Reading, Part 2 *(30 questions, 25 minutes)*

Directions: Read the passages below and the questions relating to them. Choose the best answer from among the four given for each question, and mark the corresponding space on your answer sheet.

Read the following passage and answer questions 21–25.

The Texas Rangers are probably the best known, or at least the most mythologized, group of law officers in American history. Numerous references to the Texas Rangers can be found in novels, television, and film, and the Texas Rangers baseball team was named for them. Though they are usually portrayed in popular culture as a band of renegade quickshooters because of their storied history, they actually have been a part of the Texas Department of Public Safety since 1935. Their duties today are largely focused on detective work, and they have some of the best crime labs in the United States. Direct law enforcement is under the control of the Highway Patrol; however, the Texas Rangers' legacy lives on as the force that took down Sam Bass, John Wesley Hardin, and Bonnie and Clyde in the Old West.

21 As it is used in the passage, what does the word <u>storied</u> mean?

  A   legendary

  B   having multiple floors

  C   for sale

  D   factual

22 According to the passage, which of the following would a Texas Ranger probably not be responsible for today?

  J   tracking down crime suspects

  K   analyzing evidence that is taken from a crime scene

  L   compiling facts about multiple crimes to find ones that might be related

  M   stopping and ticketing speeding drivers

23 The passage mentions a specific example of the Texas Rangers being immortalized in which of the following venues?

  A   novels

  B   film

  C   radio

  D   sports

24 It can be inferred from the passage that the Texas Rangers

  J   caught some very high-profile criminals in the past

  K   are one of the best-paid police forces in history

  L   have been a separate police force for less time than they have been part of the Texas Department of Public Safety

  M   still wear the same uniform that they wore when they were originally formed

25 The author's main purpose in writing this passage is to

  A   debunk myths about the Texas Rangers' past

  B   detail how some of the most notorious criminals in the Old West were caught

  C   contrast the Texas Rangers' current role with their past reputation

  D   trace the lineage of Texas Ranger clothing and gear

Reading, Part 2 *(continued)*

Read the following passage and answer questions 26–30.

Until 1980, Mount St. Helens, a volcanic mountain between Portland, OR and Seattle, WA, had been dormant since the mid-1800s. But over a two-day period starting on March 25th, it erupted with a series of 174 shocks registering at least 2.6 on the Richter scale, culminating in an explosion of ash that left a crater in the mountain 250 feet wide. Ash was spewed as high as 7,000 feet into the air and fell not only on the surrounding area, but also as far away as Bend, OR and Spokane, WA.

Among the immediate consequences of the eruption were a disruption of air travel in the region, power blackouts caused by ash collecting in electrical circuits, and numerous road closures, including Highway 90. Nearby cities such as Yakima were plunged into near-darkness for several days due to fine ash suspended in the atmosphere.

26 The passage implies that in a natural disaster such as an earthquake or volcano, the Richter scale measures

   J   amount of lava released
   K   amount of energy released
   L   death toll
   M   financial consequences

27 One can tell that the 1980 eruption of Mount St. Helens was very powerful because

   A   it spewed ash high into the air
   B   it left a large crater in the mountain
   C   many smaller shocks preceded it
   D   all of the above

28 What was limited in areas near Mount St. Helens after the explosion?

   J   travel
   K   visibility
   L   access to electricity
   M   all of the above

29 It can be inferred from the passage that Bend, OR and Spokane, WA are

   A   unlike Portland and Seattle
   B   considered far away from Mount St. Helens
   C   very close to Yakima
   D   not nearby any volcanoes

30 What is the best topic sentence for this passage?

   J   The 1980 explosion of Mount St. Helens caused the loss of many jobs.
   K   Before the 1980 explosion, Mount St. Helens was a big mountain.
   L   The 1980 explosion of Mount St. Helens started on March 25.
   M   The 1980 explosion of Mount St. Helens was huge in scale.

Reading, Part 2 *(continued)*

Read the following passage and answer questions 31–35.

It wasn't very long ago that environmentalists were a frequent target of public ridicule; however, now the idea that pollution and carbon produced by humans can have a big impact on Earth's environment is much more widely accepted. One reason for this could be that eco-friendliness has been taught in many schools for so long now that today's young adults grew up with an awareness of environmental issues that their parents didn't have. Another reason could be that the amount of media attention devoted to these issues has increased, thanks in part to celebrities and other public figures who have espoused this cause. Of course, still another reason could be that on a global scale, world leaders are taking more steps than ever before to lessen humanity's negative impact on air, water, climate, and animal populations. Whatever the reason, environmental issues are coming to the forefront as a topic of serious public debate.

31 Which of the following is mentioned as a possible reason for increasing acceptance of environmentalism?

  A scientists who talk to the media about their doubts regarding global warming

  B celebrities who speak out about the environment

  C new scientific evidence that supports earlier findings

  D all of the above

32 The author states that humans can have a negative impact on

  J the air and water

  K the climate

  L animals

  M all of the above

33 With which of the following statements would the author be most likely to agree?

  A Environmentalism is easy to ridicule because it is based on unproven science.

  B Everyone now agrees that environmental issues are important.

  C Media attention is not usually helpful to environmentalists.

  D World leaders are taking more steps than they have in the past to protect the environment.

34 As used in the passage, what does the word <u>espoused</u> mean?

  J married

  K refused

  L accepted

  M promoted

35 The author probably feels

  A hopeful that answers will be found to environmental problems

  B despondent that more is not being done to help the environment

  C glad that environmental concerns are being taken less seriously than before

  D angry that people are not educated better about environmental issues

Reading, Part 2 *(continued)*

Read the following passage and answer questions 36–40.

Lemurs are small primates native to Madagascar and its surrounding islands. There are about 50 species of lemur of varying sizes, and all but one live in trees and use all four limbs to climb and leap from tree to tree, using their long tails for balance. (Ring-tailed lemurs are the exception; they live primarily on the ground.) They eat mainly plants and some insects, but the tiny dwarf and mouse lemurs also eat some smaller animals. Lemurs also differ in their living habits. Some of them are nocturnal, and some are active during the day. Nocturnal lemurs usually live alone, while diurnal lemurs tend to live in groups.

Most of the existing species of lemur are considered endangered or threatened. Some larger species of lemur have already gone extinct, before lemurs were as protected as they are now by anti-hunting laws. However, the survival of many remaining lemurs is still threatened by deforestation.

36 Some lemurs are diurnal. This means they

J   are active during the night
K   are active during the day
L   live primarily in trees
M   live alone

37 According to the passage, one benefit of a lemur's long tail is

A   it helps them carry their young
B   it helps them move easily in trees
C   it helps them ward off predators
D   it helps them pick food

38 According to the passage, deforestation

J   is a bigger threat than hunting
K   cannot be stopped in Madagascar
L   only affects one species of lemur
M   threatens the lemurs' ability to survive

39 According to the passage, Madagascar and some surrounding islands

A   are the only places on Earth where the lemurs have not died off
B   are lemurs' natural habitats
C   are where lemurs were transplanted to protect them from hunting
D   are entirely covered with rainforests

40 The author's intent in writing this passage was

J   to extol how entertaining it can be to watch lemurs
K   to outline the precise scientific classifications of lemurs
L   to tell about the living habits and threats faced by lemurs
M   to tell about lemurs' unusual societal structure

Reading, Part 2 *(continued)*

Read the following passage and answer questions 41–45.

Margarine, a butter substitute marketed today for cholesterol-conscious eaters, has a long and controversial history. It was created in response to a prize being offered in 1869 by Emperor Napoléan Boneparte for a butter substitute that could be produced cheaply for the soldiers and lower classes. The winner was a substance called oleomargarine, invented by French chemist Hippolyte Mège-Mouriés. The name was eventually shortened to margarine.

The dairy industry reacted with vigorous force against the margarine trade in many countries; the sale of margarine was banned or heavily taxed by most U.S. states almost as soon as it was introduced. However, the most effective measure taken against margarine has been to control the color. Margarine is nearly white by nature, which makes it less appealing to consumers who are used to yellow butter. Prohibitions on selling colored margarine existed well into the 20th century in the United States, though margarine producers fought back by selling color tablets that could be worked into the margarine at home.

41 According to the passage, who would be a likely consumer of margarine in Napoléan's day?

 A the French navy
 B the royal classes
 C visiting dignitaries
 D citizens of Pennsylvania

42 According to the passage, who would most likely object to margarine being widely available to consumers in the United States?

 J a corn farmer
 K a policeman
 L a sharecropper
 M a dairy farmer

43 According to the passage, which of the following makes margarine less appealing?

 A the ban on its sale and production
 B its color
 C its French origins
 D its taste and texture

44 The author is probably a

 J student writing a research paper on margarine
 K dietician writing an article about the dangers of margarine
 L heart patient writing a plan for lowering his cholesterol
 M chemist writing an analysis on the production of margarine

45 Which of the following is the best title for the passage?

 A Margarine: A Colorful Past
 B Dietary Guidelines for Lowering Cholesterol
 C The Dangers of Artificial Foods
 D Napoléan's Big Contest

Reading, Part 2 *(continued)*

Read the following passage and answer questions 46–50.

Anna May Wong was a Chinese-American actress from 1922 to her death in 1961. Born and raised in Los Angeles, she fell in love with movies at an early age and started asking filmmakers to be cast in movies that were being filmed often in the same neighborhood where she grew up. Her first part in a movie was as an uncredited extra, carrying a lantern along with 300 other girls in *The Red Lantern*.

Her first leading role was in *The Toll of the Sea*, which was loosely based on the story of Madame Butterfly. Her acting received rave reviews that normally would have launched a young actress's career, but her ethnicity proved a stumbling block, mainly due to laws against minorities playing in romantic roles opposite Caucasian actors. Unfortunately, this pattern continued throughout her career. The most severe disappointment was when Wong was passed over for the leading part of O-lan in the film adaptation of Pearl S. Buck's novel, *The Good Earth*. Luise Rainer, the studio's choice for O-lan, won an Academy Award for the role.

46 According to the passage, Anna May Wong's first part in a movie

  J   won her critical acclaim
  K   made her very financially successfully
  L   did not even give her a listing in the movie credits
  M   attracted the attention of filmmakers in her neighborhood

47 According to the passage, Luise Rainer

  A   should not have won an Academy Award
  B   was chosen to play O-lan instead of Anna May Wong
  C   was passed over in favor of Anna May Wong for several choice roles
  D   should have refused the part of O-lan in The Good Earth

48 With which of the following would the author of the passage most likely agree?

  J   If Anna May Wong had not been of Chinese descent, her acting career would have been more successful.
  K   Anna May Wong deserved an Academy Award for her role in *The Toll of the Sea*.
  L   Audiences at the time were not prepared to see a Chinese-American actress in a leading role.
  M   Anna May Wong was content with her acting career.

49 The passage could best be described as a

  A   film critique
  B   brief biography of one actress
  C   cameo appearance
  D   rant against casting directors of the early 1900s

50 Which of the following is the best topic sentence for this passage?

  J   Many minorities in early Hollywood did not have enough opportunities to play major roles.
  K   Although Anna May Wong got good reviews in her earlier roles, critics later panned her work.
  L   Anna May Wong's career was limited because of her ethnicity and the laws of her time.
  M   Many teenagers who grow up in Los Angeles get to play minor roles in Hollywood movies.

Written Expression, Part 1 *(40 Questions, 25 minutes)*

Directions: This is a test of how well you can find errors in a piece of writing. The directions below tell what type of mistake may be present. If no mistake is made, choose the last answer.

For questions 1–10, look for mistakes in usage or expression.

1

- A   Though we are both fast
- B   swimmers, Mary has to work
- C   much harder at it than me.
- D   (*No mistakes*)

2

- J   Chris has practicing piano for hours. He
- K   probably would play all day, but we have
- L   a concert to attend in the afternoon.
- M   (*No mistakes*)

3

- A   Ray, who makes money in the summers
- B   by mowing lawns, is attending college
- C   full-time in the fall and spring.
- D   (*No mistakes*)

4

- J   Cheryl ran quick to get
- K   ice cream before
- L   the store closed.
- M   (*No mistakes*)

5

- A   This bookstore has one copy of our
- B   favorite book. Darcy saw it before I
- C   did, so she swears the book is her's.
- D   (*No mistakes*)

6

- J   Lifting the phone on the first
- K   ring, Tara had a suspicion that
- L   the caller had bad news.
- M   (*No mistakes*)

7

- A   Beth loves to dance, but Angie
- B   says she would rather watch
- C   movies than dancing any day.
- D   (*No mistakes*)

8

- J   Normally Sheila never gets up before
- K   6 AM in the morning, but at camp
- L   everyone must wake up at 5 every day.
- M   (*No mistakes*)

9

- A   Representative Thomas tried to write a perfect
- B   bill for all of those involved, but in the end
- C   compromise was chosen on some issues.
- D   (*No mistakes*)

10

- J   The basketball teams congratulated
- K   each other in the end they didn't want
- L   to show bad sportsmanship.
- M   (*No mistakes*)

Written Expression, Part 1 *(continued)*

For questions 11–20, look for mistakes in punctuation.

11

A The novel offered a fictional, but realistic
B view into the lives of settlers in the
C pre-Revolutionary War colonies.
D *(No mistakes)*

12

J The gymnastics team won medals
K in all three of the events it entered:
L mat, vault, and balance beam.
M *(No mistakes)*

13

A There are now over 6.5 billion people
B on Earth which is an increase of about
C 1.5 billion from just 30 years ago.
D *(No mistakes)*

14

J The principal instructed the eighth-graders
K to remain in the assembly hall, graduation
L plans were to be announced.
M *(No mistakes)*

15

A Steve and Mary went to the beach this
B morning, therefore, they were already
C sunburned by the time the soccer game
   started.
D *(No mistakes)*

16

A When Meredith was in fifth grade,
B she wrote to Maya Angelou to ask what
C exactly a poet laureate does?
D *(No mistakes)*

17

A Kevin can be a suspicious person.
   When he
B answers the phone and someone asks if
   Kevin is
C there, he responds with "Who wants to
   know?"
D *(No mistakes)*

18

J Kelli is quitting drama club next
   semester
K because, she is taking Chinese and will
   have
L to study harder than she usually does.
M *(No mistake)*

19

A Reggie's essay listed the following
   reasons for applying
B to this school; academic excellence, a
   superior
C basketball program, and proximity to
   his house.
D *(No mistakes)*

20

J My brother who is named Marty was
   always
K at the top of his class. Therefore,
   following
L in his footsteps is sometimes difficult.
M *(No mistakes)*

Written Expression, Part 1 *(continued)*

For questions 21–30, look for mistakes in spelling.

21

- A Ronald is definately the best
- B quarterback this school has
- C had in the past 10 years.
- D *(No mistakes)*

22

- J Miners used to bring canarys into
- K the mines to judge when the air
- L quality was getting dangerous.
- M *(No mistakes)*

23

- A The principal reason we're not going
- B to the ball game is that the parking
- C has become too expensive.
- D *(No mistakes)*

24

- J The chess team had to forfeit the tour-
nament
- K because alot of the members were also
- L participating in a debate tournament.
- M *(No mistakes)*

25

- A The position of club treasurer
- B requires good judgment and
- C excellent math skills.
- D *(No mistakes)*

26

- J The obstacle course Larry built was
- K so difficult that one mistep could
- L easily result in an injury.
- M *(No mistakes)*

27

- A The voters wouldn't acknowledge it, but in this
- B case a slightly higher tax would save them money
- C due to an improvement in government services.
- D *(No mistakes)*

28

- J Jack also plays baseball and
- K swims competitively, but he
- L enjoys unning most of all.
- M *(No mistakes)*

29

- A Charlie usually receives average grades
- B in math and science, but all of his English
- C teachers praise his writeing.
- D *(No mistakes)*

30

- J Melinda is a very shy person, but some of
- K her classmates think she is wierd because
- L she doesn't participate in any clubs.
- M *(No mistakes)*

Written Expression, Part 1 *(continued)*

For questions 31–40, look for capitalization *mistakes.*

31
- A Joan thinks she might major in English
- B when she goes to college, but Jan
- C is going to study Economics.
- D *(No mistakes)*

32
- J After titling his first novel Points Of The
- K Sun, Mike started sending copies of
- L the manuscript to publishers.
- M *(No mistakes)*

33
- A The first family vacation that I
- B remember is a long road trip to
- C the top of Pikes peak in Colorado.
- D *(No mistakes)*

34
- J My neighbor has very loud dogs;
- K Yesterday I heard them barking
- L all the way down the street.
- M *(No mistakes)*

35
- A My Mom has the coolest job of any parent
- B I know. She is a marine biologist studying
- C dolphins and other sea creatures.
- D *(No mistakes)*

36
- J Mohammed Ali was one of the greatest boxers
- K in history, but he is known as much for his
- L charismatic image as his skill in the ring.
- M *(No mistakes)*

37
- A When Neil Armstrong landed on the
- B moon, he said, "that's one small step
- C for man; one giant leap for mankind."
- D *(No mistakes)*

38
- J Yolanda was born on Tracy Street, but
- K by the time her parents moved away,
- L it was known as County road 23.
- M *(No mistakes)*

39
- A It was with great seriousness that Rebecca
- B told us she would henceforth be known as
- C Her Royal Highness, Princess of Everything.
- D *(No mistakes)*

40
- J few writers in the world have
- K achieved the kind of success that
- L Mark Twain did while alive.
- M *(No mistakes)*

Written Expression, Part 2 *(10 questions, 15 minutes)*

Directions: Choose the answer containing the word, phrase, or sentence that is better than the others.

For questions 41 and 42, choose the best answer based on the following paragraph.

¹Funnel cake, a staple of outdoor summer activities, originated in the Pennsylvania Dutch region of the United States. ²Depending on the region in which a person grew, one may or may not have seen funnel cake in concession stands as a child. ³Chances are, though, almost everyone who has been to a baseball game or carnival has seen elephant ears or fried dough, which are similar. ⁴The difference between these desserts and funnel cake is that funnel cake is made with batter, not dough. ⁵The batter is poured into hot oil, where it is cooked very quickly in a circular pattern. ⁶Then it is generally covered with powdered sugar or chocolate and served hot on a paper plate.

41 Which of the following is the best way to revise sentence 5?

A   The batter is poured in a circular pattern into hot oil, where it is cooked very quickly.

B   The batter is poured very quickly into hot oil, where it is cooked in a circular pattern.

C   The batter is poured very quickly into hot oil in a circular pattern, where it cooks.

D   *(No change)*

42 Which of the following is the best concluding sentence for this paragraph?

J   If you've never had one, you're really missing out.

K   It's a delicious treat, and large enough to share with at least one friend.

L   best memories of the county fair include funnel cake.

M   Fried dough, on the other hand, may be covered with a variety of other toppings including cheese and pizza sauce.

Written Expression, Part 2 *(continued)*

For questions 43 and 44, choose the best answer based on the following paragraph.

[1]Learning how to play the guitar can be very enjoyable, but it is also physically difficult. [2]Playing chords accurately and clearly requires you to press the strings very firmly against the fretboard, which can be very painful until your fingertips have built up enough calluses. [3]Naturally, this requires a great deal of practice, which can be very painful. [4]In the meantime, uncalloused fingers will turn red and blister. [5]In addition, gripping the fretboard that tightly requires you to build up strength in your hand, which cannot be accomplished overnight.

43 Which of the following is the best title for the essay?

 A   Treating Injuries Caused by Playing the Guitar

 B   Learning to Play Guitar Like a Pro

 C   The Difficulty of Learning to Play Guitar

 D   Playing Guitar by Ear

44 Which of the following is the best way to combine sentences 3 and 4?

 J   Naturally, this requires a great deal of practice, which can be very painful; in the meantime, uncalloused fingers will turn red and blister.

 K   Naturally, this requires a great deal of practice, which can be very painful, but in the meantime, uncalloused fingers will turn red and blister.

 L   Naturally, this requires a great deal of practice, which can be very painful, because in the meantime, uncalloused fingers will turn red and blister.

 M   Naturally, this requires a great deal of practice, and uncalloused fingers will turn red and blister, and it's all very difficult and painful.

Written Expression, Part 2 *(continued)*

For questions 45–47, choose the best answer based on the following paragraph.

¹My favorite musical of all time is *West Side Story*. ²It is a modern retelling of *Romeo and Juliet*, the famous play by William Shakespeare that tells of two teenagers from warring families who fall in love. ³In *West Side Story*, the teenagers are associated with different gangs in 1950s New York City. ⁴Tony is a former leader of the Jets, a Caucasian gang that rules the streets. ⁵Bernardo, Maria's older brother, he's the leader of an immigrant Puerto Rican gang called the Sharks. ⁶As tensions between the two groups heat up, Tony and Maria fall in love and plan to run away to get married. ⁷But the violence that surrounds them eventually engulfs even Tony and Maria, and Tony is killed at the end. ⁸My favorite song in the musical is a ballad called "Maria", which Tony sings as he wanders through the streets after meeting Maria.

45 Which of the following sentences could best be removed without detracting from the paragraph?

A   1

B   4

C   7

D   8

46 Which is the best way to rewrite sentence 2?

J   Change "that" to "which".

K   Change "from warring families who fall in love" to "who fall in love even though they come from warring families".

L   Change "the famous play by William Shakespeare" to "William Shakespeare's famous play"

M   *(No change)*

47 Which of the following is the best way to rewrite the underlined part of sentence 5?

A   Maria is the younger sister of Bernardo,

B   Maria being Bernardo's sister,

C   Bernardo who is Maria's older brother

D   *(No change)*

Written Expression, Part 2 (continued)

For questions 48–50, choose the best answer based on the following paragraph.

[1]There are many compromises to living in a city apartment rather than a house. [2]Space is the most obvious one, since most apartments are considerably smaller than houses. [3]Privacy can be another. [4]Even if one lives alone, people who share a building can hear each other closing doors, walking up stairs, and moving furniture around. [5]Though houses <u>offer relaxation</u> from the sounds of neighbors in the building, they also come with their own tradeoffs. [6]Lawn care, for example, is generally not something that is expected of apartment dwellers, but homeowners and even tenants of rental homes generally have to do some lawn maintenance in the summer months. [7]That requires equipment, time, and effort.

48 Which of the following is the best way to combine sentences 2 and 3?

   J   Space being the most obvious one, since most apartments are considerably smaller than houses, privacy can be another.

   K   Space is the most obvious one, most apartments being considerably smaller than houses, but privacy can be another.

   L   Space is the most obvious one, so most apartments are considerably smaller than houses, and privacy can be another.

   M   Space is the most obvious one, since most apartments are considerably smaller than houses, and privacy can be another.

49 Which of the following is the best way to write the underlined part of sentence 5?

   A   provide freedom
   B   have relief
   C   give alleviation
   D   *(No change)*

50 Which of the following is the best way to write sentence 7?

   J   That requires time and equipment, and it takes effort too.

   K   That requiring time, equipment, and effort.

   L   Requiring time, and equipment and effort.

   M   *(No change)*

Mathematics, Part 1 *(32 questions, 33 minutes)*

Directions: Choose the best answer from the four given for each problem.

1 Which of the following numbers is prime?

A   3
B   9
C   36
D   75

2 Marcia works for an ice cream shop and she needs to distribute a large bucket of ice cream into 2-quart containers for individual sale. If the bucket holds 5 gallons of ice cream and there are 4 quarts in a gallon, how many individual containers will she be able to make?

J   5
K   10
L   20
M   40

3 Based on the table, how many more votes did the People's National Party receive than all other groups?

Parties	Votes	%	Seats
People's National Party	383,887	52.2	35
Jamaica Labor Party	346,860	47.2	25
Other	3,881	0.5	0
Total	734,628		60

A   37,027
B   33,146
C   40,908
D   29,265

4 Dan and Stephanie are making cookies for a school bake sale. If they are making two-thirds as many oatmeal raisin cookies as chocolate chip and they are making 60 oatmeal raisin cookies, how many cookies are they making in all?

J   80
K   90
L   150
M   180

5 What is the greatest common factor of 9 and 36?

A   3
B   4
C   9
D   36

6 $15^2 =$

J   30
K   60
L   225
M   1500

7 $\dfrac{3}{8}$ written as a decimal is _____.

A   0.25
B   0.375
C   0.625
D   2.67

8 Based on the following chart, approximately how many more visitors went to Times Square in 2007 than 2005?

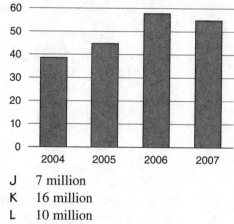

■ Annual Visitors to Times Square (in Millions)

J   7 million
K   16 million
L   10 million
M   3 million

Mathematics, Part 1 *(continued)*

9 Linda is buying a remnant of fabric that is marked $12.00, but there is a sale at the fabric store and everything is 30% off. How much will the remnant cost? Assume there is no sales tax.

   A $3.60
   B $4.00
   C $8.00
   D $8.40

10 Using the chart below, determine which year the greatest increase in demand for rentals occurred.

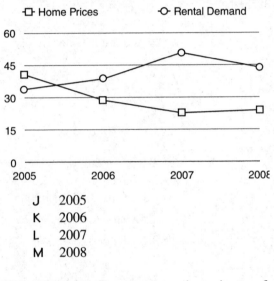

   J   2005
   K   2006
   L   2007
   M   2008

11 What is the least common denominator of $\frac{1}{4}$, $\frac{2}{3}$, and $\frac{5}{8}$?

   A   6
   B   8
   C   12
   D   24

12 Danny is counting birds in his yard for his science project. If last Saturday he counted 25 birds and today the number of birds increased by 20%, what is the number of birds he counted today?

   J   30
   K   35
   L   40
   M   45

13 What total percent of quizzes and tests count toward the final grade in Mr. Amirkhanian's biology class?

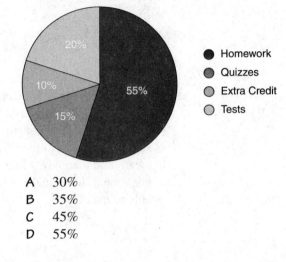

   A   30%
   B   35%
   C   45%
   D   55%

14 Which age group showed the greatest increase in watching television regularly on the Internet in one year? Use the chart below.

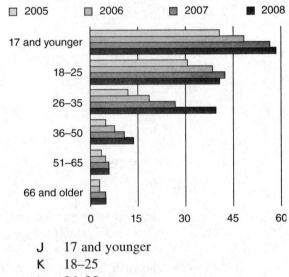

   J   17 and younger
   K   18–25
   L   26–35
   M   51–65

Mathematics, Part 1 *(continued)*

15 Jamie's parents give her $10 for every A on her report card and $5 for every B. If she received $30 for her report card today and she made one A, how many Bs did she make?

A   2
B   3
C   4
D   5

16 $4 - (-10) =$

J -6
K 6
L -14
M 14

17 How many quarters did it take the iSong Music Store to reach 2 billion downloads per quarter? Use the chart below.

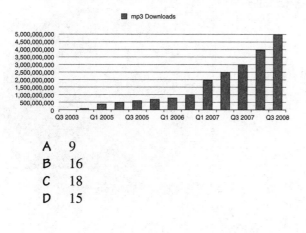

A   9
B   16
C   18
D   15

18 Ben, Ryan, and Scott tracked their improvement in playing disc golf over the summer. Who showed the best improvement in their score from May to August? (Lower numbers are better.)

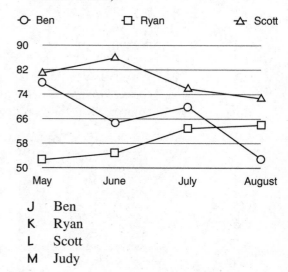

J   Ben
K   Ryan
L   Scott
M   Judy

19 Willie volunteers at the library after school for 10 hours per week. If he reshelves books for three-quarters of that time and spends the rest of the time reading to kindergarten students, how much time does he spend each week reading to kindergarten students?

A   2 hours
B   2.5 hours
C   5 hours
D   7.5 hours

20 What is the fraction equivalent of 40%?

J $\dfrac{1}{5}$

K $\dfrac{2}{5}$

L $\dfrac{2}{20}$

M $\dfrac{5}{8}$

Mathematics, Part 1 *(continued)*

21 Darla's theater group is setting up chairs for a local production. If they are expecting 120 people and each row fits eight chairs, how many rows of chairs will they need?

A   8
B   12
C   15
D   20

22 Which of the top five tallest steel roller coasters is approximately 90% as tall as the number 1 Kingda Ka roller coaster?

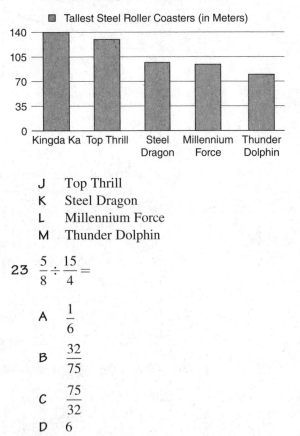

J   Top Thrill
K   Steel Dragon
L   Millennium Force
M   Thunder Dolphin

23 $\dfrac{5}{8} \div \dfrac{15}{4} =$

A $\dfrac{1}{6}$

B $\dfrac{32}{75}$

C $\dfrac{75}{32}$

D   6

24 Michelle and Rhonda take two different paths through a canyon. If Rhonda's path is 5,167 feet and Michelle's path is 7,298 feet, how many feet longer is Michelle's path?

J   1,091 ft
K   2,131 ft
L   3,036 ft
M   12,465 ft

25 Jorge and Sarah are going out to eat. They order a large pizza with three premium toppings, two large sodas, and split an order of spumoni ice cream. How much is their total for the meal?

Pizzas (premium toppings 60¢ each)	Drinks	Sides and Dessert
Medium $14.99	Iced Tea $1.50	Salad $2.99
Large $18.99	Soda $1.75 (50¢ more for large)	Spumoni Ice Cream $1.99
Extra Large $22.99	Coffee $1.25	Bread Sticks $2.75

A $27.28
B $26.28
C $30.37
D $31.37

26 Gina kept track of her monthly expenses with this chart. What is the total percent spent on all items except rent and food?

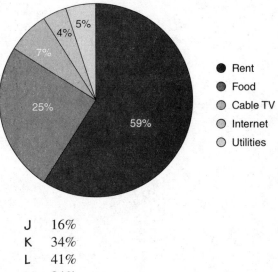

J   16%
K   34%
L   41%
M   84%

27 It takes Ludwig 45 minutes to paint a single figurine. At this rate, how long will it take him to paint 10 figurines?

A   2.5 hours
B   5 hours
C   7.5 hours
D   450 hours

Mathematics, Part 1 *(continued)*

28 2.45 =

J $\dfrac{2}{45}$

K $2\dfrac{9}{20}$

L $2\dfrac{5}{9}$

M $2\dfrac{4}{5}$

29 Arturo is buying CDs at a music store. One CD costs $9.85. If two CDs together cost $15.45, how much did the second CD cost? Assume there is no sales tax.

A $3.60
B $4.60
C $5.60
D $6.60

30 Heather bikes the course shown below every Saturday morning. If the entire course is 18 miles, what is the length of the unlabeled leg of the course?

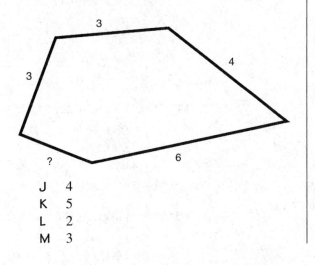

J 4
K 5
L 2
M 3

31 Mary Ellen saves $5 from her allowance each week to put toward a game console. If it will take her 30 weeks at this rate to have enough for the console, how much does the console cost? Assume there is no sales tax.

A $6
B $35
C $100
D $150

32 0.000067 written in scientific notation is _____.

J 6.7×10^6
K 6.7×10^5
L 6.7×10^{-6}
M 6.7×10^{-5}

Mathematics, Part 2 *(18 Questions, 7 minutes)*

Estimation

Directions: For questions 33–50, estimate the answer; no scratch work is allowed. Do not try to calculate exact answers.

33 The closest estimate of 18×312 is _____.

    A   60
    B   600
    C   6,000
    D   60,000

34 The closest estimate of $1.06 + 7.83$ is _____.

    J   8
    K   9
    L   10
    M   11

35 The closest estimate of $623 - 335$ is _____.

    A   100
    B   200
    C   300
    D   400

36 The closest estimate of $454 \div 29$ is _____.

    J   15
    K   150
    L   1,500
    M   15,000

37 The closest estimate of 37×52 is _____.

    A   200
    B   2,000
    C   20,000
    D   200,000

38 The closest estimate of $297 + 613$ is _____.

    J   900
    K   1,000
    L   1,100
    M   1,200

39 The closest estimate of $1,043 - 459$ is _____.

    A   500
    B   600
    C   700
    D   800

40 The closest estimate of 32×7.97 is _____.

    J   2.4
    K   240
    L   2,400
    M   24,000

41 The closest estimate of $512 \div 48$ is _____.

    A   10
    B   100
    C   1,000
    D   10,000

42 The closest estimate of $709 - 214$ is _____.

    J   5
    K   50
    L   500
    M   5,000

43 The closest estimate of 51×694 is _____.

    A   350
    B   3,500
    C   35,000
    D   350,000

44 The closest estimate of $1,875 + 5,263$ is _____.

    J   6,000
    K   7,000
    L   8,000
    M   9,000

45 The number 72.856 rounded to the nearest tenths place is _____.

    A   72.000
    B   72.800
    C   72.860
    D   72.900

Mathematics, Part 2 *(continued)*

46 The number 645.7845 rounded to the nearest hundredths place is _____.

J   600.0000
K   645.0000
L   645.7800
M   645.7850

47 The number 382.8726 rounded to the nearest tens place is _____.

A   380.0000
B   382.0000
C   382.9000
D   390.0000

48 The number 283.456 rounded to the nearest hundreds place is _____.

J   283.000
K   283.460
L   290.000
M   300.000

49 The closest estimate of $(654 - 247) \div 51$ is _____.

A   8
B   80
C   800
D   8,000

50 Rhandi is buying some blank CDs for $4.95 and a computer cable for $10.75. If she gives the clerk a $20 bill, what is the closest estimate of the change she will receive?

J $3.00
K $4.00
L $5.00
M $6.00

Ability, Part 1 *(40 Questions, 25 minutes)*

Directions: In questions 1–20, the first three figures are alike in certain ways. From the five answer choices, select the figure that is most like the first three figures in the same ways.

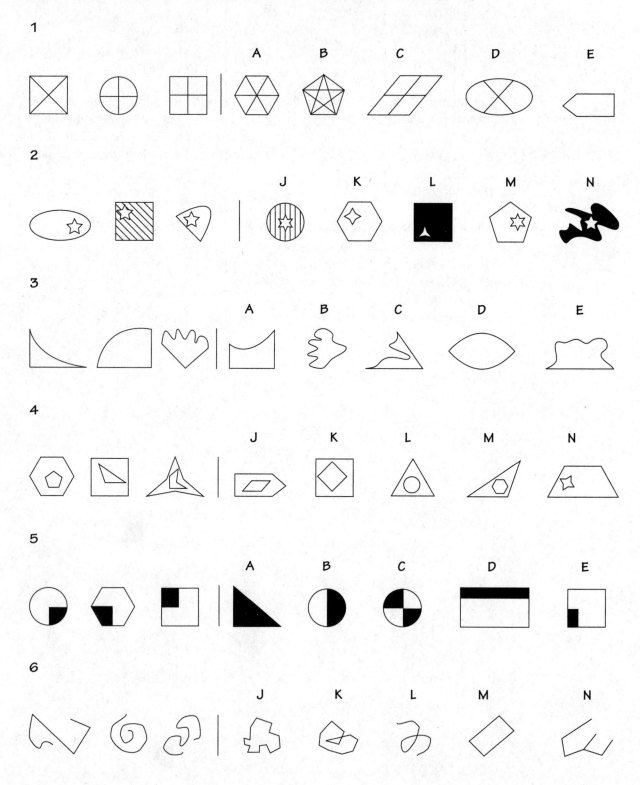

Ability, Part 1 *(continued)*

7

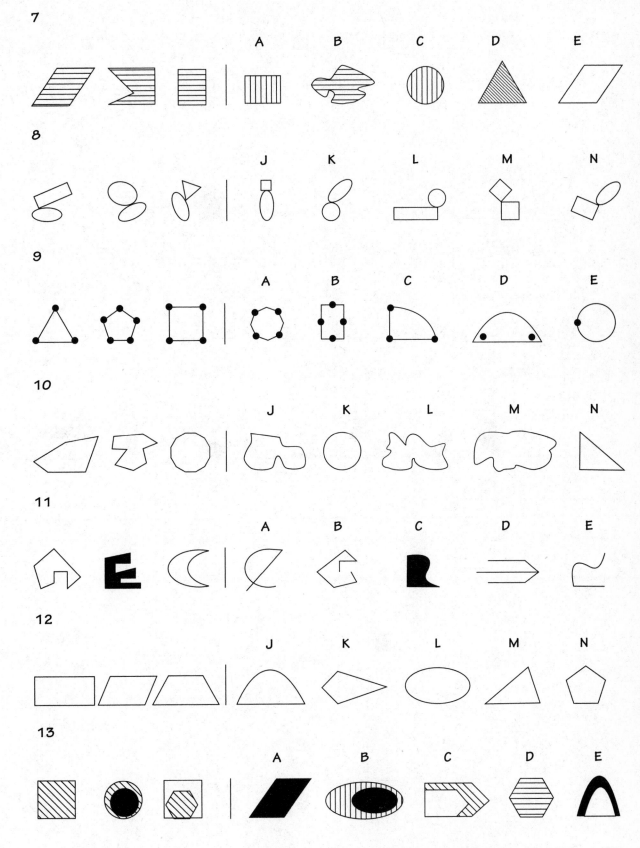

8

9

10

11

12

13

Ability, Part 1 *(continued)*

14

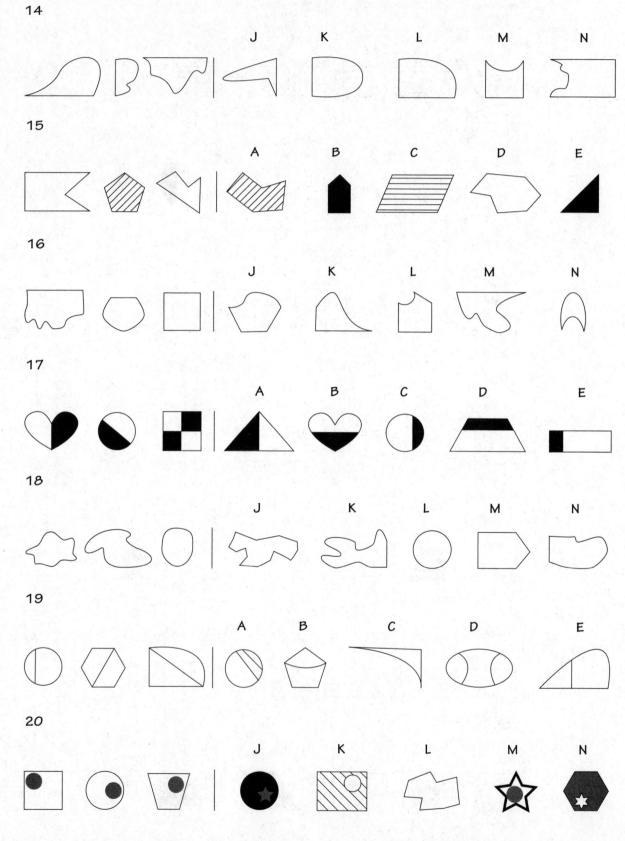

15

16

17

18

19

20

Ability, Part 1 *(continued)*

Directions: Find the figure that completes the puzzle.

21

22

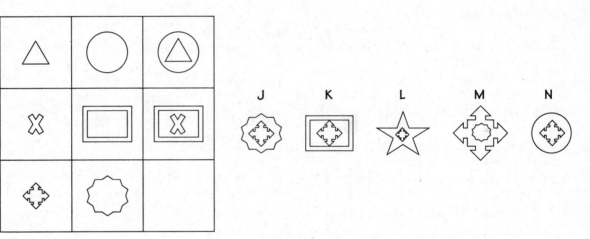

23

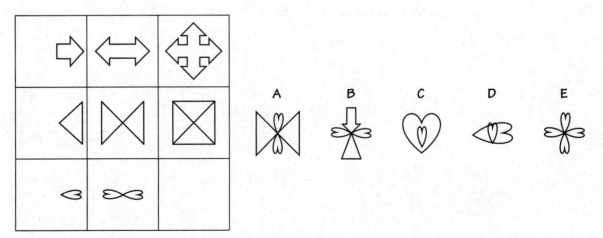

Ability, Part 1 *(continued)*

24

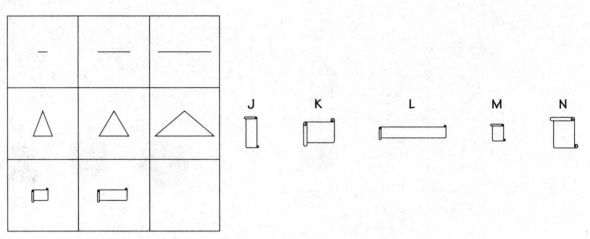

25

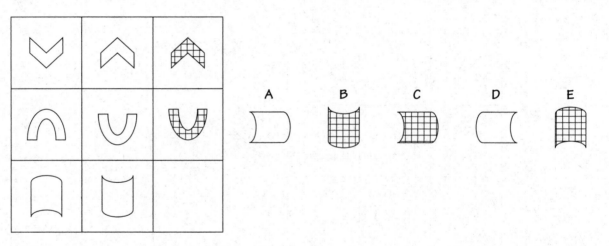

26

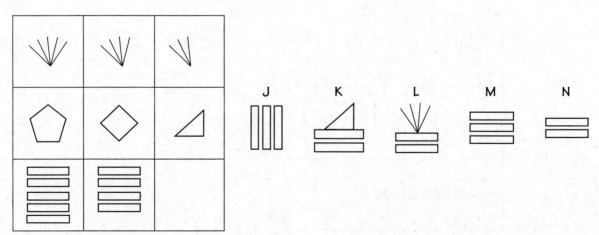

Ability, Part 1 *(continued)*

27

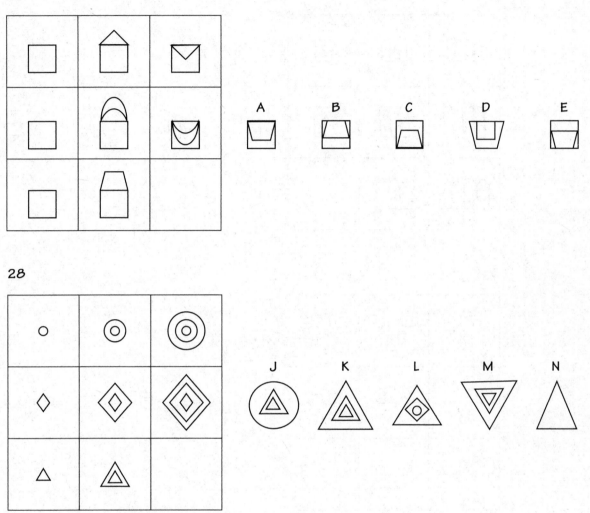

28

29

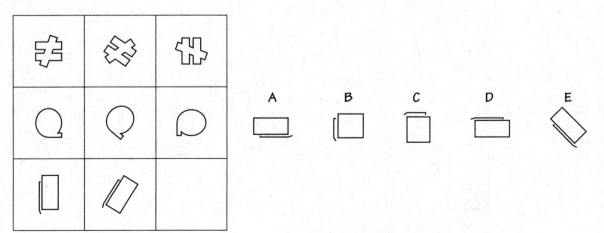

Ability, Part 1 *(continued)*

30

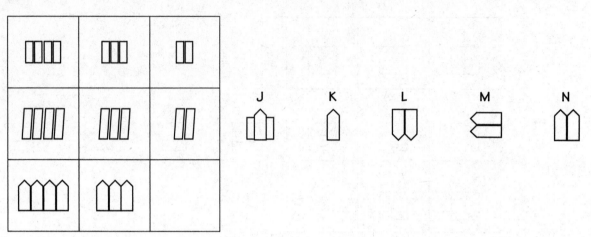

31

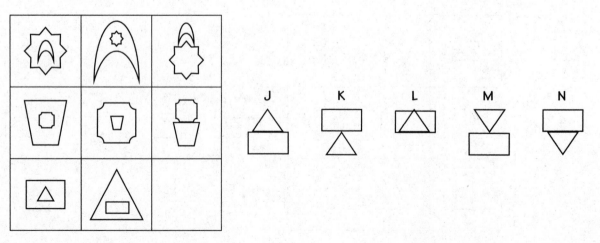

32

Ability, Part 1 *(continued)*

33

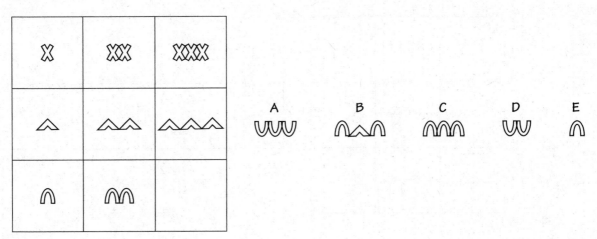

34

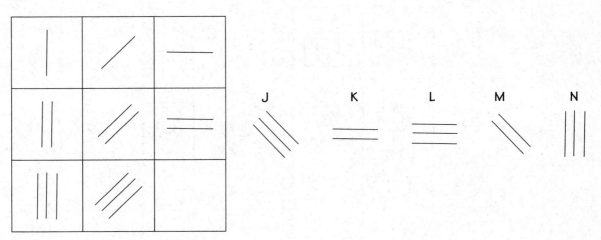

35

Ability, Part 1 (continued)

36

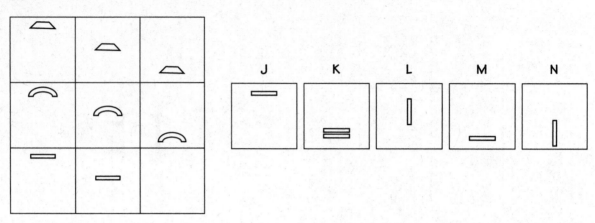

37

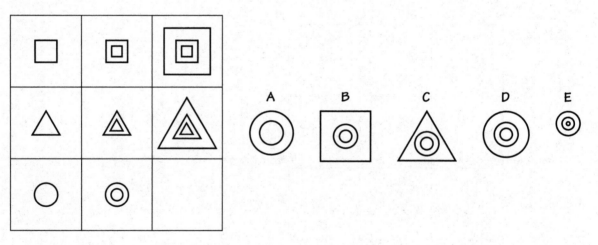

38

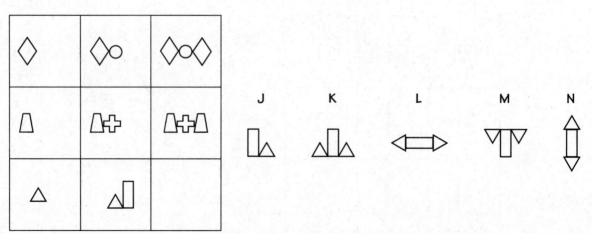

Ability, Part 1 *(continued)*

39

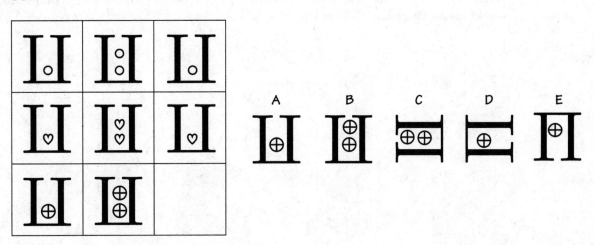

40

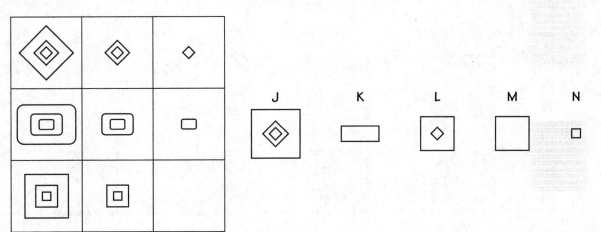

Ability, Part 2 *(10 Questions, 7 minutes)*

Directions: In questions 41–50, in the top line, a piece of paper is folded, and one or more holes are punched through all the layers. Select the figure in the bottom row that shows how the punched paper would appear unfolded.

41

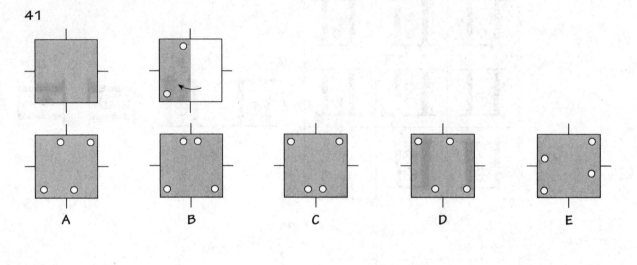

42

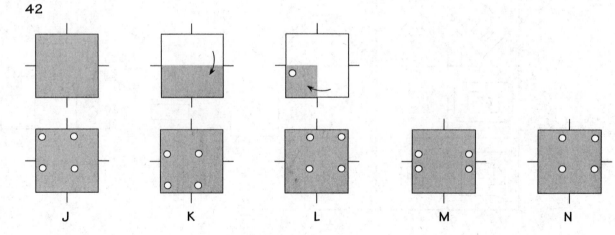

43

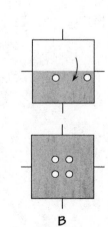
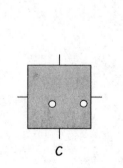
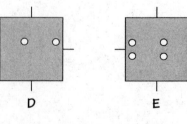

Ability, Part 2 *(continued)*

44

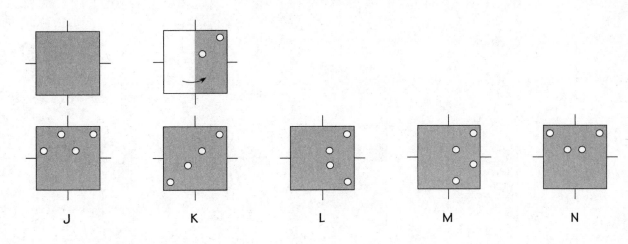

J   K   L   M   N

45

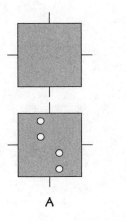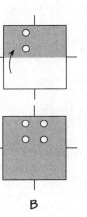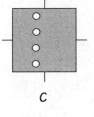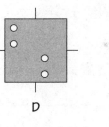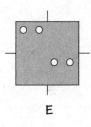

A   B   C   D   E

46

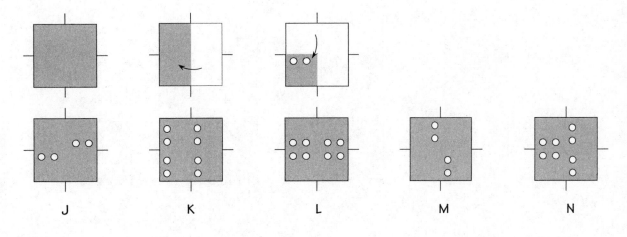

J   K   L   M   N

Ability, Part 2 (continued)

47

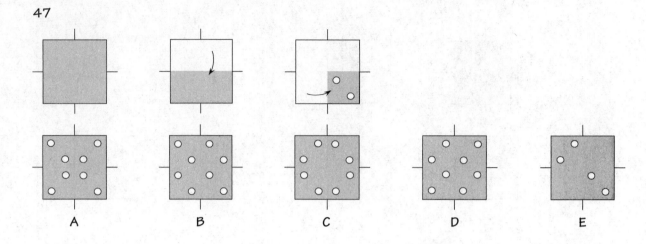

A   B   C   D   E

48

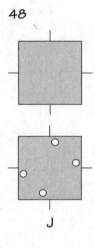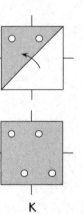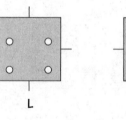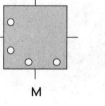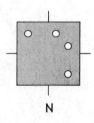

J   K   L   M   N

49

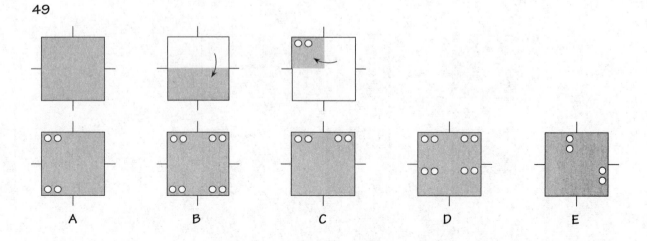

A   B   C   D   E

Ability, Part 2 *(continued)*

50

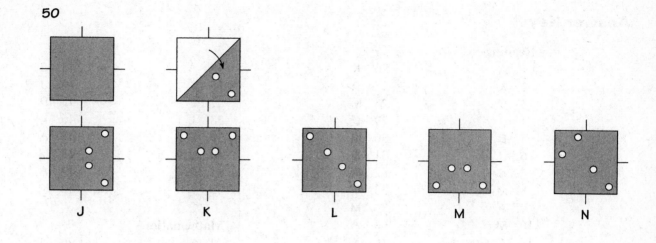

TACHS PRACTICE TEST 1

Answer Key

Reading

1. A	26. K
2. K	27. D
3. D	28. M
4. J	29. B
5. B	30. M
6. J	31. B
7. C	32. M
8. M	33. D
9. A	34. M
10. M	35. A
11. C	36. K
12. J	37. B
13. C	38. M
14. J	39. B
15. B	40. L
16. L	41. A
17. A	42. M
18. K	43. B
19. C	44. J
20. M	45. A
21. A	46. L
22. M	47. B
23. D	48. J
24. J	49. B
25. C	50. L

Written Expression

1. C	18. K
2. J	19. B
3. D	20. J
4. J	21. A
5. C	22. J
6. M	23. D
7. C	24. K
8. K	25. D
9. C	26. K
10. K	27. D
11. A	28. L
12. M	29. C
13. B	30. K
14. K	31. C
15. B	32. J
16. C	33. C
17. D	34. K

35. A	43. C
36. M	44. J
37. B	45. D
38. L	46. K
39. D	47. A
40. J	48. M
41. A	49. A
42. K	50. M

Mathematics

1. A	26. J
2. K	27. C
3. B	28. K
4. L	29. C
5. C	30. L
6. L	31. D
7. B	32. M
8. L	33. C
9. D	34. K
10. L	35. C
11. D	36. J
12. J	37. B
13. B	38. J
14. L	39. B
15. C	40. K
16. M	41. A
17. A	42. L
18. J	43. C
19. B	44. K
20. K	45. D
21. C	46. L
22. J	47. A
23. A	48. M
24. K	49. A
25. A	50. K

Ability

1. C	7. B
2. N	8. J
3. C	9. C
4. J	10. N
5. D	11. C
6. N	12. K

TACHS PRACTICE TEST 1

Answer Key *(continued)*

Ability *(continued)*

13. C	23. E	33. C	42. M
14. K	24. L	34. L	43. A
15. B	25. B	35. B	44. N
16. M	26. M	36. M	45. C
17. A	27. A	37. D	46. L
18. L	28. K	38. K	47. A
19. E	29. D	39. A	48. N
20. M	30. N	40. N	49. B
21. C	31. E	41. B	50. L
22. J	32. J		

TACHS PRACTICE TEST 1

Answers and Explanations

Reading

1. **A** To burgeon means to bloom or flourish.

2. **K** Cryptic means mysterious or coded.

3. **D** Decadent means self-indulgent or luxurious.

4. **J** Eclectic means deriving ideas from a broad or diverse range of sources.

5. **B** To forgo is to decline to take.

6. **J** An ideology is a system of belief.

7. **C** Illicit means unauthorized, but not necessarily illegal.

8. **M** Infamous looks like the opposite of famous, but it really means notorious, or famous for something bad.

9. **A** To mediate is to help people try to settle a conflict, but it doesn't necessarily mean the conflict is resolved.

10. **M** To mollify means all of the listed definitions.

11. **C** Partisan means biased. Another common phrase, bi-partisan support, means support from both sides.

12. **J** Pensive means contemplative or brooding.

13. **C** To renounce is to abandon or give up a belief.

14. **J** Sanguine means content or cheerful.

15. **B** To spawn is to create or generate.

16. **L** Terse means brief or concise. Don't confuse terse with tense, which means nervous or anxious.

17. **A** Venal means corrupt or willing to be bribed.

18. **K** A vocation is a job or career. Don't confuse vocation with vacation!

19. **C** Ironic means paradoxical, or happening in a way that is different from what one would expect.

20. **M** Compliant means agreeable or obedient.

21. **A** "Legendary" is the only answer choice that is supported by the passage, which mentions, among other statements, how the Texas Rangers were mythologized.

22. **M** The passage mentions that today's Texas Rangers focus on detective work and direct law enforcement is under the Highway Patrol. Therefore, giving speeding tickets would not be a focus for the Rangers.

23. **D** The specific example given is that the Texas Rangers baseball team is named after the police force. Novels and film are only mentioned abstractly, and radio is not mentioned at all.

24. **J** The passage stated that the Texas Rangers were responsible for catching Bonnie and Clyde, John Wesley Hardin, and Sam Bass. If you are not familiar with these stories, you can still see the implication in the last sentence, as these arrests made the Texas Rangers' legacy.

25. **C** The bulk of the passage is spent drawing contrasts between the Texas Rangers' mythology and their current job responsibilities.

26. **K** The passage states that the Richter scale measures the "shocks" felt before the big explosion, so **K** is the best answer. None of the other answers were even mentioned in the passage.

Answers and Explanations *(continued)*

27. **D** All of the answers were mentioned in the passage, and all of them are indicators of a big explosion.

28. **M** All of the answers were mentioned in the passage in the last paragraph. Roads and airports were closed, which would limit travel; visibility was limited in Yakima; and there were power outages, which would limit access to electricity.

29. **B** The passage mentions that ash fell "as far away as Bend, OR and Spokane, WA," so **B** is the best choice. None of the other answers are supported by the passage.

30. **M** Most of the details in the passage support the topic sentence in answer choice **M**, so it is the best answer. Answer choices **J** and **K** are not supported by the passage and **L** is a minor detail, not the topic of the passage.

31. **B** Answer choice **B** is the only detail that is mentioned in the passage.

32. **M** All of the answer choices are mentioned in the passage as negative effects that humanity has on the environment, which some global leaders are attempting to change.

33. **D** Answer choice **D** is almost stated in the passage, but none of the other answers are supported.

34. **M** Espoused most nearly means promoted, because it is something that helps the cause. "Accepted" is close but is not as strong as "promoted."

35. **A** The overall tone of the passage is positive and speaks about measures that are being taken to help the environment, so **A** is the best choice.

36. **K** Diurnal is mentioned as the opposite of nocturnal, and nocturnal is contrasted to "active during the day," so that is the best definition of diurnal.

37. **B** Answer choice **B** is the only answer choice that is supported by the passage; none of the others are mentioned.

38. **M** The last sentence of the passage states that deforestation is a threat to lemurs' survival.

39. **B** The first sentence of the passage states that lemurs are native to Madagascar and its surrounding islands. None of the other answer choices are supported by the passage.

40. **L** Answer choice **L** encompasses the main points of the passage. The other answer choices are either too specific or not mentioned.

41. **A** The passage states that Napoléan created the contest so that the French armed forces and lower classes could have a less expensive butter substitute, so **A** is the best answer. Clearly, royal classes and visiting dignitaries would not fall into those categories, and there is no support for the idea that margarine was exported to the United States and not under a ban at that time.

42. **M** The passage states that the dairy industry fought margarine's availability, so **M** makes the most sense.

43. **B** The passage states that margarine is nearly white in color, which makes it unappealing to consumers; so much so that banning the production of yellow-colored margarine was the most effective way to slow its popularity.

44. **J** Answer choice **J** makes the most sense because the article is factual and does not express any of the points of view that **K** and **L** would be likely to have. It also has no scientific analysis, which would be present if **M** were correct.

45. **A** Answer choice **A** reflects that the passage is a history of margarine and also makes reference to "color," which was mentioned in the passage. Answer choices **B** and **C** are completely outside the scope of the passage,

Answers and Explanations (continued)

and **D** is too specific to be the title of the passage as a whole.

46. **L** According to the passage, her first part in a movie was "as an uncredited extra," so **L** is the best choice. Answer choices **J** and **M** are mentioned in the passage, but not in reference to her first role, and **K** is not mentioned at all.

47. **B** Answer choice **B** was the only detail mentioned in the passage; the author expressed no opinions about what should have happened. Answer choice **C** is not mentioned.

48. **J** The author mentions that Anna May Wong's ethnicity was a stumbling block, so **J** is the best answer. Be careful; answer choice **L** sounds good but is not very well supported, as the passage makes no mention of *audiences* objecting to Anna May Wong.

49. **B** Answer choice **B** is the best supported of the answer choices; while the author clearly has a perspective on the casting during Anna May Wong's acting days, the passage cannot accurately be described as a rant against casting directors.

50. **L** Answer choice **L** sums up the ideas expressed in the passage. Answer choice **J** is also good, but is more broad than the material covered by the passage. The other two answer choices are not mentioned in the passage.

Written Expression

1. **C** The word *I* should be used instead of *me*, because the pronoun is actually being used as a subject. The sentence implies, "Mary has to work harder than *I do*."

2. **J** The verb is not complete. The first line should *say has been*, not just *has*.

3. **D** The sentence is correct as written.

4. **J** The word *ran* is being described. *Ran* is a verb, therefore the adverb *quickly* is needed instead of the adjective *quick*.

5. **C** The word *hers* never takes an apostrophe; it is always a personal pronoun.

6. **M** The sentence is correct as written.

7. **C** The verb *dancing* is not parallel with *watch* (which is the verb it is being compared to). The correct word to use here is *dance*.

8. **K** The phrase *6 AM in the morning* is redundant.

9. **C** The phrase *compromise was chosen* is passive.

10. **K** The sentence is a run-on; the two complete thoughts should be split into separate sentences.

11. **A** The comma after *fictional* is not necessary.

12. **M** There are no punctuation mistakes.

13. **B** The word *which* should have a comma before it.

14. **K** The sentence is a comma splice because there are two complete sentences separated by only a comma. Substituting a semicolon or breaking the sentence up into two separate sentences would make it correct.

15. **B** When *therefore* is used in the middle of a sentence without the word *and*, it must be preceded by a semicolon and followed by a comma.

16. **C** The sentence is a statement, not a question. It should end with a period.

17. **D** There are no punctuation mistakes.

Answers and Explanations (continued)

18. **K** No comma is needed after *because*.

19. **B** A colon is needed instead of a semicolon to introduce a list.

20. **J** The phrase *who is named Marty* is non-essential information in the sentence and should be set off with commas.

21. **A** The correct spelling is *definitely*.

22. **J** The correct spelling is *canaries*.

23. **D** There are no spelling mistakes.

24. **K** The correct spelling is *a lot*.

25. **D** There are no spelling mistakes.

26. **K** The correct spelling is *misstep*.

27. **D** There are no spelling mistakes.

28. **L** The correct spelling is *running*.

29. **C** The correct spelling is *writing*.

30. **K** The correct spelling is *weird*.

31. **C** Fields of study should not be capitalized unless they are the names of languages, such as *English*, or titles of specific classes, such as *Economics 101*.

32. **J** Small and unimportant words in titles, such as *of* and *the* should not be capitalized.

33. **C** All important words in proper nouns, such as place names, should be capitalized. *Pikes Peak* would be correct.

34. **K** The first word after semicolons should not be capitalized unless they are capitalized for another reason, such as a person's name.

35. **A** *Mom* should only be capitalized when it is being substituted for a name; it is not a proper noun in the phrase *my mom*.

36. **M** There are no capitalization mistakes.

37. **B** Full sentences that are quoted inside of other sentences should start with a capital letter.

38. **L** All parts of a street name should be capitalized (unless they are unimportant words such as *of*).

39. **D** There are no capitalization mistakes.

40. **J** The first word in a sentence should always be capitalized.

41. **A** Answer choice **A** most clearly states how the batter is poured, where it is cooked, and how quickly it is cooked. All the other answer choices introduce logical mistakes in the sentence.

42. **K** Answer choice **K** follows the logical flow of the paragraph best: from cooking to serving to eating.

43. **C** Most of the paragraph discussed the difficulties of playing guitar, so answer choice **C** is the most natural title. The other titles are not covered at all in the paragraph.

44. **J** The two sentences go in the same direction but do not have a causal relationship, so that eliminates answer choices **K** and **L**. **M** is very wordy and awkward, so **J** is the best choice.

45. **D** Sentence 8 is off topic from the rest of the paragraph, so it can most easily be removed without taking anything away from the topic of the paragraph.

46. **K** Even though answer choice **K** lengthens the sentence, it more clearly represents the relationship that the author is trying to express. The sentence as is implies that the families fall in love, and the remaining answer choices do nothing to fix this problem.

Answers and Explanations *(continued)*

47. **A** Answer choice **A** creates a sentence that is phrased similarly to the sentence before and does not have any grammatical problems. Answer choice **B** creates awkward construction, while **C** creates a run-on and **D** creates a fragment.

48. **M** Answer choice **M** is the only sentence that connects the two sentences with a "same direction" conjunction: the word *and*. Answer choice **J** creates a comma splice.

49. **A** Answer choice **A** is the best phrased of the answer choices; all of the others are awkwardly or incorrectly worded.

50. **M** The sentence is correct as is. Answer choice **J** introduces awkward wording, **K** has an incorrect verb, and **L** is a fragment.

Mathematics

1. **A** Three is the only prime number among the answer choices. Nine is divisible by three; 36 is divisible by 2, 3, 4, 6, 9, and 18; and 75 is divisible by 3, 5, 15, and 25.

2. **K** If there are four quarts in a gallon and the bucket holds five gallons, it holds 20 quarts total. Dividing 20 quarts into 2-quart containers gives 10 containers.

3. **B** The other two parties combined get 350,741 votes. Subtracting 350,741 from 383,887, you would get 33,146.

4. **L** Dan and Stephanie are making two-thirds as many oatmeal raisin as chocolate chip cookies, and they're making 60 oatmeal raisin cookies. Sixty is two-thirds of 90, so they are making $60 + 90 = 150$ cookies total.

5. **C** The largest number that both 36 and 9 are divisible by is 9, so that is the greatest common factor.

6. **L** $15^2 = 15 \times 15 = 225$. Be careful; don't get this confused with 15×2, which would give you 30.

7. **B** To convert a fraction to a decimal, we would need to divide out the fraction; $\frac{3}{8}$ is the same as $8\overline{)3}$, which divides out to 0.375.

8. **L** In 2005, about 45 million visited Times Square, compared to 55 million in 2007; 55 million − 45 million = 10 million.

9. **D** To calculate 30% of $12, we would multiply 12×0.3, which equals $3.60. But be careful; that's how much to subtract from the original amount, so the answer is $12.00 − $3.60 = $8.40.

10. **L** From 2005 to 2006, the demand for rentals increased from about 32 to about 40. From 2006, the demand increased from about 40 to 50, which is a greater increase. Demand decreased the following year, so the greatest increase was in 2007.

11. **D** The smallest of the answer choices that is divisible by all of the denominators (4, 3, and 8) is 24.

12. **J** To calculate 20% of 25, we would multiply 25×0.2, which equals 5. Again, be careful; that is the amount to add to the original 25, so the answer is $25 + 5 = 30$.

13. **B** Quizzes count for 15% and tests count for 20%, giving a total of 35% for quizzes and tests.

14. **L** The 26–35 age group showed the biggest increase, from 2007 to 2008.

15. **C** The report card had one A, so you can subtract $10 from the $30 total. That means Jamie got $20 for her Bs, and since she gets $5 for every B and $20 \div 5 = 4$, she got four Bs.

Answers and Explanations *(continued)*

16. **M** The two subtraction signs cancel out, giving you $4 + 10 = 14$.

17. **A** The iSong Music Store reached 2 billion downloads in Q1 2007, which is 9 quarters from the beginning of the data shown.

18. **J** Eyeballing the line chart shows that Ben's score improved the most from May to August. Scott's score improved more gradually, Ryan's score got worse, and Judy is not on the chart at all.

19. **B** Willie reshelves books for three-quarters, or $\frac{3}{4}$, of the 10 hours he spends at the library. That means he reshelves for $\frac{3}{4} \times 10 = 7.5$ hours, leaving $10 - 7.5 = 2.5$ hours for reading to kindergarten kids.

20. **K** To convert a percent to a fraction, just put the percent over 100 and reduce from there. $\frac{40}{100}$ reduces to $\frac{2}{5}$.

21. **C** Since there are 120 chairs to fit into eight rows, you would calculate $120 \div 8 = 15$.

22. **J** 90% of 140 is about 130, and the only roller coaster in the vicinity of 130 is the Top Thrill.

23. **A** Remember, to divide by a fraction, flip the second one and multiply. That gives you $\frac{5}{8} \times \frac{4}{15}$, which reduces to $\frac{1}{2} \times \frac{1}{3}$. Multiply straight across the top and bottom and you get $\frac{1}{6}$.

24. **K** To calculate how many feet longer Michelle's path is, just take the difference between the two paths; $7,289 - 5,167 = 2,131$, so **K** is the correct answer.

25. **A** The pizza should be $\$18.99 + \$1.80$ for three premium toppings. Sodas come to $\$2.25$ each. One order of spumoni ice cream is $\$1.99$. Add $\$18.99 + \$1.80 + \$2.25 + \$2.25 + \$1.99$ and you get $\$27.28$.

26. **J** The items that are not rent and food are Cable TV, Internet, and Utilities, which are 7%, 4%, and 5%, respectively. Adding them up gives a total of 16%.

27. **C** Ludwig can paint one figurine in 45 minutes, which means he can paint 10 figurines in 450 minutes. Since the answer choices are in hours, you must divide by 60 to figure out how many hours that equals; $450 \div 6 = 7.5$ hours.

28. **K** Since 2 is a whole number (in front of the decimal), all you have to convert is the .45 into a fraction. The decimal 0.45 is the same as $\frac{45}{100}$, so you just need to reduce from there. $\frac{45}{100}$ reduces to $\frac{9}{20}$, so $2\frac{9}{20}$ is the correct answer.

29. **C** To find the difference between the total and the first CD, subtract. $\$15.45 - \$9.85 = \$5.60$, so the second CD costs $\$5.60$.

30. **L** The legs of the course that you can see are 3, 3, 4, and 6. They add up to 16, and the course is 18 miles total, so the remaining leg must equal 2 because $18 - 16 = 2$.

31. **D** Mary Ellen needs to save $5 for 30 weeks, so $5 \times 30 = 150$, which is the total cost of the console.

32. **M** You would have to move the decimal point five places to the right to create 6.7 from .0000067, so $.0000067 = 6.7 \times 10^{-5}$.

33. **C** Round 18 to 20 and 312 to 300, and you get $20 \times 300 = 6,000$.

Answers and Explanations *(continued)*

34. **K** Round 1.06 to 1 and 7.83 to 8, and you get $1 + 8 = 9$.

35. **C** Round 623 to 600 and 335 to 300, and you get $600 - 300 = 300$.

36. **J** Round 454 to 450 and 29 to 30, and you get $450 \div 30 = 15$.

37. **B** Round 37 to 40 and 52 to 50, and you get $40 \times 50 = 2{,}000$.

38. **J** Round 297 to 300 and 613 to 600, and you get $300 + 600 = 900$.

39. **B** Round 1043 to 1000 and 459 to 400, and you get $1{,}000 - 400 = 600$.

40. **K** Round 32 to 30 and 7.97 to 8, and you get $30 \times 8 = 240$.

41. **A** Round 512 to 500 and 48 to 50, and you get $500 \div 50 = 10$.

42. **L** Round 709 to 700 and 214 to 200, and you get $700 - 200 = 500$.

43. **C** Round 51 to 50 and 694 to 700, and you get $50 \times 700 = 35{,}000$.

44. **K** Round 1,875 to 2,000 and 5,263 to 5,000, and you get $2{,}000 + 5{,}000 = 7{,}000$.

45. **D** The question asks for the tenths place, or one place after the decimal. The number 5 means round up, so the correct answer is 72.900.

46. **L** The question asks for the hundredths place, or two places after the decimal. The number 4 means round down, so the correct answer is 645.7800.

47. **A** The question asks for the tens place, not the tenths place. The number 2 means round down, so the correct answer is 380.0000.

48. **M** The question asks for the hundreds place, not the hundredths place. The number 8 means round up, so the correct answer is 300.0000.

49. **A** Round 654 to 650, 247 to 250, and 51 to 50, and you get $(650 - 250) \div 50 = 400 \div 50 = 8$.

50. **K** Round $4.95 to $5 and $10.75 to $11, and you get $20 - (\$5 + \$11)$, or $\$20 - \$16 = \$4$.

Ability

1. **C** All figures are split into four equal and congruent parts.

2. **N** All figures contain a five-pointed star shape.

3. **C** All figures have two straight sides and one curved side.

4. **J** All figures contain a shape in the middle that has one fewer side than the shape on the outside.

5. **D** All figures have one quarter of their area shaded in.

6. **N** All figures are completely open.

7. **B** All figures have horizontal stripes.

8. **J** All figures have an ellipse on the bottom.

9. **C** All figures have a dot on each of the corners.

10. **N** All of the sides of the figures are straight.

11. **C** All figures are completely closed.

12. **K** All figures have exactly four sides.

13. **C** All figures have only diagonal stripes.

Answers and Explanations (continued)

14. **K** All figures have one straight side and one curved side.

15. **B** All figures have exactly five sides.

16. **M** All figures have a straight side on top.

17. **A** All figures have one-half of their area shaded in.

18. **L** All figures have no straight sides.

19. **E** All figures contain exactly one straight line inside.

20. **M** All figures contain a gray shaded circle.

21. **C** The figures get darker as you move from left to right. The missing figure is in the row of hearts, so it should be a solid black heart.

22. **J** The first two columns show different shapes, and the right column shows the first shape inside the second shape.

23. **E** Each of the figures in the left column is joined by its mirror image in the middle column. The right column shows the center figure joined by top and bottom identical mirror images so that there are four of the original figure, each pointing in a different direction.

24. **L** Each figure in the left column is longer in the middle column and longer still in the right column.

25. **B** Each figure in the left column is flipped upside down in the middle column and then has stripes added in the right column.

26. **M** Each figure in the left column has five parts (five lines, five sides, five rectangles). In the middle column these figures have four parts and in the right column they have only three parts.

27. **A** Each square in the left column has another shape added on top in the middle column. In the right column, the top shape is inverted inside the square, as if folded down.

28. **K** Each figure in the left column is surrounded by a second similar figure in the middle column and then surrounded by a third similar figure in the right column.

29. **D** Each figure in the left column is rotated 45° to the right in the middle column and then rotated another 45° to the right in the right column.

30. **N** There are four identical figures lined side-by-side in the left column. In the middle column there are only three, and in the right column there are only two.

31. **E** Each figure in the left column has a shape on top of the line and an identical one beneath it. In the middle column the top has an extra identical figure added, but the bottom is left the same. There is still another identical figure added on top in the right column.

32. **J** Each figure in the left column has a smaller different figure within its center. In the middle column the positions are switched and the inside shape is now the outside (larger) shape. In the right column, the original small inside shape is now on top of the original large outside shape.

33. **C** The figure in the left column is doubled in the middle column and tripled in the right column.

34. **L** The vertical line in the top left column is tilted to the right in the middle column and then horizontal in the right column. As you move down the rows, the number of lines increases from one to three, so the missing figure should be three horizontal lines.

35. **B** The top horizontal line on the top left figure has been removed in the middle column, and then the middle horizontal line has been removed in the right column. As you move down the rows, the size of the figures increases.

Answers and Explanations *(continued)*

36. **M** The position of each figure in the left column decreases as you move from left to right, so the missing figure should be a thin rectangle oriented horizontally in the bottom of the box.

37. **D** Each figure in the left column has a smaller version of the same shape inside it in the middle column. In the right column, there is a larger version of the shape added to the outside so that there are three of the same shape, each inside the other.

38. **K** Each figure in the left column is joined by a different figure to its right in the middle column. In the right column, another figure identical to the first one is added to the right of the other two.

39. **A** Each figure in the left column has a sort of bin containing one small object. There are two of the objects in the bin in the middle column, then back to only one in the right column.

40. **N** Each figure in the left column is a set of three of the same shapes in three different sizes, one inside the next. In the middle column, the largest of the shapes has been removed. In the right column, only the smallest shape remains.

41. **B** The paper is folded once and punched once near the fold on the top, so there should be two holes close to the fold on the top.

42. **M** The paper is folded twice and punched near the outside edge, so there should be four holes near the outside edges.

43. **A** The paper is folded once and punched twice near the fold, so there should be four holes near the fold. **A**, **B**, and **E** are the only ones that meet this criteria. The holes should all be on the right side of their quarter of the paper, so **A** is the only one left.

44. **N** The paper is folded once and two holes are punched in the upper half, so there should be four holes in the upper half. Only **J** and **N** meet this criteria. The holes should mirror each other, so only **N** is left.

45. **C** The paper is folded once and punched twice on the left side, so there should be four holes on the left side.

46. **L** The paper is folded twice and two holes are punched, so there should be eight holes in the paper, meaning that **J** and **M** can be eliminated. All of the holes should be near the fold, so **L** is the best answer.

47. **A** The paper is folded twice and two holes are punched, so there should be eight holes in the paper, which eliminates **E**. The holes should mirror each other, so **B** and **D** can also be eliminated. There should be a hole near each corner and one near the middle of each quarter of the page, so **A** is the best choice.

48. **N** The paper is folded twice and punched twice along an outside edge, so **M** and **N** are the best answers. Only **N** is rotated the same way the original paper is, so it is correct.

49. **B** The paper is folded twice and punched twice, so there should be eight holes, which eliminates **A**, **C**, and **E**. All of the holes should be along the outside edges, so **B** is the better of the remaining answers.

50. **L** The paper is folded once and two holes are punched, so there should be four holes total: one near the center and one near the outside of each diagonal half. This eliminates all answers except **L**.

TACHS PRACTICE TEST 2

Answer Sheet

Directions: For each answer that you select, blacken the corresponding oval on this sheet.

Reading, Part 1

1. (A) (B) (C) (D)
2. (J) (K) (L) (M)
3. (A) (B) (C) (D)
4. (J) (K) (L) (M)
5. (A) (B) (C) (D)
6. (J) (K) (L) (M)
7. (A) (B) (C) (D)
8. (J) (K) (L) (M)
9. (A) (B) (C) (D)
10. (J) (K) (L) (M)
11. (A) (B) (C) (D)
12. (J) (K) (L) (M)
13. (A) (B) (C) (D)
14. (J) (K) (L) (M)
15. (A) (B) (C) (D)
16. (J) (K) (L) (M)
17. (A) (B) (C) (D)
18. (J) (K) (L) (M)
19. (A) (B) (C) (D)
20. (J) (K) (L) (M)

Reading, Part 2

21. (A) (B) (C) (D)
22. (J) (K) (L) (M)
23. (A) (B) (C) (D)
24. (J) (K) (L) (M)
25. (A) (B) (C) (D)
26. (J) (K) (L) (M)
27. (A) (B) (C) (D)
28. (J) (K) (L) (M)
29. (A) (B) (C) (D)
30. (J) (K) (L) (M)
31. (A) (B) (C) (D)
32. (J) (K) (L) (M)
33. (A) (B) (C) (D)
34. (J) (K) (L) (M)
35. (A) (B) (C) (D)
36. (J) (K) (L) (M)
37. (A) (B) (C) (D)
38. (J) (K) (L) (M)
39. (A) (B) (C) (D)
40. (J) (K) (L) (M)
41. (A) (B) (C) (D)

42. (J) (K) (L) (M)
43. (A) (B) (C) (D)
44. (J) (K) (L) (M)
45. (A) (B) (C) (D)
46. (J) (K) (L) (M)
47. (A) (B) (C) (D)
48. (J) (K) (L) (M)
49. (A) (B) (C) (D)
50. (J) (K) (L) (M)

Written Expression, Part 1

1. (A) (B) (C) (D)
2. (J) (K) (L) (M)
3. (A) (B) (C) (D)
4. (J) (K) (L) (M)
5. (A) (B) (C) (D)
6. (J) (K) (L) (M)
7. (A) (B) (C) (D)
8. (J) (K) (L) (M)
9. (A) (B) (C) (D)
10. (J) (K) (L) (M)
11. (A) (B) (C) (D)
12. (J) (K) (L) (M)
13. (A) (B) (C) (D)
14. (J) (K) (L) (M)
15. (A) (B) (C) (D)
16. (J) (K) (L) (M)
17. (A) (B) (C) (D)
18. (J) (K) (L) (M)
19. (A) (B) (C) (D)
20. (J) (K) (L) (M)
21. (A) (B) (C) (D)
22. (J) (K) (L) (M)
23. (A) (B) (C) (D)
24. (J) (K) (L) (M)
25. (A) (B) (C) (D)
26. (J) (K) (L) (M)
27. (A) (B) (C) (D)
28. (J) (K) (L) (M)
29. (A) (B) (C) (D)
30. (J) (K) (L) (M)
31. (A) (B) (C) (D)
32. (J) (K) (L) (M)
33. (A) (B) (C) (D)

34. (J) (K) (L) (M)
35. (A) (B) (C) (D)
36. (J) (K) (L) (M)
37. (A) (B) (C) (D)
38. (J) (K) (L) (M)
39. (A) (B) (C) (D)
40. (J) (K) (L) (M)

Written Expression, Part 2

41. (A) (B) (C) (D)
42. (J) (K) (L) (M)
43. (A) (B) (C) (D)
44. (J) (K) (L) (M)
45. (A) (B) (C) (D)
46. (J) (K) (L) (M)
47. (A) (B) (C) (D)
48. (J) (K) (L) (M)
49. (A) (B) (C) (D)
50. (J) (K) (L) (M)

Mathematics, Part 1

1. (A) (B) (C) (D)
2. (J) (K) (L) (M)
3. (A) (B) (C) (D)
4. (J) (K) (L) (M)
5. (A) (B) (C) (D)
6. (J) (K) (L) (M)
7. (A) (B) (C) (D)
8. (J) (K) (L) (M)
9. (A) (B) (C) (D)
10. (J) (K) (L) (M)
11. (A) (B) (C) (D)
12. (J) (K) (L) (M)
13. (A) (B) (C) (D)
14. (J) (K) (L) (M)
15. (A) (B) (C) (D)
16. (J) (K) (L) (M)
17. (A) (B) (C) (D)
18. (J) (K) (L) (M)
19. (A) (B) (C) (D)
30. (J) (K) (L) (M)
31. (A) (B) (C) (D)
32. (J) (K) (L) (M)

Answer Sheet *(continued)*

Mathematics, Part 2

33. (A) (B) (C) (D)
34. (J) (K) (L) (M)
35. (A) (B) (C) (D)
36. (J) (K) (L) (M)
37. (A) (B) (C) (D)
38. (J) (K) (L) (M)
39. (A) (B) (C) (D)
40. (J) (K) (L) (M)
41. (A) (B) (C) (D)
42. (J) (K) (L) (M)
43. (A) (B) (C) (D)
44. (J) (K) (L) (M)
45. (A) (B) (C) (D)
46. (J) (K) (L) (M)
47. (A) (B) (C) (D)
48. (J) (K) (L) (M)
49. (A) (B) (C) (D)
50. (J) (K) (L) (M)

Ability, Part 1

1. (A) (B) (C) (D) (E)
2. (J) (K) (L) (M) (N)
3. (A) (B) (C) (D) (E)
4. (J) (K) (L) (M) (N)
5. (A) (B) (C) (D) (E)
6. (J) (K) (L) (M) (N)
7. (A) (B) (C) (D) (E)
8. (J) (K) (L) (M) (N)
9. (A) (B) (C) (D) (E)
10. (J) (K) (L) (M) (N)
11. (A) (B) (C) (D) (E)
12. (J) (K) (L) (M) (N)
13. (A) (B) (C) (D) (E)
14. (J) (K) (L) (M) (N)
15. (A) (B) (C) (D) (E)
16. (J) (K) (L) (M) (N)

17. (A) (B) (C) (D) (E)
18. (J) (K) (L) (M) (N)
19. (A) (B) (C) (D) (E)
20. (J) (K) (L) (M) (N)
21. (A) (B) (C) (D) (E)
22. (J) (K) (L) (M) (N)
23. (A) (B) (C) (D) (E)
24. (J) (K) (L) (M) (N)
25. (A) (B) (C) (D) (E)
26. (J) (K) (L) (M) (N)
27. (A) (B) (C) (D) (E)
28. (J) (K) (L) (M) (N)
29. (A) (B) (C) (D) (E)
30. (J) (K) (L) (M) (N)
31. (A) (B) (C) (D) (E)
32. (J) (K) (L) (M) (N)
33. (A) (B) (C) (D) (E)
34. (J) (K) (L) (M) (N)
35. (A) (B) (C) (D) (E)
36. (J) (K) (L) (M) (N)
37. (A) (B) (C) (D) (E)
38. (J) (K) (L) (M) (N)
39. (A) (B) (C) (D) (E)
40. (J) (K) (L) (M) (N)

Ability, Part 2

41. (A) (B) (C) (D) (E)
42. (J) (K) (L) (M) (N)
43. (A) (B) (C) (D) (E)
44. (J) (K) (L) (M) (N)
45. (A) (B) (C) (D) (E)
46. (J) (K) (L) (M) (N)
47. (A) (B) (C) (D) (E)
48. (J) (K) (L) (M) (N)
49. (A) (B) (C) (D) (E)
50. (J) (K) (L) (M) (N)

Reading, Part 1 (20 Questions, 10 minutes)

Directions: For questions 1–20, decide which of the four answer choices is closest in meaning to the underlined word(s). Choose the best answer.

1 <u>Terminate</u> employment
   A begin
   B end
   C kill
   D expire

2 <u>Sedentary</u> lifestyle
   J exciting
   K dull
   L lazy
   M athletic

3 Acted with <u>valor</u>
   A bravery
   B worth
   C inconsistency
   D stubbornness

4 A <u>succulent</u> fruit
   J sour
   K rotten
   L sweet
   M juicy

5 A <u>futile</u> attempt
   A ridiculous
   B difficult
   C ineffective
   D successful

6 <u>Facilitate</u> the meeting
   J assist
   K develop
   L prevent
   M lead

7 A safe <u>haven</u>
   A begin
   B end
   C kill
   D refuge

8 <u>Scarce</u> resources
   J expensive
   K insufficient
   L common
   M abundant

9 <u>Strident</u> criticism
   A excessive
   B undeserved
   C harsh
   D appropriate

10 To <u>muster</u> support
    J lose
    K gather
    L decrease
    M utilize

11 View with <u>trepidation</u>
    A loathing
    B fear
    C delight
    D curiosity

12 Lively <u>banter</u>
    J loud arguing
    K light exercise
    L spiteful teasing
    M playful remarks

13 A <u>lucrative</u> venture
    A speculative
    B interesting
    C dangerous
    D profitable

14 <u>Hover</u> above
    J flit about
    K rise quickly
    L hang suspended
    M remain still

Reading, Part 1 *(continued)*

15 <u>Dire</u> need
  A   urgent
  B   pessimistic
  C   trivial
  D   common

16 <u>Dispatch</u> assistance
  J   send off
  K   accept
  L   forbid
  M   request

17 <u>Irascible</u> temperament
  A   pleasant
  B   irritable
  C   unreliable
  D   giddy

18 Tremors <u>subsided</u>
  J   began in earnest
  K   became less active
  L   did not register
  M   shook violently

19 <u>Clarify</u> the response
  A   doubt
  B   repeat
  C   make clear
  D   question

20 <u>Formidable</u> opponent
  J   equal
  K   inspiring envy
  L   worthy
  M   causing fear

Reading, Part 2 *(30 questions, 25 minutes)*

Directions: Read the passages below and the questions relating to them. Choose the best answer from among the four given for each question, and mark the corresponding space on your answer sheet.

Read the following passage and answer questions 21–25.

Antibiotic drugs can save lives. But some germs get so strong that they can become resistant to the drugs, which causes the drugs to be less effective. Germs can even pass on resistance to other germs. Antibiotics normally work by killing germs called bacteria, or by stopping the bacteria from growing. If the antibiotic does not stop or kill all of the bacteria, then only the strongest ones are left to grow and spread. A person can get sick again and this time the germs are harder to kill. The more often a person uses an antibiotic, the more likely it is that the germs will become resistant to it. This can make some diseases very hard to control.

21 The author's main purpose is to

   A   educate people about a new kind of bacteria

   B   warn people of the dangers of overusing antibiotic drugs

   C   convince people to stop using antibiotic drugs

   D   teach people about how sicknesses are developed

22 The author most likely feels that antibiotic drugs

   J   are not powerful enough

   K   are dangerous

   L   can cure any illness

   M   should be used only when necessary

23 According to the passage, which of the following is a function of antibiotic drugs?

   A   killing viruses

   B   resisting germs

   C   stopping the growth of bacteria

   D   healing an open wound

24 A doctor would be most likely to prescribe antibiotic drugs to treat

   J   rhinovirus, the virus that causes the "common cold"

   K   tuberculosis, a bacterial infection of the lungs

   L   a spiral fracture of the arm

   M   schistosomiasis, a parasitic infection

25 In the context of the passage, the word resistance most likely means

   A   the act of withstanding or opposing

   B   the act of refraining or abstaining from

   C   the act of complying or conforming

   D   the act of spreading throughout a system

Reading, Part 2 *(continued)*

Read the following passage and answer questions 26–30.

Long ago, the mice had a general council to consider what measures they could take to outwit their common enemy, the Cat. Some said this, and some said that; but at last a young mouse got up and said he had a proposal to make, which he thought would meet the case. "You will all agree," said he, "that our chief danger consists in the sly and treacherous manner in which the enemy approaches us. Now, if we could receive some signal of her approach, we could easily escape from her. I venture, therefore, to propose that a small bell be procured, and attached by a ribbon round the neck of the Cat. By this means we should always know when she was about, and could easily retire while she was in the neighborhood.

This proposal met with general applause, until an old mouse got up and said: "That is all very well, but who is to bell the Cat?" The mice looked at one another and nobody spoke. Then the old mouse said: "It is easy to propose impossible remedies."

26 Belling the Cat is an "impossible remedy" because

   J   no mouse is tall enough to reach the neck of the Cat

   K   the Cat would see the mouse coming and eat it

   L   it is too dangerous for a mouse to approach the Cat so closely

   M   the mice do not have a bell

27 This passage would most likely appear in which of the following sources?

   A   a veterinary journal

   B   an autobiography

   C   a science fiction magazine

   D   a collection of fables

28 As it is used in the passage, the word <u>retire</u> means

   J   leave the area

   K   stop working

   L   go to sleep

   M   attack

29 The mice held a general council to

   A   find a way to keep themselves safe from the Cat

   B   develop a plan to drive the Cat away

   C   decide who would be responsible for feeding the Cat

   D   appoint one mouse to deal with the problem of the Cat

30 The chief danger of the Cat is its

   J   sharp claws

   K   many teeth

   L   swift pounce

   M   silent approach

Reading, Part 2 *(continued)*

Read the following passage and answer questions 31–35.

The neighborhood of Porto Praya, viewed from the sea, wears a desolate aspect. The volcanic fires of a past age and the scorching heat of a tropical sun have in most places made the soil unfit for vegetation. The country is hilly, and the country is bounded by an irregular chain of mountains. The island would generally be considered uninteresting; but to anyone used to an English landscape, the sight of a totally bare land is new and exciting. One could hardly find a single green leaf on the wide lava plains; yet flocks of goats, together with a few cows, manage to live there. It does not rain very often, but during a short portion of the year heavy torrents fall, and immediately afterwards plants spring up out of every crevice. These plants soon dry out and become hay on which the animals live. It has not now rained for an entire year.

When the island was discovered, the land around Porto Praya was clothed with trees. The reckless destruction of these trees has made the land almost totally sterile. The same has happened in St. Helena and at some of the Canary Islands. The broad, flat-bottomed valleys are covered only with thickets of leafless bushes. Few living creatures inhabit these valleys. The commonest bird is a kingfisher (*Dacelo Iagoensis*), which tamely sits on the branches of the castor oil plant and eats grasshoppers and lizards. It is brightly colored, but not so beautiful as the European species; in its flight, manners, and place of habitation, which is generally in the driest valley, there is also a wide difference.

31 The author notes which of the following differences between the English kingfisher and the species observed on the island?

A   their relative size
B   the location in which they live
C   the colors of their feathers
D   their diet

32 When first discovered, the land around Porto Praya was

J   sterile
K   forested
L   grassy
M   desolate

33 According to the passage, *Dacelo Iagoensis* is

A   the person who discovered Porto Praya
B   the capital of Porto Praya
C   the most common bird in Porto Praya
D   the English kingfisher

34 What is the chief source of food for the goats and cows near Porto Praya?

J   grasshoppers and lizards
K   livestock feed provided by their owners
L   plants that have dried into hay
M   the kingfisher birds

35 Desolate, in the context of the passage, means

A   volcanic
B   hilly
C   sad
D   bare

Reading, Part 2 *(continued)*

Read the following passage and answer questions 36–40.

John Fitzgerald Kennedy was born on May 29, 1917, in Brookline, Massachusetts, the son of Joseph Patrick Kennedy, a bank president, and Rose Fitzgerald. John Kennedy attended Canterbury School and Choate boarding school, both in Connecticut. After graduating from Choate in 1936, Kennedy went to Harvard University. His senior thesis, entitled *Why England Slept*, about why Great Britain was not prepared for war, was later published in book form. Kennedy graduated *cum laude* from Harvard in 1940 and entered the Navy, where he was made a lieutenant and commander of a patrol torpedo boat.

When Kennedy returned from the War, he became a Democratic Congressman in 1947 and served until 1953 when he was elected to the Senate, where he served until 1961. He married Jacqueline Bouvier on September 12, 1953. Kennedy wrote *Profiles in Courage* in 1956, an account of courageous political acts by eight United States Senators. It won the Pulitzer Prize for history.

In 1960, Kennedy became the youngest person ever to be elected to the office of President of the United States. He was the thirty-fifth President and the first Roman Catholic president. He had only been in office for a little more than 1,000 days when he was shot and killed by an assassin on November 22, 1963, in Dallas, Texas. He is remembered today as a man of courage, intellect, and honor.

36 Which of the following is NOT mentioned as an achievement of John F. Kennedy?

  J   writing a book
  K   becoming President of the United States
  L   serving in the United States Navy
  M   being awarded the Nobel Peace Prize

37 An assassin is most likely

  A   a person who murders a political figure
  B   someone hired to kill someone else's enemy
  C   a soldier who kills an enemy soldier
  D   a person who kills another for religious reasons

38 Kennedy was unique as President because he was

  J   the first president of the Jewish faith
  K   the first Democratic president
  L   the youngest person ever elected to that office
  M   the only president to have been killed in office

39 How does the author most likely feel about John F. Kennedy?

  A   The author questions Kennedy's historical importance.
  B   The author admires Kennedy for his many achievements.
  C   The author praises Kennedy for his foreign policy.
  D   The author does not express positive or negative opinions toward Kennedy.

40 Which of the following would be the best title for this passage?

  J   *JFK's Achievements*
  K   *Kennedy's Military Might*
  L   *The 35th President's Legacy*
  M   *JFK: A Presidency Cut Short*

Reading, Part 2 *(continued)*

Read the following passage and answer questions 41–45.

Eating spoiled food can make you sick. Food can be spoiled even if it looks and smells all right. Germs cause food to go bad. You can't see, smell, or feel germs. It takes one to three days to get sick from eating spoiled food. One way to keep from getting food-based illnesses is to keep your kitchen clean.

Wash hands and counters often because germs can spread in the kitchen. They can get onto cutting boards, counters, sponges, forks, spoons, and knives. You can fight germs by washing your hands with hot, soapy water. Do this before touching food. Do it after using the bathroom, changing diapers, or touching pets. Wash your cutting boards, counters, dishes, forks, spoons, and knives. Use hot, soapy water and do this after working with each food item. Use plastic cutting boards. Do not use wood cutting boards. It is easier for germs to hide in wood. Wash all boards in hot, soapy water after use. Boards can go into the dishwasher too. Use paper towels to clean up kitchen counters and tables. If you use cloth towels, wash them often in the hot cycle of the washing machine or in hot, soapy water.

41 With which of the following statements would the author most likely agree?

- A If you keep your kitchen clean, you will never get sick.
- B Wood cutting boards will make you sick.
- C You might eat spoiled food without knowing it.
- D Washing in cold, soapy water is not effective.

42 Each of the following is mentioned as a way to fight germs EXCEPT:

- J washing hands
- K cleaning counters
- L using plastic cutting boards
- M wearing gloves

43 The intended audience for this passage is most likely

- A small children
- B healthcare workers
- C employees of an office cleaning company
- D people who prepare food in the household

44 According to the passage, you should wash your hands after

- J changing a diaper
- K taking out the trash
- L preparing food
- M brushing your teeth

45 According to the passage, wood cutting boards should not be used because

- A germs can hide in the wood
- B we need to preserve our forests
- C wood absorbs smells
- D wood cannot be washed in the dishwasher

Reading, Part 2 *(continued)*

Read the following passage and answer questions 46–50.

Before the accession of Queen Victoria, the Industrial Revolution had made England the richest nation in the world. The introduction of coal and the steam engine made this vast development of manufacturing possible in the latter part of the eighteenth century. Hand in hand with industrial development went the increase of population from less than thirteen million in England in 1825 to nearly three times as many at the end of the period.

The introduction of the steam railway and the steamship, in place of the lumbering stagecoach and the sailing vessel, broke up the old stagnant and stationary habits of life and greatly increased the amount of travel. The invention of the electric telegraph in 1844 brought the cities of Europe into contact with each other. The modern newspaper carried full accounts of the doings of the whole world and could reach citizens within a few hours. No less striking was the progress in public health and the increase in human happiness due to the enormous advances in the sciences of medicine, surgery, and hygiene. Indeed, these sciences in their modern form virtually began with the discovery of the facts of bacteriology about 1860, and the use of antiseptics fifteen years later. These developments helped fight the frightful epidemics which had previously plagued Europe.

46 The author of the passage is probably
   J   an historian writing a book about Queen Victoria
   K   a student writing a research paper on the Industrial Revolution
   L   a mechanical engineer, writing a patent application
   M   a politician, arguing for stricter environmental protection laws

47 According to the passage, one beneficial invention of the Industrial Revolution was the
   A   printing press
   B   stagecoach
   C   electric telegraph
   D   surgical anesthesia

48 Which of the following is mentioned as a possible reason for an increase in travel?
   J   People had become bored with their daily lives.
   K   Newspapers showed people new places they could visit.
   L   The faster travel speed offered by steam engines.
   M   The Industrial Revolution offered jobs in far-away cities.

49 As used in the passage, what does the word plagued mean?
   A   consumed
   B   troubled
   C   infected
   D   spanned

50 With which of the following statements would the author be most likely to agree?
   J   Queen Victoria started the Industrial Revolution in order to urge progress.
   K   The Industrial Revolution provided Europe with many new beneficial inventions.
   L   Prior to the Industrial Revolution, there were no machines in England.
   M   The Industrial Revolution put an end to the agricultural lifestyle.

Written Expression, Part 1 *(40 Questions, 25 minutes)*

Directions: This is a test of how well you can find errors in a piece of writing. The directions below tell what type of mistake may be present. If no mistake is made, choose the last answer.

For questions 1–10, look for mistakes in usage or expression.

1
- A   Every morning Erlene tends her
- B   garden. She weeded, watered,
- C   and picks the ripe vegetables.
- D   *(No mistakes)*

2
- J   Working as a professional
- K   fisherman is very exciting.
- L   Britt is never bored with his job.
- M   *(No mistakes)*

3
- A   Sergeant Eichenberg retired out of
- B   the police force after twenty-five
- C   years of distinguished service.
- D   *(No mistakes)*

4
- J   The "Best in the West" restaurant
- K   award has been won by Chez Vicki
- L   for the four years past.
- M   *(No mistakes)*

5
- A   After reading for an hour,
- B   Ryan's book seemed too difficult
- C   for him to read without assistance.
- D   *(No mistakes)*

6
- J   If I were to win the lottery,
- K   I would be using half the money
- L   to set up a scholarship fund.
- M   *(No mistakes)*

7
- A   Andy is obsessed with astronomy, the
- B   science that deals with the material
- C   universe beyond the Earth's atmosphere.
- D   *(No mistakes)*

8
- J   Preston's hobbies include woodworking,
- K   painting portraits, and the transformation
- L   of everyday objects into sculpture.
- M   *(No mistakes)*

9
- A   Playing basketball gave Carolyn a
- B   sense of pride and leadership skills
- C   that helped her when she is class
       president.
- D   *(No mistakes)*

10
- J   Alfredo went swift to answer the door
- K   because he was expecting a package
- L   that he had ordered to arrive.
- M   *(No mistakes)*

Written Expression, Part 1 *(continued)*

For questions 11–20, look for mistakes in punctuation.

11

A David likes taking a
B bath, after he has been outside
C playing in the mud all morning.
D *(No mistakes)*

12

J There are two things Adam always takes
K when he goes to visit his grandpa:
L his blanket and his backpack.
M *(No mistakes)*

13

A Rhonda after working in the garden
B went inside to put away the supplies,
C wash her hands, and make lunch.
D *(No mistakes)*

14

J Mrs. Baumgardner called her
    mother-in-law
K Mrs. Meinhart to ask how to
L get to the new shopping mall?
M *(No mistakes)*

15

A The town of Denton, which has a
B population of 12,000, is near the southern
C border of Chicago, IL.
D *(No mistakes)*

16

J "Who is there"? Chris asked.
K Val replied, "Me!" and stepped
L out into the living room.
M *(No mistakes)*

17

A It is too cold to stay outside. We should
B go inside and play cards, or work the
C new jigsaw puzzle we bought at the
    store.
D *(No mistakes)*

18

J "Can I go with you to the zoo
K today," Elena asked?
L "Sure," Matthew replied.
M *(No mistakes)*

19

A Bruce shook his head and
B cleared his throat. He had been
C fighting a cold; for weeks now.
D *(No mistakes)*

20

J In this year's marathon, Cheri
K ran for just over 20
L miles which is more than she ran
    last year.
M *(No mistakes)*

Written Expression, Part 1 *(continued)*

For questions 21–30, look for mistakes in spelling.

21

- A Kelly could not stomach
- B cleaning up the mess her
- C colleagues had made in the laboratory.
- D *(No mistakes)*

22

- J Empulsive behavior is normal
- K for Shannon to exhibit since
- L she is barely three years old.
- M *(No mistakes)*

23

- A It is better to remain anonomous
- B when contributing to charity;
- C doing it for fame is arrogant.
- D *(No mistakes)*

24

- J It is commonplace for Amy
- K to mispell a word occasionally
- L when she is writing swiftly.
- M *(No mistakes)*

25

- A It is critical that the United
- B States maintain certain
- C trade embargos against Cuba.
- D *(No mistakes)*

26

- J Graham crackers are a nutritious
- K and delicious snack, especially
- L when paired with fresh fruits.
- M *(No mistakes)*

27

- A Colin participates in a local
- B recycling program at his parocial school
- C that benefits the neighborhood shelter.
- D *(No mistakes)*

28

- J Caleb presented a small trincket
- K for Angelina's perusal
- L and, he hoped, her approval.
- M *(No mistakes)*

29

- A Monique's vivacious personality
- B allows her to interact with people
- C who have varied interests.
- D *(No mistakes)*

30

- J Without harmonious cooperation and
- K immediate action on the part of governments,
- L a worldwide cataclysm is emminent.
- M *(No mistakes)*

Written Expression, Part 1 *(continued)*

For questions 31–40, look for capitalization *mistakes.*

31

A Buying stock in a company such as
B WINK, inc. can be risky since the
C company has been accused of fraud.
D *(No mistakes)*

32

J My favorite song is titled
K "A Day In The Sun." I
L play it every Saturday.
M *(No mistakes)*

33

A Mrs. Furse said, "you should
B take a jacket in case you get
C cold at Hanks Park."
D *(No mistakes)*

34

J In November, Jeremiah took
K a trip to Bell's Farm for
L the Fall festival and hayride.
M *(No mistakes)*

35

A If you wish to apply for the position
B of Treasurer, you will need to speak to
C Mr. Elkins, the Chairperson of the
   committee.
D *(No mistakes)*

36

J The governors and lieutenant governors
K held a special session in Washington,
   D. C.,
L with Governor Bailey presiding.
M *(No mistakes)*

37

A Next semester I will take
B math, english, and social
C studies classes at Kenzie Prep.
D *(No mistakes)*

38

J My favorite flavors of cake are: Vanilla,
K chocolate, and strawberry. I also
L like Boston cream pie.
M *(No mistakes)*

39

A Dirk and Ross are the best
B coaches at St. Anthony's.
C They make basketball fun.
D *(No mistakes)*

40

J Dear Mrs. Week,
K The grade you gave me in World
   history is
L unfair; I received an A in Texas
   History.
M *(No mistakes)*

Written Expression, Part 2 *(10 questions, 15 minutes)*

Directions: Choose the answer containing the word, phrase, or sentence that is better than the others.

For questions 41 and 43, choose the best answer based on the following paragraph.

¹High up the Rewa, at the village of a chief, Mongondro by name, John Starhurst rested at the end of the second day of the journey. ²In the morning, attended by Narau, he expected to start on foot for the smoky mountains that were now green and velvety with nearness. ³Mongondro was a sweet-tempered, mild-mannered little old chief, short-sighted and afflicted with elephantiasis, and no longer inclined toward the turbulence of war. ⁴He received the missionary with warm hospitality, gave him food from his own table, and even discussed religious matters with him. ⁵Mongondro was of an inquiring bent of mind, and pleased John Starhurst greatly by asking him to account for the existence and beginning of things. ⁶When the missionary had finished his summary of the Creation according to Genesis, he saw that Mongondro was <u>deeply affected</u>.

41 Which of the following is the best way to separate sentence 3 into two sentences?

A   Mongondro was a sweet-tempered, mild-mannered little old chief. He was short-sighted and afflicted with elephantiasis, and no longer inclined toward the turbulence of war.

B   Mongondro was short-sighted and afflicted with elephantiasis. He was a sweet-tempered, mild-mannered little old chief who was no longer inclined toward the turbulence of war.

C   Mongondro was a sweet-tempered, mild-mannered little old chief, short-sighted. He was afflicted with elephantiasis, and no longer inclined toward the turbulence of war.

D   Mongondro was sweet-tempered. He was a mild-mannered little old chief, short-sighted and afflicted with elephantiasis, and no longer inclined toward the turbulence of war.

42 Which of the following is the best way to write sentence 1?

J   John Starhurst rested at the end of the second day of the journey high up the Rewa, at the village of a chief, Mongondro by name.

K   At the village of a chief named Mongondro, high up the Rewa, at the end of the second day of the journey John Starhurst rested.

L   John Starhurst rested at the end of the second day of the journey high up the Rewa, at the village of a chief named Mongondro.

M   *(No change)*

43 Which of the following is the best way to write the underlined part of sentence 6?

A   very moved
B   visibly upset
C   markedly confused
D   obviously delighted

Written Expression, Part 2 *(continued)*

For questions 44 and 45, choose the best answer based on the following paragraph.

[1]Molière is considered one of the greatest writers of comedy in Western literature. [2]Comedy began in the Greek theater and is essentially a conflict between two opposing societies. [3]Comedy typically features elements of surprise, incongruity, dramatic irony, repetitiveness, and the effects of opposing expectations. [4]Molière's works fuse all these elements in biting satire. [5]Political satire also began in the Greek theater, and Molière is considered a master satirist. [6]His plays *Le Misanthrope*, *Tartuffe*, *Don Juan*, and *Le Malade imaginaire* remain some of the most frequently performed plays in the modern theater.

44 Which of the following is the best way to combine sentences 3 and 4?

    J   Comedy typically features elements of surprise, and incongruity and dramatic irony, repetitiveness, and the effects of opposing expectations and Molière's works fuse all these elements in biting satire.

    K   Comedy typically features elements of surprise, incongruity, dramatic irony, repetitiveness, and the effects of opposing expectations but Molière's works fuse all these elements in biting satire.

    L   Molière's works fuse all the typical elements of comedy into biting satire: surprise, incongruity, dramatic irony, repetitiveness, and the effects of opposing expectations.

    M   Molière's works fuse all the typical elements of comedy–surprise, incongruity, dramatic irony, repetitiveness, and the effects of opposing expectations–into biting satire.

45 Which of the following would be the best title for this piece of writing?

    A   *The Greek Roots of Molière's Comedies*

    B   *The Political Satire of Molière*

    C   *Molière and Tartuffe*

    D   *Molière, King of Comedy*

Written Expression, Part 2 *(continued)*

For questions 46–47, choose the best answer based on the following paragraph.

[1]The Red wolf (*Canis rufus*) is a North American <u>canid</u> which once roamed throughout the southeastern United States and is a glacial period survivor of the Late Pleistocene epoch. [2]Based on fossil and archaeological evidence, the original red wolf range extended throughout the Southeast, from the Atlantic and Gulf coasts, north to the Ohio River Valley and central Pennsylvania, and west to central Texas and southeastern Missouri. [3]Historical habitats included forests, swamps, and coastal prairies, where it was an apex predator. [4]The red wolf became extinct in the wild by 1980. [5]1987 saw a reintroduction in northeastern North Carolina through a captive breeding program, and the animals are considered to be successfully breeding in the wild.

46 Which of the following is the best way to write sentence 4?

J The red wolf had become extinct in the wild by 1980.

K By 1980, the red wolf was extinct in the wild.

L The red wolf, becoming extinct in the wild, by 1980.

M *(No change)*

47 Which of the following would be the best sentence to add to the end of the paragraph?

A The red wolf pup begins life with a slate or dark gray pelt with auburn-tinged fur visible on its head.

B With a little help from humans, perhaps the species will survive and be removed from the endangered list.

C In May 2011, an analysis of red wolf, Eastern wolf, gray wolf, and dog genomes revealed that the red wolf was 76–80 percent coyote and only 20–24 percent gray wolf, suggesting that the red wolf is actually much more coyote in origin than the Eastern wolf.

D After the reintroduction, the newly bred red wolves are doing well in the wild.

Written Expression, Part 2 (continued)

For questions 48–50, choose the best answer based on the following paragraph.

[1]The apartheid system in South Africa was a massive system of legalized segregation, repression, and domination by the white minority, first British and then later Afrikaner. [2]Long before the system was enacted formally–following the 1948 elections with the passage by the new Afrikaner government of increasingly restrictive and repressive legislation–the Blacks (and other "coloured" people) suffered unofficial discrimination. [3]During the early 1960s, opposition against apartheid among Blacks and few whites begins to show its first buds. [4]The political activity of the opposition parties (Mandela's African National Congress and the Pan-African Congress) was banned in 1961, but continued unofficially and occasionally became violent. [5]After political activism failed, the ANC formed a military wing to begin armed resistance. [6]Two years later, Mandela was imprisoned. [7]He was not released for 28 years (Mandela was later the first president of the new, post-apartheid, South Africa).

48 Which of the following is the best way to write sentence 2?

J   The system was enacted formally following the 1948 elections with the passage by the new Afrikaner government of increasingly restrictive and repressive legislation, but the Blacks (and other "coloured" people) suffered unofficial discrimination long before that.

K   The system was enacted formally following the 1948 elections by the new Afrikaner government passing increasingly restrictive and repressive legislation, but the Blacks (and other "coloured" people) suffering unofficial discrimination long before that.

L   Long before the system was enacted formally–after the new Afrikaner government passes in 1948 increasingly restrictive and repressive legislation–the Blacks (and other "coloured" people) suffered unofficial discrimination.

M   *(No change)*

49 Which of the following is the best way to combine sentences 6 and 7?

A   Mandela was imprisoned two years later and was not released for 28 years until be became the first president of the new, post-apartheid, South Africa.

B   Two years later, Mandela was imprisoned and was not released for 28 years (Mandela was later the first president of the new, post-apartheid, South Africa).

C   Mandela, who would later become the first president of the new, post-apartheid, South Africa, was imprisoned two years later and was not released for 28 years.

D   Two years later, Mandela was imprisoned and not released for 28 years, yet but was later the first president of the new, post-apartheid, South Africa.

50 Which of the following sentences could be deleted without significantly affecting the meaning of the passage?

J   1
K   2
L   5
M   7

Mathematics, Part 1 *(32 questions, 33 minutes)*

Directions: Choose the best answer from the four given for each problem.

1 If $p = -1$, then $p + p^2 - p^3 + p^4 - p^5 =$

A -1
B 0
C 1
D 3

2 One out of every 10 apples has a worm. At this rate, how many worms will there be in 60 apples?

J 1
K 6
L 10
M 16

3 $\dfrac{1}{6} + \dfrac{1}{8} = \dfrac{a}{b}$

In the equation above, if a and b are positive integers and the sum is in its simplest reduced form, what is the value of b?

A 7
B 14
C 24
D 48

4 What is the area of a circle with a diameter of 6?

J 3p
K 6π
L 9π
M 12π

5 10,000 people took a survey about their detergent preferences. The results are shown below. How many people preferred Brand B?

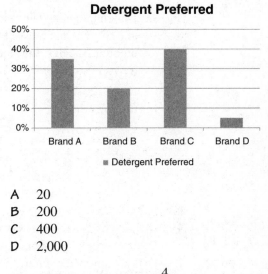

Detergent Preferred

A 20
B 200
C 400
D 2,000

6 The decimal equivalent of $\dfrac{4}{5}$ is

J 0.47
K 0.5
L 0.57
M 0.67

7 Based on the chart below, how many more people live in Webster in 2011 than did in 2008?

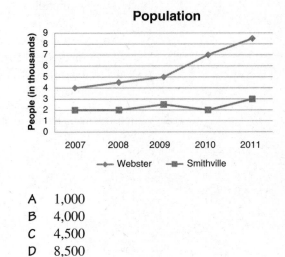

Population

A 1,000
B 4,000
C 4,500
D 8,500

Mathematics, Part 1 *(continued)*

8 What is the greatest prime factor of 24?

J 2

K 3

L 12

M 24

9 Isabella bought four bracelets for $3, $6, $4, and $9. The tax rate is 8%. What is the total amount Isabella paid, including tax?

A $1.76

B $22.00

C $22.08

D $23.76

10 What is $12\frac{4}{5} \times 6\frac{1}{4}$?

J 72

K $75\frac{1}{3}$

L $78\frac{2}{5}$

M 80

11 Wendy's pizza crust recipe is shown in the chart below. If Wendy uses 6 cups of flour, how many teaspoons of salt will she need?

Flour	3 cups
Salt	1½ teaspoons
Yeast	1 teaspoon
Water	½ cup

A 1½

B 2

C 3

D 4½

12 Which fraction is equivalent to the decimal 0.125?

J $\frac{1}{8}$

K $\frac{3}{8}$

L $\frac{5}{4}$

M $\frac{25}{2}$

13 Based on the chart below, what percent of Noah's monthly budget is spent on rent and utilities?

Monthly Budget

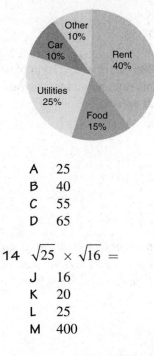

A 25

B 40

C 55

D 65

14 $\sqrt{25} \times \sqrt{16} =$

J 16

K 20

L 25

M 400

15 Kim has 12 marbles in a bag. Each marble is either red or blue and there are 5 red marbles in the bag. If she chooses one marble at random, what is the probability that it will be a blue marble?

A $\frac{5}{12}$

B $\frac{1}{2}$

C $\frac{7}{12}$

D $\frac{2}{3}$

Mathematics, Part 1 *(continued)*

16 What is the measure of angle *x*, in degrees?

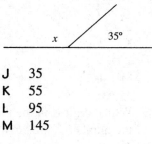

J   35
K   55
L   95
M   145

17 $2.376 - 1.894 =$
A   0.482
B   0.582
C   1.582
D   4.27

18 If $x^2 - 4x > 10$, which of the following is a possible value for *x*?
J   6
K   4
L   0
M   −1

19 Kai is 3 years older than Aaron. Four years from now, the sum of their ages will be 13. How old is Aaron now?
A   8
B   5
C   4
D   1

20 According to the graph below, what percent of Mrs. Voelkle's class received a grade lower than a C?

Math Grades

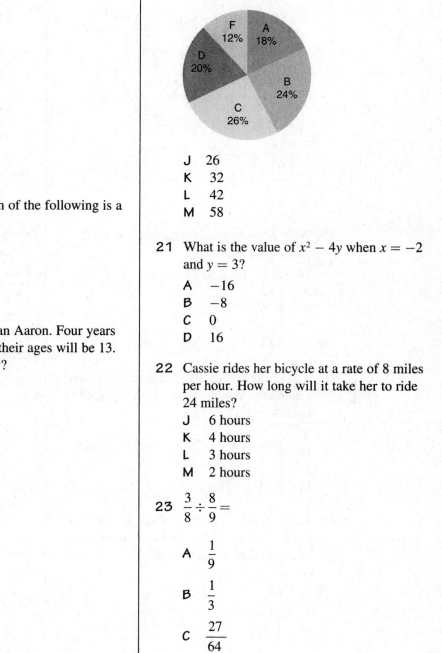

J   26
K   32
L   42
M   58

21 What is the value of $x^2 - 4y$ when $x = -2$ and $y = 3$?
A   −16
B   −8
C   0
D   16

22 Cassie rides her bicycle at a rate of 8 miles per hour. How long will it take her to ride 24 miles?
J   6 hours
K   4 hours
L   3 hours
M   2 hours

23 $\dfrac{3}{8} \div \dfrac{8}{9} =$

A $\dfrac{1}{9}$

B $\dfrac{1}{3}$

C $\dfrac{27}{64}$

D $\dfrac{8}{9}$

Mathematics, Part 1 *(continued)*

24 According to the graph below, 23 people like ONLY rock music and 14 people like ONLY country music. If there were 100 people surveyed, how many people like BOTH rock and country?

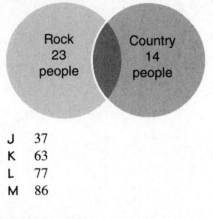

J   37
K   63
L   77
M   86

25 What is the average (arithmetic mean) of the data set below?

{9, 12, 11, 10, 8, 7, 2}
A   8.43
B   8.76
C   9
D   9.12

26 x and y are consecutive prime integers with a sum of 8. Which of the following could be the value of x?

J   3
K   4
L   7
M   8

27 Randy is building a rectangular garden with sides 4 feet and 6 feet. What is the total area of the garden, in square feet?

A   6
B   10
C   20
D   24

28 If $x + 12 = 15$ and $x + y = 7$, what is the value of y?

J   1
K   2
L   3
M   4

29 Which digit is in the thousandths place in the number 1,432.5678?
A   8
B   7
C   6
D   1

30 According to the chart, which student had the largest increase in average score from September to November?

Student	Sep. average score	Oct. average score	Nov. average score
Marisa	76	82	82
Kalee	93	97	95
Lori	85	89	98
Amee	81	98	84
Zane	79	79	75
John	91	93	96

J   John
K   Kalee
L   Lori
M   Marisa

Mathematics, Part 1 *(continued)*

31 If the hypotenuse of a right triangle has a length of 5 inches and one leg of the triangle has a length of 3 inches, how long is the other leg?

A 3
B 4
C 5
D 6

32 Laura ships her cupcakes all over the country for $3.00 each, plus a flat fee of $2.50 for shipping. If she receives an order for 12 cupcakes, what is the charge?

J $66.00
K $38.50
L $36.00
M $14.50

Mathematics, Part 2 *(18 Questions, 7 minutes)*

Estimation

Directions: For questions 33–50, estimate the answer; no scratch work is allowed. Do not try to calculate exact answers.

33 Jim goes to a garage sale and buys a table for $20, a chair for $7.95, and a lamp for $12.75. What is the closest estimate of his total?

   A $40.00
   B $41.00
   C $42.00
   D $43.00

34 The closest estimate of $\sqrt{20}$ is

   J 3.5
   K 4
   L 4.5
   M 5

35 If point x lies between -3 and -2 on the number line and point y lies between 7 and 8, what is the closest approximation of $x - y$?

   A 7
   B 14
   C 24
   D 48

36 The number 12.563 rounded to the nearest hundredth is _____.

   J 12
   K 12.56
   L 12.6
   M 13

37 The closest estimate of $38.14 + 12.89$ is _____.

   A 49
   B 50
   C 51
   D 52

38 If Bob wants to leave a 10% tip on a meal that cost $35.00, how much will he pay in total?

   J $35.00
   K $35.10
   L $37.00
   M $38.50

39 The closest estimate of $711 - 418$ is _____.

   A 300
   B 350
   C 400
   D 450

40 The closest estimate of 82×71 is _____.

   J 5,600
   K 6,300
   L 6,375
   M 56,000

41 The closest estimate of $9.763 + 24.342$ is _____.

   A 30
   B 33
   C 34
   D 36

42 The closest estimate of $352 \div 71$ is _____.

   J 4
   K 5
   L 15
   M 50

43 The closest estimate of $(33 + 58) \div 89$ is _____.

   A 0.1
   B 1
   C 9
   D 10

Mathematics, Part 2 *(continued)*

44 The closest equivalent of $\dfrac{8x}{9}$ is

- J   0.5x
- K   0.89
- L   x
- M   2x

45 What is the closest estimate of 19% of 304?

- A   6
- B   25
- C   40
- D   60

46 $\sqrt{80} \times \sqrt{8} =$

- J   3
- K   8
- L   10
- M   27

47 The number 32,458.2349 rounded to the nearest hundreds place is _____.

- A   32,500
- B   32,460
- C   32,458
- D   32,458.23

48 What is the closest approximation of the measure of angle *x*, in degrees?

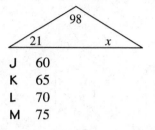

- J   60
- K   65
- L   70
- M   75

49 Kathy sees a blouse priced at $24.50 on sale for 10% off. What is the closest estimate of the sale price of the blouse?

- A $2.50
- B $10.50
- C $20.50
- D $22.50

50 What is the closest estimate of $4.8^2 - 3.2^2$?

- J   1
- K   9
- L   16
- M   25

Ability, Part 1 *(40 Questions, 25 minutes)*

Directions: In questions 1–20, the first three figures are alike in certain ways. From the five answer choices, select the figure that is most like the first three figures in the same ways.

Ability, Part 1 (continued)

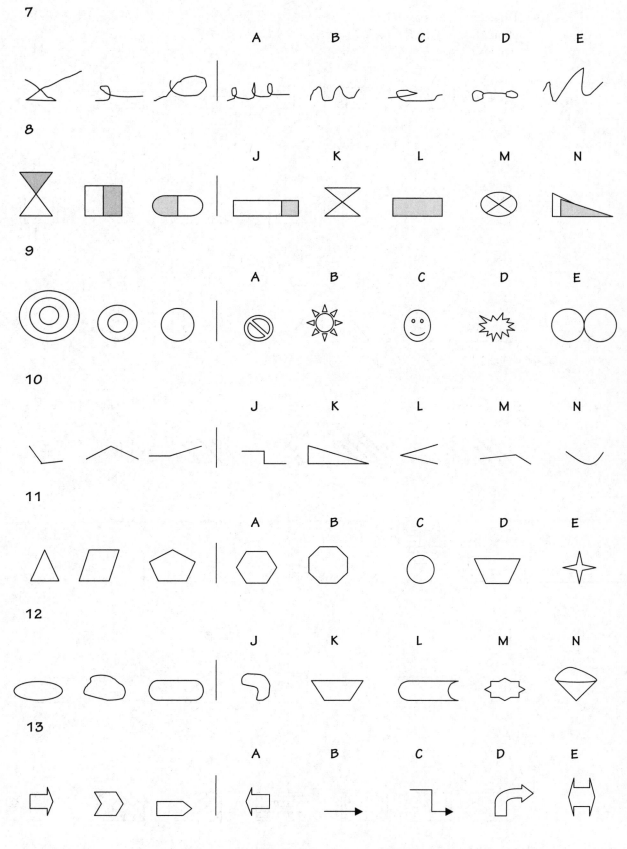

7   A   B   C   D   E

8   J   K   L   M   N

9   A   B   C   D   E

10   J   K   L   M   N

11   A   B   C   D   E

12   J   K   L   M   N

13   A   B   C   D   E

Ability, Part 1 *(continued)*

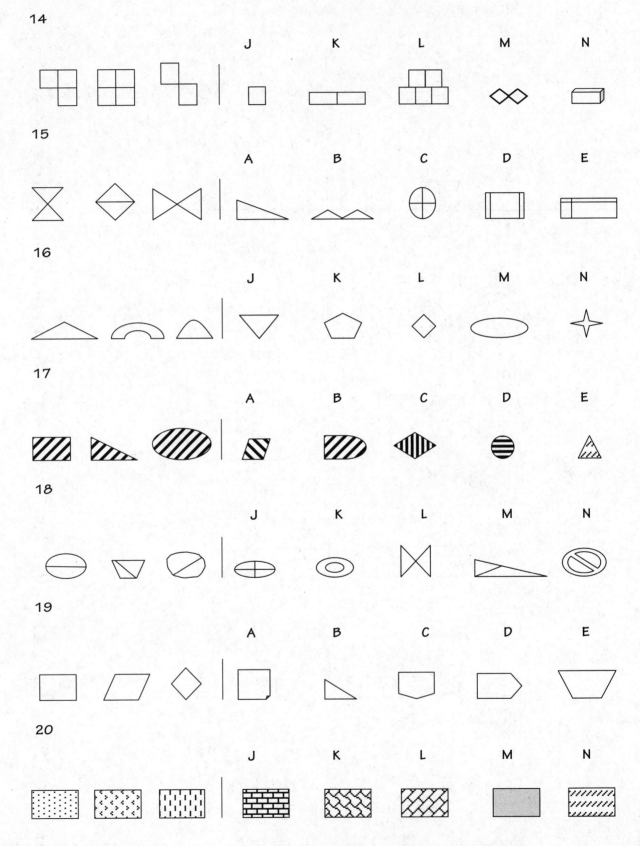

Ability, Part 1 *(continued)*

Directions: Find the figure that completes the puzzle.

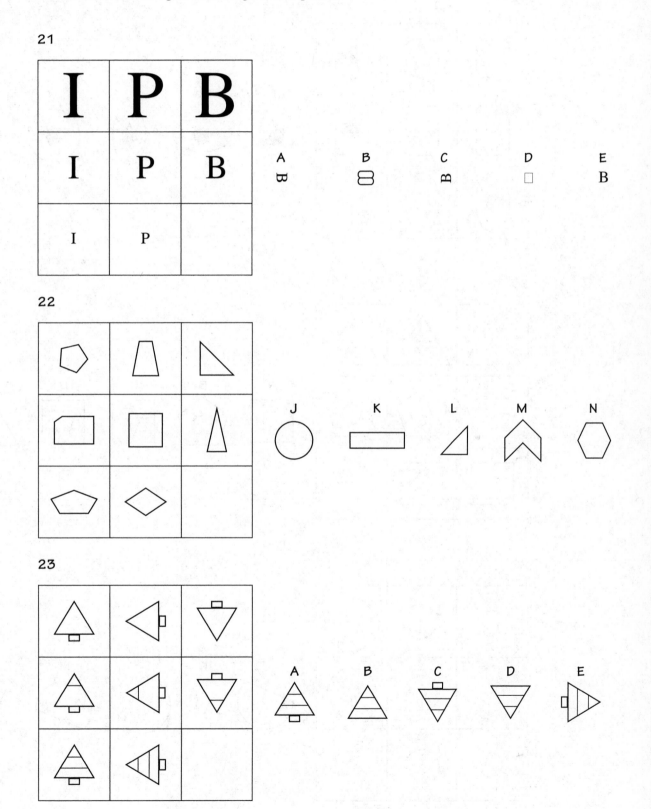

21

22

23

Ability, Part 1 *(continued)*

24

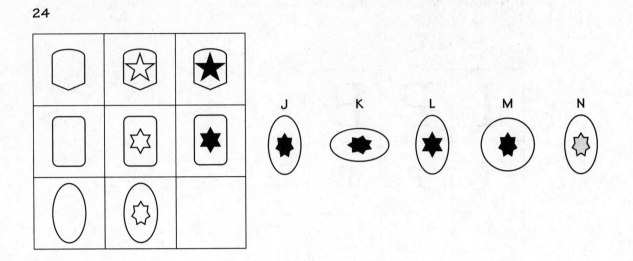

25

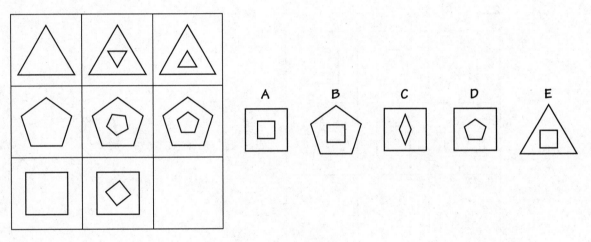

26

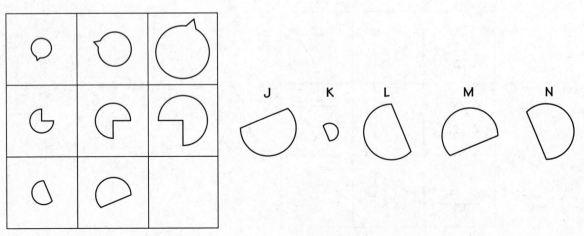

Ability, Part 1 *(continued)*

27

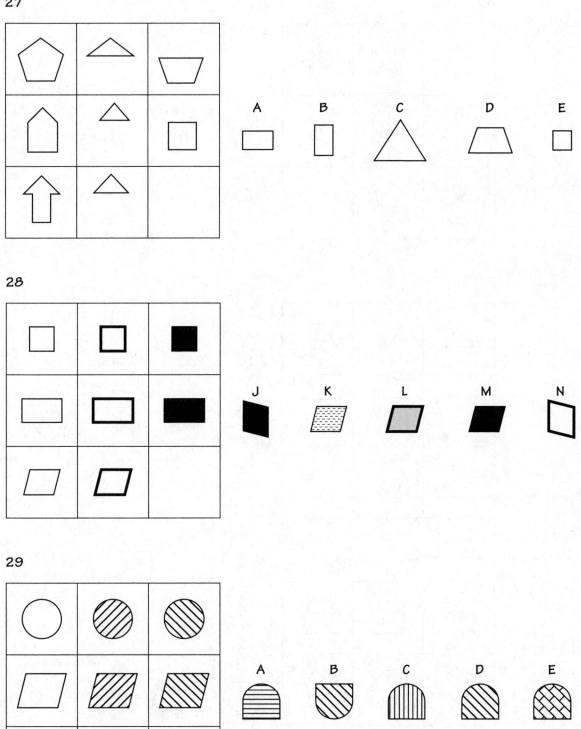

28

29

Ability, Part 1 *(continued)*

30

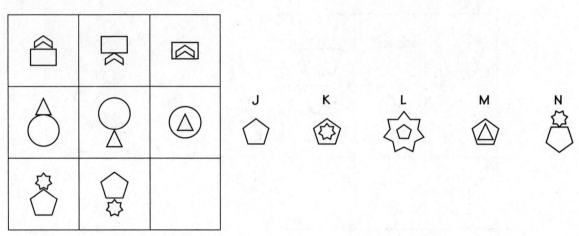

31

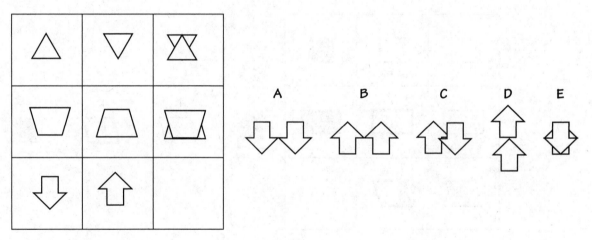

32

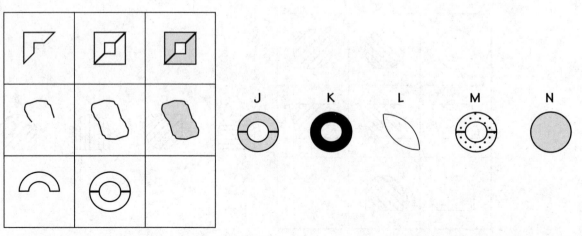

Ability, Part 1 *(continued)*

33

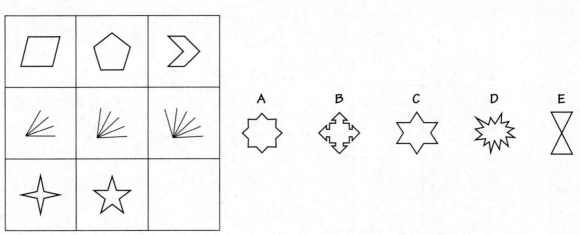

34

35

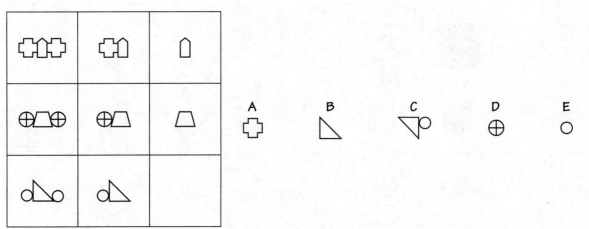

Ability, Part 1 *(continued)*

36

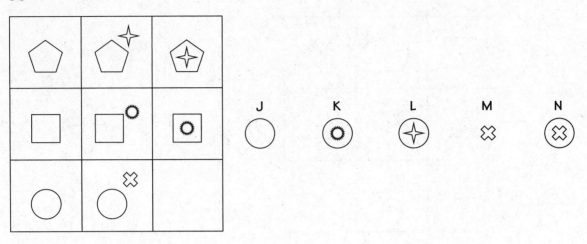

37

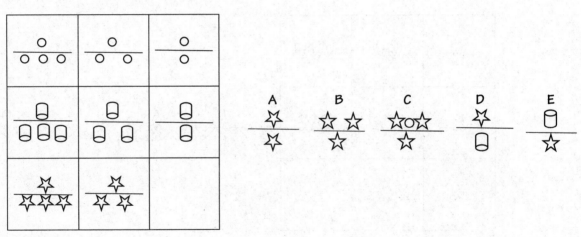

38

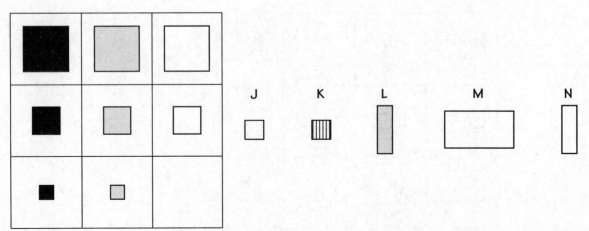

Ability, Part 1 *(continued)*

39

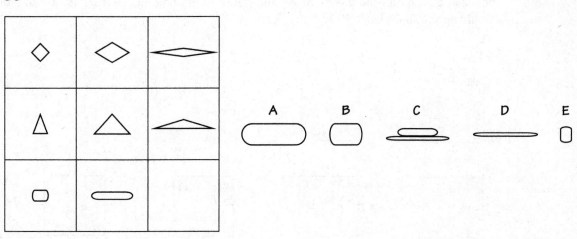

40

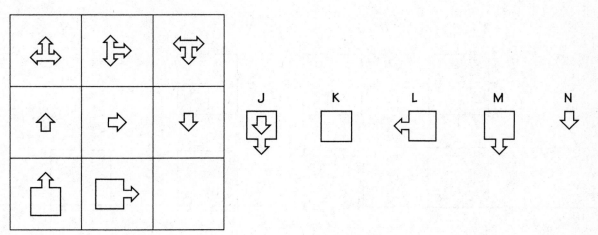

Ability, Part 2 *(10 Questions, 7 minutes)*

Directions: In questions 41–50, in the top line, a piece of paper is folded, and one or more holes are punched through all the layers. Select the figure in the bottom row that shows how the punched paper would appear unfolded.

41

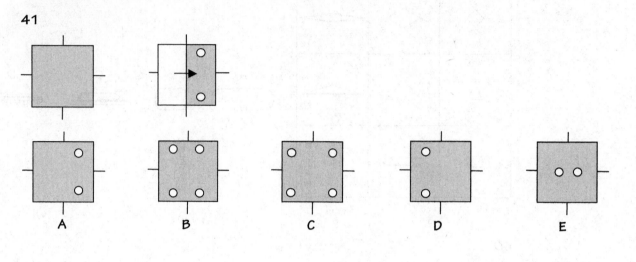

A   B   C   D   E

42

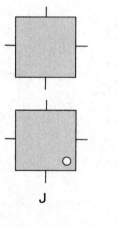

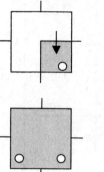
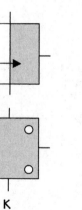
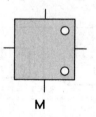
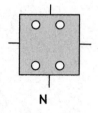

J   K   L   M   N

43

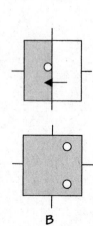
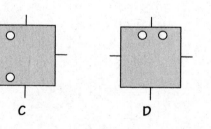
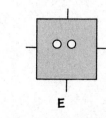

A   B   C   D   E

Ability, Part 2 *(continued)*

44

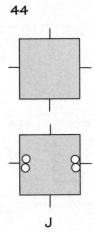 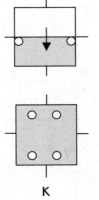 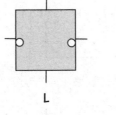 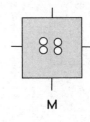 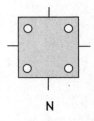

J   K   L   M   N

45

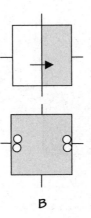 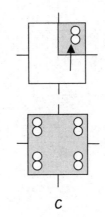 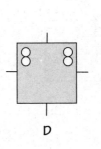 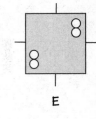

A   B   C   D   E

46

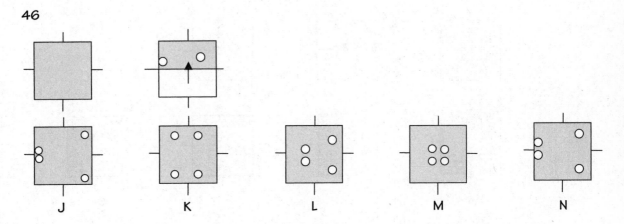

J   K   L   M   N

Ability, Part 2 (continued)

47

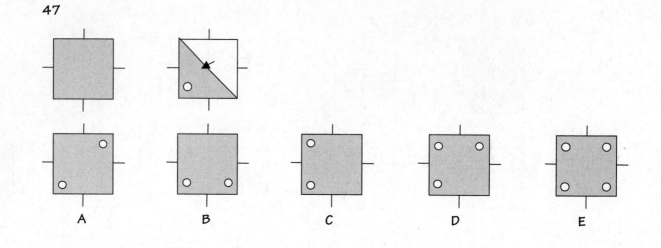

48

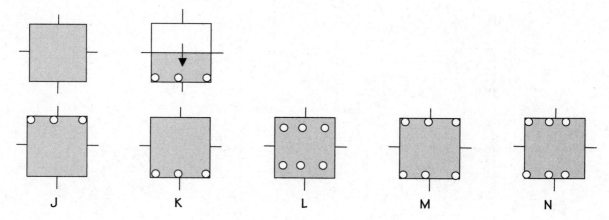

49

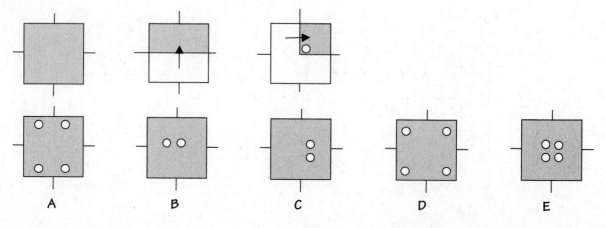

Ability, Part 2 *(continued)*

50

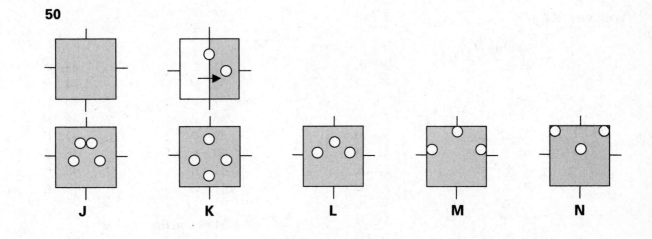

TACHS PRACTICE TEST 2

Answer Key

Reading

1. B	26. L	35. C	43. A
2. L	27. D	36. M	44. M
3. A	28. J	37. B	45. D
4. M	29. A	38. J	46. M
5. C	30. M	39. D	47. B
6. J	31. B	40. K	48. J
7. D	32. K	41. B	49. C
8. K	33. C	42. L	50. L
9. C	34. L		
10. K	35. D	**Mathematics**	
11. B	36. M	1. D	26. J
12. M	37. A	2. K	27. D
13. D	38. L	3. C	28. M
14. L	39. B	4. M	29. B
15. A	40. J	5. D	30. L
16. J	41. C	6. L	31. B
17. B	42. M	7. B	32. K
18. K	43. D	8. K	33. B
19. C	44. J	9. D	34. L
20. M	45. A	10. M	35. D
21. B	46. K	11. C	36. K
22. M	47. C	12. J	37. C
23. C	48. L	13. D	38. M
24. K	49. B	14. K	39. A
25. A	50. K	15. C	40. J
		16. M	41. C
Written Expression		17. A	42. K
1. B	18. K	18. J	43. B
2. M	19. C	19. D	44. L
3. A	20. L	20. K	45. D
4. L	21. D	21. B	46. M
5. B	22. J	22. L	47. A
6. K	23. A	23. C	48. J
7. D	24. K	24. K	49. D
8. K	25. C	25. A	50. L
9. C	26. M		
10. J	27. B	**Ability**	
11. B	28. J	1. B	7. C
12. M	29. D	2. J	8. N
13. A	30. L	3. A	9. E
14. L	31. B	4. L	10. M
15. D	32. K	5. D	11. A
16. J	33. A	6. K	12. J
17. B	34. L		

TACHS PRACTICE TEST 2

Answer Key *(continued)*

Ability *(continued)*

13.	D	23.	C	33.	C	42.	K
14.	L	24.	J	34.	L	43.	E
15.	B	25.	A	35.	B	44.	J
16.	K	26.	N	36.	N	45.	C
17.	B	27.	B	37.	A	46.	N
18.	M	28.	M	38.	J	47.	A
19.	E	29.	D	39.	D	48.	M
20.	N	30.	K	40.	M	49.	E
21.	E	31.	E	41.	B	50.	L
22.	L	32.	J				

TACHS PRACTICE TEST 2

Answers and Explanations

Reading

1. **B** *Terminate* means to bring to an end.

2. **L** *Sedentary* means "accustomed to sit or rest a great deal or to take little exercise." The best match for this is *lazy*.

3. **A** *Valor* means bravery.

4. **M** *Succulent* means juicy.

5. **C** *Futile* means useless or ineffective.

6. **J** To *facilitate* is to assist or help forward.

7. **D** A *haven* is a place of refuge or shelter.

8. **K** *Scarce* means rare or insufficient.

9. **C** *Strident* means harsh or abrasive.

10. **K** *Muster* means to gather or summon together.

11. **B** *Trepidation* is a feeling of fear.

12. **M** *Banter* is an exchange of light-hearted remarks or playful teasing.

13. **D** *Lucrative* means profitable.

14. **L** To *hover* is to hang fluttering or suspended in the air.

15. **A** A *dire* need is one that is urgent or desperate.

16. **J** To *dispatch* is to send off or away with speed.

17. **B** *Irascible* means easily angered or irritable.

18. **K** To *subside* is to become quiet or less active.

19. **C** To *clarify* is to make clear.

20. **M** A *formidable* opponent causes fear or apprehension.

21. **B** The passage is about the dangers of overusing antibiotic drugs.

22. **M** The author says that antibiotic drugs can save lives, but can be dangerous if overused. Therefore, the author would feel that antibiotics should be used with caution.

23. **C** The passage says that antibiotic drugs kill bacteria or stop the growth of bacteria.

24. **K** The passage says antibiotics are used to treat bacterial infections, so only tuberculosis would be treated with antibiotics.

25. **A** *Resist* means withstand or oppose. It can also mean refrain or abstain from, but this does not fit with the context of the passage.

26. **L** The solution is "impossible" because the mice are too afraid of the Cat.

27. **D** This story is a fable.

28. **J** In this context, *retire* means to withdraw or leave the area.

29. **A** The council was held to find a way to keep the mice safe from the Cat. Choices B and D are too specific.

30. **M** The passage says that the chief danger is the Cat's "sly and treacherous manner."

31. **B** The author says that the "place of habitation" is different.

32. **K** When the island was first discovered, it was "clothed with trees."

Answers and Explanations *(continued)*

33. **C** *Dacelo Iagoensis* is the species of king-fisher observed on the island. The author says it is the most common bird on the island.

34. **L** The passage says that the animals eat plants that have dried out and become hay.

35. **D** *Desolate* means bare.

36. **M** The passage does not say that Kennedy was awarded the Nobel Peace Prize.

37. **A** An assassin is someone who murders a political figure.

38. **L** Kennedy was the youngest president and the first Catholic president.

39. **B** The author's tone is positive. The passage is about Kennedy's many accomplishments and the author seems to admire him.

40. **J** The passage is about the accomplishments of John F. Kennedy, and it is not limited to his military or presidential achievements, so the best title would be *JFK's Achievements*.

41. **C** The passage says that "Food can be spoiled even if it looks and smells all right," so you might not know you were eating spoiled food. Choice A is too extreme. Choice D is not supported by the passage since cold water is not discussed.

42. **M** While wearing gloves might prevent the spread of germs, it is not mentioned in the passage.

43. **D** The passage is written for people who pre-pare food in a home setting.

44. **J** The passage says to wash your hands after changing a diaper (as well as after touching pets or going to the bathroom). The passage says you should wash your hands *before* preparing food.

45. **A** The passage says that it is easier for germs to hide in wood.

46. **K** The passage provides general information on the Industrial Revolution and might have been written by a student.

47. **C** The electric telegraph is mentioned as an advance of the Industrial Revolution.

48. **L** The passage cites the introduction of the steam railway and the steamship as a reason for increased travel.

49. **B** In the context of the passage, *plagued* means troubled or bothered.

50. **K** The author would agree that the Industrial Revolution provided Europe with many new beneficial inventions.

Written Expression

1. **B** The sentence is in present tense so each verb should be in present tense. The verbs in this part are in past tense.

2. **M** The sentence is correct as written.

3. **A** *Retired out of* is an incorrect idiom. The correct way to say this is *retired from*.

4. **L** The adjective *past* should come before its modifier. The correct construction is *past four years*.

5. **B** This sentence has a misplaced modifier. Ryan's book was not reading–Ryan was.

6. **K** This part of the sentence has a verb error. It should be *I would use*.

7. **D** The sentence is correct as written.

8. **K** Items in a list must be parallel in form. The hobbies should be listed as woodwork-ing, painting, and *transforming*.

9. **C** The verb tense is not consistent in this sen-tence. *Gave* and *helped* are both in past tense, so this part should read *when she was class president*.

Answers and Explanations *(continued)*

10. **J** *Swift* is used as an adverb here, so it should be *swiftly*.

11. **B** The comma in this part of the sentence is not necessary.

12. **M** There are no punctuation mistakes.

13. **A** The descriptive phrase *after working in the garden* should be set off by commas.

14. **L** This sentence is a statement, not a question, so it should end with a period.

15. **D** There are no punctuation mistakes.

16. **J** Punctuation marks should go inside quotations, so this part of the sentence should read *"Who is there?" Chris asked.*

17. **B** There should not be a comma here.

18. **K** The question mark should go inside the quotation and the sentence should end with a period.

19. **C** A semicolon is not appropriate here. No punctuation is needed.

20. **L** The phrase *which is more than she ran last year* should be separated from the rest of the sentence by a comma.

21. **D** There are no spelling mistakes.

22. **J** The correct spelling is *impulsive*.

23. **A** The correct spelling is *anonymous*.

24. **K** The correct spelling is *misspell*.

25. **C** The correct spelling is *embargoes*.

26. **M** There are no spelling mistakes.

27. **B** The correct spelling is *parochial*.

28. **J** The correct spelling is *trinket*.

29. **D** There are no spelling mistakes.

30. **L** The correct spelling is *imminent*.

31. **B** The entire company title should be capitalized, including the abbreviated *Inc.*

32. **K** Small, unimportant words in titles, such as *in* and *the* should not be capitalized.

33. **A** A complete sentence that is quoted inside another sentence should begin with a capital.

34. **L** Do not capitalize names of seasons, unless part of a title.

35. **C** *Chairperson* should only be capitalized if it is used as a title.

36. **M** There are no capitalization mistakes.

37. **B** *English* should be capitalized because it comes from the proper noun *England*.

38. **J** Do not capitalize the first word in a list after a colon, unless it is a proper noun.

39. **D** There are no capitalization mistakes.

40. **K** Specific course titles should be capitalized.

41. **B** Answer choice B separates this sentence into two parts by grouping the physical descriptions into one sentence and the character descriptions into another. This is a logical way to split the sentence and the phrasing is clear and direct, unlike in the other choices.

42. **L** The most direct phrasing of the sentence would be with the subject (John Starhurst) first, and then the verb. Choices J and L both do this, but the simple phrasing of *chief named Mongondro* is preferred in choice L. The arrangement of modifiers in choice K is confusing.

Answers and Explanations *(continued)*

43. **A** Very *moved* means approximately the same as *deeply affected*.

44. **M** The typical elements of comedy are extraneous information in this sentence, so it would be best to set that information apart from the main sentence. Choice M does this with dashes. Choice J repeats *and*, which is awkward. Choice K uses *but*, which is the wrong conjunction. Choice L puts the list of comedy elements too far from the noun.

45. **D** This essay is a general introduction to Molière and his comedy writing, so *Molière, King of Comedy* would be the best title. The other choices are too specific to apply to the passage as a whole.

46. **M** No change is needed to this sentence. It is simple and direct. Choices J and K have verb tense problems and choice L is a fragment.

47. **B** Choice B presents a good conclusion for the paragraph and is connected well to the preceding sentence. Choices A and C present new information that is not directly connected to the previous information and choice E is a repetition of previously mentioned information.

48. **J** The sentence as written is a bit difficult. Setting the extra information off by dashes is awkward here due to the length of the phrase set off. Choice J avoids this difficulty. Choices K and L have problems with verb tense.

49. **C** Answer choice C presents the information about Mandela's presidency set off by commas, as extra information should be. Choice D has two conflicting conjunctions and the other choices are awkward.

50. **L** Only sentence 5 could be deleted without losing significant information. The ANC and violence are also mentioned in sentence 4.

Mathematics

1. **D** If $p = -1$, then the equation becomes $-1 + (-1)^2 - (-1)^3 + (-1)^4 - (-1)^5$. Use Order of Operations to do the exponents first and you get $-1 + 1 - (-1) + 1 - (-1)$. Add the terms to get 3.

2. **K** Set up a proportion: $\dfrac{1}{10} = \dfrac{x}{60}$. Cross multiply to solve for x. $10x = 60$. $\dfrac{60}{10} = 6$. So there would be 6 worms out of 60 apples.

3. **C** In order to add fractions, they must have the same denominator. The least common multiple of 6 and 8 is 24, so use that common denominator $\dfrac{4}{24} + \dfrac{3}{24} = \dfrac{7}{24}$. Then you will have. The value of b is 24.

4. **M** The area of a circle is πr^2. For a circle with a diameter of 6, the radius is 3, so the area is $\pi 3^2 = 9\pi$.

5. **D** Brand B was preferred by 20% of the 10,000 people. $10,000 \times 0.2 = 2,000$.

6. **L** $\dfrac{4}{7}$ is the same as $4 \div 7 = 0.57142857$.

7. **B** According to the chart, 8,500 people live in Webster in 2011. There were 4,500 in 2008, for an increase of 4,000.

8. **K** The prime factorization of 24 is $2 \times 2 \times 2 \times 3$. The greatest prime factor is 3.

9. **D** The price of the items is $3 + 6 + 4 + 9 = 22$. To find the tax, multiply 22 by .08 to get $1.76. Add the tax to the price to get $22 + 1.76 = 23.76$.

10. **M** First, convert the improper fractions. $12\dfrac{4}{5} = \dfrac{64}{5}$ and $= 6\dfrac{1}{4} = \dfrac{25}{4}$. Now simplify the terms:

$$\dfrac{64}{5} \times \dfrac{25}{4} = \dfrac{64 \times 25}{5 \times 4} = \dfrac{64 \times 25}{4 \times 5}$$

$$= \dfrac{64}{4} \times \dfrac{25}{5} = 16 \times 5 = 80$$

Answers and Explanations *(continued)*

11. **C** For every 3 cups of flour, she will need $1\frac{1}{2}$ teaspoons of salt. Since she will double the amount of flour, she must also double the amount of salt. $1\frac{1}{2} \times 2 = 3$.

12. **J** 0.125 written as a fraction would be $\frac{125}{1000}$. That can be simplified to $\frac{1}{8}$.

13. **D** Noah spends 40% on rent and 25% on utilities, for a total of 65%.

14. **K** $\sqrt{25} = 5$ and $\sqrt{16} = 4.5 \times 4 = 20$.

15. **C** If there are 5 red marbles and 12 total marbles, then there must be 7 blue marbles. The probability of drawing a blue marble is 7 blue out of 12 total or $\frac{7}{12}$.

16. **M** There are 180 degrees in a line. $180 - 35 = 145$.

17. **A** Line up the decimal points to add:

    $$\begin{array}{r} 2.376 \\ -\ 1.894 \\ \hline .482 \end{array}$$

18. **J** Plug in each of the answer choices for x to see which one produces a true statement. Choice J gives you $6^2 - 4(6) > 10$, which simplifies to $36 - 24 > 10$ or $12 > 10$. This is a true statement.

19. **D** The easiest way to do this problem is to plug in the answer choices for Aaron's age. For choice D, if Aaron is 1 now, then Kai is 4. In 4 years, Aaron will be 5 and Kai will be 8. The sum of 5 and 8 is 13, so that choice works.

20. **K** The only grades lower than C are D and F. The class has 20% D and 12% F, for a total of 32% lower than a C.

21. **B** If $x = -2$ and $y = 3$, then $(-2)^2 - 4(3) = 4 - 12 = -8$.

22. **L** Set up a proportion. Cassie rides her bicycle at a rate of $\frac{8\ miles}{1\ hour}$. She needs to go 24 miles, so $\frac{24\ miles}{21\ hour}$. Cross multiply to solve for x: $8x = 24$. $\frac{24}{8} = 3$ hours.

23. **C** To divide fractions, flip the second fraction and multiply. $\frac{3}{8} \times \frac{9}{8} \times \frac{27}{64}$.

24. **K** If the total is 100, then subtract 23 and 14 from 100 to get 63 people who like both.

25. **A** To find the average, add the numbers and then divide by the number of terms. $9 + 12 + 11 + 10 + 8 + 7 + 2 = 59$. There are 7 terms, so divide 59 by 7 to get 8.43.

26. **J** In order to have a sum of 8, the consecutive prime integers must be 3 and 5.

27. **D** To find the area of a rectangle, multiply the length and width. $6 \times 4 = 24$.

28. **M** Solve the first equation for x. $x + 12 - 12 = 15 - 12$, so $x = 3$. Then plug in the value of x into the second equation to get $3 + y = 7$. $y = 4$.

29. **B** The digit 7 is in the thousandths place. If you said 1, then you were probably thinking of the *thousands* place.

30. **L** Lori's average score increased from 85 to 98, for an increase of 13 points. No other student increased as much.

31. **B** Use the Pythagorean Theorem to solve: $a^2 + b^2 = c^2$. For this triangle, you would have $3^2 + b^2 = 5^2$. $9 + b^2 = 25$. $b^2 = 25 - 9$. $b^2 = 16$. $b = 4$.

32. **K** 12 cupcakes at $3 each would be $36. Add the shipping fee of $2.50 and the total charge will be $38.50.

Answers and Explanations *(continued)*

33. **B** The items add up to $40.70, so the closest estimate would be $41.00.

34. **L** $\sqrt{16} = 4$ and $\sqrt{25} = 5$, so $\sqrt{20}$ is approximately 4.5.

35. **D** If x is between -2 and -3 and y is between 7 and 8, then you can estimate x to be -2.5 and y to be 7.5. $x - y$ will be $-2.5 - 7.5 = -10$.

36. **K** The question asks for the hundredths place, or two places after the decimal. Since the next digit after that is a 3, you round down and the correct answer is 12.56.

37. **C** Round the numbers to $38 + 13 = 51$.

38. **M** 10% of $35.00 would be $3.50, so the total paid would be $38.50.

39. **A** Round the numbers to 700 and 400 to get $700 - 400 = 300$.

40. **J** Round the numbers to 80 and 70 to get $80 \times 70 = 5600$.

41. **C** Since the answer choices are close together, be careful here. $9 + 24$ would be 33 but you have enough left over from the decimals to add another 1 and get 34.

42. **K** Round the numbers to 350 and 70 to get $350 \div 70 = 5$.

43. **B** Round the numbers to 30, 60, and 90 to get $30 + 60 = 90$. $90 \div 90 = 1$.

44. **L** $\frac{8}{9}$ is close to 1, so the best estimate is $1x$ or simply x.

45. **D** Round 19 to 20 and 304 to 300. 20% of 300 is 60.

46. **M** Round $\sqrt{80}$ to $\sqrt{81} = 9$ and $\sqrt{8} = \sqrt{9} = 3$. $9 \times 3 = 27$.

47. **A** The digit 4 is in the hundreds place. Since the next digit is a 5, round up to get 32,500.

48. **J** Round the given measures to 100 and 20. Since there are 180 degrees in a triangle, angle x must be close to 60 degrees.

49. **D** Round the price to $25.00. 10% of 25 is 2.5, so the discounted price would be $25.00 − $2.50 = $22.50.

50. **L** Round the numbers to 5 and 3. $5^2 = 25$ and $3^2 = 9$. $25 − 9 = 16$.

Ability

1. **B** Each figure has exactly two straight sides.

2. **J** Each figure is made up of three straight line segments, not forming a closed shape.

3. **A** Each figure is a closed shape made of straight line segments.

4. **L** Each figure is filled with a grid pattern.

5. **D** Each figure is a three-dimensional solid.

6. **K** Each is a closed figure with some number of small circles inside.

7. **C** Each curvy line has one loop and open ends.

8. **N** Each figure has half its area shaded.

9. **E** Each figure is made up of circles.

10. **M** Each figure is an obtuse angle (greater than 90 degrees).

11. **A** The figures have an increasing number of sides: 3, then 4, then 5. The next figure should have six sides.

12. **J** The figures have no angles.

Answers and Explanations *(continued)*

13. **D** Each figure is an enclosed arrow pointing to the right.

14. **L** Each figure is made up of square blocks.

15. **B** Each figure is made up of two triangles.

16. **K** Each figure has a flat base.

17. **B** Each figure has upward diagonal stripes.

18. **M** Each figure is divided by one straight line.

19. **E** Each figure is a quadrilateral.

20. **N** Each rectangle is patterned with individual elements: dots, arrows, dashes. The matching figure is patterned with individual diamonds, as opposed to a connected pattern.

21. **E** The vertical line in the top left column has a loop added to its upper right side in the middle column. In the right column, another loop has been added to the bottom right. As you move down the rows, the size of the figures decreases.

22. **L** The figures in the left column each have five sides. The figures in the middle column each have four sides and the figures in the right column have three sides. The missing figure should have three sides as well, and only answer choice L does.

23. **C** The figures in the left column are each rotated 45° to the left in the middle column. They are rotated another 45° to the left in the right column. As you move down the rows, each figure has a line added to it.

24. **J** Each figure in the left column has a star added to its center in the middle column. In the right column, the star is colored black. As you move down the rows, the figures become more rounded and the star has an additional point in each row. This means that the missing figure will be an oval with a

black seven-point star. Only choice J has that figure in the correct orientation.

25. **A** Each figure in the left column has a smaller similar figure added to its center in the middle column, but the smaller figure is not in the same orientation as the larger figure. In the right column, the smaller figure has been rotated to be in the same orientation as the larger figure.

26. **N** The figures in the left column are each rotated 45° to the right in the middle column, and they are larger than they were in the left column. They are rotated another 45° to the left and increased even more in size in the right column.

27. **B** The boxes in the left column each contain a different shape. The boxes in the middle column show only the top portion of the original figure. The boxes in the right column show only the bottom portion of the original figure. Therefore, the missing figure should be the bottom portion of the arrow: a tall rectangle.

28. **M** The figures in the left column are repeated in the middle column, but with a bolder outline. In the right column, they are solid black.

29. **D** The left column has three different shapes. In the middle column, each figure has stripes that go up in a diagonal from left to right. In the right column, each figure has stripes that go down in a diagonal from left to right.

30. **K** In the left column, each box has a set of two figures, one on top of the other. In the middle column, the order of the objects is switched, and the bottom one is now on top. In the right column, the figure that was originally on top is now inside the other figure.

31. **E** Each figure in the left column is shown upside down in the middle column. In the right column, the original figure is overlaid on top of the middle figure.

Answers and Explanations *(continued)*

32. **J** Each figure in the left column is shown with its mirror image in the middle column. In the right column, the same figure as in the middle column is shaded gray.

33. **C** Each figure in the left column has four parts (four sides, four lines, four points on the star). In the middle column these figures have five parts, and in the right column they have six parts.

34. **L** The figure in the left column is made up of three identical shapes. In the middle column, there are two of these shapes, and in the right column there is only one.

35. **B** In the left column, each box contains a row of three shapes, with the outside two shapes identical to each other. In the middle column, one of the outside shapes has been removed. In the right column, the other outside shape has been removed, so that only the shape that was originally in the middle of the set remains.

36. **N** Each figure in the left column has a small, different figure to its upper right in the middle column. In the right column, the smaller shape is inside the larger one.

37. **A** In the left column, there is one shape above the line and three identical ones below the line. In the middle column, there is still one shape on top, but now there are two below the line. In the right column, there is one shape on top and one on bottom.

38. **J** Each square in the left column is colored solid black. The squares in the middle column are colored gray. In the right column, the squares are shown with no color. As you move down the rows, the figures get smaller. This means that the missing figure will be a small square with no color.

39. **D** The figures flatten out and get longer as you go across the columns. This means that the missing figure will be a long, flat oblong.

40. **M** Each figure in the left column has been rotated to the right by 45° in the middle column. In the right column, the same figure is rotated another 45° to the right.

41. **B** The paper is folded once and a hole is punched on the bottom middle and the top middle. When the paper is unfolded, there will be two holes along the bottom and two along the top. Choice C has the correct number of holes, but they are in the corners.

42. **K** The paper is folded twice and a hole is punched near the corner. When the paper is unfolded, there will be four holes, one in each corner. Choice N has the correct number of holes, but they are near the center of the edges.

43. **E** The paper is folded once and a hole is punched just above the center right. When the paper is unfolded, there will be two holes just above the center.

44. **J** The paper is folded once. One a hole is punched along the left center and one hole is punched along the right center. When the paper is unfolded, there will be four holes, two on the left center and two on the right center.

45. **C** The paper is folded twice and two holes are punched near the corner. When the paper is unfolded, there will be eight holes, with two near each corner.

46. **N** The paper is folded once and two holes are punched: one centered on the right side and one on the left side near the center edge. When the paper is unfolded, there will be four holes: two centered on the right side and two on the left near the center edge.

47. **A** The paper is folded once on the diagonal and a hole is punched in the lower left corner. When the paper is unfolded, there will be a hole in the lower left corner and a hole in the upper right corner.

Answers and Explanations *(continued)*

48. **M** The paper is folded once and three holes are punched along the bottom edge. When the paper is unfolded, there will be a total of six holes: three along the bottom edge and three along the top edge.

49. **E** The paper is folded twice and a hole is punched near the center. When the paper is unfolded, there will be four holes, all grouped near the center.

50. **L** The paper is folded once. One hole is punched on the right edge and one hole is punched directly on the fold. When the paper is unfolded, there will be a hole on the left edge, a hole on the right edge, and a hole in the upper center where the fold was punched.